Contents

2 **Maps of Principal Sights**

6 **Regional Driving Tours**

8 **Distance Chart**

9 **List of Maps and Plans**

10 **Fall Foliage Tours**

14 **Introduction**

New England's Natural Environment – Time Line – Economy – New England and the Sea – Population – Architecture – Sculpture – Furniture – Painting – Folk Art – Literature – Culinary Traditions – Further Reading

Sights

42 **Connecticut**

74 **Maine**

110 **Massachusetts**

216 **New Hampshire**

246 **Rhode Island**

268 **Vermont**

298 **Practical Information**

Calendar of Events – Planning the Trip – When to Go – International Visitors – Getting There and Getting Around – Accommodations – Basic Information – Sports and Recreation

317 **Index**

About this guide

In the **Sights** section of this guide, selected towns, regions and attractions are presented in alphabetical order within chapters for each of the six New England states. Each **Entry Heading** is followed by the latest available population figure, map reference and local tourist office telephone number, if applicable. In the text, useful information such as location, address, opening hours, admission charges and telephone number appears in *italics*. **Symbols** indicate camping ⚠, on-site eating facilities ✗, and wheelchair access ♿. On-site parking 🅿 is indicated for sights in the cities of Boston, Hartford, New Haven, Newport and Portland. In Boston, the Ⓣ symbol indicates the closest subway stop. The Kids symbol highlights sights of special interest to children. Many entries feature **digressions**, entertaining breaks from sightseeing marked in the guide by a purple bar; a numbered dot ❶ is a map reference. Cross-references to sights described appear in SMALL CAPITALS: consult the **Index** for the appropriate page number.

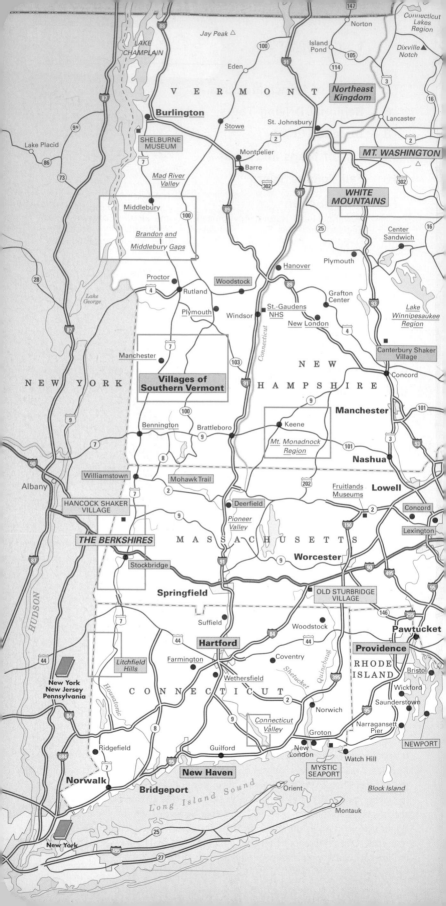

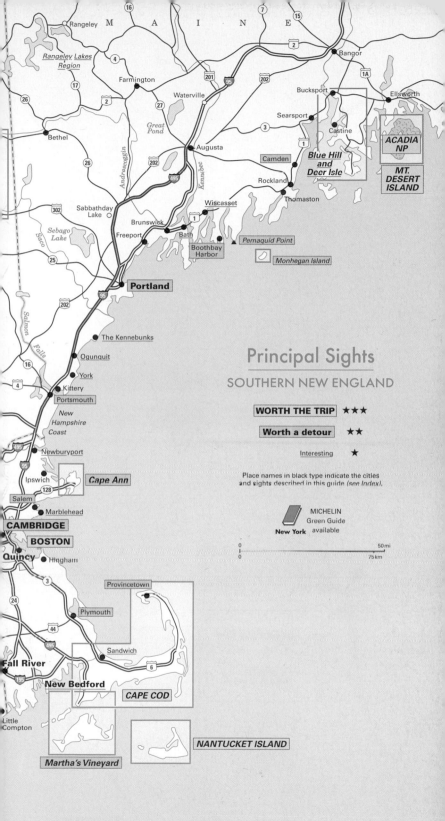

MAINE

16
7
15
Rangeley

Rangeley Lakes
Region

4

2

Bangor

201
95
202

1A

Farmington

27

Waterville

Bucksport
Searsport

Ellsworth

17

26

Great
Pond

3

Castine

ACADIA
NP

Bethel

26

202

Augusta

Camden

Blue Hill
and
Deer Isle

MT.
DESERT
ISLAND

495

Rockland

1

Sebago
Lake

302

Sabbathday
Lake

Wiscasset

Thomaston

Brunswick

Freeport

Bath

Pemaquid Point

25

Boothbay
Harbor

Monhegan Island

Portland

95

202

The Kennebunks

Ogunquit

16

York

4

Kittery

Portsmouth

New
Hampshire
Coast

Principal Sights

SOUTHERN NEW ENGLAND

495

95

Newburyport

Ipswich

128

Cape Ann

Salem

Marblehead

CAMBRIDGE

BOSTON

Quincy

Hingham

3

Provincetown

24

Plymouth

44

Sandwich

495

Fall River

195

6

New Bedford

CAPE COD

Little
Compton

NANTUCKET ISLAND

Martha's Vineyard

WORTH THE TRIP ★★★

Worth a detour ★★

Interesting ★

Place names in black type indicate the cities
and sights described in this guide (see Index).

MICHELIN
Green Guide
available

New York

0   50 mi
0   75 km

A T L A N T I C   O C E A N

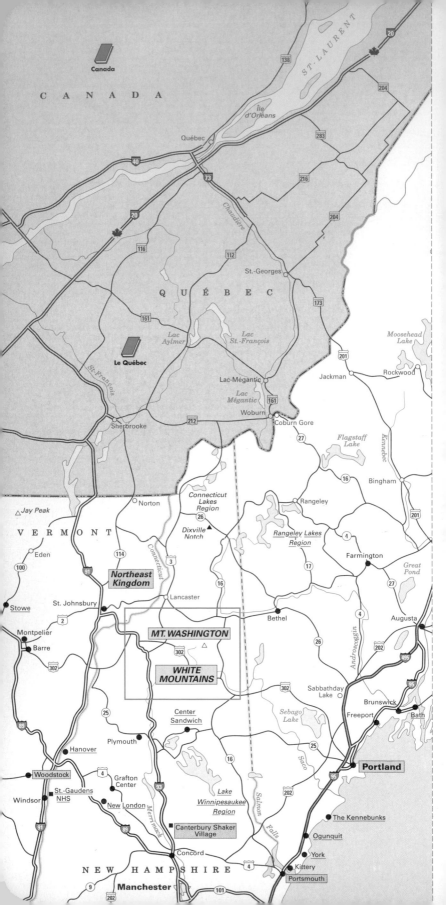

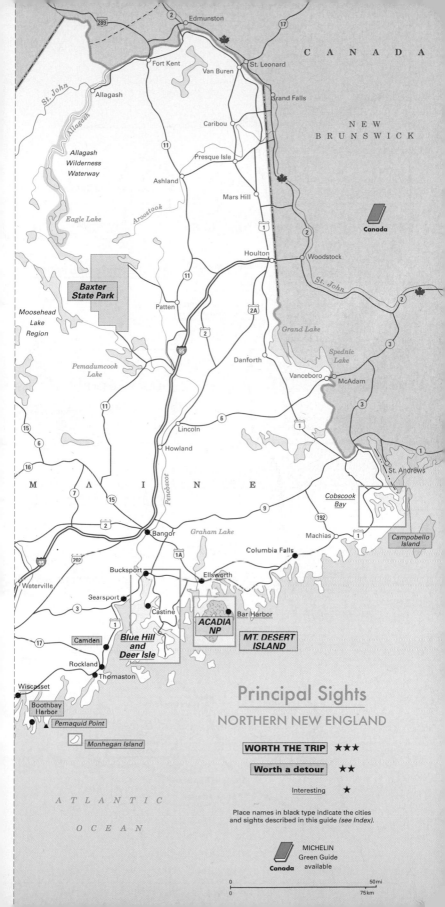

CANADA

Edmunston

Fort Kent

Van Buren

St. Leonard

Allagash

Grand Falls

NEW
BRUNSWICK

St. John

Caribou

*Allagash
Wilderness
Waterway*

Presque Isle

Ashland

Eagle Lake

Mars Hill

Aroostook

Canada

Houlton

Woodstock

**Baxter
State Park**

St. John

*Moosehead
Lake
Region*

Patten

Grand Lake

*Pemadumcook
Lake*

Danforth

*Spednic
Lake*

Vanceboro

McAdam

Lincoln

St. Andrews

Howland

M A I N E

Penobscot

*Cobscook
Bay*

Bangor

Graham Lake

Machias

Waterville

Bucksport

Columbia Falls

Ellsworth

*Campobello
Island*

Searsport

Castine

Bar Harbor

**Blue Hill
and
Deer Isle**

**ACADIA
NP**

**MT. DESERT
ISLAND**

Camden

Rockland

Thomaston

Wiscasset

Boothbay
Harbor

Pemaquid Point

Monhegan Island

Principal Sights

NORTHERN NEW ENGLAND

WORTH THE TRIP	★★★
Worth a detour	★★
Interesting	★

Place names in black type indicate the cities
and sights described in this guide *(see Index).*

Canada MICHELIN
Green Guide
available

ATLANTIC

OCEAN

0   50mi
0   75km

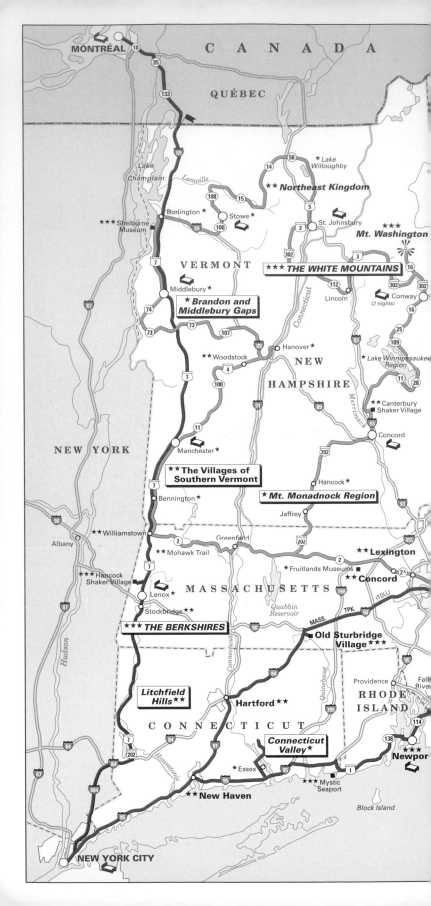

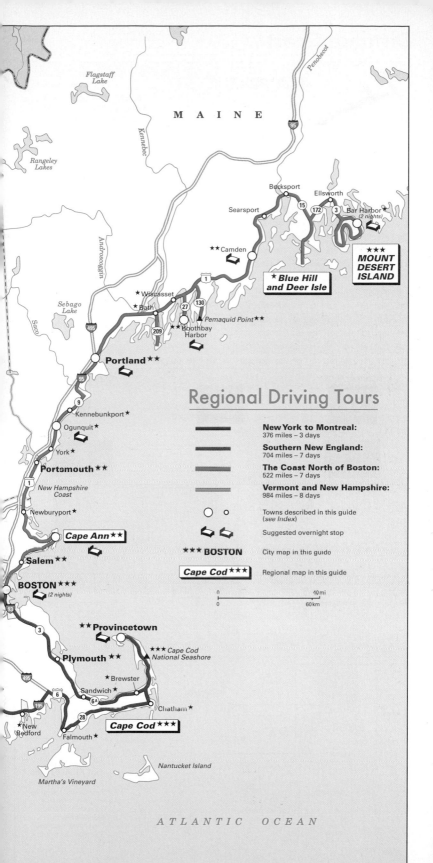

MAINE

Flagstaff Lake

Rangeley Lakes

95

Bucksport

15   Ellsworth

Searsport   172   3   Bar Harbor
(2 nights)

★★ Camden

★★★
MOUNT
DESERT
ISLAND

★ **Blue Hill
and Deer Isle**

Androscoggin

Sebago Lake

1

★ Wiscasset   130

★ Bath   27

▲ Pemaquid Point ★★

209   ★★ Boothbay
Harbor

Saco

495

Portland ★★

95

9

Kennebunkport ★

Ogunquit ★

York ★

Portsmouth ★★

*New Hampshire
Coast*

1

Newburyport ★

Regional Driving Tours

New York to Montreal:
376 miles – 3 days

Southern New England:
704 miles – 7 days

The Coast North of Boston:
522 miles – 7 days

Vermont and New Hampshire:
984 miles – 8 days

○   ○   Towns described in this guide
(see *Index*)

⬑   ⬑   Suggested overnight stop

★★★ BOSTON   City map in this guide

Cape Cod ★★★   Regional map in this guide

0	40mi
0	60km

Cape Ann ★★

Salem ★★

BOSTON ★★★
(2 nights)   93

3

★★ **Provincetown**

★★★ *Cape Cod
National Seashore*

Plymouth ★★

★ Brewster

Sandwich ★   6A

495   6

195   28

Chatham ★

★ New
Bedford

Falmouth ★   **Cape Cod ★★★**

Nantucket Island

Martha's Vineyard

ATLANTIC   OCEAN

Kennebec

Penobscot

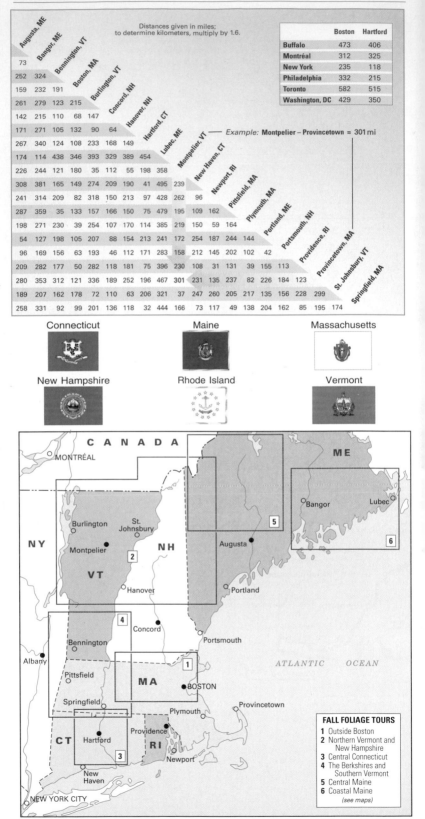

Distances given in miles; to determine kilometers, multiply by 1.6.

	Boston	Hartford
Buffalo	473	406
Montréal	312	325
New York	235	118
Philadelphia	332	215
Toronto	582	515
Washington, DC	429	350

Example: **Montpelier – Provincetown = 301 mi**

Distance chart (diagonal labels: Augusta, ME / Bangor, ME / Bennington, VT / Boston, MA / Burlington, VT / Concord, NH / Hanover, NH / Hartford, CT / Lubec, ME / Montpelier, VT / New Haven, CT / Newport, RI / Pittsfield, MA / Plymouth, MA / Portland, ME / Portsmouth, NH / Providence, RI / Provincetown, MA / St. Johnsbury, VT / Springfield, MA):

```
 73
252 324
159 232 191
261 279 123 215
142 215 110  68 147
171 271 105 132  90  64
267 340 124 108 233 168 149
174 114 438 346 393 329 389 454
226 244 121 180  35 112  55 198 358
308 381 165 149 274 209 190  41 495 239
241 314 209  82 318 150 213  97 428 262  96
287 359  35 133 157 166 150  75 479 195 109 162
198 271 230  39 254 107 170 114 385 219 150  59 164
 54 127 198 105 207  88 154 213 241 172 254 187 244 144
 96 169 156  63 193  46 112 171 283 158 212 145 202 102  42
209 282 177  50 282 118 181  75 396 230 108  31 131  39 155 113
280 353 312 121 336 189 252 196 467 301 231 135 237  82 226 184 123
189 207 162 178  72 110  63 206 321  37 247 260 205 217 135 156 228 299
258 331  92  99 201 136 118  32 444 166  73 117  49 138 204 162  85 195 174
```

Connecticut

Maine

Massachusetts

New Hampshire

Rhode Island

Vermont

FALL FOLIAGE TOURS
1 Outside Boston
2 Northern Vermont and New Hampshire
3 Central Connecticut
4 The Berkshires and Southern Vermont
5 Central Maine
6 Coastal Maine
(see maps)

List of Maps and Plans

9

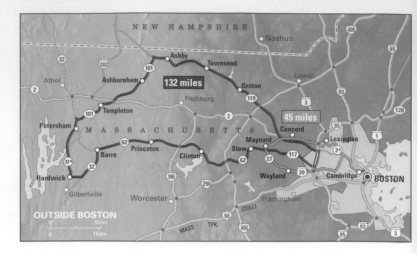

OUTSIDE BOSTON

132 miles

45 miles

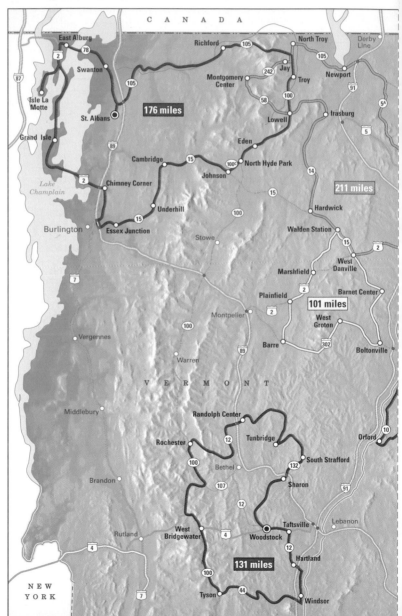

176 miles

211 miles

101 miles

131 miles

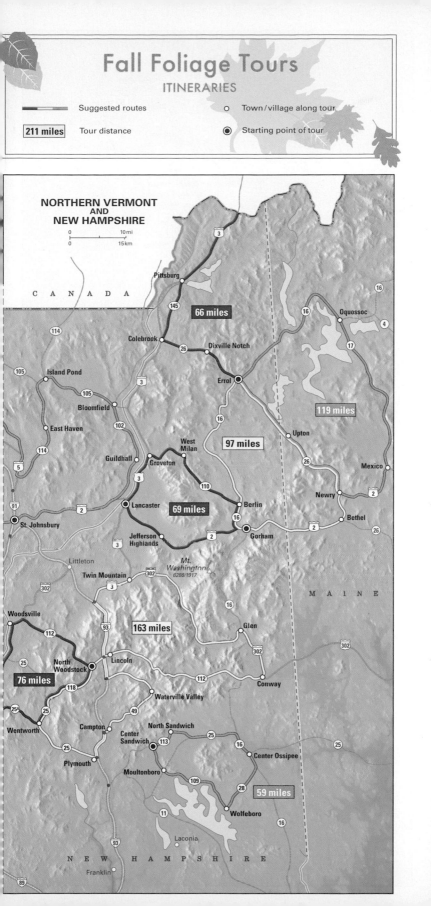

Fall Foliage Tours

ITINERARIES

Suggested routes

○ Town/village along tour

| 211 miles | Tour distance

◉ Starting point of tour

NORTHERN VERMONT AND NEW HAMPSHIRE

0 — 10mi
0 — 15km

CANADA

Pittsburg

66 miles

Colebrook — Dixville Notch

Island Pond

Bloomfield

East Haven

Guildhall

West Milan

Groveton

Errol

119 miles

Upton

97 miles

Mexico

Lancaster

69 miles

Berlin

Newry

Bethel

St. Johnsbury

Jefferson Highlands

Gorham

Littleton

Twin Mountain

Mt. Washington
6288/1917

MAINE

Woodsville

Glen

163 miles

North Woodstock

Lincoln

76 miles

Waterville Valley

Conway

Wentworth

Campton

North Sandwich

Center Sandwich

Plymouth

Moultonboro

Center Ossipee

59 miles

Wolfeboro

Laconia

NEW HAMPSHIRE

Franklin

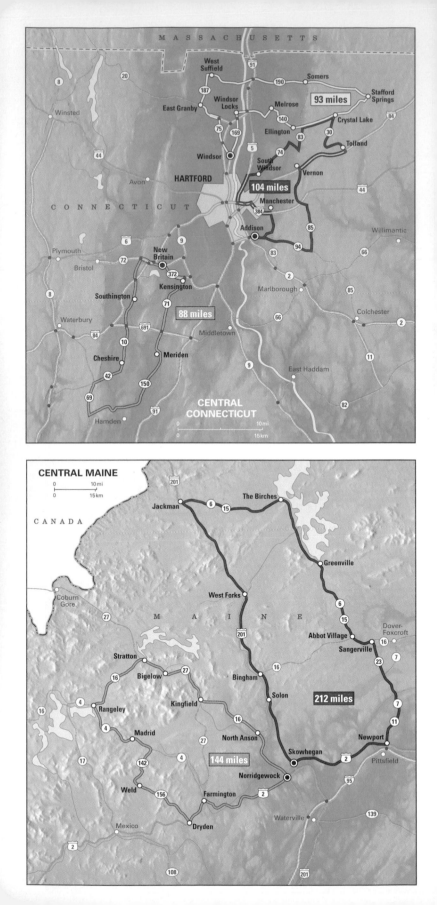

MASSACHUSETTS

West
Suffield

190   Somers

93 miles   Stafford
Springs

187   Windsor
Locks   Melrose

East Granby   140   Crystal Lake

75   169   83   30   Tolland

5   74
Windsor   Ellington
Vernon

HARTFORD   104 miles   44

South
Windsor

Manchester

384

Avon

CONNECTICUT   Addison   85

Willimantic

6   9   94

Plymouth   New
Britain   83   66

72   372

Bristol   Kensington   Marlborough   85

Southington   71   66   Colchester

8   691   88 miles   Middletown   2

Waterbury   10   Meriden

84   9   East Haddam   11

Cheshire
42   150

69   82

91   CENTRAL
CONNECTICUT

Hamden   0   10mi
0   15km

Winsted
8   20

44

CENTRAL MAINE   0   10mi
0   15km

201

CANADA   Jackman   6   15   The Birches

Greenville

Coburn
Gore   27   West Forks   6
15

MAINE   201   Abbot Village   Dover-
Foxcroft

Stratton   Sangerville   16   7

Bigelow   27   16   23

16   Kingfield   Bingham   212 miles   7

4   Rangeley   16   Solon   7
11

4   Madrid   16   North Anson   Newport

17   142   4   Skowhegan   2   Pittsfield

Weld   156   Farmington   2   95

144 miles   Norridgewock   139

Mexico   Dryden   Waterville

2   108   201

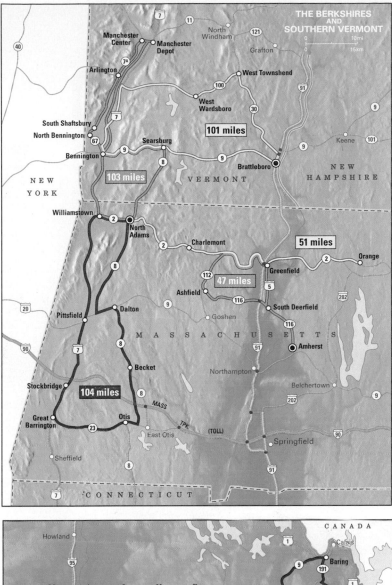

0   10mi
0   15km

101 miles

103 miles

51 miles

47 miles

104 miles

NEW
YORK

VERMONT

NEW
HAMPSHIRE

M A S S A C H U S E T T S

C O N N E C T I C U T

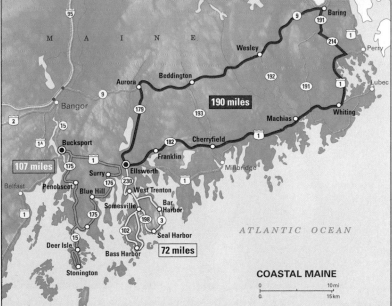

CANADA

M A I N E

190 miles

107 miles

72 miles

ATLANTIC OCEAN

COASTAL MAINE

0   10mi
0   15km

Introduction To New England

"New England is the authorized version of America: her land and people chapter and verse for more than three hundred years."

Poet David McCord
Address in 1960 at
Old Sturbridge Village

Ken Burris / Shelburne Museum

New England's Natural Environment

Framed by the White Mountains to the north and the Green Mountains to the west, New England's gently rolling hills and valleys taper off to an irregular rockbound coastline edged with sandy beaches to the south. Vast woodlands coupled with an extensive river and stream system complete the picture.

The region's major mountain ranges are remnants of higher peaks that were formed 300 million to 500 million years ago. Much younger in geologic age, the numerous ponds, lakes, U-shaped valleys and winding ridges owe their existence to the Laurentide ice sheet and associated glaciers that covered this portion of the North American continent until about 10,000 years ago.

Formation of New England – During the Paleozoic era (240 million–570 million years ago), the earth's crust, composed largely of gneiss, was submerged beneath inland seas. Layers of sediment accumulated on the sea floor until the Eurasian and North American tectonic plates collided, causing the earth's crust to heave upward. Consequently, the sea floor buckled along the Canadian Shield and rose above the water as a mass of parallel folds. The intense heat and pressure accompanying the uplift and folding of these peaks (ancestors of the Green Mountains and the Taconic Range) transformed the sedimentary sandstone and limestone into metamorphic rocks, consisting primarily of schist and marble.

During the same era, domes of Precambrian, largely granitic rock pushed upward into the folded sections of rock, forming New Hampshire's Presidential Range. These ancient mountains probably reached the elevations of the present-day Alps or Himalayas. Since then, erosion has worn the mountains down to a dissected plain. Repeated uplifts and cycles of erosion, coupled with the scouring by subsequent glaciers, created the principal features of New England's landscape.

A Glaciated Landscape – The last of four stages of continental glaciation that occurred during the first part of the Quaternary epoch ended some 10,000 years ago. About 1.5 million years ago, at the dawn of the Pleistocene Period, the climate became increasingly colder and snow accumulated, spawning the beginning of the most recent Ice Age. The weight of the top layers of snow, compacted by repeated melting and refreezing, eventually compressed the lower tiers into crystalline ice.

When the ice reached a thickness of 150ft to 200ft, the lower layer, no longer able to support the intense pressure, began to spread. Moving southeastward from the Labrador peninsula in Canada to Long Island, New York, the enormous Laurentide ice sheet stretched across the northeastern part of the Appalachians and came to a halt along a line roughly parallel to New England's present southern coastline.

Glaciers scoured the walls and floors of narrow valleys, widening them into U-shaped valleys called notches. Abrasive materials stuck to the bottom of the ice chiseled and striated the granite and other bedrock. Boulders, now scattered across New England, were plucked from exposed mountainsides. Glacial detritus formed natural dams, often blocking valleys and creating ponds and waterfalls as the ice dissipated. Large isolated blocks of ice left in the wake of receding glaciers eventually melted, giving rise to the kettle lakes (named for their rounded shape) that dot the region.

Near the coast, sticky clay deposits left by the glaciers formed low-lying oval hills (known as drumlins) such as Boston's Bunker Hill and World's End in HINGHAM. When the ice finally melted, it left behind enormous moraines consisting of unsorted rock fragments ranging from huge boulders to tiny clay particles. The formation of **Cape Cod, Martha's Vineyard, Nantucket, Block Island** and Long Island has been attributed to these prominent ridges of debris, which remained above sea level when the ocean invaded the low-lying land.

Major Geographic Features

Appalachian Mountains – The Appalachians, extending about 1,600mi from Canada's St. Lawrence Valley to Alabama, form the spine of New England. Several parallel ranges with a primarily north-south orientation make up the northeastern Appalachian system.

The White Mountains – These once heavily glaciated mountains, characterized by rocky, cone-shaped summits and U-shaped valleys, claim the highest peak in the northeastern US: Mt. Washington (6,288ft).

The Green Mountains – The most prominent peaks in Vermont form a north-south ridge through the center of the state. Composed of ancient metamorphic rocks, including Vermont's rich marble deposits, this mountain chain extends into Massachusetts, where it is known as the Berkshires.

The Taconic Range – Extending along the common border of New York and Massachusetts, and into southern Vermont, this range, comprised primarily of schist, includes Mt. Equinox in Vermont and Mt. Greylock in Massachusetts.

The Monadnocks – Several isolated mountains, called monadnocks, the remnants of ancient crystalline rock more resistant to erosion than the surrounding rock strata, dominate the countryside. Mt. Monadnock in New Hampshire exemplifies this type

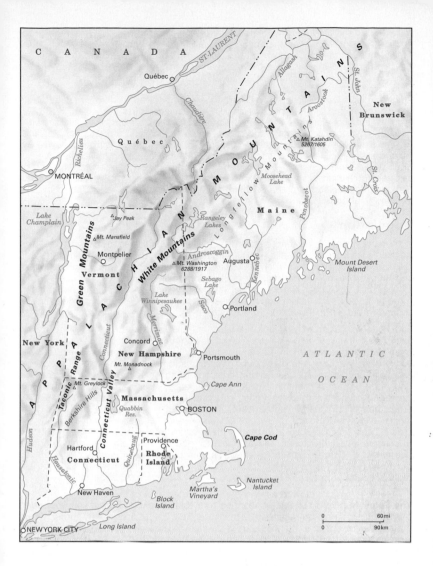

of relief; its name has been adopted by geographers to describe similar formations found elsewhere. Other monadnocks include Mts. Katahdin and Blue in Maine, Mts. Cardigan and Kearsage in New Hampshire, and Mts. Wachusetts and Greylock in Massachusetts.

The Connecticut Valley – New England is bisected by this 400mi-long, north-south incision carved by the Connecticut River. The valley follows a fault that is punctuated by several craggy basalt ridges (Mts. Sugarloaf and Holyoke) rising above the valley floor in Massachusetts and north of New Haven, Connecticut. The valley's abundance of fossils (PIONEER VALLEY) reflects its rich geologic past.

The Coast – In the north the coast is jagged and indented, with countless peninsulas and bays following a northwest-southeast orientation, a vivid reminder of the direction of the Laurentide ice sheet. Melting glacial waters, together with a rising sea level, inundated this land, hiding most of the glacial landforms and creating a coastline of elongated bays and hundreds of offshore islands. South of PORTLAND, Maine, the broad, flat coastal plain gives way to sandy beaches. The estuaries and lagoons of quiet water protected by barrier beaches have given rise to vast salt marshes that provide food and resting grounds for birds and waterfowl in the Atlantic Flyway. Farther south, enormous accumulations of sand cover the glacial moraines of Cape Cod and the islands, creating the landscape that typifies the Cape.

Climate – Mark Twain once observed that "there is a sumptuous variety about the New England weather, that compels admiration—and regret. ...In the spring I have counted 136 different kinds of weather inside of 24 hours." This varied climate results from the fact that the region lies in a zone where cool, dry air from Canada meets warm, humid air from the southeast. Annual precipitation averages 42in, and the seasons are sharply defined.

Winter is cold, particularly in the north, where temperatures can range from –10°F to 10°F (–23°C to –12°C) and the annual snowfall in the mountains ranges from 90 to 100in. A period of variable temperatures, **spring** in New England is brief. In the north, the two- to three-week interval between winter and summer, when the snow melts and the ground thaws, is known as "mud season." Flooding can make driving on country roads hazardous during this time.

A pattern of hazy or foggy days alternating with showers and followed by clear weather characterizes the humid **summer**. Daytime temperatures peak at 90°F (32°C); evenings are cool along the coast, in the mountains and near the lakes. **Autumn**, with its sunny days and cool nights, is the season when "leaf lookers" travel to New England to view the spectacular fall foliage. A cool spell in late September is often followed by **Indian summer**, a milder period when the leaves take on their most brilliant color.

Northeasters, coastal storms accompanied by high tides, heavy rain (or snow in winter) and gale-force winds, can occur at any time of year, especially off the coast of Maine. Temperatures for northern and southern New England vary and are affected by differences in altitude.

Vegetation

With more than 70 percent of the region's surface covered by woodland, New England's landscape is appealing in the summer for its thick cover of green, and even more so in the fall for its blazing leaf colors. The forests consist of a combination of deciduous trees and evergreens. The most common deciduous trees are beech, birch, hickory, oak, and sugar or rock maple. Among the conifers, the white pine is found throughout southern New England, while hemlock, balsam fir and spruce forests abound in the north. The latter are exploited by large paper-making companies.

Fall Foliage – Dramatic and unforgettable, the blazing New England foliage transforms the countryside into a palette of vivid golds (birches, poplars, gingkos), oranges (maples, hickories, mountain ash) and scarlets (red maples, red oaks, sassafras and dogwoods), framed by the dark points of spruce and fir trees. What makes the scene especially impressive are the flaming crimsons of the maple trees that cover New England. The Indian summer climate, with its crisp, clear sunny days followed by increasingly longer and colder nights, catalyzes the chemical reaction that halts the production of chlorophyll in the leaves, and causes the previously concealed pigments—yellowish carotene, brown tannin, and red anthocyanin—to appear.

Leaves begin to change color in the northern states in mid-September and continue to change until mid-October, and until late October in the south. However, the first two weeks in October remain the most glorious period, when bright color blankets the New England landscape. In all six states, information centers provide foliage reports by telephone *(p 311)*. *Driving itineraries for selected foliage tours begin on p 10.*

The Sugar Maples – Capable of adapting to a cold climate and rocky soil, the sugar or rock maple is found throughout Vermont and New Hampshire. In early spring, when the sap begins to rise in the maple trees, farmers insert a tube, from which a bucket is suspended, into the trunk. The sap that collects in the bucket is transferred to an evaporator in a nearby wooden shed called a sugarhouse, where it is boiled down into

New England's Fall Foliage

syrup. It takes about 40 gallons of sap to produce one gallon of syrup. Modern technology has simplified this process; now, plastic tubes lead directly from the tree to the sugarhouse. *Visitors are welcome at many of New England's sugarhouses p 312.*

Marshes and Bogs – Because of its glacial origin, the soil in New England is often swampy. Vast marshlands, distinguished by tall grasses and reedy plants, line the region's coast. Bogs, wetlands characterized by the high acid content of the soil, support plants such as sedges, heaths, orchids, Labrador tea, sphagnum moss and, in low-lying sandy areas, cranberries. Dead matter that accumulates in the bog is prevented from decaying because of the acidic environment, and over a period of time this material is transformed into peat. Gradually the surface of the bog may be covered with a thick, soggy mat of sphagnum moss. Peat deposits will support trees and shrubs, and eventually vegetation will fill in the bog, converting it into dry, forested land.

Wildflowers – By late spring the mantle of snow has almost disappeared and the flowers in the woods, along the roadside and in the fields and mountains burst into bloom. The magnificent **rhododendron** and **laurel** bushes lend pink accents to the dark green woods. During the summer the roadsides are alternately tinted with the orange of the flowering **Turk's-cap lily**, the yellow of the tall-stemmed **goldenrod**, the pale blue of the multitude of tiny **asters** and the purplish hue of broad, swaying patches of **lupine**. Hundreds of species of more familiar wildflowers, including buttercups, daisies, sunflowers, Queen Anne's lace and lily of the valley, adorn the fields and grassy meadows. In moist, marshy areas, look for the delicate **lady's slipper**, a small pink or white member of the orchid family, and the greenish **Jack-in-the-pulpit**, so named because of the curved flap that gives the flower its appearance of a preacher in a pulpit.

Wildlife

There are virtually no forms of wildlife unique to New England, yet several species are typical of the region's fauna.

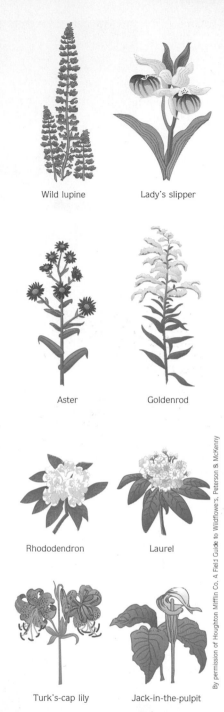

Wild lupine

Lady's slipper

Aster

Goldenrod

Rhododendron

Laurel

Turk's-cap lily

Jack-in-the-pulpit

The Forests – The **white-tailed deer**, the favorite game of hunters, is found in many parts of New England. This species of deer, characterized by its white, bushy tail, inhabits the northern spruce and fir forests together with **black bears** and **moose**. The region's largest mammal, the moose boasts an enormous set of antlers and may be encountered in the middle of forest roads.

In ponds and streams, colonies of **beavers** toil, felling trees with their teeth to build dams. Their structures often create deep ponds or cause flooding in low-lying areas. Swampy zones are thus created where trees cannot survive; dead tree trunks identify these ponds.

Among the other forest inhabitants are the masked **raccoon**, the **porcupine** with its protective bristly quills, the black-and-white-striped **skunk**, and the **red squirrel**. The **chipmunk**, a member of the squirrel family, is a small mammal that frequents settled areas as well as woodlands.

Puffins

The Coast – **Seagulls** and **terns** are ever-present along the coast, always searching for food on boats, on the beaches, in inlets and marshes and on the piers that line the waterfront. The **great cormorants** are larger in size and live principally on the rocky sea cliffs that they share with several species of seals.

Coastal marshes serve as the feeding and resting grounds for hundreds of species of birds. Located along the Atlantic Flyway, broad stretches of salt marshes, such as those west of Barnstable Harbor on Cape Cod, are frequented by large numbers of bird-watchers during the spring and fall migrations. Flocks of Canada geese, their graceful V-formation a familiar sight in the New England sky during migratory seasons, rest in these tranquil areas. **Puffins** may also be seen.

Beaver

Time Line

Exploration

1000	Norse sailors reach the shores of present-day Newfoundland.
1492	Christopher Columbus lands on the island of San Salvador.
1497	**John Cabot** explores the coast of North America. English claims to land in the New World are based on his voyages.
1509	Henry VIII becomes king of England.
1524	**Giovanni da Verrazzano** explores the coast of North America for France.
1534	Henry VIII establishes the Church of England.
1558	Elizabeth I accedes to the English throne.
1602	English explorer **Bartholomew Gosnold**, sailing south along the New England coast, names Cape Cod, the Elizabeth Islands and Martha's Vineyard.
1604	The Frenchmen **Samuel de Champlain** and **Pierre de Gua, Sieur de Monts**, founders of Acadia (New France), establish a colony on the island of St. Croix and explore the Maine coast.
1605	Capt. **George Weymouth** returns to England from Maine with five American Indians.
1607	Virginia Colony, the first permanent English settlement in North America, is established at Jamestown. **Sir John Popham** and **Sir Ferdinando Gorges** finance an expedition to start a colony on the coast of Maine.
1608	Samuel de Champlain founds Quebec City.
1613	The Jesuits establish a mission on Mt. Desert Island, Maine.
1614	**Capt. John Smith**, sailing for a group of London merchants, returns to England with a cargo of fish and furs. The term "New England" is used for the first time in his account of the voyage, *A Description of New England*. Dutch navigator Adrian Block names Block Island.

Colonization

1620	The Pilgrims arrive on the **Mayflower** and establish Plymouth Colony, the first permanent English settlement in New England.
1625	Charles I becomes king of England.
1626	Roger Conant leads a group to Cape Ann and organizes the Puritan colony of Salem.
1630	**Boston** is founded by Puritans led by **John Winthrop**.
1635	**Thomas Hooker** leads a group of settlers from Massachusetts Bay Colony to the Connecticut Valley and founds Hartford Colony.
1636	**Harvard College** established. **Roger Williams** flees the intolerance of Massachusetts Bay Colony and establishes Providence, Rhode Island.
1638	**Anne Hutchinson** and William Coddington found Portsmouth, Rhode Island.
1638-39	The Connecticut Valley towns of Hartford, Windsor and Wethersfield join to form Connecticut Colony.
1653	Oliver Cromwell is appointed lord protector of England.
1660	The Restoration and accession of Charles II.
1662	A royal charter unites the New Haven and Connecticut colonies.
1689	Accession of William III and his wife, Mary.
1702	Anne becomes queen of Britain.
1713	By the Treaty of Utrecht, France cedes Acadia, Newfoundland and the Hudson Bay territory to Britain.
1714	George I accedes to the British throne.
1763	The Treaty of Paris ends the French and Indian War (1756-63). France cedes Canada and territories east of the Mississippi to Britain.

Independence

1765	Passage of the **Stamp Act**, a direct tax levied by Britain on the American colonies without the consent of the colonial legislature.
1766	Stamp Act is repealed.
1767	Parliament passes the **Townshend Acts**, which levy duties on colonial imports of tea, paper and glass.
1770	The majority of the Townshend Acts are repealed, but the tax on tea remains. Friction between the colonists and the British leads to the Boston Massacre.

Craig Aines/f/STOP PICTURES

Revolutionary Reenactment, Portsmouth, New Hampshire

1773	In response to the British refusal to repeal the tax on tea, colonists stage the Boston Tea Party at Boston Harbor.
1774	Parliament passes the five **Intolerable Acts**, four of which were directed against the citizens of Massachusetts in retaliation for the Boston Tea Party the previous year. Colonists who oppose Britain's policies hold the **First Continental Congress**.
1775	Outbreak of the **American Revolution**: April 18 – Ride of Paul Revere. April 19 – Battles of Lexington and Concord. May 10 – Siege of Fort Ticonderoga by Ethan Allen and the Green Mountain Boys, along with Benedict Arnold and his men. June 17 – Battle of Bunker Hill. July 3 – Washington is appointed commander in chief by the Continental Congress.
1776	March 17 – British troops evacuate Boston. July 4 – **Declaration of Independence** is adopted.
1777	Battle of Bennington. Vermont declares its independence and adopts its own state constitution.
1780	French forces led by General Rochambeau arrive in Newport, Rhode Island, to aid the American revolutionaries.
1781	Colonists defeat British troops led by General Cornwallis at Yorktown, Virginia.
1783	End of the American Revolution; Britain recognizes the independence of the 13 colonies.
1788	Ratification of the US Constitution. Connecticut, Massachusetts and New Hampshire are admitted to the Union as the fifth, sixth and ninth states, respectively.
1789	**George Washington** is chosen as the first president of the US. The French Revolution begins.
1790	Rhode Island becomes the 13th US state.
1791	Vermont, the last New England colony to join the Union, is admitted as the 14th state in the US.

19C and 20C

1812	US declares war on Britain.
1814	The Treaty of Ghent ends the War of 1812 on Christmas Eve.
1815	The defeat of French emperor Napoleon Bonaparte at the Battle of Waterloo on June 19 leads to his abdication and exile.
1820	Maine enters the Union as the 23rd state.
1837	Queen Victoria begins her 64-year reign.
1845	Famine strikes Ireland.
1851-52	Harriet Beecher Stowe's novel **Uncle Tom's Cabin** appears in serial form in the abolitionist paper **The National Era**.

1861-65	**Civil War**
1865	John Wilkes Booth assassinates President Lincoln at Ford's Theatre in Washington, DC, on the night of April 14.
1905	The Treaty of Portsmouth, ending the Russo-Japanese War, is signed at the Portsmouth Naval Base in Kittery, Maine.
1914-18	**World War I**
1917	US declares war on Germany.
1921	Italian immigrants Nicola Sacco and Bartolomeo Vanzetti are tried for murder in Dedham, Massachusetts.
1929	Stock market crash signals the start of the Great Depression.
1932	Franklin Delano Roosevelt is elected 32nd president of the US.
1939-45	**World War II**
1941	US declares war on Japan following the December 7 attack on Pearl Harbor.
1944	Bretton Woods Conference is held in New Hampshire.
1954	World's first nuclear-powered submarine is constructed at Groton, Connecticut.
1961	At age 43, John F. Kennedy from Massachusetts becomes the youngest man ever to be elected US president.
1963	President Kennedy is assassinated in Dallas, Texas, on November 22.
1966	Massachusetts state attorney general Edward W. Brooke is the first African American elected to the US Senate since Reconstruction.
1976	The Liberian tanker **Argo Merchant** runs aground near Nantucket Island and spills 7.5 million gallons of crude oil into the North Atlantic.
1980	Boston celebrates its 350th anniversary.
1983	**Australia II** wins the America's Cup by defeating the American yacht **Liberty** in the best of seven races off the coast of Newport, Rhode Island.
1985	Vermont voters elect the nation's first foreign-born woman governor, Madeleine M. Kunin.
1988	Democratic candidate Michael Dukakis, former governor of Massachusetts, loses the US presidential election to George Bush. Dukakis receives 46 percent of the nation's popular vote.
1990	Twelve works of art, valued at $100 million, are stolen from the Isabella Stewart Gardner Museum in Boston.
1991	Bridgeport, Connecticut, becomes the largest US city to file a petition of bankruptcy. The city's petition is denied.
1992	Mashantucket Pequot Indians open Foxwoods, a resort casino in Ledyard, Connecticut.
1993	The Norman Rockwell Museum at Stockbridge opens in western Massachusetts.
1994	**Harvard University**, the most generously endowed of private universities ($6 billion), launches largest fund-raising drive in the history of higher education.
1995	Boston's Museum of Fine Arts restructures to reduce its $4.5 million deficit. **Boston Garden**, one of the oldest sports arenas in the nation, is torn down and replaced by a new sports and entertainment complex, the FleetCenter. Part of the largest public works project in the US ("The Big Dig"), Boston's new Ted Williams Tunnel opens to commercial traffic, connecting the city to Logan Airport.
1997	From its Charlestown berth, the **USS Constitution**, America's oldest commissioned warship afloat, sails under its own power for the first time in 116 years.
1998	The worst ice storm of the century hits the Northeast, killing trees and causing power outages in Maine, New Hampshire and Vermont.
1999	The Massachusetts Museum of Contemporary Art (MASS MoCA) opens in a renovated factory in North Adams. Festivals throughout New England celebrate the arrival of the new millennium.
2000	The first US census of the new century is conducted, revealing the growth patterns of the towns and cities of New England as well as the nation.

Economy

The economic evolution of New England paralleled that of the area's mother country. A period of intense agricultural activity was followed by maritime prosperity and then industrialization, which formed the backbone of the economy through the 19C and into the 20C. After World War II the region fell into an economic slump, due to the movement of many of its factories to the South. As a result New England turned to new, diversified, high-value industries, such as electronics, as its principal sources of revenue.

Industry

In the 19C profits accumulated from trade, shipping and whaling, and the influx of immigrants from Europe and Canada, which provided the large labor force needed for industrialization, fostered New England's growth into one of the world's leading manufacturing centers.

The Mill Towns – The region's many waterways compensated for the lack of raw materials and fuel by providing the power necessary to operate factory machinery. Mill towns, supporting factories that specialized in a single product, sprung up on the banks of rivers and streams. Textiles and leather goods were made in Massachusetts and New Hampshire, precision products such as clocks and firearms were manufactured in Connecticut, and machine tools were produced in Vermont. The large manufacturing centers in the Merrimack Valley—**Lowell**, Lawrence and **Manchester**—developed into world leaders in textile production. Strings of brick factories, dwellings and stores still dominate these cities.

During the 20C most of these industries moved south to the Sun Belt, but the region remained a leader in the manufacture of woolen cloth. The production of machine tools and fabricated metals has now replaced textiles, and the shoe industry is important in New Hampshire and Maine.

The New Industries – The rebirth of New England after World War II was linked to the development of its research-oriented industries, which could draw on the region's excellent educational institutions and highly trained personnel. These new industries, located essentially in the Boston area (on Route 128), in southern New Hampshire and in HARTFORD, contributed to advances made in space and computer technology and electronics. Their existence gave rise to the production of high-value goods, such as information systems, precision instruments and electronic components, and provided an increasing number of jobs. **Boston**, known for its medical research firms, is also home to producers of medical instruments and artificial organs.

Agriculture

Despite the poor soil and rocky, hilly terrain, subsistence farming was an important activity until the mid-19C. In the spring settlers cleared land to ready it for planting. The mounds of rock they removed from the soil were used to build the low stone walls that appear to ramble aimlessly through the woods. Farming reached a peak in New England between 1830 and 1880 with 60 percent of the region under cultivation. After 1880 the opening of the fertile plains south of the Great Lakes drew farmers westward. They abandoned their farms, and the forests gradually reclaimed the land. Today only six percent of the surface of New England continues to be devoted to agriculture, while 70 percent of the region's land (90 percent in Maine and 80 percent in New Hampshire) remains covered with woodlands. Despite this fact, certain areas have been successful in cultivating single-crop specialties.

Dairy and Poultry Farming – The major portion of income from agriculture is provided by dairy and poultry farming. The region's dairy farms supply milk products to the sprawling urban areas of southern New England. Dairy farms, well suited to the terrain, predominate in Vermont, where large red barns with their shiny aluminum silos dominate the landscape.

Poultry farming is practiced throughout the region. Connecticut and Rhode Island focus on raising chickens. In fact, Rhode Island is famous for raising a breed of chicken called the Rhode Island Red. Vermont's turkey farms—their buildings well lit, temperature-controlled and equipped with modern machinery—are busiest during the holiday seasons, particularly around Thanksgiving.

Specialty Crops – Shade-grown **tobacco** is raised in the fertile Connecticut River Valley. Firm and broad-leafed, this tobacco, grown beneath a layer of netting and hung in large sheds to dry, is used as the outer wrapping of cigars. Fruit is cultivated in many areas: apple, peach and pear orchards extend along the banks of LAKE CHAMPLAIN and abound on the sunny slopes of New Hampshire, in the Connecticut and Nashua Valleys and in Rhode Island. Maine leads all other states in production of **blueberries**, and the sandy bogs on CAPE COD and in nearby areas yield the nation's largest crop of **cranberries**, the small, red berries traditionally served as part of the Thanksgiving Day feast.

Maine's other specialty crop is potatoes, grown in the fertile soil of Aroostook County. The state's potato industry ranks third in size after Idaho's and Washington's.
In the fall, visitors to rural New England can purchase locally raised **pumpkins**, **gourds** and **Indian corn** at roadside stands.

Forests – Despite the enormous area that they cover, New England's deciduous and coniferous forests are not significant as sources of income because of large-scale deforestation of the region throughout the 19C. Today vast tracts of land are under federal and state protection. Only the commercial timberlands owned by the large paper companies in northern Maine and New Hampshire constitute important sources of revenue. A major portion of the timber harvested is processed into wood pulp for the mills in

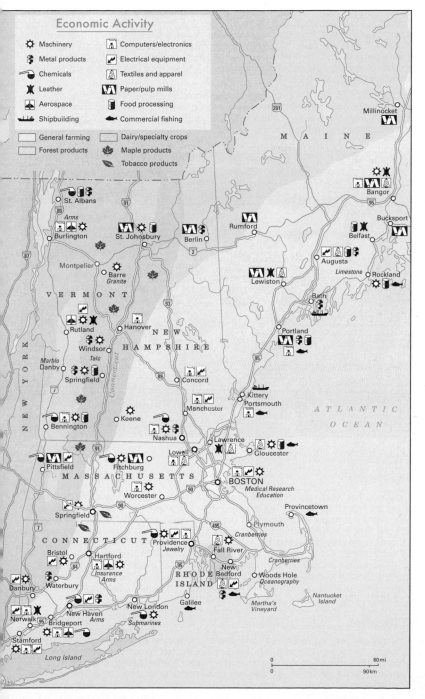

Maine (Millinocket, **Bucksport**, Woodland, Rumford) and New Hampshire (Berlin), with Maine's factories ranking among the world's leading paper producers. Other plants and mills transform timber into a variety of wood products, including lumber, veneer, furniture and boxes. The production of **maple syrup** is a traditional springtime activity in Vermont, New Hampshire and Maine.

Fishing

As early as the 15C, European fishermen were drawn to the rich fishing grounds off the coast of New England. These shallow, sandy banks (such as George's Bank), extending 1,500mi east to west off Cape Cod, teemed with fish. The fishing industry was so vital to New England that fishermen were exempt from military service, and Massachusetts Bay Colony adopted the cod as its symbol.

Commercial fishing has been especially important to the ports of GLOUCESTER, NEW BEDFORD and Boston. Modern techniques of filleting, freezing and packaging fish, and larger, more efficient vessels have made New England a leader in the packaged and frozen seafood industry. However, the region's fishing industry has seen dramatic curtailment over the past three decades, stemming from overfishing (particularly of cod, flounder, tuna and haddock), pollution and insufficient conservation. More recently, stringent federal regulations have been proposed to reduce stock depletion.

Lobstering ranks as an activity approaching an art in Maine, where it is practiced by thousands of Down East lobstermen, who can often be observed in a variety of craft, checking their traps in the offshore waters. Maine lobster is a delicacy that is available in markets across the nation.

John Lazenby/f/STOP PICTURES

Unloading Lobster

Insurance

Insurance has been an important business in New England since the 19C, when investors offered to underwrite the risks involved in international shipping. Every boat that sailed out of port represented a gamble; it could return with valuable cargo, or it could sink, eliminating forever all hopes of profit. With the decline of sea trade, the insurance industry expanded to include losses due to fire, and the center of the industry shifted inland. Hartford, Connecticut, a national insurance center, is the seat of a substantial number of insurance companies. The modern office towers built in Boston to serve as headquarters of the John Hancock and Prudential insurance companies are the tallest structures in New England, symbolizing the importance of this industry to the economy.

Education

Traditionally renowned as a national center of culture and learning, New England is home to four prestigious Ivy League universities (Harvard, Yale, Brown and Dartmouth) and two choice preparatory schools (Phillips Exeter Academy in Exeter, New Hampshire, and Phillips Academy in Andover, Massachusetts). The concentration of schools, academies and some 258 institutions of higher learning in the six-state area makes education a significant contributor to the economy. Small businesses in cities (**Worcester, New Haven, Providence**), towns (**Middlebury, Hanover, Brunswick, Amherst**) and regions (**Pioneer Valley, Greater Boston**) depend on the revenue generated by the schools within their borders. In Massachusetts, where education is a major source of income, the state's 80 private colleges alone have generated $10 billion in revenue.

Tourism

Tourism ranks with manufacturing as one of New England's major industries. Mountain and seaside resorts in New England have been welcoming visitors for over a century, and with the growing popularity of winter sports since the 1940s, the region has developed into a year-round vacation area. Fine handicrafts, fashioned by artisans working in New Hampshire, Vermont and along the coast, abound throughout New England. Their sale depends to a great extent on tourists.

New England and the Sea

New England has been closely related to the sea ever since the colonists turned from the rocky soil to the offshore waters for their food. At first the colonists erected weirs, similar to those used to this day by the Indians in Maine to snare fish near the shore. Not until the mid-17C did Yankee vessels sail in large numbers to the Grand Banks, the fishing grounds off the southern coast of Newfoundland, which teemed with cod, haddock and pollack. The Sacred Cod, hanging in the Massachusetts State House in BOSTON, symbolizes the important role played by the cod fisheries in the history of Massachusetts. New England's fisheries became the backbone of the region's trade with Europe, and boatyards sprang up along the coast from Connecticut to Maine to construct fishing and cargo vessels.

Fisheries, trade and shipbuilding prospered, reaching their zenith in the mid-19C. The south (Connecticut, Rhode Island and southeastern Massachusetts) was home to the Yankee whaling fleet; ports along the northern coast of Massachusetts and New Hampshire led the trade with the Orient (the China trade) and the shipbuilding industry. With its protected inlets and thick forests, the Maine coast focused on wooden shipbuilding. Between 1830 and 1860, nearly one-third of the boats launched in the US were built in Maine.

Small coastal villages grew into sophisticated urban centers, as merchants, shipmasters and sea captains accumulated great wealth and built the handsome Federal and Greek Revival homes that still stand in SALEM, NANTUCKET, PORTSMOUTH, NEWBURYPORT, NEW BEDFORD, PROVIDENCE and other seaport cities.

Several large museums preserve New England's seafaring past. MYSTIC SEAPORT and the whaling museums in New Bedford, Nantucket and Sharon recall the Yankee whaling tradition. In Salem the PEABODY ESSEX MUSEUM presents the story of New England's trade with the Orient, and the MAINE MARITIME MUSEUM and the PENOBSCOT MARINE MUSEUM portray the history of shipbuilding in Maine.

Whaling

During the 19C whale oil was used to light homes and streets across America and Europe. New Bedford and Nantucket, leading whaling centers, were busy day and night with vessels arriving, departing or preparing for whaling voyages. Herman Melville's novel *Moby Dick* (1851) vividly re-creates New England's whaling days.

A Prized Catch – Since history has been recorded, man has been fascinated by this warm-blooded, air-breathing mammal that roams the world's oceans. The order Cetacea, to which all whales belong, includes the largest animal that has ever lived, the blue whale. A mature blue whale can attain a length of 100ft and weigh up to 150 tons. Whales can be divided into two groups: toothed and toothless (baleen).

Toothed whales are predators that feed on fish. Averaging 63 tons, the **sperm whale** was the species on which New England's whaling industry depended. This animal was hunted in large numbers because it was a source of rare products. Spermaceti, a solid waxy substance, was used to make fragrant candles. Obtained in liquid form from a cavity in the whale's head, sperm oil provided fuel for oil-burning lamps. One male sperm whale yielded more than 1,800 gallons of oil. Ambergris, a substance found in the intestines of the whale, was used commercially in the manufacture of perfumes.

Baleen whales, such as the **right whale** (considered the "right whale to hunt" since it floated when it was dead) live on plankton sifted out of

Scrimshaw - Whale's Tooth

Courtesy Mystic Seaport Museum

27

the sea by their long, comb-like sheets of baleen, a horny material that hangs from the roof of the animal's mouth. The plastic of the 19C, flexible baleen furnished the raw material for corset and umbrella stays, buggy whips and a variety of other products.

A Meteoric Industry – Indians were hunting whales long before the first settlements were established. The colonists learned how to hunt inshore whales by observing the Indians. They built tall watchtowers and set up large black cauldrons, called try-pots, in which the whale fat was melted down, on the beaches. In the 18C the discovery of sperm whales in deep ocean waters led to the construction of larger vessels that were outfitted for long ocean voyages. By 1730 Yankee whalemen had moved the tryworks from the beaches to the decks of whaling vessels so they could process whales at sea.

In the late 18C Nantucket boasted a fleet of 150 whaling vessels; in its heyday, New Bedford was the home port of nearly 400. NEW LONDON, PROVINCETOWN, Fairhaven, MYSTIC, STONINGTON and EDGARTOWN also launched fleets. Shipyards turned out sturdier ocean-going vessels, factories manufactured spermaceti candles, tons of baleen were dried in the fields and thousands of barrels of whale oil were stored along the wharves. Whale ships built, owned and commandeered in New England sailed the oceans from Greenland to the North Pacific, from the Azores to Brazil, and from Polynesia to Japan. Many languages could be heard as seamen from international ports-of-call walked the streets of New England's waterfront districts.

The decline of the whaling industry in New England was precipitated by the discovery of petroleum in Pennsylvania in 1859 and the loss of nearly half of New England's whaling fleet during the Civil War years. In 1861 the Union Navy purchased 39 whale ships to form the "Stone Fleet," a group of vessels that were loaded with blocks of granite and sunk in the harbors of Savannah, Georgia, and Charleston, South Carolina, to prevent blockade runners from entering those channels. The Confederate ship *Shenandoah* destroyed an additional 21 whaling vessels in the north Pacific Ocean in 1865. After the war New England sent out fewer and fewer whalers. In 1971, whale hunting was finally outlawed in the US.

Maritime Commerce

New England's maritime commerce with Africa, Europe and the West Indies brought prosperity to many of its coastal ports in the early 18C, but not until after the Revolution, when Americans were free to trade with the Orient, did Boston, Providence, Portsmouth, Salem and other cities develop into rich centers of the China trade.

China Trade – Boats sailing to the Far East rounded Cape Horn, then generally made detours to ports along the way to obtain returns—goods that could be traded in China for silk, porcelain and tea. Furs were acquired along the northwest Pacific coast, sandalwood from the Sandwich Islands, and the delicacy *bêche-de-mer* (sea grub) from the Polynesian Islands. Later, when opium replaced furs as returns, boats called at ports in India and Turkey to barter for the illicit drug before continuing to China.

Other exotic products obtained along the route were pepper purchased in Sumatra, sugar and coffee from Java, cotton from Bombay and Madras, ivory from Zanzibar, spices from Indonesia and gum arabic from Oman.

Until 1842 **Canton** was the only Chinese port open to foreign trade. Vessels anchored about 10 miles outside the city at **Whampoa Reach**. Several weeks or even months could be spent visiting shops and factories and bartering with Chinese merchants before the foreign vessel, filled with a cargo of luxury items, set sail for home.

The museums and historical houses of New England exhibit countless examples of Chinese decorative arts and furnishings brought back to America from the Orient during the years of the China trade.

Ice: A Unique New England Industry – The ice trade developed in the 19C when ice was harvested north of Boston and in Maine, and shipped to the southern states, the West Indies and as far away as Calcutta to be used for refrigeration. Ice was harvested in the winter, when the rivers, lakes and ponds were frozen over. Snow was cleared with the aid of oxen or horses. The ice field, marked off into squares, was cut into blocks weighing up to 200lbs each. Packed in sawdust and stored in nearby ice-houses until the first thaw, the ice was then transported by boat to its destination. Boats with specially constructed airtight hulls were used to prevent the ice from melting. The ice business prospered until the introduction of mechanical refrigeration in the late 19C.

Shipbuilding

The wooden sailing vessel has been the basis of New England's shipbuilding tradition since 1607, when the pinnace *Virginia* was built by the short-lived Popham colony on the banks of the Kennebec River in Maine.

Early Days – As the colonists established their first settlements, shipyards began to dot the coast. At first they built small, one-masted ketches and fishing sloops, followed in the early 18C by two- and three-masted schooners capable of crossing the Atlantic. The schooner enjoyed a long and glamorous career in the waters off the New

England coast. When English dominance of American trade led to widespread smuggling by the colonists, it was the schooner, with its simple rigging, ease-of-handling, and ability to evade British revenue ships, that carried many an illicit cargo safely into port. During the American Revolution, armed, privately owned schooners (privateers) were authorized by the Continental Congress to capture enemy vessels. The schooner remained in service as a cargo carrier until the end of World War I.

Age of the Clipper Ship – With the opening of Chinese ports in the 1840s, Americans clamored for Chinese goods. Knowing that American customers would pay high prices for the freshest teas from the Orient, shrewd shippers demanded faster vessels to transport this perishable commodity in the shortest possible time. The clipper—derived from the word *clipper*, which was used to describe any person or thing that traveled quickly—was designed to meet their needs. Between the mid-1840s and the mid-1850s, these three-masted vessels, with their lean hulls, narrow bows and acres of canvas sails, became famous for the great speeds they could attain. During the California Gold Rush, clippers—with names such as *Lightning, Flying Cloud* and *Eagle Wing*—carried miners and supplies from the Atlantic coast, around Cape Horn, to San Francisco, and sailed the long ocean routes to the Orient.

The major boatyards working to turn out these ships were located in New York, BOSTON, and BATH, Maine, and the master designer was **Donald McKay** of East Boston. Of the approximately 100 vessels that made the voyage around Cape Horn in less than four months, 19 of them, including the *Flying Cloud*, were built by McKay. The first ship to round the Cape to San Francisco in under 90 days, the *Flying Cloud* set a record of 89 days on her maiden voyage in 1851, and repeated it three years later. Her record has never been surpassed by a ship under sail.

Last Sailing Ships – From the 1850s to the early 1900s, the ports of Maine specialized in the production of commercial wooden sailing vessels: the **down-easter** and the **great schooner**. The down-easter, a three-masted square-rigger, had the long, clean lines of a clipper, and could attain comparable speeds. Unlike the clipper, the down-easter had a large, deep hull that offered greater carrying space and made it a more profitable means of transporting cargo.

The down-easters and two- and three-masted schooners were used in shipping until the 1880s, when boat builders discovered that four-masted schooners, though larger, cost little more to operate. The construction of the great schooners—four-, five- and six-masted vessels—followed. These ships hauled large bulk cargoes (coal, lumber, granite, grain) from the East Coast, around Cape Horn and up to the West Coast. Striving to compete with the steamboat, Maine shipyards turned to the production of a small fleet of steel four-, five- and six-masters. The days of sail were numbered, however; the efficient, regularly scheduled steamer triumphed.

Population

New England's population of 13 million inhabitants is unevenly distributed; the majority live in the southern half of the region, where the largest cities (BOSTON, WORCESTER, PROVIDENCE, SPRINGFIELD, HARTFORD and NEW HAVEN) are found. The large waves of immigrants who arrived in the 19C brought with them a diversity of cultures that is still reflected in the ethnic character of the population today.

The Many Faces of New England – The **Indians** of the Algonquin Nation were the first to inhabit the region. They were woodland Indians, who farmed, hunted, fished and camped along the coast. Their numbers had already been greatly reduced by disease and tribal warfare when the Europeans settled here in the 17C. The largest group, the **Narragansett** tribe of Rhode Island, was virtually wiped out by the English colonists in the Great Swamp Fight during King Philip's War. Similarly the **Pequot** tribe of Connecticut was decimated by colonists and enemy tribes in the Pequot War of 1637. Today the Mashantucket Pequot Indians operate a number of successful enterprises near MYSTIC. Present-day descendants of the **Passamaquoddy** and **Penobscot** tribes live on reservations at Pleasant Point and Old Town in Maine. The circular traps, or weirs, that they constructed offshore to trap fish are visible as you drive along the north coast of Maine. Members of the **Wampanoag** tribe make their home on CAPE COD and MARTHA'S VINEYARD.

Descendants of the 17C and 18C Puritan settlers dominated New England's population until the mid-19C. Hard work, frugality and "Yankee ingenuity"—the talent for making the best of any situation—characterized these early New Englanders, some of whom amassed great fortunes in trade and shipping, and later in industry and finance. The population remained basically homogeneous until the 1840s, when the potato famine in Ireland caused thousands of **Irish** to emigrate to New England, where they found work in the mills. The **Italians** followed in the 1870s, and at the end of the 19C **French Canadians**, attracted by jobs in the region's factories, began to settle here. Communities of **Portuguese** fishermen from the Azores developed in coastal ports such as Gloucester, PROVINCETOWN and QUINCY, while successive waves of immigrants brought **Swedes, Russians** and other **Eastern Europeans** to the cities and factory towns. As Boston's **African-American** community vacated the North End for Beacon Hill, the Irish, followed by the Jews and eventually the Italians, made the North End their home. Each ethnic group formed its own cohesive neighborhood, where the unity of language, culture and religion drew them together. Irish, Italians and Jews tended to settle in or near the large cities, while the Portuguese continue to reside in the coastal areas, maintaining traditions, such as the celebration of the blessing of the fleet *(see Calendar of Events)*. French names are common in New Hampshire, Maine and Vermont, where French Canadians form a significant part of the population. People of Swedish, Russian and Eastern European extraction chose to live in Maine and the rural areas. The majority of the region's black and **Hispanic** populations reside in southern New England.

Architecture

New England's identity is justifiably architectural: it is indeed the classic calendar image of white-spired churches, trim red barns and weather-beaten farmhouses, well preserved by a cold climate and fierce pride in local history. Best known for its Colonial architecture, the region nevertheless retains a rich heritage of building traditions from all periods, ranging from practical Indian dwellings to the magnificent seaside estates of the Gilded Age and the visually striking high rises of Postmodernism. In the 20C New England's prestigious universities attracted such leading modernists as Walter Gropius, Le Corbusier, Eero Saarinen, Philip Johnson and I.M. Pei who, in turn, reshaped the architectural tenor of such cities as BOSTON, CAMBRIDGE and NEW HAVEN and placed New England in the forefront of contemporary design.

Native American – The traditional Algonquin dwelling was not the familiar tepee of the Great Plains but the **wigwam**, a domed or conical hut made of bent saplings covered with reed mats or bark. Quick and easy to build, these snug shelters were adopted as temporary housing by the first Massachusetts colonists until they could construct timber-framed homes. Wigwams built in the traditional manner may be seen at Salem's Pioneer Village and at the Institute for American Indian Studies in LITCHFIELD HILLS.

Early Colonial – The prevailing early-Colonial dwelling was the two-story post-and-beam house, a post-Medieval form characterized by a steeply pitched roof originally designed to support thatch. Several examples dating from about 1660 to 1720 still exist in Connecticut (Buttolph-Williams House in WETHERSFIELD) and in the early Massachusetts Bay town of IPSWICH (Parson Capen House) and at Plimoth Plantation in PLYMOUTH. Settlers of these areas came almost exclusively from East Anglia, a region in southeast England where wood construction was common. Finding an unlimited timber supply in the new country, they logically continued a building technique that was already familiar. The typical house plan comprised two large, multipurpose rooms with exposed beams and a massive center chimney hugged by a narrow stairway leading to chambers above. Clad in shingles or clapboard siding, the exterior featured small casement windows with diamond-shaped glass panes imported from England. Often intersecting gables provided more space to the second story (Iron Works House *p 149*), which might have a slight overhang, or jetty, trimmed with decorative pendants (Stanley-Whitman House *p 46*). When the steep roof extends almost to the ground over a rear kitchen lean-to, the house is known as a **saltbox** (Fairbanks House *p 152*). Built low to brace against shoreline winds, the smaller, one-and-a-half-story **Cape Cod cottage**, another common early-Colonial house type, features a pitched or bowed roof.

Early Colonial

The heavy hand-hewn framing pieces used in the construction of houses were numbered (Roman numerals can still be spotted on attic rafters). The pieces, usually of pine or oak, were fitted on the ground and then lifted into place in an all-hands effort called a "raising." By court decree all 17C New England villages were laid out according to a similar plan, with the houses set around a parklike central **green**, or common, to provide protection against Indians and assure close proximity to the **meetinghouse**, the largest building in a settlement. A deliberate departure from the traditional Anglican church, the Puritan meetinghouse was an original architectural form—a square wooden structure with a hipped roof and crowning belfry (Old Ship Church in HINGHAM). It served both as church and town hall, reflecting the close ties between politics and religion in the 17C.

Georgian – This term generally refers to an English architectural style developed by such noted architects as Christopher Wren and James Gibbs and popularized in America from about 1720 until the Revolution (during the reigns of Kings George II and III) largely through pattern books and British-trained builders. The Georgian style was inspired by the new fashion for Italian Renaissance architecture—especially that of Andrea Palladio. Based primarily on the design principles of ancient Rome, this style incorporated the Classical orders, especially Doric, Ionic and Corinthian.

Georgian

Dignified and formal, the high-style Georgian house proved ideally suited to the tastes of a growing mercantile class. Mansions in wood, stone or brick soon appeared in every major port city. Crowned by a pitched, hipped or gambrel roof, the house featured a symmetrical facade accentuated with even rows of double-hung windows. Often a central projecting pavilion front with a Palladian window and a pedimented portico graced the entryway. Heavy quoins (stone or wood blocks) typically marked the corners, and the elaborate front door was topped by a round-arched fanlight and a sculptural pediment.

A central-hall plan with end chimneys accommodated larger rooms (now with specific uses such as dining and music), robust wood carving and plaster decoration, and colorful paint treatments. In rural farm towns the Georgian house frequently retained the old center-chimney plan but boasted ornate exterior features, such as the heavy swan's-neck door pediments used in the Connecticut River Valley (DEERFIELD). Several Georgian public buildings were designed by **Peter Harrison** (1716-75), perhaps America's most important colonial architect. Harrison's Redwood Library in NEWPORT is based on a Roman temple. His Touro Synagogue, also in Newport, and King's Chapel in Boston are notable for their interior paneling.

During this period many New England churches gained their familiar front towers and steeples, often adapted from the published designs of Wren (Trinity Church *p 257*) or Gibbs (First Baptist Church in America *p 263*).

Federal – Popular from about 1780 to 1820, this British Neoclassical style, sometimes called Adam style, was first adopted in America by an affluent merchant class, primarily Federalists who retained close trade ties to England even after the Revolution. Bostonian **Charles Bulfinch** (1763-1844) was New England's best-known Federal-period architect, responsible for Beacon Hill's Massachusetts State House and Harrison Gray Otis House. Another proponent of the Federal style, **Samuel McIntire** (1757-1811) designed several public buildings and houses in SALEM. His Gardener-Pingree House is typical of the 19C seaport town's many elegant three-story Federal houses built of narrow, butter-smooth bricks with low, hipped roofs crowned by handsome cornice-line balustrades.

Federal

Like its Georgian counterpart, the high-style Federal mansion, often with bowed or rounded walls (Gore Place *p 149*) was symmetrical, and its central door was topped by a Palladian window (Harrison Gray Otis House in Boston). But the overall appearance was far lighter and more conservative, with proportions elongated, exterior decoration reduced and fanlights flattened from half-rounds into ellipses.

The style is most notable for its refined interior decor, influenced by the work of British architect **Robert Adam**. Oval and round rooms were introduced, along with graceful freestanding staircases and exquisitely decorated fireplace mantels and surrounds, carved with delicate garlands, urns, wheat sheaves and other classical motifs inspired by recent discoveries at Pompeii and Herculaneum. Extremely popular, Federal-style design eventually spread to even the most modest of farm- and village houses and churches throughout New England (look for the telltale elliptical front-door fanlight).

Greek Revival – Coinciding with several popular English books on Greek archaeology, the Greek Revival style came to America via England and was popular here from about 1820 to 1845. While the Georgian and Federal styles were based on Roman prototypes, the new architectural mode adhered to ancient Greek orders and design principles, notable for squarer proportions, a more monumental scale and less surface ornament. Imitative of Greek temples, buildings in the style were almost always white and usually featured the so-called "temple front." This two-story portico with Doric, Ionic or Corinthian columns supported an unbroken triangular pediment at the roof line.

Among the educated elite the Greek Revival style represented a symbolic link between the republic of ancient Greece and the new American nation. It was adopted for many impressive public buildings, including marble or granite courthouses, banks, libraries (Providence's Athenaeum), churches (Church of the Presidents *p 203*) and temples of

Greek Revival

trade (Providence's Arcade), as well as for domestic architecture. Elegant Greek Revival-styled mansions appeared in affluent towns and seaports (Whale Oil Row *p 68*).

Among the major designers of the period were **Alexander Parris** (Quincy Market in Boston) and **Robert Mills** (Custom House *p 193*.) **Asher Benjamin**, who wrote some of the most influential builder's handbooks in America, designed many New England churches (Boston's Old West Church) and fine Bostonian homes (Nos. 54-55 Beacon St.). Through handbooks such as his, the style was also adopted for simple clapboard farm- and village houses throughout the region. On more modest farmhouses the triangular roof gable was turned to face front and the corner boards suggested the columns.

19C Vernacular – A distinctive feature of rural New England is the **covered bridge** (WEST CORNWALL and WINDSOR). In 1820 noted New Haven architect Ithiel Town (Center and Trinity Churches in NEW HAVEN) patented the **lattice truss**, the interwoven framework visible on the inside of the bridge. The roof, of pine or spruce, was designed to protect the structural elements from harsh weather. The **connected farm**, a complex of attached houses, barns and animal sheds prevalent in northern New England in the mid-19C, developed as old outbuildings were moved from farm property and added to the main residence. The attached buildings commonly housed cottage industries such as canning and weaving, which were important supplements to farm income.

Along the coast, 19C **lighthouses** mark harbor entrances and dangerous shoals. These structures originally included a tower and beacon, first lit with oil lamps and parabolic reflectors, as well as housing for the keeper, who was often a US customs agent. The keeper's role has now been lost to automation. Occupying dramatic sites, some decommissioned 19C lighthouses have been converted to private homes, but many lights can be visited by the public (Sheffield Island in NORWALK; Owl's Head in ROCKLAND).

Still visible in many industrial towns are 19C **textile mills**, originally powered by water turbine (steam power became common in the 1850s). Manned largely by cheap immigrant labor, mills were designed as self-contained complexes and typically included railroads, parks, canals, churches and employee housing. Punctuated by rhythmic rows of windows and an occasional clock tower or smokestack, these granite- or brick-walled buildings, usually five or more stories, can stretch for miles along a riverfront. Some complexes now contain museums (the National Historic Park in LOWELL); others have been converted to house small business and retail outlets (Lowell's Amoskeag Manufacturing Complex).

Victorian Eclecticism – During the Victorian era (1837-1901), classical design was abandoned in favor of a broad range of styles, many inspired by the dark, romantic architecture of Medieval Europe. Pointed-arch windows, steeply pointed gables and gingerbread cornice boards are hallmarks of the picturesque **Gothic Revival** style (Kingscote *p 255*) also seen in board-and-batten **Carpenter's Gothic** villas and cottages (Roseland Cottage *p 73*). Other Victorian-era styles include **Italianate** (square towers, flat or low-pitched roof and broad porch; Victoria Mansion *p 102*); **Second Empire** (mansard roof, ornate cornice and round dormers; Boston's Old City Hall); and **Queen Anne** (turrets, spindlework, asymmetrical porches, bay windows and gingerbread trim; Oak Bluffs (MARTHA'S VINEYARD). In the early 1870s Boston architect **Henry Hobson Richardson** developed Romanesque Revival (also known as Richardsonian Romanesque), a distinctly American style rooted in the Medieval architecture of France and Spain. His masterpiece, Trinity Church in Boston, incorporates the characteristic squat columns, round arches and heavy, rough-cut stone. Favored for seaside resorts were the **Shingle** style (dark wood shingles, towers and piazzas, steeply pitched roofline and asymmetrical facade; Newport's Hammersmith Farm and Casino and **Stick** style (gabled roof, rustic woodwork with diagonal bands, contrasting paint colors, decoratively shaped shingles; Newport's Art Museum and Mark Twain House in HARTFORD).

Turn of the Century – Late in the 19C architects trained in the academic principles of the prestigious École des Beaux-Arts in Paris rejected the eccentric Victorian styles in favor of "correct" interpretations

Italianate

of historic European architecture, notably French Baroque, English Neoclassicism and Italian Renaissance (Renaissance Revival). Typical of the highly decorative **Beaux-Arts** style are great estates such as Newport's the Breakers and Marble House by the fashionable society designer **Richard Morris Hunt**, and grandiose public buildings (Boston Public Library). Both were modeled on Italian Renaissance palaces. Beaux-Arts buildings are typically of stone (marble or granite) and feature ornate statuary, heavy facade ornamentation and rows of paired columns alternating with arched windows.

Developing at the same time was the **Colonial Revival** style, which drew on America's own Colonial architecture, reinterpreted on a larger scale. A Palladian window, classical columns, swan's-neck pediments and a large entry portico are typical features. Promoted by such pretigious architectural firms as **McKim, Mead and White** (Rhode Island State House), the style was used primarily for neo-Georgian town houses and country estates from about 1900 to 1920 (North and South Streets in LITCHFIELD).

Contemporary Architecture – New England attracted many of the European architects who brought the **International style** to America in the 1930s, including **Walter Gropius** (1883-1969), founder of the German design school known as the **Bauhaus**. Representative of **early Modernism**, which rejected ornament and historical references and embraced machine-age technology and materials, is the 1938 Gropius House *(p 172)*, a streamlined cubic design incorporating the then-new materials of glass block, acoustical plaster and chrome. Among other innovative modernist works is **Eero Saarinen's** 1955 M.I.T. Chapel in CAMBRIDGE. Its brick cylindrical shape presents a distinct contrast to the chaste white wooden church of the New England green. The heir of early Modernism was the so-called **glass box** design, ubiquitous in the 1960s in the construction of multistoried urban apartments and public buildings. An unusual example is the 1963 Beinecke Library at Yale University by **Gordon Bunshaft** of **Skidmore, Owings and Merrill**, designed with self-supporting walls of translucent marble. Many glass boxes appeared in New Haven, Boston and other New England cities during periods of widespread urban redevelopment that resulted in the demolition of older buildings. In concert with the growing preservation movement of the last two decades, innovative design programs have, however, helped save endangered structures and rehabilitate the blighted market and waterfront districts in such cities as Boston, Salem, NEWBURYPORT, NORWALK and BURLINGTON.

Since the early 1970s innovators Robert Venturi, Robert Stern, Philip Johnson and others have developed **Postmodernism**, a movement promoting a deliberate return to ornament. Familiar historical motifs such as the classical pediment are often playfully exaggerated, used as the dominant crowning element of a building, for example. The Palladian window is simplified, even caricatured, or the classical column is reduced to a plain shaft, topped by a ball rather than a traditional capital. Unexpected exterior color combinations are another feature. In recent years New England campuses and city skylines, notably Boston (222 Berkeley Street and 500 Boylston Street), Providence and Hartford, have become national showcases for buildings in the style, which emphasizes scale, compatible materials and the relationship of a building to its neighbors.

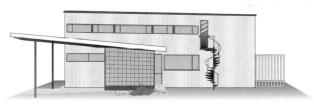

International Style

Sculpture

Sculpture consisted predominantly of folk art—shop and trade signs, weather vanes, figureheads—until the 19C, when American sculptors, studying in Italy and at the Ecole des Beaux-Arts in Paris, were exposed to the grandeur of classical sculpture. New Hampshire-born **Daniel Chester French** (1850-1931) and **Augustus Saint-Gaudens** (1848-1907), who lived his later years in New Hampshire, trained abroad and exerted a strong influence on American sculpture from the period following the Civil War until the early 20C. Each obtained numerous public commissions for war memorials and statues during his lifetime. French became known early in his career for his statue the *Minute Man* (Concord, MA), while the monumental seated *Lincoln* (Lincoln Memorial in Washington, DC) is recognized as his most impressive achievement. Saint-Gaudens executed delicate, bas-relief portrait plaques and monumental sculptures, such as the Shaw Memorial in Boston, for which he is best remembered.

Although both spent much of their careers in Italy, Boston native **Horatio Greenough** (1805-52) and Vermont-born **Hiram Powers** (1805-73) aided significantly in establishing Neoclassicism in American sculpture. Powers' *The Greek Slave* (1843) was the most popular sculpture of its time both in the US and in Europe.

John Rogers (1829-1904) of Salem studied in Rome, though briefly. Influenced by the American scene, Rogers modeled small sculptured clay groups depicting events of historical and topical interest *(The Slave Auction)* and everyday living *(Checkers at the Farm)*. His 80 "Rogers groups" as they were known were reproduced by the thousands and gained immediate popularity. Born in Cambridge, Massachusetts **Anna Hyatt Huntington** (1876-1973) studied in Boston with **Henry Hudson Kitson**, whose former studio is located in the Berkshires. Her first exhibition, held at the Boston Arts Club, showcased over 40 sculptures of animals. Working in Europe as well as in the US, Huntington garnered many prestigious awards for her sculpture. She is known primarily for the anatomical precision of her life-size animal and human figures.

In more recent times, award-winning sculptor **Louise Nevelson** (b. 1900), who was born in Russia, grew up in Rockland, Maine. After studying in New York City and Munich, she traveled in Central America; her early sculptures reveal the influence of that country's sculpture in her characteristic blockish, interlocking pieces. By the mid-1950s, she had developed the style for which she is best known: open boxes of monochromatically painted wood (often black, sometimes white), stacked to form a freestanding wall. Her work may be seen at the Farnsworth Art Museum in Rockland. Well-known sculptors **Sol Lewitt** (b. 1928) and **Nancy Graves** (b. 1940) were born in New England (Hartford, Connecticut and Pittsfield, Massachusetts respectively).

Among other New England locations, sculptural works (particularly contemporary sculpture) are on view at the DeCordova Sculpture Park in Lincoln, Massachusetts and the sculpture garden at the Aldrich Museum of Contemporary Art in Ridgefield, Connecticut, as well as on the campuses of Yale University and Massachusetts Institute of Technology.

Furniture

American furnishings were influenced from colonial days through the 19C by European, and particularly English, designs. Carpenters in rural villages copied the pieces the colonists had brought with them across the ocean, or reproduced from memory the furniture they had known in England. Early American cabinetmakers turned to imported style manuals as guides to making contemporary furniture.

Pilgrim – Furniture made between 1620 and 1690—tables, chairs, Bible boxes and chests—is heavy and rectilinear, reflecting the Medieval influences of the English Tudor and Jacobean styles. Oak is the principal wood used. The Connecticut-made Hadley, Guilford and Sunflower chests ornamented with carved and painted floral designs or geometric motifs are characteristic of this period.

William and Mary – This style was in vogue from 1689 to 1702 during the reign of William of Orange and his wife, Mary. The Flemish influence and contact with the Orient introduced such techniques as japanning (floral or scenic designs on lacquered wood surfaces) and turning (wooden pieces shaped on a lathe). Japanned highboys, chests with bold turnings, and chairs with caned or leather backs were popular during these years.

William and Mary

Queen Anne – Curved lines, such as the gracefully shaped cabriole leg, are a stylistic feature of furniture made between 1720 and 1750. Maple, walnut and cherry are the woods typically used; decoration is minimal. A Queen Anne chair is distinguished by its cabriole legs and vase-shaped back splat.

Queen Anne

The **Windsor chair**, unrelated to the Queen Anne style, was imported from England in the early 18C and remains popular in America. The Windsor is defined by its spindles inserted between a plank seat and curved upper railing. The comb back, bow back and writing table are variations of the original low-back Windsor.

Chippendale – London cabinetmaker Thomas Chippendale borrowed elements of French rococo and Chinese art in creating the wide range of furniture forms illustrated in his design manuals. Pieces from 1750 to 1785 are generally fashioned of mahogany, with curved legs (ending in the ball-and-claw foot) and chair backs pierced with lacy fretwork. Adornment consists of rich carving, elaborate brasses and finials. The **Goddard and Townsend** families of Newport were among the most celebrated cabinetmakers working in this style. Their blockfront case pieces, carved with a shell motif, are adaptations of Chippendale's designs.

Windsor

Federal – Inspired by British architect **Robert Adam** and English cabinetmakers **George Hepplewhite** and **Thomas Sheraton**, the style that won favor from 1785 to 1815 is defined by light, straight lines and refined decoration: veneers, inlay and marquetry in contrasting woods. The square, tapered leg—fluted, reeded or ending in a spade foot— is common. Chair backs in the Hepplewhite style resemble a variety of shapes, including an oval, shield, heart or wheel; Sheraton chair backs are rectilinear. Cabinetmakers working in the Federal style included John and Thomas Seymour and John and Simeon Skillin of Boston. The eagle, adapted from the Great Seal of the US, is a popular motif. Looking glasses with gilt frames surmounted by a flat cornice or a delicate urn and floral sprays, and shelf and mantel clocks produced by New England clockmakers, relieve the restrained classical interiors. The girandole mirror, ornamented with an eagle, was a favorite accessory.

Chippendale

Empire – Imported from Europe, this heavy, massive style, popular from 1815 to 1840, was inspired by Greek and Egyptian antiquity. Bronze, gilt, winged and caryatid supports, lion's-paw feet, rolled backs on chairs, and sofas with upswept ends typically distinguish this style.

Hepplewhite

Victorian – Furniture of the period between 1840 and the late 19C, inspired by a variety of styles including Gothic, Elizabethan, Renaissance and French rococo, is heavy and ornate. Upholstered chairs and sofas are overstuffed, and velvet coverings are typical. Balloon-back and fiddleback chairs, and tables with marble tops were popular.

Shaker Furniture – Produced primarily from 1800 until the middle of the 19C, Shaker chairs, tables and cupboards, simple and functional, are admired for their clean, pure lines and superb craftsmanship. Shaker chairs are recognized by their ladder backs, and seats made of rush, cane, splint or woven webbing.

Painting

From the beginning of the colonial period to the late 17C, painting was appreciated primarily for its practical uses for trade signs and portraiture. The artist often sketched only the face of his subject from life, then completed the remainder of the picture in a stylized manner. Highlighting this genre of portrait, which is appealing for its simplicity and charm, is the painting *Mrs. Elizabeth Freake and Baby Mary* that now hangs in the Worcester Art Museum in Massachusetts.

18C Development – The arrival of Scottish painter **John Smibert** (1688-1751) in America in 1729 initiated the era of professional painting. At his Boston studio Smibert instructed his students in the art of portraiture as it was practiced in Europe. His works, such as *Bishop Berkeley and his Entourage* (Yale University Art Gallery, New Haven), served as models for the Americans who studied with him, including Newport artist **Robert Feke** (1705-50) and **John Singleton Copley** (1738-1815), America's first important portraitist. Copley painted the well-known persons of his day (*Paul Revere*, Museum of Fine Arts, Boston), rendering his subjects amazingly lifelike by paying keen attention to detail and surface texture.

Gilbert Stuart (1755-1828) was the most important American painter of the period. Although he is best remembered for his portraits of George Washington, Stuart in fact painted only three portraits of the president from life, using these as models for his later works.

In the late 18C many Americans traveled to London in order to study with their countryman **Benjamin West** (1738-1820), who was born in Springfield, Massachusetts, and became a leader of the Neoclassical movement. **Samuel F. B. Morse** (1791-1872), a fine portraitist before he devoted himself to the invention of the telegraph, studied with West, as did **Ralph Earl** (1751-1801), who spent seven years in London, yet retained the simplicity of his native American folk style. It was also under West's guidance that **John Trumbull** (1756-1843), son of the governor of Connecticut, executed a series of historical paintings (*The Battle of Bunker Hill; Signing of the Declaration of Independence*, Yale University Art Gallery) that ultimately made Trumbull famous. He was later commissioned by Congress to decorate the rotunda of the Capitol in Washington, DC.

19C – Until the 1800s demand was primarily for portraits, with folk artists such as **William Matthew Prior** (1806-73) and **Erastus Salisbury Field** (1805-1900) active at mid-century. Following the American Revolution, the opening of the West led to an increased awareness of the vast scale and beauty of the nation, and the American scene became a popular theme for artists. Painters of the **Hudson River school** in the 1820s followed the lead of **Thomas Cole** and **Albert Bierstadt** by setting up their easels outdoors and painting directly from nature. Their favorite New England subjects were THE WHITE MOUNTAINS and the CONNECTICUT VALLEY. Born in HARTFORD, **Frederic Edwin Church** (1826-1900), whose major works were of New England landscapes, studied with Cole. The sea was a source of inspiration for other artists. **Fitz Hugh Lane** (1804-65), living in Gloucester, illustrated in soft, glowing tones the serene beauty of the sea and the offshore islands. New Bedford artist **William Bradford** (1823-92), fascinated by maritime themes and the northern lights, depicted the rising and setting of the arctic sun, and whalers sailing among icebergs (New Bedford Whaling Museum).

Beginning in the 1860s, Americans began to live and study abroad for longer periods of time. **James McNeill Whistler** (1834-1903), a native of Lowell, became known in London for his delicate riverscapes of the Thames. **William Morris Hunt** (1824-79), influenced by the French schools, opened a studio in Boston where he introduced artists to the principles of naturalism as reflected in the landscape paintings of the Barbizon school. Some years later, Italian-born **John Singer Sargent** (1856-1925) traveled extensively in Europe and won acclaim as the portraitist of the international social set. The grace and elegance he imparted to his subjects made him the most sought-after artist of his day. The career of the self-taught watercolorist and master of the naturalist movement, **Winslow Homer** (1836-1910), began during the Civil War, when Homer served as an illustrator for *Harper's Weekly.* He is known for the large canvases of the sea that he painted during many summers at Prout's Neck, Maine.

20C – In the present century several painters, each with their own distinctive style, have been identified with New England. **Grandma Moses** (1860-1961), who did not begin to paint until she was in her 70s, illustrated themes associated with rural New England *(Sleigh Ride; Sugaring-Off)*. The vivid coloration and charm of her works, a collection of which can be seen at the Bennington Museum in Vermont, are reminiscent of America's folk artists.

Norman Rockwell (1894-1978), for many years an illustrator for the *Saturday Evening Post*, painted a chronicle of American life. Rockwell's vision of the persons and events he depicted was always tempered by his warmth, keen attention to detail and sense of humor. His principal works can be viewed in STOCKBRIDGE. Born in 1917, **Andrew Wyeth** has spent several summers in Maine, where he painted his dramatic canvases exploring the relationship between man and nature. Wyeth's compositions, executed in a lucid, realistic style, are simple and uncluttered, as is his celebrated painting *Christina's World*. The Farnsworth Art Museum in ROCKLAND exhibits a large group of his works.

Worcester Art Museum, gift of Mr. & Mrs. Albert W. Rice

Mrs. Elizabeth Freake and Baby Mary (c.1674)
Artist Unknown

Folk Art

In rural New England, isolated from the mother country, necessities for dai
were handmade by the farmers themselves or by tradesmen who received a mo
fee for their services. The tools, household utensils, cloth, weather vanes and furn-
ture they produced revealed the tastes, flair and loving attention to detail of their
creators. Today these items are admired for their unsophisticated charm, and for the
picture of early rural American life they present.

Quilts – Quilted bed coverings, consisting of a top and bottom layer of cloth stitched
together with sheets of cotton or wool batting in between, were essential during the
long, cold New England winter. Often finished in a geometric or floral motif, the quilt
became one of a rural household's few decorative accessories. Because of the scarcity
of material, quilts were often fashioned from scraps of leftover cloth. These patch-
work quilts were either **pieced** (scraps were cut into geometric shapes and sewn
together) or **appliqued** (small pieces of cloth were sewn onto a broad layer of cloth to
form a specific design).

Quilting had a pleasant social aspect as well: the **quilting bee**. When the top layer of a
quilt was completed—perhaps it was a **wedding quilt** for a young woman planning to
be married, or a **freedom quilt** to be presented to a young man on his 21st birthday—
the women gathered at one house to stitch the quilt together. The assembly was often
the most difficult part of making the quilt, and after the quilting bee, the quilters
would hold a party to celebrate its completion.

Stencils – This early decorative technique, which uses paint and pre-cut patterns to
embellish furniture, implements, cloth, floors and walls, brightened the interiors of
many homes. Wall stenciling added color to the otherwise plain white plaster or
wooden plank surfaces, and in the 19C it was a low-cost alternative to expensive
imported wallpapers. The painter could choose from a large selection of motifs: geometric figures, flowers, baskets of fruit, or the symbolic eagle (liberty), pineapple
(hospitality), willow (immortality) or heart and bells (joy). The popular "fancy" chair,
produced by **Lambert Hitchcock** at his factory in Riverton, in the LITCHFIELD HILLS area of
Connecticut, was decorated with hand-painted stenciling.

Weather Vanes – When most New Englanders farmed or went to sea, weather vanes
were important as indicators of changes in the weather. The simple profile of a
weather vane, carved from wood or cut from metal, topped most buildings of any
significant height. A weather vane made to crown a church spire might be in the
shape of a cockerel or fish, the symbols of early Christianity. In rural areas the silhouette of a cow, horse or sheep rose above farm buildings, while along the coast,
the whale, clipper ship and mermaid were popular. New England's famous grasshopper weather vane, atop the cupola of Boston's Faneuil Hall, has been the symbol
of the port of Boston since the 18C. The **whirligig**, a carved three-dimensional figure
with paddlelike arms, was a whimsical variation of the weather vane. Large
whirligigs indicated wind speed and direction, while smaller ones served as children's
toys.

Figureheads, Trade Signs and Shop Figures – During the age of sailing, carvers
sculpted figureheads, sternboards and other accessories for new vessels. A small
figure representing the wife or daughter of the ship's owner ordinarily adorned a
whaling vessel, while figures (generally female) with windblown hair were carved
as graceful extensions of the prows of clipper ships *(see the collections in the maritime museums in Mystic, CT; New
Bedford, Nantucket and Salem, MA;
and Shelburne, VT).*

Ship carvers also produced trade signs
and shop figures. These brightly
painted, hand-carved signs and figures,
an early form of advertising, illustrated
the specialty of a shop: a mariner hold-
ing a sextant was associated with a nautical instrument maker, and a sign bearing a large boot indicated a cobbler's
shop. The streets of the Old Port Exchange in PORTLAND are lined with such
eye-catching signs. Among the large
number of **cigar store figures** produced in
the 19C, the most familiar was the image of the Indian, a reminder that tobacco was a native product. Ranging
from 2ft to 7ft in height, the cigar store
Indian usually wore a headdress of tobacco leaves that were often mistaken
for feathers.

Courtesy Mystic Seaport Museum

Ship Figureheads

:ss – Until the mid-19C most glass manufactured in New England was in the form , window glass and glass containers. Handmade glassware was a luxury only a few .ould afford. However, Deming Jarves and his workmen at **Sandwich** made available, for the first time, attractive glassware at affordable prices. The factory at Sandwich became famous for pressed glass with patterns that resembled lace. Despite large-scale production of pressed glass, the art of glassblowing continued to thrive. Of the numerous glass factories operating in New England during the 19C, those in Massachusetts—the New England Glass Co., Boston and Sandwich Glass Co. and Mount Washington Glass Co.—were unrivaled for the beauty of their products. Items varied from tableware to decorative art glass *(described below)* and may be seen at the Glass Museum in SANDWICH, Old Sturbridge Village and the Bennington Museum in Vermont.

Burmese Glass – This opaque glass, in hues ranging from coral pink to yellow, was made between 1885 and 1895 by Mount Washington Glass Co. Pink coloring was made possible by gold in the glass mixture.

Peachblow – The making of this glass employed a technique similar to that used for Burmese glass, but featured shades from opaque white to rose. Soft matte, satiny finishes result from an acid bath. Peachblow, made by the New England Glass Co. (1886-88), was known as Wild Rose.

Lava Glass – This shiny black glass, the first American art glass, was invented and patented by Mount Washington Glass Co. in New Bedford. The first pieces of lava glass were made from volcanic pumice.

Amberina – Ranging from pale amber to rich ruby in color, this transparent glass was dubbed Amberina by the New England Glass Co. and Rose Amber by the Mount Washington Glass Co. The amber-glass mix contained a small amount of gold, which, upon reheating a portion of the glass, resulted in a ruby color.

Pomona – The designs and frosted appearance of this expensive, transparent glass were originally achieved by covering the piece with wax, scratching through the wax with an etching device, then applying acid, which ate through the glass to create the frosted effect. Designs were stained, then the piece was fired at a high temperature.

Scrimshaw – Perfected by New England sailors in the 19C, scrimshaw, the art of etching the surface of the teeth or jawbone of a whale, or the tusks of a walrus, is considered by some the only art form indigenous to America. The tooth or tusk was allowed to dry, then the surface was polished with shark skin, and the picture or design to be etched—whale hunts, detailed ship replicas, port scenes—was incised onto the bone with a jackknife or sail needles. Ink, soot or tobacco juice was applied for color. The scrimshander's skill was reflected in the intricately detailed ornamentation of jagging wheels (used to crimp the edges of pie crusts), bird cages, inlaid boxes and other items. Exceptional scrimshaw collections can be found at the whaling museums in New Bedford, Nantucket and Sharon.

Decoys – Wooden decoys sculpted and painted to resemble geese, ducks, shorebirds and waterfowl have been used since colonial times to lure birds within range of the hunter. The practice originated with the Indians, who used heaps of mud, reeds and skins filled with grass to attract waterfowl. By the 19C decoy-making had developed into an art form. Craftsmen portrayed birds with increasing realism, taking into consideration the natural conditions where the decoys would be used. In Maine, where the sea is rough and the wind strong, decoys were large and heavy, and had a flat bottom and low head to ensure stability; in Massachusetts Bay, where the waters are calmer, the decoys were lighter. Purely decorative decoys, such as the shorebirds and miniatures carved and painted by **A. Elmer Crowell** of Massachusetts, illustrate the more elegant forms of this art. Craftsmen along the coast from Cape Cod to Maine still engage in producing these lures. The Shelburne Museum *(see Entry Heading)* owns a fine collection of over 1,000 decoys, including examples of Crowell's work.

Gravestones – The Puritans, who found little time for the frivolities of art during their daily life, have left outstanding examples of the skill of their early stonecutters in the rows of gravestones that stand in New England's old burial grounds. The designs were initially symbolic and plain. In the 17C the hourglass, sun, scythe, winged skull, hearts and cherubim (symbols for life, death and resurrection) were typical motifs. Throughout the 18C realistic portraits and detailed scenes of the death of the deceased became popular. The romantic tendencies of the 19C were represented by extensive use of the weeping willow and the urn, classical symbols for death.

The old cemeteries in BOSTON, LEXINGTON, NEWBURYPORT and SALEM, NEW LONDON and NEWPORT contain splendid examples of gravestone art.

Michelin Green Guides are updated periodically... do you have the latest edition?

38

Literature

The literature produced in the colonies in the 17C and 18C consisted primarily of histories and religious writings: sermons, pamphlets, diaries and journals. The *History of Plimoth Plantation* by William Bradford, governor of Plimoth Plantation between 1621 and 1657; and a journal account of life in the Massachusetts Bay Colony written by its first governor, John Winthrop (1588-1649), remain the principal records of this period. The clergyman **Cotton Mather** (1663-1728) wrote hundreds of sermons, scientific tracts and treatises including his monumental *Ecclesiastical History of New England*.
Inventor, statesman, philosopher and scientist **Benjamin Franklin** (1706-90), of Boston, was highly regarded at home and abroad for his satire of British policies in America. His *Poor Richard's Almanac* was found in most New England homes.

Coming of Age – In the 19C a literature distinctly American in theme, idea, character and setting emerged in New England. The transcendentalist movement, based on belief in the mystical union of all nature, gained popularity under the leadership of **Ralph Waldo Emerson** (1803-82), who lectured throughout the US. His essay *Nature* (1836) states the ideals and principles of transcendentalism.
Henry David Thoreau (1817-62), a disciple of Emerson, put the tenets of transcendentalism into practice by living a solitary existence for two years at Walden Pond in CONCORD. *Walden* recounts his life in the woods. Transcendentalism inspired experiments in communal living such as Brook Farm near Boston and in central Massachusetts (FRUITLANDS MUSEUMS). The voice of this movement was sounded in the literary magazine *The Dial*, which Emerson and Margaret Fuller founded in 1840. Bronson Alcott, whose daughter **Louisa May Alcott** (1832-88) became famous for her novel *Little Women*, contributed to *The Dial*.
Attracted by transcendentalism, **Nathaniel Hawthorne** (1806-64) lived at Brook Farm for a brief time. As a writer, he helped establish the short story and the psychological novel as significant American literary forms. Hawthorne's Puritan ancestry is reflected in the gloomy atmosphere and moralistic themes of his short stories and novels such as *The House of the Seven Gables* and *The Scarlet Letter*, a symbolic study of the effects of sin on the human soul. Influenced by Hawthorne's technique, **Herman Melville** (1819-91) wrote his masterpiece *Moby Dick* while living in THE BERKSHIRES.
Many writers supported the abolitionist movement. **William Lloyd Garrison** (1805-79) published the anti-slavery newspaper *The Liberator* for more than three decades until the adoption of the 13th Amendment. The best-selling novel *Uncle Tom's Cabin* by **Harriet Beecher Stowe** (1811-96) exposed the cruelties of slavery.
With the expansion of the nation came a heightened awareness of regional differences, and the introduction of a literary genre depicting local color, scenery and speech. Hartford resident **Mark Twain** (1835-1910) was a master of the new regional literature. His most popular works, *Tom Sawyer* and *Huckleberry Finn*, portrayed life on the Mississippi River. The novel *The Country of the Pointed Firs* by **Sarah Orne Jewett** (1849-1909) presents a poetic account of the people and countryside of Maine.
History was a favorite subject of New Englanders. Although nearly blind, Salem native **William Hickling Prescott** (1796-1859) wrote several volumes about Spanish history; **George Bancroft** (1800-91), a Massachusetts teacher, produced the *History of the United States*, the first major work of its kind. A 10-volume study by **Francis Parkman** (1823-93) of the conflict between England and France in the New World spans four decades. Bostonian **Henry Adams** (1838-1918) described the shaping of the nation's character in his nine-volume history. In 1828 **Noah Webster** (1758-1843), a native of New Haven, published the first *American Dictionary of the English Language*.

20C – In the 20C the American theater won international acclaim through the works of playwright **Eugene O'Neill** (1888-1953), whose close association with the Provincetown Players began in 1916 when his play *Bound East for Cardiff* was produced in PROVINCETOWN. New England was the setting for his *Desire Under the Elms*, *Mourning Becomes Electra* and the Pulitzer Prize-winning *Beyond the Horizon*. Other New England authors include native-born John P. Marquand, Kenneth Roberts, William Dean Howells and Jack Kerouac as well as writers who adopted New England as their second home, including Edith Wharton, Pearl Buck, Norman Mailer, Alexander Solzhenitsyn. Harvard graduate **John Updike**, perhaps best known for his novels *Rabbit Run*, *Rabbit Redux* and Pulitzer-Prize winning *Rabbit is Rich* (1981) and *Rabbit at Rest* (1990), moved to IPSWICH in the 1960s. He used New England as the setting for much of his later fiction, including *The Witches of Eastwick* (1984). A 1985 best-seller *The Beans of Egypt, Maine*, by Carolyn Chute, offers a fictional account of rural life in the state. Maine native and best-selling author **Stephen King**, a master of the horror genre, was born in PORTLAND. The prolific writer has used New England, and in particular Maine, as the background for many of his short stories and novels, such as *Salem's Lot*, *It*, and most recently *The Girl Who Loved Tom Gordon* (1999). Hanover, New Hampshire resident Bill Bryson has attracted more attention to the popular Appalachian Trail with his humorous best-seller *A Walk in the Woods* (1998), and Pulitzer Prize-winning Tracy Kidder, author of *House*, has written about the small town life of NORTHAMPTON in his book *Home Town* (1998).

Poetry – **Henry Wadsworth Longfellow** (1807-82), born in PORTLAND, taught modern languages at Harvard. One of the most widely read poets of his day, Longfellow chose American folk heroes, such as Hiawatha, Evangeline, Paul Revere and Miles Standish, as the subjects of many of his poems. Longfellow's contemporary **John Greenleaf Whittier** (1807-92) was a spokesman for the abolitionist cause and wrote poetry that portrayed life in rural, pre-industrialized New England.

Emily Dickinson (1830-86), an Amherst resident who remained a recluse most of her life, wrote verses rich in lyricism and sensitivity. Best known for his poems about nature, **Robert Frost** (1874-1963) lived on a farm in New Hampshire from 1901 to 1909, and later spent his summers in Vermont. His verse, inspired by New England's people and landscapes, exhibits a refreshing simplicity, as illustrated in his poem *Stopping by the Woods on a Snowy Evening*. Originally from Massachusetts, **Amy Lowell** (1874-1925) moved to England in 1913, where she met Ezra Pound and became a leader of the Imagist movement, which experimented with creating concrete images, free of the unrestrained imagery and sentimentality that characterized 19C verse.

The poetry of **e.e. cummings** (1894-1962), a native of CAMBRIDGE, is distinguished by his unconventional use of typography and punctuation. Another New England-born poet whose work has made a significant impact on modern poetry is **Robert Lowell** (1917-77), whose early verse reflects New England's historical and ethical traditions.

Culinary Traditions

New England has a well-deserved reputation for simple, hearty fare, but the cuisine here can also be remarkably varied. In addition to shellfish, the region boasts delicious game meat, including venison and grouse; farmland produce; good local wines; and regional specialties ranging from maple syrup and Vermont cheddar cheese to saltwater taffy and **Boston cream pie** (actually a custard-filled cake glazed with chocolate). Country inns and taverns serve traditional Yankee fare, while waterfront **clam shacks**, dockside lobster pounds and shoreline dinner halls offer the best in seafood dining experience.

Native American Traditions – Many local dishes trace their roots to the New England Indians, who were the first to make maple sugar, **cranberry sauce**, **Johnnycakes** (these fried cornmeal patties are popular in Rhode Island) and **Indian pudding**, a hot dessert of molasses, cornmeal, cinnamon and nutmeg. Slow-cooked **Boston baked beans** flavored with molasses and salt pork also derive from a native recipe, as does their traditional accompaniment, **brown bread**, made with equal parts of rye and wheat flour and cornmeal, and steamed in a tin can rather than baked.

Fish and Shellfish – Brook trout is a popular freshwater fish, while swordfish and tuna (grilled with lemon), **bluefish** and **striped bass** (baked or broiled) are saltwater favorites; straight from the fisherman's catch, these fish are so fresh that they need little seasoning. **Lobster**, found in the cold waters off Rhode Island, Massachusetts and Maine, was so common in the 1600s that it was considered one of the lowliest menu items. Now scarce, it is the king of shellfish, served baked or boiled with lemon and butter, in rich stews, bisques and pies, hot and buttered on a bun (lobster roll) or chilled with mayonnaise (lobster-salad roll).

Blue mussels grow in clusters around shoreline rocks; try these tender mollusks steamed in wine and herbs or grilled with garlic. Equally popular are **clams**, harvested by rake from the sandy bottoms of warm-water bays and salt ponds. They are delicious steamed with butter, batter-fried, deep-fried in light, puffy **fritters** (a Rhode Island specialty) or baked and stuffed with bread crumbs and seasonings. Varieties include the thin-shelled, long-necked steamer; large hardshelled quahogs (KOE-hogs); and littlenecks and cherrystones, two types of young quahogs eaten raw on the half shell with lemon and a cocktail sauce

Larry Lefever/Grant Heilman Photography

Boiled Lobster

spiced with horseradish. Fall and winter are the seasons for **bay scallops** (sautéed in butter and lemon) and **oysters** (raw on the half shell).

The famous New England **clambake** is another Indian custom. To make this all-in-one shoreline meal—served up from a beach-dug pit—potatoes, onions, unhusked corn, chicken, lobsters and clams are layered in seaweed over charcoal-heated stones for hours of slow steaming. (The classic clambake typically feeds up to 100 people, but restaurants offer a smaller version cooked in a steamer pot.)

Chowders and Stews – Thought to have originated with settlers from the Channel Islands, **chowders** are thick, slow-simmered soups made from milk and vegetables. Corn chowder is a regional specialty. Fish chowder usually features cod or haddock; steamers or quahogs, potatoes and onions (never tomatoes) are key ingredients of **clam chowder** (made in Rhode Island with clear clam-juice broth rather than milk). The **New England boiled dinner** is an autumn dish of corned beef (brisket cured in salt brine) and stewed, late-season garden vegetables (turnips, beets, cabbage and carrots). The dish, traditionally made on Monday, simmered all day while the wash was being done; leftovers went into **red flannel hash** (named for the beets) for meals the rest of the week.

Fresh Produce – Seasonal favorites include fiddlehead ferns (spring), and strawberries (early summer), savored in strawberry shortcake. Maine is famous for its blueberries; indeed, no trip to New England is complete without sampling blueberry pancakes, pie, muffins or a type of pudding called **blueberry slump**. Late summer produces vine-ripened tomatoes, corn on the cob and pumpkins (used for soups and pies). Add to these classic farmstand offerings preserves made from wild beach plums and Concord grapes. In autumn, stop at a pick-your-own orchard for cider and some of the best apples grown in the US (Cortland, Granny Smith, Macoun and McIntosh).

Maple Syrup – Come early spring, maple trees are tapped for sap, which is cooked down into a sweet syrup used for baking and as a topping for pancakes, waffles and ice cream. Vermont and New Hampshire lead New England in maple syrup production. The best quality is Grade A light amber, followed by Grade A medium and dark ambers.

Further Reading

Non-Fiction

Adventure Guide to New England by Stephen Jermanok *(MacMillan, Inc., 1996)*
Appalachian Mountain Club guidebooks *(Appalachian Mountain Club)*
Boston Globe Historic Walks in Old Boston
by John Harris *(Globe Pequot Press, 2000)*
Fifty Hikes in New England series by state *(Countryman Press, Inc., 1996)*
Home Town by Tracy Kidder *(Random House, 1998)*
Long Trail Guide *(Green Mountain Club, 1997)*
New England: Land of Scenic Splendor *(National Geographic Society, 1994)*
Recommended Country Inns: New England
by Elizabeth Squier *(Globe Pequot Press, 1999)*
A Walk in the Woods by Bill Bryson *(MacMillan, Inc., 1999)*

Fiction

The Bostonians by Henry James (1886)
Captains Courageous by Rudyard Kipling (1897)
The Country of the Pointed Firs by Sarah Orne Jewett (1896)
The Crucible by Arthur Miller (1953)
Ethan Frome by Edith Wharton (1911)
The House of the Seven Gables by Nathaniel Hawthorne (1851)
The Last Puritan by George Santayana (1935)
The Late George Apley by John P. Marquand (1937)
Moby Dick by Herman Melville (1851)
The Outermost House by Henry Beston (1928)
The Scarlet Letter by Nathaniel Hawthorne (1850)
Two Years Before the Mast by Richard Henry Dana (1840)

Connecticut

Area: 4,845sq mi
Population: 3,287,116
Capital: Hartford
Nickname: The Constitution State
State Flower: Mountain laurel

This rectangle extending about 90 miles east to west and 55 miles north to south bears the name of the river that divides it almost in half: the Connecticut, an Indian word meaning "beside the long tidal river." Small colonial villages scattered throughout the state offer a pleasing contrast to the densely populated industrialized centers in the Hartford region and to the cities of Stamford, Bridgeport, Stratford and New Haven on the south shore. The affluent communities in southwestern Connecticut's Fairfield County (Greenwich, Ridgefield, New Canaan) are, in essence, "suburbs" of New York City.

The state is predominantly rural; two-thirds of its woodlands are included in the state park and forest system. To the south, on the shores of Long Island Sound, sandy beaches separate the former whaling ports of New London, Mystic and Stonington. The idyllic Litchfield Hills, rising in the northern part of the state, are an extension of the Green Mountains and the Berkshire Hills.

The Constitution State – Connecticut's first settlers were staunch Puritans who found the atmosphere in Boston too liberal. They arrived from Massachusetts in 1633 by the Connecticut River and within two years had founded the towns of Hartford, Windsor and Wethersfield.

In 1638 these towns joined to form Hartford Colony, later to become Connecticut Colony. The Fundamental Orders of Connecticut, statutes drawn up and adopted January 14, 1639, as the basis of government in Hartford Colony, is the first constitution drafted in the New World—thus the state's nickname, the Constitution State.

Economy – Benefiting from the wide range of products developed by the state's inventors, Connecticut has traditionally been a prosperous manufacturing center, and for over a decade, it ranked first in the nation in per capita income. Mechanical innovations introduced by Connecticut clockmakers *(p 57)* made clockmaking one of the state's earliest industries and put a clock in almost every home in America.

In the 19C the production of firearms became an important business. The Colt .45 revolver, developed by Hartford entrepreneur **Samuel Colt**, and the Winchester rifle were made in Connecticut. During the same period, **Eli Whitney** manufactured his revolutionary new cotton gin in New Haven and introduced the use of standardized parts at his firearms factory nearby. Danbury became known for its hats, Torrington and Waterbury for brass items, and Meriden for its fine silverware.

Connecticut continues to obtain a great part of its income from industry. Electrical goods, tools, chemicals, plastics, jet engines, helicopters and nuclear submarines are its leading products. The Electric Boat Division of General Dynamics at Groton builds submarines for the nation's fleet. A number of corporations (General Electric, Union Carbide, Xerox) and insurance companies maintain headquarters in the state.

Larry Lefever/Grant Heilman Photography

Locally marketed poultry, fruit and dairy products are major sources of agricultural income. Broadleaf tobacco, used for cigar wrapping, is shade-grown in the Connecticut and Farmington Valleys. Picturesque tobacco sheds identify these flat regions.

BRIDGEPORT

Population 141,686
Map of Principal Sights
Tourist Office ☎ 800-866-7925

This heavily industrialized and populated center on Long Island Sound was the home of **Phineas T. Barnum** (1810-91), the colorful showman-promoter. A statue of Barnum, a former mayor of Bridgeport, surveys the harbor from Seaside Park at the end of Main Street. Manufacturing, government, service industries and wholesale and retail activities support the local economy. Prominent among the city's educational institutions is the **University of Bridgeport**.

SIGHT

Barnum Museum – 🏛 *820 Main St. Open year-round Tue-Sat 10am–4:30pm, Sun noon–4:30pm. Closed major holidays. $5.* ♿ ☎ *203-331-9881. www. barnummuseum.org.* This ornate building is as eccentric as its creator; the circus memorabilia it houses reflects Barnum's exuberant personality. Barnum's world-famous three-ring circus toured America and Europe in the 19C and won acclaim as "The Greatest Show on Earth." Highlights include costumes and furnishings that belonged to Tom Thumb, the first major star attraction of the circus, and the **Brinley Miniature Circus** of more than 3,000 hand-carved figures. A contemporary wing features temporary exhibits on art and American popular culture.

EXCURSION

Ferry to Port Jefferson, Long Island, NY – *Departs from Bridgeport Harbor year-round Mon–Sat 6:30am–9:30pm (10pm Fri), Sun 7:30am–10pm. One-way 1 hr 15min. Reservations suggested. $32.50 (car & driver). ✗ Bridgeport & Port Jefferson Steamboat Co.* ☎ *203-335-2040. www.pagelinx.com.*

CONNECTICUT VALLEY★

Map of Principal Sights
Tourist Office ☎ 860-347-0028

Wide, shallow and bordered by unspoiled countryside, the Connecticut River flows into a multitude of coves and boat harbors as it ends its more than 400mi journey downstream to Long Island Sound. Villages such as Old Lyme and Old Saybrook have retained their early character thanks to a sandbar at the mouth of the river that has always prevented deep-draft vessels from entering these waters.

There are two ways to explore the valley: by land, following the itinerary below through small riverside towns; or by river, taking a cruise from East Haddam, Deep River or Essex. In the summer ferry rides *(3 hrs, p 45)* from Haddam to Long Island are available.

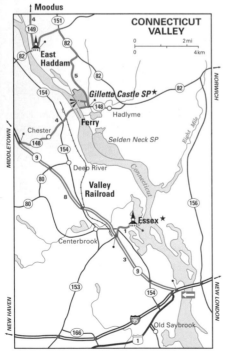

DRIVING TOUR

Allow 4 hrs. 26mi.

From I-95, Exit 69 (Old Saybrook), take Rte. 9 to Exit 3 in the direction of Essex.

★**Essex** – Established in 1645, Essex developed into an important shipbuilding center by the early 18C, and in 1775 produced Connecticut's first warship, the *Oliver Cromwell.* Today Essex attracts a sophisticated summer crowd who berth their yachts and cabin cruisers at local marinas. The town's main street consists of interesting shops, art galleries and the Old Griswold Inn, which has been operating since 1776. A former warehouse at Steamboat Dock houses the **Connecticut River Museum**, with maritime exhibits that include a model of the *Oliver Cromwell (67 Main St.; open year-round Tue–Sun 10am–5pm; $4;* ♿ ☎ *860-767-8269; www.connix. com/~crm).*

Essex Steam Train and Riverboat – 🧒 *Exit 3 off Rte. 9. Train departs from Essex Station mid-Jun–early Sept daily 10:30am–4:30pm (weekends 6pm). May–early Jun Wed–Fri 1:30pm & 3pm, weekends noon, 1:30pm & 3pm. Mid-Sept–Oct Wed–Sun 10:30am–4:30pm. Limited service rest of the year. Train to Chester (round-trip 1 hr) with connecting river cruises from Deep River to East Haddam (train & cruise: round-trip 2 hr 30min). Commentary. $10 (train only), $16 (train & cruise). ✗ (riverboat) Valley Railroad Co. ☎ 860-767-0103. www.valleyrr.com.* Rides on the railroad's early-20C steam train afford views of the valley landscape and the Connecticut River.

From Essex take Rte. 9 to Exit 6, then Rte. 148 to the ferry that crosses the river.

Chester-Hadlyme Ferry – *Departs from Chester Apr–Nov Mon–Fri 7am–6:45pm, weekends & holidays 10:30am–5pm. Closed Thanksgiving Day. One-way 5min. $2.25 (car & driver). State Bureau of Aviation & Ports. ☎ 860-443-3856.* During the crossing there is a good view of Gillette Castle, perched high on a hilltop above the east bank.

Old Griswold Inn

Main St., Essex. ☎ 860-767-1776. This cozy inn, established in 1776, is known for prime rib, seafood, meat pies and its own sausages as well as its Hunt Breakfast—a Sunday buffet of traditional English entrées, including creamed chipped beef, smoked bacon and fried Perdue chicken *(11am–2:30pm)*. The lunch menu features Yankee pot roast, shepherd's pie, steamed littleneck clams, welsh rarebit and other stout fare. Dine in the library amid a collection of marine art or in the Covered Bridge Room to a backdrop of Currier and Ives steamboat prints. The dark-panelled taproom, built in 1734 as a one-room schoolhouse, is warmed by a potbellied stove.

Take Rte. 148, then turn left, following the signs for Gillette Castle.

★**Gillette Castle State Park** – *Park open daily year-round. Castle hours limited due to renovation. Call for hours. ✗ ☎ 860-526-2336.* The castles of the Rhine Valley inspired the design of this bizarre stone castle built in 1919 by actor **William Gillette**, who drew up the plans for the castle and decorated each of the 24 rooms himself. Furniture that slides on metal tracks and other devices were developed by Gillette, who had a fascination for gadgetry. The 190-acre estate offers splendid **vistas★** of the Connecticut River and the valley below. *Picnic areas and hiking trails are available.*

Take Rte. 82 to East Haddam.

East Haddam – This small town with beautiful old homes is proud of its little red **schoolhouse** where Nathan Hale once taught, and of being the site of the **Goodspeed Opera House**, a Victorian-style opera house dating from the era when New York-to-Connecticut steamers called at East Haddam. *Musicals are presented from Apr–Dec. Ticket information ☎ 860-873-8668.*

River cruises (one-way 3hrs) operate between Marine Park in Haddam (2.5mi north of East Haddam, on the other side of the river) and Long Island, New York, late Jun–Labor Day Tue–Thu & weekends 9am. $22.50 ($15 one-way). ✗ ⅖ Camelot Cruises ☎ 800-522-7463.

Follow Rte. 149, which offers good views of the river before turning northeast.

Moodus – Facing the Moodus green is the **Amasa Day House** (1816), which contains well-preserved examples of the floor stenciling laid over a century ago *(visit by 45min guided tour only, Jun–Aug Wed–Sun 1pm–5pm; closed major holidays; $2; ☎ 860-873-8144).*

COVENTRY

Population 9,820
Map of Principal Sights
Tourist Office ☎ 860-928-1228

This small town in rural northeastern Connecticut was the birthplace of the American patriot **Nathan Hale** (1755-76).
A schoolteacher by profession, Hale was commissioned an officer in the Connecticut militia at the outbreak of the Revolutionary War. After participating in several military operations in New England, he volunteered for the perilous mission of gathering intelligence about the British troops on Long Island. Young Hale was discovered by the British and hanged as a spy on September 22, 1776. The last words he spoke on the scaffold, "I only regret that I have but one life to lose for my country," are among the most memorable in the annals of American history.

SIGHTS

Nathan Hale Homestead – *2299 South St. Visit by guided tour (1 hr) only. mid-May–mid-Oct daily 1pm–4pm. Closed major holidays. $4.* ☎ *860-742-8996.* Nathan Hale never lived in this 10-room dwelling, which was built in October 1776 by his father on the site of the home where Hale was born. The family homestead until 1832, the house contains Hale family memorabilia and period furnishings.

Caprilands Herb Farm – *534 Silver St. Open year-round daily 10am–5pm. Closed Jan 1, Easter Sunday, Thanksgiving Day, Dec 25.* ☎ *860-742-7244.* More than 300 different types of herbs are cultivated on the 20 acres of this farm, which has been the family estate of Adelma Grenier Simmons (1903-1997) since 1929. Visitors are free to wander through the restored 18C barn, the specialty gardens and the greenhouse. The 18C farmhouse is the setting for a daily luncheon and lecture program *(Apr–Dec; $20; check-in 11:30am; reservations required).*

■ Connecticut Impressionist Art Trail

Childe Hassam, John Twachtman and Albert Pinkham Ryder were among the many American masters who, captivated by the beauty of Connecticut, made the state their outdoor "studio" during the 19C. Follow the Art Trail to visit any or all of 12 sites that showcase the work of American painters experimenting with the momentary effects of light and color. *For a color brochure with map, contact Southeastern Connecticut (☎ 800-863-6569) or Greater Hartford (☎ 800-793-4480) Tourism Districts.*

Bruce Museum – *One Museum Dr., Greenwich* ☎ *203-869-0376.* Represents several artists who painted in Cos Cob and Greenwich, an area particularly important to the development of the American Impressionist movement.

Bush-Holley House Museum – *39 Strickland Rd., Cos Cob* ☎ *203-869-6899.* Takes visitors back to the 19C, when this Colonial saltbox was a gathering place for Hassam, Twachtman and others.

Weir Farm National Historic Site – *735 Nod Hill Rd., Wilton* ☎ *203-834-1896.* Preserves the bucolic landscapes that once inspired American Impressionist J. Alden Weir. The farm is the only national park in Connecticut.

Yale University Art Gallery – *1111 Chapel St., New Haven* ☎ *203-432-0600. See Entry Heading New Haven.*

Florence Griswold Museum – *96 Lyme St., Old Lyme* ☎ *860-434-5542.* Presents the studio of William Chadwick and a collection of works by artists belonging to the famous 19C Lyme art colony.

Lyman Allyn Art Museum – *625 Williams St., New London* ☎ *860-443-2545. See Entry Heading New London.*

William Benton Museum of Art – *University of Connecticut at Storrs* ☎ *860-486-4520.* Showcases works by Emil Carlsen, Mary Cassatt, J. Alden Weir and Louis Comfort Tiffany.

Hartford Steam Boiler Inspection and Insurance Co. – *One State St.* ☎ *860-722-5473; call for appointment.* A private executive gallery featuring more than 100 American Impressionist artworks.

Wadsworth Atheneum – *600 Main St., Hartford* ☎ *860-278-2670. See Entry Heading Hartford.*

Hill-Stead Museum – *35 Mountain Rd., Farmington* ☎ *860-677-9064. See Entry Heading.*

New Britain Museum of American Art – *56 Lexington St., New Britain* ☎ *860-229-0257. See Entry Heading Hartford.*

Mattatuck Museum – *144 W Main St., Waterbury.* ☎ *203-753-0381.* The state's only museum devoted exclusively to Connecticut history and artists.

When planning your trip to New England and during your touring,
use Michelin Map 473 to New England (and the Hudson Valley).
  –Easy-to-fold large format map
  –Detailed road network with distances and interchanges
  –Places of interest: amusement parks, ski areas, wineries, national and
   state parks and monuments
  –Comprehensive index of more than 6,500 cities, towns and villages

FARMINGTON★

Population 20,608
Map of Principal Sights
Tourist Office ☎ 860-527-9258

Beautiful 18C and 19C residences line the streets of this elegant HARTFORD suburb on the Farmington River. Several of these early structures on Main Street are part of a well-known school for girls, **Miss Porter's School**.

SIGHTS

★**Hill-Stead Museum** – *35 Mountain Rd. Visit by guided tour (1 hr) only. May–Oct Tue–Sun 10am–5pm. Rest of the year Tue–Sun 11am–4pm. Closed major holidays. $7. ☎ 860-677-9064. www.hillstead.org.* In 1900 Theodate Pope, one of America's early female architects, worked with the firm of McKim, Mead and White to design this Colonial Revival country house for her father, the wealthy industrialist Alfred Atmore Pope. The design of the sunken garden is based on a plan by Beatrix Jones Farrand. Hill-Stead's attractive furnishings and European and Oriental objets d'art lend a pleasant, lived-in atmosphere to this museum that is set on 150 acres. Pope's interest in the Impressionists led him to purchase a large number of the works of art displayed, especially the fine paintings by Monet *(Haystacks)*, Manet *(The Guitar Player)*, Degas *(The Tub; Jockeys)* and several canvases by Whistler and Mary Cassatt.

Stanley-Whitman House – *37 High St. Visit by guided tour (40min) only. May–Nov Wed–Sun noon–4pm. Rest of the year weekends noon–4pm. Closed major holidays. $5. ☎ 860-677-9222.* The influence of the European building styles on American Colonial architecture is seen in this house (c.1720) with its overhang, decorative pendants and central chimney. Inside there are furnishings and handcrafted items of the period.

GROTON

Population 9,837
Map of Principal Sights
Tourist Office ☎ 860-444-2206

This small industrial city on the east bank of the Thames River, opposite NEW LONDON, is the home port of the US Atlantic submarine fleet. Above the river on the grounds of **Fort Griswold State Park** rises the **Groton Monument**, a stone obelisk that commemorates the patriots who were killed when British troops captured Fort Griswold *(p 67)* in 1781.

The US Naval Submarine Base *(not open to the public)* contains more than 270 buildings; subs are berthed and repaired at the Lower Base beside the river. Sailing vessels, merchant ships, tugboats and sightseeing boats also ply the waters of Groton's busy deep water harbor. Boatyards on the Thames turn out many different types of ships, but it is Groton's largest employer, the Electric Boat division of General Dynamics—builder of the world's first nuclear-powered submarine that is best known. Each year, in June, the Thames River is the site of the colorful Yale-Harvard regatta.

SIGHT

Historic Ship Nautilus – 🔲 *Berthed at a pier adjacent to the Submarine Base. From I-95 Exit 86 take Rte. 12 north, then follow the signs. Open mid-May–late Oct Wed–Mon 9am–5pm, Tue 1pm–5pm. Rest of the year Wed–Mon 9am–4pm. Closed Jan 1, Thanksgiving Day, Dec 25 & first week in May. ☎ 860-694-3558 or 800-343-0079. www.ussnautilus.org.* With the launching in 1954 of the *Nautilus*, the world's first nuclear-powered vessel, submarine technology entered the atomic age. The *Nautilus* established new submerged records for speed, distance and underwater endurance and in 1958 became the first submarine to reach the North Pole.

Decommissioned in 1980, the 320ft ship is now the principal attraction at the USS Nautilus/Submarine Force Museum complex. The torpedo room, control room and other sections of the vessel may be viewed.

Exhibits in the **Submarine Force Museum** present the story of underwater navigation, the *Nautilus* and life aboard a sub. Operational periscopes allow visitors to practice sighting.

GUILFORD

Population 19,848
Map of Principal Sights
Tourist Office ☎ 860-347-0028

In 1639 Minister Henry Whitfield arrived here with 25 families and bought the land that became Guilford from the Menunketuck Indians. Commerce and the fishing, milling and shipbuilding industries developed in this small town, which grew rapidly because of its location on the main road between New York City and Boston. Guilford's 18C and 19C homes and lovely green reflect its early prosperity.

SIGHTS

Henry Whitfield State Museum – *248 Old Whitfield St. Open Feb–mid-Dec Wed–Sun 10am–4:30pm. Rest of the year by appointment only. Closed major holidays. $3.50.* ☎ *203-453-2457.* In a land where wood was plentiful, Reverend Whitfield, inspired by the dwellings of northern England, built his home of stone. The first dwelling (1639) built in Guilford, it served as a garrison and meeting hall. Restored to its 17C appearance and decorated with 17-19C furnishings, the house is the oldest stone dwelling in New England.

■ The Thimble Islands

Legend has it that Captain Kidd buried treasure on one of the 365 Thimble Islands, which lie off the coast of Connecticut between Guilford and Branford, at Stony Creek. First charted in 1614, the islands range in size from a few boulders to several acres of farmland. Many are privately owned and hold just a single shingled beach cottage, complete with the requisite turrets and verandahs. Boat tours of the islands *(45min)* on the **Sea Mist II** *(*☎ *203-481-3345)* and the **Volsunga IV** *(*☎ *203-488-8905)* leave from Stony Brook town dock mid-May to Columbus Day.

Hyland House – *84 Boston St. Visit by guided tour (45min) only, Jun–Labor Day Tue–Sun 10am–4:30pm. Mid-Sept–mid-Oct weekends only 10am–4:30pm. Closed Columbus Day. $2.* ☎ *203-453-9477.* This typical "saltbox," built in the late 17C, is furnished with American antiques of the period. The parlor is noteworthy for its fine wood paneling.

Thomas Griswold House – *171 Boston St. Visit by guided tour (30min) only, Jun–Oct Tue–Sun 11am–4pm. Rest of the year by appointment only. $2.* ☎ *203-453-3176.* Inhabited by five generations of the same family (1774-1958), this beautifully restored classic saltbox house features its original double-batten door (solid vertical planks held by horizontal boards) constructed for defense against Indian attacks. Two fireplaces are restored to their original dimensions. The period rooms contain furniture from the 18C to the 19C. Note in particular two fine examples of the "Guilford" corner cabinet.

> "You can always tell the Irish,
> You can always tell the Dutch,
> You can always tell a Yankee;
> But you cannot tell him much."
>
> Eric Knight, from *All Yankees Are Liars*

HARTFORD★★

Population 139,739
Map of Principal Sights
Tourist Office ☎ 860-527-9258

Rising beside the Connecticut River, this Yankee city and state capital, has been nicknamed "the Insurance Capital of the Nation." The headquarters of numerous insurance companies are located here, making Hartford a major national center for insurance and related services. The downtown holds a tight cluster of skyscrapers, a sprawling convention center and indoor shopping mall, several landmark buildings and some striking examples of 1980s architecture such as One Corporate Center.

Historical Notes

From Good Hope to the Connecticut Colony – Hartford's location on a waterway navigable to the sea led the Dutch to establish a trading post, named Fort Good Hope, on this site in 1633. Because of the region's abundant supply of furs and timber, Puritans from the Massachusetts Bay Colony settled in the area two years later. Their village grew quickly, and in 1638 it joined with Wethersfield and Windsor to form

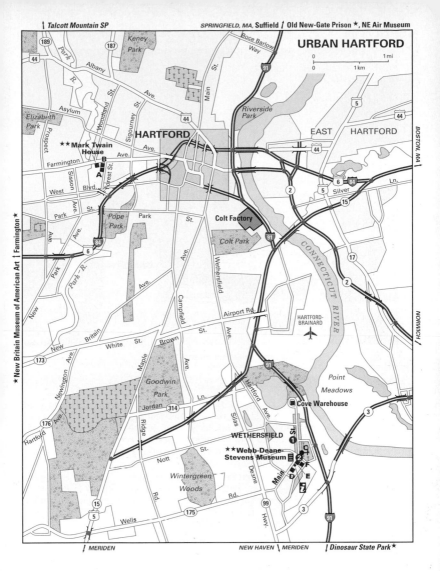

Hartford Colony. The **Fundamental Orders of Connecticut**, the governing document drawn up by members of Hartford Colony in 1639, is regarded as the New World's first constitution. In 1662 Hartford Colony became the Colony of Connecticut.

An Insurance Center – Hartford's insurance industry originated in the 18C when a group of men agreed to cover a shipowner's losses if his vessel did not return home safely. As shipping began to decline in the 19C, the industry shifted from marine to fire insurance. On October 31, 1835, more than 600 buildings were destroyed by fire in New York City. The enormous number of claims filed forced many New York insurance firms into bankruptcy. On a snowy winter night, the astute president of the Hartford Fire Insurance Co. traveled to New York to assure his policyholders that their claims would be honored. The company promptly paid the claims, and its business boomed. Its consistently good record in the wake of subsequent disasters in BOSTON and Chicago gave rise to the city's sobriquet "Insurance Capital of the Nation." The approximately 40 insurance companies located in Greater Hartford today employ over 10 percent of the labor force throughout the metropolitan area.

Today's Economy – Manufacturing plays an important role in the city's economy. Pratt and Whitney Aircraft, the Colt Industries (the Colt revolver credited with "winning the West" was manufactured in Hartford during the 19C) and producers of typewriters, precision instruments and computers are located in the Greater Hartford region. The blue, star-speckled, onion-shaped dome of the **Colt factory** is a landmark visible from I-91.

Extensive revitalization of Hartford's downtown area during recent decades includes the construction of new shopping and business complexes, notably Constitution Plaza and the Civic Center. The landmark Cheney Building, renamed The Richardson in honor of the renowned architect who designed it in 1877, now houses a shopping mall and apartments.

49

State Capitol from Bushnell Park

Fred M. Dole/f/STOP PICTURES

DOWNTOWN *4 hrs. Map p 52.*

Hartford Civic Center – *Trumbull St. Visitor information booth.* Completed in 1975, this concrete-and-glass structure is Connecticut's major convention center and the entertainment hub of Hartford. In addition to the 14,500-seat coliseum, the assembly hall and 10,000sq ft of exhibition space, the complex has an enclosed shopping mall, adjacent hotel and underground parking facilities. A pedestrian walkway links the center to CityPlace.

Diagonally across from the Civic Center, on Church Street, a simple elongated building (1977) with a smooth, patterned exterior houses the award-winning **Hartford Stage Company**. *Performances are presented by the company in its 489-seat theater Sept–Jun. For specific information ☎ 860-527-5151. www.hartfordstage.org.*

① Max Downtown
CityPlace. ☎ *860-522-2530.* Ask local residents and Max is usually mentioned top-of-mind as a favorite place to dine. Its American and Continental menu of beef, veal, fish and fowl offerings, served in an upscale milieu, is sure to please. The "GarBar,"a cigar room, has been established for clientele who enjoy a puff. *Reservations advised.*

City Place – *185 Asylum St.* This is Connecticut's tallest building, a 39-story office-retail tower (1984) with setbacks and a granite-and-glass exterior that blends well with its surroundings. Designed by Skidmore, Owings and Merrill, CityPlace contains an atrium where exhibits and concerts are offered year-round.

★**Old State House** – *800 Main St. Open year-round Mon–Fri 10am–4pm, Sat 11am–4pm. Closed major holidays. Visitor center has maps and brochures for Hartford and the state.* ♿ ☎ *860-522-6766.* This elegant Federal-style building (1792) with its graceful staircases, arches, balustrades and classical pediments was designed by Charles Bulfinch, the architect of the statehouses of Maine and Massachusetts. The legislative chambers on the second floor contain original furnishings. Don't miss the small Steward's Museum containing international curiosities and taxidermic animals, also on the second floor.

★**Constitution Plaza** – The modern 12-acre plaza completed in the 1960s provided Hartford with new office buildings, shops and an open mall, and added a striking landmark to the city's skyline: the **Phoenix Mutual Life Insurance Building**. This elliptical, glass-sheathed tower is referred to as "the Boat" because of its shape. The plaza is the site of the Hartford Festival of Light, an annual lighting display held every evening from late November to the first of January.

Travelers Tower – *1 Tower Square.* This building is the home of the Travelers Insurance Co., which began, as its name suggests, by insuring travelers. In 1864 the company's first policyholder insured his life for $5,000 "against accident while on a four-block walk home for lunch from his place of business." For this he paid a premium of two cents.

From the **observation deck** there is a **view★★** of the Hartford region *(visit by 30min guided tour only, mid-May–mid-Oct Mon–Fri 10am–3pm; closed major holidays; advance 1-day reservation suggested; 100 steps to climb;* ☎ *860-277-4208; www.travelers.com).*

■ **The Charter Oak**

The independence of the Hartford Colony was guaranteed by the Royal Charter of 1662. In 1687, however, the royal governor, Edmond Andros, demanded the return of the charter. According to legend, during a meeting that took place one evening to discuss the matter, someone suddenly extinguished the candles and, in the darkness, fled with the document. The charter was hidden in an oak tree where it remained until Sir Edmond returned to England a few years later. The tree, which became known as the Charter Oak, fell during a storm in the 19C. A variety of items made from the oak are on view in the city's museums. The number of objects supposedly made from the tree is so large that it prompted **Mark Twain** to remark there is "a walking stick, dog collar, needle case, three-legged stool, bootjack, dinner table, tenpin alley, toothpick, and enough Charter Oak to build a plank road from Hartford to Salt Lake City." The original charter remains intact and is on display with the Fundamental Orders at the **State Library**.

★★**Wadsworth Atheneum** – *600 Main St. Open year-round Tue–Sun 11am–5pm. Closed Jan 1, Jul 4, Thanksgiving Day, Dec 25. $7.* ✕ ⅄ ☎ *860-278-2670. www.wadsworthatheneum.org.* Founded in 1842, this formidable museum, whose initial collection consisted of landscapes by such artists as John Trumbull, Frederic Edwin Church and Thomas Cole, now houses some 50,000 works spanning more than 5,000 years. In addition to paintings by the Hudson River school, highlights include European porcelain, 19C European paintings and the comprehensive Nutting collection of 17C American furniture.

The present structure of five connected buildings is the result of several additions to the original Gothic Revival edifice, completed in 1844, to house the library and art gallery established by Daniel Wadsworth. Donations and bequests funded subsequent additions to the original structure: the Colt Wing (1907), Morgan Memorial (1910), Avery Memorial (1934) and Goodwin Wing (1969). An interesting blend of traditional and modern architecture styles, the complex comprises the museum, a theater and an art library.

Main Floor – The Hilles Gallery is devoted to changing exhibits. The Huntington Gallery features the museum's collection of modern **European paintings and sculpture**. On display are paintings by Picasso, Mondrian and Dali as well as sculpture by Giacometti, Calder, Hepworth and David Smith, among others. In **Avery Court** an 8ft-tall figure of Venus, sculpted in the 16C by Pietro Francavilla, graces the indoor fountain. The MATRIX Gallery is reserved for temporary exhibits of contemporary art. **Morgan Great Hall** and adjacent galleries feature Asian, Greek, Roman and Egyptian antiquities, European Medieval and Renaissance works and 17-19C European and American painting and sculpture. The Costume and Textiles exhibit is also here. Among the highlights of the American section in the Great Hall are the historic subjects and genre paintings by Benjamin West and John Trumbull *(Signing of the Declaration of Independence).*

Second Floor – The Amistad and Fleet Galleries of African-American Art present selections from the museum's collection of art and artifacts from the 18C to the 20C. Several rooms in the Morgan Wing are devoted to 17C and 18C painting. Among the prominent Spanish, Italian, French and Dutch masters represented in the collection are Caravaggio *(Ecstasy of Saint Francis),* Hals, Rubens, Zurbaran *(Saint Serapion),* Boucher, Chardin, Van Dyck and Goya *(Gossiping Women).*

The museum's comprehensive collection of **Meissen**, Sèvres, Worchester and other porcelain is exhibited in the Continental Porcelain Gallery in the Morgan Wing. Collections of English silver and ceramics are also located on this floor.

American Collection – Second- and third-floor galleries in the Avery Wing contain the museum's collection of American art spanning the early colonial period to the 20C. Included are portraits by John Singleton Copley *(Mrs. Seymour Fort),* Ralph Earl *(Chief Justice Oliver Ellsworth and His Wife),* Rembrandt Peale and Thomas Eakins. These galleries also house a spectacular group of landscape paintings by members of the **Hudson River school**, including Cole *(Mount Etna from the Ruins of Taormina)*, Bierstadt *(In the Mountains–Yosemite Valley)* and Church, as well as more recent works by noted 20C artists such as Andrew Wyeth *(Chambered Nautilus)*.

Displayed in the galleries on the second floor is the distinguished **Wallace Nutting collection** of early American Colonial furniture. Note the elaborately carved chests, ironwork, and domestic implements and utensils gathered by this retired Congregationalist minister (1861-1941), who greatly admired the furniture of the Pilgrim century and acquired the items found in these galleries to serve as models for his furniture reproduction company. Author of more than 20 books on antique furniture, he restored half a dozen houses including the Wentworth-Gardner House *(p 232)*, the Saugus Iron works House *(p 149)* and the Webb House *(p 72)*.

Rounding out the American section is the Hammerslough collection of silver with its great variety of forms, including porringers, saltcellars, skewers and strainers.

Third Floor – This floor houses selections from the collection of **19C European paintings**, one of the museum's major strengths. Canvases by Monet *(Beach at Trouville)*, Renoir *(Monet Painting in his Garden at Argenteuil)*, Toulouse-Lautrec *(Jane Avril Leaving the Moulin Rouge)* and Degas are presented together with works by Manet, Ingres, Delacroix *(Bathing Women)*, Cézanne, Vlaminck, Vuillard and Bonnard. Traveling exhibits are mounted in the Austin Gallery.

Outside the museum, in Burr Mall between the Atheneum and the Municipal Building, is the giant, red stabile **Stegosaurus (1)** by Alexander Calder. On the triangular open space diagonally across from the Atheneum, note Carl Andre's controversial sculpture **Stone Field (2)**, a group of 36 boulders arranged in a geometrical pattern.

★**Connecticut State Capitol** – *210 Capitol Ave. Open Apr–Oct Mon–Fri 8am–5pm, Sat 10:15am–2:15pm. Rest of the year Mon–Fri 7am–6pm. Closed major holidays.* ✗ ⅗ 🅿 ☎ *860-240-0222.* This array of turrets, finials, gables, porches and towers, designed by Richard Upjohn, was the talk of the town when it was built in 1879. Rising above heavily sculpted walls, the capitol's golden dome overlooks **Bushnell Park**, designed originally by Frederick Law Olmsted.

The hand-painted columns, elaborate stenciling, courtyards, stained-glass windows, marble floors and balconies of the **interior** all produce a startling effect. The capitol houses the legislative chambers and offices of state officials. Legislative offices are located in the five-story **Legislative Office Building**, which is joined to the capitol by both a terraced walkway and an underground concourse.

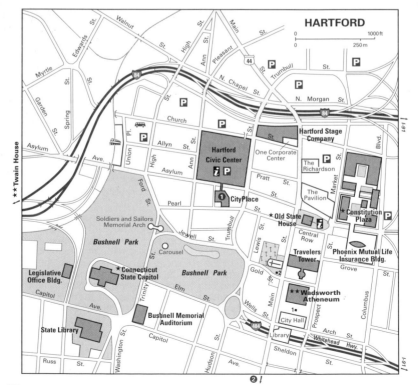

State Library – *231 Capitol Ave. Open year-round Mon–Fri 9am–5pm. Closed major holidays.* ✗ ⅙ ☎ *860-566-4777. www.cslib.org.* This building, across from the capitol, houses the State Library *(east wing)*, the state's Supreme Court *(west wing)* and the State Museum *(center wing)*. Museum exhibits include Colt firearms, revolving displays of Connecticut history and the Fundamental Orders of Connecticut *(p 49)*.

Bushnell Memorial Auditorium – *Trinity St. and Capitol Aves.* Concerts, opera, ballet, films and plays are presented in this brick Colonial-style building erected in 1930 as a memorial to Rev. Horace Bushnell (1802-76).

ADDITIONAL SIGHTS *2 hrs. Map p 49.*

★★**Mark Twain House** – *351 Farmington Ave. Take I-84 west to Exit 46. Turn right on Sisson Ave., then right on Farmington. Visit by guided tour (1 hr) only, Memorial Day–mid-Oct & Dec Mon–Sat 9:30am–5pm, Sun 11am–5pm. Rest of the year Mon, Wed–Sat 9:30am–5pm, Sun noon–5pm. Closed major holidays. $9.* ▣ ☎ *860-493-6411. www.hartnet.org/twain.* Today a memorial to the well-known author, this delightful house was one of the comfortable Victorian dwellings that stood on **Nook Farm**, a "nook" of woodland beside the north branch of the Park River. In the 19C a community of writers lived in this pastoral setting, including Mark Twain and Harriet Beecher Stowe, whose homes have been restored and may be visited.

Mark Twain House

Twain commissioned this whimsical Stick-style Victorian pile in 1874. During his residency in this house (1874-91), he wrote seven of his most successful works, including *The Adventures of Tom Sawyer* (1876) and *The Adventures of Huckleberry Finn* (1884). Outside, a profusion of open porches, balconies, towers, brackets and steeply pitched roofs give the structure a free, irregular shape. Inside, the splendid decoration done in 1881 has been restored: note in particular the silver stenciling, elaborately carved woodwork and exquisite wall coverings.

Harriet Beecher Stowe Center (**A**) – *77 Forest St. Visit by guided tour (1 hr) only, Jun–Columbus Day & Dec Mon–Sat 9:30am–5pm, Sun noon–5pm. Rest of the year Mon, Wed–Sat 9:30am–5pm, Sun noon–5pm. Last tour 1 hr before closing. Closed major holidays. $6.50* ▣ ☎ *860-525-9317. www.hartnet.org/~stowe.* Near the

---

■ Mark Twain

As everyone knows, Mark Twain was the pen name of Samuel Clemens (1835-1910), who was born in Florida, Missouri. Humorist nonpareil and inveterate observer of humanity, Twain derived his alias from riverboat jargon. During a stint as a Mississippi River boat pilot, he had learned that "mark twain" was the call for a water depth of two fathoms. A high-spirited and good-natured individualist, Twain smoked 20 cigars a day, slept backward in his bed in order to face its carved headboard, and did most of his best writing in the Billiard Room of his Hartford home. New inventions intrigued him—he owned the first private telephone in Hartford. His hospitality was legendary, and he counted among his closest friends Gen. William Tecumseh Sherman and Rudyard Kipling.

2 Modern Pastry Shop, Inc.

422 Franklin Ave. ☏ *860-296-7628.* It's worth the drive to South Hartford to the Italian neighborhood located along Franklin Avenue, where there's a wide choice of dining establishments. But if time is short, stop at this bakery for cannoli and espresso. Try a custard filled (with either chocolate or vanilla) or the traditional ricotta cheese-filled cannoli. If you're still hungry, an assortment of cookies (almond paste, butter and chocolate), cakes, tortes, pies and over 30 Italian and French pastries awaits you.

Twain house stands a simple Victorian cottage, which was the writer's home from 1873 until her death (1896). Stowe, whose novel *Uncle Tom's Cabin* led to an unprecedented attack on slavery, wrote several novels about New England.

Lacy gingerbread motifs adorn the plain facade. The light, airy interior contains furnishings that belonged to Stowe.

Next door is the handsome **Day House** (**B**) *(also featured on the tour)*, which contains the Nook Farm research library and changing exhibits. Katharine S. Day was Stowe's grandniece and a prime force in preserving the farm's structures.

EXCURSIONS

★**Wethersfield** – *5mi south of Hartford by I-91. See Entry Heading.*

★**Dinosaur State Park** – 🄺🄸🄳🅂 *10mi south of Hartford, in Rocky Hill. West St.* *Take I-91 to Exit 23, turn left at the light. Open year-round Tue–Sun 9am–4:30pm. $2.* ♿ ☏ *860-529-8423. www.dinosaurstatepark.org.* The park offers a good opportunity to observe, intact and at their original site, more than 500 dinosaur tracks. The size of the impressions and the 4ft-long pace suggest that the two-legged dinosaurs that made these tracks were probably 8ft tall and about 20ft long. A full-scale model of *Dilophosaurus*, the dinosaur considered the best match for these tracks, and a model of Coelophysis, some skeletal remains of which have been found in the Connecticut Valley, are part of the exhibit. A geodesic dome constructed in 1978 protects the excavated site and accompanying displays. In the casting area, visitors may make plaster casts of actual tracks *(open May–Oct daily 9am–3:30pm; visitors must provide their own materials; call for information).*

★**Farmington** – *10mi west of Hartford by I-84. See Entry Heading.*

★**Old New-Gate Prison and Copper Mine** – *14mi northeast of Hartford, in East Granby. Take I-91 north to Rte. 20 west. Turn right onto Newgate Rd. Open May–Oct Wed–Sun 10am–4:30pm. $4.* ☏ *860-653-3563. Rubber-soled shoes advised.* This former copper mine was worked until the mid-18C when financial setbacks induced the owners to sell the property to the colonial government. The government transformed the mine into the state's first prison in 1773. Here, robbers, counterfeiters, horse thieves and, later, Tories and British prisoners of war were held captive. Walking through the cold, damp mine tunnels buried deep within the earth, visitors can imagine the despair of those prisoners who, as a precaution against escape, were forced to sleep in these sunless subterranean passageways.

★**New Britain Museum of American Art** – *15mi southwest of Hartford, in New Britain. 56 Lexington St. Take I-84 to Exit 35 onto Rte. 72 east. Take Exit 8. Turn left at traffic light onto Lake St. At the stop sign, turn right and then immediate left onto Lexington St. Open year-round Tue–Fri noon–5pm, Sat 10am–5pm, Sun noon–5pm. Closed major holidays. $4.* ♿ ☏ *860-229-0257. www.nbmaa.org.* The holdings of this small museum illustrate trends in American art from the colonial period to the present. The 18C portraitists (Trumbull, Stuart, Smibert), the Hudson River school, the eight artists of the Ashcan school (including Sloan, Henri, Luks) and such renowned 19C and 20C masters as Homer, Whistler, Wyeth and Cassatt dominate the collection. Thomas Hart Benton's series of murals *Arts of Life in America* (1932), painted originally for the Whitney Museum of American Art in New York City, has been permanently installed here. *"Looking at Art,"* a museum publication ($5) available at the museum shop, is helpful for viewing the collection.

Talcott Mountain State Park – *8mi northwest of Hartford. Leave Hartford on Rte. 189, then follow Rte. 185 to park entrance. Grounds open year-round daily 8am–dusk. Tower open Labor Day–Oct daily 10am–5pm; late Apr–early Sept Thu–Sun 10am–5pm.* ☏ *860-242-1158.* A trail *(1.3mi)* leads up to the Heublein Tower, which affords a sweeping **view**★ across the Farmington Valley to Hartford, and south to Long Island Sound.

New England Air Museum – 🧒 *14mi northeast of Hartford, in Windsor Locks. Bradley International Airport. Take I-91 north to Rte. 20 west, then Rte. 75 north. Open year-round daily 10am–5pm. Closed Thanksgiving Day & Dec 25. $6.75.* ♿ ☎ *860-623-3305. www.neam.org.* Located in two spacious buildings on the west side of Bradley airport, the museum displays some 70 aircraft, which trace the history of aviation. Among the earliest exhibits is the 1909 Blériot XI, one of the first to be produced on a broad scale. Developments of later decades are high-lighted by a large number of military aircraft. Helicopters are also on view; note the large Sikorsky Seabat used for rescue missions in Antarctica.

Suffield – *18mi north of Hartford by I-91 north, Rte. 20 west, then Rte. 75 north. See Entry Heading.*

LITCHFIELD HILLS★★

Map of Principal Sights
Tourist Office ☎ 860-567-4506

The area known as the Litchfield Hills, situated in Connecticut's northwest territory just south of Massachusetts' Berkshire Hills, covers some 1,000sq mi of countryside and woodland—much of it preserved as state parks and wildlife sanctuaries. Some 30 towns, distinguished by pristinely preserved Main Streets and 18C homes, dot the Litchfield Hills. Comely country inns and B&Bs, antique shops, art galleries and craft stores greet visitors to this tranquil corner of New England.

The broad **Housatonic River** quietly traverses the thickly wooded and hilly extreme north-west section of Connecticut, between the foothills of the Taconic Mountains and the Berkshire Hills. The beauty of Housatonic Valley and its proximity to New York have made Litchfield Hills a favorite of artists, writers and businesspeople.

Historical Notes – The area experienced a brief period of prosperity in the 18C when iron ore was discovered in the Litchfield Hills. Forges were built and operated until coal-fields were discovered in Pennsylvania. Ruins of the old furnaces still remain in several villages, although they are usually hidden by the woods that have grown up around them. Today Litchfield Hills is a peaceful landscape, with no raucous entertainment districts, glaring neon signs or noisy highways. Quiet country roads lead to the small colonial villages, across covered bridges and through parks and forests. Trails (including the **Appalachian Trail**) crisscrossing the region's parks and forests are used by skiers in the winter and hikers during the milder seasons. Alongside these trails, streams and falls mark the path of the Housatonic as it flows downstream to Long Island Sound.

Housatonic River

★★LITCHFIELD

A photographer's paradise in Indian summer when the trees are afire with color, Litchfield is a small, reserved New England village with broad streets and stately clapboard dwellings dating from the 18C.

The nation's first law school and first institution of higher learning for women (Miss Pierce's School) were established in Litchfield during this early period. In the 19C the railroad and industrial development bypassed the center of town, a fact that accounts for Litchfield's having one of the loveliest and best-preserved ensembles of early American architecture in Connecticut.

White Flower Farm

Rte. 63, 3mi south of Litchfield. ☎ *860-567-8789.* Exploring this quintessential Connecticut landscape of tree-shaded lanes, meadows and perennial gardens is more like visiting a botanical park than a working nursery. Among the highlights of the self-guided walking tour are the rose arbor, a spring cottage garden, an all-white moon garden and a greenhouse display of lush tuberous begonias. The 63-acre farm sells every imaginable type of bulb, perennial, shrub and ornamental species. The small shop stocks garden books, stationery and cards, pottery, candles and other gift items. Make your purchases here at the nursery or order through the beautifully illustrated free catalog.

The Green – North, South, East and West Streets meet at the green, dominated by Litchfield's **First Congregational Church**. Nearby, the **Litchfield Historical Society Museum★** organizes exhibits related to life in 18C and 19C Litchfield *(7 South St.; open mid-Apr–Nov Tue–Sat 11am–5pm, Sun 1pm–5pm; $5, includes admission to Tapping Reeve House;* ♿ ☎ *860-567-4501).* Many handsome dwellings can be found along **North** and **South Streets**; most are privately owned and are accessible to the public only during the historic homes tour in mid-July.

Tapping Reeve House and Law School – *82 South St. Same hours as Historical Society; combined admission fee.* ☎ *860-567-4501.* The home of Tapping Reeve, founder of the nation's first law school (1775), stands near the one-room schoolhouse where he taught classes. A recently installed interactive exhibit traces the school's history, 19C student life in Litchfield and other related topics.

★White Memorial Foundation and Conservation Center – *2mi west of Litchfield by Rte. 202 west. Grounds open daily year-round.* ☎ *860-567-0857.* Varied vegetation and landscapes abound on this 4,000-acre preserve, which is owned and operated by the White Memorial Foundation. A map of the center's hiking trails and historic buildings may be purchased at the museum *(open year-round Mon–Sat 9am–5pm, Sun noon–4pm; closed major holidays; $4;* ♿ *)* or Foundation office *(on the grounds).*

DRIVING TOUR: ALONG THE RIVER *3 hrs. 24mi. Map below.*

This itinerary follows Route 7, once a major route linking Montreal and New York City, from Bulls Bridge along the Housatonic River north to West Cornwall. Three state parks are included in the tour as well as the towns of Kent and West Cornwall.

Begin at Bulls Bridge, 3mi north of Gaylordsville on Rte. 7. Turn left onto Bulls Bridge Rd., which passes over a covered bridge that spans the Housatonic River. After crossing a second bridge, turn right onto Schaghticoke Rd.

Schaghticoke Road – *The first mile of this narrow road is largely unpaved.* The road follows the river as it winds through wooded terrain that is offset by patches of gnarled ledges and rock formations bordering the riverbed. After 1mi, the road arrives at the Schaghticoke Indian Reservation and passes an old Indian burial ground. The inscription on one of the stones reads simply: "Eunice-Mauwee – A Christian Indian Princess 1756-1860."

The road passes the buildings of **Kent School**, a prestigious private secondary school (525 students).

Turn left onto Rte. 341.

Macedonia Brook State Park – *Follow Rte. 341 for 1mi, then turn right and follow the signs. Open year-round daily 8am–dusk.* ⚠ *(seasonal)* ☎ *860-424-3200. http://dep.state.ct.us/rec.* The park, with its rocky gorge, streams, and brook, offers camping, fishing and hiking.

Take Rte. 341 to Kent.

Kent – Nestled among the hills bordering the Housatonic River, Kent is the home of artists and craftspeople whose works are often displayed in shops in the village center.

★**Sloane-Stanley Museum** – *On Rte. 7, 1mi north of junction of Rtes. 7 & 341. Open mid-May–Oct Wed–Sun 10am–4pm. $3.50.* ☎ *860-927-3849.* Located near the ruins of the Old Kent Furnace (19C), this museum contains a fine collection of early American wooden and iron tools, acquired and arranged artistically by American artist Eric Sloane (1905-85). A video *(30min)* on Sloane is available for viewing.

Follow Rte. 7 north.

Kent Falls State Park – *Entrance on Rte. 7. Open year-round daily 8am–dusk. $5-$8/car.* ☎ *860-424-3200. http://dep.state.ct.us/rec.* Steps to the right of the falls lead to a point from which the cascades can be viewed from above. From this point, one can cross the bridge and descend to the parking lot by following a path *(30min)* through the woods.

Route 7 passes through the hamlet of **Cornwall Bridge**, where the local general store is a welcome sight to hikers on the Appalachian Trail.

Housatonic Meadows State Park – *Entrance on Rte. 7. Open year-round daily 8am–dusk.* ⚠ *(seasonal)* ☎ *860-424-3200. http://dep.state.ct.us/rec.* The **Pine Knob Loop Trail** *(round-trip 2 hrs from the parking lot on the west side of Rte. 7)* leads to the summit of **Pine Knob** (1,160ft) where there are views into the Housatonic Valley.

Return to Rte. 7 and continue north to West Cornwall.

★**West Cornwall** – This tiny village with several shops and restaurants is known for its picturesque **covered bridge**, built in 1864 and recently restored.

ADDITIONAL SIGHTS

★**American Clock and Watch Museum** – *In Bristol. 100 Maple St. Take I-84 to Exit 31. Follow Rte. 229 to the right for 3mi. Turn left on Woodland St. Open Apr–Nov daily 10am–5pm. Closed Thanksgiving Day. $3.50.* ☎ *860-583-6070.* In the 19C America's clockmaking industry was centered in the Bristol area, where in 1860 alone, more than 200,000 clocks were produced. The neighboring towns of Terryville and Thomaston were named for Connecticut clockmakers **Eli Terry** and **Seth Thomas**. By using standardized wooden parts, Terry made it possible to turn out a moderately priced time-piece. His innovation, the small, compact **shelf clock**, was easily carried by Yankee peddlers *(p 58)* who sold thousands of these lightweight timepieces in states east of the Mississippi.

Most of the clocks and watches in the museum's collection were produced in Connecticut. The annex contains novelty clocks and timepieces easily identified by their shape: acorn, banjo and tall case clocks.

★**Bellamy-Ferriday House and Garden** – *In Bethlehem, via Rtes. 63 and 61. On the green. Visit by guided tour (30min) only, May–Oct Wed, Fri & weekends 11am–4pm. Closed major holidays. $5.* ☎ *203-266-7596.* This two-story clapboard Georgian-style house, graced with a Palladian portico, was built about 1745 and enlarged and embellished over the next 200 years. The interior includes vernacular furnishings from the area.

Housatonic Hangouts

By the time the doors open every morning at 8am, Patsy Stroble and her crew of bakers have been up for hours preparing the linzer tarts, croissants, miniature cheesecakes and giant sugar cookies that make tiny **Stroble Baking Co.** *(14 N. Main St. in Kent* ☎ *860-927-4073)* a local landmark. If you arrive early enough, the muffins and bread will still be warm; the coffee is always hot. Stroble's also offers sandwiches, salads, homemade soup and cold drinks.

April is the time to shoot the rapids on the Housatonic River. Just when the waters are wildest, trained guides from **Clarke Outdoors** *(163 Rt. 7 in West Cornwall* ☎ *860-673-6365)* offer class IV-V white-water rafting trips through the Bulls Bridge Gorge *(call for reservations).* For a calmer paddle in summer or autumn, rent a canoe or kayak and travel a 6mi stretch of flat water; you can pull up on shore by the covered bridge in West Cornwall to take a lunch break in the village. A shuttle returns upriver at the end of the run.

Hickory Stick Bookshop
Rte. 47 in the center of Washington. ☎ 860-868-0525. Although one of the many nationally known authors living in Litchfield Hills—including Philip Roth and Arthur Miller—might be on hand for a signing, the real draw at this welcoming bookstore is the vast selection of current books, plus the personal service. People come from all over the state to browse the well-stocked sections on fiction, photography, nature, cooking, sports, music, biography, history, reference, poetry and drama. There is also an attention-grabbing children's corner as well as a great choice of stationery, greeting cards and gifts.

Dotted with white barns and orchards, the grounds feature a 1912 garden with lilacs, peonies, magnolias and roses in season.

Institute for American Indian Studies – *In Washington. 38 Curtis Rd. Take Rte. 199 south 2mi to Curtis Rd. and follow signs to the institute. Open Apr–Dec Mon–Sat 10am–5pm, Sun noon–5pm. Rest of the year Wed–Sat 10am–5pm, Sun noon–5pm. Closed major holidays. $4. ☎ 860-868-0518.* This small museum in a peaceful woodland setting honors the culture and history of Connecticut Indians. Exhibits include archaeological artifacts, handcrafted splint baskets and a longhouse room.
A short nature trail leads to a re-created Algonquin encampment, complete with a longhouse and several **wigwams**.

Hitchcock Chair Factory – *Rte. 20, in Riverton. Factory store open year-round Mon–Fri 10am–5pm, Sat 10am–6pm, Sun noon–5pm. Closed Easter Sunday, Thanksgiving Day & Dec 25. ♿ ☎ 860-379-4826. www.hitchcockchair.com.* Lambert Hitchcock's chair factory, established here in the early 19C, turned out thousands of rush-seated "fancy" hand-stenciled chairs that were sold throughout the country. Restored in 1946, the factory is again producing chairs, tables and chests in the Hitchcock tradition.

Glebe House Museum and Jekyll Garden – *In Woodbury. Hollow Rd. off Rte. 6. Open Apr–Nov Wed–Sun 1pm–4pm. $5. ☎ 203-263-2855.* In 1783 a group of Anglican clergy met here and elected Samuel Seabury (1729-1796) the first bishop in the colonies (he had to travel to Scotland to be ordained). Considered the birthplace of the Episcopal Church in this country, the restored c.1750 gambrel-roof dwelling built on a **glebe** (land set aside for the parish priest) reflects the Revolutionary period.
Surrounding the house, Colonial Revival perennial borders brim with lupines and hollyhocks. They were planted in the 1990s in accordance with plans designed for the property in the 1920s by English garden designer Gertrude Jeckyll, but not implemented at the time.

■ The Yankee Peddler and the Nutmeg State

No figure of Connecticut lore better personifies the New Englander's reputation for driving a hard bargain than the Yankee peddler. A term of many incarnations, **Yankee** derives from a pejorative *(Janke)* introduced here by 17C Dutch traders on the Connecticut River, and by 1800 the word was used as a verb specifically meaning "to cheat." As the western frontier opened up in the 19C, Yankee became synonymous with the peripatetic **Connecticut salesmen** who set out for remote rural areas with wagons and wicker baskets full of locally made tin utensils, clocks, penny banks, shoes, mousetraps, baskets—and the occasional broken watch, stagnant barometer and magic nostrum said to cure everything from bunions to head colds.
In the 1830s a series of essays satirizing the proverbially dishonest Connecticut peddler by Canadian writer Thomas Haliburton included the apparently false accusation that crafty Yankee salesmen were also passing off **wooden nutmegs** to unsuspecting housewives. Cheap and plentiful, nutmegs were imported in quantity from the West Indies to Connecticut ports, and it is doubtful that anyone would bother to carve wooden imitations when the real thing was so easily accessible. Nevertheless, the story stuck. One entrepreneur did sell wooden nutmegs as Connecticut souvenirs at the 1876 Philadelphia Centennial Exhibition—claiming each and every one was made from Hartford's famed Charter Oak, which had fallen down in a storm some 20 years earlier. For their own part, Connecticut residents took characteristically perverse pleasure in the sobriquet "Nutmeg State" and adopted it as their own.

MYSTIC SEAPORT★★★

Map of Principal Sights

The village of **Mystic**, on the Mystic River, has been a shipbuilding center since the 17C. Today Mystic is known primarily as the site of Mystic Seaport, a museum-village that re-creates the atmosphere of America's maritime past. This living replica of a 19C waterfront community features tall ships, a village center and a working shipyard, all of which add to the authenticity of the setting. Museum buildings house extensive collections of marine art and artifacts, providing visitors with insight into New England's seagoing past.

Historical Notes – In the 1850s clipper ships were built in Mystic's boatyards, which lined the 6mi Mystic River. At about the same time, whaling became a major industry on the coast and Mystic's fleet grew to include some 18 whaling ships. (The only wooden whaler remaining in this country, the *Charles W. Morgan*, is the centerpiece of Mystic Seaport today.) By the 1880s, however, shipbuilding declined and continued to decline into the 20C, endangering Mystic's (and America's) maritime heritage. Three individuals residing in the town established the Marine Historical Assn. in 1929 in an effort to preserve Mystic's maritime past. The museum has grown from a collection of nautical memorabilia displayed in a renovated mill to a complex of some 60 buildings covering 17 acres, formerly the site of timber ponds and shipbuilding yards. In 1978 the name Mystic Seaport was adopted and today the popular attraction is maintained as a private, nonprofit educational facility.

VISIT *1 day*

Kids *From I-95 Exit 90, follow Rte. 27 south. Open Apr–Oct daily 9am–5pm. Rest of the year daily 10am–4pm. Closed Dec 25. $16. Schedule of daily events and map are available at entrance.* ✖ ☎ *860-572-5315. www.mysticseaport.org.*

Begin your visit at the visitor center at the main entrance. A video *(shown continuously)* offers a good introduction to the seaport.
The 1908 steamboat **Sabino** makes trips *(30min)* on the river *(mid-May–mid-Oct daily 11am–4pm, every hour on the hour; $3.50 in addition to museum admission; &.)*.

The Village and Waterfront – The heart of the village is the waterfront. Along the wharves and adjacent streets are shops and businesses commonly found in a 19C seaport: the bank, printer, tavern, ship's chandlery, the shops of the craftsmen who worked to outfit the vessels, and the ropewalk—the incredibly long cordage company building where the miles of rope necessary for rigging large vessels were made.
Youngsters will particularly enjoy the **Children's Museum**, where they may participate in games and shipboard activities that were popular during the sailing era.
Three impressive, fully rigged sailing vessels are moored at the waterfront.

The Charles W. Morgan – The *Morgan*, sole survivor of America's 19C whaling fleet, has been declared a National Historic Site. During some 80 years of service, the *Morgan* made 37 voyages, a number of which lasted three to four years. Visitors may board the ship to examine the crew's quarters and gigantic try-pots, the cauldrons used to melt whale fat.

The Joseph Conrad – This Danish-built training vessel (1882) has sailed under the Danish, British and American flags. Property of Mystic Seaport, the *Conrad* now serves its original function as a training ship.

The L.A. Dunton – This graceful schooner, built in 1921, typifies the fishing vessels that once sailed from New England to the Grand Banks off Newfoundland in the 1920s and 30s.

Mystic Seaport

Fred M. Dole/f/STOP PICTURES

Kitchen Little

81-1/2 Greenmanville Ave.
☏ *860-536-2122.* Located near Mystic Seaport, this tiny, waterside eatery is well known for its huge and inventive breakfasts *(6:30am–2pm),* with egg dishes called the Mystic Melt, the Portuguese Fisherman or the Kitchen Sink. There's also pancakes, French toast and other morning staples. Lunch portions are hearty too. If indoor seating is not available, share a picnic table outside at the rear with the seagulls.

Henry B. du Pont Preservation Shipyard – All kinds of boats from the seaport's vast collection are restored here. Visitors may observe craftsmen at work from a platform on the second level.

Mystic River Scale Model – The exhibit features a large model of Mystic as the village appeared in 1853.

Stillman Building – The three-story building contains outstanding collections of **ship models** and **scrimshaw**. A film *(10min)* dating from 1917 depicts the rigors of a whale hunt. Beginning in the summer of 2000, a 6,700sq ft exhibit will highlight the nation's historic and contemporary connections to its rivers, lakes and oceans.

Wendell Building – This building houses the seaport's rich collection of wooden **ship figureheads**.

ADDITIONAL SIGHT

★★ **Mystic Aquarium** – 🔲 *55 Coogan Blvd. in Mystic. Open Jul–Labor Day daily 9am–6pm. Rest of Sept–Jun daily 9am–5pm. Closed Jan 1, Thanksgiving Day, Dec 25. $15.* ✗ ♿ ☏ *860-572-5955. www.mysticaquarium.org.* More than 6,000 sea creatures, including four-eyed fish and Australian mudskippers, make their home in this "institute for exploration." A six-year, $52 million renovation and expansion has resulted in one of the largest and most ecologically minded aquariums in the nation. Living specimens of marine animals and plants are grouped into some 45 major exhibits demonstrating aquatic communities, habitat and adaptation. In the new **Ocean Planet Pavilion**, bonnethead sharks prowl a 30,000 tank shared with 500 exotic fish, while the **Sunlit Seas** exhibits feature species that thrive in ecosystems such as estuaries and coral reefs. Atlantic bottlenose dolphins, known for their sunny dispositions, play in the World of the Dolphin tank *(daily demonstrations in the theater).* Conceived by eminent oceanographer Dr. Robert Ballard, the **Challenge of the Deep** exhibit "submerges" visitors below the ocean surface to explore the diverse sea life, the resting place of the Titanic and the shipwreck of an ancient Roman vessel. Outside, African black-footed penguins, endangered Steller's sea lions, northern fur seals and graceful beluga whales can all be found in settings constructed to resemble their natural habitats.

EXCURSIONS

★★ **Mashantucket Pequot Museum** – 🔲
7mi northeast of Mystic. From I-95, take exit 92, then Rte. 2 west and follow signs to museum. Open Memorial Day–Labor Day daily 10am–7pm. Rest of the year Wed–Mon 10am–6pm. Last admission 1 hr before closing. Closed Jan 1, Thanksgiving Day, Dec 25. $10. ✗ ♿ ☏ *860-396-6800. www.mashantucket.com.* This tribally owned-and-operated musem is devoted to the history and culture of the Mashantucket Pequot Indians, a southeastern Connecticut tribe who have lived continuously on the 3,000-acre reservation granted to them by the Connecticut Colony in 1666. The Pequots were nearly exterminated in the Pequot War of 1637, in which colonists and Mohegan, Narragansett and Niantic Indians attacked and set fire to a major Pequot settlement. Set on the original reservation, the glass and concrete facility (1998) incorporates a futuristic design that pays homage to nature by embracing woodland views and integrating stone and gurgling streams into the modern structure. Nearby, an earlier Pequot enterprise, the **Foxwoods Resort Casino**, was developed after the tribe received federal recognition and funding in 1983.

Abbott's Lobster in the Rough

117 Pearl St., Noank (2.5mi southwest of Mystic via Rte. 215). ☏ *860-536-7719.* The large parking lot is a clue that Abbott's is indeed a popular place to eat. This rambling lobster shack is right on the waters of Fishers Island Sound and the views are great, especially while you're consuming some of the best lobster around. So dress casually and head for the large outdoor menu board to choose your lobster by weight. Or try the Hot Lobster Roll (1/4lb on a toasted bun) or the generous Seafood Feast (chowder, shrimp, steamers, mussels, lobster with slaw, chips and drawn butter). It's ok to bring your own beer or wine since alcoholic beverages are not served on the premises.

Inside the museum, dioramas, interactive videos, films, campfire aromas and recorded bird songs create a multisensory experience that focuses on day-to-day life from prehistoric times to the present. Off the entry hall is the entrance to a 185ft tower that permits views of the reservation. The self-guided tour begins in the dramatic 60ft high glass atrium known as the Gathering Space, then progresses by ramp, escalator or elevator to exhibits underground. On level one, visitors pass through a simulated glacial crevasse on an exploration of the ice age; a life-size, computer-animated diorama of a caribou hunt illustrates the rigors of nomadic existence. The highlight of the museum is the indoor 16C **Pequot Village**, a 22,000sq ft re-creation of a native dwelling site, complete with wigwams, cornfields, pond and canoe. Surrounding the village are three interpretive galleries showcasing artifacts of 16C and 17C Pequot life; videos capture the painstaking process of making arrowheads, wampum, wigwams and clothing. Level two is devoted to reservation life from the 17C to the present.

★**Stonington** – *4mi east of Mystic on Rte. 1, then Rte. 1A.* This is one of the prettiest coastal villages in Connecticut. The early character of this former shipbuilding center is preserved by the lovely old homes lining Stonington's tree-shaded streets. From the stone lighthouse, there is a view to Fishers Island, which is privately owned.

Randall's Ordinary
Rte. 2, North Stonington. ☎ *860-599-4540.* This country inn and restaurant is situated on a peaceful 200-acre farm, established in 1685. Prepared in an open hearth fireplace by staff in period costume, the colonial fare is served as a prix fixe meal with choice of scallops, duck or angus steak, for example. Shaker herb or butternut squash soup, bread baked in the beehive oven and a variety of vegetables accompany the entrée, all presented on handsome pottery crafted in Bennington, Vermont. From the tiny adjoining tap room, a barmaid serves Madeira wine, ale or cider. Apple crisp, or bread pudding based on a recipe said to be from Thomas Jefferson, complete the repast.

Old Lighthouse Museum – *7 Water St. Open Jul–Aug daily 10am–5pm. May–Jun & Sept–Oct Tue–Sun 10am–5pm. Rest of the year by appointment only. $4.* ☎ *860-535-1440.* Seasonal exhibits in the old lighthouse are nostalgic reminders of Stonington's days as a shipbuilding center and sealing and whaling port. Artifacts date from the 17-19C and include portraits, whaling tools and scrimshaw. Visitors may climb to the lighthouse tower for a view encompassing three states: Rhode Island, New York and Connecticut.

NEW HAVEN★★

Population 130,474
Map of Principal Sights
Tourist Office ☎ 203-777-8550

Seen from I-95, New Haven appears to be a city of manufacturing facilities and tall office towers, such as the unusual cylindrical-towered **Knights of Columbus Building** framed by the red basalt ridges of East Rock and West Rock Parks. Only by leaving the interstate and driving toward the green can visitors discover the serene residential streets (Whitney Avenue, Hillhouse Avenue, Prospect Street), a quaint commercial district (College and Chapel Streets) and the ivy-covered buildings of Yale University.

Historical Notes

The first planned city in America was founded in 1638 by a group of Puritans led by the Rev. John Davenport and Theophilus Eaton. New Haven was at first an independent colony. Efforts to develop the settlement's economy were unsuccessful, and in 1662 New Haven was made part of Connecticut Colony.

In the 18C New Haven's founders realized their dream when the colony flourished because of its deepwater harbor. The War of 1812 brought an end to this prosperous period in New Haven, as it did in other ports throughout New England.

The face of the town changed forever with the arrival of the railroad in the 19C. Industry and manufacturing developed, and immigrants came by the thousands to work in Connecticut's clock, firearms and carriage factories. One of the many innovative men in New Haven was **Eli Whitney**, who is recognized as the father of mass production. Whitney introduced the use of standardized parts as the basis of the assembly line in his arms factory outside the city.

By the mid-20C, burdened by the problems of unplanned industrial growth and increasing competition from the suburbs, the city rapidly deteriorated. Projects focusing on the revitalization of the downtown area, as well as the suburbs, were undertaken in the 1960s, resulting in the rehabilitation and construction of schools, homes and parks. Today New Haven is a blend of both traditional and modern architectural styles.

■ A Cultural Center

The presence of Yale University, with its museums, libraries and programs of music, theater and dance, has made New Haven a prominent cultural center. The wide range of fine shops and restaurants adds to the city's cosmopolitan flavor. The New Haven stage, once a proving ground for Broadway productions, has become well known in its own right.

Long Wharf Theater – *222 Sargent Dr. ☎ 203-787-4282*. Located in a former warehouse, this theater has been the recipient of a Tony Award.

Shubert Performing Arts Center (**1**) – *Map p 63. 247 College St. ☎ 203-624-1825*. The Shubert's varied program of performances includes Broadway-bound productions, Broadway road shows and concerts.

Palace Performing Arts Center (**2**) – *Map p 63. 246 College St. ☎ 203-789-2120*. Musicals and classical and popular concerts are presented at this 2,037-seat concert hall, formerly the Roger Sherman Theater.

Yale Repertory Theater (**3**) – *Map p 63. 1120 Chapel St. ☎ 203-432-1234*. The "Rep" focuses on plays written by young playwrights and on modern interpretations of the classics.

New Haven Symphony Orchestra – *70 Audubon St. ☎ 203-776-1444*. One of the finest in the nation, the city's resident symphony orchestra performs at Woolsey Hall (**G**) on the Yale campus.

Concerts are also staged at the **Yale School of Music** (**4**) *(map p 63)* ☎ *203-432-4157*.

★★★YALE UNIVERSITY *1 day. Map p 63.*

This Ivy League school is one of the oldest and most distinguished institutions of higher learning in the US. The university was founded in 1701 by a group of Puritan clergymen who wished to provide Connecticut with an educational institution where young men could be trained to serve the church and state. The school they established, known at first as the Collegiate School, was located in Saybrook. In 1716 the school was moved to the New Haven green, and two years later the Collegiate School was renamed Yale for its benefactor, the wealthy merchant **Elihu Yale**.

Organization – The university's 10,600 students, 4,000 faculty members, and staff represent a community of over 25,000 persons. Undergraduates are divided among 12 colleges, each of which has its own library, dining room, dormitories, social activities and athletic programs. Graduate programs are offered by Yale's schools of Art,

Architecture, Divinity, Drama, Forestry and Environmental Studies, Arts and Sciences, Law, Medicine, Music, Nursing and Management.

Yale gained university status in 1887, long after its Medical School (1810) and Law School (1824) were established. The nation's first Ph.D. degrees were awarded by Yale in 1861 and, before the turn of the century, women were admitted to the Ph.D. program. Women have been admitted to the undergraduate school since 1969.

Architecture – The architectural diversity that characterizes the Yale campus is dominated by the **Gothic** style, with its Medieval turrets, spires, massive towers, leaded stained glass and cathedral-like stone buildings. The **Georgian** influence is also significant, although the facades of most of these handsome structures are visible only from their courtyards.

Harkness Tower, Yale University

Michael Marsland/Yale University

In the 1920s and 30s, **James Gamble Rogers** designed Harkness Tower (1921), Sterling Memorial Library (1930), Pierson and Davenport Colleges (1932) and several other campus structures and spaces while serving as Yale's consulting architect. Because of his considerable impact on Yale's design, he has been called "the architect of Yale University." Since the 1950s Yale has commissioned leading architects of the day to design the university's more recent, modern structures: **Louis Kahn** (the Yale Art Gallery and the Yale Center for British Art); **Paul Rudolph** (School of Art and Architecture); **Eero Saarinen** (Morse and Ezra Stiles Colleges, the Yale Co-op and the Ingalls Hockey Rink); **Philip Johnson** (Kline Biology Tower) and **Gordon Bunshaft** (Beinecke Rare Book and Manuscript Library).

Walking Tour

Begin at the visitor center on Elm St.

Visitor Center – *149 Elm St. Open year-round Mon–Fri 9am–4:45pm, weekends 10am–4pm. Closed Jan 1, Thanksgiving Day, Dec 24, 25 & 31. Guided tours (1 hr 15min) of the campus available Mon–Fri 10:30am & 2pm, weekends 1:30pm; ☎ 203-432-2302. www.yale.edu.* Here visitors can obtain a fact booklet and other brochures about the university, its buildings, collections and campus sculpture. Staff members are available to answer questions.

*Proceed to Phelps Gate (**A**) on College St. Enter the Old Campus.*

Old Campus – This is the site of Yale's earliest college buildings. **Connecticut Hall** (**B**) is the university's oldest structure. A statue of Nathan Hale, a Yale alumnus, stands in front of this simple Georgian hall where Hale lived as a student.

Cross the Old Campus and exit onto High St.

Across High Street is the landmark **Harkness Tower** (**C**) (1920), a 221ft Gothic Revival bell tower heavily ornamented with carved figures of famous Yale alumni, among them Noah Webster and Eli Whitney.

Turn left on High St., pass under an arch, then turn right onto Chapel St.

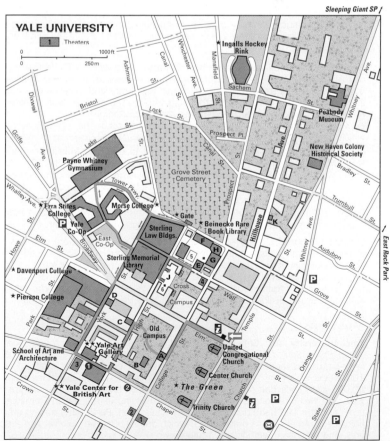

The **Yale University Art Gallery**, Louis Kahn's first major work, stands facing his last creation, the **Yale Center for British Art**. Both buildings present interesting conceptions of museum architecture from the point of view of building materials, light and the use of space. *Descriptions of the museums' collections pp 64-66.*

Continue to York St.

The former Gothic Revival-style church on the left is the **Yale Repertory Theater** (**3**) *(p 62)*, home of the Yale Repertory Company, a professional acting troupe at in residence at the university. Diagonally opposite stands Paul Rudolph's high-rise **School of Art and Architecture**. Seemingly seven stories tall, the building actually has 36 levels that are visible only from the interior.

Turn right onto York St. and continue about halfway down the street.

★**Pierson and Davenport Colleges** – These elegant Georgian buildings hidden beyond the colleges' Medieval-style, street-side facades may be seen from the courtyards. On the opposite side of the street stands **Wrexham Tower** (**D**), designed after the church in Wales where Elihu Yale is buried.

Cross Elm St. and continue on York St. At no. 306 York St., walk through the narrow passageway on the left.

★**Morse and Ezra Stiles Colleges** – Saarinen's design for this ensemble of contemporary buildings was inspired by an Italian hill town. A continuous play of light and shadows is created throughout the day by the maze of stone passages with their vertical planes, geometric forms and sharp angular turns.

Nearby is another of Saarinen's works, the **Yale Co-op** (now known as the West Co-op, since an adjacent building, the East Co-op, has been constructed).

On Tower Parkway, across the street from Morse and Ezra Stiles Colleges, is the **Payne Whitney Gymnasium**, one of Yale's cathedral-like structures.

Continue along Tower Pkwy., which becomes Grove St., to High St.

Note the massive Egyptian Revival-style **gate**★ at the entrance to Grove Street Cemetery. Its architect, **Henry Austin**, was responsible for several of the 19C houses on Hillhouse Avenue *(p 66)*.

Return via Grove St. to York St. Turn left onto York St., then left onto Wall St.

Sterling Law Buildings – Law students live in this group of buildings similar in design to the English Inns of Court where students during the 16-18C studied law. Portraits of police and robbers have been carved in stone above the windows.

Cross High St.

★**Beinecke Rare Book and Manuscript Library** – *121 Wall St.* The exterior walls of this library (1961, Gordon Bunshaft) are composed of a granite framework fitted with translucent marble panels. Enter the library and observe the unusual effect produced by the sunlight streaming through the marble slabs. A **Gutenberg Bible** and changing exhibits are displayed on the mezzanine.

Isamu Noguchi's **sculptures** (**5**) of geometric shapes anchor the sunken courtyard, which fronts the library.

Facing the library are several buildings erected to celebrate Yale's bicentennial: **Woodbridge Hall** (**E**) offices, the **University Dining Hall** (**F**) and **Woolsey Hall** (**G**) auditorium. The rotunda, **Memorial Hall** (**H**), contains a large group of commemorative plaques. On the plaza, near Woodbridge Hall, note Alexander Calder's red stabile *Gallows and Lollipops*.

Return to the corner of Wall and High Sts. and turn left onto High St. A number of small statues ornament the rooftops of buildings along this street.

Sterling Memorial Library – *120 High St.* This is Yale's main library, yet at first glance its stained-glass windows, frescoes and archways suggest a cathedral.

The **Cross Campus Library** (**J**), located beneath Cross Campus *(to the left)*, was built underground to allow the green to remain intact. Gracing the Cross Campus entry plaza is a granite **fountain sculpture** (**6**) honoring Yale women by **Maya Lin**, a former Yale student and designer of Washington DC's Vietnam Veterans Memorial.

Museums

★★**Yale University Art Gallery** – *1111 Chapel St. Open year round Tue–Sat 10am–5pm, Sun 1pm–6pm. Closed major holidays.* ♿ ☎ *203-432-0600. www.yale.edu/artgallery.* This gallery was founded in 1832 with a gift of some 100 works of art by the patriot artist **John Trumbull**. Today selections from an 80,000-piece collection ranging from early Eqyptian times to the present are displayed in two interconnected units: a 1928 building in the Italian Romanesque style, and the 1953 addition designed by Louis Kahn. Particularly strong are the holdings of American decorative arts, which are centered on colonial and federal eras, and American painting and sculpture.

Ground Floor – The collection of ancient art features a Mithraic shrine *(Temple to the Sun God)* with elaborate paintings and reliefs from **Dura-Europos**, an ancient Roman town in Syria. A selection of Greek, Etruscan and Egyptian vases and sculpture includes *Leda and the Swan* (370 BC), a Roman copy of a Greek original attributed to Timotheos. Equally noteworthy are the stone, clay, and jade artifacts in the growing **pre-Columbian** collection. The group figurines provide glimpses into the daily life of the period.

First Floor – Special exhibits and contemporary art are found on this floor. Noteworthy in the Sculpture Hall is Richard Serra's site-specific *Stacks* (1990), two steel monoliths placed 60ft apart. The Albers Corridor features a rotating selection of the gallery's 74 paintings and 110 prints by the German-born artist Joseph Albers, who chaired Yale's art department for 10 years (1950-60).

Second Floor – In addition to Impressionist paintings, the 19C collection includes works by Manet *(Young Woman Reclining in Spanish Costume)*, Courbet *(Le Grand Pont)*, Van Gogh *(Night Cafe)*, Millet, Corot, Degas and Matisse.

In the section devoted to early modern art, the visitor will find works by Marcel Duchamp *(Tu'm)*, Stella *(Brooklyn Bridge)*, Magritte *(Pandora's Box)* and Dali *(The Phantom Cart)* and canvases by Tanguy, Ernst, Klee and Kandinsky.

The Ordway Gallery contains changing exhibits of 20C art. Paintings by Picasso *(Coquillages sur un piano; Femme assise)*, Renoir *(Mount St. Victoire)*, Pollock *(No. 4)*, Rothko *(No. 3, 1967)* and de Kooning are featured.

The collection of **African art** comprises masks, and ceremonial and royal objects.

Third Floor – The **Jarves collection** of early Italian painting (13-16C) includes such jewels as da Fabriano's *Madonna and Child* and Ghirlandaio's *Portrait of a Lady with a Rabbit*. The adjacent galleries, devoted to European art, contain the Medieval collection. Among the European paintings are portraits by Holbein and Hals, an oil sketch by Rubens, Correggio's *Assumption of the Virgin*, and the *Allegory of Intemperance* attributed to Hieronymus Bosch.

The **Garven collection** of colonial and early-19C Americana is arranged didactically for the university's teaching purposes. Furniture, silver, pewter and ironware are used to illustrate the development of American art forms and their relationship to the society that produced them.

On view in the gallery of American paintings and sculpture from the 19C and 20C are masterpieces by, among others, Eakins, Homer, Church, Cole, Remington, Hopper and O'Keeffe. One section of the gallery displays works of John Trumbull including the original paintings *The Battle of Bunker Hill* and *Signing of the Declaration of Independence*, used as models for copies later produced by Trumbull for the Capitol in Washington DC. Hiram Powers' sculpture *The Greek Slave* is also on display.

Fourth Floor – The Asian galleries feature Japanese sculpture and Chinese bronzes, ceramics and paintings spanning the period from the 12C BC to the present.

★★**Yale Center for British Art** – *1080 Chapel St. Open year-round Tue–Sat 10am–5pm, Sun noon–5pm. Closed major holidays. ♿ P ☎ 203-432-2800. www.yale.edu/ycba.* The most comprehensive collection of British art outside the United Kingdom is housed in this center. In 1966 Paul Mellon, benefactor of the National Gallery in Washington DC, donated to Yale his collection of British art—more than 60,000 works, including 1,300 paintings, 10,000 drawings, 20,000 prints, and 20,000 rare books. Louis Kahn drew the plans for a new building to house the collection, which opened to the public in 1977. Kahn's design allows natural light to enter through numerous skylights and filter down through three- and four-story open

1 Scoozzi

1104 Chapel St. ☎ 203-776-8268. From the Yale Center for British Art, head up the street and down the stairs to this seemingly subterranean trattoria and wine bar for *insalate*, pasta and risotto that offer the perfect nourishment for museum hopping. A shaded courtyard and fast, friendly service complement the inventive cuisine, making the entire dining experience a satisfying one.

2 Union League Cafe

1032 Chapel St. ☎ 203-562-4299. Treat yourself to a bit of New Haven history and great cuisine at this French-inspired brasserie located just off the green. The graciously restored Sherman Building sits atop the homesite of Roger Sherman, a signer of the Declaration of Independence who served as the city's first mayor. Housed inside, Union League offers patrons an elegant yet relaxed setting for enjoying Old and New World delicacies at reasonable prices. Specialties range from artichokes in a basil and saffron sauce, whole wheat crepes with smoked salmon and sevruga caviar to succulent tenderloin of beef accompanied by the requisite potato gratin Dauphinois. Save room for house-made ice cream, tarts or mousse for dessert.

courts to the display areas. The museum also organizes large, often provocative temporary shows of British art (both contemporary and historical), as well as related lectures and film screenings.

The Collection – The collection, which surveys the development of English art during and after the Elizabethan period, includes sporting paintings, town and marine views, portraits and "conversation pieces" (informal group portraits) dating primarily from 1700 to 1850.

The **fourth floor** houses paintings and sculpture that have been installed chronologically to provide a survey of British art from the late 16C through the early 19C. Several rooms on this floor are reserved for the works of **Gainsborough**, **Reynolds**, **Stubbs**, **Turner** and **Constable**. On the **second floor** is a selection of 19C and 20C paintings and sculpture.

Peabody Museum – 🔳 *170 Whitney Ave. Open year-round Mon–Sat 10am–5pm, Sun noon–5pm. Closed major holidays. $5.* ♿ 🄿 ☎ *203-432-5050. www.peabody. yale.edu.* Yale's natural history museum showcases a famous collection of **dinosaurs** *(1st floor)* featuring a horned dinosaur, the first *Stegosaurus* ever mounted and the fossil of an *Apatosaurus* (67ft long, 35 tons). The 10ft *Archelon* (75 million years old) is the largest turtle in the world. The fossil skeleton of *Deinonychus*, a species discovered in 1964, sports a wicked, sickle-shaped claw. Rudolph Zallinger's mural *The Age of Reptiles* depicts the dinosaurs and plant life that existed 70 million to 350 million years ago. The first floor also houses a collection of mammals, primates and artifacts representing the cultures of Mesoamerica, the Plains Indians and New Guinea. Minerals and rocks, a bird hall and dioramas of North American flora and fauna can be found on the third floor. The second floor is reserved for special exhibits.

Yale Collection of Musical Instruments (**K**) – *15 Hillhouse Ave. Open Sept–Jun Tue–Thu 1pm–4pm. Closed Thanksgiving Day, Dec 25 and during university recesses. $1. A series of concerts is held annually featuring restored instruments from the collection.* ☎ *203-432-0822.* The collection consists of more than 800 instruments representative of the traditions of Western European music from the 16C to the 19C.

ADDITIONAL SIGHTS *Map p 63*

★**The Green** – When New Haven was a Puritan colony, the town was laid out as a giant square subdivided into nine smaller squares. The center square, the green, was reserved for the use of the entire community as pastureland, parade ground and burial ground, and has remained the heart of the downtown district over the years. Different architectural styles are represented by the three early 19C churches on the green: **Trinity Church** (Gothic Revival), **Center Church** (Georgian), **United Congregational Church** (Federal).

Hillhouse Avenue – Most of the beautiful mansions on this street were built in the 19C by wealthy industrialists and merchants and are now owned by Yale University. Architectural styles include Federal, Greek Revival, Renaissance Revival and even Hindu.

★**Ingalls Hockey Rink** – *Prospect St.* This lantern-shaped rink (1957) was designed for Yale by the Finnish-born architect Eero Saarinen.

New Haven Colony Historical Society – *114 Whitney Ave. Open Sept–Jun Tue–Fri 10am–5pm, weekends 2pm–5pm. Rest of the year Tue–Fri 10am–5pm, Sat 2pm–5pm. Closed major holidays. $2.* ♿ 🄿 ☎ *203-562-4183.* Antique pewter, china and toys dating from the period of the New Haven Colony are among the items on display in the society's 11 galleries.

East Rock Park – *Follow Orange St. Cross Mill River and turn left, then bear right. The road leads to the summit parking lot. Open mid-Apr–Oct daily 8am–dusk. Rest of the year weekends & holidays only 8am–dusk.* 🄿 ☎ *203-946-6086.* From the summit of this basalt ridge there is a **view**★★ of the entire New Haven area. In the distance stretches Long Island Sound.

EXCURSIONS

Shore Line Trolley Museum – 🔳 *5mi east of New Haven, in East Haven, by I-95. 17 River St. Take Exit 51, turn right onto Hemingway Ave., then left onto River St. Open Memorial Day–Labor Day daily 10:30am–4:30pm. May, Sept, Oct & early–mid-Dec weekends only 10:30am–4:30pm. Apr & Nov Sun only 10:30am–4:30pm. Closed Thanksgiving Day, Dec 25. $5. A 3mi trolley excursion takes riders along the Connecticut shore between the museum and Short Beach.* ♿ 🄿 ☎ *203-467-6927. www.bera.org.* The museum is primarily the work of volunteer trolley buffs who have restored one-third of the nearly 100 street, subway and elevated railway cars on the grounds.

Sleeping Giant State Park – *6mi from New Haven. Take Whitney Ave. (Rte. 10) to Hamden and turn right on Mt. Carmel Ave. Open year-round daily 8am–dusk. Trail maps and information available at ranger headquarters.* 🄿 ☎ *203-789-7498.* The park has picnic facilities and more than 30mi of trails around the Giant. **Tower Path** *(round-trip 1 hr 30min)* leads to the highest point in the park, where, from a stone tower, there are good **views**★★ of the region.

NEW LONDON

Population 28,540
Map of Principal Sights
Tourist Office ☎ 860-444-2206

Located on a harbor at the mouth of the Thames River, New London has always depended on the sea for its livelihood. Home to the US Coast Guard Academy, the city still has ties with the sea today.

Historical Notes – New London's deepwater port was a haven for privateers during the Revolution, a fact that led to the British attack on New London and GROTON in 1781. During this assault, led by Benedict Arnold, **Fort Trumbull** *(not open to the public)* and **Fort Griswold** fell to the enemy, and nearly all of New London was destroyed by fire. In the mid-19C the city was a principal whaling port. Elegant homes built from the profits of whaling still stand in neighborhoods that have remained residential, despite the development of onshore industries.

Starr Street

© Paul Rocheleau

The shipping industry and the US Naval Submarine Base located across the Thames are major contributors to the local economy. Scientists and engineers at the Naval Underwater Systems Center, on the grounds of Fort Trumbull, develop technology related to modern undersea warfare.

Some 1,600 men and women attend Connecticut College, a four-year, liberal arts school located near the Coast Guard Academy. Revitalization of the downtown area has included the renovation of several 19C Greek Revival houses on **Starr Street** and the 19C Union Railroad station (designed by H.H. Richardson).

SIGHTS *4 hrs. Map p 68.*

★**Hempsted Houses** – *Hempstead & Jay Sts. Visit by guided tour (1 hr) only, mid-May–mid-Oct Thu–Sun noon–4pm. $4. ☎ 860-443-7949.* Built in 1678, the timber-framed Joshua Hempsted House is a splendid example of 17C American architecture. The walls are insulated with seaweed and pierced with tiny leaded casement windows. Inside, the low-ceilinged rooms contain fine primitive American furnishings. The granite Nathaniel Hempsted House was built by Joshua's grandson in 1759. The interior features an unusual projecting bake oven.

★**Lyman Allyn Art Museum** – *625 Williams St. Open year round Tue–Sat 10am–5pm, Sun 1pm–5pm. Closed major holidays. $4. ✗ ♿ ☎ 860-443-2545. http://lymanallyn.conncoll.edu.* This small museum established by a bequest of the Allyn family specializes in paintings by Connecticut artists and in the decorative arts of the state. Attractively arranged furnishings, paintings, sculpture and decorative arts, dating from classical civilizations to the present, complement the **American collection** (1680-1920), housed in the Palmer Galleries *(1st floor).*

United States Coast Guard Academy – Kids *15 Mohegan Ave. Open year-round daily 9am–dusk. ♿ ☎ 860-444-8270. www.cga.edu. Contact the academy for special events and parade dates.* The academy, a four-year military college that trains officers for the Coast Guard, began in 1876 when the schooner *Dobbin* was chosen to serve as a floating training school to prepare cadets for the Revenue Marine (which later evolved into the Coast Guard). The *Dobbin* was succeeded by several other ships until the early 20C, when the academy was established at Fort Trumbull. In 1932 the academy moved to its present site beside the Thames.

Visitor Center – *Open May–Oct Wed–Sun 10am–5pm. Apr weekends only 10am–5pm.* Begin your visit here by viewing a video about the life of the cadets.

Coast Guard Museum – *In Waesche Hall. Open year-round Mon–Fri 9am–4:30pm, Sat 10am–5pm, Sun noon–5pm. Closed major holidays.* The museum's exhibits deal with the history of the Coast Guard.

The Waterfront – The academy's training vessel, the **Eagle**★, is occasionally berthed at the waterfront. German-built, the *Eagle* (1936) is a graceful, three-masted square-rigger used for cadet training cruises to Europe and the Caribbean in the summer. *When in port, the* Eagle *may be visited by guided tour. ☎ 860-444-8595.*

Connecticut College Arboretum – *Williams St. Open year-round daily dawn–dusk.* ☎ *860-439-5020. http://arboretum.conncoll. Map of arboretum available at entrance.* This 750-acre preserve consists of three major plant collections. Covering 20 acres, the Native Plant Collection features shrubs, trees and wildflowers indigenous to eastern North America. The main trail *(2mi)* circles a marsh; two optional loops lead to a bog and hemlock forest. A variety of woody plants occupy the 3-acre Caroline Black Garden. The Campus Landscape comprises 120 acres with over 200 trees from different parts of the world.

Ye Towne's Antientest Buriall Place – *Huntington St. Enter from Hempstead St.* This old burial ground has many early New England slate tombstones carved with winged angels, skulls and crossbones, geometric patterns and other designs.

Whale Oil Row – *105-119 Huntington St.* These four white mansions with their imposing columns are typical of the Greek Revival residences constructed by wealthy merchants and seamen in the 19C.

Monte Cristo Cottage – *325 Pequot Ave. South on Howard St., then turn left on Pequot Ave. (in the direction of Ocean Beach). Open Memorial Day–Labor Day Tue–Sat 10am–5pm, Sun 1pm–5pm. Mid-Sept–Oct by appointment only. $4.* ☎ *860-443-5378.* The unpretentious two-story frame dwelling looking out on the Thames was the boyhood summer home of playwright **Eugene O'Neill** (1888-1953).

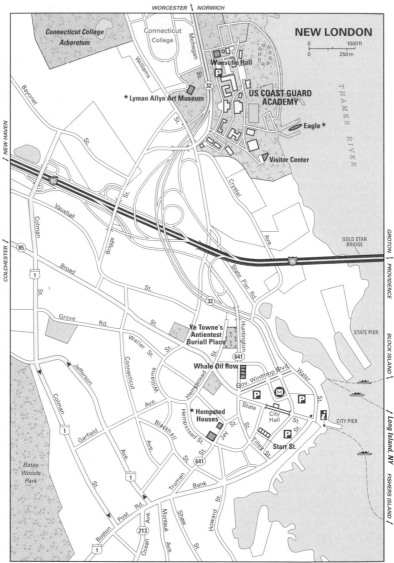

The cottage was the setting for his two most autobiographical works: *Long Day's Journey into Night* and *Ah, Wilderness!* A short *(18min)* film serves as an introduction to the years the O'Neills spent here.

Ferry to Orient Point, Long Island, NY – *Departs from New London ferry dock. Late May–Labor Day daily 7am–9:45pm. Rest of the year daily 7am–8:45pm (winter 7pm). Closed Dec 25. One-way 1 hr 20min. $32 (car & driver). Reservations required.* ✗ *Cross Sound Ferry* ☎ *860-443-5281. www.longislandferry.com.*

EXCURSIONS

Ocean Beach – *5mi south of New London on Ocean Ave.* This wide, sandy beach, edged with a pleasant boardwalk, offers an amusement arcade, miniature golf, archery, swimming and boating.

Eugene O'Neill Theater Center – *6mi south of New London, in Waterford. 305 Great Neck Rd. Take Bank St., then turn left at Ocean Ave. and continue to Rte. 213 (Niles Hill Rd.). Performances Jun–late Aug.* ✗ & *For schedule* ☎ *860-443-5378. www.eugeneoneill.org.* Named in honor of the 20C playwright Eugene O'Neill, the center is devoted to the development of new talent for the American stage. Activities on the center's 10-acre grounds include the National Playwrights Conference and the National Music Theater Conference. The center also sponsors the National Theater Institute and the National Critics Institute.

NORWALK

Population 78,331
Map of Principal Sights
Tourist Office ☎ 800-866-7925

The spirit of this once lively 19C seaport is alive in **SoNo** (an acronym for South Norwalk) on the Norwalk River, where the restored Victorian buildings along Washington Street between Main and Water Streets house attractive restaurants, shops and galleries.

Cruises leave from Hope Dock for the historic 1868 **Sheffield Island Lighthouse** *(late Jun–Labor Day Mon–Fri 11am & 1:30pm, weekends & holidays 10am, 12:30pm & 3pm; May–late Jun & rest of Sept weekends & holidays only 12:30pm & 3pm; one-way 30min; commentary; $12;* ✗*; Norwalk Seaport Assn.* ☎ *203-838-9444; www.seaport.org).*

SIGHTS

★**Maritime Aquarium** – Kids *10 Water St. Open Jul–Labor Day daily 10am–6pm. Rest of the year daily 10am 5pm. Closed Thanksgiving Day, Dec 25. $8.25.* ✗ & ☎ *203-852-0700. www.maritimeaquarium.org.* A renovated 19C brick warehouse on the river houses this two-story complex, which features an aquarium with Long Island Sound habitats, shark and seal tanks, demonstrations of boatbuilding and an IMAX theater.

Lockwood-Mathews Mansion Museum – *295 West Ave. Visit by guided tour (1 hr) only, Jun–Labor Day Tue–Fri 11am–3pm, weekends 1pm–4pm. Rest of Sept–Dec & Mar–May Tue–Fri 11am–3pm, Sun 1pm–4pm. Last tour 1 hr before closing. Closed major holidays. $5.* ☎ *203-838-9799. www.norwalk.com.* The three-story, turreted, dormered Victorian summer home of LeGrand Lockwood was designed in about 1864 in granite with a mansard roof. The 50-room interior, including an art gallery, children's theater and Moorish sitting room, boasts marble floors and mahogany and walnut woodwork crafted by Italian artisans. The grand staircase alone, with 266 balusters, reportedly cost $50,000.

EXCURSION

New Canaan – *10mi north of Norwalk, via Rte. 123.* This choice suburb in Connecticut's Fairfield County has been an art center since the early 20C when artists founded the **Silvermine Guild of Artists** here. The guild maintains a complex of studios, galleries, classrooms and a photography lab on Silvermine Road *(east of Rte. 123).* Highlighting its program of events is the annual exhibition **The Art of the Northeast**.

Consult the legend on the inside front cover for an explanation of symbols and colors appearing on maps throughout this guide.

NORWICH

Population 37,391
Map of Principal Sights
Tourist Office ☎ 860-444-2206

Situated where the Yantic and Shetucket Rivers meet to form the Thames, Norwich has been an important industrial center since the 18C. The city's historic district, radiating out from a prim triangular **green**, has a fine group of early dwellings.

SIGHT

Leffingwell Inn – *348 Washington St. Visit by guided tour (1 hr) only, Apr–late Nov Tue–Sun 1pm–4pm. Rest of the year by appointment only. Closed major holidays. $5.* ☎ *860-889-9440.* This dwelling was the site of many political meetings during the Revolution. Restored and converted into a museum, the house contains furnishings, silver and other products made by Norwich craftsmen.

EXCURSION

Uncasville – *5mi south of Norwich by Rte. 32.* Named for the Mohegan sachem **Uncas**, the town of Uncasville is still home to members of the Mohegan tribe. In the 17C Uncas made an alliance with the colonists, who agreed to help him and his braves resist any attacks by the powerful Narragansett Indians of Rhode Island. During the last major battle between the two tribes in 1643, Uncas captured and killed Miantonomo, the chief of the Narragansetts.

Tantaquidgeon Indian Museum – *Rte. 32. Open May–Sept Tue–Sun 10am–3pm. Contribution requested.* ♿ ☎ *860-848-9145.* This small museum was built by John Tantaquidgeon, a descendant of the Mohegan chief Uncas. Items traditionally made and used by the Mohegans, and gifts from other Indian tribes, are among the exhibits.

RIDGEFIELD

Population 6,363
Map of Principal Sights
Tourist Office ☎ 203-743-0546

Although Ridgefield lies just an hour's drive from the hustle and bustle of Manhattan, this charming town, with its tree-shaded avenues, shops and mansions, retains a distinctly New England character.

SIGHTS

Keeler Tavern Museum – *132 Main St. Visit by guided tour (45min) only, Feb–Dec Wed & weekends 1pm–4pm. Closed major holidays. $4.* ☎ *203-438-5485.* The Keeler Tavern operated as an inn from colonial days through the early 20C. During the Battle of Ridgefield, April 27, 1777, a cannonball lodged in the wall post, where it remains to this day. This fact accounts for the tavern's nickname, the Cannonball House.

> ### Hay Day Country Farm Market
> *21 Governor St.* ☎ *203-431-4400.* A feast for the eyes as well as the palate, this emporium for garden produce and gourmet picnic supplies is more than its name implies. In addition to an astounding selection of fresh fruit and vegetables, the store offers meat, seafood, breads, cheeses, confections, condiments and gifts. If you're overwhelmed by the selection and artful displays, take a restorative espresso break in the cafe, where a rack of daily newspapers is on hand. *There is also a Westport Hay Day, 1385 Post Rd. East, and a Greenwich Hay Day, 1050 E. Putnam Ave., Riverside.*

Aldrich Museum of Contemporary Art – *258 Main St. Open year-round Tue–Sun noon–5pm (Fri 8pm). Closed Easter Sunday, Thanksgiving Day, Dec 25. $5.* ♿ ☎ *203-438-4519. www.aldrichart.org.* Changing exhibits of contemporary art are presented in this handsome Colonial dwelling. The **sculpture garden** displays changing works by such sculptors as Sol LeWitt, Tony Smith and others *(open year-round daily dawn to dusk).*

> "The very warm heart of 'New England at its best,' such a vast abounding Arcadia of mountains and broad vales and great rivers and large lakes
> and white villages embowered in prodigious elms and maples. It is extraordinarily beautiful and graceful and idyllic—for America."
>
> Henry James' impression of Connecticut, May 1911

SUFFIELD

Population 11,427
Map of Principal Sights
Tourist Office ☏ 860-763-2578

The Connecticut River forms the eastern boundary of this small, countrified town established in 1670. Well-preserved houses border Main Street, together with the brick buildings of Suffield Academy, a private preparatory school.
Agriculture has been the principal local activity. Tobacco growing was the major industry until World War II. Broadleaf tobacco continues to be grown here, though much farmland has been converted to dairies, nurseries and industrial parks.

SIGHT

Hatheway House – *55 S. Main St. Visit by guided tour (1 hr) only, May–Oct Wed & weekends 1pm–4pm. Rest of the year by appointment. Closed major holidays. $4. ☏ 860-668-0055.* The house, actually three structures in one, owes its present size to Oliver Phelps, a merchant and land speculator who acquired the property in 1788. Phelps enlarged the main section of the house (c.1760) by adding a single-story structure to the south end. About 1795 Phelps had the Federal-style north wing built. The central section is simple and functional, furnished with William and Mary and Queen Anne pieces. In contrast, the Federal wing is elegant, decorated with Adamesque ornamentation and fine Hepplewhite, Sheraton and Chippendale furnishings. The original 18C hand-blocked French wallpapers in the Federal wing add a special touch to the house.

WETHERSFIELD★

Population 25,651
Map p 49
Tourist Office ☏ 860-527-9258

Unspoiled by industry throughout the 20C, Wethersfield is a pleasant HARTFORD suburb. Approximately 200 dwellings in the town's picturesque historic district, Old Wethersfield, date from the 17C and 18C. A number of these houses, built by wealthy merchants and shipowners, have been restored.
Established in 1634 along a natural harbor in the Connecticut River, Wethersfield was an important center of trade until the 18C, when floods changed the course of the river, leaving only a cove at the original harbor site. This change drastically affected the town's commercial activity, which decreased rapidly until, by the late 18C, farming had replaced trade as the economic mainstay.

★★OLD WETHERSFIELD *3 hrs*

Main Street – This wide street is lined with attractively restored houses. The monumental double doors with carved swan's-neck pediments seen on many of the 18C facades are distinctive to the Connecticut River Valley. The 1764 brick **Congregational Meetinghouse** (**C**) adjoins an early burial ground that contains tombstones dating from the 17C.

★★Webb-Deane-Stevens Museum – *211 Main St. Visit by guided tour (1 hr) only, May–Oct Wed–Mon 10am–4pm. Rest of the year weekends only 10am–4pm. Closed Jan 1, Thanksgiving Day, Dec 25. $8. ☏ 860-529-0612. www.webb-deane-stevens.org.* Owned by the National Society of the Colonial Dames of America, these three houses allow a study in architectural styles and decorative arts from 1752 to 1840, and a comparison of the lifestyles of a wealthy merchant, a politician and a modest craftsman.

① Comstock, Ferre & Co.
263 Main St. ☏ 860-571-6590. This venerable seed company dates back to 1820, reputedly the oldest in the country. Its retail seed business and garden center began in 1958. Today a large selection of bedding plants, shrubs and flowers as well as the famous seeds, available in packets or bulk, attract backyard gardeners and growers alike. Old-fashioned wooden pull-down seed bins line the interior of the 18C structure, and an adjoining gift shop brims with crafts and keepsakes. The center is an especially colorful place to browse in fall, when pumpkins and squash, cornstalks and chrysanthemums surround decorative country-bumpkin scarecrows dressed in denim overalls.

2 The Standish House

222 Main St. ☎ *860-257-1151.* Located across from the First Congregational Church in the heart of Old Wethersfield, this cheery eatery offers à la carte dining at lunch and dinnertime. Appetizers include caramelized beet root with chive sour cream, warm duck liver salad or asparagus crepes, as well as lobster bisque and New England bouillabaisse. Entrées such as Shrimp St. Jacques, roasted veal sweetbreads or Lazy Man's Lobster My Way (picked lobster meat sautéed with spinach and leeks) compete for attention. On Sundays a traditional morning breakfast is available. The coffee shop features an espresso bar, homemade pastries and gift baskets.

Webb House – This elegant Georgian residence (1752), built by the prosperous merchant Joseph Webb Sr., was the scene of a four-day conference in May 1781 between Gen. George Washington and the French Count Rochambeau. Plans for the Yorktown campaign, which led ultimately to the defeat of the British in the American Revolution, were discussed by the two military leaders during this time.

The house contains a fine collection of period furnishings and decorative arts. Highlights include the south parlor where Washington and Rochambeau met (note the Colonial Revival mural c.1916 that depicts Revolutionary events) and the bedchamber used by General Washington, who lodged at the Webb House during his stay in Wethersfield. The bedroom features the original flocked wool wallpaper, which Washington admired and noted in his diary.

Deane House – This house was built in 1766 for Silas Deane, an American diplomat who traveled to France during the Revolution to negotiate arms and equipment for the Continental Army. While abroad, Deane became involved in business deals that aroused suspicions about his loyalty, and he was accused of treason. He returned home and spent the rest of his life attempting, unsuccessfully, to clear his name. The entry hall is notable for the splendid side stairway with its carved cherry balusters, stained to imitate more expensive mahogany. The off-center stairway is unusual for a house of its period.

Stevens House – Isaac Stevens was a leather worker who built this house in 1788 for his bride. The dwelling passed by marriage to the Francis family, many of whose possessions are on view. Among the typical mid-19C furnishings are the Hitchcock chairs *(p 58).* The modest interiors make an interesting contrast to those of the more richly embellished Webb and Deane Houses.

Wethersfield Museum (D) – *Keeney Memorial Center, 200 Main St. Open year-round Tue–Sat 9am–4pm, Sun noon–4pm. Closed major holidays. $3.* ♿ ☎ *860-529-7161. www.wethhist.org.* A former schoolhouse, this Victorian-era brick building (1893) serves as a visitor center and features a thematic exhibit that brings Wethersfield's history alive with interactive displays and artifacts ranging from a tiny arrowhead to a massive Connecticut Valley doorway. Two galleries are devoted to changing art exhibits.

Hurlbut-Dunham House (E) – *212 Main St. Visit by guided tour (45min) only, early Jul–Labor Day Thu–Sat 10am–4pm, Sun 1pm–4pm. Mid-May–Jul 4 & rest of Sept–mid-Oct Sat 10am–4pm, Sun 1pm–4pm. Closed major holidays. $3.* ☎ *860-529-7161. www.wethhist.org.* During the early 1900s Jane and Howard Dunham, a prominent Wethersfield couple, traveled the world to collect furnishings for the gracious brick house that had been in their family since 1875. The house passed to the Wethersfield Historical Society with the Dunham belongings intact. It has been restored to reflect the period of 1907-1935. Rococo Revival wallpapers, trompe l'oeil cornices and crystal chandeliers are among the featured appointments.

★**Buttolph-Williams House** (F) – *249 Broad St. Visit by guided tour (30min) only, May–Oct Mon, Wed–Mon 10am–4pm. Closed major holidays. $3.* ☎ *860-529-0612.* This center-chimney house (c.1720), distinguished by oak clapboards, casement windows and a hewn overhang, is considered to be one of the most faithful restorations of an early Colonial dwelling in Connecticut. Particularly evocative of the Pilgrim era, the house served as the inspiration for the popular children's book *The Witch of Blackbird Pond* (1958) by Elizabeth George Speare.

Cove Warehouse – *At Cove Park overlooking the cove. Open early Jul–Labor Day Thu–Sat 10am–4pm, Sun 1pm–4pm. Mid-May–Jul 4 & rest of Sept–mid-Oct Sat 10am–4pm, Sun 1pm–4pm. $1.* ☎ *860-529-7161. www.wethhist.org.* Goods that arrived by sea in the 17C were stored in Wethersfield's seven warehouses before they were transported inland. About 1700, floods demolished six of the warehouses, leaving only Cove Warehouse intact. The structure houses an exhibit on the town's maritime trade between 1650 and 1830.

WOODSTOCK

Population 6,008
Map of Principal Sights
Tourist Office ☎ 860-928-1228

Woodstock's village green is set in the sparsely populated northeast section of the state. Facing the green is the summer residence known as Roseland Cottage.

SIGHT

Roseland Cottage – *Visit by guided tour (1 hr) only, Jun–mid-Oct Wed–Sun 11am–5pm. Last tour 1 hr before closing. $4. ☎ 860-928-4074.www.spnea.org.* This handsomely landscaped and furnished board-and-batten cottage was built by New York publisher Henry Bowen in 1846. The site became famous in the 19C for the spectacular Independence Day celebrations held here by Bowen. The festivities included fireworks, dancing and parties and were attended by such distinguished guests as Presidents Grant, Hayes and McKinley.

"I like the sound of world museum.
Perhaps because the word root refers less
to an actual collection of things than to the
musing, cogitating, and reflecting that one does
while beholding a collection"

Eric Sloane, A museum of Early American Tools 1964

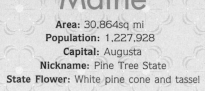

Maine

Area: 30,864sq mi
Population: 1,227,928
Capital: Augusta
Nickname: Pine Tree State
State Flower: White pine cone and tassel

Equal in surface area to the combined size of the other five New England states, Maine is a vast, thickly forested region fringed with a 3,500-mile coastline. The origin of the name Maine is uncertain. Attributed by some historians to the Maine region in western France, the name is believed by others to derive from "the main," a term used by fishermen to distinguish the mainland from the offshore islands. Maine is also referred to as **Down East** because of the winds that carry sailing vessels eastward along this section of the coast.

Glaciers sculpted the irregular, deeply indented coastline that characterizes Maine. Moving southeast across the land, then retreating northwest, the ice chiseled out elongated peninsulas and headlands. Offshore, hundreds of islands, the peaks of submerged mountains, dot the water. Pine trees grow on the islands, along the shore and across the interior to the north, giving the state its nickname.

A Succession of Owners – The Maine coast was explored by the Vikings in the 11C and several centuries later by European fishermen. In 1604 Pierre du Gua, Sieur de Monts, and Samuel de Champlain established a small colony on an island in the St. Croix River from which they set out the following year to found the Acadian territory. An English settlement, the Popham Colony, was established at the mouth of the Kennebec River in 1607; then in 1635 the English monarch Charles I gave the region of Maine to Sir Ferdinando Gorges, appointing him "Lord of New England." From this time on, the coast was the scene of constant battles between the French and the English. In 1677 the Massachusetts Colony bought Maine from the descendants of Sir Gorges, and the region remained under the jurisdiction of Massachusetts until 1820, when Maine was granted statehood under the conditions of the Missouri Compromise.

Economy – The state of Maine has a diversified economy. In the early days the state's wealth depended on its forests. Timber was harvested to supply masts for the Royal Navy during the colonial period, when all pine trees 24 inches or greater in diameter belonged to the Crown. In the 19C wooden **shipbuilding** in Maine peaked at Wiscasset, Bath and Searsport, where boatyards turned out four-, five- and six-masted vessels. Today the forests supply important **paper** and **pulp mills** at Jay, Millinocket, Rumford, Westbrook and Woodland.

Fishing, especially **lobstering**, is a major industry; more than 50 percent of the nation's lobster catch comes from Maine. In the many small fishing ports along the coast, thousands of colorful buoys float on the surface of the water, marking the location of traps set by lobstermen. The state leads the US in the sardine-packing industry, producing some 75 million tins of sardines each year. An annual catch of 35,000 metric tons of Atlantic herring nets fishermen $5 million.

Dianne Dietrich Leis

Textiles, shoes and boots are also Maine-made products. Maine farmers raise the nation's third-largest crops of potatoes, as well as 98 percent of the country's blueberries.

75

AUGUSTA

Population 21,325
Map of Principal Sights
Tourist Office ☎ 207-623-4559

Situated on the banks of the Kennebec River, Maine's capital is a bustling industrial and residential city. Government, industry and tourism are Augusta's major businesses. The capital district, located in the State Street area on the west bank of the Kennebec River, includes the State House, the State Museum and other attractions.

The river and its adjacent woodlands have been a source of wealth to Augusta ever since the 17C, when the Pilgrims established a trading post on its east bank. In the 18C and 19C the Kennebec River served as an important avenue for boat traffic, as well as a source of ice in winter. Wood cut from the forests bordering the river also contributed to the region's prosperity.

SIGHTS *1 day*

State House – *State and Capitol Sts. Open year-round Mon–Fri 8am–5pm. Closed major holidays.* & ☎ *207-287-2301.* The domed capitol building is best viewed from the riverside park across from the front entrance of the State House. Constructed between 1829 and 1832 according to the designs of the eminent Boston architect Charles Bulfinch, the major portion of the State House was later remodeled and enlarged. Despite this change, the columned facade and other Bulfinch characteristics were preserved. The House, Senate and Executive chambers are all located in the State House.

Blaine House – *192 State St. Visit by guided tour (20min) only, year-round Tue–Thu 2pm–4pm.* & ☎ *207-287-2121.* Built for a Bath sea captain in the 1830s, this Colonial mansion was the home of James G. Blaine (1830-93), congressman, secretary of State and presidential candidate in 1884. The house has served as the governor's mansion since 1919. The tour includes public and family rooms on the main floor.

Maine State Museum – *State St. Open year-round Mon–Fri 9am–5pm, Sat 10am–4pm, Sun 1pm–4pm. Closed Jan 1, Easter Sunday, Thanksgiving Day, Dec 25.* & ☎ *207-287-2301.* This modern building houses the State Library and Archives, as well as the State Museum. Exhibits on the history, life and environment of Maine and its residents are on view in the museum's three levels. Dioramas, period rooms, artifacts and equipment tell the story of state industries, past and present, such as agriculture, lumbering and shipbuilding. **Made in Maine** includes mill and factory machinery plus more than 1,000 samples of products manufactured in the state. Archaeological artifacts document the life of the area's first inhabitants and an interactive display traces early exploration routes. Maine's geographical and political history from the early 17C to 1842 is also featured.

Old Fort Western – *16 Cony St. Open Jul 5–Aug Mon–Fri 10am–4pm, weekends 1pm–4pm. May–Jul 4 & Sept–Columbus Day daily 1pm–4pm. $4.50.* ☎ *207-626-2385. www.oldfortwestern.org.* This was the site of the trading post built by the Plymouth Pilgrims in the 17C. In 1754 Fort Western was erected at this riverside location as a defense against Indian raids. The reconstructed blockhouses and stockades, and the restored 14-room barracks furnished with antiques, appear as they did during the 18C. The fort was never attacked; for the most part it served as a supply depot for other garrisons farther up the river. Today costumed guides re-create the fort's history.

BANGOR

Population 33,181
Map of Principal Sights
Tourist Office ☎ 207-947-0307

This bustling city on the west bank of the Penobscot River faces the Maine woods in one direction and the sea in the other. Located at the crossroads of two major interstate and several US highways and local routes, Bangor teems with traffic, both commercial and personal. Its international airport serves as a refueling station for airlines flying North America–Europe routes and as a port of entry for flights arriving in the US.

Situated at the terminus of the log drives from the north, and near an outlet to the sea, Bangor developed into an international export center for timber in the 19C. Crews of lumberjacks felled trees in the winter, drove them downriver in the spring, and spent the remainder of their time—and most of their pay—during the off-season in Bangor. Tough and rowdy, these expert woodsmen called themselves "the Bangor Tigers." When the "Tigers" were in town, the taverns, grog shops and brothels in the district dubbed Devil's Half-Acre seldom had a quiet night or day. **Paul Bunyan**, a legendary character created by a Michigan newspaperman, typifies the Bangor Tiger. Late-20C legend **Stephen King** maintains a winter home in Bangor. This modern-day master of the horror story, whose popular novels have been made into high-grossing films, was born in PORTLAND. Maine's oldest bookshop, Betts Bookstore, on Main Street in Bangor, specializes in King titles.

SIGHTS

Paul Bunyan Statue and Park – *Main St.* A gigantic **statue** (31ft) of Paul Bunyan stands on lower Main Street in a park near the Bangor Civic Center overlooking the Penobscot River. The residents of Bangor presented the statue as a gift to the city in 1959. *Visitor center located in the Chamber of Commerce at 519 Main St., adjacent to the park. A self-guided walking tour map of Bangor's historic buildings is available from the visitor center or from the Bangor Historical Society, 159 Union Street* ☎ *207-942-5766.*

★**Cole Land Transportation Museum** – 🧒 *405 Perry Rd. From I-95 take Exit 45B. Turn left at first light, then left onto Perry Rd. Open May–mid-Nov daily 9am–5pm. $3.* ☎ *207-990-3600. www.colemu seum.org.* Housed in a cavernous building on the outskirts of town, over 200 vehicles, primarily from the state of Maine, illustrate a cross section of past modes of transportation and industry. Snowplows, fire engines, farm machinery, locomotives and boxcars, vintage automobiles, construction and military vehicles, wagons, sleighs and a variety of nonvehicular transport such as bicycles and baby carriages are organized by category within the 38,000sq ft exhibit area. Among the highlights are a prairie schooner bound for the Oregon Territory in the 1840s, a 1925 trailer with a camper tent, and an ice cutter used to extract ice from a pond in LaGrange, Maine.

Pilots
1528 Hammond St. ☎ *207-942-6325.* Billing itself as a grill restaurant, Pilots is a long-time, local attraction, favored for its seafood and steaks. Try the Grill Special 10oz steak or the light-cut roast prime rib. Native Maine clams, shrimp, scallops and coast haddock as well as lobster (broiled, sautéed, baked) are also featured, with a menu note that the lobster is delivered daily. Pilots is open for lunch and dinner.

City Limits
735 Main St. ☎ *207-941-9888.* Contained within a large, white house built by a family of shipbuilders in 1809, this restaurant offers an ambitious menu of beef, poultry, seafood and Italian dishes. Its fisherman's platter serves up scallops, clams, Maine and Gulf shrimp, crab meat and haddock with french fries and onion rings. Greek scallops, lobster fettuccine alfredo and seafood linguine are other tempting choices. Lunch items are equally diverse: try the Deer Isle crabmeat sandwich on a toasted roll, City Limits' homemade lasagna or the hot steamed lobster entrée.

BATH★

Population 9,799
Map of Principal Sights
Tourist Office ☎ 207-443-9751

Named for its sister city in England, Bath has been a shipbuilding center since the 18C, when its coveted location on a channel to the sea provided the town with advantages over other regional boatbuilding centers.

The port once owned a fleet of merchant vessels that sailed regularly to the West Indies, California and the Far East. Boatyards along the Kennebec River turned out square-riggers, down-easters *(p 29)*, and some of the largest schooners ever constructed. The buildings of the **Maine Maritime Museum** and the graceful old homes on Washington Street date from this time. The **Bath Iron Works** (BIW), on the west bank of the Kennebec River, has been building ships since 1893 and is Maine's largest private employer. The launching of a new tanker, container ship, frigate or cargo vessel is still a major event at BIW.

★★MAINE MARITIME MUSEUM

Devoted to preserving Maine's maritime heritage, the museum maintains a historic shipbuilding complex and offers boatbuilding programs that employ traditional skills used in constructing wooden sailing craft. The **Maritime History of Maine**★ exhibit, housed in the **Maritime History Building** overlooking the Kennebec River, fills two adjoining galleries and introduces 400 years of Maine seafaring, commerce and shipbuilding. Also on view is an exhibit of Maine's family fleets, as well as changing displays of maritime art and artifacts.

Visit

Kids *243 Washington St. Open year-round daily 9:30am–5pm. Closed Jan 1, Thanksgiving Day, Dec 25. $8.* ☎ *207-443-1316. www.bathmaine.com. Boat rides (50min) on the Kennebec River late Apr–Oct ($8 in addition to museum admission).*

The Buildings – Today five of the original buildings remain. In the former **Mold Loft** (1917) and **Mill and Joiner Shop** (1899), shipbuilding tools, power machinery, old photographs and illustrated explanations of the making of a wooden ship tell the story of the Percy and Small Shipyard and the great vessels turned out here. The **Paint and Treenail Shop** (1897), where treenails (wooden pegs used in ship construction), paints and stains were produced, contains exhibits on the trades related to shipbuilding. Note the re-created 19C shipyard office and the scale model of Donnell Cordage Co. (1843), along with its 1,000ft-long ropewalk. Originally this company stood at the south end of Bath. Caulking to seal the seams of wooden vessels was prepared in the 1899 **Caulker's Shed**.

From the second floor of the **Boatshop**, visitors can observe participants in the museum's program constructing and restoring wooden boats. On the floor below, there are displays of small craft from the museum's collection.

Percy and Small Shipyard – Large wooden schooners were the specialty of the Percy and Small Shipyard, which operated on this site from 1897 to 1920. The six-masted, 3,720-ton *Wyoming*, the largest wooden sailing vessel ever to fly the US flag, was built here.

The Waterfront – Frequently berthed along the riverbank, the schooner *Sherman Zwicker* was built in Nova Scotia in 1942 and worked the cod and haddock fisheries on the Grand Banks off Newfoundland until 1968. Visitors can board this ship when it is in port. From the boat's deck there is a good view of the lighthouse at Doubling Point and of the Bath Iron Works, including its 400ft crane, capable of hoisting a weight of some 220 tons.

Near the excursion boat dock, a comprehensive exhibit of the state's 200-year lobstering history, **Lobstering and the Maine Coast**, is presented in a reconstructed sail loft that was floated down on a barge from north Bath. Special features include four restored lobster boats and a film *(17min)*, written in the 1950s by **E.B. White**, about the lobstering industry.

EXCURSION

★**Popham Beach** – *16mi south of Bath on Rte. 209.* Situated at the tip of a fingerlike peninsula reaching into the ocean, this resort village lies between the Kennebec River and the sea. One of the earliest English settlements in the New World was established at Popham Beach in 1607. The colony lasted only one year, but in that time its residents succeeded in building the first English ship constructed in America, the 30-ton pinnace *Virginia*.

At the northern tip of Popham Beach, **Fort Popham**, the granite fortress overlooking the point where the Kennebec meets the Atlantic Ocean, was built during the Civil War to prevent Confederate vessels from sailing upriver to Bath. Modified over the years, the fort was also used during the Spanish-American War and both world wars. Nearby, at **Popham Beach State Park**, a broad sandy beach—rare for this part of the coast—lies on the ocean side of the point *(open mid-Apr–Oct daily 9am–dusk; $2; ☎ 207-389-1335)*.

BAXTER STATE PARK★★

Map of Principal Sights

Dominated by the state's highest peak, **Mt. Katahdin** (5,267ft), Baxter State Park is a densely forested rectangular tract of land (204,733 acres) in the heart of the Maine wilderness. The park is named for **Percival Proctor Baxter** (1876-1969), who devoted the greater part of his life and fortune to acquiring this land, which he ultimately deeded to the people of Maine under the condition that the park be preserved "forever in its natural wild state."

In accordance with Baxter's wishes, the park has remained primarily a wildlife sanctuary for deer, moose, bear and other denizens of the north country. The roads are narrow and unpaved *(speed limit 15-20mph)*, camping facilities are primitive, and there are no motels, shops or restaurants within the park boundaries. While only a few scenic attractions can be observed from the road, the park's 175mi trail system, which includes the northern section of the Appalachian Trail, leads to points that afford spectacular views of this remote region. Because of the unique circumstances underlying the establishment of Baxter State Park, the park is administered independently of other state parks. Headquarters are in Millinocket. *For access and orientation, see "Visiting Northern Maine" p 93.*

■ **Mt. Katahdin** – A giant granite monolith, Katahdin (an Indian name meaning "the greatest mountain") has long figured in local Indian mythology. One Abnaki legend tells of Pamola, a deity with the wings and claws of an eagle, the arms and torso of a man, and the enormous head of a moose, who lived on the peak of Mt. Katahdin. Whenever he was angry, Pamola cast violent rainstorms, lightning and thunder onto the lands below. The park today offers good opportunities for hiking and camping.

Baxter Peak is the highest of Katahdin's four summits, the others being Hamlin Peak, Pamola Peak and South Peak. Observed from the east, the **Great Basin**, a bowl-shaped formation scoured out of the mountain by glacial activity, is Katahdin's most distinguishable feature. Seen from the west, the **Knife Edge**, a narrow, serrated granite ridge that joins Pamola and South Peaks, cuts a jagged profile across the sky.

VISIT *1 day*

Open mid-May–mid-Oct daily 6am–10pm. Rest of the year call for hours. $8 non-resident vehicle fee. △ ☎ *207-723-5140.*

The main entrances to the park lead to Park Road, the only route through the park; it is not a sightseeing route but does pass several scenic points of interest, such as **Abols Falls** and the **Slide Dam**. *It is necessary to hike to see the other sights and views in the park.*

Hiking Trails – *Before starting out, hikers should register and check with the ranger in the area as to weather and trail conditions. Stephen Clark's book* Baxter Park and Katahdin *is a comprehensive guide to the park trails. Most trails are in the south section of the park. Baxter's trails are blazed blue; white blazes mark the Appalachian Trail (AT).*

Sandy Stream Pond Trail – *Southeast section of the park. 1.5mi. Begin at Roaring Brook Campground.* After .5mi, a short spur to the left leads to Big Rock where there is a good view of Katahdin's Great Basin and Hamlin Peak.

South Turner Mountain Trail – *4mi. Begin at Sandy Stream Pond Trail.* After .5mi, where a fork leads left to Russell Pond Trail, take the right fork and follow the blue blazes to the summit. The trail becomes difficult as it ascends the steep, boulder-covered slope of the mountain. The view from the summit of Katahdin and the surrounding region is worth the effort.

Chimney Pond Trail – *Ascent 3.5mi. Begin at Roaring Brook Campground.* Chimney Pond, located on the floor of the Great Basin, is the site of one of the park's many campgrounds.

Appalachian Trail – *Southwest section of the park. 1mi hike from Daicey Pond to Big Niagara Falls.* Follow the white-blazed trail. After 1mi you will see **Little Niagara Falls**. Continue a short distance to **Big Niagara Falls**.

Hunt Trail – *10.5mi (8-10hrs). Begin at Katahdin Stream Campground.* Follow the white blazes. This is one of the popular trails to the top of Katahdin. Allow a full day for the climb and descent. Only those in excellent physical condition should attempt this long, demanding hike. A pleasant, much shorter hike *(1mi)* on this trail leads to **Katahdin Stream Falls**.

EXCURSION

Patten – *8mi east of the park by the Park Rd., then Rte. 159.* This small agricultural community straddles the border between the rich potato fields of Aroostook County and the forests of northern Maine. High-powered diesel trucks hauling wood pulp and logs are a familiar sight on local roads. Lumbering is an important business in Patten, even though the era of lumber camps and river drives has long since ended.

At the **Lumberman's Museum** *(.5mi west of Patten on Rte. 159)*, exhibits ranging from crooked knives to steam log-haulers, a sawmill and reconstructed lumber camps tell the story of the lumberjack's life. The 1820 bunkhouse replicates the type shared by as many as a dozen woodsmen during the lumbering season *(open Jul–Aug Tue–Sun 10am–4pm; mid-May–Jun & Sept–Columbus Day Fri–Sun 10am– 4pm; $3.50; ☎ 207-528-2650).*

For visitor information in Maine, plan a stop at the Maine Tourism Association on Route 95/1 north of the New Hampshire line (open Jun–Sept daily 8am–6pm; rest of the year daily 9am–5pm; closed Jan 1, Easter Sunday, Thanksgiving Day & Dec 25; ☎ 207-439-1319; www.mainetourism.com).

BETHEL

Population 2,329
Map of Principal Sights
Tourist Office ☎ 207-824-2282

Bethel's distinguished inn, prep school and carefully preserved houses situated near the village green are enhanced by the town's magnificent setting in the White Mountains. Bethel offers opportunities for hunting, fishing, golf, rock-hounding in the abandoned mines in the area, and excursions into the White Mountains. The nearby **Sunday River Resort** is a popular winter ski area.

Permanent settlement in the area dates from 1774, when a sawmill and then a grist-mill were established on a brook flowing into the Androscoggin River. In 1796 the town was incorporated and named Bethel, a Biblical term meaning "house of God." With the arrival of the railroad in 1851 connecting the community to Portland and then to Montreal, the timber industry began to dominate Bethel's economy. Lumber and dairy products are major sources of area income today. *Mill tours (2hrs, Tue & Thu from 10am) at Mead Corp., 35 Hartford St. in Rumford (about 20mi northeast of Bethel) enable visitors to see how paper is made. Combined forest and mill tours 7:30am–3pm; call for specific dates* ☎ *207-369-2045.*

Today a National Historic District, the village of Bethel is a quiet residential hamlet, attracting visitors to the recreational facilities of the Bethel Inn and Country Club, co-ed students to its **Gould Academy** and skiers to the slopes of Sunday River Resort. *A walking-tour brochure for the village is available from the Bethel Historical Society* ☎ *207-824-2908.*

Bethel Inn & Country Club

Broad St., ☎ *207-824-2175.* This ensemble of large yellow houses and service buildings fronts the village green or common. The inn welcomes the public at breakfast, lunch and dinnertime. In the main dining room morning fare is served from the bounteous buffet or a substantial menu. It's also the evening setting for inn specialties and traditional New England dishes such as maple-walnut scented venison medallions, broiled marinated duck breast or pan-sautéed salmon. Dinner is served in the Mill Brook Tavern as well, where Mexican night is held once a week *(Thu).* Lunch can be enjoyed in the tavern or on the screened terrace, overlooking the 18-hole golf course. A weekly lobsterbake *(Tue)* is available on the terrace. *Dinner reservations required; last seating 8:45pm.*

SIGHT

Moses Mason House – *On the village green. Visit by guided tour (30min) only, Jul–Labor Day Tue–Fri 1pm–4pm. Rest of the year by appointment. $2.* ☎ *207-824-2908.* Built c.1813 for a prominent physician and his family, the house features nine rooms furnished to the period. Highlights include the colorful folk-art **murals** (c.1835) adorning the central staircase, an indoor privy and a pictorial bookcase built by the doctor himself.

EXCURSIONS

★**Grafton Notch State Park** – *25mi northwest of Bethel by Rte. 26. Open year-round daily dawn–dusk. Rest of the year call for hours. $1.* ☎ *207-824-2912 or 207-624-6080 (off season).* The road heads through the Bear River Valley and into Grafton Notch State Park, an unspoiled area in the White Mountains. The drive through the park offers views of the notch dominated by **Old Speck Mountain** (4,180ft) to the west and **Baldpate Mountain** to the east. Several picnic areas near the road are designated.

Screw Auger Falls – The falls tumble over slabs of rock into shallow pools.

Mother Walker Falls – *1mi north of Screw Auger Falls.* Old Speck is visible from this small waterfall.

★**Evans Notch** – *18mi southwest of Bethel. Follow Rte. 2 west for 10mi, then turn left onto Rte. 113.* The drive through Evans Notch *(Gilead to North Chatham)* in White Mountain National Forest offers **views** of the Cold River Valley, one of the valleys of the White Mountains.

Admission prices shown in this guide are the single adult price only. Discounts may be available for senior citizens, children, students, military and other categories.

BLUE HILL and DEER ISLE★

Map of Principal Sights
Tourist Office ☏ 207-667-5584

The quiet, wind-swept peninsula that reaches from Route 3 down to Stonington seems to have been overlooked by modern civilization. Small, secluded villages and cozy inlets harboring lobster boats nestle in woodlands that hug the water's edge. Views of Penobscot Bay and Mt. Desert Island are especially striking on a clear day, when the blue sky frames the dark green spruces.

DRIVING TOUR *1 day. 96mi circuit from Bucksport.*

Bucksport – This small town lies on the east bank of the Penobscot River at the point where **Verona Island** divides the river. Bucksport's main street, lined with shops and the **Jed Prouty Tavern**, runs parallel to the river. At the northern end of Bucksport, a large paper company employs an innovative technique that prevents the noxious odors associated with papermaking from being released into the air. Across the river, **Fort Knox★**, a massive granite structure, guards the entrance to the Penobscot.

From Bucksport take Rte. 1/3 north, then turn right onto Rte. 175 south. Continue straight to Rte. 166, then Rte. 166A to Castine.

Castine – Tranquil tree-lined streets and stately 18C and 19C Georgian and Federal houses belie this town's tumultuous past. Established as a trading post by the Plymouth Pilgrims (1629), the vulnerable port community on the Penobscot peninsula was controlled by the British until Frenchman Baron de St. Castine seized it in 1667. Renamed for the baron, the town subsequently fell to the Dutch, then reverted to British control. Castine's future as an American settlement was determined when the 1783 Treaty of Paris established the St. Croix River as the eastern boundary between the US and British-held Canada. **Fort George**, built by the British in the 18C, and the American stronghold **Fort Madison** (1811) were occupied by the British during the War of 1812.

Lining the **village green** *(Court St. just off Main St.)* are the 1790 Unitarian Church and Ives House (1840), later home to poet Robert Lowell. The large brick buildings on Pleasant Street belong to the Maine Maritime Academy, founded in 1941 and specializing in marine studies. The academy's 499ft training vessel, the **State of Maine**, can be boarded when the ship is in port. Designed as a passenger-cargo ship, the vessel was later used for troop transport in the Korean and Vietnam Wars *(visit by 30min guided tour only, mid-Jul–Aug Mon–Fri 10am–noon & 1pm–4pm; mid-Sept–mid-Dec & Feb–mid-Apr weekends only 10am–noon & 1pm– 4pm; closed academic & major holidays; ☏ 207-326-4311; www.mainemaritime.edu).*

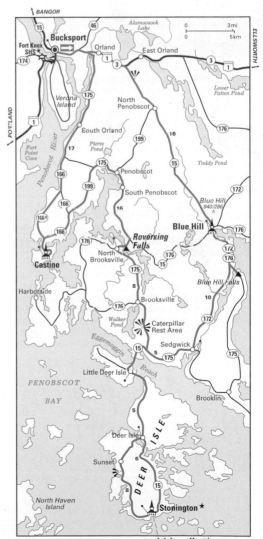

Take Rte. 166, then Rte. 199 north around the east side of the peninsula. At Penobscot, take Rte. 175 south.

Reversing Falls – Five miles south of South Penobscot, near North Brooksville, there is a picnic area where an unusual phenomenon can be seen, a reversing falls. At this point the waterway is very narrow. When the tide changes, the narrow passage creates a bottleneck, causing the water to rush in (or out, depending on whether the tide is rising or falling) with such great force that a series of falls is formed. The best view of the reversing falls is from the bridge on Route 175.

Continue south on Rte. 175 to Rte. 176/15.

From the **Caterpillar Hill Rest Area** in Brooksville, there is a spectacular **panorama**★★ of Deer Isle, Penobscot Bay, and Camden Hills and the bay islands.

At the junction of Rtes. 175 and 15, cross the bridge to Little Deer Isle, then continue to Deer Isle. Rte. 15 passes through the village of Deer Isle and follows the eastern shore to Stonington.

★**Stonington** – This tranquil fishing village at the tip of the peninsula typifies the picturesque towns along the coast. Stonington's quarries supplied the granite used in the construction of public buildings and monuments throughout the US; today most of the quarries lie abandoned. Hoisting machinery can be seen on the offshore islands. Boats to **Isle au Haut**★, in Acadia National Park, leave from Stonington.

Continue along the western shore of the island. A beautiful view unfolds upon approaching the town of Sunset. After Sunset head east and take Rte. 15 north. Cross the bridge to Little Deer Isle and pick up Rte. 175 east in Sargentville.

In Sedgwick turn left onto Rte. 172. At the town of Blue Hill Falls turn right onto Rte. 175. Cross two bridges to Blue Hill Falls, a reversing falls similar to the one at North Brooksville (above). Return to Rte. 172 and continue to Blue Hill.

Blue Hill – Named for the hill that dominates the town and yields a hearty annual blueberry harvest, this pretty village is home to many craftsmen, including a well-known assembly of potters. A trail *(from the village drive north on Rte. 172 and turn left across from the fairgrounds; continue .8mi to trail marker)* leads to the top of Blue Hill (940ft), where you can look out across Blue Hill Bay to Mt. Desert Island.

A summer school for chamber music is held in the village; artist-faculty concerts are presented regularly at Kneisel Hall *(late Jun–mid-Aug Fri evenings, Sun afternoons ☎ 207-374-2811; www.hypernet.com/kneisel.html).*

Take Rte. 15 north.

The road climbs, passes along the base of Blue Hill, then descends to Route 1/3, offering beautiful **views** as it leads north.

■ Retired Skippers Race

The first Retired Skippers Race was held off the coast near Castine in 1952 to boost circulation of a flagging local newspaper. The inventive editor challenged two retired skippers—one from Bucksport and one from Deer Isle—to a duel on the water. The race has continued to attract retirees and other sailing enthusiasts for nearly 50 years, from the original 2 to some 40 entrants today. Contestants must be at least 65 years of age (the previous requirement of Maine residency has been dropped). Although retired skipper status is not mandatory, several of the sailors have been shipmasters. Each August racers depart from the Castine Harbor bell buoy to sail a triangular course toward Isleboro in Penobscot Bay. The race usually lasts about 2-3 hours, depending on winds and other weather conditions.

BOOTHBAY HARBOR★★

Population 2,347
Map of Principal Sights
Tourist Office ☎ 207-633-2353

Boothbay Harbor lies at the tip of one of the craggy peninsulas that extend into the sea from the deeply indented, mid-coast section of Maine. Protected headlands sheltering deep natural anchorages make the region a major boating center and a favorite summer resort.

The popular New England festival **Windjammer Days** takes place at Boothbay Harbor in late June. During the three-day celebration, two- and three-masted schooners parade through the harbor and residents hold community suppers, concerts, a pageant and a street parade.

VISIT

The Town – Small shops line the streets leading down to the wharves, and motels, hotels and inns are found in the snug coves and along the rugged stretches of shore such as **Ocean Point★** *(5mi east of Boothbay Harbor via Rte. 96)*. Lobstering is the principal activity of the local fishermen, who can be observed practically year-round gathering shiny, green-brown lobsters from the wooden traps set below the water's surface. Restaurants and lobster wharves feature the fresh-caught delicacy broiled, stuffed, boiled or made into lobster salad.

Cruising the Bay and Islands – Boothbay Harbor serves as the departure point for a number of different cruises in the bay as well as day trips to Monhegan Island. Cruises depart from several piers in the center of town *(along Commercial St.)* and vary from one to several hours in duration. *For information contact the following companies: Cap'n Fish's Boat Cruises at Pier 1 ☎ 207-633-3244; Balmy Days II at Pier 8 ☎ 207-633-2284; and Islander Cruises at Pier 6 ☎ 207-633-2500.*

BRUNSWICK

Population 14,683
Map of Principal Sights
Tourist Office ☎ 207-725-8797

This attractive community, with its wide avenues, is the home of Bowdoin (BO-din) College. Shade trees and handsome mansions line Federal Street and other streets nearby. Small manufacturing plants and the US Naval Air Station are the chief contributors to the local economy.

The Bowdoin campus, in the heart of Brunswick, radiates outward from the town's pleasant green, which was laid out by citizens in the early 18C. Construction of a hydroelectric dam was begun in 1979 in the vicinity of the falls of Androscoggin River and was completed in 1981. The falls were the major power source in the 19C for the town's lumbering and textile industries.

SIGHTS

Bowdoin College – Established in 1794, this well-regarded small liberal arts college spreads over 110 acres and enrolls some 1,400 students. Bowdoin counts among its alumni authors Nathaniel Hawthorne and Henry Wadsworth Longfellow; explorers Robert Peary and Donald MacMillan; and the nation's 14th president, Franklin Pierce. Harriet Beecher Stowe wrote *Uncle Tom's Cabin* while she and her husband, a professor at Bowdoin, lived in Brunswick.

The college is named for James Bowdoin, a former governor of Massachusetts (1785-87). The Bowdoins were a French family who arrived in Maine in the 17C and rose to prominence during the colonial period. Grateful to their new country, they endowed the college with land, money and old master drawings from their personal art collection.

★ **Bowdoin College Museum of Art** – *Walker Art Building. Open year-round Tue–Sat 10am–5pm, Sun 2pm–5pm. Closed major holidays & Dec 25–Jan 1. ♿ ☎ 207-725-3275. www.bowdoin.edu/cwis/resources/museums.* This 19C building was designed by Charles Follen McKim of the prestigious architectural firm McKim, Mead and White. On the main floor, selections from the museum's group of early American portraits include works by Gilbert Stuart, Robert Feke, John Smibert, Joseph Blackburn and John Singleton Copley. Other first-floor galleries contain 19C and 20C American paintings as well as a selection of European works and Greek and Roman antiquities. Asian art is displayed downstairs. Memorabilia, graphics and works by Winslow Homer are displayed annually *(mid-May–mid Aug only)*.

Peary-MacMillan Arctic Museum – *Open year-round Tue–Sat 10am–5pm, Sun 2pm– 5pm. Closed major holidays & Dec 25–Jan 1. ♿ ☎ 207-725-3416. www.bowdoin.edu/dept/arctic.* This museum is dedicated to Adm. Robert Peary, credited with being the first man to reach the North Pole (1909), and his assistant Donald MacMillan. The major part of the collection consists of clothing, instruments, tools and record books of the Peary and MacMillan expeditions. Other exhibits include art and artifacts from cultures native to the Arctic and natural history specimens of the wildlife found there.

Sights described in this guide are rated:
    ★★★   *Worth the trip*
    ★★   *Worth a detour*
    ★   *Interesting*

CAMDEN★★

Population 4,022
Map of Principal Sights
Tourist Office ☎ 207-236-4404

Set at the foot of the Camden Hills, overlooking the island-speckled waters of Penobscot Bay, Camden is one of the loveliest towns on the New England coast. The pleasant lifestyle of its residents is reflected in the attractive village center and waterfront. Restaurants, galleries, and shops decorated with flower-filled window boxes abound in the business district, and nearby streets are lined with large houses.

Camden's earliest trade was shipbuilding: the first schooner made here was launched in 1769. Woolen mills elbowed in around 1900 and thrived here through World War II. But it was the steamboat that ushered in monied summer visitors in the early 1900s. The mansions that these wealthy seasonal residents built still fill the streets around the town center. In the harbor sleek yachts are anchored amid the tall two-masted windjammers, which offer a variety of pleasure cruises in season *(for information & schedules, contact the Maine Windjammers Assn. ☎ 207-374-5400)*.

Beyond the landscaped setting of the Camden Public Library is **Bok Amphitheatre**, where concerts are presented outdoors against the backdrop of the bay. The nearby waterfront park is an ideal place from which to watch the harbor's activity.

View of Camden from Mt. Battie

SIGHTS

★★**Camden Hills State Park** – *Rte. 1 north of Camden. Open mid-May–mid-Oct daily 9am–dusk. Rest of the year call for hours. $2.* ⚠ ☎ *207-236-3109 or 207-236-0849 (off season).* A road *(1mi)* leads to the top of **Mt. Battie** (800ft), where a spectacular **view★★★** of Camden's harbor, Penobscot Bay and the bay islands unfolds. This tranquil scene inspired Maine-born poet Edna St. Vincent Millay to write her first volume of verse, *Renascence*, in 1917. The park also includes a 25mi network of trails that provide good hiking in summer and cross-country skiing in winter.

Bayview Street Dining

Camden's colorful waterfront is the big draw for residents and tourists alike, especially when it comes to eating. Three good choices for a dinner that won't disappoint are the marina-side **Waterfront** restaurant *(☎ 207-236-3747)*, with its superb seafood servings (such as haddock stuffed with shrimp, crabmeat and spinach), efficient service and open-air terrace. Also at water's edge is **Atlantica** *(☎ 207-236-6019)*, which offers up creative marine and land selections with an international twist (Korean barbeque, Indonesian scallop stir-fry or Eggplant Napoleon) in a lively setting. **Rathbones** *(☎ 207-236-3272)* fetes diners with inventive fowl, meat and fish dishes (cardamon and pistachio-crusted haddock or truffle sautéed lobster) in intimate, elegant rooms asplash with red-painted, art-adorned walls and highbacked ocher cloth-covered chairs; begin with chilled cream of fiddle head soup and end with Godiva mousse cake or orange ginger crème brûlée.

Returning to the center of Camden by Route 52 affords another good view of the Camden Hills as they slope down to Megunticook Lake.

Old Conway House – *1mi south of Camden on Rte. 1. Visit by guided tour (1hr) only. Jul–Aug Tue–Fri 10am–4pm. Jun & Sept by appointment. $3.* & ☎ *207-236-2257. www.mint.net/~chmuseum.* This group of buildings includes an 18C farmhouse with antique furnishings and a barn containing a collection of carriages and farm equipment. Also on site is a restored sugarhouse (1820) and a small museum featuring artifacts and memorabilia of Camden and Rockport.

EXCURSION

Rockport – *3mi south of Camden by Rte. 1.* This seaside hamlet, formerly known for its lime industry, is a picturesque, relaxing spot. Ruins of the lime kilns can be viewed in Marine Park near the harbor.

The Lobster Pound

Rte 1, 5mi north of Camden in Lincolnville Beach. ☎ *207-789-5550.* Situated right on the beach, this popular, rambling restaurant offers diners great views and delicious seafood for lunch and dinner. Family-owned for three generations, the complex has a separate picnic area *(open in summer)* for more casual dining and take-out. Appetizers include clam chowder, lobster stew or steamed clams. Steaks, chicken and roast turkey take a back seat to Maine shrimp, soft-shell clams, haddock, Atlantic scallops, as well as swordfish and halibut—blackened, broiled or charbroiled. Center stage, however, is the lobster dinner selection: the whole boiled (up to 2lbs), the coastal (1-1/8lb and includes dessert), the complete (add chowder) or the shore deluxe (full dinner with 1-1/2lb lobster accompanied by clams or mussels). You can select your lobster from the saltwater tank and watch as it's prepared for your table.

CAMPOBELLO ISLAND (Canada)★★

Map of Principal Sights

Campobello Island, at the mouth of the Bay of Fundy, is linked to Lubec, Maine, by the Franklin Delano Roosevelt Memorial Bridge. An international agreement signed by the US and Canada in 1964 established an international park dedicated to Franklin Delano Roosevelt on Campobello Island.

Historical Notes – Discovered in the 17C by Samuel de Champlain and Sieur de Monts, the island was named in 1767 for the governor of Nova Scotia, William Campbell—*campo bello* (Italian for "beautiful pasture") calling to mind the island's scenery. In the late 19C the island was again discovered, this time by wealthy Bostonians and New Yorkers, such as the Roosevelts, who bought land and subsequently built summer cottages here. Land developers were quick to use the island's frequent thick fogs to their advantage, advertising that "basking in the fog was as healthy for the body as basking in the sun."
Easily accessible from the mainland, Campobello Island receives many visitors attracted by the international park and the island's wild, unspoiled beauty. In the offshore waters, circular **weirs**, composed of nets strung on stakes, trap fish according to an ancient Indian method.

VISIT

Campobello Island is part of the Canadian province of New Brunswick. US citizens must present personal identification (such as a birth certificate or voter registration card, and photo identification) at the border. It is advisable to carry proof of citizenship with you. This Canadian time zone is 1hr later than Maine.

★★**Roosevelt Campobello International Park** – *Grounds open daily year-round. Buildings open late May–mid-Oct daily 9am–5pm.* & ☎ *506-752-2922.* **Franklin Delano Roosevelt** (1882-1945), whose four terms as president of the US were unprecedented in the nation's history, spent his early summers at Campobello. He continued to vacation on the island with his wife, Eleanor, and their children until August 1921 when, following a swim in the icy waters of the Bay of Fundy, he was suddenly stricken with polio. Almost completely paralyzed, FDR began a long period of convalescence during which he gradually regained his strength. Unfortunately he remained partially paralyzed for the rest of his life.
Turning his energies toward politics, Franklin was elected governor of New York in 1929 and within four years was elected to the first of four terms he would serve as president. FDR did not return to the island until 1933, 12 years after the onset of his tragic illness. Then, as on the several other occasions when he visited the island before his death, he stayed only for a brief time. The Hammer family donated the Roosevelt cottage and property to the government in 1963 to serve as a park in FDR's memory.

Visitor Center – Films are shown as an introduction to Campobello and Roosevelt's life on the island.

Roosevelt Cottage – The 34-room house facing Eastport across the bay is modestly furnished. Many personal mementos, such as FDR's hat, fishing rod, family photos and letters, recall the vacations the Roosevelts spent at Campobello.

Drives in the Park – The vast 2,800-acre park exhibits a variety of magnificent landscapes, including forests, bogs, cliffs, lakes and beaches. The humid seaside climate favors dense, rich vegetation. From **Friars Head** *(south of the visitor center turn right at the sign marked Picnic Area)* there is a view west of Lubec and the Maine coast. A sweeping vista along the shore of **Herring Cove** to **Herring Cove Head** is visible from **Con Robinson's Point** *(follow Glensevern Rd. east to the end)*. At **Lower Duck Pond** a pebble beach borders the rocky shore. The island's woodlands, dubbed "fog forests," are often enshrouded in a thick mist.

East Quoddy Head Lighthouse – *A short distance north of Wilson's Beach, take the gravel road.* The lighthouse and its picturesque surroundings look out on Head Harbor Island.

COBSCOOK BAY★

Map of Principal Sights
Tourist Office ☎ 207-853-4644

Emptying into **Passamaquoddy Bay**, Cobscook Bay is a natural basin that is almost entirely landlocked. The coastal fishing towns of Eastport and Lubec, separated by less than 3mi of water but nearly 40mi apart by land, stand sentinel over the channels linking the two bay areas. The exceptionally high tides (18-24ft) for which this bay and its neighboring shores are known so impressed the local Indians that they named it Cobscook, meaning "boiling waters."

During the 1930s the US and Canada joined forces in the **Passamaquoddy Tidal Power Project** to provide power for local farms and industry by harnessing the energy released by the tides of Passamaquoddy and Cobscook Bays. The project called for the construction of a dam or series of dams that would link several of the islands to the mainland. Construction began in 1935 but was abandoned after a short time, leaving several thousand workers unemployed and bankrupting the city of Eastport. As a result of the energy crisis of the 1970s and 80s, interest in the Passamaquoddy Tidal Power Project revived for a time.

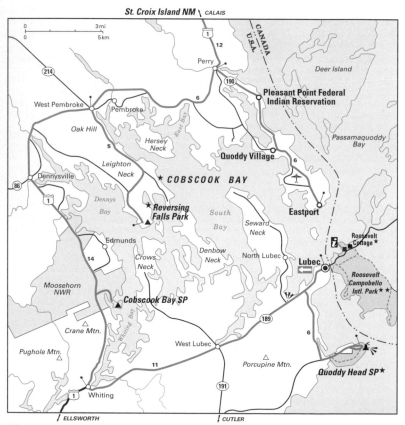

DRIVING TOUR *1/2 day. 76mi. Map 86.*

Lubec – During the 17C and 18C, this small fishing port was a center for goods smuggled into the US from Canada. Ships authorized to sail to Europe set out from Lubec and returned several days later with cargoes of rum, sugar and other staples. The record-breaking time of these highly profitable round-trip "transatlantic voyages"—in fact only short trips to Canada where goods were available at low prices—was never questioned. By the late 1800s, 20 sardine-packing factories had been established in Lubec, forming the basis of the town's economy. Only two of these factories remain.

From Lubec the Franklin Delano Roosevelt International Bridge provides access to the International Park on Campobello Island.

★**Quoddy Head State Park** – *6mi south of Lubec. Follow Rte. 189 4mi to the gas station and turn left at the sign. Open mid-May–mid-Oct daily 9am–dusk. Rest of the year call for hours. $1.* ☏ *207-733-0911 or 207-941-4014 (off season).* Red-and-white-striped **Quoddy Head Lighthouse**, marking the easternmost point of the US, is in the park. From the lighthouse there is a view of the island of Grand Manan in New Brunswick, Canada.

A coastal **footpath** *(round-trip 1hr 15min)* beginning at the parking lot *(to the right of the lighthouse, arriving from Rte. 189)* affords a superb **view** of the sea and the granite ledges.

Leave Lubec on Rte. 189 heading west. Outside Lubec the road climbs to a point that offers a view of Passamaquoddy Bay and the harbor. At Whiting take Rte. 1 north.

Cobscook Bay State Park – *Open mid-May–mid-Oct daily 9am–dusk. Rest of the year call for hours. $2.* ☏ *207-726-4412.* The park contains campsites located on the shores of Cobscook Bay. Here, tall stands of evergreens, growing out of crevices in the coastal ledges, dominate the island-speckled waters of the bay.

Continue on Rte. 1. In West Pembroke take the unmarked road on the right (opposite Rte. 214) and follow signs for Reversing Falls Park.

★**Reversing Falls Park** – This is one of the best places from which to admire Cobscook Bay's pine-covered islands and secluded coves. Twice daily, with the change of tides, the current is so strong in one area that the rushing waters form a .5mi-long falls.

Return to Rte. 1. Continue through Perry, then take Rte. 190 south.

Pleasant Point Federal Indian Reservation – Homes of the Passamaquoddy Indian tribe dot the landscape of this small community. One of the dozen tribes that originally inhabited Maine, the Passamaquoddy Indians now number about 2,500 throughout the state. They depend primarily on fishing for their livelihood and have constructed a network of weirs to trap fish in the offshore waters.

Most of the Indians at Pleasant Point are Catholic, and the celebration of special occasions combines Christian religious rituals with the traditional ceremonies and native costumes of the Passamaquoddy tribe.

Between Pleasant Point and Quoddy Village, Route 190 passes over one of the dams constructed as part of the Passamaquoddy Tidal Power Project.

Quoddy Village – This hamlet is enhanced by the absence of industry, crowds and pollution. Spacious dwellings, built in the 1930s to house workers on the tidal project, have been remodeled to provide comfortable, modern living space.

Eastport – This small community, the easternmost city in the US, is located on Moose Island between the entrances to Cobscook and Passamaquoddy Bays. Exceptionally high tides invade the shore at Eastport, making it necessary for the city's wharves to be built on unusually tall piles.

The sardine-canning industry flourished here between 1875 and the 1920s, together with the production of fish meal and pearl essence (a liquid derived from herring scales and used to add iridescence to artificial pearls). Today the aquaculture industry is a major economic activity. A recent project to develop cargo facilities along the waterfront has once again made Eastport an operational deep-water port and stimulated the city's economy.

Return to Rte. 1 and turn right at Perry.

St. Croix Island National Monument – This island off the ruddy shores of the mainland was the site of a colony established in 1604 by a group of 75 men led by Samuel de Champlain and Sieur de Monts. The severe winter resulted in the death of a number of the colonists, and the following year the colony moved across the Bay of Fundy to Nova Scotia. The island was later significant in setting the St. Croix River as the boundary line separating the US and Canada.

COLUMBIA FALLS

Population 552
Map of Principal Sights

Columbia Falls functioned as one of the numerous shipbuilding and lumbering centers on the coast in the 19C.

SIGHT

Ruggles House – *Take Rte. 1 to sign for Columbia Falls. Turn onto this road and follow it .25mi. Visit by guided tour (30min) only, Jun–mid-Oct Mon–Sat 9:30am–4:30pm, Sun 11am–4:30pm. $3.50 contribution requested.* ☎ *207-483-4637 or 207-483-4689.* Built in 1818, this house was one of the finest dwellings in the village. Though modest in size, the house boasts a handsome exterior and bright, comfortable rooms. The hand-carved wain-scoting, fireplaces and cornices were, according to legend, executed by an Englishman whose hand was guided by an angel.

ELLSWORTH

Population 5,975
Map of Principal Sights
Tourist Office ☎ 207-667-2617

Ellsworth, both a traditional coastal village and a small modern city, is graced with the attractive First Congregational Church and Scandinavian-inspired City Hall. The business district, destroyed by fire in 1937, has been rebuilt, while older dwellings still occupy the nearby residential areas.

SIGHT

Black Mansion – *West Main St. Visit by guided tour (1hr) only, Jun–mid-Oct Mon–Sat 10am–5pm. Closed major holidays. $5.* ☎ *207-667-8671. http://ellsworthme.org/cbmm.* The Georgian elegance of this brick mansion is reflected in its harmoniously proportioned columns and balustrades, its tall chimneys and symmetrical single-story wings. There is no entranceway on the street side of the house. The interior contains period furnishings and personal possessions of the house's former residents, the Black family.

FARMINGTON

Population 7,436
Map of Principal Sights
Tourist Office ☎ 207-778-4215

This farming community serves as the shopping center for the vacation areas of the Belgrade Lakes to the south, the Rangeley Lakes to the west, and the Sugarloaf and Saddleback Mountain ski areas. Farmington became known for its famous resident **Lillian Norton** (1857-1914), the celebrated opera star.

SIGHT

Nordica Homestead – *From Farmington Center take Rte. 4 north and turn right onto Holley Rd. Open Jun–Labor Day Tue–Sat 10am–5pm, Sun 1pm–5pm. $2.* ⏏ ☎ *207-778-2042.* Known particularly for her Wagnerian roles, American soprano Lillian Norton attended Boston's New England Conservatory of Music. She performed in cities throughout the world, from Paris to New York City. As a result of a shipwreck near Java, she died during her world farewell tour. Her home has been transformed into a museum, named after Norton's stage name, Lillian Nordica. Exhibits on her life and career are presented here.

FREEPORT

Population 6,905
Map of Principal Sights
Tourist Office ☎ 207-865-1212

A favored shopping spot, this small town is the home of **L.L. Bean**, the famous sporting goods mail-order enterprise, as well as 120 brand-name factory outlets and stores established in Freeport over the past several years.

During Freeport's early days, the logs for ships' masts and spars were harvested from the surrounding forests and shipped to England from the town's open harbor, or "free port." In 1820 Freeport earned its sobriquet, "Birthplace of Maine," when the treaty agreeing to separate Maine from Massachusetts—and subsequently granting Maine statehood—was signed in a local tavern here.

Today the tranquil anchorage in South Freeport *(at the end of Pine St.)* harbors a mix of pleasure boats and fishing vessels and the town's well-manicured Main Street caters to the tourist, instead of to the lumber trade.

SIGHTS

Desert of Maine – *I-95 Exit 19, then 2mi west on Desert Rd. Open early May–mid Oct daily 8:30am–5pm. $6.75.* ⚠ ♿ ☎ *207-865-6962. www.desertofmaine.com.* Once a densely wooded area, these 500 acres are now covered with sand dunes that began to appear in the 18C, after a farmer made a large clearing in the woods to provide his animals with grazing land. Wind and rain eroded the topsoil, gradually exposing the sandbed, which had lain hidden below. Over the years the wind has shaped and reshaped the sandy expanse into dunes that now spread across the formerly wooded landscape.

★**Wolfe's Neck Woods State Park** – *5mi from the center of Freeport. From Rte. 1 turn right onto Bow St., then right onto Wolfe's Neck Rd. Open Memorial Day–Labor Day daily 9am–dusk. Rest of the year daily 9am–6pm. $1 (Memorial Day–Labor Day $2).* ♿ ☎ *207-865-4465 or 207-624-6080 (off season).* The beauty and calm of the park's wooded picnic sites and trails overlooking Casco Bay offer a pleasant diversion from the shop-lined streets of Freeport village. The Casco Bay Trail *(.5mi),* which provides close-up views of Googins Island, is especially scenic.

■ L.L. Bean

On Main St. at Bow St.; ☎ *800-221-4221.* The L.L. Bean factory store in the center of Freeport features clothing, foot gear and equipment for outdoor sports. It is not unusual to see the company's parking lot crowded at 3am or 4am since the store is open 24 hours a day year-round, as it has been since 1951 when its founder tired of customers knocking on his door before dawn. Outdoorsman and inventor **Leon Leonwood Bean** (1872-1967) began his merchandising empire in 1912 making and selling hunting boots. His success led him to expand his enterprise into a mail-order business specializing in outdoor clothing and equipment. The modest factory showroom blossomed over time into a megastore, where five levels—including an indoor trout pond—now display equipment for nearly every outdoor sport imaginable. Whether your fancy runs to hiking, fishing, camping, hunting, skiing, snowshoeing or kayaking (to name just a few), you can outfit yourself here.

THE KENNEBUNKS★

Population 14,029
Map of Principal Sights
Tourist Office ☎ 207-967-0857

Many artists and writers frequent the popular resort villages of the Kennebunk region: **Kennebunk, Kennebunkport★, Kennebunk Beach, Goose Rocks, Arundel** and **Cape Porpoise.** Kennebunkport is said to be the setting of *Arundel,* a novel by Kenneth Roberts, a native of the region. More recently, the town has gained renown as the site of the summer home of George Bush, 41st president of the US (1989-93).

The magnificent elm trees, white houses and churches in Kennebunk and Kennebunkport date back to the prosperous shipping days of the 19C. From 1766 until 1879, some 20 shipyards at Kennebunk Landing produced hundreds of wooden sailing vessels. In later years, from the late 19C through the early 20C, the 5mi stretch of Maine coast from Kennebunk Beach to Cape Porpoise reigned as a fashionable resort area, with dozens of grand hotels and summer mansions providing lodging for visitors.

Today Kennebunk contains many year-round homes and businesses. An architectural tour *(p 90)* of the historical district provides an introduction to the buildings in this village. Kennebunkport's shopping area, Dock Square, harbors a variety of small shops.

SIGHTS

Wedding Cake House – *In Kennebunk on Rte. 9A. Not open to the public.* According to legend, the captain who lived in this house was about to be married when he was unexpectedly called to sea. Although the wedding took place, there was not enough time to bake and decorate a traditional wedding cake. To console his wife the captain promised he would have the house "frosted like a wedding cake" upon his return. His vow resulted in the addition of the lacy gingerbread trim ornamenting the house and barn.

Brick Store Museum – *117 Main St. in Kennebunk. Open early Jun–Labor Day Tue & Thu–Sat 10am–4:30pm, Wed 1pm–8pm. Rest of Sept–Dec Tues–Sat 10am–4:30pm. $5.* ♿ ☎ *207-985-4802. www.cybertours/brickstore.com.* Formerly a general store, this brick structure (1825) and three adjacent 19C buildings have been renovated to house the museum. Galleries are devoted to decorative arts and marine collections, as well as to changing exhibits related to local history. One of the restored buildings, the nearby 1803 Taylor-Barry House *(24 Summer St./Rte. 35)*, is formerly a shipmaster's home. *An architectural walking tour (1hr 30min) of the Kennebunk Historic District is conducted by museum guides Jun–Sept Wed 7pm & Fri 1pm. $4. Self-guided tour booklet ($5) is available at the museum shop.*

Seashore Trolley Museum – 🏬 *In Kennebunkport. From Kennebunk take Rte. 1 north 3mi to Log Cabin Rd., turn right and continue east about 2mi. Open Memorial Day–mid-Oct daily 10am–5pm. May 1–23 & Oct 22–30 weekends only 10am–5pm. $7. ☎ 207-967-2800. www.trolleymuseum.org.* The 3.5mi ride on a restored electric trolley car will be a new experience or a nostalgic one for visitors. After the tour, stroll through the car barns to see the antique trolley cars and watch artisans at work in the painstaking restoration process.

Cape Porpoise – *From Kennebunkport, take Rte. 9 north 2mi.* The indented shores of Cape Porpoise shelter a fishing village that becomes a pleasant resort during the summer months.

Goose Rocks Beach – *From Kennebunkport, take Rte. 9 north 4mi. Turn right at the sign for beach. Motels provide guests with beach sticker required for parking.* Salt marsh grasses frame this inviting 2mi sandy beach.

KITTERY

Population 9,372
Map of Principal Sights
Tourist Office ☎ 207-439-7545

Shipbuilding, fishing and tourism are the mainstays of this village located just north of the New Hampshire line. Private boatyards turn out pleasure craft, adding to the town's role as a shipbuilding center.

Kittery has been associated with shipbuilding ever since the British began constructing warships here in 1647. In 1778 Adm. John Paul Jones' ship, the *Ranger*, built in Kittery, carried the news to France of General Burgoyne's surrender and received the first salute ever given an American ship by a foreign power. The Portsmouth Naval Base and Shipyard, established on Seavey Island in the Piscataqua River in 1800, has been the most important business in Kittery since the 19C.

A drive along the tree-shaded Route 103 leading to the 18C settlement of Kittery Point affords glimpses of the river and some of the area's original Colonial homes.

SIGHT

Fort McClary State Historic Site – *On Rte. 103 east of Kittery in Kittery Point. Open Memorial Day–Sept daily 9am–8pm. $1. ☎ 207-384-5160.* A hexagonal-shaped blockhouse is all that remains of the 17C fort first christened Fort William and afterward renamed for Maj. Andrew McClary, who was killed at the Battle of Bunker Hill. The blockhouse is situated in a calm, waterfront park setting.

EXCURSIONS

★ **Hamilton House** – *9mi west of Kittery by Rte. 236 to S. Berwick, turn left opposite junction with Rte. 91. Continue to road's end. Bear left, then take first right onto Vaughan's Lane. Visit by guided tour (45min) only, Jun–mid-Oct Wed–Sun 11am–5pm. $4. ☎ 207-384-2454.* This Georgian mansion and its riverside gardens were the setting for much of Sarah Orne Jewett's novel *The Tory Lover*. The house (1785), built for the merchant Jonathan Hamilton, contains hand-carved archways, cornices and molding. Japanned and painted furnishings, as well as murals of the local countryside, adorn the first floor.

Sarah Orne Jewett House – *In South Berwick, 10mi north of Kittery on Rte. 236. Same hours & admission as Hamilton House.* This was the home of 19C novelist **Sarah Orne Jewett** (1849-1909). Jewett's novels *The Country of the Pointed Firs* (1896), an expression of her admiration for Maine and its people, and *The Tory Lover*, set in Berwick during the Revolution, are American classics. The house is arranged as it was when the author lived here.

> ■ **Kittery's Outlet Malls**
>
> *From I-95, take Exit 3 to Coastal Rte. 1. ☎ 800-548-8379. www. thekitteryoutlets.com.* More than 120 outlet stores cluster along a 1.5mi stretch of Route 1 in Kittery, offering shoppers a wide range of items such as clothing, shoes, crystal, silver, housewares and furnishings. Designers Anne Klein, Liz Claiborne, Ralph Lauren, Tommy Hilfiger and other well-known manufacturers are represented.

MONHEGAN ISLAND★★

Population 88
Map below

This rocky island, 10mi off the mainland, appears from the distance like a large whale floating on the surface of the ocean. From a closer point you can see Monhegan's steep cliffs dropping sharply to the sea.

Ledge markings discovered on Manana, the islet across the harbor from Monhegan, are considered by some as evidence that the Vikings landed here in the 11C. Several centuries later Monhegan served as a fishing station for European fishermen.

The island's small year-round population earns its living from fishing and lobstering. A law prohibiting fishermen from trapping lobsters in Monhegan waters between June 25 and January 1 allows Monhegan lobsters to grow bigger and thus bring a better price. In the summer Monhegan is a haven for artists and tourists. The island's magical beauty and 17mi of trails attract hikers and photographers. *Trails are numbered and can be identified by tiny wooden blocks placed on tree trunks where two or more trails meet. Allow 4hrs for trails described.*

PRACTICAL INFORMATION .... Area Code: 207

Getting There – From **Portland** to all ferry departure points, take I-295 north to I-95 north to Rte. 1 north: to **Port Clyde** (81mi), take Rte. 1 north to Rte. 131 south; to **New Harbor** (57mi), take Rte. 1 north to Rte. 130 south to Rte. 32; to **Boothbay Harbor** (49mi), take Rte. 1 north to Rte. 27 south.

International and domestic flights to **Portland International Airport** ☎ 774-7301. Major rental car agencies *(p 306)*. Closest Amtrak **train** station: South Station, Boston ☎ 800-872-7245. Greyhound **bus** station: Portland ☎ 800-231-2222.

Ferry Schedule *2- to 3-month advance reservation strongly suggested.*

Departs From	Schedule	Duration (one-way)	Adult Fare (round-trip)	Company
Port Clyde	May–Oct. daily; rest of the year Mon, Wed & Fri only	1hr	$25	Monhegan Boat Line ☎ 372-8848
New Harbor	mid Jun–Sept daily; mid-May–early Jun & early Oct–mid-Oct, Wed & weekends only	1hr	$26	Hardy Boat Cruises ☎ 800-278-3346
Boothbay Harbor	Memorial Day–Sept, once daily; first 2 wks of Oct, weekends only	1hr 30min	$29	Balmy Days Cruises ☎ 633-2284

Visitor Information – Monhegan Island is easily visited by foot or bicycle. No cars or public transportation available on the island; bicycles prohibited on trails. For more information, contact the Maine Tourism Assn., PO Box 396, Kittery ME ☎ 207-439-1319. www.mainetourism.com.

Accommodations – Lodging information available from Maine Tourism Assn. *(above)*. Accommodations on Monhegan Island are limited; advance reservations required (summer season 3- to 4-month advance reservation recommended). No camping allowed.

Recreation – **Swimming** at Swim Beach only, near the village of Monhegan. Seventeen miles of **hiking** trails. **Birding** at Lobster Cove. **Harbor seals** usually can be seen at half-tide on Duck Rock.

Monhegan Harbor at Sunrise

SIGHTS

Burnt Head – Follow Trail 4 to Burnt Head for a **view★★** of the White Head cliffs.

★★**White Head** – From Burnt Head follow Trail 1, which straddles the ledges and an evergreen forest. White Head's 150ft cliffs are generally blanketed with seagulls.

Cathedral Woods – Trail 12 runs along Long Swamp to Cathedral Woods, an inland forest of evergreens towering above lush undergrowth of fern and moss.

★**Monhegan Lighthouse** – From the top of Lighthouse Hill there is a **panorama** of Monhegan, the harbor and Manana. The lighthouse keeper's house has been transformed into a **museum** that displays photographs, artifacts and prints related to animal, plant and human life on the island *(open Jul–Aug daily 11:30am–3:30pm, Sept daily 12:30pm–2:30pm; $2 contribution requested)*. There is also an exhibit relating to Ray Phillips (1897-1975), the hermit of Manana, whose house still stands on the island's hillside.

MOOSEHEAD LAKE REGION

Map of Principal Sights
Tourist Office ☎ 207-695-2702

This remote inland body of water, New England's largest lake (117sq mi), is dotted with hundreds of islands and surrounded by timberlands that reach as far as the Canadian border. Numerous bays and coves indent the lake's 350mi shoreline, making it look from the air like a wide set of antlers.

The region has been a paradise for sportsmen since the 19C. Easy-to-reach ponds and lakes, as well as isolated lakeshore sporting camps *(accessible only by plane)*, attract fishermen and hunters. Canoe and raft trips, including those on the Allagash Wilderness Waterway, begin on the shores of Moosehead Lake.

Every year in May, the region is the setting for **MooseMainea**, a month-long celebration featuring moose-themed events and activities.

SIGHTS

Greenville – Situated at the southern end of Moosehead Lake, Greenville is a resort center, headquarters for two large paper companies and a major outfitting center for sportsmen heading into the north country. Winter skiing is offered at Big Squaw Mountain Ski Area outside Greenville. Lily Bay State Park, north of town, has a beach and facilities for camping, boating and picnicking. Lily Bay Road, north of Greenville, provides access to Lily Bay State Park.

Mt. Kineo – Rising abruptly from the waters of Moosehead Lake, Mt. Kineo reaches an altitude of 1,806ft. There is a good view of Kineo from Route 6/15 just north of Rockwood. Kineo was well known among the many tribes that journeyed to this flint mountain to obtain the hard, durable stone needed to make weapons, tools and other implements.

Allagash Wilderness Waterway – *74mi north of Greenville.* The 92mi Allagash Wilderness Waterway offers experienced canoeists a magnificent stretch of white water in the heart of a wilderness area. *For access and orientation, see p 93.*

Visiting Northern Maine .... Area Code: 207

The following information is offered to facilitate access and orientation to this remote area of the state:

Getting There – The Moosehead Lake area is accessed from Greenville, the Katahdin region from Millinocket. From **Bangor** to **Greenville** (72mi): Rte. 15 north. From **Quebec City** to **Greenville** (219mi): I-73 south to Rte. 173 south to Rte. 6/15. From **Bangor** to **Millinocket** (71mi): I-95 north to Rte. 11 south. From **Quebec City** to **Millinocket** (329mi): I-73 south to Rte. 173 south to Rte. 201 south to Rte. 16 east to Rte. 6/16 to Rte. 11 north. International and domestic flights to **Bangor International Airport** ☎ 947-0384. Major rental car agencies *(p 306)*. Greyhound **bus** station: Bangor ☎ 800-231-2222.

Getting Around – Public roads in northern Maine are scarce. Lumber companies maintain private roads, many of which are open to the public and operate like toll roads; 4-wheel drive vehicles recommended. Lumber trucks have right-of-way on logging roads. Many areas are accessible only by seaplane or canoe.

Seaplanes – Moosehead Lake area: **Folsom's Air Service** PO Box 507, Moosehead Lake, Greenville ME 04441-0507 ☎ 695-2821; **Currier's Flying Service** PO Box 351, Greenville Junction ME 04442 ☎ 695-2778; **Jack's Flying Service** PO Box 338, Greenville ME 04441 ☎ 695-3020. Katahdin region: **Katahdin Air Service Inc.** PO Box 171, Millinocket ME 04462 ☎ 723-8378; **Scotty's Flying Service** RR 1 Box 256, Patten ME 04765 ☎ 528-2626.

Visitor Information – For access to designated wilderness areas and detailed topographic maps, contact **North Maine Woods** PO Box 425, Ashland ME 04732 ☎ 435-6213. www.northmainewoods.org. **Allagash Wilderness Waterway**: Maine Department of Conservation, Bureau of Parks & Lands, State House Station 22, Augusta ME 04333 ☎ 287-3821. www.state.me.us. Visitors entering the Allagash Waterway must register at the Telos-Chamberlain entrance, or at the Churchill Dam, Umsaskis Lake or Michaud Farm checkpoints. **Guide Services**: for a free directory, contact Maine Professional Guides Assn., PO Box 847, Augusta ME 04332 ☎ 549-5631.

Moosehead Lake Area – **Moosehead Vacation & Sportsmen's Assn.** PO Box MTG, Rockwood ME 04478 ☎ 534-7300. **Moosehead Lake Region Chamber of Commerce** visitor center: Rte. 15. Mailing address: PO Box 581, Greenville ME 04441 ☎ 695-2702. www.mooseheadlake.org.

Katahdin Region – **Katahdin Area Chamber of Commerce** visitor information kiosk operates seasonally on Rte. 11; mailing address: 1029 Central St., Millinocket ME 04462 ☎ 723-4443. www.katahdinmaine.com.

Accommodations – Accommodations range from motels to historic inns and bed and breakfasts concentrated in Greenville and Millinocket. **Sporting camps** are located in Greenville, Rockwood and Millinocket. Camping at Lily Bay State Park, Baxter State Park and private campgrounds; reservations required. **Camping** information: **Maine Forest Service** PO Box 1107, Greenville ME 04441 ☎ 695-3721. Accommodation information also available from agencies listed above.

John Gerlach/Dembinsky Photo Assocs.

Recreation – Fishing, ice fishing and hunting are bountiful throughout the region (contact Maine Fisheries and Wildlife for seasons and information: 41 State House Station, Augusta ME 04333 ☎ 287-8000). **White-water rafting** throughout area. **Cross-country** rentals and trail maps available in Greenville and Millinocket. **Snowmobiling** on Interstate Trail System, rental and trail information available. Most **supplies** available in Greenville and Millinocket. *Contact organizations listed above for more information regarding recreation in northern Maine.*

MOUNT DESERT ISLAND★★★

Map of Principal Sights
Tourist Office ☎ 207-276-5040

Measuring 108sq mi and cut almost in half by the fjord **Somes Sound**, Mt. Desert Island remains an unspoiled region of pink granite mountains, dark forests and freshwater lakes. Pointed evergreens, emerging from rocky ledges that fall away from the shore, recall the description of Mt. Desert as "the place where the mountains meet the sea." The major portion of **Acadia National Park** is located here.

Historical Notes

The island was once the summer campgrounds of the Penobscot and Passamaquoddy Indians. In September 1604 French explorer **Samuel de Champlain** and **Sieur de Monts**, grantee of Acadia (the French territory that extended from present-day Montreal to Philadelphia), anchored in what is now **Frenchman Bay**. Champlain's impression of the largest island in the bay as a line of seven or eight mountains with rocky, treeless summits led him to name the island Isle des Monts Deserts. Nine years later a group of Jesuits established a settlement on this island. Their colony existed only a month before being destroyed by the British.

During the 150 years that followed, the Acadian territory was a constant battlefield for the English and the French. In the late 17C the governor of Canada gave Mt. Desert Island to the Frenchman **Antoine de la Mothe Cadillac**, who spent only one summer there before heading west and founding the city of Detroit. Following the defeat of the French at Quebec in 1759, English colonists began to settle on the coast in increasingly large numbers. The English dominated the island until after the Revolution, when the boundary between the US and Canada was established by the Treaty of Versailles (1783).

In the mid-19C the area's beauty was discovered by artists. The enthusiasm expressed in their writings and paintings enticed the wealthy to vacation on Mt. Desert Island. Elegant summer "cottages" were built, and Bar Harbor developed into a resort community similar to Newport, while Northeast and Southwest Harbors became popular yachting centers.

View from Cadillac Mountain

★BAR HARBOR

Located on Mt. Desert Island, Bar Harbor is the major gateway to Acadia National Park and a departure point for ferries to Nova Scotia (☎ *888-249-7245*).

During the late 19C and early 20C, Bar Harbor was second only to Newport as a playground of the wealthy. Summer residents arrived by rail and steamship, and spacious Victorian-style hotels provided them with comfortable lodging facing the sea. Affluent families such as the Rockefellers, Astors and Vanderbilts built cottages that became legendary for their magnificence. In one mansion the center of the dining room floor opened to allow the banquet table to descend. The table then reappeared, completely prepared for the next course! Only a handful of these residences still stand; the remainder were destroyed by a fire that swept Bar Harbor in 1947.

PRACTICAL INFORMATION .... Area Code: 207

Getting There – From **Portland** (127mi). take I-95 east to Rte. 1 north to Belfast. then Rte. 1/3 north to Ellsworth. then Rte. 3 south; from **Bangor** (46mi). take Rte. 1A south to Ellsworth then Rte. 3 south. International and domestic flights to **Bangor International Airport** ☏ 947-0384. Major rental car agencies *(p 306)*. Closest Amtrak **train** station: South Station. Boston ☏ 800-872-7245. Greyhound **bus** station: Bangor. service to Bar Harbor (Cottage and Kennebunk Sts.) late Jun–early Oct ☏ 800-231-2222.

Getting Around – Mt. Desert Island is best visited by car. although some sights are accessible by bicycle (rentals available in island towns) and foot. **Shuttle** service between Ellsworth and Mt. Desert Island towns *(year-round Mon–Fri)*: Downeast Transportation, PO Box 914, Ellsworth ME 04605 ☏ 667-5796. Year-round **ferry** service to Cranberry Isles departs from Northeast Harbor (Beal & Bunker, PO Box 33, Cranberry Isles ME 04625 ☏ 244-3575); to Swans Island from Bass Harbor (Maine State Ferry Service, PO Box 114, Bass Harbor ME 04653 ☏ 244-3254). Other companies offer periodic crossings from both harbors. contact chambers of commerce *(below)*. **Acadia National Park Tours** depart from Cottage St. in Bar Harbor mid-May–Oct daily, PO Box 794, Bar Harbor ME 04609 ☏ 288-9899. **Carriage tours** *(1–2hrs)* of the park depart from Wildwood Stables mid-Jun–mid-Oct ☏ 276-3622.

Visitor Information – Bar Harbor Chamber of Commerce visitor center: 93 Cottage St. Mailing address: PO Box 158, Bar Harbor ME 04609 ☏ 800-288-5103. **Mt. Desert Chamber of Commerce** visitor center: Sea Street Marina, Northeast Harbor *(late May–mid-Oct)*. Mailing address: PO Box 675, Northeast Harbor ME 04662 ☏ 276-5040. **Acadia National Park** visitor center, Hulls Cove entrance, open mid-Apr–Oct; rest of the year park headquarters at Eagle Lake (Rte. 233, 3mi west of Bar Harbor). Mailing address: Superintendent, Acadia National Park, PO Box 177, Bar Harbor ME 04609 ☏ 288-3338. www.nps.gov/acad.

Accommodations – Information available from **Bar Harbor** *(above)*. **Southwest Harbor** (reservation service) ☏ 244-9264 and **Northeast Harbor** ☏ 276-5040 Chambers of Commerce. Accommodations include modest hotels. bed and breakfasts and rental cottages. **Camping** *(year-round)* in Acadia National Park (reservations for Blackwoods Campground ☏ 800-365-2267); other campgrounds located near other island towns. contact chambers of commerce *(above)*.

Recreation – In Acadia National Park: **swimming** at Echo Lake and Sand Beach; **hiking** and **cross-country skiing** (120mi of trails); **biking** restricted to carriage roads (57mi). Fishing licenses and rental equipment available in island towns. Whale-watching *(p 312)* and scenic cruises depart from Bar Harbor and Northeast Harbor. Most specialty **shopping** and supplies in Bar Harbor. *Contact the chambers of commerce listed above for more information regarding shopping and recreation on Mt. Desert Island.*

Today hotels, motels and guest houses line the road approaching the business district; in the center of town there are many fine shops and restaurants. During the winter, numerous lodgings and shops close down and a quiet atmosphere prevails. A large part of the year-round population works at Jackson Laboratory.

★★★ACADIA NATIONAL PARK *Map p 96*

Open year-round. Hiking, boating, fishing, swimming and winter sports. Park visitor center is located 3mi north of Bar Harbor on Rte. 3 (hours below). $10/vehicle/7 days. ⚠ ✕ ☏ *207-288-3338. www.nps.gov/acad.*

Acadia National Park is located primarily on Mt. Desert Island, with smaller sections on Isle au Haut and **Schoodic Peninsula** across Frenchman Bay. Each year the park attracts some four million visitors.

The idea for a park was born when a group of Mt. Desert's summer residents put into motion a drive to protect the island's natural environment. Thanks to their efforts, more than 5,000 acres on Mt. Desert Island had been set aside as a nature preserve by 1913. These lands, donated to the US government in 1916, were declared a national park three years later. In 1929 the park was permanently named Acadia after the historic French territory.

Over one-third of the park's 35,000 acres—33,000 of which are located on Mount Desert Island—were donated by John D. Rockefeller Jr. It was Rockefeller who was responsible for the creation of 50mi of carriage paths in the eastern end of the island. The park's main attraction, **Loop Road**, parallels a spectacular section of open coast with expansive views and climbs to the top of Cadillac Mountain. Bordering the temperate and subarctic zones, the park contains a rich variety of flora and fauna. Some 500 species of flowers, shrubs, trees and nonflowering plants grow in the region, and about 300 species of birds have been sighted here over the years.

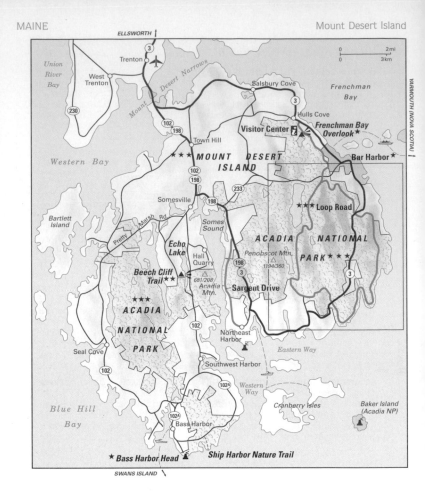

SWANS ISLAND

★★★Loop Road *4hrs. Circle drive 29mi. Map p 97.*

The many scenic outlooks, turnoffs and parking areas along this coastal road afford vistas ranging from sweeping seascapes to panoramas of pink granite mountains and island-studded waters. *Road may be fogbound in morning hours.*

Begin at the visitor center on Rte. 3.

Visitor Center – *Hulls Cove. Open mid-Apr–Oct daily 8am–4:30pm.* ☎ *207-288-3338.* This modern building, rustic in appearance, faces Frenchman Bay.

Follow signs for Loop Road .6mi to Frenchman Bay Overlook.

★**Frenchman Bay Overlook** – From the overlook there is an unobstructed **view** to Schoodic Peninsula and across Frenchman Bay. An orientation table aids in identifying the many small, rounded islands in the bay.

The road passes through a forest and by an open meadow and skirts a marsh where beaver dams can be seen. In the early evening you might observe beavers at work.

Loop Rd. is a one-way road from the Spur Rd. entrance to just south of Jordan Pond. After 3mi turn right for Sieur de Monts Spring.

Sieur de Monts Spring – The spring and surrounding area constituted one of the first parcels of land set aside as part of the nature preserve that became Acadia National Park. The spring was named for de Monts, leader of the 1604 expedition to North America.

The **Nature Center** nearby displays exhibits related to the park *(open May–Sept daily 9am–5pm).* In the **Wild Gardens of Acadia**, regional trees, flowers and shrubs are arranged according to their natural habitat: marsh, bog, beach or mountain.

Abbe Museum (**M**) – *Open Jul–Aug daily 9am–5pm. Mid-May–Jun & Sept–late Oct daily 10am–4pm. $2.* ♿ ☎ *207-288-3519. www.abbemuseum.org.* Dioramas and prehistoric artifacts (Stone Age tools, pottery) in this small pavilion evoke the life of Maine's earliest inhabitants, who occupied the Frenchman Bay and Blue Hill Bay areas prior to European colonization.

Return to Loop Rd.

To the left stand the buildings of **Jackson Laboratory**, internationally known for its role in cancer research. The cliffs of Champlain Mountain loom on the right. Along the road, scenes typical of Acadia come into view: pink granite peaks, tall evergreens and natural roadside rock gardens.

Follow signs to Sand Beach.

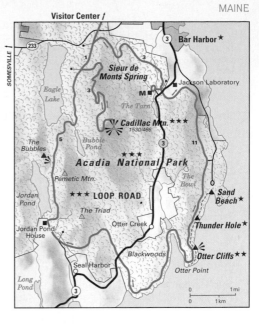

★ **Sand Beach** – Composed of coarse sand, the only saltwater beach in the park provides a pleasant swimming spot for those who don't mind the bracing water temperatures (50°F to 60°F in summer).

To see some spectacular scenery, walk **Shore Path** *(1.8mi)* from the upper parking level along the rocky coast past Thunder Hole to the end of Otter Point.

★ **Thunder Hole** – *Parking on the right.* Over the years the ocean has burrowed into the rock here. At high tide—and especially after a storm—the surf crashes through this narrow chasm with a thunderous roar.

Continue .3mi on Loop Rd.

★★ **Otter Cliffs** – The next stop takes in these sheer cliffs (110ft above the ocean) just north of Otter Point. Here, on the highest Atlantic headlands north of Rio de Janeiro, dramatic **views**★★ encompass the splintered coast and vast sea beyond.

Loop Road winds around Otter Point and Otter Cove, intersects with the road to Seal Harbor, then follows the shore of **Jordan Pond**, which lies below the cliffs of Penobscot Mountain.

At the northern end of the pond, note the large boulder balanced precariously atop one of the two rounded hills known as **The Bubbles**. For a closer look, stop at The Bubbles parking area.

Continue on Loop Rd. for 1.4mi and turn right at sign for Cadillac Mountain.

★★★ **Cadillac Mountain** – The 3.5mi drive to the top of Cadillac Mountain (1,530ft) affords views of Eagle Lake—the largest body of freshwater in the park—Bar Harbor and the islands below. Named for Antoine de la Mothe Cadillac, the proprietor of Mt. Desert Island in the late 17C, the mountain ranks as the highest point on the Atlantic Coast. Easy **Summit Trail**, which winds for less than 1mi around the barren mountaintop, offers breathtaking **panoramas**★★★ of Frenchman Bay and the park.

Return to Loop Rd., then turn right to complete the circle.

Other Areas of the Park

★★ **Schoodic Peninsula** – *From Mount Desert Island, take Rte. 3 north to Rte. 1. Follow Rte. 1 north to West Gouldsboro and turn right onto Rte. 186. Just past Winter Harbor, look for signs to Acadia National Park and turn right. Road becomes one-way at park entrance.* Two thousand acres of Acadia National Park occupy the southern tip of this promontory, which juts out from the mainland east across the bay from Mount Desert Island. Scenery along the park road encompasses a kaleidoscope of tall stands of fir trees rimmed with pink granite ledges and encircled by the blue waters of the bay. From Schoodic Head there are vistas across the bay to Mount Desert Island.

★ **Isle au Haut** – *Map p 81. Boats depart from Stonington mid-Jun–early Sept Mon–Sat 7am, 10am, 11:30am & 4:30pm, Sun 11:30am. Rest of the year Mon–Sat only; call for departure times. One-way 45min. $12. Isle au Haut Co.* ☎ *207-367-5193. To Duck Harbor mid-Jun–early Sept only Mon–Sat 10am & 4:30pm. The boat stops at Isle au Haut Harbor, an anchorage for pleasure craft.* Located south of Stonington on Deer Isle, tiny Isle au Haut measures just 6mi long and 3mi wide. The island is private, except for the 2,800 acres of woodland that belong to Acadia National Park. To best sample its beauty, spend some time hiking the web of trails that traverse the park. The boat to Duck Harbor affords closer access to the dramatic Western Head trail that rounds the western tip of the island.

ADDITIONAL SIGHTS *Map p 96*

★★**Beech Cliff Trail** – *From Somesville take Rte. 102 south, turn right, then left onto Beech Hill Rd. and continue to the end of the road.* This easy trail *(round-trip 30min)* leads to the crest of Beech Cliff, where magnificent **views**★★ reach from Echo Lake to Acadia Mountain, rising above the opposite shore of Somes Sound.

★**Bass Harbor Head** – *At the end of Rte. 102A, 4mi south of Southwest Harbor.* Towering above the rocky shore of this remote headland, Bass Harbor Head **light-house** (1858) makes a delightful subject for a camera or an artist's paintbrush, especially at sunset.

Sargent Drive – *Between Northeast Harbor and Rte. 3/198. Passenger cars only.* For views of the East Coast's only true fjord—a deep glacial valley now flooded by the ocean—take Sargent Drive as it traces the eastern shore of Somes Sound.

Echo Lake – Swimming is permitted in this freshwater lake that lies at the foot of Beech Cliff.

Ship Harbor Nature Trail – *Rte. 102A; east of Bass Harbor. To walk the complete loop (1hr), take a right at the first fork, then bear right at the sign for Ship Harbor Loop.* Such natural wonders as a potbellied tree and an exposed root system resembling a tall modernistic sculpture line this trail, which follows the ledges along the coast of Ship Harbor, then enters a spruce forest. Take this walk at high tide.

OGUNQUIT★

Population 974
Map of Principal Sights
Tourist Office ☎ 207-646-2939

In the Algonquin language, *ogunquit* means "beautiful place by the sea." The artists who discovered this coastal fishing village undoubtedly agreed with the description, for by the turn of the century many painters and writers had come to live and work close to Ogunquit's rocky shores.

Works by members of the town's present-day artists' colony are exhibited in galleries scattered throughout the village, including the **Ogunquit Art Association Gallery** on Route 1 south of Ogunquit Square and the rustic **Barn Gallery** on Shore Road. Overlooking the sea, the small, modern **Museum of American Art** *(Shore Rd., .5mi south of Perkins Cove ☎ 207-646-4909)* showcases the work of 20C American artists. During the summer a different play is presented every week at the **Ogunquit Playhouse** *(☎ 207-646-1805)*.

SIGHTS

★**Perkins Cove** – *From Rte. 1, take Shore Rd. and follow signs to cove. Parking is limited.* This charming man-made anchorage harbors dozens of quaint boutiques and craft shops as well as several seafood restaurants. A footbridge across the entrance to the cove can be raised to allow boats to pass. Perkins Cove is also the departure point for a variety of excursion and fishing boats. *Boats can be hired for deep-sea fishing or for breakfast, cocktail, and lobstering cruises. For a modest fee, tourists are welcome to join local lobstermen as they set out to gather the day's catch.*

★**Marginal Way** – *Parking available at Perkins Cove and Israel's Head lighthouse.* Beginning at Perkins Cove, this scenic coastal footpath follows the windswept promontory called Israel's Head and ends near the center of town. Originally a cattle path for a local farmer, Marginal Way now provides visitors with striking **views**★ of the rocky coast and Perkins Cove.

EXCURSION

Wells – Located on the stretch of sandy beach that extends from Kittery to Portland, Wells has been a summer resort since the last century. **Wells Auto Museum** **Kids** on Route 1 displays some 80 antique automobiles dating from 1900 to 1963 as well as motorcycles and bicycles. Children will enjoy the collection of antique toys and bicycles *(open Memorial Day–Columbus Day daily 10am–5pm; $5; &* ☎ *207-646-9064)*.

PEMAQUID POINT★★

Carved by glaciers centuries ago, the gnarled ledges at Pemaquid Point are especially spectacular for their pegmatite formations—long, narrow bands of black and white rock that jut into the sea. The point is renowned for its lighthouse, which rises on the bluff above and stands guardian over this dramatic section of coastline.

Located south of Damariscotta, this peninsula was one of the first regions on the coast to be settled. The artifacts excavated at the site of colonial Pemaquid provide evidence that the area was colonized in the 17C. The point was probably a station for European fishermen in the 15C and 16C.

SIGHTS *1/2 day*

★**Pemaquid Point Lighthouse Park** – *At the end of Rte. 130 near Bristol. Open late May–mid-Oct daily 9am–5pm (Jul & Aug 6pm). $1.* & ☎ *207-677-2492.* Commissioned by President John Quincy Adams in 1827, Pemaquid Point Lighthouse *(interior closed to the public)* helped sailors—as it still does today—avoid the jagged rocks that divide the opening between Muscongus and John's Bays. From this site stretches a magnificent **view**★★ of the rocky, splintered coastline, with the stone lighthouse reflected in shallow pools left by the surf as it recedes.

In the adjoining former lightkeeper's cottage, the **Fishermen's Museum** contains photographs, fishing gear, lobster buoys and other items related to the life of the fisherman *(open late May–mid-Oct Mon–Sat 10am–5pm, Sun 11am–5pm; rest of the year by appointment; contribution requested;* & ☎ *207-677-2494).*

The small art gallery across the parking lot displays changing exhibits of local artists' work during the summer months.

Pemaquid Point Lighthouse

Pemaquid Beach – *From the lighthouse take Rte. 130, then turn left on Snowball Rd. (follow sign to beach).* It is unusual to find such a beautiful sandy beach along this rugged section of the coast. Take time for a picnic, or a walk along the shore.

★**Colonial Pemaquid State Historic Site** – *Continue past Pemaquid Beach on Snowball Rd.* Foundations of 17C homes and a cemetery dating back to 1695, survive to tell the story of Maine's first permanent settlement. Surveying John's Bay is a replica of the stone tower of **Fort William Henry**, erected in 1692 to fortify the northeastern edge of England's territory. The fort fell to the French—who destroyed it—in 1696, and 33 years later Fort Frederick replaced it. Near the fort an archaeological **museum** contains dioramas of the original settlement and artifacts excavated from the cellar holes just outside *(open Memorial Day–Labor Day daily 9am–5pm; $1;* ✕ ☎ *207-677-2423).*

★**Christmas Cove** – *13mi west of Colonial Pemaquid. Take Rte. 130 north. Turn left onto Harrington Rd. and continue to Rte. 129. Turn left onto Rte. 129 and drive south to the cove.* Rocky headlands and offshore islands shelter this small waterfront settlement. The tranquil cove was named by Capt. John Smith, who is said to have anchored in this snug harbor on Christmas Eve of 1614, during his expedition along the New England coast.

PORTLAND★★

Population 64,358
Map of Principal Sights
Tourist Office ☎ 207-772-5800

The largest city in Maine, Portland is located on Casco Bay, known for its picturesque Calendar Islands. The city is an important oil and fishing port and the financial, cultural and commercial center of northern New England's major metropolitan area. It is also the departure point for the Prince of Fundy Line ferry to Nova Scotia.

Practical information... Area Code: 207

Getting There – From **Boston** (109mi): I-93 to I-95 north. Canadian and domestic flights to **Portland International Airport** ☎ 774-7301. Taxi service *($10–$13 to downtown)* and hotel courtesy shuttles. Major rental car agencies *(p 306)*. Closest Amtrak **train** station: South Station, Boston ☎ 800-872-7245. Greyhound **bus** station: 950 Congress St. ☎ 800-231-2222. **Ferry** service from **Nova Scotia** May–Oct (11hrs): Prince of Fundy Cruises, 468 Commercial St., Portland ME 04101 ☎ 800-341-7540.

Getting Around – Public parking lots are located throughout the city; first hour free at Park & Shop lots with validation stamp from local businesses. Many sights are easily visited by foot. **Greater Portland Transit** bus lines offer transport within Portland and outlying areas ☎ 774-0351.

Visitor Information – **Convention and Visitors Bureau of Greater Portland** visitor center: 305 Commercial St., Portland ME 04101 ☎ 772-5800. www.visitportland.com.

Accommodations – Accommodations include economy and moderate hotels *($50–$130/day)* and bed and breakfasts *($55–$115/day)*; information available from Convention and Visitors Bureau *(above)*. Portland **Hostel** *(May–late Aug)*: Portland Hall, 645 Congress St., Portland ME 04101 ☎ 874-3281. *Average prices for a double room.*

Recreation – **Shopping** at Old Port Exchange and Congress St.; outlet stores in FREEPORT. Self-guided **walking tours** with map of historic areas *($1)*, and guided tours *($8)* early July–early Oct by **Greater Portland Landmarks**, 165 State St. ☎ 774-5561. **Hiking** on Eastern Promenade, Back Cove Trail and Western Promenade. **Biking** on Peaks Island shoreline, rentals available. **Swimming** at Crescent Beach State Park. *Contact Convention and Visitors Bureau for more information regarding shopping and recreation in Portland.*

Historical Notes

Resurgam: "I shall rise again" – True to its motto, *Resurgam*, Portland has risen like a phoenix from its ashes after being almost entirely destroyed on three different occasions. During the early 17C, the English established a trading post here, and by 1658 the village of Falmouth had sprung up on the site. Abandoned in the 1670s after Indian raids caused the inhabitants to flee, the village was resettled in 1716 and supported itself by its mast trade with England. Falmouth's strong anti-Loyalist sentiments led the British to bombard the town in October 1775, as an example to the other colonies. Following the war, the few hundred colonists who remained in Falmouth gradually rebuilt the city, and in 1786, ten years after the birth of the nation, they renamed it Portland.

Prosperity Attained – The city was the capital of Maine between 1820 and 1832. Mansions lined High and State Streets, and the railroad linking Montreal and Portland was completed in the mid-19C. Portland had grown into a prosperous shipping center by July 4, 1866, when a fire swept through the downtown area, leveling most of the buildings in the business district and destroying one-third of the city. From these ashes rose the city's rich group of Victorian structures.

After having experienced a period of decay during the early 20C, Portland underwent a major economic and cultural rebirth in the 1970s and 80s. The city is responsible for shipping petroleum products to Canada via the Portland pipeline. Renewal of such areas as the Old Port Exchange generated new interest in Portland as a business center in the 1970s. This trend has continued, sparked by construction projects including One City Center, the expansion of the Bath Iron Works into Portland and the development of an 18-acre fishing pier.

SIGHTS *1 day. Map p. 101.*

The metropolitan area, cutting into Casco Bay, is rimmed with pleasant parks and strolling paths. The Eastern and Western Promenades, both designed by the nation's preeminent landscape architect, Frederick Law Olmsted, offer panoramic views of the bay and the surrounding region. Portland's skyline is best viewed from the walking path around Back Cove.

Old Port Exchange – The warehouses, offices and shops in this old waterfront district were run-down and deteriorating rapidly when, in the early 1970s, several persons decided to open a few small restaurants and shops in the area. Their immediate success encouraged other merchants to move into the district and renovate neighboring buildings into attractive specialty shops, professional offices and living space.

A stroll along Middle, Exchange, and Fore Streets will allow you to admire the window displays, art galleries and craft shops and to try some of the dozens of restaurants. The 19C architecture is interesting for its diversity of styles and decorative brickwork, including keystones, cornices and coursing.

Exchange Street – Encompassing nos. 103-107, this **block** (**A**) is inspired by the Italianate style; the **building** (**B**) on the corner of Middle and Exchange Streets has a trompe l'œil mural. Several of the windows, though they appear to be part of the mural, are actually real.

Middle Street – The mansard roof reveals the French influence on this elaborately arched and arcaded **block** (**C**), which includes nos. 133-141.

Fore Street – No. 373, the **Seaman's Club** restaurant (**D**), displays the Gothic Revival style; the **Mariner's Church** (**E**), no. 368, with its tall windows and triangular pediment, illustrates the Greek Revival style. A good example of the Second Empire style, the **Custom House** at no. 312 reflects the maritime wealth of 19C Portland.

Portland Museum of Art – *7 Congress Sq. Open Memorial Day–Columbus Day daily 10am–5pm (Thu & Fri 9pm). Rest of the year Tue–Sun 10am–5pm (Thu & Fri 9pm). Closed Jan 1, Thanksgiving Day, Dec 25. $6.* ✗ & ☎ *207-773-2787. www.portlandmuseum.org.* The museum, founded in 1882, is the largest and oldest public museum in Maine. Its original quarters were the McLellan-Sweat House, to which an extension, the L.D.M. Sweat Memorial, was added in 1911. The most recent addition to the complex is the brick and granite Charles Shipman Payson Building (designed by Henry N. Cobb of I.M. Pei and Partners in 1983), which adjoins the earlier structures and now houses the museum's collection. A facade composed of an arresting blend of circles, rectangles and other forms, and an interior boasting gallery spaces illuminated by domed clerestories are noteworthy features of the building.

The Collections – More than 13,000 works, including decorative and fine arts, compose the museum's holdings. The museum's strength is its collection of 19C and 20C American art, and in particular the **State of Maine** collection of paintings, sculpture and prints by artists associated with Maine. Winslow Homer *(Weatherbeaten)*, Andrew Wyeth *(Broad Cove Farm, Cushing, Maine)*, Edward Hopper *(Pemaquid Light)* and John Marin *(Deer Isle Series: Mark Island Lighthouse)* are among the artists

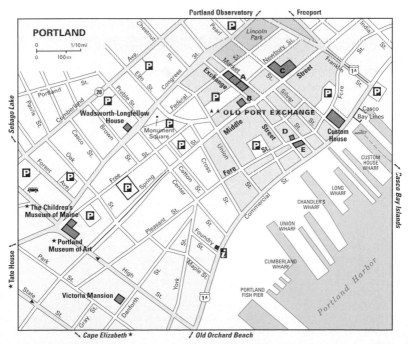

represented who drew their inspiration from the Maine landscape. The collection, which began in 1888 with Benjamin Akers' sculpture *Dead Pearl Diver*, has grown steadily and has been enriched by the gifts of 17 canvases by Homer; a collection of Impressionist and Postimpressionist works in 1991; and in 1996 the Noyce Collection of 66 paintings and sculptures by such artists as George Bellows, N.C. Wyeth, Jamie Wyeth, Fitz Hugh Lane and Childe Hassam.

Several galleries contain sections devoted to American glass *(lower level)*, and American and English ceramics and decorative arts *(4th floor)*. Highlighting the displays are cases of Portland glass, Federal-period paintings and furniture and the Pepperrell collection of silver presented to Maine-born Sir William Pepperrell, leader of the successful siege in 1745 of the French fortress of Louisbourg. A regular schedule of changing exhibits supplements the permanent collection.

★**Children's Museum of Maine** – **Kids** *142 Free St. Open Jun–early Sept daily Mon–Wed & Fri–Sat 10am–5pm, Thu 11am–5pm, Sun noon–5pm. Rest of the year open Wed & Fri–Sat 10am–5pm, Thu 11am–5pm, Sun noon–5pm. $5.* ઠ ☎ *207-828-1234. www.childrensmuseumofme.org.* Children of all ages will find something to amuse them in this 17,250sq ft museum located next to the Museum of Art. On the first level, Maine Street, USA, kids can experience the daily routines of a farm, supermarket, bank and fire department. The second level is devoted to hands-on science exhibits ranging from a model space shuttle to a weather station. Highlight of the third level, the **Camera Obscura★** projects a panoramic view of Portland.

Victoria Mansion (Morse-Libby House) – *109 Danforth St. Visit by guided tour (45min) only, May–Oct Tue–Sat 10am–4pm, Sun 1pm–5pm. Nov–Dec Tue–Sat 11am–5pm, Sun 1pm–5pm. Closed Jul 4 & Dec 25. $6.* ☎ *207-772-4841. www.portlandarts.com/victoriamansion.* Designed by the architect Henry Austin for wealthy local hotelier Ruggles Morse, this brownstone mansion (c.1860) reflects the sumptuous detail and decor characteristic of the Italianate style. The lavish interior, which includes trompe l'oeil murals, elaborately carved woodwork and stained glass, suggests that of a luxury hotel.

Wadsworth-Longfellow House – *489 Congress St. Visit by guided tour (45min) only, Jun–Oct daily 10am–4pm. $5.* ☎ *207-879-0427. www.mainehistory.org.* This 1785 brick dwelling—the first built in Portland—was the childhood home of **Henry Wadsworth Longfellow**. Longfellow's simple narrative poems, recounting legends from America's past, won him fame across the nation and abroad. After his death he was the first American to be memorialized in the Poet's Corner in Westminster Abbey. Furnishings and memorabilia of the poet and his family are on display.

★**Tate House** – *1270 Westbrook St. Drive west on Congress St., turn right on St. John St., then left on Park Ave. At I-295 overpass, continue on Congress St. to Westbrook St. Visit by guided tour (1hr) only, mid-Jun–Sept Tue–Sat 10am–4pm, Sun 1pm–4pm. Oct Fri & Sat 10am–4pm, Sun 1pm–4pm. Closed Jul 4 & Labor Day. $5.* ▣ ☎ *207-774-9781.* Located in Stroudwater beside the Fore River, this unusual gambrel-roofed dwelling (1755) was the home of George Tate, the king's mast agent. Tate's duties included making shipping arrangements for trees selected as masts for Royal Navy ships. All trees higher than 74ft and at least 24in at the base were marked as royal property, not to be felled by colonists. The trees were transported by oxen and then by ships custom-built to ferry the masts to England. The attractively furnished interior contains fine paneling, cornices, doorways and furniture that recall those in an 18C London town house.

Portland Observatory – *138 Congress St., northeast of downtown. Observatory closed for restoration til spring 2000. Call for hours and entry fee.* ☎ *207-774-5561. www.portlandlandmarks.org.* Last surviving 19C signal tower on the Atlantic Coast, this octagonal, shingled observatory dates back to 1807. Prior to the days of the telephone and telegraph, shipowners used this vantage point to signal (with flags) to Portlanders that ships were entering the harbor. Climb the 102 steps to the upper deck for a beautiful **view** of Portland and Casco Bay.

EXCURSIONS

Casco Bay Islands – *Cruises depart from Maine State Pier. For information & reservations Casco Bay Lines* ☎ *207-774-7871. www.cascobaylines.com.* The Bailey Island Cruise *(late Jun–mid-Sept daily 10am; round-trip 5hr 45min; commentary; $14.50; ✕ ઠ ▣)* allows for a stopover *(2hrs)* at Bailey Island. The US Mail Boat Cruise stops at several islands, but passengers are not permitted to disembark because of time constraints *(mid-Jun–Labor Day daily 10am & 2:15pm; rest of the year daily 10am & 2:45pm; round-trip 3hrs; $9.75; ✕ ઠ ▣).* As the boat leaves the harbor, note the large storage tanks for the oil pipeline to Montreal, and Fort Gorges, a 19C granite structure.

Calendar Islands – The islands in Casco Bay are so numerous that 17C explorer John Smith dubbed them the "Calendar Islands," since it seemed to him that there was one for each day of the year. Current counts range from 130 to 220, but Smith's

label endures nonetheless. Today, although only several of the islands are populated, their history remains steeped in tales of pirates and other colorful characters.
From the boat the houses and shops on heavily populated **Peaks Island** and the
beaches of **Long Island** are visible. The population of **Great Chebeague**, the largest
of the Calendar Islands (3mi wide and 5mi long), increases from 400 in winter to
some 3,000 during the summer. The solitary stone tower on **Mark Island** commemorates shipwrecked sailors; the tower contains food and water and serves as
a shelter in the event that anyone is shipwrecked in nearby waters. At **Bailey Island**
note the granite cribwork bridge constructed to allow the surf to pass freely
through the openings.

★**Cape Elizabeth** – *10mi south of Portland. Take Rte. 77 to S. Portland. At the
library turn right onto Cottage Rd., which becomes Shore Rd.* Cape Elizabeth's
wild and rocky shoreline provides a scenic excursion from Portland.

★**Portland Head Light** – *Take Shore Rd. north to the lighthouse, which is located at Fort
Williams.* This was the first lighthouse built on the East Coast after the Revolution.
In an effort to reduce construction costs, builders used materials from the local shores
and fields. The 300,000-candlepower electric light is visible 16mi offshore. From the
deck of the tower there is a **view**★ of Casco Bay. In the former lightkeeper's quarters, a **museum** details the history of the lighthouse and of adjacent Fort Williams.

Two Lights – This tiny community is named for the two lighthouses standing side
by side on this southeastern section of the cape: the Cape Elizabeth Light and its
inactive twin. Forty acres of shoreline surround **Two Lights State Park**, ideal for picnicking and fishing *(access via Rte. 77 South to Two Lights Rd.; open year-round
daily 9am–dusk; $2; ☎ 207-799-5871).*

Crescent Beach State Park – *Access via Rte. 77/Bowery Beach Rd. Open Memorial
Day–Columbus Day daily 9am–dusk. Rest of the year call for hours. $2.50. ✗
☎ 207-799-5871.* The park lies just west of Two Lights and has one of the best
sand beaches in Maine.

Freeport – *20mi north of Portland by Rte. 1 or Rte. 295 (I-95). See Entry Heading.*

Old Orchard Beach – *12mi southwest of Portland by Rte. 1 and Rte. 9 East.*
Americans and Canadians have been summering at this first stretch of saltwater beach
south of Montreal for more than 100 years. Motels, cottages, trailer parks and restaurants front the broad, 7mi-long beach and carnival rides animate the pier in summer.

Sebago Lake – *20mi north of Portland by Rte. 302.* Portlanders who enjoy swimming, boating and fishing favor Sebago Lake, the second-largest inland body of
water in Maine after Moosehead Lake. **Sebago Lake State Park** *(25mi from Portland
by Rte. 302)*, bordering the lake, has picnic areas, campsites and a sandy beach
*(open May–mid-Oct daily 9am–dusk; rest of the year call for hours; $2.50; ⚠
☎ 207-693-6613, or 207-693-6231 off season).*

Shaker Village and Museum – *In Sabbathday Lake, 20mi north of Portland. Take
I-95 to Exit 11, then Rte. 26 north 8mi. Open Memorial Day–Columbus Day
Mon–Sat 10am–4:30pm. $6. ☎ 207-926-4597.* This hilly lakeside property is the
site of the Sabbathday Lake Shaker Village, the last active Shaker community in
America. Founded in the late 18C by Shaker missionaries, the settlement continued
to exist throughout the 19C and 20C, a period when most other Shaker villages
became extinct. Although there are less than a dozen Shakers now living here, the
principles of Shakerism, "hands to work and hearts to God," and a strong devotion to the Shaker religion continue to guide their lives. The Shakers occupy a
number of the buildings on site, most of which can be viewed only from the
outside. With its granite trim and delicate wooden porch, the **Brick Dwelling House**
appears elegant when contrasted with the simple white clapboard structures found
throughout the village. Inside, simple furnishings and examples of clothing illustrate the Shakers' uncomplicated way of life. Shaker industries and inventions are
depicted in the **Meeting House**, the first building (1794) erected in the village and
still used for worship today.

■ Poland Spring

3mi north of Sabbathday Lake by Rte. 26. This mountain and lake hamlet
became famous in the 19C after a man who had been seriously ill drank from
the spring on Ricker's Hill and quickly regained his health. A small factory
was established to bottle the water, and a lavish hotel complex, including
the Poland Spring House, developed near the spring. The resort, which
burned down in 1975, catered to businessmen and dignitaries who came
"to take the waters." Poland Spring water is still bottled at a factory on
Ricker's Hill and sold in stores and supermarkets around the world. From
the hill it is possible to look out onto the mountains in the southern part of
the state.

RANGELEY LAKES REGION★

Map of Principal Sights
Tourist Office ☎ 207-864-5571

Nestled in the mountains of western Maine, this region contains an abundance of lakes and ponds, the largest being the lakes of the Rangeley chain. Spectacular mountain and lake panoramas unfold along Routes 4 and 17, and for those who prefer the solitude of the woods, there are trails leading to quiet brooks and mountaintops.

Scenic turnoffs on Route 17, south of Oquossoc, afford **views★★★** of the area's largest lakes. There are also rewarding views from Route 4 between Oquossoc and the village of **Rangeley**. Possibilities for warm-weather activities include tennis, golf, swimming, canoeing, mountain climbing and fishing, especially for trout and salmon in the spring. Ski areas have been developed at **Saddleback** and **Sugarloaf Mountains**.

SIGHTS

Rangeley Lake State Park – *From Rte. 4 or 17, take Southshore Dr. and follow signs to park. Open mid-May–Sept daily 9am–dusk. Rest of the year call for hours. $2. ⚐ ☎ 207-864-3858 or 207-624-6080 (off season).* This park on the south shore of Rangeley Lake includes a beach area with boat ramps, docks and secluded campsites.

★★**Eustis Ridge** – *26mi north of Rangeley by Rte. 16. Turn left onto Rte. 27. After 3mi turn left onto the unmarked road.* From this vantage point there is a **view** of the region. Route 27 continues to the Canadian border through unspoiled countryside.

★**Mt. Blue State Park** – *31mi southeast of Rangeley by Rte. 4, then Rte. 142. Open mid-May–Oct 1 daily 9am–dusk. Rest of the year call for hours. $2. ⚐ ☎ 207-585-2347 or 207-585-2261 (off season).* This 1,273-acre park on the shores of **Lake Webb★** offers varied recreation in a pretty setting. From the **State Park Beach Road** there are mountain and lake vistas.

ROCKLAND

Population 7,972
Map of Principal Sights
Tourist Office ☎ 207-596-0376

Commercial center for mid-coast Maine, Rockland bustles as a modern seaport and leading exporter of lobsters. (Rockland's **Lobster Festival** offers an opportunity to savor fresh seafood caught along this area of the coast.) Light industry, commerce and tourism also contribute to the local economy.

Rockland is home port to Maine's large fleet of **windjammers**. During the summer months, visitors can cruise Penobscot Bay on one of these tall-masted schooners *(for information, contact the Maine Windjammer Assn. ☎ 800-624-6380)*.

■ Maine Lobster Festival

Early August. ☎ 800-562-2529. For over 50 years, this exciting five-day festival has been held each year in Rockland to celebrate the state's lobster and maritime heritage. Lobster-eating contests, a 10K race, live music, marine exhibits, arts and crafts shows, a parade and beauty pageant are featured activities. And of course there's plenty of lobster—nearly eight tons—as well as other seafood, prepared to be consumed. Those brave enough can attempt to run the **Lobster Crate Race** atop a "path" of 50 bobbing crates partially submerged in cold harbor waters. The winner is the contestant who crosses the most crates without falling into the sea. There's a lobster diaper derby and cod fish carry for the kids, among other games. Average attendance the last few years has topped 65,000.

SIGHTS

★★**Farnsworth Art Museum** – *356 Main St. (at Elm St.). Open Memorial Day–Columbus Day daily 9am–5pm. Rest of the year Tue–Sat 10am–5pm, Sun 1pm–5pm. For hours of Homestead & Olson House see below. Closed Jan 1, Easter Sunday, Thanksgiving Day & Dec 25. Admission fee varies seasonally. ♿ ☎ 207-596-6457. www.midcoast.com/~farnswth.* Possessing a collection of more than 8,000 works, this museum is earning a reputation for its holdings of 19C and 20C American art, especially its growing number of paintings by **Newell Convers, Andrew and Jamie Wyeth**. Recent renovations and additions have catapulted the Farnsworth from a modest gallery for Maine art to a nationally acclaimed center for the study of Maine artists, particularly the three generations of Wyeth painters. The complex comprises the main museum building and adjoining Wyeth Study Center, the Farnsworth Homestead, and the new Wyeth Center in downtown Rockland, and, in the nearby village of Cushing, the Olson House.

Established with money from the estate of local businesswoman Lucy Farnsworth (1838-1935) in memory of her father, the museum opened to the public in 1948. The Farnsworth mounted its first major exhibit of works by Andrew Wyeth (b. 1917) in 1951 and held subsequent retrospectives of art by Andrew's father, famed illustrator N.C. Wyeth (1882-1945) and Andrew's talented son, Jamie Wyeth (b. 1946). In 1992 the museum was given Olson House, which figured prominently in Andrew Wyeth's painting *Christina's World*. In 1998 the museum unveiled its Wyeth Center, housed in a renovated 19C church, primarily to showcase the Andrew and Betsy Wyeth collection of Maine-related art. (The state has been a summer home for the Wyeth family since the 1930s). The museum has plans to convert a store on Main Street into exhibit space for contemporary art.

Main Museum – Galleries on level two and four focus on American art from the colonial period to the present with an emphasis on works related to Maine. Early works include those by such American masters as Thomas Eakins, Winslow Homer, Fitz Hugh Lane and Gilbert Stuart. American Impressionists Childe Hassam, John Twachtman and Maurice Prendergast are also represented. The Hadlock Gallery *(level 4)* is devoted solely to paintings by Andrew Wyeth; highlights include *Her Room*, *Turkey Pond* and *Road to Friendship*. Featured on level six are works, among others, by Ashcan school artists, and paintings and sculpture by **Louise Nevelson**, who resided in Rockland. Note her work titled *The Endless Column* (1969, painted wood).

Wyeth Center – Located in a c.1870 meetinghouse, the 3,500sq ft center contains three galleries, which feature landscapes and paintings of animals by Jamie Wyeth, with a few works by N.C. and Andrew. Mounting all three family members' work under one roof permits comparison and contrast of the styles, subjects and vision of these artists. (The center's stark, white clapboard exterior has, in fact, been depicted by Jamie Wyeth.)

Farnsworth Homestead – *Open Memorial Day–Columbus Day daily 10am–noon & 1pm–4pm.* Completed in 1850, this stately Greek Revival residence reflects the wealth of its owner, Rockland entrepreneur William Farnsworth. His daughter Lucy *(above)*, who lived here until her death in 1935, stipulated in her will that the family home be opened to the public. Rooms in the house are furnished with original Victorian pieces belonging to the Farnsworth family and dating from about 1876.

Olson House – *In Cushing. Directions on back of admission ticket. Open Memorial Day–Columbus Day daily 11am–4pm.* Located almost 15mi from the museum, in the village of Cushing, this house, immortalized in Andrew Wyeth's *Christina's World*, is open to the public part of the year. Eerie and intriguing, the house and its former inhabitants provided inspiration to Wyeth for nearly 30 years. His wife, Betsy, described the dwelling as "a weathered ship stranded on a hilltop," and that is exactly how it remains: unpainted, unfurnished and undecorated save for reproductions of Wyeth paintings done here (including *Christina's World*) along with the artist's own recollections on how they came about.

Vinalhaven and North Haven Island Ferries – *Depart from foot of Main St., Rockland: to Vinalhaven Apr–Oct daily 7am–4:30pm; rest of the year daily 7am–3:15pm; one-way 1hr 15min; $9 round-trip ($26/car & driver); to North Haven year-round daily 9:30am, 2pm & 5pm; one-way 1hr; $9 round-trip*

Art Museum Neighbors

Across the street from the Farnsworth, stop in for press-pot coffee and a pre-owned paperback at **Second Read** *(328 Main St. ☎ 207-594-4123)*. This cafe/bookstore encourages eaters to read and readers to eat, simultaneously. Lots of hardly worn soft and hardbacks at reduced prices fill the ceiling-high shelves, enticing those at the coffee bar (lattes, espresso, mochas and *macchiatos*) and bistro tables to browse and buy. Lunch creations range from PB&J sandwiches to hummus and tabouli. *Caprese* is a summer specialty: tomatoes, pesto and mozzarella grilled on house bread. A huge selection of homebaked desserts awaits first-course survivors.

In the immediate vicinity, **Cafe Miranda** *(15 Oak St. ☎ 207-594-2034)* offers creative cuisine in a casual, eclectic atmosphere. A clever blending of Asian, Italian, Mexican, New England and Continental ingredients makes this fusion food a real treat. Try the saffron risotto and roasted mussels, the smoked salmon avocado burrito or the Soft-shell Crabs Chinois stir-fry. Focaccia accompanies the meal. *Open for dinner only.*

($26/car & driver); no service Jan 1 & Dec 25, limited service Thanksgiving Day; ⟁ *: Maine State Ferry Service* ☎ *207-596-2202. www.state.me.us/mdot/opt/ ferry/ferry.htm.* These boats cruise among the serene tree-clad Fox islands in Penobscot Bay, the region that is the setting of Sarah Orne Jewett's novel *The Country of the Pointed Firs* (1896). Largest of these islands at 14mi long, quaint **Vinalhaven** was incorporated in 1789. Lobster boats anchor in quiet inlets, and fishing sheds, with their stacks of lobster traps and brightly painted buoys, dot the island. Several of Vinalhaven's abandoned granite quarries provide a place to swim and fish in the summer. From the northern end of the island there is a view across the water to **North Haven**, a small quiet island with many summer residents.

EXCURSIONS

Owl's Head Transportation Museum – 𝗞𝗶𝗱𝘀 *2mi south of Rockland by Rte. 73. On grounds adjacent to Knox County airport. Open Apr–Oct daily 10am–5pm. Rest of the year daily 10am–4pm. Closed Jan 1, Thanksgiving Day, Dec 25. $6.* ⟁ ☎ *207-594-4418. www.ohtm.org.* Complemented by antique automobiles, bicycles, motorcycles and engines, the museum's core collection of aircraft dates from the early 20C. Demonstrations of automobiles and airplanes from the collection are held at special summer events on the museum grounds. *Call for events schedule.*

Owl's Head Lighthouse – *4mi south of Rockland. From Rte. 73, follow signs to Owl's Head State Park.* The tiny community of Owl's Head is known for its lighthouse, which is perched atop a 100ft cliff overlooking West Penobscot Bay.

Thomaston – *3mi south of Rockland via Rte. 1.* This yachting center, a village of attractive old homes and churches, is the site of Maine State Prison. Adjacent to the prison, on Route 1, is a showroom where woodenware made by the inmates is sold. Dragon Products, a cement plant located outside the village center, employs a large number of Thomaston's residents.

Montpelier – *Rte. 1 at the junction of Rte. 131. Open late May–mid-Oct Tue–Sat 10am–4pm, Sun 1pm–4pm. $4.* ☎ *207-354-8062.* The stately white mansion replicates the original residence built in 1794 by Gen. **Henry Knox** (1750-1806), an aide to General Washington during the Revolution. In the winter of 1775-76, Knox led an expedition that carried 59 cannons from Fort Ticonderoga to Boston. This equipment was used against the British the following spring, forcing them to evacuate Boston. Later appointed the nation's first secretary of War (1785-94), Knox was a wealthy landowner when he resigned his government post and settled in Thomaston. The original mansion fell into disrepair after Knox's death and was torn down in 1871 to make way for the railroad. Opened to the public in 1931, the replica Federal-style dwelling contains graceful oval rooms, a freestanding staircase flanking an arched doorway, and antique furnishings including Knox family pieces and a mirrored bookcase reportedly owned by Marie Antoinette.

SEARSPORT

Population 2,603
Map of Principal Sights

Located near the head of Penobscot Bay, this seafaring town boasts the second busiest harbor in the state. Searsport serves as a major export center for the potato crop raised to the north in Aroostook County.

For years the village was a boatbuilding center and home to more than 10 percent of the nation's deepwater shipmasters in the 19C. Searsport mariners sailed trade routes to the other side of the world, making the name of their hometown one of the most familiar in the ports of the Orient, Africa, Europe and the Caribbean. The beautiful dwellings built for these seamen still line the streets near the waterfront.

SIGHT

★**Penobscot Marine Museum** – *Church St. Open Memorial Day–mid-Oct Mon–Sat 10am–5pm, Sun noon–5pm. $6.* ☎ *207-548-2529. www.penobscotmarinemuseum. org.* A complex of eight structures on the site includes several restored sea captains' homes, the former Town Hall, the Phillips Memorial Library and the adjoining Douglas and Margaret Carver Memorial Art Gallery. Exhibited throughout the buildings, the museum's rich collection of marine paintings, models and artifacts illustrates the era of sail and trade.

The **Fowler-True-Ross House** (c.1837) contains wall hangings, furniture, tableware and Oriental objets d'art that Searsport captains brought back to New England from their travels. The barn attached to the **Nickels-Colcord-Duncan House** features an exhibit on Penobscot Bay fisheries and a display of small craft. Ship models, half-models, shipbuilding tools, Oriental trade objects and a permanent exhibit on the large wooden ships built in Maine in the 19C fill the 1845 **Town Hall**. Displays on the first floor of the **Captain Merithew House** (c.1826) focus on 19C industry along Penobscot Bay. Rooms on the second floor feature paintings by Thomas and James Buttersworth, ship models and watercolors, among other items. In the Art Gallery, don't miss the ostrich eggs skillfully etched with whaling scenes.

EXCURSION

*★**Fort Knox State Historic Site** – In Bucksport, 10.5mi north of Searsport on Rte. 1. Map p 81. Open May–Oct daily 9am–dusk. Rest of the year call for hours. $2. ☎ 207-469-7719.* The tense political situation between the US and Great Britain in 1840, which arose as a result of the New England-Canada boundary dispute, led to a decision by the American military to build a fort along the Penobscot River. Although the dispute was settled before work on the fort began, construction was nevertheless initiated. Named for Gen. Henry Knox, chief of artillery under General Washington during the Revolution, the fort, never completed, served as a military training ground during the Civil War. The enormous granite fortress, with its archways, buttresses and winding staircases, is a model of 19C American military architecture. From the top of the ramparts there is a view of the town of Bucksport and the river.

Periwinkles Bakery

225 W. Main St. (Rte 1). ☎ 207-548-9910. Ask residents of Searsport, and they'll tell you it's hard to resist Periwinkles. Billed "a sweet retreat," this roadside bakery beckons early risers with its Green Mountain coffee and fresh scones, pastries, croissants and English sausage rolls. Noontime nibblers turn in for homemade soups, sandwiches, pizza or quiche, topped off with blueberry pie or pecan squares. The tiny tea room tempts tourists and locals alike with creamy cheesecakes and chocolate delights alongside an invigorating cup of tea. *High tea is offered Sunday afternoons by reservation.*

WISCASSET★

Population 3,339
Map of Principal Sights

An appealing town with broad, tree-lined streets, Georgian mansions, antique shops and restaurants, Wiscasset was once the home of wealthy merchants and shipmasters. Prior to 1807 the town reigned as America's busiest international port north of Boston. Wiscasset's shipyards, built on the banks of the Sheepscot River, turned out clipper ships that carried lumber and ice to the West Indies and returned laden with the staples necessary for daily living. But in 1807 Congress passed President Jefferson's Embargo Act, which forbade all international trade to and from American ports in reaction to trade restrictions enforced by Britain and France. This legislation paralyzed Wiscasset's sea trade.

SIGHTS

★★**Musical Wonder House** – **Kids** *18 High St. Visit by guided tour (30min) only, late May–Oct daily 10am–5pm. $7.50 (1hr tour $15). ☎ 207-882-7163. www.musicalwonderhouse.com.* This Georgian dwelling contains a superb collection of some 1,000 19C and 20C antique mechanical instruments, including player pianos, gramophones and music boxes, all in working order. Constructed primarily to reproduce melodies by means of metal discs or cylinders, these machines, enclosed in handcrafted boxes or cabinets, were highly treasured by their owners as works of art. The Regina Orchestral Corona, which changes discs automatically; the Harpe Aeolienne music box; the Emerald polyphon with its hand-tuned silver bells; and the Regina Sublima drum table, a Louis XV-style table decorated with hand-painted scenes, all play tunes as rich as their names imply.

Nickels-Sortwell House – *Corner of Main and Federal Sts. Visit by guided tour (45min) only, Jun–mid-Oct Wed–Sun 11am–5pm. $4. ☎ 207-882-6218. www.spnea.org.* This Federal-style mansion (1807), with its well-proportioned facade and entry, fronts Main Street. Built for a Wiscasset shipmaster in 1807, the house was later owned by Massachusetts mayor Alvin Sortwell. Period furnishings on display belonged to the Sortwell family. Note the graceful **elliptical staircase** illuminated by a third-floor skylight.

Lincoln County Museum and Old Jail – *133 Federal St. Visit by guided tour (30min) only, Jul–Aug Tue–Sun 11am–4:30pm. $2. ☎ 207-882-6817.* This grim jail (1809), with its granite walls up to 41in thick, was built when the whipping post and other forms of public punishment were no longer effective in dealing with problems arising in the rapidly growing villages on the coast. About 40 prisoners could be housed in the cells on the original two floors; the third floor was added later to accommodate debtors and the insane.

EXCURSION

Fort Edgecomb – *1mi southeast of Wiscasset. Take Rte. 1 across the Sheepscot River, then turn right. Open Memorial Day–Labor Day daily 9am–5pm. $1.* ☎ 207-882-7777. Overlooking a narrow passage on the Sheepscot River, this octagonal-shaped, wooden blockhouse (1809) protected Wiscasset during the War of 1812. Today its picnic grounds command a view of the river and Westport Island.

YORK★

Population 9,818
Map of Principal Sights
Tourist Office ☎ 207-363-4422

York is splintered into so many separate villages that Mark Twain once wryly observed, "It is difficult to throw a brick ...in any one direction without disabling a postmaster." Today the area known to locals as "the Yorks" includes historic **York Village**, dating from colonial times; **York Harbor**, a low-key resort at the mouth of York River; **York Beach**, an oceanfront amusement and swimming area; and the sheltered beach of **Cape Neddick**.

Historical Notes – In 1624 the Pilgrims established a trading post at Agamenticus, the present-day site of York. The small settlement that grew up around the trading post was chosen by **Sir Ferdinando Gorges**, the proprietor of Maine, as the capital of his vast New World territory. In 1641 Sir Gorges gave the village a city charter and renamed it Gorgeana in his honor. Gorges' dreams of developing "the main" (later Maine) were never realized; the Massachusetts Bay Company assumed control of this section of the coast in 1652 and reorganized Gorgeana as the town of York.
Although York was completely destroyed by a raiding party during the French and Indian War, the town developed into a busy port and became the county seat by the dawn of the American Revolution. Since the 19C York residents have preserved the early colonial charm of their town.

★★COLONIAL YORK *1/2 day*

From Rte. 1, take Rte. 1A. Turn right at First Parish Church onto Lindsay Rd.

A group of early structures flanks the village green, offering visitors a glimpse of colonial times. On the north side of Route 1A stands the 18C **First Parish Church**, with its cock weather vane, and the **Town Hall**, which served for a time as the York County courthouse. Across Route 1A, surrounding the old cemetery, are properties belonging to the Old York Historical Society, which are open to the public: the Jefferds' Tavern; an 18C schoolhouse; the Emerson-Wilcox House; and, rising from the top of a small hill, the Old Gaol, an 18C jail *(open mid-Jun–mid-Oct Tue–Sat 10am–5pm, Sun 1pm–5pm; $7 payable at Jefferds' Tavern; closed major holidays;* ☎ *207-363-4974. www.oldyork.org).*

The Lobster Barn

Rte 1, in York. ☎ *207-363-4721.* This longtime roadside restaurant features casual dining in a rustic, low-ceilinged interior furnished with wooden booths and tables. Seafood is its specialty: lobster cooked a variety of ways, clams, crab, shrimp, scallops, steamers, haddock, swordfish and casseroles. Also on the menu are prime rib, steaks, chicken and hamburgers. Don a bib and try the one-pound boiled lobster dinner complete with coleslaw or baked potato, homemade bread and salad. For dessert, order a New England classic: Indian pudding. In the summer months **Lobster in the Rough**, a 200-seat pavilion, is open for outdoor dining behind the barn.

Old Burying Ground – Surrounded by a low stone wall, this cemetery is interesting for its 17C tombstones. Note the grave covered with a large horizontal stone, placed there, according to legend, to stop a "witch" from leaving the tomb. In actuality, the spouse of the deceased put the block there to protect the grave from wandering cattle.

Jefferds' Tavern and Schoolhouse – This tavern, built in Wells in 1754, served as a wayside station on the Portsmouth-Portland stage route. The large, cozy taproom contains plank floors and a wooden bar. Rooms on the floor above were set aside for women and children, who ordinarily did not congregate downstairs with the men. The one-room schoolhouse (1745) provides insight into early schooling in Maine.

Old Gaol – Originally a stone dungeon, built in 1719 to serve the entire province of Maine, this jail was enlarged soon after to include several cells and provide living quarters for the jailer and his family. Small openings cut in the thick stone walls allow shards of sunlight to enter the cool, damp cells.

Emerson-Wilcox House – Built in 1742 as a private dwelling, this large house served over the years as a general store, tailor shop, tavern, post office and home. The tavern catered to travelers on the Post Road, as well as to local residents and the occupants of the Old Gaol. The interior contains period rooms that offer glimpses into York's past as well as American textiles dating from 1745.

Follow Lindsay Rd. to Sewall's Bridge beside the York River.

Nearby are the George Marshall Store (now a gallery used for local exhibits) and a fishermen's shed covered with lobster buoys.

John Hancock Warehouse – *Same hours as above.* This warehouse is one of several coastal warehouses owned by John Hancock, Revolutionary War patriot, signer of the Declaration of Independence and prosperous merchant. It is the only remaining commercial building from York's colonial period. Exhibits here document local life and industry during the 18C.

Across the bridge, the inviting red Colonial dwelling beside the river was the home of **Elizabeth Perkins** (1869-1952), one of York's prominent residents.

ADDITIONAL SIGHTS

York Harbor – *Follow Rte. 1A south of York Village.* This landlocked boating center is a haven for small craft. Beautiful homes grace the harbor's tree-covered shores. The **Sayward-Wheeler House** contains the family heirlooms, including Queen Anne and Chippendale furnishings, of a prosperous trader and his descendants *(79 Barrell Lane Ext.; visit by 45min guided tour only, Jun–mid-Oct weekends 11am–5pm; $4; ☎ 603-436-3205; www.spnea.org).*

Route 1A leads past **Long Sands Beach**, which stretches 2mi from York Harbor to Nubble peninsula and is bordered by summer cottages.

★**Nubble Light** – *Leave Rte. 1A and turn right onto Nubble Rd.; continue to the tip of Cape Neddick.* From the shore there is a good view of Nubble Lighthouse (1879) and the offshore island it occupies; the Isles of Shoals lie in the distance.

York Beach – This summer resort on the shores of Short Sands Beach offers an assortment of busy concession stands, eating places and souvenir shops. Several hotels built during the last century stand near the beach like a group of distinguished dowagers proudly surveying their waterfront domain.

Baily Island, Maine

Massachusetts

Area: 7,838sq mi
Population: 6,016,425
Capital: Boston
Nickname: Bay State
State Flower: Mayflower

Extending from the Atlantic Ocean to the border of New York state, Massachusetts provides a cross section of the region's varied topography. The tree-covered Berkshire Hills in the west gradually slope down to the fertile meadows of the Connecticut Valley in the center of the state. Miles of sandy beach lie south of Boston, while to the north the coast is irregular and rocky. The state is rectangular in shape, except for the southeast section that juts into the ocean, adding hundreds of miles to the Massachusetts coastline.

Birthplace of American Independence – New England's earliest permanent settlements were in Massachusetts. In search of religious freedom, the Pilgrims established Plymouth Colony in 1620, followed within 10 years by the Puritans, who founded Boston. As the population expanded and prospered, the British parliament's taxation policies placed an increasing financial burden on the colonists. Angered by England's policy of "taxation without representation," and inspired by the oratory of **Samuel Adams**, **James Otis** and **John Hancock**, the colonists reacted by staging the **Boston Tea Party**, which, along with the **Boston Massacre** in 1770, proved to be the prelude to the confrontations at Lexington and Concord, and the ensuing battle for American independence.

Economy – For two centuries Massachusetts earned its living from the sea by fishing, whaling and trade. Great fortunes were made in the China trade, and when maritime commerce declined in the 19C, this wealth provided the capital needed for the shift to industrialization.

With the advantages of an abundance of waterpower and the increasing waves of immigration that provided a large labor force, the Berkshires, the southern section of the coast and the Merrimack Valley were soon dotted with many small industrial centers, or "mill towns." Massachusetts developed into a prominent manufacturer of textiles and leather goods. By 1850 **Lowell**, the first planned industrial city in the nation, was the world's leading producer of textiles. In the 20C these industries migrated to the South and were supplanted by the manufacture of electronics, machine tools and electrical equipment. Today Massachusetts' most important source of revenue is its **"brain power,"** represented by the state's excellent educational institutions and technological and financial services industries.

Massachusetts continues to lead the New England states in commercial fishing, with Gloucester and New Bedford ranking among the nation's major ports. Agriculturally, the Bay State's **cranberry crop**, cultivated in the regions of Cape Cod and Plymouth, is the nation's largest.

Cranberry Harvest in Carver

John Lazenby/f/STOP PICTURES

111

THE BERKSHIRES★★★

In westernmost Massachusetts lies a valley watered by the streams of the Housatonic River and bordered by the foothills of the Taconic and Hoosac Ranges. This region, the Berkshires, is a mix of small 19C mill towns and comfortable residential communities that blend gracefully with their surroundings.

Many wealthy New Yorkers and Bostonians have second homes in the Berkshires. Attractive in summer for its refreshing climate and cultural offerings, in the fall for its splendid foliage and in the winter for skiing, this versatile region also offers hiking, fishing, golf and other sports.

Historical Notes

The Mohegans – The Mohegans once lived on the banks of the Hudson River and journeyed to the Housatonic Valley, "the place beyond the mountains" as they called it, to hunt. In time, reduced in number by disease and warfare, they abandoned the lowlands for the thickly wooded hills, where they lived peacefully until the arrival of the colonists in the 18C. Devoted to Christianizing the Indians, the colonists established STOCKBRIDGE in 1734 as an Indian mission on land granted for this purpose by the General Court.

To the north lived the **Mohawks**, enemies of the Mohegans and the French, and allies of the British. One of the major routes traveled by pioneers migrating to the Midwest from the eastern colonies followed an old Indian trail *(p 187)* blazed by the Mohawks through the Appalachian Mountains to the Great Lakes.

From Agriculture to Industry – The early settlers farmed the land, but after the Revolution, many farms were abandoned as their owners moved westward to the fertile plains region. In New England the migration westward was accompanied by a transition from farming to industry. The Berkshires developed into a major manufacturing center, and **mill towns**—small factory communities such as North Adams, Pittsfield, Dalton and Lee, with their monotone rows of brick mill buildings—sprang up throughout the region. The railroad followed, linking the valley towns to the rest of the state after the construction of the Hoosac Tunnel in 1875.

★★GREAT BARRINGTON REGION

Great Barrington – Great Barrington is the commercial center for the many vacation homes on the outskirts of this pleasant town. The Great Barrington Rapids, once the site of Mohegan camps, were the major power source for local mills in the 18C. It was here, on the banks of the Housatonic, that the inventor William Stanley demonstrated for the first time the use of alternating current. On March 20, 1886, Great Barrington became one of the first cities in the world to have its streets and homes lit by electricity.

Touring the Berkshires

Accommodations – Several hotels and a variety of inns and bed and breakfasts can be found in the Berkshires. For lodging information, contact the Berkshire Visitors' Bureau ☎ *413-443-9186 or 800-237-5747 (US and Canada)*.

Entertainment and Recreation – Allow several days to follow the excursions described below and to attend at least one of the music or dance festivals held in the summer. Included among these events are the **Tanglewood Music Festival** *(☎ 413-637-1600 summer; ☎ 617-266-1492 year-round)* and the **South Mountain Concert Festival** *(☎ 413-442-2106)*. The **Jacob's Pillow Dance Festival** brings together international performers of ballet, modern dance and mime *(Jun–Aug ☎ 413-243-0745). See Calendar of Events.* Summer theater is offered at the **Berkshire Playhouse** in Stockbridge and at the **Williamstown Theater** in WILLIAMSTOWN. Classical Shakespearean theater is presented in Lenox at **The Mount**, once the summer home of novelist Edith Wharton (1862-1937).
In winter, there is skiing at **Butternut Basin**, **Brodie Mountain** and **Otis Ridge**.
The map in this section covers only the southern part of the Berkshires. For attractions in the northern part of the region, see **Mt. Greylock** and **Williamstown**.
For more information on festivals in the Berkshires, contact the Berkshire Visitors' Bureau (above).

One-Day Itinerary in the Berkshires – From the south, take Route 7. Stop in **Stockbridge** and follow the itinerary between Stockbridge and Lenox . Visit the **Hancock Shaker Village** outside Pittsfield, then the **Clark Art Institute** in Williamstown.

Bartholomew's Cobble – *11mi south of Great Barrington. Take Rte. 7 south, then Rte. 7A to Ashley Falls; take Rannapo Rd., then Weatogue Rd. Open year-round daily 9am–5pm. $3.* ☎ *413-229-8600. www.thetrustees.org.* This natural rock garden covered with a variety of trees, wildflowers and ferns rises above the Housatonic River. The **Ledges Trail** *(round-trip 45min)* through the Cobble follows the river. At station 17, cross the road and continue on Hulburt's Hill Trail to an open pasture on Miles Mountain (1,050ft) with a view of the Housatonic Valley.

★**Bash Bish Falls** – *16mi southwest of Great Barrington. Follow Rte. 23 west to South Egremont, then Rte. 415 at the pond, then immediate right onto Mt. Washington Rd., East St., West St. and Bash Bish Falls Rd. From the parking area, a steep trail marked with blue triangles and white blazes leads to the falls. Down the road 1mi there is another parking area; from there, a longer, but easier, path leads to the falls. These steep slopes can become icy and dangerous in fall, winter and spring. Open year-round daily dawn–dusk.* ☎ *413-528-0330.* Bash Bish Brook flows over a 275ft gorge, creating a 50ft waterfall and natural pool in this forest setting.

> **John Andrew's Restaurant**
> *Rte. 23 South Egremont.* ☎ *413-528-3469.* It's worth the drive to this somewhat isolated house in South Egremont for the elegant, understated decor and rarefied cuisine. Superbly prepared and presented entrées, low-key jazz and a peaceful country setting greet diners here. Try the sautéed duck breast with balsamic and maple glaze or the grilled pork chop served with ragout of sweet potato and pearl onion-wild mushroom phyllo. For dessert, sample the chocolate pot de crème, the pistachio brûlée or the rhubarb crisp with ginger and lemon gras ice cream. *Reservations advised.*

★**Monument Mountain** – *4.5mi north of Great Barrington on Rte. 7. From the parking area on the west side of Rte. 7, two trails lead to the summit. The easier trail, the Indian Monument Trail (ascent 1hr), begins to the left, 600yds south along the highway, and enters the woods, where a sign points right to Indian Monument (a cairn about 100yds off the trail). Turn right and continue, always selecting the right spur. The second, more difficult trail (ascent 45min) begins to the right of the parking area and is blazed with round white markers.* From the rocky summit, named Squaw Peak for an Indian maiden who leaped to her death from this point, the visitor can behold a **panorama**★ of the Berkshires. A cairn at the base of the mountain is said to mark the grave of the Indian maiden *(directions above).*

■ The Grand Estates

Favorable descriptions of the Berkshires, written in the mid-19C by Nathaniel Hawthorne, Henry Ward Beecher and others, attracted wealthy families to summer here. These families built the handsome residences that still punctuate the countryside outside Great Barrington, Lee, Lenox and Stockbridge. At the beginning of the 20C, Lenox alone could count 75 of these magnificent properties, including Tanglewood and the estate of Andrew Carnegie, the richest man in the Berkshires.

Increased taxes, spiraling costs and the Great Depression brought an end to the luxuries of the era, and most of the estates were abandoned or sold and converted into schools or resorts. A growing number of former estates are now operated as year-round inns.

★TYRINGHAM VALLEY

From Great Barrington take Rte. 23 to Monterey, then turn left onto Tyringham Rd., which becomes Monterey Rd.

Tyringham – This charming valley town was the site of a community of Shakers in the 19C. The valley's scenic landscape attracted many artists, including Henry Kitson, sculptor of the Lexington *Minuteman*, at the beginning of the 20C. Kitson's former studio, the picturesque **Gingerbread House**★, is an art gallery and museum called Santarella *(open late May–Oct daily 10am-4:30pm; $4;* ☎ *413-243-3260). Continue on Main St., then Tyringham Rd. to Rte. 20.*

Lee – In the mid-19C five paper factories operated in this mill town. During the same period, rich marble deposits were discovered beneath a section of land that had been considered worthless because it was too poor to farm. Lee marble was quarried and used in the construction of the Capitol in Washington, DC and in other public buildings, making the name of this small town famous.

★★★FROM STOCKBRIDGE TO LENOX

★★**Stockbridge** – *See Entry Heading.*

In Stockbridge take Pine St. opposite the Red Lion Inn. Turn left onto Prospect St. (Mahkeenac Rd.) and drive along the lakeshore of Stockbridge Bowl; continue on Hawthorne Rd. At the junction of Hawthorne Rd. and Rte. 183 there is a good view of the lake.

★**Tanglewood** – Tanglewood is the summer home of the Boston Symphony Orchestra and the site of one of the nation's most famous musical events, the **Tanglewood Music Festival** *(p 112)*. More than 300,000 music lovers attend every year. The festival was inaugurated in 1934 with concerts by the New York Philharmonic Symphony. In 1936 the New York Philharmonic was replaced by the Boston Symphony Orchestra, which has presented the summer series of concerts ever since.

Tanglewood, formerly the residence of the Tappan family, was given to the Berkshire Festival Society in 1937 to serve as the festival's permanent home. Buildings on the 500 acres include the main house; the 5,000-seat Koussevitzky Music Shed, designed by Eliel Saarinen; and the 1,180-seat Seiji Ozawa Hall, opened in 1994.

From the gardens there is a **view** of the body of water called **Stockbridge Bowl** and **Hawthorne Cottage** *(not open to the public)*, a replica of the dwelling where Nathaniel Hawthorne lived for 18 months while writing *The House of the Seven Gables* (1851) *(see Entry Heading Salem).*

Take Rte. 183 to Lenox.

★**Lenox** – Surrounded by estates that have been transformed into schools and resorts, Lenox, with its inviting inns and restaurants, is a delightful place to stay.

Take Rte. 7 north and turn left opposite the Quality Inn onto West Dugway Rd.; then bear left at the fork on West Mountain Rd.

Pleasant Valley Wildlife Sanctuary – *3mi north of Lenox. Open Jul–Columbus Day Mon–Fri 9am–5pm, weekends 10am–4pm. Rest of the year Tues–Fri 9am–5pm, weekends 10am–4pm. Closed Jan 1, Thanksgiving Day, Dec 25. $3. Trail map available at office.* ☎ *413-637-0320. www.berkshires@massaudubon.org.* The refuge has 7mi of trails that lead through fields and woodlands revealing vegetation typical of the region. A beaver colony occupies the string of ponds in the valley, and their dams are visible.

PITTSFIELD AREA

Pittsfield – Pittsfield is a commercial center and the capital of the Berkshires. The **Berkshire Museum**, which includes a small aquarium, exhibits fine European and American paintings and sculpture, and history and science displays *(39 South St.; open Jul–Aug Mon–Sat 10am–5pm, Sun 1pm–5pm; rest of the year Tue–Sat 10am–5pm, Sun 1pm–5pm; closed Jan 1, Thanksgiving Day, Dec 25; $6;* ♿ ☎ *413-443-7171; www.berkshiremuseum.org).*

Pittsfield State Forest – *Entrance on Cascade St., 3mi from the Park Square rotary; take West St., turn right on Churchill St., then left on Cascade St. Open year-round daily 8am–8pm. $2/car.* ⚠ ♿ ☎ *413-442-8992.* This area offers year-round opportunities for hiking, skiing and other recreation.

Dakota

1035 South St. (Rte. 7), Pittsfield ☎ *413-499-7900.* Enjoy seafood or steaks—or even bison from this restaurant's own Vermont farm—in a rustic, re-created hunting lodge interior, complete with ceiling-hung canoe, moose heads and Indian pottery. Wood-grilled shrimp, farm-raised trout and Atlantic salmon are available from the menu as well as prime rib, sirloin and chicken. Selections from a sizable salad bar complete your dinner along with homebaked wholegrain bread. You won't have room for dessert.

Arrowhead – *780 Holmes Rd. From Park Square, drive east on East St.; turn right onto Elm St., then right onto Holmes Rd. Visit by guided tour (45min) only, May–Oct daily 9:30am–5pm. Rest of the year by appointment. $5.* ♿ ☎ *413-442-1793. www.mobydick.org.* Arrowhead, the home of Herman Melville, is being restored to reflect the atmosphere of the era when he lived here (1850-63). Melville wrote a number of his most important works at Arrowhead including his masterpiece, *Moby Dick.* The kitchen with its huge fireplace bearing an inscription from Melville's *I and My Chimney,* the upstairs study with its view of Mt. Greylock, and the remaining rooms all contain furnishings owned by the Berkshire County Historical Society, which maintains the house.

★★★**Hancock Shaker Village** – *3mi west of Pittsfield by Rte. 20. See Entry Heading.*

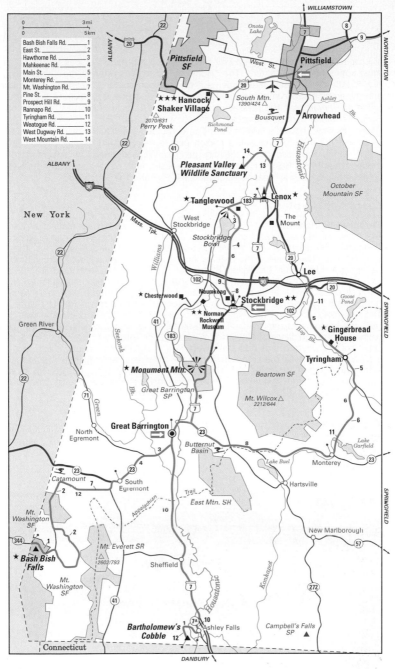

BOSTON★★★

Population 574,283
Map of Principal Sights
Tourist Office ☎ 617-536-4100

Massachusetts' historical capital city has earned a reputation as one of the nation's most appealing urban centers. The "Hub," as Bostonians refer to their hometown, is the "cradle of American independence," a renowned center of learning and culture, and the administrative and financial nexus of New England. Its proximity to CAMBRIDGE, home of Harvard and the Massachusetts Institute of Technology, has contributed to Boston's role as a cultural mecca.

Boston is New England's largest city. The combined populations of the metropolitan area total 4.7 million. Over half a million people representing diverse ethnic cultures reside within the 46sq mi of the city proper. While offering the advantages of a modern metropolis, Boston has retained a pleasant human scale, evident in its historic neighborhoods such as Beacon Hill, the Back Bay and the North End.

Historical Notes

European Settlement – In 1630 about 1,000 Puritans led by **John Winthrop** arrived on the coast of Massachusetts to establish a settlement for the Massachusetts Bay Company. Disenchanted with the living conditions in SALEM and CHARLESTOWN, they set their sights on the peninsula the Indians named Shawmut, then inhabited by an eccentric Anglican clergyman, **Rev. William Blackstone**. The Englishman welcomed the Puritans, who proceeded to establish a permanent settlement on the small peninsula. When the Puritans tried to make Blackstone a member of their church, he sold them his remaining 50 acres and left for the more peaceful atmosphere of Rhode Island.

The new colony, known as Trimountain because of its hilly topography, was soon renamed Boston after the town in Lincolnshire from which many of the Puritans hailed. Under the firm guidance of Governor Winthrop, the settlement developed as a theocratic society where church and state were one. A rigid moral code was enforced and a pillory was built on the common to punish offenders, among them the carpenter whose price for constructing the pillory was deemed too high. Because of its maritime commerce and shipbuilding, Boston rapidly became the largest town in the British colonies—a distinction it held until the mid-18C.

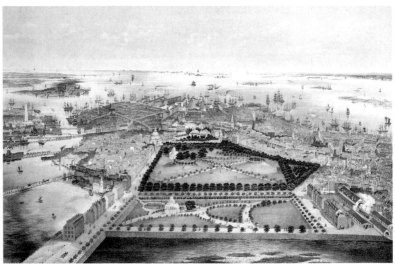

Boston Athenaeum

Bird's-Eye View of Boston (1850)

Cradle of American Independence – In an attempt to replenish the Crown's coffers in the wake of the costly French and Indian War, the British parliament voted to enforce high taxes and harsh trade regulations against the American colonies. This policy enraged the colonists, who, as British citizens, claimed that their rights to representation were being denied. Following the passage of the **Stamp Act** (1765), a tax on publications and official documents in Massachusetts, public reaction became violent. Mobs roamed the streets, the governor's mansion was burned and a boycott was organized. Although parliament repealed the Stamp Act the following year, renewed demonstrations erupted in 1767 with the passage of the **Townshend Acts**, which regulated customs duties. England responded immediately by sending troops to

116

enforce British law. The colonists, especially those who were forced to lodge and feed soldiers, grew increasingly hostile. Steadily mounting tensions eventually exploded into clashes between Bostonians and the British.

The **Boston Massacre** was the first of these clashes. On March 5, 1770, a group of Bostonians gathered near the State House to protest recent events. When a British officer answered the insults of a member of the crowd with the butt of his musket, the crowd became abusive and the guard was called out. Several Redcoats, provoked by the civilians, loaded their weapons and fired, killing five men. Political activist **Samuel Adams** seized on this incident to rally the citizens to his cause.

Three years later the **Boston Tea Party** further aggravated the situation. By 1773 parliament had repealed all the Townshend Acts except the tax on tea, which gave the East India Company a monopoly to sell tea in the colonies. This tax so angered colonists that in November 1773 Bostonians refused to allow the captains of three of the company's tea-laden ships to unload their cargo. At a well-attended meeting held December 16, 1773, in the Old South Meeting House, an attempt was made to resolve the issue. When British compromise was not forthcoming, Samuel Adams concluded with his famed cue: "This meeting can do nothing more to save the country." Thereupon 90 Bostonians disguised as Indians fled the building with a war cry, trailed by a large crowd, and proceeded to board the ships and dump the tea into the harbor. In retaliation England closed the Port of Boston and invoked punitive measures that served only to further unite the colonists against the British. Colonial militia were organized and began training on village greens.

The Ride of Paul Revere – In April 1775 Gen. Thomas Gage dispatched 800 British soldiers to the outlying towns of CONCORD and LEXINGTON to seize the colonists' stash of arms and arrest patriot leaders **John Hancock** and Samuel Adams. The patriots, forewarned by their network of spies, were prepared. According to a prearranged plan, on the night the British began to march to Concord the sexton of Old North Church signaled the direction they took by hanging two lanterns in the steeple. In the meantime Paul Revere safely crossed the river to Charlestown and set out to Lexington on horseback to warn Hancock and Adams. Thanks to the legendary ride by Revere, William Dawes and Dr. Samuel Prescott, the militia was ready when the British arrived at Lexington, and later at Concord.

The Siege of Boston and the Battle of Bunker Hill – Following events at Lexington and Concord, the British retreated to Boston, where they were surrounded by rebel forces. While the British eyed the strategic heights around Boston, colonial leaders, informed of the British plan to fortify Bunker Hill in Charlestown, hastened to occupy nearby Breed's Hill before the arrival of the British. On June 17, 1775, when the British awoke and discovered an American redoubt had been built on Breed's Hill during the night, a force of 5,000 soldiers was sent out to capture the site. Although the colonists' position was defended by only 1,500 militiamen, the British failed in their first two attempts to secure the fort. They then set fire to Charlestown and launched the third and final attack against the rebels. Colonial leader William Prescott, aware that his men were low on ammunition, gave his famous order: "Don't fire until you see the whites of their eyes!"

The British succeeded in capturing the fort, but in doing so, they lost over 10 percent of all the British officers killed during the Revolution. Though it took place on Breed's Hill, this struggle is known by the misnomer the Battle of Bunker Hill.

The British Evacuation – During the early months of 1776, the supplies captured by the colonists at Fort Ticonderoga were hauled across New England to Boston. American artillery began to bombard Boston on March 2. By March 5 the colonists had fortified Dorchester Heights to the south with the cannons from the fort and the British were forced to accept a compromise. The colonial troops peacefully reclaimed Boston, and British General Howe and his men were permitted to evacuate the city unharmed. Soon after, General Washington made a triumphant entry into Boston, which saw little subsequent war activity as the theater of operations shifted to New York, Pennsylvania and the southern colonies.

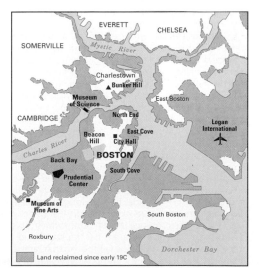

Land reclaimed since early 19C

19C: "Cutting Down the Hills to Fill the Bays" – Modern Boston is the product of transformations wrought by two centuries of prodigious landfill projects. Familiar place names such as Back Bay, the South End and Dock Square recall features of the area's original 783-acre landmass, which has increased almost fourfold through landfill alone since the early 19C. *See map p. 117.*

The Puritans who settled Shawmut found an irregularly shaped peninsula joined to the mainland by a natural causeway (the "neck") stretching along a section of present-day Washington Street. On the western side rose a three-peaked ridge (Trimountain) dominated by Beacon Hill. Extending south of Beacon Hill, the tract purchased from Reverend Blackstone was set aside as "Common Field," and remains parkland to this day as the Boston Common. The eastern shore facing the harbor was indented by Town or East Cove, which divided the residential North End from commercial and public sectors that burgeoned in the vicinity of the harbor, the original South End.

Over the course of the 19C, Boston's population increased dramatically, rising from 18,000 in 1790 to 54,000 in 1825. By the turn of the century, it totaled over half a million. The pressing need for more living space prompted a flurry of landfill projects that forever transformed the city's topography. These ambitious programs, characterized by noted historian Walter Muir Whitehill as "cutting down the hills to fill the bays," involved hauling colossal quantities of earth into the waters around the city, thus transforming the spindly peninsula into an extension of the mainland. The filling in of the waters on either side of the narrow neck was crucial to the city's growth, for it enabled a network of railroad lines to penetrate the downtown area. Boston's great 19C transformation began with the development of the Beacon Hill district in the early 19C. In the following decades the areas on the peninsula's east and south sides were filled in, leading to the expansion of the waterfront area and the creation of the residential district now called the South End. The century's most spectacular landfill project took place in the insalubrious Back Bay on the neck's north side. This 40-year project increased the city's area by 450 acres and resulted in one of the nation's finest planned residential districts. After the Great Fire of 1872 leveled 776 buildings downtown, many residents and churches resettled in the fashionable Back Bay, precipitating the development of the downtown as a commercial district. Landfill projects continued to increase the city's area throughout the 19C and into the present century, particularly around Charlestown and East Boston, site of Logan International Airport.

The city's system of public parks, parkways and tree-shaded malls, designed in the 19C by the nation's premier landscape architect, **Frederick Law Olmsted**, encircles the city with a nearly continuous swath of greenery. The so-called **Emerald Necklace** begins at Boston Common and stretches southwest along the Public Garden, Commonwealth Avenue, the Fenway, Jamaica Park, the Arborway, Arnold Arboretum and Franklin Park.

The New Boston – By the mid-20C Boston was deteriorating. Rising property taxes, the exodus of businesses to the suburbs or out of state and the general population decline had taken their toll. Faced with problems associated with urban blight, the city reacted by establishing the **Boston Redevelopment Authority** in 1957. Under the leadership of **Edward Logue**, BRA inaugurated a program aimed at "revitalizing" one-fourth of the city. The plan generated much controversy since it mandated the bulldozing of entire neighborhoods, including Scollay Square and the adjacent Jewish and Italian enclave known as the West End.

The architect **I.M. Pei**, who had trained at the Massachusetts Institute of Technology, was among the experts called upon in the 1960s to draw up designs for the new **Government Center** on the site of Scollay Square, Boston's bawdy entertainment district. This $260 million project called for an enormous brick-paved expanse showcasing the award-winning City Hall building alongside several contemporary structures of varying architectural merit and a 19C commercial building (the Sears Crescent). In the following decades Pei contributed to reshaping Boston's built environment by executing such important commissions as the John Hancock Tower, the Kennedy Library and the West Wing of the Museum of Fine Arts.

A major renewal project of the 1960s, the mixed-use Prudential Center created controversy, largely because it failed to create a human scale compatible with surrounding Back Bay neighborhoods. More successful was the 1970s renovation of the Faneuil Hall Marketplace, which dramatically revived the ambience of downtown Boston by injecting new vitality into the city's historic heart.

In the 1980s the **Financial District**, long established in the vicinity of Federal and Congress Streets, began expanding in the direction of the rejuvenated harbor district. The waterfront's redevelopment, which was boosted by the rehabilitation of the adjacent Faneuil Hall area, has reestablished Boston's historic link to the sea. In the near future this area will be further enhanced with the dismantling of the unsightly, traffic-clogged Central Artery that has long severed the waterfront and the North End from the downtown proper. The Central Artery/Tunnel project, begun in the early 1990s, calls for the construction of an underground highway beneath the site of the current expressway as well as a new harbor tunnel to provide more efficient access to the airport. Upon its completion around the year 2005, this ambitious public works program, estimated to cost $10 billion, is expected to alleviate Boston's infamous traffic snarls and create over 150 acres of new parkland.

Boston Today

Bostonians – Reflecting various waves of immigration, Boston's population is quite diverse. The "proper Bostonian," or **Brahmin**, descends from New England's early Puritan settlers who shared a common language and culture, and whose close-knit society set Boston apart by the 19C as the city where "the Lowells talk only to the Cabots, and the Cabots talk only to God." Stereotyped as refined, conservative and Harvard-educated, the proper Bostonian today represents an ever-decreasing percentage of the city's population.

Boston's large **Irish** population began arriving by the thousands in the wake of the 1840s potato famine. Penniless yet hardworking, the Irish integrated into mainstream American life, and many succeeded in rising to positions in local and federal government. One of Boston's most famous Irish Americans was former US president John Fitzgerald Kennedy.

Toward the end the century, many **Italian** immigrants, particularly from southern Italy, settled in Boston. The Italians eventually replaced the Irish and Jewish populations in the North End and the now-destroyed West End.

The **African-American** community, once concentrated on Beacon Hill, represents a large presence in Roxbury and the adjacent neighborhoods of Dorchester and Mattapan. Boston is home to one of the oldest black communities in the US. The first blacks were brought to colonial Boston as slaves from the West Indies in 1638, just eight years after the colony's establishment. A growing number of freed blacks settled in the North End. Many of them worked as barbers, sailors, laborers and coachmen and many, including **Crispus Attucks**, an assassinated hero of the Boston Massacre, served in the Revolution. In the 1780s the slave trade was legally abolished in Massachusetts— a reflection of the state's staunch abolitionist position. In the 19C, with the dedication of the African Meeting House on Beacon Hill, the black community moved to the north slope of the Hill in search of improved living conditions. Better housing, job opportunities and schools led blacks to gradually move out to Cambridge, the Back Bay and the South End.

Boston's rapidly growing **Hispanic** population has settled in pockets such as the South End, Jamaica Plain and East Boston. It is estimated that these and other minority groups, such as Asians, now make up about one-third of the city's population. In the 1970s and 80s, Boston became a national testing ground for controversial busing policies. In an attempt to provide quality education for students of all socioeconomic classes and particularly blacks, the federal government attempted with limited success to integrate the city's public schools.

Each year the area's colleges and universities draw a new influx of students and professors from across the country and abroad. The large **student population**, estimated in recent years at over 200,000, lends great diversity to the area's social and cultural fabric. Students reside on and around the numerous urban and suburban campuses scattered throughout the area, and they constitute a particularly strong presence in large sections of Cambridge, Brookline and Allston-Brighton.

Economy – Since the days of the Bay Colony, shipping and trade have been the mainstays of Boston's economy. Following a period of decline in the early 20C, modernization of the port's services and of the 25mi of docking space in the 1950s and 60s increased the amount of cargo the port could handle. Today, however, Boston is not among the 20 top-ranking ports in the country.

A similar surge of growth was experienced in the business sector, particularly in the insurance industry. Insurance giants Prudential and John Hancock have established a towering presence in the Back Bay through the construction of the area's two tallest skyscrapers. Boston financiers, guardians of the Yankee fortunes made in shipping and industry, continue to generate a large share of New England's economic activity from their offices in the Financial District.

Industrially, a new era was born in the 1950s with the construction of Route 128, a circumferential highway outside the downtown area, and the emergence along this highway of about 700 research and development firms. Boston is a recognized world leader in this field; its universities are training grounds for scientists and research specialists, especially in electronics and computer technology. Boston is also a world leader in health care; the city's medical facilities, notably **Massachusetts General Hospital**, are internationally recognized centers of research and treatment. The nationwide recession of the 1980s dealt a serious blow to Boston's economy as evidenced by sky-rocketing unemployment and a sagging real-estate market. Signs of recovery were apparent in the 1990s, however, and, by the end of the decade, Boston's financial and high-tech industries were booming. A new 600,000sq ft convention center, estimated to cost $700 million, is slated to open at the end of the year 2003; area hotel accommodations are expected to grow concomitantly.

A Cultural Hub – *For the locations of theaters and concert halls see map p 121.* By the 19C Boston had become a gathering place for intellectuals and writers, earning the sobriquet "the Athens of America." Well-heeled and cultivated Bostonians traveled extensively, returning home with treasures that initiated the collections of the Museum of Fine Arts, the Isabella Stewart Gardner Museum and the museums of Harvard University. In 1881 philanthropist Henry Lee Higginson founded the **Boston Symphony Orchestra**. Today the BSO and the **Boston Pops**, with its repertoire of lighter music, perform seasonally in Symphony Hall. In the summer the Pops presents free concerts on the Charles River Esplanade. The heart of the **Theater District** lies in the area near Tremont and Stuart Streets. Boston is a testing ground for Broadway productions. The Colonial Theater, the Shubert Theater and the Wilbur Theater present musicals and comedies. Dramas are staged at the Charles Playhouse and at numerous university theaters, such as Boston University's Huntington Theatre and the American Repertory Theatre in Harvard Square. Performances by the **Boston Ballet Company** occur seasonally at the Wang Center.

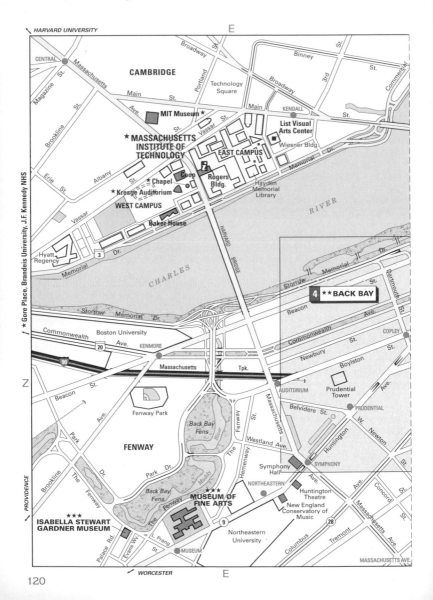

Education – A principal concern of the Puritans was the establishment of a sound educational system. Ever since the founding of Boston Public Latin School (c.1630), the first public school in America, and Harvard College (1636), the first college in the colonies, Boston has remained a leader in the field of education. The metropolitan area's roster of some 68 colleges and universities includes Harvard, Massachusetts Institute of Technology, Boston University, New England Conservatory of Music, Boston College, Brandeis University, Tufts University and Wellesley College.

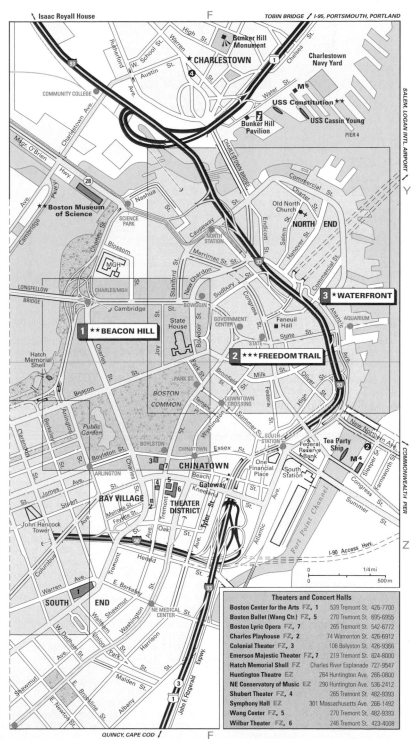

Theaters and Concert Halls		
Boston Center for the Arts FZ, 1	539 Tremont St.	426-7700
Boston Ballet (Wang Ctr.) FZ, 5	270 Tremont St.	695-6955
Boston Lyric Opera FZ, 7	265 Tremont St.	542-6772
Charles Playhouse FZ, 2	74 Warrenton St.	426-6912
Colonial Theater FZ, 3	106 Bolyston St.	426-9366
Emerson Majestic Theater FZ, 7	219 Tremont St.	824-8000
Hatch Memorial Shell FZ	Charles River Esplanade	727-9547
Huntington Theatre EZ	264 Huntington Ave.	266-0800
NE Conservatory of Music EZ	290 Huntington Ave.	536-2412
Shubert Theater FZ, 4	265 Tremont St.	482-9393
Symphony Hall EZ	301 Massachusetts Ave.	266-1492
Wang Center FZ, 5	270 Tremont St.	482-9393
Wilbur Theater FZ, 6	246 Tremont St.	423-4008

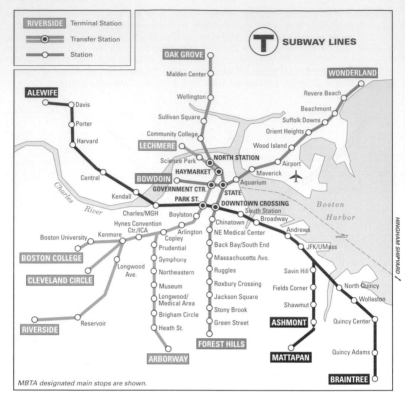

RIVERSIDE Terminal Station
Transfer Station
Station

T SUBWAY LINES

MBTA designated main stops are shown.

★★① BEACON HILL *Map p 126*

Historically the home of Boston Brahmins and the city's early black community, the "Hill" preserves an Old World ambience undisturbed by the bustle of the surrounding metropolis.

A Remarkable Transformation – Today's Beacon Hill is the only remnant of the three peaks comprising the Trimountain ridge. Its name derives from the primitive beacon that the Puritans raised on its summit in 1634 to warn of invasion. From 1795 to 1798 preeminent architect Charles Bulfinch oversaw the erection of his golden-domed State House on the Hill's southern slope. Construction of this grand building spurred Bulfinch, Harrison Gray Otis and their business associates to create an elegant residential district on a nearby tract purchased from painter John Singleton Copley. From 1799 until the mid-19C, these developers transformed the entire face of the Trimountain area: Beacon Hill's summit was lowered 60ft and the two neighboring peaks were leveled, creating abundant landfill for the surrounding marshlands; the present street system was laid out; and the charming enclave of English-style brick residences that we know as Beacon Hill came into being.

The sunny south slope, between Pinckney Street and the Common, became the bastion of Boston's affluent society and the center of its respected intellectual and artistic community, whose members included Daniel Webster, Julia Ward Howe and the Alcotts. The more modest north slope, spilling into Cambridge Street, became the center of Boston's black community in the 19C, many of whom worked for the well-to-do on the the Hill. Today Beacon Hill reigns as one of Boston's most desirable addresses. A stroll along its serene streets lined with gas lamps and brick facades transports the visitor to a bygone era.

An Architectural Showcase – Created almost entirely in the first half of the 19C, Beacon Hill constitutes a living museum of the period's architectural heritage, showcasing the works of the city's leading 19C architects. The work of Charles Bulfinch is well represented by the State House and some 15 Federal-style town houses found primarily on the fashionable south slope. Beacon Hill houses designed by architects Asher Benjamin and Alexander Parris reflect the Greek Revival style in vogue in the 1820s.

The Hill's streetscape is noteworthy for its extraordinary visual unity, resulting from the predominant use of brick, a uniform three- to four-story building height, and harmonious blending of flat and bowed facades. Quaint service lanes are lined with

PRACTICAL INFORMATION .... Area Code: 617

Getting There

By Air – International and domestic flights to **Logan International Airport**, 2mi northeast of downtown ☎ 800-235-6426 (ground transport information). Taxi service to downtown *($18–$20)*; commercial shuttles *($8)*; major rental car agencies *(p 306)*. Massachusetts Bay Transportation Authority (MBTA) Blue Line service from airport. Airport Water Shuttle (between Logan and Rowes Wharf) ☎ 330-8680 or 800-235-6426.

By Bus and Train – Greyhound **bus**: South Station ☎ 800-231-2222; Peter Pan: 700 Atlantic Ave. ☎ 800-237-8747. Amtrak **train**: South Station ☎ 800-872-7245; suburban trains North and South Stations ☎ 722-3200.

Getting Around

By Public Transportation – Commuter **ferry** service between Long Wharf and Charlestown Navy Yard **Boston Harbor Cruises** ☎ 227-4321.

Subway and Buses – The MBTA operates underground and surface transportation in the greater Boston area. Stations are indicated by the Ⓣ symbol at street level. Most MBTA lines operate Mon–Sat 5:15am–12:30am, Sun 6am–12:30am. **Subway** fare $.85, **bus** fare $.60 *(exact fare required)*. MBTA Visitor Passports are good for 1 *($5)*, 3 *($9)* or 7 *($18)* days of unlimited travel on all MBTA subway and local bus lines, available at some stations and hotels. Subway maps are available at the main stations; MBTA system maps *($2.50)* can be purchased at the Globe Corner Bookstore, 1 School St. *For route and sales information* ☎ *222-3200.*

By Car – Use of public transportation or walking is strongly encouraged within the city as roads are often congested and street parking may be difficult. Parking garages generally charge $5–$15/day. Some facilities give "early-bird" discounts *(25-50%)* before 10:30am. Construction of the Central Artery/Tunnel Project will divert traffic for the next few years; for information on road closures and detours ☎ 228-4636.

By Taxi

By Taxi	☎		☎
Checker Taxi	536-7000	Red Cab	734-5000
Green Cab	628-0600	Town Taxi	536-5000

General Information

Visitor Information – **Greater Boston Convention and Visitors Bureau**: 2 Copley Place, Suite 105, Boston MA 02116. ☎ 800-888-5515. www.bostonusa.com. **Boston Common** visitor center: Tremont and West Sts. *(open Mon–Fri 8:30am–5pm, weekends 9am–5pm)* ☎ 800-888-5515. **National Park Service** visitor center: 15 State St. *(open mid-Jun–Labor Day daily 9am–6pm; rest of the year Mon–Fri 9am–5pm; closed Jan 1, Thanksgiving Day, Dec 25)* ☎ 242-5642. www.nps.gov/bost.

Accommodations – Reservation services: **Citywide Reservation Services** 839 Beacon St., Boston MA 02115 ☎ 267-7424; **Host Homes of Boston**, PO Box 117, Waban Branch, Boston MA 02468 ☎ 244-1308 or 800-600-1308; **Bed and Breakfast Cambridge & Greater Boston**, PO Box 1344, Cambridge MA 02238 ☎ 720-1492 or 800-888-0178. *Boston Travel Planner* available *(free)* from the Convention and Visitors Bureau *(above)*. Accommodations range from elegant downtown hotels *($195–$495/day)* to budget motels *($75–$130/day)*. Most bed and breakfasts are in residential areas of the city *($60–$125/day). Average prices for a double room.*

Local Press – Daily news: *Boston Globe* (morning), Thursday entertainment section; *Boston Herald* (morning). Weekly entertainment: *Boston Phoenix*.

Foreign Exchange Offices – **Travelex World Wide Money** has currency exchange offices located in Logan International Airport ☎ 800-445-0295. **Thomas Cook Currency Services** (☎ 800-287-7362) and **American Express Travel Services** (☎ 800-297-3429) have exchange offices in the city.

Useful Numbers

Useful Numbers	☎
Police/Ambulance/Fire	**911**
Police (non-emergency)	343-4240
Dental Emergency *(24hrs)*	508-651-3521
Medical Emergency Inn-House Doctor *(24hrs)*	859-1776
CVS Pharmacy *(daily 7am–midnight)*	523-1028
Main Post Office 25 Dorchester Ave. *(24hrs)*	654-5327
Weather	936-1234

© Justine Hill

Sightseeing – **Old Towne Trolley Tours** *(daily year-round; no service Thanksgiving Day, Dec 25)* offers 1hr 40min narrated tours *($23)* of the city; visitors can board at major attractions along the route ☎ 269-7150. **Cruises**: departures from Long Wharf – **Boston Harbor Cruises** ☎ 227-4321, **Schooner Liberty Tall Ship** ☎ 742-0333; departures from Commonwealth Pier – **Spirit of Boston Harbor Cruises** *(Memorial Day–late Sept)* ☎ 748-1450. **Whale-watching cruises** *p 312.*

Entertainment – Consult the arts and entertainment sections of local newspapers for schedule of cultural events and addresses of principal theaters. Tickets for local events: **Bostix Ticket Booth** (Faneuil Hall Marketplace) offers half-price tickets for selected events on the day of the performance (purchases must be made in person, cash only) ☎ 723-8915 or **Ticketmaster** ☎ 931-2000.

Sports – Tickets for major sporting events can be purchased at the venue, or through Ticketmaster outlets *(see Entertainment above)*. The 26mi Boston Marathon, run every year from Hopkinton to the Back Bay, takes place on Patriots' Day *(3rd Mon in Apr)*.

SPORT/TEAM	SEASON	VENUE
⚾ Major League Baseball Red Sox (AL)	Apr–Oct	Fenway Park
🏈 Professional Football New England Patriots (NFL)	Sept–Dec	Foxboro Stadium
🏀 Professional Basketball Celtics (NBA)	Oct–Apr	FleetCenter
🏒 Professional Hockey Bruins (NHA)	Sept–Apr	FleetCenter

Shopping in Boston

In this area...	you will find...
Downtown	**Downtown Crossing** – major department stores including Macy's, Filene's and Filene's Basement (renowned for its great bargains). **Faneuil Hall Marketplace** – a lively cluster of specialty shops and eateries in a historic setting. **Haymarket** – outdoor farmers' market.
Back Bay	**Copley Place** – boutiques, restaurants, Neiman-Marcus department store. **Prudential Center** – apparel and specialty stores, Lord & Taylor and Saks Fifth Avenue department stores. **Newbury Street** – antique shops, galleries and boutiques.
Beacon Hill	**Charles Street** – antique shops and galleries.
Cambridge	**Harvard Square** – trendy shops, record stores, boutiques. **Cambridge Side Galleria** – over 100 apparel and specialty stores.

Peter Vanderwarker

Acorn Street, Beacon Hill

former stables and servants' quarters, while intimate culs-de-sac evoke a sense of mystery. The Hill's designation as a historic district in 1955 and the determination of residents to safeguard its precious architectural heritage have been instrumental in the preservation of this urban jewel. *Beacon Hill's private gardens are revealed to the public in May by special tour. For information:* ☎ *617-227-4392.*

Walking Tour *2hrs (not including guided tours).* Ⓣ *Park St.*

Visitors are advised to exercise caution in inclement weather as brick sidewalks can be very slippery.

Begin at the corner of Park and Tremont Sts. and walk uphill on Park St.

Gently sloping Park Street provides a pleasant approach to the gold-domed State House crowning **Beacon Street★**. Writer Oliver Wendell Holmes dubbed Beacon "the sunny street that holds the sifted few." The row of stately edifices forming the Hill's southern facade offers coveted views of Boston Common. Beyond the Common, this fashionable thoroughfare stretches west into the Back Bay *(p 135)* and points beyond.

Turn right on Beacon St.

★**Boston Athenaeum** – *10 1/2 Beacon St. Closed for 18-month renovation beginning summer 1999. Otherwise open Jun–Aug Mon–Fri 9am–5:30pm (Mon 8pm). Rest of the year Mon–Fri 9am–5:30pm (Mon 8pm), Sat 9am–4pm.* ♿ ☎ *617-227-0270. www.bostonathenaeum.org.* This venerable Boston institution was established in 1807 as one of the nation's first private lending libraries. Later in the century numerous important works from the Athenaeum's art trove formed the core of the Museum of Fine Arts' world-class collection. The library's present home on Beacon Hill was built in the 1840s to accommodate its growing holdings, which today total some 750,000 volumes and works of art. Walking through the hallowed reading rooms packed with leather-bound volumes and fine sculptures, paintings and prints, visitors are ushered into a rarefied atmosphere of tradition and erudition. Works by Gilbert Stuart, Thomas Sully and Jean-Antoine Houdon highlight the collection. The art gallery *(2nd floor)* features changing exhibits from the collection. Several rooms and terraces provide lovely **views** of the Old Granary Burying Ground.

★★**State House** – *Corner of Park and Beacon Sts. Open year-round Mon–Fri 10am–4pm, Sat 10am–3:30pm. Closed Jan 1, Thanksgiving Day, Dec 25.* ♿ ☎ *617-727-3676.* The golden dome of Massachusetts' capitol building dominates Beacon Hill, enduring as a cherished Boston landmark for nearly two centuries. Completed in 1798 by Charles Bulfinch, the original brick edifice, fronted by a projecting portico, was extended in 1895 and 1916 by large additions to its sides

125

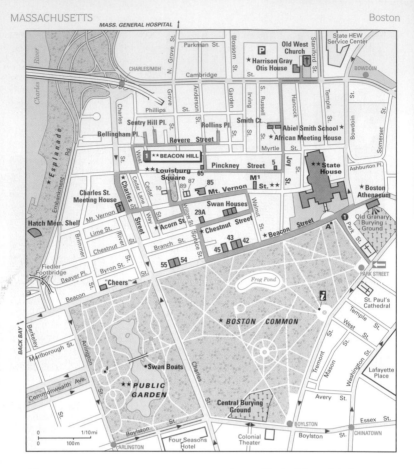

1 Curious Liquids

22-B Beacon St. ☎ *617-720-2836.* Rare is the cafe that offers copious light, funky decor, great music and even better coffee. Rarer still does that cafe anchor a block known for centuries as the home of the cultural elite, and boast views of two of the most venerable landmarks in the city (Boston Common and the State House). Maybe that's where the "curious" in Curious Liquids comes in. Frequented by politicos, locals and bicycle couriers alike, this beloved neighborhood java joint is great for a morning jolt. Take a seat in one of the mismatched chairs upstairs, with its high ceilings and bright yellow walls, or ensconce yourself downstairs in the book-lined subterranean enclave that's a perfect retreat from the bustling world outside.

and rear. Most of the original ornamentation and design of the interior spaces specified by Bulfinch have been left intact. Statues on the front lawn depict Anne Hutchinson, banished from the 17C colony for her theological views; Mary Dyer, hanged for her Quaker beliefs; orator Daniel Webster; and Horace Mann, a pioneer in American education.

The main entrance of the State House leads into **Doric Hall**, named for its rows of Doric columns. In the 19C addition the **Senate Staircase Hall**, with its marble walls and floors, displays paintings immortalizing Paul Revere's ride, James Otis' oratory against the Writs of Assistance, and the Boston Tea Party. Paintings in the **Hall of Flags**, which was built to house a collection of Civil War battle flags, portray the Pilgrims on the *Mayflower*, John Eliot preaching to the Indians, and the scene at Concord Bridge on April 19, 1775.

The main staircase leads to the **Third Floor Hall**, dominated by Daniel Chester French's statue of Roger Wolcott, governor of Massachusetts during the Spanish-American War. The Senate Chamber, Senate Reception Room, Governor's Office and House Chamber occupy this floor. Before leaving the domed House Chamber, note the **Sacred Cod**, a gilded, carved-wood symbol of the fish that supported Massachusetts' early fishing industry.

Upon exiting the State House, cross Beacon Street to admire the **Shaw Civil War Monument★** (**A**), a bronze relief by Augustus Saint-Gaudens that honors Col. Robert Gould Shaw and the 54th Massachusetts Colored Infantry, the Union's first regiment of free black volunteers. Shaw was killed in 1863 during the Union assault on Fort Wagner in South Carolina.

Continue walking down Beacon St.

Among the street's noteworthy buildings are the exclusive Somerset Club at **nos. 42-43**, a double-bowed granite structure whose right half is attributed to Alexander Parris (1819), and **no. 45** (1808), the last of three houses that Bulfinch designed and built for Harrison Gray Otis on Beacon Hill.

Cross Spruce St.

The handsome pair of bowfront Greek Revival houses at **nos. 54-55** are attributed to Asher Benjamin, architect of the Charles Street Meeting House and the Old West Church *(both described later on the tour)*. The state chapter of the National Society of Colonial Dames occupies no. 55.

Return to the corner of Beacon and Spruce Sts., turn up Spruce and take a right on Chestnut St.

As you pass narrow Branch Street on the left, note the modest buildings that once housed servants.

★**Chestnut Street** – This picturesque street presents a fine assortment of houses reflecting architectural styles dating from 1800 to 1830. **No. 29A** (1800, Charles Bulfinch) features distinctive purple glass in its bowfront. Other examples of the Hill's famed 18C purple window panes—resulting from the glass' manganese dioxide content—may still be seen in a few other dwellings on the Hill (including 63-64 Beacon St.). The graceful trio at nos. 13-17, known as the **Swan Houses** (c.1805), further illustrates Bulfinch's preference for a restrained Federal style.

Continue one block up Chestnut St., turn left on Walnut St. and continue one block to Mt. Vernon St.

★★**Mt. Vernon Street** – Qualified by writer Henry James as "the only respectable street in America," this gracious thoroughfare boasts some of the Hill's finest residences. At no. 55 stands the **Nichols House Museum★** (**M¹**), the Hill's only residence open to the public *(visit by 30min guided tour only May–Oct Tue–Sat noon–5pm; rest of the year Mon, Wed, Sat noon–5pm; closed Jan & major holidays; $5; ☎ 617-227-6993)*. Designed by Bulfinch in 1804, the house preserves the possessions and spirit of a colorful Beacon Hill lady, Miss Rose Standish Nichols. The spacious interior contains late-19C and early-20C furniture carved by Nichols herself, as well as Flemish tapestries, needlepoint, ancestral paintings, and sculptures she collected on her many trips abroad.

On the way downhill, pause to admire the freestanding edifice at **no. 85** (1802) set back some 30ft from the street line. Faced with slender pilasters and topped by a wooden balustrade and an octagonal tower, this handsome residence was the second of three mansions Bulfinch designed for Harrison Gray Otis. Bulfinch also conceived the neighboring mansions at nos. 87 and 89.

★★**Louisburg Square** – Named in honor of the victorious siege of the French fortress at Louisbourg (Nova Scotia, Canada) led by the Massachusetts militia in 1745, this select enclave epitomizes Beacon Hill's refined lifestyle. The appearance of the elegant Greek Revival bowfront row houses and the small private park have changed little since their creation in the 1830s and 40s. Writer Louisa May Alcott lived in no. 10 from 1880 until her death eight years later. Christmas Eve caroling on the square is a cherished Bostonian tradition.

Leave the square via Willow St. and turn right onto Acorn St.

★**Acorn Street** – This romantic cobblestone passage is the most photographed street on the Hill.

At the end of Acorn St., turn right on West Cedar St., then left on Mt. Vernon St. to Charles St.

★**Charles Street** – Antique shops, art galleries and coffee shops line the Hill's bustling commercial thoroughfare. At the corner of Mt. Vernon Street stands the **Charles Street Meeting House** (c.1807), designed by Asher Benjamin. This popular forum for 19C abolitionists William Lloyd Garrison, Frederick Douglass and Sojourner Truth was converted into offices in the 1980s.

Continue one block on Charles St. and turn right on Pinckney St.

Pinckney Street – This lovely, sloping street was the dividing line between the affluent neighborhood on the sunny south slope and the more modest community on the north slope.

Turn left on West Cedar St. After one block, go right on Revere St.

Revere Street – The street's left side is interrupted by a series of intimate private courts: **Bellingham Place**, **Sentry Hill Place** and **Rollins Place**. At Rollins Place the white "house" at the end of the court is not a house at all, but rather a decorative wall at the head of a drop.

Walk back to Anderson St. and turn left.

The imposing brick edifice (1824) crowning the corner of Pinckney and Anderson Streets (**no. 65**) formerly housed the Phillips Grammar School (1844-61), the city's first racially mixed school.

Continue uphill on Pinckney St.

The small clapboard house at **no. 5**, built for two black men in the 1790s, is one of the Hill's oldest surviving structures.

Turn left onto Joy St.

Joy Street – This long street descends the north slope of the Hill, the center of Boston's historic black community from the late 18C to the 19C.

Smith Court – This small cul-de-sac was the heart of the black community following the Revolution. Many of its residents worked for wealthy families who lived on the elite south slope. At no. 46 Joy Street stands the **Abiel Smith School★** (1834), an elegant pedimented structure that housed the city's first black school, the first publicly funded school for black children in the country. Recently renovated, the building today contains a restored schoolroom and exhibits on African-American history.

Behind the school stands the nation's oldest remaining black church, the **African Meeting House★** *(may be closed for renovation during 2000; otherwise open year-round Mon–Fri 10am–4pm; closed Jan 1, Thanksgiving Day, Dec 25; ☎ 617-742-5415; www.nps.gov/boaf).* Built in 1806 by black Baptists disenchanted with the discrimination encountered in the white churches, this handsome brick edifice provided a forum for supporters of the anti-slavery movement.

For most of the 20C, the meetinghouse served as a synagogue. Today it is preserved as a privately owned historic site managed by the National Park Service. The lower floor houses the Museum of Afro-American History, a small showplace for exhibits on themes relating to New England's black community. The meetinghouse proper occupies the upper floor. *For more information on Beacon Hill's African-American history, obtain the free brochure describing the Black Heritage Trail, which identifies 14 historically significant sites (most of which are included on the present walking tour herein) from the Boston African-American National Historic Site, 14 Beacon St., Suite 506, Boston MA 02108; ☎ 617-742-5415; www.nps.gov/boaf.*

At the foot of Joy St., cross busy Cambridge St.

★Harrison Gray Otis House – *141 Cambridge St. Visit by guided tour (45min) only, year-round Wed–Sun 11am–5pm (on the hour; last tour 4pm). Closed major holidays. $4. ☎ 617-227-3956. www.spnea.org.* The house (1796) was the creation of two men who permanently influenced Boston's urban landscape: architect Charles Bulfinch and Harrison Gray Otis, lawyer, speculator and politician. The first of three houses Bulfinch designed for Otis on Beacon Hill, this Federal-style dwelling reflects the refined taste of the upper classes during the early years of the Republic. A second-story Palladian window softens the facade. Exquisite period furniture, ornate moldings, hand-blocked borders and a freestanding staircase adorn the interior.

The house serves both as a museum and as the headquarters of the Society for the Preservation of New England Antiquities. Founded in 1910, the society administers more than 30 house museums in five states.

Old West Church – Complementing its Federal-style neighbor, the Otis House, this handsome structure with its strong vertical lines was designed by Asher Benjamin in 1806. In 1775 British troops razed the original meetinghouse that stood on this site when they suspected the patriots of using its steeple to signal American troops.

For an abrupt return to the 20C, glance across Staniford Street at the State Health, Education and Welfare Service Center (1970, Paul Rudolph), a sprawling concrete complex that replaced six blocks of tenement buildings in the bulldozed West End district. The facade on Staniford and Merrimac Streets features a dramatic exterior staircase.

★★★ ② THE FREEDOM TRAIL *1 day. Map p 129. Ⓣ Park St.*

The following walk includes most of the historical monuments along the Boston section of the Freedom Trail, a popular itinerary linking major Revolutionary and other sites of the Boston National Historical Park *(see Charlestown for additional Freedom Trail sights).* The route is indicated on the pavement by red brick or a painted red line.

Begin at the visitor center on Boston Common at Tremont and West Sts. (open year-round Mon–Sat 8:30am–5pm, Sun & holidays 9am–5pm; closed Thanksgiving Day & Dec 25; ☎ 617-536-4100; www.bostonusa.com).

Downtown

★**Boston Common** – *Map p 126.* This 50-acre park in the heart of the city has belonged to the people of Boston since the 1630s, when Reverend Blackstone sold the tract to the Puritans. Designated by these early Bostonians as "Common Field" forever reserved for public use, this Boston landmark has served over the centuries as pastureland, military training ground, public execution site, rallying ground and concert venue.

Lacking a formal landscape scheme, the park's hilly terrain is crisscrossed by tree-lined paths linking downtown to Beacon Hill and the Back Bay. The **Central Burying Ground** (1756), fronting Boylston Street, contains the unmarked grave of the pre-eminent early American portraitist Gilbert Stuart *(p 35).*

Proceed to the corner of Tremont and Park Sts. and follow the Freedom Trail red line for the rest of the tour.

★**Park Street Church** – *Open mid-Jun–Aug Tue–Sat 9am–3pm. Closed Jul 4.* ☎ *617-523-3383. www.parkstreet.org.* The graceful, 217ft wooden steeple of this brick edifice (1809, Peter Banner), inspired by the work of English architect Christopher Wren, is one of Boston's loveliest landmarks. The church carillon chimes the melodies of familiar hymns on the hour. William Lloyd Garrison delivered his first anti-slavery speech in this meetinghouse in 1829, and "America" (My Country 'tis of Thee) was sung for the first time here on July 4, 1831.

★**Old Granary Burying Ground** – Named for the 17C granary that once stood nearby, this burial ground contains the remains of the great Revolutionary War orators James Otis and Samuel Adams, as well as Paul Revere and Crispus Attucks, who was killed in the Boston Massacre. An obelisk in the center of the cemetery honors Benjamin Franklin's parents.

★**King's Chapel** – *Corner of Tremont and School Sts. Open mid-Jun–Labor Day Mon & Thu–Sat 10am–4pm. Rest of the year by appointment. Contribution requested.* ♿ ☎ *617-227-2155.* New England's first Anglican church, this granite edifice (1754, Peter Harrison) replaced the original wooden chapel built on the site in the 1680s. The central tower was wrapped in a wooden Ionic colonnade in the 1780s but never received its steeple due to lack of funds. Only nine years after the British evacuation of Boston, the structure was reborn as the first Unitarian church in

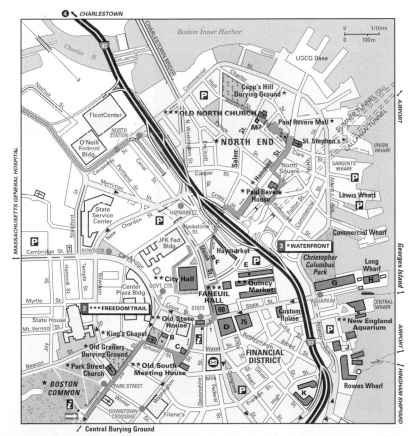

America. Enter the church to admire its outstanding Georgian **interior**. The adjoining **burying ground★**, Boston's oldest, is the final resting place of John Winthrop (the colony's first governor) and John Alden (son of Priscilla and John).

Old City Hall (**B**) – *45 School St.* Constructed on the site of America's first public school (c.1630), this stately granite building (1865) is Boston's finest example of the Second Empire style. Its architect, Arthur Gilman, is also credited with planning the Back Bay. The structure was converted to commercial use in the late 1960s following completion of the present City Hall. A statue of Benjamin Franklin, who was born nearby, graces the left side of the forecourt.

Old Corner Bookstore (**C**) – *Corner of Washington and School Sts.* This restored 18C brick commercial building, now operating as a bookstore specializing in Boston-related publications, has figured prominently in Boston's publishing world. Over the centuries it has housed the publisher of New England literati Longfellow, Emerson and Hawthorne, as well as the offices of the *Atlantic Monthly* and the *Boston Globe*.

★★Old South Meeting House – *Washington and Milk Sts. Open Apr–Oct daily 9:30am–5pm. Rest of the year daily 10am–4pm. Closed Jan 1, Thanksgiving Day, Dec 24 & 25. $3.* ♿ ☏ *617-482-6439.* Noted orators Samuel Adams and James Otis led many of the protest meetings held at Old South prior to the Revolution. The momentous rally that took place on the evening of December 16, 1773, gave rise to the Boston Tea Party.

Sporting a plain brick facade and a tower surmounted by a wooden steeple, the edifice was inspired by the designs of Christopher Wren. Its expansive interior was transformed by the British into a riding stable during the siege of Boston.

The story of the structure's history is told through interpretive displays, artifacts and recordings of passionate speeches and private conversations that are audible at various points throughout the interior.

★★Old State House – *Washington and State Sts. Open year-round daily 9am–5pm. Closed Jan 1, Thanksgiving Day, Dec 25. $3.* ♿ ☏ *617-720-3290. www.boston-history.org.* Boston's oldest public building (1713) was the British government headquarters in the colonies until the Revolution and was the site of several crucial events. In 1770 the Boston Massacre erupted on this site. On July 4, 1776, the colonies declared their independence in Philadelphia. Two weeks later the Declaration of Independence was read from the balcony here, inciting the crowds to topple and burn the lion and unicorn—symbols of the British Crown—perched on the building's gables (reproductions now adorn the building). The Massachusetts government met in this building until the new State House was completed in 1798; the Old State House was later converted into shops and subsequently housed the city government. In 1881 the Bostonian Society was founded to maintain the site as a museum devoted to Boston's history.

Inside, two floors accessed by a spiral staircase feature excellent exhibits on the city, past and present. The historic balcony can be seen from the Council Chamber.

To the rear of the State House, note the circle of cobblestones embedded in the traffic island in the busy intersection of Congress and State Streets, marking the actual Boston Massacre **site** (**1**). This vantage point affords a dizzying look at several of the skyscrapers dwarfing the Old State House. Standing sentinel over State Street are two noteworthy 20C towers: on the left, **60 State Street** (1977, Skidmore, Owings

Old State House

Peter Vanderwarker

Dianne Dietrich Leis

Faneuil Hall Marketplace

and Merrill), and on the right, **Stock Exchange Place** (**D**) (1984, Peabody and Stearns), which integrates part of the existing granite structure. Almost hidden behind Stock Exchange Place is Boston's most exuberant modern tower: **75 State Street**★ (1988, Skidmore, Owings and Merrill), distinguished by upper stories boldly adorned in multicolored granite and more than 3,500sq ft of gold leaf. Farther down State Street rises the tower of another enduring Boston landmark, the **Custom House** (base: 1840s, A. B. Young; tower: 1910s, Peabody and Stearns).

After negotiating the intersection of Congress and State Streets, turn around to admire the east facade of the Old State House against the dramatic backdrop of a looming black metal tower (One Boston Place).

★★**City Hall** – *Open year-round Mon–Fri 8:30am–5:30pm. Closed major holidays.* ♿ ☎ *617-635-4500.* On the left emerges the rear of City Hall *(best viewed from the plaza reached via the stairs flanking the building).* Rising from its brick base, this top-heavy concrete pile has remained one of Boston's controversial architectural statements since its completion in 1968. The nationally acclaimed edifice by Kallman, McKinnell and Knowles recalls the works of the influential Modernist Le Corbusier and helped to bring the so-called Brutalist style to prominence in the US. The architecturally minded will enjoy exploring the vast public spaces on the lower floors. City council meetings may be observed from the fifth-floor galleries *(Wed 4pm).*

★★★**Faneuil Hall** – *Dock Sq., main entrance facing Quincy Market. Open year-round daily 9am–5pm. Closed Jan 1, Thanksgiving Day, Dec 25.* ♿ ☎ *617-242-5689. www.thefreedomtrail.org.* Presented to Boston in 1742 by wealthy merchant Peter Faneuil, this revered landmark served as the town meeting hall throughout the Revolutionary period. Among the noted American leaders who have addressed groups assembled here over the years are Samuel Adams, Wendell Phillips, Susan B. Anthony and John F. Kennedy. Damaged by fire in 1762, the building was reconstructed according to the original plans drawn by John Smibert. In 1806 a major renovation supervised by Charles Bulfinch doubled the building's size.

Faneuil Hall's cupola is crowned with the grasshopper weather vane commissioned by Peter Faneuil in 1742. Modeled after the gilded bronze weather vanes that top the Royal Exchange in London, the grasshopper has symbolized the Port of Boston since the 18C. A statue of Samuel Adams stands in front of the building.

A staircase leads up to the large meeting hall on the second floor, where George P.A. Healy's painting *Daniel Webster's Second Reply to Hayne* covers the front wall. The **Ancient and Honorable Artillery Company**, America's oldest military organization, maintains a museum of historical arms, uniforms, flags and paintings on the third floor *(open year-round Mon–Fri 9am–5pm; closed major holidays;* ♿ ☎ *617-227-1638).*

★★**Quincy Market** – *Behind Faneuil Hall.* The lively Faneuil Hall Marketplace complex, known as Quincy Market after its principal edifice, exemplifies the successful revitalization of a formerly blighted urban area. Run-down market buildings and warehouses have been restored, and the renewed commercial complex has become one of the most popular sections of the city. Bostonians and tourists alike flock day and night to its numerous restaurants, outdoor cafes, and specialty shops.

The heart of the development consists of three granite buildings constructed in 1825 by Alexander Parris. The centerpiece, Quincy Market proper, is a long arcade in the Greek Revival style. Glass enclosures from the 1970s restoration flank its sides and contain dozens of small shops and eateries. The North and South Street buildings adjoining Quincy Market house more elegant stores. In North Market is the popular family-style restaurant **Durgin Park** (**E**).

Union Street – During the late 18C this street was lined with taverns and pubs. The Duke of Orleans, later King Louis-Philippe of France, lived for several months on the second floor of the venerable institution **Ye Olde Union Oyster House** (**F**) (still in operation as a restaurant), where he gave French lessons to earn his keep.

Cross Blackstone St. to Haymarket, site of a colorful farmers' market on weekends, and continue through the pedestrian tunnel and into the North End. (Follow the signs during Central Artery project construction.)

★NORTH END

Severed from the rest of the city by an elevated expressway, which is to be replaced by an underground expressway during the Central Artery project, this colorful district has been continuously inhabited since 1630. Throughout the 17C and 18C, the North End reigned as Boston's principal residential district and included a community of free blacks. Irish and Jewish immigrants who settled here in the 19C eventually moved on, replaced by Southern Italian immigrants, who have maintained a strong presence here. Rooftop gardens; shops bulging with fresh meats, poultry and vegetables; and restaurants and cafes that serve home-cooked pasta, pizza, pastries and espresso crowd **Hanover**★ and **Salem Streets**, the main thoroughfares. The local community continues to celebrate numerous saint's days throughout the year *(schedules of feasts are posted in storefronts and churches)*. These lively events feature religious processions, outdoor entertainment and an abundance of food sold by street vendors.

★**Paul Revere House** – *19 North Sq. Open mid-Apr–Oct daily 9:30am–5:15pm. Jan–Mar Tue–Sun 9:30am–5:15pm. Rest of the year daily 9:30am–4:15pm. Closed Jan 1, Thanksgiving Day, Dec 25. $2.50. ☎ 617-523-2338. www.paulrevere-house.org.* This two-and-a-half-story wooden clapboard house is the only extant 17C structure in downtown Boston. The dwelling was already 90 years old when the silversmith Paul Revere bought it in 1770. The house was the starting point of Revere's historic ride to Lexington on April 18, 1775. Furnishings include items owned by the Revere family.

Paul Revere Mall

★**St. Stephen's Church** – *Hanover and Clark Sts. Open year-round daily 7am–dusk.* Skillfully positioned at a bend on Hanover Street and aligned with the Paul Revere Mall across the street, this former Congregational meetinghouse, built in 1806, was renamed in the 1860s by the Catholic diocese of Boston, which purchased it to meet the spiritual needs of the North End's immigrant population. Of the five churches designed by Charles Bulfinch in Boston, St. Stephens is the only one still standing. The well-preserved stark interior is flanked with a delicate colonnade supporting a balcony.

★**Paul Revere Mall** – This intimate brick plaza links St. Stephen's and the Old North Church. Beyond Cyrus Dallin's equestrian **statue** (**2**) of Paul Revere looms the spire of the Old North Church. A series of bronze plaques set into the sidewalls traces the role of the North End's residents in Boston's history.

★★★Old North Church (Christ Church) – *Entrance at 193 Salem St. Open Jun–Oct daily 9am–6pm. Rest of the year daily 9am–5pm. Closed Thanksgiving Day & Dec 25 (except for services). $2 donation requested.* ♿ ☎ *617-523-6676. www. oldnorth.com.* It was here, on the evening of April 18, 1775, that the sexton displayed two lanterns in the steeple to signal the departure of the British from Boston by boat, on their way to Lexington and Concord. A century later this church was immortalized by Longfellow in his poem *Paul Revere's Ride.* Built in 1723, Old North was surmounted by a spire that was destroyed and replaced twice following violent storms. The present spire dates from 1954. Inside, the box pews, the large windows and the pulpit, from which President Gerald Ford initiated the celebration of the nation's bicentennial, are characteristic features of New England's colonial churches. The four wooden cherubim near the organ were among the bounty captured from a French vessel. Replicas of the famous lantern can be seen in the combination gift shop and **museum** (**M²**) adjacent to the church.

★Copp's Hill Burying Ground – *Open year-round daily 9am–5pm.* ☎ *617-635-4505.* This cemetery contains the graves of noted Bostonians, including three generations of the prominent Mather family: Increase Mather (1639-1723), minister and Harvard president; Cotton Mather (1663-1728), churchman and writer; and his son, Rev. Samuel Mather (1706-85). *The Mather plots are located in northeast corner near Charter St. gate.* Also interred here are the remains of hundreds of black Bostonians who settled in the North End in the 18C.

Return to Hanover St. to taste some Italian specialties or simply take in the local color. Note that the red line of the Freedom Trail continues to Charlestown.

★ ③ THE WATERFRONT *3 hrs, not including cruise. Map p 129.* ⓣ *Aquarium.*

During Boston's long period of maritime prosperity, sailing ships brimming with exotic cargoes frequented the busy harbor. To accommodate the port's burgeoning shipping industry, the original harborfront was dramatically transformed in the first half of the 19C via a landfill project that added more than 100 acres. After 1900 Boston's shipping activities sharply declined, precipitating the deterioration of the waterfront area. The construction of two traffic arteries (Atlantic Avenue in the 1860s and the elevated Central Artery in the 1950s) severed the area from the rest of the city.

Long-awaited rehabilitation of this historic area did not begin in earnest until the 1960s. Renovation of several wharf buildings injected new commercial and residential activity, and the 1970s the Quincy Market restoration created a crucial link between downtown and **Christopher Columbus Park** (1976), a popular harborside promenade extending from Commercial Wharf to Long Wharf. A flurry of new residential and hotel complexes in the 1970s and 1980s significantly enhanced the waterfront's cachet while giving new texture to Boston's skyline. The latest addition is the $112 million, 16-story World Trade Center Hotel (1998). From the harbor there is a commanding view of the new 10-story **federal courthouse** (1998). The waterfront's historic link to downtown will at last be reestablished in the 21C when an underground expressway replaces the unsightly Central Artery. To learn more about the massive project, stop by the **Big Dig Visitor Center** located near the New England Aquarium. Exhibits include engineering displays, a scale model and videotapes about what has been called the largest highway construction project in American history.

Sights

★★New England Aquarium – **Kids** *Central Wharf. Open Jul–Labor Day Mon–Fri 9am–6pm (Wed & Thu 8pm), weekends 9am–7pm. Rest of the year Mon–Fri 9am–5pm, weekends 9am–6pm. Closed Thanksgiving Day, Dec 25. $10.50.* ☎ *617-973-5200. www.neaq.org.* This large aquarium, the first of its kind in the nation, displays wonders of the underwater world in simulated natural environments. Interpretive panels, demonstrations and special exhibits help foster understanding of the 600 species of fish, invertebrates, mammals, birds, reptiles and amphibians found around the world. Opened in 1969, the aquarium's original structure, a Brutalist concrete block (Cambridge Seven Assocs.), was greatly expanded and given a much-needed facelift in 1998 by the firm Schwartz/Silver. Fronted by a shimmery new stainless-steel entryway, the recently completed West Wing (the first of a four-phase, $100 million renovation/expansion) features an outdoor seal area and five times more gallery space for special exhibits. A large-format theater and 75,000sq ft of new permanent exhibit space are expected to open in 2000 and 2002 respectively.

Dominating the center of the aquarium is a four-story, cylindrical **ocean tank** containing a re-creation of a Caribbean coral reef. As visitors descend the ramp encircling the 200,000 gallon tank, they can watch sharks, sea turtles, moray eels and the many species of fish that inhabit this glass-enclosed world as well as some 3,000 corals and sponges. In the Edge of the Sea tidepool, youngsters are invited to handle crabs, sea stars and urchins. A glass-enclosed lab permits observation of routine and emergency care of sea creatures. Sea lion shows take place daily aboard the **Discovery**, a vessel berthed next to the aquarium.

② The Barking Crab

Map p 121 Sleeper St. ☎ *617-426-2722.* Look at a map and you can see that Boston nestles right up to the bay. Look for a waterfront eatery, though, and you're likely to end up hungry, unless you know where to go. The city's only rough-and-ready clam shack is a relative newcomer to Boston, but it's already a fixture for its fresh (sometimes live) seafood and authentic atmosphere. The long, rickety wooden building overlooking Fort Point Channel used to be an open-air fish market. Now the interior is festooned with lobster traps, life preservers and buoys, while an adjacent tent *(heated in winter)* is filled with picnic tables to accommodate overflow crowds. And there *are* crowds, especially in summer when the tent flaps are raised for alfresco dining. Favorites include the Lonely Crab (a fresh Dungeness with dipping butter), beer-battered fish and chips, and inventively prepared swordfish and tuna specials—but landlubbers will find plenty to munch on too.

Boston Tea Party Ship and Museum – 🎫 *Map p 121* (**FZ**). *Congress St. Bridge. Open Jun–Aug daily 9am–6pm. Sept–Nov & Mar–May daily 9am–5pm. Closed Thanksgiving Day. $8.* ☎ *617-338-1773. www.historictours.com.* A full-size replica of the brig *Beaver,* one of the original tea ships that was boarded by marauding "Indians" on December 16, 1773, is berthed at the pier on Congress Street. The museum alongside the ship features pictures, documents, a model of 18C Boston and a video *(12min)* that illustrate the Boston Tea Party and events leading to the Revolution.

The Wharves – Constructed in the 1830s, the granite buildings on **Commercial Wharf** and **Lewis Wharf** were renovated in the 1960s into modern harborfront offices and luxury apartments. The original **Long Wharf** (1710) stretched like a monumental avenue from the Custom House Tower some 2,000ft into the harbor to service large craft unable to anchor closer to the shore. Over the centuries its length was halved and its row of shops and warehouses demolished. The low-scale profile of the brick **Marriott Hotel Long Wharf** (**G**) (1982, Cossutta and Assocs.) harmonizes well with the traditional architecture of the waterfront. Occupying a fine site on the wharf's edge, the granite **Custom House Block** (**H**) (1837, Isaiah Rogers) has been converted into a mixed-use commercial and residential complex. Long Wharf is the docking point for boats offering sightseeing cruises of the harbor and its islands, as well as a water shuttle to the Charlestown Navy Yard.

As seen from the harbor, the sprawling multi-use complex (1987, Skidmore, Owings and Merrill) known as **Rowes Wharf** functions as a dramatic waterfront facade for the downtown area. The brick complex, comprising the luxury Boston Harbor Hotel, residences and offices, was designed to harmonize with its surroundings, as evidenced by its three wharf-like extensions and the maximum 15-story height. The monumental entrance arch offers waterfront access and views of the harbor. Note the delightful airport water-shuttle pavilion capped by an attractive dome.

Immediately north and east of Rowes Wharf loom two ensembles—both by eminent contemporary architects—that contrast markedly with the scale and style of the waterfront's traditional architecture: **Harbor Towers** (**J**) (1971, I.M. Pei and Partners), a pair of 40-story concrete blocks, and **International Place** (**K**) (1987, Burgee and Johnson), a 2.6-acre complex dominated by a graceless cylindrical tower.

Cruises – Sightseeing cruises and excursion boats (Provincetown, Nantasket) that depart from the waterfront *(p 124)* are a wonderful way to see the harbor and view the Boston skyline.

Georges Island – *Depart from Long Wharf late May–Labor Day daily 10am–5pm. Mid-Sept–mid-Oct daily 10am–4pm. Round-trip 1hr 30min. Commentary. $7.50.* 🍴 ♿ *Boston Harbor Cruises* ☎ *617-227-4321.* This 28-acre island, inhabited during colonial times and later fortified due to its strategic location, is a public recreation site with picnic areas at the water's edge. Dominating the island is well-preserved Fort Warren, used during the Civil War to incarcerate some 2,000 Confederate military prisoners. Among those held were James Mason and John Slidell, Confederates who figured prominently in the **Trent Affair**. The two had embarked for England aboard the British steamer *Trent* to solicit funds for the Confederate cause. En route, they were taken prisoner by the Union. The Union's disregard for diplomatic convention so incensed Britain that it threatened to join the war on the Confederate side. The Union, however, bent to British demands and released the men.

The fort's observation tower offers **views** of the Boston skyline and the many islands and islets composing the Boston Harbor Islands, which are now a national park. *Free water taxis run from Georges Island to several nearby islands during the summer season.*

Whale-Watching Cruises – Several cruises are available *(p 124).*

★★④ BACK BAY *Map p 138*

Hailed by architectural critic Lewis Mumford as "the outstanding achievement in American urban planning for the 19C," the fashionable Back Bay presents contrasting faces. Its well-preserved historic district of 19C town houses lies in the shadow of a bustling high-rise sector that exemplifies the best and the worst of 20C planning.

Long-term Reclamation – The Back Bay was once an expanse of mud flats submerged at high tide by the Charles River estuary. In the early 19C, construction of a 1.5mi tidal mill dam along present-day Beacon Street disrupted the area's natural drainage, creating acres of foul swampland. By mid-century this threat to public health and the need for additional housing provided the impetus for the most ambitious of Boston's landfill projects. From 1857 to the 1890s, more than 450 acres—contained within the present-day boundaries of the Charles River, the Public Garden, Huntington and Massachusetts Avenues—were reclaimed. For over 30 years, 3,500 carloads of earth a day were dumped into the swamp.

A Grand Plan – Architect Arthur Gilman's master plan called for five east-west axes, the grandest being Commonwealth Avenue, a wide Parisian-style boulevard divided by a central planted mall. To the north, Copley Square functioned as the principal public space and a grand setting for prominent civic institutions. Stately rows of four- and five-story mansions and town houses, punctuated by towering churches, sprung up along the rectilinear streets.

The Back Bay's early residential architecture reflects contemporary French tastes, as evidenced by the omnipresent mansard roof, the controlled building height and a unified streetscape. As construction progressed, architects adopted the period's prevailing revival styles (Gothic, Chateauesque, Richardsonian Romanesque, Italian Renaissance, Georgian), as exemplified in buildings erected after the 1870s in the area west of Dartmouth Street.

The Back Bay's east end near the Public Garden, boasting tony boutiques, watering holes and the area's finest residences, has a decidedly upscale flavor. The Kenmore Square area attracts a mixed crowd of students and young urban dwellers to its funky shops, bookstores and the Tower Records megastore *(360 Newbury St.)*. Art enthusiasts will enjoy gallery hopping along Newbury Street and viewing a show at the Institute of Contemporary Art. The riverfront Esplanade to the north functions as a playground and outdoor entertainment forum.

Large-scale Contrast – South of the fast-paced Boylston Street corridor, the Back Bay takes on a dramatically different appearance. Monumental redevelopment schemes of varying quality, such as the Prudential Center, Copley Place and the Christian Science Center, create a decidedly 20C scale and flavor. Here, buildings of cement and steel offer a striking counterpoint to the low-scale brick universe of the 19C residential streets.

Walking Tour
1/2 day. ⊤ Copley.

★★Copley Square – Named for painter John Singleton Copley, the Back Bay's principal public square showcases some of the city's most celebrated architectural treasures. The former railroad yard was transformed into the Back Bay's civic center in the 1870s and

Trinity Church and Copley Square

135

80s with the construction of Boston's finest 19C public buildings. Today the square's east end is dominated by the contrasting silhouettes of massive Trinity Church and soaring John Hancock Tower. To the south rises the sober limestone facade of posh Copley Plaza Hotel (1912), designed in the Renaissance Revival style by Henry J. Hardenbergh, architect of New York's Plaza Hotel. The handsome 19C facade of the Boston Public Library graces the west side, while the New Old South Church, in the northwest corner, adds exoticism to the ensemble.

★★**Trinity Church** – *Copley Sq. Open year-round daily 8am–6pm. Closed Patriots' Day. Contribution requested.* ☎ *617-536-0944. www.trinitychurchboston.org.* Recognized as the masterpiece of architect Henry H. Richardson, this imposing granite and sandstone pile (1877) initiated the popular style known as Richardsonian Romanesque in America. Richardson studied at the Ecole des Beaux-Arts in Paris, where he was impressed by the power and richness of the Romanesque style. His successful designs for Trinity Church reveal this influence. A massive central tower, inspired by one of the towers of the Old Cathedral in Salamanca, Spain, dominates the church; the west porch, influenced by the church of St.-Trophime in Arles, France, is carved with statues and friezes representing biblical figures.

Richardson chose John La Farge to oversee the decoration inside. The lavishly painted walls, murals, paneled ceilings and small lunettes above the high, tower windows, are among the best works executed by La Farge. Intricately carved scenes depicting the life of Christ and the figures of past preachers adorn the pulpit, dedicated in 1916. The richly decorated chancel, designed in 1938, appears to be illuminated solely by light reflecting from the metal leaf that covers the ceiling.

★★**John Hancock Tower** – *Enter on St. James Ave.* This striking 60-story slab, sheathed in 10,344 units of half-inch thick tempered glass, was designed by I.M. Pei. Since its completion, Hancock Tower (1975) has reigned as New England's tallest skyscraper. The unusual rhomboid shape creates a variety of profiles, depending on one's vantage point. From the opposite side of Boylston Street, the tower appears one dimensional. From other angles it is a gigantic mirror reflecting the sky and its venerable neighbors, notably Trinity Church and the old John Hancock Building (1947), whose pyramidal summit is topped by a functioning weather beacon.

Observatory – *Open Apr–Oct daily 9am–11pm. Rest of the year Mon–Sat 9am–11pm, Sun 9am–6pm. Last ticket sold 1hr before closing. $5.* ⅃ ☎ *617-247-1977. www.observatory@jhancock.com.* From the 60th floor, sweeping **views**★★★ of the city and its environs unfold. Touch screens allow visitors to zoom in and identify landmarks. An insightful commentary on Boston's history is narrated by eminent architectural historian Walter Muir Whitehill, and a topographic map is used to recount the city's exciting Revolutionary times in a presentation titled "Boston 1775" *(16min).*

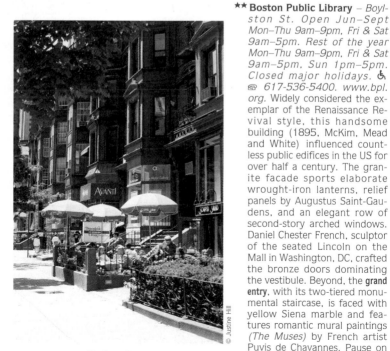
Newbury Street
© Justine Hill

★★ **Boston Public Library** – *Boylston St. Open Jun–Sept Mon–Thu 9am–9pm, Fri & Sat 9am–5pm. Rest of the year Mon–Thu 9am–9pm, Fri & Sat 9am–5pm, Sun 1pm–5pm. Closed major holidays.* ⅃ ☎ *617-536-5400. www.bpl.org.* Widely considered the exemplar of the Renaissance Revival style, this handsome building (1895, McKim, Mead and White) influenced countless public edifices in the US for over half a century. The granite facade sports elaborate wrought-iron lanterns, relief panels by Augustus Saint-Gaudens, and an elegant row of second-story arched windows. Daniel Chester French, sculptor of the seated Lincoln on the Mall in Washington, DC, crafted the bronze doors dominating the vestibule. Beyond, the **grand entry**, with its two-tiered monumental staircase, is faced with yellow Siena marble and features romantic mural paintings *(The Muses)* by French artist Puvis de Chavannes. Pause on the landing to view the peaceful **courtyard** *(accessible from ground floor)*, a popular haven for readers and lunchers. Recently renovated **Bates Hall** *(2nd floor)*, a reading room with a barrel-vaulted ceiling, shelters long oak tables topped with green-glass brass lamps. Visitors may wander through the cavernous rooms on the upper floors to admire murals executed by Edwin Abbey *(Quest of the Holy Grail; delivery room, 2nd floor)* and John Singer Sargent *(Judaism and Christianity; 3rd-floor corridor)* and the library's Joan of Arc collection *(Cheverus Room, 3rd-floor)*.

Fronting Boylston Street, the stark granite addition to the library was designed by renowned architect Philip Johnson as a contemporary complement to the venerable McKim, Mead and White edifice.

Across Boylston Street rises the picturesque **New Old South Church** (1874, Cummings and Sears), replete with a lofty bell tower, a Venetian-style cupola and a profusion of Italian Gothic detailing. The Boston Marathon ends at this church.

Turn right on Exeter St. and right on Newbury St.

★**Newbury Street** – Originally a quiet residential street, Newbury now reigns as the city's most exclusive shopping district. Converted town houses sport glass storefronts showcasing the city's finest boutiques, antique shops, specialty stores and cafes.

The block between Exeter and Dartmouth Streets boasts a cluster of art galleries and a lively street scene, making it one of the Back Bay's most pleasant pockets. Anchoring the corner of Newbury and Exeter, the fortress-like **Exeter Street Theatre Building** (**L**) (1884, Hartwell and W.C. Richardson)—originally the First Spiritualist Temple, later a popular movie house and now a bookstore—clearly shows the influence of H.H. Richardson's nearby Trinity Church. The intersection at Newbury and Dartmouth, engulfed in a steady flow of vehicular and foot traffic, offers numerous visual delights: the former **Boston Arts Club** (**N**) (1881, W. R. Emerson), whose graceful hexagonal corner turret plays off the looming tower and cupola of the adjacent New Old South Church; the former **Hotel Victoria** (1886), with its Moorish window detailing; and a humorous trompe-l'œil **mural** (**3**) crowded with prominent Boston personalities *(wall facing parking lot)*.

Turn left on Dartmouth St. and continue to Commonwealth Ave.

★★**Commonwealth Avenue** – Inspired by the grand boulevards laid out in late-19C Paris under Napoléon III, this 200ft-wide thoroughfare was reputedly the address of choice for Boston's new rich. Today "Comm Ave," as it is known locally, retains much of its former grandeur and still connotes elegant living.

3 Sonsie
327 Newbury St. ☎ *617-351-2500*. High-rent Newbury Street, with its profusion of international design boutiques, sports a number of cafes and outdoor eateries, but none is more popular or more ingeniously versatile than Sonsie. In the morning, white-aproned staff glide between the marble tables and wicker chairs to deliver espressos, cappuccinos and croissants, while lunchtime pastas, grilled sandwiches and brick-oven pizzas provide the fuel needed for the day's shopping splurge. Dinner can be either casual in the cafe, where the floor-to-ceiling window-doors (folded back in summer) provide ample opportunities for people-watching, or more intimate in the restaurant, with its cozy booths, linen tablecloths and artful Mediterranean decor. And in true European style, the well-appointed bar serves everything from *macchiatos* to martinis all day long.

On the southwest corner *(no. 160)* extends the sprawling **Vendome** (1871, W. G. Preston), once the Back Bay's most luxurious hotel and temporary home to such celebrities as Oscar Wilde, Mark Twain, Sarah Bernhardt and Ulysses S. Grant. This Second Empire behemoth, with regrettable upper-story transformations, was converted into condominiums in the 1970s. Facing the Vendome from its corner lot across the mall *(306 Dartmouth St.)*, the outwardly restrained **Ames-Webster Mansion** (1872-82) *(not open to the public)* preserves a lavish reception room considered by many as the Back Bay's most impressive interior space.

Cross to the planted mall and continue east one block.

Commonwealth Avenue's pleasant **mall**, lined with elm trees and punctuated by commemorative statues, offers a good vantage point to view a characteristic sampling of Back Bay houses on either side of the wide avenue.

Just before reaching the next corner, glance to the right for a view of **First Baptist Church**★ (1872), a pivotal work by H.H. Richardson. The **frieze** adorning the upper portion of the bell tower is attributed to Frédéric-Auguste Bartholdi, designer of the Statue of Liberty. Note the trumpeting angels and figures representing the Sacraments, whose faces are reputedly modeled after well-known contemporaries such as Longfellow, Emerson and Hawthorne.

Turn left on Clarendon St. and right on Marlborough St.

Marlborough Street – The most tranquil of the Back Bay's five east-west axes, this generously shaded residential street lined with brick sidewalks and gas lamps exudes a romantic 19C ambience. At the end of the block on the right, note the bold concrete **First and Second Church** (1971, Paul Rudolph), which incorporates the tower and other remnants from the original 19C church that burned in 1968.

Turn left on Berkeley St. and right on Beacon St.

★**Beacon Street** – Favored by Boston's old rich in the 19C, this distinguished thoroughfare is flanked by grand town houses, many converted to colleges and cultural institutions. North-side residences are prized for their views of the Charles River. The **Gibson House**★ *(no. 137)*, built in 1859, has retained its Victorian flavor and offers a rare glimpse into the lifestyle of an affluent Back Bay family. Elaborate woodwork, 15ft ceilings, imported carpets, "leather" wallpaper and scores of curios attest to the family's tastes and financial means *(visit by 1hr guided tour only, May–Oct Wed–Sun 1pm–3pm, on the hour; rest of the year weekends only, 1pm–3pm, on the hour or by appointment; closed major holidays; $5; ☎ 617-267-6338).*

Continue to the corner of Beacon and Arlington Sts.

At this point TV fans will enjoy making a detour to the nearby Bull and Finch Pub *(84 Beacon St.; map p 126)* to glimpse the familiar stone and brick facade popularized in the successful 1980s television series **"Cheers."**

Near the corner of Beacon and Arlington Streets, the Fiedler footbridge leads to the Charles River **Esplanade**★ *(map p 126)*. Landscaped in the early 1930s, this delightful waterfront park extending over 10mi attracts joggers, in-line skaters, cyclists, picnickers and sailing enthusiasts. Outdoor performances given at the **Hatch Memorial Shell** are popular in summertime.

Return to the corner of Beacon and Arlington Sts. Continue on Arlington St.

Arlington Street – This elegant thoroughfare fronting the Public Garden boasts some of the Back Bay's earliest structures, such as the sandstone Second Empire mansion at **no. 12** (1860, Arthur Gilman), where society matron Mrs. Montgomery Sears entertained leading artists of the day. On the other side of Commonwealth Avenue rises the 1981 addition to the venerable Ritz-Carlton Hotel.

Cross to the Public Garden.

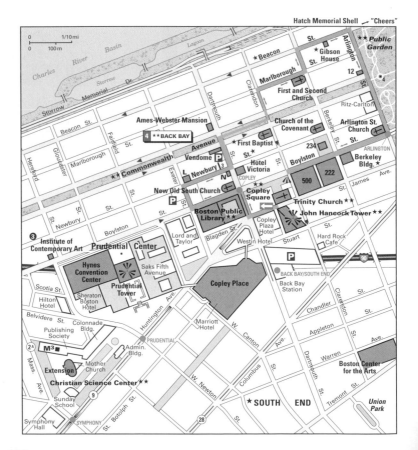

★★Public Garden – *Map p 126*
Entering from the Arlington Street gate, the eye is drawn to the equestrian **statue (4)** of George Washington (1878, Thomas Ball), which extends its gaze along the perfectly aligned Commonwealth Avenue. This 24-acre rectangular park, bounded by a handsome cast-iron fence, was reclaimed from the swampy Back Bay in the 1830s for the purpose of creating a botanical garden. Today the popular retreat charms visitors with its flowering parterres, tree-lined footpaths and commemorative statuary. First

Swan Boats, Boston Public Garden

launched in the 1870s, the beloved **swan boats** ply the tranquil waters of an artificial pond traversed by a whimsical suspension bridge and bordered with weeping willows. The "Make Way for Ducklings" statue grouping in the northeast section re-creates the title characters of Robert McCloskey's classic children's book.

Continue to the corner of Arlington and Boylston Sts.

Standing sentinel over this heavily trafficked intersection is the sandstone **Arlington Street Church** (Arthur Gilman). Begun in 1859, it holds the distinction of being the first building erected in the Back Bay. The church's Unitarian congregation takes pride in its long tradition of social and political activism.

Turn right onto Boylston St.

Boylston Street – Returning to this much-transformed 19C thoroughfare, the visitor is struck by the abrupt change in scale created by the imposing 20C buildings that line its south side. The festive **Berkeley Building★** (1905, Codman and Despredelle), a white terra-cotta and glass extravaganza topped by an obelisk-studded parapet, enlivens the corner lot at no. 420. Across the street at **234 Berkeley Street** stands the French-style stone and brick edifice (1863, W. G. Preston) that originally housed the Museum of Natural History. A glance north toward Newbury Street will reveal the massive Gothic Revival **Church of the Covenant** (1867, Richard M. Upjohn), whose 236ft tower prevails as a familiar landmark.

The block between Berkeley and Clarendon Streets accommodates an oddly matched pair of high rises designed by prominent Postmodern architects: **222 Berkeley Street** (1991, Robert Stern) playfully refers to Boston architectural tradition (note for example the miniature State House dome capping the Boylston Street entrance); the more ostentatious **500 Boylston Street★** (1988, Burgee and Johnson), crowned with an oversize fanlight element and a row of urns, now figures as a prominent element of the Boston skyline.

From the corner of Boylston and Clarendon, pause to admire the striking **view★** of the glass Hancock tower mirroring the fragmented forms of the old Hancock Building and Trinity Church.

Additional Sights in the Back Bay

Copley Place – *Access via the Westin Hotel on southwest corner of Copley Sq.* Occupying an irregularly shaped site between the Back Bay and the South End, this controversial 9.5-acre, $500 million multi-use complex (1984, Architects Collaborative) comprises two luxury hotels (Westin and Marriott), four office buildings, an upscale mall (Neiman-Marcus and 100 shops and restaurants), apartments, a multiscreen cinema and a 1,500-car garage.

Glass-covered pedestrian bridges link the complex to the Prudential Center and to the Westin Hotel, whose undistinguished facade closes the southwest corner of Copley Square.

Prudential Center – *Access from Boylston St.* One of Boston's major urban renewal projects of the 1960s, this 32-acre complex (Luckman and Assocs.), built at a cost of $150 million, has been widely criticized for its uninspired architecture and alienating public spaces. The center was built over the railroad freight yards that long divided the Back Bay from the South End. Clustered around the 52-story **Prudential Tower**, "the Pru" comprises apartment high rises, the Sheraton Boston Hotel, a convention center, shops including major department stores (Lord and Taylor, Saks Fifth Avenue), restaurants and parking facilities. A long-awaited renovation begun in the 1980s has succeeded in infusing new life into the complex: an attractive shopping mall (more than 50 shops and eateries) now connects the various buildings, and the entire complex is linked with the surrounding streets and with the tony Copley Place by means of sleek arcades and bridges. In 1999 construction began on space for some 70 additional shops *(expected completion date 2001)*. The enlarged **Hynes Convention Center** sports a handsome colonnade on its Boylston Street facade.

Skywalk, an observation deck on the 50th floor of the tower, offers good **views** of the surroundings *(access from lower mall; at information desk turn right, then right again to glass doors for tower elevators; open year-round daily 10am–10pm; closed Jul 4, Thanksgiving Day, Dec 25; $4;* ♿ 🅿 ☎ *617-859-0648).*

■ Bookish Boston

Although Cambridge reputedly leads the nation in bookstores per capita, Boston's ranking in the bibliophile department is pretty high as well. **Avenue Victor Hugo Book Shop** *(339 Newbury St.)* and the **Brattle Book Shop** *(9 West St.)* are among the city's best choices for used, rare and antiquarian tomes. Both have floor-to-ceiling shelves and that musty, dust-and-paper smell partic-ular to such dog-eared places. **Trident Booksellers and Cafe** *(338 Newbury St.)* is a small shop focusing on new titles; it maintains a big section of review copies for sale at half price. The **Globe Corner Bookstore** *(500 Boylston St.)* specializes in travel literature and stocks a good selection of maps to many countries. And for readings by some of the world's best-known writers, try the British chain **Waterstone's** *(Quincy Marketplace)* or the venerable **Boston Public Library** *(Boylston St.).*

★★**Christian Science Center** – *From Prudential Center, take Huntington Ave. Exit.* This stunning ensemble houses the world headquarters of the Christian Science Church. The Christian Science religion was founded in 1866 by New Hampshire native Mary Baker Eddy following a serious injury from which she quickly recovered after medi-tating on a Gospel account of one of Jesus' healings. Eddy believed she had discovered the science of man's true relation with God, and that through the practice of Christian Science the individual could learn to overcome the ills that challenge mankind. After extensive study of the Bible, she published *Science and Health with Key to the Scriptures*, the textbook of Christian Science. In 1879 Eddy and her students estab-lished the Church of Christ Scientist, which was reorganized as the First Church of Christ Scientist (The Mother Church) in 1892. The Christian Science Publishing Society was later founded to help carry the religion's word around the globe.

Today weekly public services are held during which passages from the Bible and texts written by Mary Baker Eddy are read. The *Christian Science Monitor*, an international daily newspaper published by the Church of Christ Scientist since 1908, has corre-spondents around the globe and is highly respected for its objective news coverage.

Visit – *Open year-round. Call for hours.* ♿ 🅿 ☎ *617-450-3790. www.tfccs.com.* Facing Massachusetts Avenue the grandiose **Mother Church Extension** (1906) features Renaissance-inspired elements such as the expansive entrance portico and a central dome rising 224ft. The Romanesque-style Mother Church (1894), with its rough granite facade and bell tower, is connected to the rear of the Extension. The inte-rior is adorned with mosaics and stenciled frescoes. Enter the Publishing Society building (1934) to experience the **Mapparium** (**M³**) 🅺, a 30ft walk-through glass-paneled globe that represents the worldwide scope of the church's publishing activities *(open year-round; call for hours;* ☎ *617-450-3790).*

The original complex was expanded in the 1970s by a group of architects led by **I.M. Pei.** The result is an extraordinary urban space infused with an elegant monu-mentality rarely found in 20C urbanism. Three bold concrete structures—the 26-story Administration Building, the porticoed Colonnade Building and the fan-shaped Sunday School—stand like abstract sculptures around an enormous **reflecting pool** (670ft by 100ft). The graceful rolling of the water over the pool's rounded granite edges creates the illusion of boundlessness.

THE MUSEUMS

★★★**Museum of Fine Arts** – *Map p 142* (**EZ**). *465 Huntington Ave.* Ⓣ *Museum. Open year-round Mon–Fri 10am–4:45pm (Wed–Fri 9:45pm), weekends 10am–5:45pm. Closed Thanksgiving Day, Dec 25. $12 ($10 Thu & Fri after 5pm; contribution only Wed after 4pm). Concerts Jun–Aug Wed 7:30pm, rest of the year Sun 3pm; concert information* ☎ *617-369-3770.* ⨯ ♿ 🅿 ☎ *617-267-9300. www.mfa.org.* One of the country's leading museums, the Museum of Fine Arts (MFA) houses a comprehensive collection of some 500,000 holdings organized into nine distinct departments: Art of the Ancient Americas, Africa and Oceania; Asian; Ancient Egyptian, Nubian and Near Eastern; Classical; European Decorative Arts and

Sculpture; American Decorative Arts and Sculpture; Painting; Contemporary Art; and Prints, Drawings and Photographs. Rare collections of works on paper, textiles and costumes, and musical instruments merit one gallery each, while special exhibits, including large, popular traveling shows, are displayed in the newer West Wing and four additional spaces throughout the 540,000sq ft museum. The MFA's strong film department hosts international festivals, world premieres and retrospectives of work by well-known and experimental filmmakers in the Remis Auditorium.

In the 19C Bostonians traveled abroad extensively and returned with art treasures for their private collections. These collections, together with works from the Boston Athenaeum and Harvard University, formed the core of the museum's holdings in its early years. Officially opened in 1876 in Copley Square, the museum's first building proved inadequate by the turn of the century. More spacious quarters were provided with the construction of the present Neoclassical building (1909, Guy Lowell), with its impressive portal, columns and domes, in the Back Bay Fens. The need for expansion brought about the addition of the **West Wing** (1981). Sleek and modern in character, the three-story granite structure designed by I.M. Pei and Partners features a 225ft galleria capped by a barrel-vaulted glass roof. The newer facility houses visitor services and gallery space for 20C art and traveling exhibits. *Throughout the galleries are specially commissioned sculpted seats, designed as functional works of art. Note that they are labeled: "Please be seated." Specific works mentioned below may not be on display, due to the museum's rotation policy. It is advisable to inquire in advance as to their exhibit status.*

★ **Ancient Americas, Africa and Oceania** – The art of ancient America is represented by stunning **goldwork**, including Colombian offering figurines *(tunjos)*, nose ornaments, pendants and a funerary mask from the Calima culture (AD 200-900). A collection of ceramic drinking vessels (AD 600-800) from Guatemala is decorated with bright, intricate designs. The MFA's collection of art from West and Central Africa includes works by 30 cultures south of the Sahara and north of the Kalahari Desert; many pieces are recent acquisitions and date back only to the 19C. Highlights include a wide array of wooden **masks** and dramatically posed **sculptures** used for educational and religious purposes. The art of Oceania is divided into two subgroups: Melanesia (the Pacific islands north of Australia, including Indonesia) and Polynesia (the islands that lie within the triangle bounded by Hawaii, Easter Island and New Zealand). Made of wood, fiber, feathers and shells, the Melanesian masks, totems and figurines on display are vividly painted, but not meant to endure; most are only a century old and are used during religious rites. By contrast, Polynesian art, made with materials such as hardwood, ivory, jade and bone, is more restrained and durable, with some items dating back to the 18C.

★★★ **Asian** – The Japanese and Chinese collections are exceptional. Works gathered by **Edward Morse**, **Ernest Fenollosa** and **Sturgis Bigelow** during their travels across Japan in the late 19C form the core collection. Displays also include selections from the distinguished **Hoyt Collection** of Chinese and Korean ceramics.

Japanese art began to develop in the 6C, when Buddhism arrived in Japan through Korea. Painting was a preferred medium. The MFA boasts fine examples of Japanese painting (13-18C), including rare screens and hand scrolls, such as the renowned *The Burning of the Sanjo Palace* (Heiji Monogatari Emaki), which portrays the violence of the Japanese civil wars. The decorative 17C screen *The Gay Quarters of Kyoto* presents a detailed record of the dress and activities of the times. Buddhism dominated sculpture as well; many of the museum's representations of Buddhas are displayed in a temple setting.

Highlighting the Chinese art section is an extensive collection of ceramics from the Neolithic period to the Qing dynasty (2000 BC-19C AD). Two statues are interesting for their contrasting demeanor: a graceful limestone **Bodhisattva** (6C) and the magnificent polychromed wooden statue of **Kuan Yin** (12C) in a casual pose.

The galleries are also graced by a collection of rare **Korean celadons**; painted screens and statuary depicting the Buddhist mystical traditions of Tibet and Nepal; and outstanding paintings, sculpture and glassware from India and the **Islamic cultures**. Outside, on the museum grounds, the **Japanese Garden** Tenshin-En exemplifies Karesansui-style garden art, in which the placement of large stones, plants and raked pebbles suggests natural scenes and forces.

★★ **Ancient Egyptian, Nubian and Near Eastern** – The bulk of the MFA's superb collection of Egyptian art, spanning 4,000 years of Egyptian civilization, came to the museum as a result of a 40-year MFA/Harvard expedition to Egypt and the Sudan beginning in 1905. Excavations conducted by the expedition at Giza yielded **Old Kingdom** treasures (2778-2360 BC) rivaled only by the Egyptian Museum in Cairo. Among the many pieces of sculpture excavated from the tombs and temples of Dynasty IV is **King Mycerinus** and his queen **Kha-merer-hebty II**, one of the oldest extant statues portraying a couple. Dating from the same period is the realistic portrait bust of **Prince Ankh-haf**. The expedition's digs at El Bersheh and in the Sudan produced treasures from the more recent Dynasty XII: the well-preserved paintings on the coffins of **Prince Djehutynekht and his wife**, the black granite statue of **Lady Sennuwy**, painted wooden servant models designed to serve the dead in eternity, and Meroitic jewelry from Meroë, capital of the former Kushite civilization (Ethiopia).

Treasurers from ancient Nubia (the region that is today southern Egypt and northern Sudan) include boldly painted pottery from the first Nubian Kingdom (3100-2800BC) and intricate jewelry, such as blue faience beaded necklaces and ivory inlay, from the Kerma Kingdom (2000-1500BC). A collection of nearly 80 **Shawabti figures** of King Taharka (690-640BC) and gold amulets, jewelry and finger caps recovered from the tomb of **Queen Mernua** (c.6C BC) are also on display. Two colossal statues of the Nubian kings Aspelta and Anlamani are on view on the second floor.

In the **Ancient Near Eastern** section, note the collection of cylindrical seals that were skillfully carved by Mesopotamian craftsmen.

★★ **Classical Department** – The cameos, coins, bronzes and collection of Greek vases (5C BC) were gathered by **Edward Perry Warren**, curator of the department in the late 19C and early 20C. Under his guidance the department acquired the major portion of its holdings, which include Bronze Age ceramics and Minoan seal stones; a three-sided marble bas-relief from the Greek Isle of Thasos; and the ivory and gold statue of the **Minoan Snake Goddess** (1600-1500 BC).

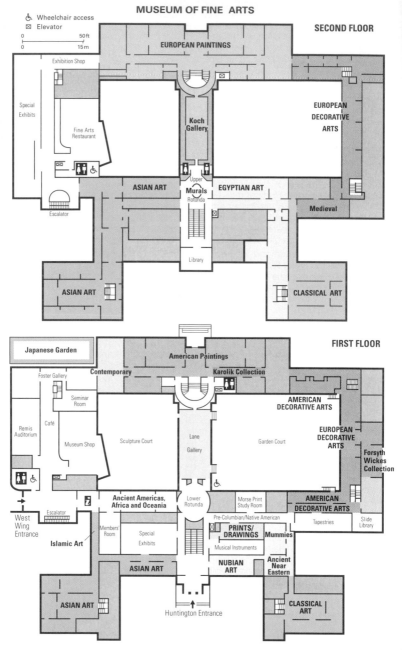

American Decorative Arts – Among the MFA's collection of **American Decorative Arts** is a large and representative group of furniture made by the early American craftsmen of Boston, New York City, Newport and Philadelphia. Many pieces are from the rich **M. and M. Karolik Collection**. The museum's extensive collection of early American silver includes the historic **Liberty Bowl** (1768) made by Paul Revere and dedicated to the members of the Massachusetts legislature who refused to rescind a letter to the colonies protesting against the Crown.

★★ **American Paintings** – The American collection is represented primarily by paintings, furnishings and silver. Portraiture dominated American painting in the 17C, as is illustrated by the portrait *Robert Gibbs*, painted by an unknown artist. Prominent among the 18C portraitists were Gilbert Stuart, whose paintings of George and Martha Washington (the *Athenaeum Portraits*) are exhibited alternately at the National Portrait Gallery in Washington, DC and at the MFA, and John Singleton Copley, who painted wealthy and noted Bostonians of his day *(Samuel Adams* and *Paul Revere)*. In the 19C painters turned their attention to nature, and in particular to the sea. The adventure, excitement and beauty of the sea were portrayed on canvas by Fitz Hugh Lane *(Boston Harbor; Owl's Head, Penobscot Bay, Maine)*, Albert Pinkham Ryder, and Winslow Homer *(Fog Warning; Lookout–"All's Well")*. During the same era John Singer Sargent and Mary Cassatt *(At the Opera)* lived abroad, drawing their inspiration from European movements. Sargent's *The Daughters of Edward Darley Boit* was influenced by *Las Meninas* of Velázquez. Recently restored, Sargent's **murals** of mythological figures, the last decorative works he completed before his death, are on view in the upper rotunda and colonnade.

In the Lane Gallery, works by Arthur Dove, Georgia O'Keeffe *(White Rose with Larkspur No. 2)*, Joseph Stella *(Old Brooklyn Bridge)*, Jackson Pollock, David Hockney, and Color Field artists Morris Louis and Jules Olitski exemplify early to mid-20C art. More recent paintings by **20C artists**, including Picasso and Frida Kahlo, are also on display. Picasso's strong anti-war sentiments are expressed in his bold, vibrantly colored *Rape of the Sabine Women*.

The **Contemporary** gallery features both selections from the museum's permanent collection and traveling exhibits often chosen to complement installations in the adjacent Foster Gallery.

European Decorative Arts – Period rooms, including an English Tudor paneled room (15C), a French Louis XVI salon and the Hamilton Palace Room, fill these galleries. Note the Medieval statues carved from wood and ivory, and the enamels,

The Daughters of Edward Darley Boit (1882) by John Singer Sargent

Courtesy Museum of Fine Arts, Boston

On the first floor, in a special suite of rooms, is the **Forsyth Wickes Collection** of 18C French furnishings, porcelain, paintings, watercolors and sculpture. The graceful red and gold lacquered writing desk was made for Queen Marie Antoinette.

★★ **European Paintings** – Principal European schools from the Middle Ages to the present are represented. A Catalonian chapel with a 12C apse fresco and 15C paintings is interesting for its Romanesque decoration. From the Flemish school note *St. Luke Painting the Virgin* (15C) by Rogier Van der Weyden. Nearby galleries display Tiepolo's *Time Unveiling Truth*, a powerful and symbolic analogy, and portraits by Rembrandt. The lovely **Koch Gallery** holds double-hung, gilt-framed works of the Spanish school, specifically, paintings by Goya, El Greco *(Fray Felix)*, Velázquez and Zurbarán *(Saint Francis)*.

Bostonians' preference for the Romantics (Delacroix), realists (Courbet), the Barbizon school (Corot), Impressionists and Postimpressionists brought a distinguished group of 19C French paintings to the MFA. Among the masters represented are Renoir *(Bal à Bougival)*, Monet *(La Japonaise; Haystacks; Rouen Cathedral)*, Degas *(Carriage at the Races)*, Manet *(Execution of Maximillian; The Street Singer)*, van Gogh *(The Postman Joseph Roulin)* and Cézanne *(Madame Cézanne in a Red Armchair)*. Gauguin's *D'où venons-nous? Que sommes-nous? Où allons-nous?* (Where Do We Come From? What Are We? Where Are We Going?) treats the eternal questions regarding mankind's life and destiny. Millet's sympathetic rendering of the peasant is illustrated in *The Sower* and in his many other works exhibited in the museum.

★★★ **Isabella Stewart Gardner Museum** – *Map p 120* (**EZ**). *280 The Fenway.* Ⓣ *Museum. Open year-round Tue–Sun 11am–5pm. Closed Thanksgiving Day, Dec 25. $9. Guided tours (1hr) available Fri 2:30pm.* ✗ ⅆ ☏ *617-566-1401. www.boston.com/gardner.*

Courtyard, Isabella Stewart Gardner Museum

John Kennard/Isabella Stewart Gardner Museum

Isabella Stewart, born in New York City in 1840, became a Bostonian when she married financier Jack Lowell Gardner. Daring and vivacious, Mrs. Gardner was a free spirit whose actions were often frowned upon by other members of Boston's staid society. Art and music were her lifelong delights, and in 1899 she initiated the construction of **Fenway Court** to house her fabulous art collection, part of which she gathered in Europe, and part of which was acquired in the US by her agents.

The galleries of Fenway Court, permanently arranged by Gardner herself, contain furnishings, textiles, paintings and sculpture from her collections. Nothing has been changed since her death (1924); the galleries, opening onto flower gardens in the courtyard, create an impression of continual summer.

Ground Floor – In the **Spanish Cloister** ceramic tiles from a 17C Mexican church cover the walls, enhancing John Singer Sargent's dramatic painting *El Jaleo*.

The **courtyard**, with its refreshing gardens, Venetian window frames and balconies brimming with fresh flowers, provides a graceful haven in the city. Classical sculptures surround an ancient Roman mosaic pavement (2C) from the town of Livia. In the **small galleries** off the courtyard is an exhibit of 19C and 20C French and American paintings, including portraits by Degas and Manet, and landscapes by Whistler, Matisse and Sargent. The Yellow Room houses *The Terrace of St. Tropez*, the first canvas by Henri Matisse ever to enter an American museum.

Second Floor – The room of **early Italian paintings** contains Simone Martini's altarpiece *Madonna and Child with Four Saints*, two allegorical panels by Pesellino, Fra Angelico's *The Dormition and Assumption of the Virgin* and Gentile Bellini's delicately executed *Turkish Artist*. The fresco of Hercules is the only fresco by Piero della Francesca outside of Italy.

The **Raphael Room** exhibits two of the Italian painter's works: a portrait of Count Tommaso Inghirami and a *pietà*. The *Annunciation* exemplifies the technique of linear perspective developed in the 15C. Other works in the room include Botticelli's *Tragedy of Lucretia* and Giovanni Bellini's *Madonna and Child*.

Adjacent to the Raphael Room, in the **Short Gallery**, is Anders Zorn's spirited painting of Mrs. Gardner at the Palazzo Barbarossa in Venice.

Continue through the Little Salon, decorated with 18C Venetian paneling and 17C tapestries, to the Tapestry Room.

The **Tapestry Room** is the setting for concerts held at Fenway Court. On an easel sits *Santa Engracia* by Bermejo (15C Spain). There are also lovely 16C tapestries.

Rubens' masterful portrayal of Thomas Howard, Earl of Arundel, and works by Hans Holbein and Anthony Van Dyck *(Lady with a Rose)* grace the **Dutch Room**.

Third Floor – From the **Veronese Room**, with its Spanish and Venetian tooled and painted leather wall coverings, enter the **Titian Room**, which contains one of Titian's masterpieces, the sensual *Rape of Europa*, painted for Philip II of Spain. In the **Long Gallery** the life-size terra-cotta statue *Virgin Adoring the Child*, attributed to Matteo Civitale, provides a beautiful example of Renaissance sculpture. On the wall above a large sideboard hangs Botticelli's *Madonna and Child of the Eucharist* (1410, the "Chigi Madonna"), which hung in the Chigi palace in Rome until the 19C. *A Young Lady of Fashion*, formerly attributed to Uccello, is characteristic of portrait art in 15C Florence. The **Gothic Room** contains a full-length portrait (1888) of Mrs. Gardner painted by her friend John Singer Sargent. Nearby is a small panel entitled *The Presentation of the Infant Jesus in the Temple*, which has been attributed to Giotto, the master of the 14C Florentine school.

★★**Children's Museum** – 🧒 *Map p 121* (**FZ M⁴**). *300 Congress St. at Museum Wharf.* Ⓣ *South Station. Open year-round daily 10am–5pm (Fri 9pm). Closed Thanksgiving Day, Dec 25. $7 ($1 Fri after 5pm).* ✕ ♿ ☎ *617-426-8855. www.bostonkids.org.* Conceived exclusively for children (but a delight to adults as well), the museum concentrates on visitor programs, teacher resources and early childhood education. Formerly located in Jamaica Plain, the museum moved to its current location in 1979. Recently (1999), the museum announced plans to expand its waterfront site through the purchase of 60,000sq ft previously occupied by the contiguous Computer Museum, which merged with the Boston Museum of Science *(below)*. The newly acquired space will house a 3,500sq ft Sesame Street exhibit, a new lobby, exhibit halls and additional eating facilities.

The complex contains four floors, three of which house interactive exhibits, many with a decidedly educational or multicultural twist, such as **Teen Tokyo** *(4th floor)*, where visitors can ride a Japanese subway car; the Supermercado *(3rd floor)* stocked with Latin American foods; and a Native American wigwam and storage area *(3rd floor)* containing artifacts of Southern New England tribes. Among other galleries, the second floor features Boats Afloat with water exhibits that invite kids to play with toy boats or pilot harbor vessels; **Science Playground**, where children can experiment with physics; and Johnny's Workbench, filled with tools and materials, ready to be used. Playspace *(3rd floor)* welcomes toddlers and preschoolers. Participatory theater shows and other displays on Boston's ethnic groups round out the mix. There's even a recycle shop, where foam, paper goods, decorative materials and other reusable items can be purchased by the bagful for kids to make their own creations.

★★**Boston Museum of Science** – 🧒 *Map p 121*(**FY**). *Rte. 28.* Ⓣ *Science Park. Open Jul 5–Labor Day daily 9am–7pm (Fri 9pm). Rest of the year daily 9am–5pm (Fri 9pm). Closed Thanksgiving Day & Dec 25. $9.* ✕ ♿ 🅿 ☎ *617-723-2500. www. mos.org.* Located in a modern building (1951) beside the Charles River, the museum invites children and adults to explore the world of science and technology through cutting-edge, hands-on exhibits. Though the museum traces its roots to the 1830 founding of the Boston Society of Natural History, it now embraces all areas of science, including computer technology, under one huge roof. In 1999, the Science Museum and Boston's **Computer Museum** announced plans to merge, resulting in the latter's move to the Science Museum location.

More than 600 interactive exhibits, a planetarium and observatory, and theater with a five-story screen greet visitors to the museum. The kaleidoscopic array of push-button displays and life-size models allows visitors to participate in activities ranging from playing with lightning produced by a Van de Graaff generator to pretending to fly through the cosmos in models of American spacecraft. Visitors can also watch new chicks hatch, hear dinosaurs roar, and peer through the world's largest magnifying glass. The most up-to-date exhibits include a solar race track, visible-music machine, a **mathematics lab** that melds classical thought with modern-day applications and a 90ft **wave tank**. Located near the wave tank, the Computer Museum's first exhibit at the Science Museum is entitled "The Virtual FishTank."

In the first-floor atrium, the **Charles Hayden Planetarium** presents programs that explore the world of stars, galaxies, pulsars, clusters, quasars and other phenomena of outer space. There are usually two or more programs daily, in addition to laser shows *($7.50, but discounted combined admission available; call for schedule).*

Institute of Contemporary of Art – *Map p 138. 955 Boylston St. Ⓣ Hynes/ICA. Open year-round Wed–Sun noon–5pm (Thu 9pm). Closed major holidays and for art installations. $6. ♿ ☎ 617-266-5152.* This Richardsonian building, which once housed a police station, has been renovated into modern gallery space. The institute presents multimedia and site-specific programs year-round that explore the trends and themes in American and international contemporary art. The stark white interior contains two levels of galleries surrounding a central, zigzagging staircase. Introductory videos complementing the exhibits are shown in the ICA theater.

★**John F. Kennedy Library and Museum** – *Map p 151. Columbia Point in Dorchester, near the University of Massachusetts. Ⓣ JFK/ UMass, .5mi from the museum; free shuttle bus available. Open year-round daily 9am–5pm. Closed Jan 1, Thanksgiving Day, Dec 25. $8. ✗ ♿ 🅿 ☎ 617-929-4523. www.cs.umb.edu/ jfklibrary.* This sleek, white concrete and glass structure, a monument to the late President John F. Kennedy, was designed by architect I.M. Pei. The building's neat, sharp lines seem to point across the harbor to the impressive view of the Boston skyline. Approximately one-third of the library building is reserved for the **contemplation pavilion**, a nine-story gray glass pavilion that contains simply an American flag, a bench and quotations from President Kennedy on the wall.

The tour begins with a film *(18min)* on the early life of JFK. In a series of exhibit bays, personal memorabilia and historic videos trace the life and accomplishments of John Kennedy. The archives on the upper floors house thousands of photos, tapes and taped interviews with people who knew him.

Fred Sieb Photography

John F. Kennedy Library

★CHARLESTOWN *Map p 121* (FY)

Located on a hill across the Charles River, Charlestown is easily recognized by its tall stone obelisk, the Bunker Hill Monument. The USS *Constitution* sits in its permanent berth at a wharf in the Navy Yard. Charlestown's colonial dwellings were destroyed by the British during the Battle of Bunker Hill and were replaced following the Revolution by the rows of Federal-style houses that line the streets leading to the monument. A large-scale renovation program begun in the 1980s transformed the Navy Yard into a waterfront complex containing luxury apartments, offices and marinas. *Ferries depart from Boston's Long Wharf to Pier 4 in the Charlestown Navy Yard year-round Mon–Fri 6:30am–8pm, Sat 10am–6pm. $1 (one-way). ♿. Boston Harbor Cruises. ☎ 617-227-4321.*

Bunker Hill Monument – *Open year-round daily 9am–5pm. Closed Jan 1, Thanksgiving Day, Dec 25.* ☎ *617-242-5641. www.thefreedomtrail.org.* This 221ft granite obelisk (1842), designed by Solomon Willard, marks the site of the American redoubt during the Battle of Bunker Hill *(p 117).* The observatory, reached by a 294-step winding stairway, offers a **view★** of Charlestown, Boston and the harbor. Exhibits and a scale model of the 1775 battle are contained in a meetinghouse made of Carrera marble.

Charlestown Navy Yard – Construction in 1800 of the US Naval Shipyard at Charlestown made this city a shipbuilding center. Thirty of the yard's 130 acres, including the site of the USS *Constitution* and its museum, were designated a part of the Boston National Historic Park after the yard was closed in 1974.

Bunker Hill Pavilion – *Visitor center open year-round daily 9am–5pm. Closed Jan 1, Thanksgiving Day, Dec 25.* ⅖ ▣ ☎ *617-242-5601. www.nps.gov/bost.* Information on the Navy Yard, Freedom Trail and Boston National Historic Park is available here. Park rangers conduct free tours of the Navy Yard *(call for schedule).* The historic Battle of Bunker Hill, as seen by an American militiaman and a British soldier, is presented in a multimedia program entitled "Whites of Their Eyes" *(20min, shown continuously).*

④ Warren Tavern

Map p 121. 2 Pleasant St. ☎ *617-241-8142.* With its low timbered ceilings, snug fireplace and long mahogany bar, this tavern may resemble an English pub, but in fact it's just as American as they come—Patriot, that is. Constructed c.1780, the structure was one of the first to be rebuilt after the British torched Charlestown in 1775. Doubling as a Masonic hall, the alehouse was a favorite of Paul Revere (whether the juicy Paul Revere Burger with sautéed mushrooms and Swiss has anything to do with the silversmith's culinary preferences is uncertain). George Washington was known to quaff a few here, too. Today Warren Tavern remains a cozy place for a sandwich or Shepard's Pie (a house specialty), or hot chocolate by the fire, after a long day on the Freedom Trail.

★★**The USS Constitution** – 🄺🄸🄳🅂 *Open year-round daily 9:30am–dusk. Closed Jan 1, Thanksgiving Day, Dec 25.* ▣ ☎ *617-242-5641. www.thefreedomtrail.org.* The USS *Constitution,* the pride of the American fleet, is the oldest commissioned warship afloat. Authorized by Congress in 1794, this 44-gun frigate designed by Joshua Humphreys and Josiah Fox was constructed from timbers provided by states from Georgia to Maine. Within four years after being built, the *Constitution* sailed to the Mediterranean at the head of the American fleet to participate in the Tripolitan War, which ended payments by American ships to the Barbary pirates. Distinguished for the role she played in the war, the *Constitution* nevertheless won her greatest victories during the War of 1812 against the British: capturing the HMS *Guerrière* and the *Java* in 1812, and simultaneously seizing the *Cyane* and the *Levante* three years later. It was during the battle with the *Guerrière,* when enemy fire seemed to bounce off her planking without causing damage, that the *Constitution* was given her nickname "Old Ironsides." By 1830, after having survived 40 military engagements, the *Constitution* was declared unseaworthy and destined for the scrap heap. Oliver Wendell Holmes' poem "Old Ironsides" aroused such strong popular sentiment in favor of the ship that funds were appropriated to rebuild it. Reconstructed in 1905, 1913 and 1973, the ship has retained only 18 percent of her original timbers. A recent $12 million overhaul readied the vessel for sailing on its 200th birthday in July 1997, its first sailing under its own power since 1881.

Berthed a short distance from the USS *Constitution* is the **USS Cassin Young,** a World War II destroyer similar to the type built here in the 1930s and 40s *(visit by 45min guided tour only, mid-Jun–Jul daily 10am–5pm; rest of the year daily 10am–4pm).*

USS Constitution Museum (M⁵) – *Pier 1. Open May–Oct daily 9am–6pm. Rest of the year daily 10am–5pm. Closed Jan 1, Thanksgiving Day, Dec 25.* ⅖ ▣ ☎ *617-426-1812.* Exhibits in the granite building (designed by Alexander Parris) trace the history of Old Ironsides from 1794 to the present.

■ **Sailing Vessels**

Sailing vessels are distinguished by the type of sail and the number of masts they carry. A **sloop** is a one-masted, fore-and-aft-rigged vessel. A **schooner** carries two or more masts; all its sails are fore-and-aft rigged.

BROOKLINE *Map p 150*

The affluent suburb of Brookline was the birthplace of **John Fitzgerald Kennedy** (1917-63), the 35th president of the US. Ever since 1870 Boston has made six attempts, unsuccessfully, to annex Brookline, one of the largest towns in Massachusetts and a pleasant residential community located only 4mi southwest of the center of the city's downtown area.

John Fitzgerald Kennedy National Historic Site – *83 Beals St. Visit by guided tour (45min) only, mid-Mar–Nov Wed–Sun 10am–4:30pm. $2. ☎ 617-566-7937.* Joseph and Rose Kennedy lived in this modest wooden house from 1914 to 1921, a period during which four of their children, including John, were born. The house is restored to its 1917 appearance.

ADDITIONAL SIGHTS

★**South End** – *Map p 138.* Situated literally and figuratively on the other side of the tracks with respect to upscale Back Bay, the long-neglected South End is on its way to becoming one of Boston's most vibrant inner-city neighborhoods. This English-style community of bowfront brick row houses developed between the 1840s and the 1870s in the newly reclaimed area along the "neck" connecting Boston's original peninsula to the mainland. After a short period of popularity, the district fell into decline, and by the end of the century, shabby rooming houses and derelict apartments abounded, inhabited largely by transients and immigrants. In recent decades pockets of the South End have undergone gentrification, attracting businesses and cultural institutions, such as the **Boston Center for the Arts** *(541 Tremont St.)*, housed in the landmark Cyclorama Building (1884). Very much in transition, the South End remains a socially and culturally mixed neighborhood. The vicinity of Tremont and Clarendon Streets best exemplifies the rejuvenation, with its meticulously restored row houses, fashionable restaurants and specialty shops. Intimate **Union Park**, the finest of the South End's remaining oval-shaped residential parks, is bordered by handsome row houses with high stoops sporting fanciful cast-iron and brownstone balustrades.

Chinatown – *Map p 121* (**FZ**). Alive with distinctive dialects, scents and traditions, this small ethnic enclave functions as the cultural and commercial hub for New England's Chinese and Chinese-American communities. Street signs displaying oriental calligraphy, pagoda-roofed telephone booths, markets overflowing with exotic foods, shops stocked with jade and porcelain and tempting eateries enliven this otherwise bleak commercial area wedged between the Theater District, the downtown shopping zone and the Massachusetts Turnpike. Beach Street, Chinatown's main thoroughfare, is spanned by a monumental **gateway** *(at Hudson St.).* Nearby **Tyler Street** boasts numerous popular restaurants serving oriental fare.
The monthlong celebration of the Chinese New Year, beginning in late January or early February, is Chinatown's major annual festival. Chinese residents traditionally hold a colorful parade on the first Sunday of their New Year.

Bay Village – *Map p 121* (**FZ**). This quaint residential enclave, tucked away in the shadow of the Park Square area and the sometimes seedy Theater District, rose on reclaimed mud flats between 1825 and 1840 as a speculative venture. Many of the two-story brick row houses along Church, Melrose and Fayette Streets have been lovingly restored to their 19C appearance.

Franklin Park Zoo – **Kids** *Map p 150. Intersection of Blue Hill Ave. and Columbia Rd. From Boston take Rte. 1 south to Rte. 203, then follow the signs. Open Apr–Sept Mon–Fri 10am–5pm, weekends 10am–6pm. Rest of the year daily 10am–4pm. $6. ✗ ♿ 🅿 ☎ 617-541-5466. www.zoonewengland.com.* Franklin Park is part of Boston's Emerald Necklace of parks. Principal attractions of the zoo include A Bird's World, housing naturalistic bird environments; a free-flight outdoor aviary *(open summer only);* the children's petting zoo, featuring informal demonstrations; and the Range, showcasing antelope, horses and other hoofed animals. The **African Tropical Forest Pavilion★** provides a sensory and educational foray into one of the planet's environmentally threatened areas. The humid climate, dense vegetation and native animal sounds give visitors a taste of life in the rain forest of equatorial Africa.

Arnold Arboretum of Harvard University – *Map p 150. Near the Zoo, at 125 Arborway, Jamaica Plain. Open year-round daily dawn–dusk. Visitor center open year-round Mon–Fri 9am–4pm, weekends noon–4pm; closed major holidays. ♿ ☎ 617-524-1718. www.arboretum.harvard.edu.* This 265-acre arboretum is an outdoor research-educational facility administered by Harvard University and the Department of Parks. Founded in 1872, the arboretum has evolved into a living museum of approximately 7,000 species of ornamental trees and shrubs. It is especially beautiful in May and June when the delicate scents of blooming lilacs, azaleas, rhododendrons and magnolias fill the air.

Suggested walks: Jamaica Plain Gate to pond area *(15min);* pond area to Bonsai House *(10min);* Bonsai House to Bussey Hill *(15min),* where there is a panorama of the arboretum.

EXCURSIONS

★★ **Cambridge** – *See Entry Heading.*

★★ **Lexington** – *11mi northwest of Boston. See Entry Heading.*

★★ **Concord** – *17mi northwest of Boston. See Entry Heading.*

Medford – *Map p 150.* This residential suburb north of Boston is the home of **Tufts University**.

Isaac Royall House – *15 George St. Visit by guided tour (45min) only, May–early Oct Wed–Sun 2pm–5pm. $3. ☏ 781-396-9032. The house has no interior lighting and may be dark on overcast days.* This gracious three-story mansion exemplifies the Georgian architectural style in vogue during the colonial period. The residence was built by wealthy British merchant Isaac Royall Sr., who moved his household (including 27 slaves) here from the West Indies in 1732. When his Loyalist son Isaac Jr. fled to Halifax in the early days of the Revolution, the house was confiscated and served as the headquarters for Gen. John Stark before the 1776 British evacuation. Inside, some of the original 18C woodwork has been preserved. Rooms are appointed with lovely period pieces, including a fine collection of 18C clocks. The two-story slave quarters beside the mansion is reputedly the only structure of its kind remaining in the northern US.

Saugus – *Map p 151.* The buildings of the Saugus Iron Works, which operated in this small town north of Boston in the 17C, were reconstructed in 1954 to appear as they did during the colonial period, when they housed one of New England's earliest industries.

★ **Saugus Iron Works** – *244 Central St. Open Apr–Oct daily 9am–5pm. Nov–Mar 9am–4pm. Closed Jan 1, Thanksgiving Day, Dec 25. ☏ 617-233-0050.* In 1646, encouraged by the government's interest in developing the natural resources of the colonies, John Winthrop Jr., the son of the governor of Massachusetts, established the first ironworks in America at Hammersmith (Saugus). Despite the advanced techniques used and the skill of the workers, the operation was a financial failure, and within 30 years it ceased to function. By this time, however, many workers had been trained, and the Saugus works had provided the impetus for the development of the iron industry in America.

Museum – Artifacts excavated at this site, including items turned out by the early ironworks and a 550lb hammerhead used in the original forge, are on display.

Iron Works House – This dwelling, the only surviving 17C structure on-site, is a good example of early Colonial architecture in America. Casement windows, batten doors, steep gables and the second-story overhang decorated with pendants underscore the Medieval character of this style.

Other buildings include the **furnace**, where the ore was transformed into liquid and cast into bars; the **forge**, with its fires and large waterwheels; the **rolling and slitting mill**, where the iron bars were flattened and cut into nail rods; and the **Iron House**, where iron products were stored before being shipped downriver to Boston or Lynn.

Waltham – *Map p 150.* Located on Boston's peripheral Route 128, this industrial center is a leading producer of electronic equipment.

★ **Gore Place** – *52 Gore St. Grounds open year round daily. Mansion: visit by guided tour (1hr) only, mid-Apr–mid-Nov Tue–Sat 11am–5pm, Sun 1pm–5pm; rest of the year by appointment. Closed major holidays. $5 (mansion). 🅿 ☏ 781-894-2798. www.goreplace.org.* This elegant Federal-style estate, located 9mi west of Boston, was the country residence of US senator and Massachusetts Gov. Christopher Gore (1758-1827). Attributed to French architect J.-G. Legrand, the house features spacious oval-shaped rooms, marble floors and an impressive spiral staircase—all well suited to the lavish entertaining for which the Gores were renowned. The finely proportioned rooms are appointed with distinctive period pieces and portraits by eminent early American artists such as Copley, Stuart and Trumbull.

Brandeis University – *415 South St.* Named for former Supreme Court Justice Louis D. Brandeis, this was the first Jewish-sponsored, nonsectarian university established in the US (1948). A strong commitment to the liberal arts underlies the program of study at Brandeis, where 3,600 students of all faiths are enrolled in 32 undergraduate and 20 graduate programs.

A harmonious, contemporary design unifies the more than 95 modern buildings on the 235-acre campus. The three chapels (Jewish, Protestant and Catholic) designed by **Max Abramowitz** exemplify this influence. The **Rose Art Museum** contains exhibits of contemporary paintings and sculpture, including works by Willem de Kooning, Robert Rauschenberg and Andy Warhol *(open Sept–Jun Tue–Sun 1pm–5pm (Thu 9pm); closed major holidays; ✗ ⛦ ☏ 617-736-3434).* Plays are presented in the **Spingold Theater Arts Center**.

Weston – *15mi west of Boston.* Pleasant, attractively landscaped homes line the streets of this growing Boston suburb.

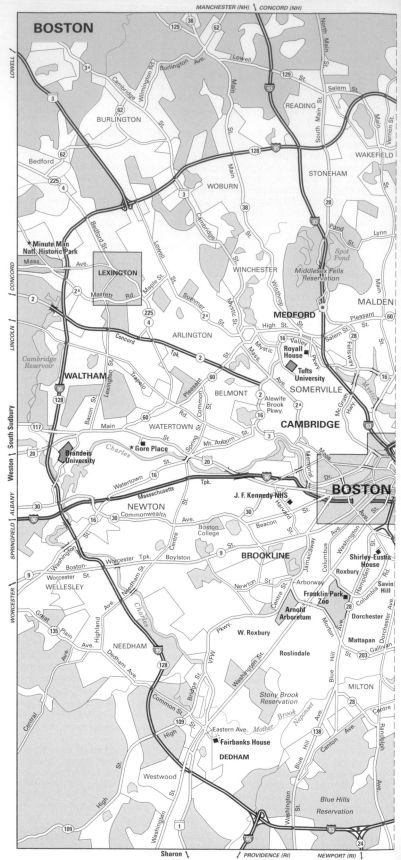

BOSTON

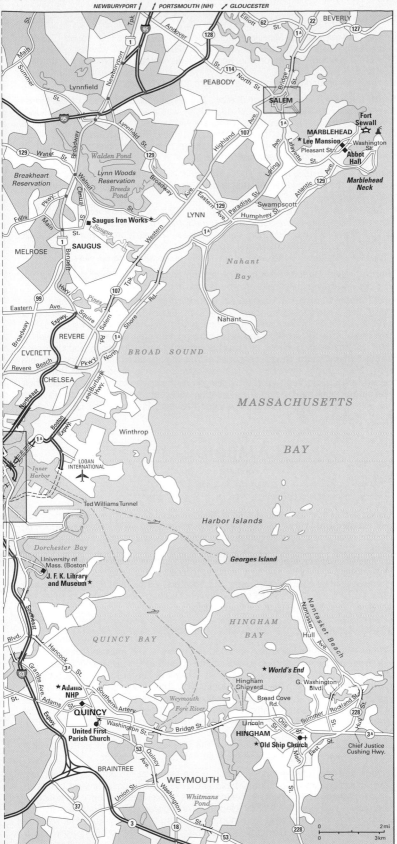

BEVERLY

PEABODY

SALEM

MARBLEHEAD
Lee Mansion
Fort Sewall
Washington St.
Abbot Hall
Marblehead Neck

Lynnfield

Walden Pond

Lynn Woods Reservation
Breeds Pond

Breakheart Reservation

Saugus Iron Works

LYNN

MELROSE

SAUGUS

Swampscott

Nahant Bay

REVERE

EVERETT

CHELSEA

Nahant

BROAD SOUND

MASSACHUSETTS

Winthrop

BAY

LOGAN INTERNATIONAL

Inner Harbor

Ted Williams Tunnel

Harbor Islands

Georges Island

Dorchester Bay

University of Mass. (Boston)

J. F. K. Library and Museum

QUINCY BAY

HINGHAM BAY

Nantasket Beach

Hull

World's End

Hingham Chipyard

G. Washington Blvd.

Adams NHP

QUINCY

United First Parish Church

Broad Cove Rd.

Weymouth Fore River

Lincoln

HINGHAM

Old Ship Church

Chief Justice Cushing Hwy.

BRAINTREE

WEYMOUTH

Whitmans Pond

Cardinal Spellman Philatelic Museum – *235 Wellesley St. Open year-round Thu–Sun noon–5pm. Closed major holidays. $5.* 🅿 ☎ *781-768-8367. www.spellman.org.* This brick building, located on the Regis College campus, is home to the Cardinal Spellman philatelic collection and other famous collections, including four million stamps from around the world. The museum library contains over 40,000 volumes.

South Sudbury – *21mi west of Boston.* The **Wayside Inn** *(20mi west of Boston on the Old Post Rd.–Rte. 20;* ☎ *508-443-1776)* was made famous by Longfellow's *Tales of a Wayside Inn.* Overnight guests are welcome at the inn, which also serves meals and allows visitors to tour the rooms, including the Longfellow Parlor, where the clock, etched panes of glass and other memorable objects described in Longfellow's poems have been preserved.

Dedham – *Map p 150.* In April 1920, this quiet community became known nationwide when the controversial murder trial of Nicola Sacco and Bartolomeo Vanzetti took place here.

Fairbanks House – *511 East St. at Eastern Ave. Visit by guided tour (50min) only, May–Oct, Tue–Sat 10am–5pm, Sun 1pm–5pm. Closed major holidays. $5.* 🅿 ☎ *781-326-1170. www.dedham.com/fairbanks.* This early wooden dwelling, built in 1636, was enlarged on several occasions as the owner's family and fortune increased. Furniture, textiles and other family possessions are on view.

Sharon – *18mi south of Boston.* This pleasing community is one of the more than 90 cities and towns that make up the Boston metropolitan area.

Kendall Whaling Museum – *27 Everett St. 1mi north of the village center. Open year-round Tue–Sat 10am–5pm, Sun 1pm–5pm. Closed major holidays. $4.* ⓖ 🅿 ☎ *781-784-5642. www.kwm.org.* Although this museum is small, its fascinating collection of artwork, artifacts and other whaling memorabilia makes the trip worthwhile. International in flavor, it displays British, Dutch, American and Japanese **paintings★** that illustrate several centuries of whaling, including the "factory ship" era of the 20C. Equally impressive is the extensive collection of **scrimshaw★**, especially the scrimshaw violin. In addition to whaling implements and tools, ship models, Inuit whaling gear and the museum's seal-hunting collection, small craft are on view: an Inuit kayak, and a whaleboat used aboard the *John R. Manta* (the last American sailing whaler).

CAMBRIDGE★★

Population 95,802
Map of Principal Sights
Tourist Office ☎ 617-441-2884

Located on the Charles River across from Boston, Cambridge is the world-renowned home of Harvard University and the Massachusetts Institute of Technology (MIT). The city consists of a maze of university buildings, commercial streets and residential neighborhoods.

Massachusetts Avenue, the state's longest thoroughfare, extends the length of Cambridge from Harvard Bridge, past MIT and through the city's center, **Harvard Square**, with its lively coffeehouses, restaurants and theaters. Between Harvard Square and the common lie quiet streets lined with colonial dwellings. **Memorial Drive** borders the Charles River, affording views of central Boston.

Historical Notes

From New Towne to Cambridge – In 1630 New Towne, the small settlement across the river from Boston, was chosen as the capital of the Bay Colony. Fortifications were built to protect the town, and six years later, when the Puritans voted to establish a college to train young men for the ministry, New Towne was selected as the site. Leaders of the Bay Colony agreed to give the college a sum of money equal to the total colony tax. In 1638, recognizing the close bond between the college and the colony, they changed the name of New Towne to Cambridge, after the English university town.

The school was called Harvard, in honor of the Charlestown pastor **John Harvard**, who died later that year, leaving half his estate and library to the college.

Cambridge and the Revolution – Following the events at Lexington and Concord, the patriots established their military headquarters in Cambridge. Harvard buildings and private homes, abandoned by fleeing Tories, were transformed into hospitals and barracks. On July 3, 1775, George Washington took command of the Continental Army on Cambridge Common, and during the months that followed, he lived in the Vassal House (Longfellow National Historic Site) on Tory Row (now Brattle Street).

Charles River and Harvard University

City of the Future – The development of modern technologies by Harvard and MIT have made the city a vital research center. The majority of the seminal research on computer processing was carried out by international scientists working in Cambridge. Since World War II, research and development industries have flourished in Cambridge and have played a key role in the growth of the industrial parks on Route 128.

■ Literary Cambridge

Cambridge developed as a publishing center in the 17C, when the first printing press in the colonies was established here by the widow of an English pastor and her assistants, the Daye brothers. A Bible in an Indian language, an almanac and the *Bay Psalm Book* were among the first works printed.

As the seat of Harvard College, Cambridge became the home of many leading educators and scholars of the day. By the mid-19C the city had developed into a center of progressive thought, attracting a circle of prominent writers, reformers and intellectuals to live, study or teach in Cambridge. Among the more famous figures associated with Cambridge are Henry Wadsworth Longfellow, Oliver Wendell Holmes, Margaret Fuller and Dorothea Dix.

★★★HARVARD UNIVERSITY *1 day. Map p 155.* Ⓣ *Harvard.*

Harvard College – The first college established in America, Harvard has been one of the nation's most prominent educational institutions since it was founded in 1636 to train young men for the leadership of church, state and trade. Its enrollment grew from 12 students to its current total of over 18,000 degree candidates. The school's affiliation with Congregationalism declined as new and more liberal programs and policies were adopted; its affiliation with the Commonwealth of Massachusetts ended in 1865, when Harvard became a private institution.

Harvard University – Harvard developed as a modern university in the 19C, as professional schools were added to the original college: Medicine (1782), Divinity (1816), Law (1817), School of Dental Medicine (1867) and Arts and Sciences (1872). Renowned teachers such as **James Russell Lowell, William James, Louis Agassiz** and **Henry Wadsworth Longfellow** introduced new fields of study into the curriculum. Harvard continued to expand in the early 20C as new laboratories, lecture halls, museums and libraries were built.

Harvard's superior academic traditions, extensive course offerings, distinguished faculty and devotion to research have made it one of the world's leading institutions of higher learning. The university library houses more than 12 million volumes, and the Fogg Art Museum is a world-class university art museum.

① Leavitt and Peirce

1316 Massachusetts Ave.
☎ *617-547-0576.* While
not as old as the university
that stands across the
street, this venerable
tobacconist facing Harvard
Yard earned the sobriquet
"the *other* college in the
square" for its 114-year
tradition of quality,
selection and service.
Legendary puffers Winston
Churchill and Franklin
Delano Roosevelt have both
graced the establishment,
which still has the tweedy,
sweetly pungent aura of a
19C men's club. Though
L&P now purveys Harvard
memorabilia and men's
accessories as well as
games, tobacco remains the
specialty, with dozens of
imported and domestic
cigarette and cigar brands
to choose from. And if you
really like the place, for the
princely sum of $2, you can
stick around all day and
play chess on the second-
floor balcony overlooking
the merchandise.

Harvard is closely associated with research facilities such as the Astrophysical
Observatory of the Smithsonian Institution and engages scholars to study and
resolve global problems relating to government, health and education.

Harvard's $6 billion endowment, the
largest of any university in the world, is
shared by the undergraduate college and
10 graduate schools: Divinity, Law, Dental
Medicine, Medical, Arts and Sciences, Business Administration, Education, Public
Health, Design, and the John F. Kennedy
School of Government. As a member of the
Ivy League, a group of prestigious East Coast
universities that also includes Yale, Dartmouth, Brown and Princeton, Harvard
does not award athletic scholarships or
academic credit for physical education
courses, but it does sponsor 40 varsity athletic teams. The university's rowing crews,
practicing on the Charles River, are a familiar sight to local residents.

Harvard Men and Harvard Women –
Some 6,600 undergraduate students attend Harvard. Women were first admitted
to the Harvard community in 1879, when
Radcliffe College was founded to provide
women with equal access to a Harvard education. Today, Harvard's undergraduate
program is completely coeducational. Students live in one of thirteen Harvard
Houses, often lovely Georgian-style buildings that surround courtyards.

The Campus

Harvard is a city within a city with 500 buildings, including more than 100 libraries,
nine museums and dozens of laboratories on 380 acres of land, primarily in
Cambridge. A variety of architectural works, from Colonial residences to public
buildings by prominent 20C figures such as Gropius (Harkness Commons and the
Graduate Center, 1950 *map p 155* (**L**)), Le Corbusier (Carpenter Center of Visual
Arts) and James Stirling (Sackler Museum), reflect Harvard's role as a cultural hub.
Begin at Harvard Information Center in Holyoke Center.

★★ **Harvard Yard** – From Massachusetts Avenue, note the **Wadsworth House** (**A**), a clapboard dwelling (1726) that was the residence of Harvard presidents until 1849.
The Yard is the oldest part of the university. Administration buildings, dormitories
and Holden Chapel, Harvard's first official chapel, are located here. To the left is

Massachusetts Hall, Harvard University

Harvard University

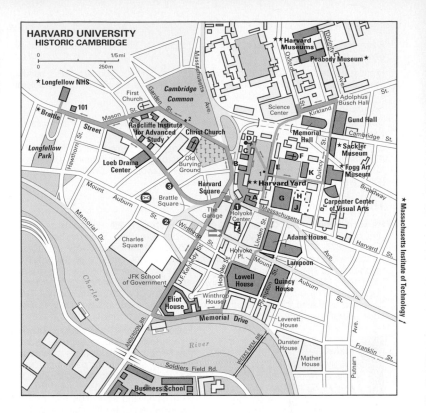

HARVARD UNIVERSITY
HISTORIC CAMBRIDGE

Massachusetts Hall (B) (1720), the oldest Harvard building still standing; across from it sits **Harvard Hall (C)** (1766). Beyond Harvard Hall is **Holden Chapel (D)**, ornamented with the blue and white Holden coat of arms. **University Hall (E)** (1815), a granite building designed by Charles Bulfinch, occupies the other side of the Yard. Daniel Chester French's **statue of John Harvard (1)** stands in front of University Hall. Because of the plaque on the statue that reads "John Harvard, founder 1638," the statue is known as the "statue of the three lies": the college was founded in 1636, John Harvard was the school's benefactor, not its founder, and the figure portrays a student who attended Harvard in 1882.

To the rear of University Hall stands **Memorial Church (F)**, dedicated to Harvard men killed in the world wars. Opposite rises the **Widener Memorial Library (G)**, with its imposing stairway. Inside, visitors can admire the Renaissance-style octagonal rotunda. Named for Harry Widener, a former Harvard student who lost his life in the *Titanic* tragedy, Widener Memorial is the largest university library in the world. Nearby is the modern **Pusey Library (H)**, where the Harvard University archives are stored; the **Houghton Library (J)** possesses Harvard's rare books and manuscripts.

*Pass in front of the Romanesque facade of **Sever Hall (K)**, the work of H.H. Richardson, and leave the Yard. Turn left onto Quincy St.*

The concrete and glass **Carpenter Center of Visual Arts** (1963), the only structure in North America designed by modern architecture pioneer Le Corbusier, features a dramatic entrance ramp and his signature sun screens; nearby is the **Fogg Art Museum**, and just beyond is the **Sackler Museum**, a contemporary L-shaped orange brick structure. Continue on to **Gund Hall** (the Graduate School of Design) with its modernistic glass-enclosed stairway. Across the way, **Memorial Hall**, a massive Victorian building topped with a square tower and pyramidal roofs, houses the Sanders Theater.

Turn left onto Kirkland St. Pass Adolphus Busch Hall, then the striking Science Center, completed in 1973 by Jackson, Sert and Assocs. Cross the Yard.

The Harvard Houses

Many Harvard students live in the elegant Georgian residences found between the Charles River and Massachusetts Avenue: **Adams House**, **Quincy House** and **Lowell House**. These houses, most of which are brick, share a similar design and have broad grassy courtyards, providing a small-college atmosphere to the sprawling university community. During the warmer months, students use the yards to prepare for class, study for exams or toss a Frisbee.

From Massachusetts Ave. turn right onto Linden St. You will pass Adams House. Cross Mt. Auburn St.

From the intersection of Linden and Mt. Auburn Streets, you can see a building that resembles a Flemish castle. This structure houses the offices of the **Lampoon**, a satirical magazine published by Harvard students.

Continue on Holyoke Pl.

Opposite rises the blue cupola of **Lowell House***; for a glimpse of the elegance that typifies the Harvard Houses, glance into its yard.*

Continue on Holyoke St., then cross the yard opposite. Turn right on Memorial Dr. The buildings of the **Business School***, on the Boston side of the Charles River, come into view. To reach Harvard Square, follow J.F. Kennedy St. On the way pass* **Eliot House** *and the "Garage," a complex of boutiques.*

The Museums *Map p 155*

★★ **Harvard Museums of Cultural and Natural History** – 🔲 *Entrances on Divinity Ave. and 26 Oxford St. Open year-round Mon–Sat 9am–5pm, Sun 1pm–5pm. Closed Jan 1, Jul 4, Thanksgiving Day, Dec 25. $5. ⅙ ☎ 617-495-3045. www.hmnh. harvard.edu.* Grouped under one roof, these four museums serve as the repository for the myriad specimens and artifacts that make up Harvard's outstanding research collections. Many of the galleries, dimly lit and packed with simple glass-and-wood display cases, have retained the old-fashioned charm of a 19C exhibition hall. Don't be fooled by the no-frills presentation; the collections merit an attentive visit. *Begin your visit of the Peabody Museum at the Divinity Ave. entrance.*

2 Rialto

On the 2nd floor of the Charles Hotel, 1 Bennett St. ☎ 617-661-5050. Consistently ranked among the Boston area's hottest restaurants, Rialto serves up epicurean elegance in a slick, snazzy decor. Cozy banquettes line the walls of the popular cocktail lounge, while around the corner in the dining room, striped lampshades and two-toned wood floors complement Deco-style glass partitions and mirrored windows. The food, prepared by an award-winning chef, derives its inspiration from southern Europe, but its style is part of the Boston gourmet *zeitgeist*: expect savory seafood dishes, pastas and game prepared with seasonal vegetables and plated with the precision of an artist. Leave room for a luscious, made-to-order dessert.

★ **Peabody Museum of Archaeology and Ethnology** – Founded in 1866 by George Peabody, this large museum displays objects and works of art brought back from early-20C Harvard-sponsored expeditions. The ground floor contains a delightful museum shop and an exhibit that explores the evolution of North American cultures to the present day. The third-floor exhibit, containing original artifacts and plaster casts of pre-Columbian monuments, interprets Latin America's archaeological heritage and the impact of European contact. The Victorian-style **Oceania** exhibit *(4th floor)* reveals a variety of exquisitely crafted artifacts from the Pacific Rim. *The other museums are accessible from the third-floor gallery.*

Mineralogical and Geological Museum – Among the numerous minerals, gemstones and meteorites featured in the three galleries, do not miss the eye-catching giant gypsum crystals from Mexico.

Botanical Museum – The world-renowned collection of **Blashka Glass Flowers**★★ occupies the museum's two galleries. Crafted in Germany by Leopold and Rudolph Blashka between 1886 and 1936, the nearly 3,000 hand-blown glass models accurately represent some 830 species of flowering plants and are prized for their scientific and aesthetic value.

Museum of Comparative Zoology – Some of the rare finds on view in the fossil collections are the 25,000-year-old Harvard mastodon, unearthed in New Jersey; a *Paleosaurus*, one of the oldest fossil dinosaurs (180 million years old); and a *Kronosaurus* (120 million years old), perhaps the largest marine reptile to have ever lived. In the adjacent galleries, scores of large glass cases enclose specimens of animals from around the globe. Note in particular the impressive North American bird collection representing 650 species.

★ **Fogg Art Museum** – *32 Quincy St. Open year-round Mon–Sat 10am–5pm, Sun 1pm–5pm. Closed major holidays. $5 (includes admission to Sackler Museum). ⅙ ☎ 617-495-9400. www.artmuseums.harvard.edu.* On entering the museum, take a moment to admire the Italian Renaissance-style courtyard. Exhibits on two levels surrounding the courtyard span all periods of Western art from the Middle Ages to the present and include notable examples of **Italian Renaissance** painting,

Impressionist and Postimpressionist painting and sculpture, and classical art. A compelling interactive exhibit on the dating and restoration of Ancient Art can be found in the Italian Renaissance gallery.

A corridor on the second floor leads to the contiguous **Busch-Reisinger Museum★**, specializing in the art of 20C German-speaking Europe. Its renowned collection, displayed on a rotating basis in six galleries, boasts works by Expressionists such as Max Beckmann and members of the Die Brücke and Der Blaue Reiter (Kandinsky, Klee, Feininger) groups. Another gallery is reserved for temporary exhibits.

★Sackler Museum – *485 Broadway. Same hours as Fogg Museum.* ♿ ☎ *617-495-9400.* A dramatic Postmodern building designed by James Stirling (1985) houses this companion museum to the Fogg. The Sackler focuses on Ancient, Near Eastern and Far Eastern Art. Asian ceramics, sculpture, Japanese prints and a noteworthy group of Chinese **bronzes** and **jades** highlight the collection. In addition, temporary exhibits on a variety of subjects are presented in the ground-floor galleries.

★HISTORIC CAMBRIDGE *2hrs. Map p 155.*

Cambridge Common – The common was the town center for more than 300 years and was the site of General Washington's main camp from 1775 to 1776. According to tradition, Washington took command of the Continental Army under the "Washington Elm" that grew on Cambridge Common until the 1920s. A plaque (**2**) and scion of the elm mark the spot where the tree once stood on the Garden Street side of the green.

Christ Church – *Zero Garden St. Open year-round daily 7:30am–6pm (Sat 3pm).* ♿ ☎ *617-876-0200. www.cccambridge.org.* The oldest church in Cambridge, this gray wooden structure, designed in 1760 by Peter Harrison, is notable for its lovely Georgian interior. Abandoned at the beginning of the Revolution, the church was later used as barracks for American troops.

Radcliffe Institute for Advanced Study (formerly Radcliffe College) – Named for Ann Radcliffe, a Harvard benefactress, Radcliffe College was chartered in 1894 to provide women access to a Harvard education. In 1943 co-instruction began and, beginning in 1963, Harvard degrees bore the seals of both institutions. The admissions offices of both Harvard and Radcliffe were joined in 1975, quotas for women were abolished and equal admission standards were established for women and men. However, in 1999 Harvard and Radcliffe announced plans to merge and thereby create a center for advanced scholarship (primarily women and gender studies), open to men and women.

In the **Radcliffe Yard** there are several buildings to note. The Federal-style **Fay House** is the first structure acquired by Radcliffe; the **gymnasium** now houses the Murray Research Center and the Rieman Center for Performing Arts. Part of the original yard, the **Agassiz House** contains a theater where playwrights Eugene O'Neill and David Mamet premiered their early works. A building at the far end of the Yard houses the **Schlesinger Library**, the most extensive library of women's studies in the country.

Before exiting the Yard and turning onto Mason Street, observe the First Church (19C) surmounted by a gilded cock weather vane made in the 17C by Deacon Shem Drowne, the artisan who crafted the grasshopper atop Faneuil Hall in Boston.

★Brattle Street – Loyalists to the British Crown, wealthy Tories built homes here in the 18C, thus the street's former name, Tory Row. The stately residences now lining Brattle Street date primarily from the 19C. Note **no. 101** (Hastings House) and **nos. 113** and **115** (these two structures belonged to Longfellow's daughters).

★Longfellow National Historic Site – *105 Brattle St. Closed for renovation until fall 2000. Otherwise call for hours.* ☎ *617-876-4491. www.nps.gov/long.* This Georgian dwelling, built in 1759 by the Loyalist John Vassall, served as the headquarters of General Washington during the siege of Boston. In the 19C **Henry**

3 Hi-Rise Pie Co.

56 Brattle St. ☎ *617-492-3003.* Tucked back from the street, in the canary-yellow 1808 Dexter Pratt House (the former abode of the village blacksmith immortalized by Longfellow) stands a humble cafe that sells some of the best baked goods in Harvard Square. Piled up next to the front counter is a cornucopia of brownies, cookies, scones and brioches (if you arrive early enough), as well as a selection of breads (brown, semolina, corn, country) baked daily at the main bakery/cafe on Concord Avenue in West Cambridge. For lunch there's a creative assortment of deli sandwiches (all on fresh bread), quiche and hearty soups. Eat upstairs in the simple but light-filled rooms or take a picnic to go. The small plaza in front is a fine place to eat on sunny day.

157

Wadsworth Longfellow lived in the house between 1837 and 1882, the period during which he wrote *Evangeline* (1847) and *The Song of Hiawatha* (1855). Today the house contains many of the Longfellows' original furnishings, including 10,000 books, artworks by such noted painters as Gilbert Stuart and Albert Bierstadt and, in the poet's study, a chair crafted from the wood of the "spreading chestnut tree," made famous by Longfellows' *The Village Blacksmith*. A small garden graces the rear of the house.

Opposite the house, **Longfellow Park** extends toward the river.

Returning to Harvard Square by Brattle Street, you will pass in front of the **Loeb Drama Center** *(no. 64)*, Harvard's modern theater, where the American Repertory Theatre performs both classical and contemporary plays.

★MASSACHUSETTS INSTITUTE OF TECHNOLOGY
Map p 120. Ⓣ *Kendall Center/MIT.*

One of the nation's premier science and research universities, Massachusetts Institute of Technology (MIT), overlooking the Charles River, spreads out on either side of Massachusetts Avenue. Inviting green spaces, broad concrete plazas and vast recreational fields interweave with a variety of architecturally styled buildings—from Neoclassical to Postmodern—testifying to the school's evolution and longevity.

Founded during the 19C in Boston's Copley Square, MIT was at first known as Boston Tech. By 1916 the school had outgrown its Copley Square site, and it was moved to its new location in Cambridge, accompanied by three days of parades, speeches and celebrations.

■ Cambridge's Bookstores

Following its bookish namesake in England, Cambridge allegedly has more bookstores per capita than any other American city. Fueled by 200,000 college students in the Boston area, these shops, for the most part, purvey a wide range of high-brow offerings, stay open late, sponsor lectures and readings and encourage browsing. In the Harvard Square area, **Harvard Book Store** *(1265 Massachusetts Ave.)* and **Wordsworth Books** *(30 Brattle St.)* are considered the best of the big independent bookstores. Harvard has a small selection of used books in the basement. Founded in 1927, **Grolier Poetry Bookstore** *(6 Plympton St.)* is one of only two stores in the US devoted singularly to poetry. Its 404sq ft display space is mostly vertical. **Schoenhof's Foreign Books** *(76-A Mt. Auburn St.)*, a linguist's mainstay since 1856, has 56,000 titles representing more than 400 languages and dialects, while the **Globe Corner Bookstore** *(28 Church St.)* specializes in travel literature and maps to many countries.

The school was established as the Massachusetts Institute of Technology in 1861 by **William Barton Rogers**, a natural scientist who stressed the practical application of knowledge as the institute's principal goal. Guided through its early years by Rogers, MIT continued to pursue its original objective in the 20C and is today a leader in modern research and development, with schools of Engineering, Science, Architecture and Planning, Management, and Humanities and Social Science. The international character of the institute is reflected in its enrollment of some 9,700 students from 50 states and 101 foreign countries, who benefit from MIT's sophisticated teaching methods and modern equipment. Scientific works published by MIT are disseminated to centers of learning and cities around the world.

East Campus – *To the right of Massachusetts Ave., arriving from Harvard Bridge.* The Neoclassical buildings along Massachusetts Avenue were designed by Welles Bosworth as part of the institute's new campus in 1916. A low dome tops the **Rogers Building** *(no. 77)*, where a visitor center stocks free maps of the campus. On the lower level a variety of ship models from the **Hart Nautical Collections**, part of the MIT Museum, can be seen *(open year-round daily 9am–8pm; & ⊛ 617-253-5942; www.mit.edu/museum)*. Contemporary art is displayed in the **List Visual Arts Center** on the main floor of the Wiesner Building, a Postmodern structure by MIT graduate I.M. Pei. The three galleries hold temporary exhibits curated with an eye toward aesthetic experimentation and political engagement *(open Oct–Jun Tue–Sun noon–6pm, Fri noon–8pm; closed major holidays; $5 contribution suggested; & ⊛ 617-253-4680. web.mit.edu/lvac/www)*. Between the Hayden Memorial Library and the Earth Sciences Center looms Alexander Calder's stabile *La Grande Voile (The Big Sail)*. Nearby stands *Transparent Horizon*, a black steel sculpture by Louise Nevelson.

Farther north on Massachusetts Ave. *(no. 265)*, the main gallery of **MIT Museum**★ **Kids** is a fun-house of eye-catching, mind-boggling art. Defying the truism that art and science don't mix, permanent exhibits include an array of stop-motion photographs, mobiles based on geometric principles, kinetic sculptures and reputedly the world's largest collection of **holograms** *(a Viewer's Guide to Holograms is available at the admissions desk). Open year-round Tue–Fri 10am– 5pm, weekends noon–5pm. Closed major holidays. $5.* & ☎ *617-253-4444. web. mit.edu/museum.*

West Campus – *To the left of Massachusetts Ave., arriving from Harvard Bridge.* The smooth-surfaced, modern Student Center houses the Tech **Coop**, the student union and restaurants. **Kresge Auditorium**★ and the **MIT Chapel**★ were designed by **Eero Saarinen** in 1956. Note the auditorium's triangular shell roof, which rests essentially on three points. The interfaith chapel, a cylindrical brick structure, is topped with an aluminum sculpture by Theodore Roszak. Inside the chapel, light enters from above, illuminating the mobile over the altar. Water in the moat casts reflections on the interior walls, creating a continual play of light and shadows. Also noteworthy is **Baker House**, a dormitory designed in 1947 by Finnish architect Alvar Aalto.

CAPE ANN★★

Map of Principal Sights
Tourist Office ☎ 978-283-1601

Salty sea air, exhilarating and clear, pervades the fishing villages, coastal estates and harbors of this rocky island north of Boston. A 32mi road (Routes 127 and 127A) rings the periphery of the island and offers stunning views of the beaches, cliffs and towns that make Cape Ann a summertime vacation mecca.

Historical Notes – The cape was explored in 1604 by Samuel de Champlain, then in 1614 by Capt. John Smith, who mapped and named the area in honor of Queen Anne, wife of James I of England. A small colony was established in 1623 at Gloucester by a group of Englishmen who had come "to praise God and catch fish." Their descendants were the generations of cape-born sailors who have made the region one of the world's largest fishing centers.

Bostonians frequent Cape Ann, seeking out its maritime atmosphere, art galleries and fine seafood restaurants. Browsing in the shops and enjoying the area's ruggedly beautiful scenery are among the popular pastimes. **Whale-watching cruises** *(p 312)* offer visitors the opportunity to observe these great mammals in their summer feeding grounds just off the coast. Camera buffs delight in the magnificent natural light, which strikes the rocky shores and transforms the landscape into a changing spectrum of color and shadows throughout the day.

★★DRIVING TOUR *1/2 day. 32mi. Map p 160.*

The itinerary follows Routes 127 and 127A around Cape Ann, passing through quaint fishing villages and offering views of the coast and the ocean.

Magnolia – This former fishing village developed into a summer resort in the 19C. Many of Magnolia's large, comfortable dwellings, built as vacation homes during that era, are now year-round residences. Shore Road follows the coast, presenting views of the modest harbor and, in the distance, the Boston skyline.

From Shore Rd. turn left onto Lexington Ave., then right onto Norman Ave., which becomes Hesperus Ave.

Hammond Castle Museum – **Kids** *80 Hesperus Ave., about 1mi northeast of town center. Open Jun–Aug Mon–Fri 9am–4pm, weekends 9am–3pm. Sept–Oct weekends only 10am–4pm. Rest of the year weekends only 9am–1pm. Closed major holidays. $6.* ☎ *978-283-2080.* Inspired by castles built in the Middle Ages, this stone castle was completed in 1929 by the eccentric inventor John Hays Hammond Jr. On one side, twin towers rise 80ft above terraced gardens, a drawbridge and an enclosed exercise yard that Hammond built for his 18 cats. Below the opposite towers lie the treacherous rocks of Norman's Woe, the setting for Longfellow's poem *The Wreck of the Hesperus.* The interior contains his collection of Medieval furnishings, paintings and sculpture. The **Great Hall**★ houses an 8,200-pipe organ Hammond constructed over a period of 20 years.

Return to Hesperus Ave., which leads to Rte. 127 (Western Ave.).

Drive by **Stage Fort Park**, site of the settlement established in 1623, then cross the drawbridge that links the cape to the mainland. To the right is Leonard Craske's statue the **Gloucester Fisherman**★ (**A**), a tribute to the thousands of Gloucestermen who have died at sea.

★**Gloucester** – The oldest seaport in the nation, Gloucester is one of the world's leading fishing ports. Its fleet of schooners, which once sailed between Virginia and Newfoundland in search of cod, halibut and mackerel, was immortalized by

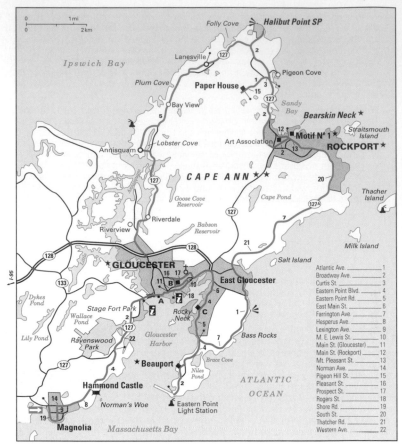

Rudyard Kipling in his novel *Captains Courageous*. Still a principal provider of fish, with its fleet of about 250 boats, Gloucester is also a distribution center for the industry. At the seafood processing plants near the waterfront, the catch of fishermen from New England, Canada, Iceland, Greenland and Scandinavia is cured, packaged and prepared for shipping to cities across the nation.

The fishermen, many of whom are of Portuguese or Italian descent, remain devoted to their traditions, and especially to the annual **Blessing of the Fleet**, which takes place during the last weekend in June on the feast of St. Peter.

Enter Gloucester by Rte. 127 (Rogers St.).

Crowning a knoll above a small park stands the austere stone house of noted 19C maritime artist Fitz Hugh Lane *(not open to the public; grounds open year-round daily dawn–dusk)*. Views from the knoll sweep across the harbor.

Turn left on Manuel E. Lewis St., left on Main St. and right on Pleasant St.

★★ **Cape Ann Historical Museum** (**B**) – *27 Pleasant St. Open Mar–Jan Tue–Sat 10am–5pm. $4. Closed major holidays.* ♿ ☎ *978-283-0455. www.cape-ann.com.* The museum is dedicated to the seafaring and artistic traditions of Cape Ann. Three levels of large, sunlit galleries trace the history of the fisheries and maritime industries here and highlight works of 19C and 20C artists attracted to the cape's light and landscape. Among the museum's holdings are works by Maurice Prendergast, John Sloan and Cecilia Beaux as well as the nation's largest collection of **seascapes** by 19C American marine painter **Fitz Hugh Lane** (1804-65). His paintings of Gloucester Harbor and of local scenes are admired for their warm, luminous colors, attention to detail and serene atmosphere. In the two rooms devoted to Gloucester's fisheries, photographs, dories and scale models of wharf buildings c.1892 are complemented by dramatic nautical paintings and Angelo Lualdi's 1915 religious icon *Our Lady of Good Voyage*, an 8ft rendition of the saint cradling a Gloucester fishing schooner.

Return to Rte. 127 (Rogers St.) by Prospect St.

You will pass the Portuguese-inspired **Our Lady of Good Voyage Church**, which is surmounted by two blue cupolas.

Follow Rte. 127 north to East Main St. and bear right.

East Gloucester – Among East Main Street's restaurants and art galleries is the **North Shore Arts Assn. (C)**, located in a weathered red barn *(197 East Main St.; open May–Oct Mon–Sat 10am–5pm, Sun noon–5pm; contribution requested;* ♿ ☎ *800-943-2255; www.shorenet/~nya/nsaa.html.* The association features the work of local artists. Opposite is **Rocky Neck**, which has been the site of an artists' colony since the 19C and is replete with small galleries.

Follow Eastern Point Rd. to Eastern Point (private). Visitors to Beauport are permitted access via the private road.

★**Beauport** – *Eastern Point Blvd., in Eastern Point. Visit by guided tour (1hr) only, mid-Sept–mid-Oct daily 10am–4pm. Mid-May–early Sept Mon–Fri 10am–4pm. Closed Memorial Day, Jul 4, Labor Day. $6.* ☎ *978-283-0800. www.spnea.org.* Overlooking Gloucester Harbor and the distant Boston skyline, this 40-room summer residence of architect-decorator Henry Davis Sleeper (1878-1934) contains an imaginative mix of period styles and decors. Sleeper wished to create in each room a different mood and character. Thus beneath the varied roofline of chimneys, turrets, spiral flues and towers, he designed a colonial Paul Revere Room, an Indian Room, a Byron Room and a China Trade Room, among others. His creations here made him one of the most celebrated decorators of his day.

At the tip of Eastern Point is **Eastern Point Light Station**, dominating a long, granite breakwater at the entrance to Gloucester Harbor.

Return along Eastern Point Blvd. to the entrance of the private road, then turn right onto Farrington Ave. and left onto Atlantic Rd.

The drive along Atlantic Road affords a good **view** of the coast and, across the water, of the twin lights on Thacher Island.

Return to Rte. 127A (Thacher Rd.), which skirts beaches, occasional salt marshes and rocky, wooded areas. Thatcher Rd. becomes South St. as you approach the town of Rockport.

★**Rockport** – *During tourist season, downtown parking is difficult to find. A shuttle bus (50¢) operates every 15min between the parking lot outside of town (free parking) and the town center.* This tranquil fishing village, which developed as an artists' colony in the 1920s, enjoyed its industrial heyday in the 19C, when granite quarried from its shores was shipped to ports as far away as South America. Rockport's art galleries and shops, found in the vicinity of Main Street, as well as the village's charming character and coastal setting, attract many visitors.

The village is especially picturesque in the late afternoon, when the set-ting sun illuminates the

Motif No. 1, Rockport

Fred Sieb Photography

sea, the granite ledges, the boats anchored offshore and the red fishing shed **Motif No. 1**★, named for the many paintings it has inspired. The shed is accessible from **Bearskin Neck**★, a small promontory where old fishing sheds have been converted into shops. Narrow walkways lead to the end of the neck, a good vantage point from which to observe the rocky shore and the harbor. On Main Street *(no. 12)*, the **Rockport Art Assn.** exhibits the works of regional artists. A public, oceanside pathway passes through private lawns and leads to Garden, North and South Beaches.

Leave Rockport on Mt. Pleasant St., then turn right onto Broadway Ave., which leads into Rte. 127 (Railroad Ave. and Granite St.). Just before Pigeon Cove turn left onto Curtis St., then left onto Pigeon Hill St.

Woodman's

Main St. in Essex,
about 6mi northwest of
Gloucester via Rte. 133.
Woodman's doesn't merely
serve up fried clams.
Lawrence "Chubby"
Woodman claims to have
invented them, back in
1914. Today this sprawling
family-style clam shack is a
North Shore fixture. Lines
of eager diners snake out
the door on summer
weekends (it's a post-
beach/post-antiquing
favorite). Once you're
inside at the order counter,
you have your choice of all
things clam: fried clams,
fried clam strips, clam
chowder, clam cakes and a
few other items, including
fresh whole lobster, corn
on the cob and award-
winning onion rings. Take
your number, find a seat
and get ready for what's
sure to be a memorable,
if greasy, feast.

Paper House – 🚸 *52 Pigeon Hill St.*
Open Apr–Oct daily 10am–5pm. Contri-
bution requested. ☎ *978-546-2629.*
The walls and furnishings are constructed almost entirely of newspapers.
It took Elis F. Stenman and his family 20
years to complete the project.

Return to Rte. 127; continue north for
almost 1mi and turn right on Gott Ave.

Halibut Point State Park – *Open*
May–Labor Day daily 8am–8pm. Rest of
the year daily dawn–dusk. $2/vehicle. ♿
☎ *978-546-2997.* From the parking lot,
numerous self-guided trails wind
through the woods and past granite
quarries *(guided 2hr quarry tour Memo-*
rial Day–Columbus Day Sat 10am) to the
northern tip of Pigeon Cove. Vantage
points on the rocky shore provide extensive **views**★ across Ipswich Bay to the
south, and as far as Maine to the north.
The Halibut Point State Park headquarters incorporates a concrete World War
II watchtower.

Continue on Rte. 127.

The coastal region between Pigeon Cove
and **Annisquam** is a succession of charming villages and rocky inlets: **Folly Cove**,
Lanesville, **Plum Cove** and **Lobster Cove**. After
Annisquam, Route 127 joins Route 128
in Riverdale.

> "After God had carried us safe to New England
> and we had...provided necessaries for our livelihood...
> one of the next things we...looked after was to advance
> learning and perpetuate it to posterity..."
>
> From *New England's First Fruits* (1943)

CAPE COD★★★

Map of Principal Sights
Tourist Office ☎ 508-362-3225

Shaped like a muscular arm curled in a flex, celebrated Cape Cod is fringed with 300mi of sandy beaches, whitewashed fishing villages, towering dunes, salt marshes and windswept sea grasses. The product of a fascinating geological and human past, the cape has been a favorite resort since the development of the automobile.

Geological Notes

During the last Ice Age, the Laurentide ice sheet extended southward from the Labrador peninsula across New England. Its glaciers terminated along a line running westward across Long Island to New York and on to Ohio and the Great Lakes. MARTHA'S VINEYARD and NANTUCKET are remnants of eroded and submerged terminal moraines, extensive arched ridges of unsorted earth and rocks deposited in front of the glaciers. As temperatures rose and the ice melted, the glaciers retreated northward, leaving behind a series of recessional moraines. At the end of the Ice Age, the rising sea flooded the land around the upstanding morainic debris, creating the peninsula now known as Cape Cod.
Wind and sea have also played a significant part in shaping the cape. Marine erosion created the tall cliffs of the Outer Cape; ocean currents, carrying sand northward, formed the Province Lands sector of Provincetown, the sandy hook at the tip of Cape Cod.

Cape Cod National Seashore

Historical Notes

Cape of the Cod – Cape Cod was named by explorer **Bartholomew Gosnold**, who landed here in 1602 and was impressed by the cod-filled waters that surrounded the peninsula. Eighteen years later, in 1620, the *Mayflower*, en route to its original destination in Virginia, anchored at the present site of PROVINCETOWN, and the Pilgrims spent five weeks exploring the region before continuing on to PLYMOUTH.
The earliest permanent settlements on the cape were established around 1630 with fishing and farming as the mainstays. In the 18C whaling grew into a principal industry on the cape, as vessels sailed out of Barnstable, Truro, Wellfleet and Provincetown to hunt. The rocky, treacherous shoals, a challenge to even the most expert seamen, posed a great danger to all shipping in these waters. Traces of several of the hundreds of vessels that sank off the cape before the construction of the CAPE COD CANAL are occasionally revealed on the beach during low tide; as the tide rushes in, they are again hidden by the shifting sands.

The Cape Today – In the summer, traffic along the cape's main thoroughfares—Routes 6 and 128—can slow to an agonizing crawl and the strip malls that flank the roads provide little diversion. Despite the numerous motels, fast food places, souvenir shops and clusters of condominiums found in or near the old fishing ports, the cape has managed to preserve pockets of its natural beauty and seafaring charm. Small colonial and fishing villages dot the North Shore (the bay side); to the east, miles of windswept dunes are protected in the Cape Cod National Seashore (CCNS). Acres of

■ **Cranberry Bogs** – Half of the nation's cranberries come from southern Massachusetts and Cape Cod, where natural conditions such as marshy areas and sandy bogs lend themselves to the production of this small red berry. Named by Dutch settlers for the likeness of its flower's stamen to a crane's beak, the cranberry is used to make juice, baked goods and jellies. It has become a staple (served as whole-berried sauce or in jellied form) in the main course of traditional Thanksgiving and Christmas dinners in America. Widespread cultivation of this fruit was begun in the early 19C, when a local resident, Henry Hall, discovered that the berries thrive best when covered with a layer of sand. Each spring sand was spread over the plants, and the berries were harvested in the fall. The process remains basically unchanged, although it is now mechanized. Festivals are held each fall on the cape and in nearby areas to celebrate the harvest of the cranberry crop from the region's bogs.

low-lying cranberry bogs and salt marshes, pine and scrub oak forests, and dozens of lakes, ponds and small, gray-shingled "Cape Cod" houses offer a pleasing relief to the sandy landscape of this peculiar Atlantic peninsula.
A large number of craftspeople live on Cape Cod. The hundreds of shops found on the roadside feature their handmade specialties: glassware, leather goods, candles, wooden decoys, fabric and pottery.

The Islands – The Cape Islands, **Martha's Vineyard**, **Nantucket** and the **Elizabeth Islands**, lie to the south. Purchased by Englishman Thomas Mayhew in 1642, the islands developed into whaling centers in the 18C and 19C and remained unspoiled by industry into the 20C. Bordered by magnificent beaches bathed by the warm Gulf Stream waters, the islands today are devoted primarily to tourism.

PRACTICAL INFORMATION .... Area Code: 508

Getting There – From **Boston** to **Sagamore Bridge** (56mi): I-93 south to Rte. 3 south, continue on Rte. 6. International and domestic flights to **Logan International Airport** (Boston) ☎ 617-561-1800 or **T.F. Green State Airport** (Providence) ☎ 401-737-4000. Major rental car agencies *(p 306)*. Closest Amtrak **train** station: Boston ☎ 800-872-7245. **Bus** station: Hyannis – Plymouth & Brockton Bus Lines ☎ 778-9767; Bonanza Bus Lines ☎ 800-556-3815. **Ferry** service from Boston to Provincetown: mid-Jun–Labor Day daily, Memorial Day–mid-Jun & early Sept–mid-Oct weekends only; 3hrs; $30; Bay State Cruises ☎ 617-748-1428. Year-round **shuttle** service between Logan Airport (Boston), Plymouth and Provincetown; Plymouth & Brockton Bus Lines (Hyannis) ☎ 778-9767.

Getting Around – Cape Cod is easily visited by car or bicycle. Bicycle rentals in most island towns, car rentals in Hyannis.

Visitor Information – **Cape Cod Chamber of Commerce** visitor center; kiosks operate seasonally at Sagamore and Bourne Bridges. 307 Main St. PO Box 790, Hyannis MA 02601 ☎ 362-3225. www.capecodchamber.org.

Accommodations – Reservation services: **Bed & Breakfast Cape Cod**, Box 1312, Orleans MA 02653 ☎ 255-3824 or 800-541-6226; **Taylor-Made Reservations**, 39 Touro St., Newport RI 02840 ☎ 401-848-0300. *Cape Cod Resort Directory* available from **Cape Cod Chamber of Commerce** *(above)*. Accommodations include economy and moderate hotels *($50–$125/day)* and bed & breakfasts *($70–$100/day)*. *Average prices for a double room.*
Rental cottages and **campgrounds** throughout the island; contact the Chamber of Commerce. **American Youth Hostel:** The Outermost Hostel, 28 Winslow St., PO Box 491, Provincetown MA 02657 ☎ 487-4378.

Recreation – Saltwater and freshwater **beaches** are located throughout Cape Cod. Most beaches are town-owned. Waters on the Atlantic Ocean are cooler than waters along the South Shore. Unlike the calmer waters of Cape Cod Bay, the ocean has a strong undertow. A parking fee *($5–$8)* is usually charged at public beaches in the summer. Ask the local tourist office or your lodging's staff about beach fees and regulations, which vary from town to town.
Bicycle trails abound *(see textbox titled "Cycling the Cape")*. Trail maps (including the 19.6mi Cape Cod Rail Trail from South Dennis to Eastham) are available at visitor centers in Eastham and Provincetown. Public **golf** courses are located in Brewster, Falmouth, Dennis and Mashpee. There is excellent **birdwatching** along the eastern peninsula.
Specialty **shopping** and supplies are available in most island towns. *Contact Chamber of Commerce for more information regarding shopping and recreation on Cape Cod.*

★★THE NORTH SHORE *1 day. 30mi. Map pp 166-167.*

Route 6A follows the North Shore (also known as the **Bay Side** because it fronts Cape Cod Bay), passing through tiny villages that were prosperous 19C ports.
From the intersection with Rte. 6, take Rte. 6A east for .5mi.

Pairpoint Glass Works – *851 Sandwich Rd. (Rte. 6A), in Sagamore. Glassblowing demonstrations May–Dec Mon–Sat 9am–6pm, Sun 10am–6pm. Rest of the year Mon–Sat 10am–5pm, Sun 11am–5pm.* &. ☎ *508-888-2344 or 800-899-0953. www.pairpoint.com.* At America's oldest glassworks, visitors may observe skilled glassblowers as they produce, then decorate, pieces of Pairpoint crystal according to the methods traditionally employed in the production of handmade glassware through the 19C.
From Rte. 6A bear right onto Rte. 130, then turn right onto Pine St.

★**Heritage Plantation of Sandwich** – *On Grove St. Description p 209.*

★**Sandwich** – *Rte. 6A. See Entry Heading.*
Cranberry bogs, then sand dunes and salt marshes are visible as Route 6A nears Barnstable. Beyond the dunes lies **Sandy Neck**, a 7mi strip of land that protects Barnstable Harbor. At one time, whalers boiled down whale blubber in cauldrons that lined the shores of **Sandy Neck Beach**, now a popular swimming area.

Barnstable – Pleasure craft have largely replaced the fishing and whaling boats that once filled Barnstable's harbor. A road on the left *(follow the Barnstable Harbor sign)* leads to the water's edge. Part of the **Trayser Museum Complex**, the custom house contains memorabilia and artifacts relating to Barnstable's maritime past *(open mid-Jun–mid-Oct Tue–Sun 1:30pm–4:30pm; contribution requested; ☎ 508-362-2092).*

Yarmouth Port – The beautiful sea captains' homes on Main Street are reminiscent of Yarmouth's era as a busy port. The **Winslow-Crocker House** (c.1780), fronting Route 6A, may be toured *(visit by 45min guided tour only, Jun–mid-Oct weekends 11am–5pm; $4; ☎ 508-362-4385; www.spnea.org).*

Dennis – Musicals, dramas and comedies are presented at the **Cape Playhouse**, a well-known summer theater. From **Scargo Hill Tower** *(from Rte. 6A turn right after the cemetery, then left onto Scargo Hill Rd.)* there is a **view** that extends from Plymouth to Provincetown.

■ Cycling the Cape

Many appealing bike paths thread Cape Cod. Here are three:
Shining Sea Bikeway *(3.1mi, Falmouth to Woods Hole)* borders the water's edge for about 1mi, otherwise it's through townscape and wetlands. *For specifics: Falmouth Town Hall ☎ 508-548-7611.* **Cape Cod Rail Trail** *(19.6mi, South Dennis to Salt Pond Visitor Center in Eastham or 25.8mi to South Wellfleet)* follows a paved, former railbed on some busy city streets, but also through forest and along the ocean; cranberry bogs may be sighted. *For specifics: Nickerson State Park ☎ 508-896-3491.* **Nauset Trail** *(1.6mi Salt Pond Visitor Center to Coast Guard Beach)* winds through the forests and marshlands of Cape Cod National Seashore to reach the beach. *Specifics: CCNS Headquarters ☎ 508-349-3785. For a fourth bike path, see Entry Heading Provincetown.* Bicycle trail maps are available at visitor centers in Eastham and Provincetown.

Bike Rentals: Cruisers, mountain and hybrid bikes (10-speeds, 3-speed), even tandems are available from companies in Falmouth, Orleans, Eastham and Provincetown. **Holiday Cycles** *(465 Grand Ave. Falmouth Heights ☎ 508-540-3549)* offers free parking for the Shining Sea Bikeway with rental. **Little Capistrano Bike Shop** *(Salt Pond Rd., Rte. 6, Eastham ☎ 508-255-6515)* rents helmets, car racks and baby seats as well as bicycles.

★**Brewster** – Extending 8mi along Cape Cod Bay, this charming resort town, first settled in the mid-17C, has preserved many of the stately residences built by prosperous sea captains in the 19C. The town's eight public beaches *(accessible from various points along Main St./Rte. 6A)* are noteworthy for the 2mi garnet-tinted flats that are uncovered at low tide.

Sydenstricker Glass Factory (**A**) – *On Rte. 6A in West Brewster. Demonstrations year-round Mon–Sat 9am–2:30pm. Closed Jan 1, Thanksgiving Day, Dec 25. ☎ 508-385-3272. www.sydenstricker.com.* The owner of this glassworks has developed an original technique in glassmaking. Two sheets of glass are used to make each item; one of the sheets is decorated, then joined to the second according to the principles used in the enameling process. The factory also produces tableware and other items.

■ The General Store

A common roadside sight on the cape, in fact throughout much of New England, is the general store: typically a two-story wood-framed, gable-roofed house painted white, with a US flag mounted on the front. It's hard not to stop at these inviting treasure troves of Americana, past and present, even just for an ice-cream bar. Foodstuffs, souvenirs, clothing, hardware, stationery, pottery, garden tools, pet supplies, beach necessities, beauty and health items—you name it, the general store's got it. **The Brewster Store** *(1935 Main St., ☎ 508-896-3744)* is just such a store, a purveyor of general merchandise that's open year-round as early as 6am.

Cape Cod Museum of Natural History (B) – 🧒 *869 Main St. (Rte 6A). Grounds open daily year-round. Museum open year-round daily Mon–Sat 9:30am–4:30pm, Sun 11am–4:30pm. Closed major holidays. $5.* ♿ ☎ *508-896-3867. www. capecodnaturalhistory.org.* This learning center featuring interactive exhibits on the fauna and geology of the cape appeals to visitors of all ages. Three **nature trails** crisscrossing the museum's 80-acre property allow exploration of typical Cape Cod landscapes, such as salt marshes, cranberry bogs and a pristine beach. Tours of Monomoy Island are conducted by museum naturalists.

New England Fire and History Museum (C) – 🧒 *1439 Main St. Open Memorial Day–Labor Day Mon–Fri 10am–4pm. Rest of Sept–Columbus Day weekends only noon–4pm. $5.* ♿ ☎ *508-896-5711.* Five buildings contain equipment and memorabilia that tell the story of the important role played by the firefighters and their volunteer companies throughout the nation's history. A diorama vividly illustrates the Great Chicago Fire of 1871. A blacksmith shop and 19C apothecary are among the buildings on the green.

Stoney Brook Mill (D) – 🧒 *1mi from Rte. 6A. Turn right onto Stoney Brook Rd. Open May–Jun Thu–Sat 2pm–5pm. Jul–Aug Fri 2pm–5pm. Contribution suggested.* ☎ *508-896-3701.* The old gristmill still grinds corn into cornmeal. From April through mid-May, the stream that runs beside the mill is the scene of an exciting natural phenomenon: a herring run. During this period, alewives (fish 10in-13in long) swim upstream to freshwater ponds and lakes to spawn. They then return downstream with their newborn fingerlings, following an instinct similar to that of the salmon.

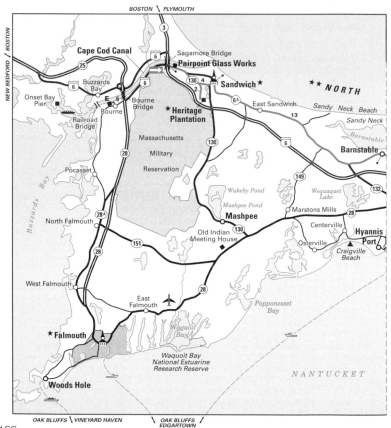

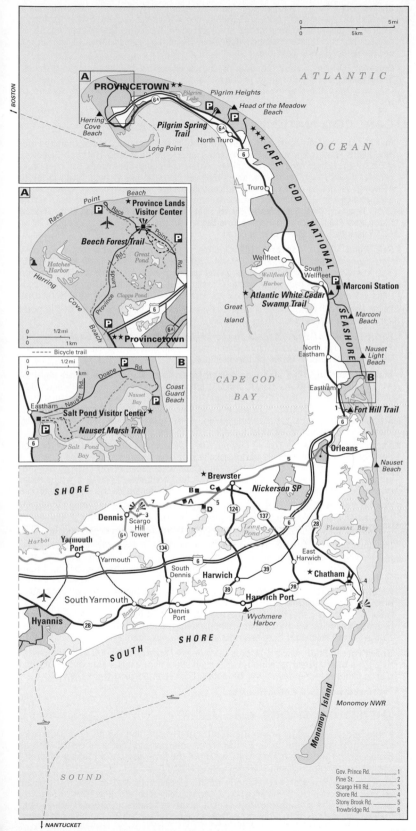

Nickerson State Park – *On Rte. 6A. Open Apr–Sept daily 8am–8pm. Oct–Mar daily dawn–dusk.* ⚠ ⬧ ☎ *508-896-3491. www.state.ma.us/dem.* Picnic grounds, bicycle rentals and a small store are located in the park, the former estate of pioneer railroad-builder Roland Nickerson. Swimming is permitted in Flax Pond, and boat rentals are available.

Orleans – Orleans is the first town on the cape where you will see ocean beaches. **Nauset Beach**, about 10mi long, protects Nauset Harbor, Pleasant Bay, Orleans and Chatham from the violent storms called northeasters that pound this section of the coast.

★★★CAPE COD NATIONAL SEASHORE *Map p 167*

In 1961 the eastern coast of Cape Cod, with its fragile dunes, cliffs, marshes and woodlands, became a federally protected area: the Cape Cod National Seashore (CCNS). Since that time bicycle trails, nature trails and dune trails for over-sand vehicles (dune buggies, four-wheel drive vehicles and jeeps) have been created, allowing visitors to enjoy the magnificent landscape. A visitor center is located at each end of the 27,000-acre seashore, and lifeguard services are available at the CCNS beaches: **Coast Guard Beach**, **Nauset Light Beach**, **Marconi Beach**, **Head of the Meadow Beach**, **Race Point Beach** and **Herring Cove Beach** *($7/day parking fee is charged at all CCNS beaches; seasonal pass is $20).*

★**Salt Pond Visitor Center** – 🔳Kids *On Rte. 6 in Eastham. Open May–Sept daily 9am–5pm. Rest of the year daily 9am–4:30pm. Closed Dec 25.* ⬧ ☎ *508-255-3421. www.nps.gov/caco.* Rangers at the center provide literature and information regarding seashore regulations, trails, facilities and programs. A large room contains exhibits on Cape Cod's history, geography, natural history and architecture.
Nauset Marsh Trail – *1mi. Access near the visitor center.* Beautiful views of the pond and marshes can be seen from the trail.

Fort Hill Trail – *1.5mi. To reach the Fort Hill parking lot from Rte. 6 take Governor Prince Rd.* The trail leaves from Penniman House and leads through open fields that afford expansive views of the marshes.

Marconi Station – The area was named for **Guglielmo Marconi**, the Italian physicist who established the transatlantic wireless station that operated here between 1901 and 1917. The first formal transmission from this station was a communication between President Theodore Roosevelt and King Edward VII on January 19, 1903. Scattered remnants of the station remain; other sections have been destroyed by shore erosion, which is especially evident along the cliffs and beach here.
★**Atlantic White Cedar Swamp Trail** – *1.25mi. The trailhead is located at Marconi Station parking lot.* The trail reveals various aspects of the vegetation on Cape Cod as it leads through the low brush, where beach grasses prevent erosion, then passes into an area of scrub oaks and pitch pines. The trail continues through a white cedar swamp before opening out onto the road that formerly led to the wireless station.

Pilgrim Spring Trail – *.5mi from the interpretive shelter near the Pilgrim Heights parking lot.* The trail leads through a section of scrub pines and brush to the site of a spring where the Pilgrims are believed to have first found drinking water in 1620.

★**Province Lands Visitor Center** – 🔳Kids *Race Point Rd. outside Provincetown. Open mid-Apr–Sept daily 9am–5pm. Oct–mid-Nov daily 9am–4:30pm.* ☎ *508-487-1256. www.nps.gov/caco.* In addition to presenting interpretive exhibits and films on the area's geography, flora and fauna, the center offers a rich program of nature walks and lectures. The observation deck atop the contemporary wooden building provides a fine **panorama★** of the dunes.
After visiting the center, follow the road to **Race Point Beach**, an expansive stretch of coast graced by the picturesque silhouette of the former lifesaving station *(open to the public)* relocated here from its original site in Chatham.

Beech Forest Trail – *1.5mi. Access from Beech Forest parking lot.* The trail passes through a beech forest threatened at certain spots by the advancing dunes. A pond that is filling in—one day it will become a bog—can be seen from the trail.

★★**Provincetown** – *See Entry Heading.*

THE SOUTH SHORE *Map pp 166-167*

Route 28 runs along the South Shore through Hyannis and Dennis Port, the major shopping centers of the cape. Extremely commercial and tourist-oriented, with its motels, shops and restaurants, this section of the cape also has a number of pretty villages, including Chatham, Harwich and Falmouth.

★**Chatham** – Protected by the sandy offshore barrier of Nauset Beach, Chatham remains an active port. Fishing boats depart daily from **Fish Pier** *(off Shore Rd.)* and return in the late afternoon. One mile south of Chatham, Shore Road leads to **Chatham Lighthouse**, which affords good **views★** of both Pleasant Bay and Nauset Beach.

Chatham Railroad Museum – Kids *Depot Rd. Open mid-Jun–mid-Sept Tue–Sat 10am–4pm. Contribution suggested.* ♿. Located in Chatham's former Victorian-style railroad depot, the museum contains locomotive models, schedules, posters, the original ticket office and other exhibits that evoke the history of railroading.

Monomoy Island – *Access by boat only. Ferry & tour information ☎ 508-945-0594.* A fierce storm in 1958 created this island. Because of the island's importance as a stopover for birds in the Atlantic Flyway, it has been established as Monomoy National Wildlife Refuge *(open year-round daily dawn–dusk).*

Harwich Port – Picturesque **Wychmere Harbor** is visible from Route 28.

Harwich – *On Rte. 39.* The white-columned buildings in the center of Harwich include the **Brooks Free Library** and the **Brooks Academy Museum** *(open early Jun–mid-Oct Wed–Sat 1pm–4pm; rest of the year by appointment; ☎ 508-432-8089; www.capecodhistory.org).* Harwich is a leading producer of cranberries.

Hyannis – Situated midway along the South Shore, this town is the major shopping center for the cape. Hyannis is also an important gateway to Cape Cod with its regularly scheduled airline and island ferry services. The small **John F. Kennedy Museum** displays photos primarily of the family's vacations on the cape *(397 Main St.; open mid-Apr–mid-Oct Mon–Sat 10am–4pm, Sun 1pm–4pm; late Oct–Dec & mid-Feb–early Apr Wed–Sat 10am–4pm; $3;* ♿ *☎ 508-790-3077).*

Hyannis Port – This fashionable waterfront resort is the site of the Kennedy family's summer compound. *(The compound is not visible from the road, nor is it open to the public.)* The **John F. Kennedy Memorial**, a bronze medallion set in a fieldstone wall, is located on Ocean Street. **Craigville Beach** *(off Rte. 28)* is a pleasant place to swim and sunbathe.

Mashpee – *On Rte. 130.* Wampanoag Indians were already living on the cape when the English settlers arrived. In the 17C Rev. Richard Bourne appealed to the Massachusetts legislature to set aside land for the Indians. In response, the lawmakers gave the large tract of land known as Mashpee Plantation to the native residents. In the 19C this parcel of land became the town of Mashpee. The **Old Indian Meeting House**, built in 1684, is the oldest meetinghouse on the cape *(Meetinghouse Rd., off Rte. 28; visit by 30min guided tour only, Jun–Labor Day Fri 10am–5pm; ☎ 508-477-1536).*

★**Falmouth** – Despite its development as a tourist town, Falmouth has retained a quaint 19C atmosphere in its village center. Lovely old homes stand near the green.

Woods Hole – Located about 2mi southwest of Falmouth, on the tip of a small peninsula, this former whaling port is a world center for the study of marine life. Two private laboratories are located here: the **Marine Biological Laboratory**, where approximately 1000 scientists and students conduct research in the field of marine flora and fauna *(visitor center at 100 Water St. open Jul–Aug Mon–Sat 10am–4pm, Sun 11am–3pm; rest of the year, call for hours; 1hr guided tours of the lab available;* ♿ *☎ 508-289-7423; www.mbl.edu)* and the **Woods Hole Oceanographic Institution**, the largest independent marine research laboratory in the US. The latter institution studies all aspects of ocean science from the sea floor to the atmosphere and also maintains a small visitor center *(15 School St.; open Memorial Day–Labor Day Mon–Sat 10am–4:30pm, Sun noon–4:30pm; rest of the year hours vary; closed Jan–Mar; $2 contribution suggested;* ♿ *☎ 508-289-2252; www.whoi.edu).* In September 1985, marine geologist Dr. **Robert Ballard**, based at Woods Hole at the time, led the team of French and American scientists who discovered the wreck of the *Titanic* off the coast of Newfoundland. In addition, the US Geological Survey's **Branch of Atlantic Marine Geology** and the **National Marine Fisheries Service**, both federal facilities, are part of the center. The **aquarium** Kids, used by the Fisheries Service in its research, may be visited *(166 Water St.; open mid-Jun–mid-Sept daily 10am–4pm, rest of the year Mon–Fri 10am–4pm;* ♿ *☎ 508-495-2001).*

Cruises – *Boats to Martha's Vineyard depart from the Steamship Authority Pier in Woods Hole. See Entry Heading Martha's Vineyard.*

Pie in the Sky Bakery

In Woods Hole, 10 Water St., next to the post office. ☎ 508-540-5475. There's something about the salty sea air that bids us rise and greet the day. Woods Hole residents are up and about early, what with the marine center's activity and the constant arrival and departure of Martha's Vineyard ferries at the Steamship Authority. So buy a newspaper and head for this pleasant bakery/cafe for coffee and morning fare. Espresso, cappuccino, fresh made muffins and pastries are served from 6:30am *(Sun 8am)*. Both outdoor and indoor seating are available. Pie in the Sky is also open for lunch.

CAPE COD CANAL *Map p 166*

Dug between 1909 and 1914, Cape Cod Canal separates Cape Cod from the rest of Massachusetts. The **Sagamore** and **Bourne Bridges** (for vehicles) and a railroad bridge that resembles London's Tower Bridge constitute the cape's only links to the mainland. The 544ft central span of the railroad bridge can be lowered in less than 3min to allow a train to cross the canal. *Cruises on the canal depart from Onset Town Pier late Jun–Labor Day Mon–Sat 10am, 1:30pm & 4pm, Sun 10am & 1:30pm. Mid-May–mid-Jun & rest of Sept–mid-Oct daily 10am & 1:30pm. Early May weekends only 10am & 1:30pm. Round-trip 2hrs & 3hrs. Commentary. $10–$13.* ✗ ☎ *508-295-3883. www.hy-linecruises.com.*

Aptucxet Trading Post Museum (**E**) – *24 Aptucxet Rd. in Bourne. From the rotary on the Cape Cod side of Bourne Bridge, follow the sign for Mashpee, then Shore Rd. Turn right onto Aptucxet Rd. and follow the signs. Open Jul–Aug Mon–Sat 10am–5pm, Sun 2pm–5pm. May–Jun & Sept–Columbus Day Tue–Sat 10am–5pm, Sun 2pm–5pm. $3.50.* ♿ ☎ *508-759-9487.* The Pilgrims established this trading post in 1627 to promote trade with both the Dutch from New Amsterdam and the Wampanoag Indians. Furs, sugar, tobacco and cloth were bought and sold here, using wampum (beads cut and polished by the Indians from shells and used as currency). The present building was reconstructed in 1930 on the foundations of the former trading post. Inside there are examples of the goods bartered. An ancient rune stone found in Bourne bears an inscription translated as: "God Gives Us Light Abundantly." A saltworks, similar to those used by early cape settlers to evaporate salt from seawater, has been built near the canal.

CONCORD★★
Population 17,076
Map of Principal Sights
Tourist Office ☎ 978-459-6150

A quiet, refined colonial town, with beautiful homes tucked amid the rustic landscape, Concord is a desirable place to live. Named in the 17C for the "concord" of peace established between the Indians and the settlers, this small town was the site, 150 years later, of a confrontation between American patriots and British soldiers that changed the course of American history forever. Concord has a distinguished literary past, having been the home, in the 19C, of intellectuals and writers such as Ralph Waldo Emerson, Nathaniel Hawthorne, Henry David Thoreau and Bronson Alcott.

Historical Notes

The Revolt Begins – On April 19, 1775, following a skirmish with colonists at LEXINGTON, the British marched to Concord. At the **Old North Bridge**, the untrained, poorly equipped farmers—called **"minutemen"** because of their readiness to take up arms to fight the British at a minute's notice—stood their ground against the Redcoats, thus triggering the American Revolution *(for an account of events on April 19, see Entry Heading Lexington).*

Transcendentalism – **Ralph Waldo Emerson** (1803-82), a native of Concord, popularized transcendentalism (a philosophical movement characterized by the belief that God exists in both man and nature) and expressed his philosophical ideas in his *Essays on Nature*, a series of lectures he delivered across the US. Other writers and thinkers, attracted by the liberal ideas and the return-to-nature philosophy inherent in transcendentalism, came to Concord to live near Emerson. Among them was **Henry David Thoreau** (1817-62), who built a cabin in the woods near Walden Pond, where he lived from 1845 to 1847. Thoreau's book *Walden* recounts the author's personal experiences during this period. **Nathaniel Hawthorne, Margaret Fuller** and others founded Brook Farm, an experimental community near West Roxbury that was envisioned as a retreat from Victorian society, and a return to a simple life. **Amos Bronson Alcott**, a proponent of transcendentalism, established his School of Philosophy adjacent to Orchard House, where his daughter **Louisa May Alcott** penned an account of her childhood in *Little Women*.
Admirers come to Concord to tour the literary shrines associated with these eminent writers: Emerson House; the Wayside, where Hawthorne lived for several years; the Alcotts' Orchard House and School of Philosophy; and Sleepy Hollow Cemetery, where many of them have been laid to rest.

SIGHTS *2hrs. Map 171.*

★**Minute Man National Historical Park** – 🈀 This park was established to commemorate events that took place April 19, 1775 along Battle Road *(Rte. 2A between Lexington and Concord)* and in Lexington, Lincoln and Concord. The 750-acre park is essentially a contiguous strip of land 4mi long, stretching over the three townships, with additional sections in Concord. A 5.5mi interpretive trail running alongside Battle Road *(Rte. 2A between Lexington and Concord)* describes the patriots' guerrilla-style attacks on British troops retreating to Bunker Hill.
Minute Man Visitor Center – *Off Rte. 2A in Lexington. May–Oct daily 9am–5pm. Rest of the year daily 9am–4pm. Closed Jan 1, Dec 25.* ♿ ☎ *978-369-6993. www.nps.gov/mima.* Exhibits and a state-of-the-art multimedia presentation entitled *The Road to Revolution (25min)* introduce visitors to the events of April 19, which occurred in the surrounding area.

★★ North Bridge Unit – A replica of the **Old North Bridge★** (**1**) marks the place where colonial farmers advanced on the British and fired the "shot heard 'round the world." Emerson immortalized the old "rude bridge" in his poem *Concord Hymn. (Brief interpretive talks are held at the North Bridge Apr–Oct, weather permitting.)* Nearby, Daniel Chester French's famous statue of the **Minute Man** honors the patriots who resisted the British at Concord. The **North Bridge Vistor Center** has exhibits and provides information regarding ranger talks and other special programs *(up the road from the North Bridge; open May–Oct daily 9am–5:30pm; rest of the year daily 9am–4pm; closed Jan 1, Thanksgiving Day, Dec 25;* ♿ ☎ *978-369-6993).*

As you leave, on the right is the **Old Manse** where Ralph Waldo Emerson, and later Nathaniel Hawthorne, lived *(visit by 45min guided tour only, mid-Apr–Oct Mon–Sat 10am–5pm, Sun noon–5pm; $5.50;* ☎ *978-369-3909; www.thetrustees.org).*

The Wayside – *455 Lexington Rd. Visit by guided tour (45min) only, May–Oct Thu–Tue 10am–5pm. Last tour 4:30pm. $4.* ☎ *978-369-6975. www. nps.gov/mima/wayside.* In 1775 this was the residence of Concord's muster master, whose job it was to gather the colonial troops together in the event of a British attack. In the next century, Wayside was the home of Nathaniel Hawthorne (who named the house), Margaret Sydney (author of *Five Little Peppers and How They Grew*), and Bronson Alcott, who at one time hoped to establish a community similar to Brook Farm *(p 170)* here.

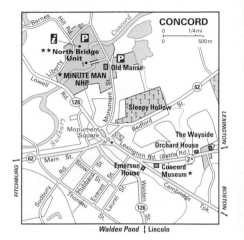

Walden Pond | Lincoln

★ Concord Museum – 🧒 *Lexington Rd. and Cambridge Tpk. Open Apr–Dec Mon–Sat 9am–5pm, Sun noon–5pm. Rest of year Mon–Sat 11am–4pm, Sun 1pm–4pm. Closed Jan 1, Easter Sunday, Thanksgiving Day, Dec 25. $6.* ♿ ☎ *978-369-9609. www.concordmuseum.org.* Arranged in 19 galleries, many of which feature authentic period pieces, this extensive collection of artifacts, documents and period rooms provides visitors with an excellent survey of Concord's rich history. Opened in 1997, the six-gallery exhibit Why Concord? traces the growth of the town from prehistoric times to the 20C and includes the interior of **Emerson's study** and the renowned **Thoreau gallery**. One of the lanterns hung in the steeple of Old North Church to signal Paul Revere on April 18, 1775; a diorama of the battle at Old North Bridge; and objects used by Thoreau at Walden Pond are on display. Upstairs, more than 1,500 objects illustrate trends in **American decorative arts** from the 17C to the 19C. Cummings E. Davis, a Concord merchant, amassed the collection in the mid-19C, mostly from local sources.

Orchard House/Home of the Alcotts – *399 Lexington Rd. Visit by guided tour (45min) only, Apr–Oct Mon–Sat 10am–4:30pm, Sun 1pm–4:30pm. Rest of the year Mon–Fri 11am–3:30pm, Sat 10am-4:30pm, Sun 1pm–4:30pm. Closed Jan 1–15, Easter Sunday, Thanksgiving Day, Dec 25. $6.* ☎ *978-369-4118. www. louisamayalcott.org.* Orchard House was the home of the Alcott family from 1858 to 1877, the period during which Louisa May Alcott wrote her autobiographical novel *Little Women* (1868). The **School of Philosophy**, built on the hillside, was operated by her father, Bronson Alcott, until the end of the 19C. It is now used for special programs that are open to the public.

Ralph Waldo Emerson House – *28 Cambridge Tpk. at Rte. 2A. Visit by guided tour (30min) only, mid-Apr–Oct Thu–Sat 10am–4:30pm, Sun 2pm–4:30pm. $5.* ☎ *978-251-2960.* The house is furnished as it was during the years that the New England writer and philosopher Ralph Waldo Emerson lived here (1835-82).

Walden Pond Reservation – *1.5mi south of Concord center on Rte. 126 (Walden St.).* Henry David Thoreau built his cabin on the shore of this lake. To reach the cabin site (marked by a cairn) from the parking lot, follow the trail signs to a granite post, where the trail turns right *(15min).* Walden Pond is now a nature preserve.

Sleepy Hollow Cemetery – *From Concord center turn right onto Rte. 62. Enter the cemetery through the second gate on the left. Follow signs for Author's Ridge. Open year-round daily 7am–dusk.* ☎ *978-318-3233. www.concordnet.org.* A short climb from the parking lot leads to **Author's Ridge**, where the Alcotts, Hawthorne, Emerson and Margaret Sydney are buried.

EXCURSION

Lincoln – *5mi southeast of Concord via Rte. 126.* This small, affluent residential town with a decidedly rural charm traces its origins to the mid-17C. Two historic homes and a museum/sculpture park can be toured.

Codman House – *Codman Rd. Visit by guided tour (45min) only, Jun–mid-Oct Wed–Sun 11am–5pm. Closed major holidays. $4. ☎ 781-259-8843. www.spnea.org.* This enchanting estate, nestled in a bucolic setting, preserves the legacy of the family that resided here for five generations. Built in 1749 by a gentleman farmer, the house was acquired in the 1790s by the Codman family, who transformed the original Georgian structure. The intimate interior reflects changing tastes of the members of this family over the centuries: Georgian woodwork, Victorian paneling, 20C stuffed chairs. The walls of several rooms are hung with paintings from the family's collection of 18C European art.
A romantic Italianate **garden** (c.1920), filled with decorative statuary and a long pool topped with water lilies, graces a quiet corner of the estate.

★**Gropius House** – *68 Baker Bridge Rd. Visit by guided tour (45min) only, Jun–mid-Oct Wed–Sun 11am–5pm. Rest of the year weekends only 11am–5pm. Closed major holidays. $5. ☎ 781-259-8098. www.spnea.org.* Walter Gropius (1883-1969), founder of the influential German school of art and architecture, the Bauhaus, and director of the Harvard School of Architecture, designed this International-style house for his family in collaboration with neighbor Marcel Breuer in 1938.
Encompassing only 2,300sq ft, the two-story structure combines New England vernacular elements such as clapboard with more modern materials such as glass block, chrome and steel. Gropius' characteristic industrial aesthetic predominates throughout, as evidenced in the use of ribbon windows and large unadorned surfaces. The free-flowing space within extends outdoors by means of large window surfaces and terraces. Evoking a sense of order and tranquillity, the interior contains furniture and accessories created at the Bauhaus, as well as family mementos and works given to the architect by Joan Miró, Josef Albers, Henry Moore and other well-known artists.

★★**DeCordova Museum and Sculpture Park** – *51 Sandy Pond Rd. Sculpture park open year-round daily 6am–10pm. Museum open year-round Tue–Sun 11am–5pm. Closed major holidays. $6 (museum). ✗ ♿ ☎ 781-259-8355. www.decordova.org.* Opened in 1950 on a lush lakeside estate bequeathed by Boston businessman Julian de Cordova, this museum is devoted to promoting appreciation for contemporary art by Americans, with particular emphasis on New England artists. The 35-acre sculpture park provides a sylvan setting for a rotation of nearly 100 monumental works, made from everything from tree bark to anodized steel by nationally and internationally acclaimed artists. A new wing, added to the original mansion-museum in 1998, doubled gallery space and now hosts 18 temporary group and individual exhibits per year, along with selections from the museum's 2,000-piece permanent collection. The Art ExperienCenter is an interactive display that explains the theory and creation of abstract art.

DEERFIELD★★

Population 5,018
Map of Principal Sights
Tourist Office ☎ 413-665-7333

Locally known as "The Street," Deerfield's mile-long main thoroughfare with its limited number of business establishments and many 18C and 19C dwellings, provides a picture of a wealthy early-American farming community. Indeed the richness of the surrounding farmlands, threaded by the Deerfield River and nestled below the Pocumtuck Ridge, makes Deerfield's **site** one of the loveliest in the state. Today the village is known for **Historic Deerfield**, a collection of restored Colonial and Federal structures intermingled with the buildings and houses of the community and open to the public as a museum.

Historical Notes – Deerfield was not always the tranquil town it appears to be today. Incorporated in 1673, Deerfield was abandoned three years later after the massacre at Bloody Brook, and again in 1704 when the village was burned down in a French and Indian attack during Queen Anne's War. A peace treaty signed in 1735 encouraged settlers to return, and during the following century the village grew into one of New England's most prosperous agricultural centers. As a result, many fine houses were built, particularly in the 1740s and 50s. The painstaking process of the renovation and redecoration of Deerfield's large Colonial and Federal structures began in 1848, the first project of its kind in the US. Of some 55 buildings in Deerfield that pre-date 1825, only two have been moved to the village from other Massachusetts locations.
Today the **Brick Church** (1824) and several buildings of **Deerfield Academy**, a prestigious prep school founded in 1797, stand on the grassy **common** near the post office, which is a replica of a Puritan meetinghouse. A little farther down the street is the well-appointed **Deerfield Inn** (1884), a popular lodging and dining spot for residents and out-of-towners. Private residences are interwoven with the museum buildings along The Street and side roads.

★★HISTORIC DEERFIELD

Strung along the broad, tree-lined thoroughfare of the town of Deerfield, secluded from the high-speed world of neighboring I-91 and Route 5/10, the restored structures of this museum complex remind us of the grandeur and practicality of the past. Their revival is due largely to the initial efforts of a few collectors and early preservationists who understood the importance of heritage. In 1870 local residents formed the Pocumtuck Valley Memorial Assn., which opened the Memorial Hall Museum ten years later. The parents of a Deerfield Academy student, Henry and Helen Geier Flynt, Historic Deerfield's founders, opened Ashley House to the public in 1948. The museum was chartered in 1952 and 10 years later some 12 houses had been renovated and opened for public tours.

A total of 14 historic buildings dating from c.1730 to 1850 are open to the public as house museums today, 13 of which are on their original sites. Many of the dwellings are topped with gambrel roofs and adorned with richly carved doorways characteristic of the Connecticut Valley style. The interiors are equally luxurious and elegant. More than 18,000 objects dating from 1600 to 1900 are on display. Special collections include the **Helen Geier Flynt Textile Museum**, the **Henry Needham Flynt Silver and Metalware Collection**, and the George A. Cluett Collection of American Furniture. Most recently the 27,000sq ft **Flynt Center of Early New England Life** (1998) was opened to house changing exhibits and the museum's visible storage of some 2,500 antiques; visitors can access information on individual pieces via an on-site computer.

Deerfield Dining

For traditional New England fare in a formal setting, the **Deerfield Inn** (☎ 413-774-5587) will not disappoint. The spacious dining room reflects the charm of the Colonial decor found throughout the inn. Here regional dishes and standard American cuisine are served with gracious Yankee hospitality. A typical à la carte meal consists of New England clam chowder; rolls served with regular, tomato/chili and basil butters; potato encrusted Atlantic salmon with garlic mashed potatoes; citric sorbet; and for dessert, Indian pudding.

In the village center of South Deerfield, the ground floor of an old house is the modern setting for **Sienna** (*68 Elm St.* ☎ *413-665-0215*), a sleek *salle à manger* with ocher and deep-red walls. An excellent evening offering would include asparagus soup with goat cheese, grilled salmon on crabmeat mashed potatoes with Hawaiian fruit salsa, accompanied by fresh sourdough bread. If you've no room for dessert, after-dinner espresso is served with complimentary biscotti.

In addition to daily tours, the museum presents public workshops, lectures and educational programs. Two research libraries focusing on the history of Deerfield and the Connecticut Valley are maintained on the grounds.

Visit *2 days*

Open year-round daily 9:30am–4:30pm. Closed Thanksgiving Day, Dec 24 & 25. $12. ✗ ⚅ ☎ *413-774-5581. www.historic-deerfield.org.*

Helpful Hints

It is not possible to see all of Historic Deerfield in one day. The admission ticket is valid for 7 consecutive days and ticket holders are encouraged to make return visits. Four buildings are open on a self-guided basis: the Sheldon-Hawks House, Henry Needham Flynt Silver and Metalware Collection, Memorial Hall Museum and the Flynt Center. The other buildings may be visited by 25min guided tours beginning at 10am (guides stand at the door 15min prior to tour times to answer questions). *Wear comfortable shoes, since buildings are some distance apart.*

Begin your visit at Hall Tavern, where a site plan and schedule of tours and daily activities are available. Plan out what you want to visit and at what times. You may want to first view the orientation film *(10min)* shown at the tavern. Throughout the day allow time for rest and refreshment. A covered seating area with vending machines is located outside at the rear of the tavern. The only place within walking distance to have lunch or dinner is The Deerfield Inn; lunch is served until 2pm. Otherwise, restaurants can be found in South Deerfield.

When Historic Deerfield has closed for the day, follow the pleasant **Channing Blake Meadow Walk** *(gate locked at 6pm)*, which is accessible from The Street. This 2/3mi interpretive trail traverses an active farm with livestock, meadows and wetlands and ends near the river *(family trail packs, containing a guidebook and activity sheets, can be rented at Hall Tavern)*. To see the Old Burying Ground, continue beyond the trail a short distance to the left.

A well-stocked museum shop is housed within the J.G. Pratt Store, located next to Deerfield Inn.

Described below are highlights of the museum.

Ashley House – The house (1730) is typical of the dwellings that were built in the Connecticut Valley in the 18C. The interior contains richly carved woodwork and beautiful furnishings. This house was the home of Parson Jonathan Ashley, a devoted Tory who, despite threats from the townspeople to bar him from the meetinghouse, persisted in his loyalty to the Crown during the Revolution.

Wright House – The light and airy Federal dwelling (1825) has American paintings, porcelain and the fine Cluett collection of Federal and Chippendale furniture.

Door of the Dwight House

Asa Stebbins House – The Stebbins House (1810), with its distinctive arched doorway, was the first Deerfield residence to have a dining room. A splendid collection of wall coverings, including 19C French wallpaper illustrating Captain Cook's voyages to the South Seas, decorates the interior of the house.

Hall Tavern – Moved to Deerfield from another location in 1950, this former tavern (1760) is now the site of Historic Deerfield's visitor center. The ballroom upstairs is embellished with stenciled designs.

Frary House/Barnard Tavern – This late-18C dwelling was later enlarged to serve as a tavern. Inside is a ballroom with a fiddlers' gallery, and rooms filled with country antiques, pewter and ceramics.

Wells-Thorn House – The house's kitchen (1720) retains its early primitive characteristics, while the refined paneling and furnishings and the use of color in the rooms built later (1751) reflect the refined tastes of its well-to-do owner.

Dwight House – The facade of this dwelling (1725) is ornamented with a handsomely carved doorway, a feature typical of Connecticut Valley architecture.

Memorial Hall – This brick building houses the museum of the **Pocumtuck Valley Memorial Assn.**, a memorial to the Pocumtuck Indians and the settlers of Deerfield. Exhibits are displayed over three floors and include a large assortment of quilts, household items, furniture, portraits, costumes, military memorabilia and period rooms. The highlight is the door from the original Indian House, the only dwelling not destroyed in the 1704 raid.

FALL RIVER

Population 92,703
Map of Principal Sights
Tourist Office ☎ 508-997-1250

The site of the famous 1892 trial of Lizzie Borden, who was accused of murdering her parents with an ax (she was ultimately acquitted), Fall River was a major textile center in the 19C and early 20C.

During the same period, luxuriant steamships of the **Fall River Line** linked New York to BOSTON and carried the wealthy to their summer cottages in NEWPORT. The city was hard hit by the Great Depression, then by the migration of the textile mills to the South and the development of synthetic fibers. Despite these setbacks, the city's textile industry survived. Textiles and clothing are still produced here, and many of the old mill buildings have found new life as factory outlets. In the mid-1960s the state's slain World War II service personnel were commemorated at Fall River's waterfront, initiating what is now a naval museum.

★BATTLESHIP COVE

In 1965 the battleship USS *Massachusetts* was moored at Fall River to serve as a permanent memorial to the 13,000 Massachusetts men and women who gave their lives in service to their country during World War II. In recent decades, several other naval ships have joined the *Massachusetts* as exhibits at this outdoor naval museum.

Visit

Kids *Exit 5 from Rte. 195 east. Open Apr–Oct daily 9am–5pm. Rest of the year daily 9am–4:30pm. Closed Jan 1, Thanksgiving Day, Dec 25. $9. ✗ ☎ 508-678-1100 or 800-533-3194. www.battleshipcove.com.*

Berthed on the waterfront next to the state pier, five vessels are permanently preserved and open to the public as a means of exploring naval history.

■ Warships

Developed in Europe, small, fast PT (Patrol, Torpedo) boats first served the US Navy in World War II. Destroyers, among the fastest ships in the navy, were originally designed to protect the fleet's battleships from enemy torpedo boats. Because of their tactical flexibility, destroyers are now used offensively as well as defensively.

PT Boat 796 – The ferocious shark painted on the hull symbolizes the threat these modest-sized boats posed to the enemy. PT boat memorabilia is displayed.

Submarine Lionfish – This World War II submarine carried 20 torpedoes and an 80-member crew. The vessel's sophisticated operating equipment, once considered classified, can be seen in the control room.

Destroyer USS Joseph P. Kennedy – The ship was named for Joseph, the eldest of the four Kennedy brothers, who was killed on a volunteer mission in World War II. A typical World War II destroyer, the *Kennedy* carried a crew of 275.

★**Battleship USS Massachusetts** – Remarkable for its enormous size (longer than two football fields) and the large crew required for operation (2,300 men), the 46,000-ton *Massachusetts* logged 225,000 miles in wartime service between 1942 and 1945 and was the first and last US battleship to fire 16in shells against the enemy. Below deck, sections of the ship have been set aside for an exhibit devoted to aviation, and for the Memorial Room honoring the Massachusetts men and women killed in World War II. Narrow corridors lead visitors past the barbershop, laundry and other service areas that were indispensable aboard a large ship.

Corvette Hiddensee – The newest ship to join the fleet at Battleship Cove (1996) is the 185ft *Hiddensee*, a Russian-made missile corvette, reputedly the only one of its kind on display in the US. Designed largely for coastal defense, the vessel served both the East German and the unified German navies.

ADDITIONAL SIGHTS

Fall River Heritage State Park Visitor Center – *Take the pedestrian bridge at Battleship Cove. Open Jun–Aug daily 10am–6pm. Sept–May daily 10am–4pm. Closed Jan1, Thanksgiving Day, Dec 25. ✗ ぬ ☎ 508-675-5759.* A slide show (30min) relating the history of the city's textile industry is shown daily. This brick riverside building has the appearance of a 19C New England mill. From the tower, visitors are treated to a sweeping view of the entire Mt. Hope Bay region.

Marine Museum – *70 Water St. Open year-round Mon–Fri 9am–5pm, weekends noon–5pm. Closed Jan 1, Thanksgiving Day, Dec 25. $4. ぬ ☎ 508-674-3533. www.marinemuseum.org.* The museum's photographs, marine paintings, prints and ship models bear witness to the region's maritime past and the Fall River Line. Accurately constructed ship models, such as the 28ft model of the *Titanic* and the 13ft 9in model of the *Puritan*, and photographs of the plush Victorian interiors found on the Fall River steamers suggest the luxury and comfort enjoyed by Fall River Line passengers.

★**Fall River Historical Society Museum** – *451 Rock St. Visit by guided tour (1hr) only, Jun–Sept & Dec Tue–Fri 9am–4pm, weekends 1pm–5pm. Apr–May & Oct–mid-Nov Tue–Fri 9am–4pm. Last tour 1hr before closing. Closed major holidays. $5. ☎ 508-679-1071. www.lizzieborden.org.* Art and artifacts from Victorian-era Fall River fill this 1843 Greek Revival mansion, a former stop on the Underground Railroad. Dating from the 1870s, the polychrome stenciling on the 14ft ceilings is among the best preserved in New England. The world's largest display of trial transcripts, police photos and family photographs from the Lizzie Borden case is on exhibit in the parlor. Upper rooms contain selections from the society's 3,000-piece costume collection, a marine exhibit and still-life paintings.

FRUITLANDS MUSEUMS★

Map of Principal Sights

Fruitlands, a 218-acre farm that is now home to four museums, tops a hill dominating the Nashua Valley. The farm once briefly hosted one of America's first Utopian communes, that of Bronson Alcott and his followers.

In 1843 Bronson Alcott, the philosopher of Concord, and the English reformer **Charles Lane** attempted to establish a Utopian community with their adherents on the 18C farm known as Fruitlands. Idealistic and reacting to the materialism of the times, they became vegetarians, wore only linen clothing and spent most of their time outdoors. Their return to nature lasted but a few months, as disillusioned members of the community left Fruitlands one by one.

VISIT *2hrs*

The farm is located on Prospect Hill Rd. in Harvard. From Rte. 2 (Exit 38A), take Rte. 110/111 toward Harvard, then take the first right on Old Shirley Rd. Follow the signs. Open mid-May–Oct daily 10am–5pm. $6. ✕ ☎ *978-456-3924. www. fruitlands.org.*

The farmhouse has been transformed into a museum of transcendentalism; other museums on the grounds treat varied aspects of early American culture. From the tea room and the terrace, there is a lovely **view** of the region, including Mts. Monadnock and Wachusett. Nature trails thread the site, offering visitors a pleasant stroll on the land bordering the museum buildings *(map available at entrance)*.

Fruitlands – The museum of transcendentalism is arranged in this 18C farmhouse. The museum exhibits mementos belonging to Emerson, Thoreau and Alcott, the philosophers and writers of the period.

Shaker Museum – This simple Shaker building (1794) was moved to Fruitlands after the Harvard Shaker Community, founded in the late 18C, was disbanded in 1919. The structure contains Shaker products and furnishings.

Indian Museum – Two statues by Philip Sears, *The Dreamer* and *He Who Shoots the Stars*, flank the entrance to the building, inviting visitors to enter and view the superb collection of North American Indian artifacts, baskets and clothing. Note the samples from Thoreau's sizable collection of arrowheads.

Picture Gallery – The primitive portraits and landscape paintings hanging in this building are representative of America's 19C itinerant portraitists and the artists of the **Hudson River school** (Cole, Church, Durand).

■ The Tea Room

A fifth attraction at Fruitlands Museums is the restaurant on the premises. The sophisticated lunch menu at The Tea Room augurs a leisurely and rewarding dining experience, inside, or outdoors on the tent-covered terrace *(heated in cooler weather)*. Chef-prepared soups, quiches, salads and crepes as well as specialty sandwiches or a "create your own" sandwich board are offered daily from 11am–3pm (on Sundays there's a brunch buffet from 10am–2pm). Start with the ginger pumpkin soup. Then choose the roasted acorn squash and vegetable melange with figs and pine nuts; the spinach and shitake mushroom crepe; or the herb-grilled chicken with lemon-poppyseed vinaigrette, roma tomatoes, toasted pecans and fresh nectarines. Tea with "decadent desserts" is served from 3pm–4pm. *Reservations advised.* ☎ *978-456-3924 ext. 224.*

Michelin Green Guides available in English
for North America include:
California
Canada
Chicago
Florida
Mexico
New England
New York City
New York, New Jersey, Pennsylvania
Quebec
San Francisco
Washington DC

HANCOCK SHAKER VILLAGE★★★

Map p 115

Hancock Shaker Village, an active Shaker community between 1790 and 1960, is today a museum village that relates the history of this sect, which for more than two centuries has practiced a form of communal living. Some 1,200 acres of farmland, meadow and woodland and more than 20 structures (those original to the site, some reconstructed and others moved from Shaker sites elsewhere) compose the museum. Exhibits and the buildings themselves interpret life as the Shakers lived it through over 10,000 objects, and demonstrations of such daily tasks such as gardening, milking cows, spinning yarn and cooking.

■ The Shakers

Origins – In the mid-18C a group of dissident Quakers in Manchester, England, came to be called "Shaking Quakers" because of their trembling and whirling during religious services. Later they were known simply as Shakers. In 1774 Shaker **Ann Lee**, an English textile worker, who had become a leader in the movement, emigrated to America with a small band of followers to avoid persecution for her religious beliefs. Her adherents considered Ann to be the female personification of Christ and referred to themselves as Believers—short for **United Society of Believers in Christ's Second Appearing**. Settling in New York, Lee and her adherents dedicated themselves to practicing and preaching the beliefs of the Shaker religion. They attracted new members wherever they went, and by the mid-19C the Shaker movement had reached its peak. The number of communities has steadily declined since the end of the 19C, although the Shaker experience in communal living never ceases to interest people from all walks of life.

The Community – Shaker life was based on the principles of community property, equality of the sexes, celibacy, separation from the outside world and public confession of sin. Men and women lived in families of 30 to 100 people who shared responsibilities equally with the Elders and Eldresses (two men and women from the village who served as the group's spiritual leaders). Duties in the field, shops and kitchen were divided among the members, and all activities in the community were governed by a rigid time schedule.
Because Shakers lived a celibate life, converts, called New Believers, were important to the community's continued existence. New Believers came from the outside world and from the Shaker society as well, since orphans adopted by the group often became permanent members of the community.
Shaker architecture exemplified simplicity, purity and functionalism. Buildings were designed to serve a specific purpose and were constructed from materials best suited to that purpose. The order and peace that guided the religious life of the Shakers inspired the designs of their buildings.

Historical Notes – Hancock Shaker Village was the third of a total of 19 Shaker communities in the US. It was founded some 14 years after Ann Lee and her followers came to the New World from England. At its peak, this community supported about 300 Shakers, who were primarily farmers operating a 3,000 acre farm, including dairy cows (Hancock is still an active farm today). But the village population was in decline by the 1930s and the Hancock Shakers razed several buildings on the site. In 1960 the property was sold to a group of Shakers who sought to preserve the sect's heritage. The core of Hancock's collection was formed by personal donations that include furniture, textiles, baskets and tools. Today the facility is operated as a nonprofit educational organization. A new $2.5 million **Center for Shaker Studies** is under construction near the entrance to the village, expected to open in the summer of 2000. It will house a visitor center, museum shop, orientation facilities and two galleries for rotating exhibits.

VISIT *3hrs*

🧒 *At the junction of Rtes. 20 and 41, 9mi north of the Massachusetts Tpk. (Exit 1). Open late May–late Oct daily 9:30am–5pm; $13.50. Visit by guided tour (1hr 30min) only, Apr–Memorial Day & late Oct–Nov 10am–3pm. Rest of the year by appointment. $10. Closed Thanksgiving Day. ✗ ☎ 800-817-1137. www. hancockshakervillage.org. A site plan and schedule of daily events are obtainable at the visitor center. Several documentary films on the Shakers are shown continuously in various buildings throughout the village. An orientation film is presented in the Poultry House.*

Brick Dwelling, Gathering Room

Hancock Shaker Village

From the current visitor center, pass the **garden tool shed**, then the **herb garden**. On the other side of Route 20 you will find the Shaker **cemetery**, a replica of the **schoolhouse**, a horse barn (1850), **ministry shop** (1874), and the **meetinghouse** (1793), which was moved to the village in 1962.

Poultry House – This former poultry house contains a small viewing room, where a film *(12min)* orients visitors to the Shaker community and exhibits on Shaker life, industry and religion.

Brick Dwelling – The community dining room, kitchens and retiring rooms were located in this structure, which also houses displays of pharmaceutical, medical and sewing artifacts from buildings that are no longer standing. Spacious, light and airy, the Brick Dwelling boasted 100 large doors, 245 cupboard doors, 369 drawers, and 95 windows with 3,194 panes of glass.

Shops – In these shops the Brothers made tinware, brooms, oval boxes and clocks; the Sisters dried herbs, wove cloth and made dairy products. Today artisans work here, reproducing Shaker crafts.

Round Stone Barn – Built in 1826, the barn is a masterpiece of Shaker architecture and functionalism. Wagons entered the third level and emptied their hay into the central haymow. On the middle level, stables radiated out from the central manger, making it easy for one person to feed the entire herd. Manure pits were located on the lower level.

■ Shaker Industries

Guided by the words of Mother Ann, "Do all your work as though you had 1,000 years to live, and as though you were going to die tomorrow," the Shakers became known for the products they made. Originally constructed solely for the use of Shakers, these items were in time marketed across the country as the sect grew dependent on the outside world for certain goods. Although the garden and seed industry was the Shakers' specialty, the Shaker label on brooms, furniture, oval boxes and other items guaranteed the highest quality. Shaker innovations, such as the pegboard, sliding cupboard and low-back chair, reflect the functionalism of the products crafted by members of this sect. Many Shaker-crafted products, including furniture, baskets and clothing, are on sale in the gift shop at Hancock Shaker Village.

Barn Complex (1910-1939) – Formerly a stable for livestock and hay storage, the barn includes the Good Room, where baked goods and beverages are served, and the fun **Discovery Room**. In the latter, visitors can make a Shaker basket, milk a "cow," weave a scarf and don period Shaker clothing, among other hands-on activities.

Nearby, the **Tan House** served as a blacksmith shop, cider room and tannery; it now functions as a cabinetmaker's workshop. The **Ice House** and the **Hired Men's Shop** are also located close to the barn.

Trustees Office and Store – Official community business was conducted in this building, which also housed the Shaker Fancy Goods Store.

Meetinghouse – The Shakers met here every Sunday for their religious services. Neatness and symmetry characterize the overall design of the structure. The meeting room, a large open hall on the first floor, provided ample space for dancing. Singing (a cappella) was customarily part of the worship as well. Of an

> ■ **Sister Olive's Ginger Cakes**
>
> | | |
> |---|---|
> | 1/2 cup butter | 1 teaspoon baking soda |
> | 1/2 cup brown sugar | 3 teaspoons ginger |
> | 1 egg, beaten | 1 teaspoon cinnamon |
> | 1/2 cup thick sour milk or cream | 1/2 teaspoon salt |
> | 3-1/2 cups flour, pre-sifted | Raisins |
> | 1 cup molasses | |
>
> Cream butter and sugar together. Add egg and beat well. Add sour milk or cream. Add molasses. Sift dry ingredients together and mix in well. Drop by teaspoons on greased cookie sheet, placing far apart. Top each with 3 raisins.
> Bake 12 minutes at 350 degrees. Yields 4-1/2 dozen cakes.
> *Source: The Best of Shaker Cooking* by Amy Bess Miller and Persis Fuller

estimated 10,000 songs attributed to the Shakers, the best known is most likely "Simple Gifts," adapted by American composer Aaron Copland for his *Appalachian Spring* ballet. The offices and living quarters of the community's spiritual leaders occupied the second floor.

Laundry and Machine Shop — The machines in this large building were at one time activated by a turbine that was powered by water flowing from a mountain reservoir to the north of the village.

> **"Let your words be few and seasoned with grace."**
> Ann Lee

HINGHAM
Population 19,821
Map p 151
Tourist Office ☎ 781-826-3136

Hingham is a lovely old settlement on Massachusetts' South Shore. This Boston suburb is graced with tree-shaded streets lined with 18C and 19C dwellings, including the **Old Ordinary**, now a museum devoted to local history.

SIGHTS

* **Old Ship Church** — *107 Main St. Visit by guided tour (30min) only, Jul–Aug daily 1pm–4pm. Rest of the year by appointment. Contribution requested.* & ☎ 781-749-1679. Built by ships' carpenters in 1681, Old Ship Church is the last remaining Puritan meetinghouse in the US. Inside, the finely crafted pulpit, galleries, columns, paneling and box pews remain unpainted, and the interior glows with the rich tones of natural wood. The church received its popular name, Old Ship, due to the curved ceiling timbers that give the roof the appearance of an inverted ship's hull.

* **World's End** — *Follow Rte. 3A to the Hingham Harbor rotary, then take Summer St. east .5mi. Turn left onto Martin's Lane and continue .75mi to sign for World's End. Open Apr–Sept daily 9am–8pm. Rest of the year daily 9am–5pm. $4.* ☎ 781-821-2977. www.thetrustees.org. *Trail access to the left of the parking lot. From the entrance bear left onto the wide gravel road; always take the left fork.* This quiet peninsula lies only 14mi from BOSTON. Gentle hillsides are covered with grassy meadows, shaded paths and wildflowers. The trail leads past Pine Hill, Planters Hill and then over the Bar (a narrow neck of land) before arriving at the "world's end," the tip of the peninsula, where there are views of Boston and Nantasket Beach.

IPSWICH
Population 11,873
Map of Principal Sights
Tourist Office ☎ 978-356-8540

This small colonial town, bordered by white sandy beaches and woodlands, attracts many artists and tourists. The popularity of Ipswich has given rise to the concentration of restaurants and shops in the center of town, and the gastronomically famous **Ipswich clam** is a regional favorite. Restored 17C and 18C dwellings line the streets of Ipswich, enhancing its centuries-old charm.

SIGHTS

Whipple House – *1 South Village Green. Visit by guided tour (45min) only, May–Oct Wed–Sat 10am–4pm, Sun 1pm–4pm. $7.* ☎ *978-356-2811.* This handsome dwelling, built by John Whipple around 1655, provides evidence of the comfort and refinement that graced the lives of many early New Englanders. The spacious rooms are decorated with enormous fireplaces and period furnishings. Note upstairs the samples of handmade lace from Ipswich, a center of lace making from the late 17C to the early 19C.

> ### Goodale Orchard Farm Store and Cider Mill
>
> *143 Argilla Rd.* ☎ *978-356-5366.* En route to Crane Beach, look for this delightful 125-acre farm amid the meadows, ponds and horse pastures of the lovely countryside. At the end of the dirt road bordered with orchard trees, produce-filled bins and fresh flower bouquets front the large 18C barn. Inside, a variety of farm-grown fruits and vegetables as well as soups and sandwiches, canned goods, herbs and homemade wines and cider are for sale. Raspberries, strawberries, blueberries and apples are there for the picking *(in season)*. Stop in for a cup of cold cider in the summer (or warm cider in the fall). *Open May til the weekend after Thanksgiving Day.*

★ **Crane Beach** – *From Rte. 1A south of Ipswich, take Rte. 133 east toward Essex. Turn left on Northgate Rd. At the end of Northgate Rd., turn right on Argilla Rd. The road ends at Crane Beach. Open year-round daily 8am–dusk. $7.50–$15/car (rates vary seasonally).* ✗ ♿ ☎ *978-356-4354. www. thetrustees. org.* This sandy beach stretches for several miles along the coast. The dunes beyond the beach are covered with a pitch pine forest and a red maple swamp. The best way to explore the area is by following the **Pine Hollow Trail** *(45min; access to the right of the parking lot).* During the summer, concerts are presented at the mansion on **Castle Hill**, the former residence of the Crane family *(concert information* ☎ *978-356-4351).*

EXCURSION

Topsfield – *7mi southwest of Ipswich by Topsfield Rd. From the center of Ipswich take Market St. to Topsfield Rd.* Topsfield was a prosperous farming village until the 19C, when it became a residential community.

Parson Capen House – *1 Howlett St., facing the green. Visit by guided tour (45min) only, mid-Jun–mid-Sept Wed, Fri & Sun 1pm–4:30pm. Other times by advance appointment. Closed major holidays. $3.* ☎ *978-887-9724. www.tiac.net/users/ tophist.* The pitched roof, central chimney, overhanging stories and hanging pendants of this Elizabethan dwelling (1683) reflect the trend toward English building traditions in American Colonial architecture.

LEXINGTON★★

Population 28,974
Map of Principal Sights
Tourist Office ☎ 781-862-1450

This thriving residential community has been historically inseparable, in the minds of most Americans, from the town of Concord since April 19, 1775, when British and colonial troops clashed at Lexington and at Concord, triggering the events that exploded into the **American Revolution**. The Revolutionary War sites and monuments preserved here allow visitors to retrace, step by step, the incidents that occurred on that day, over 200 years ago, when the British marched from BOSTON to Lexington and on to Concord.

Historical Notes

Measures and Countermeasures – Tensions between the colonists and the British increased steadily following the passage of the Stamp Act in 1765. In 1774 the colonists established their own legislative body, the Provincial Congress, with John Hancock as its president. Within a year the Congress had created a militia and stockpiled arms in Concord for the colonial troops. England reacted swiftly by dispatching troops to Boston and closing the city's port. In an attempt to put an end to the rebels' activity, General Gage, the leader of the British troops in Boston, decided to march on Concord and seize the weapons hidden there.

April 19, 1775 – Forewarned of the British soldiers' approach by Paul Revere and his riders, 77 minutemen who had spent the night of April 18 at **Buckman Tavern** in Lexington awaiting the enemy moved toward the **green** where their leader, Captain Parker, advised them: "Stand your ground and don't fire unless fired upon, but if they mean to have a war, let it begin here!" At about five o'clock in the morning, the British began to arrive, and Parker, realizing that his men were greatly outnumbered, gave the order to disperse. He was too late; a shot rang out, and during the skirmish that followed, eight minutemen were killed and ten others wounded. The British commander ordered his men to regroup and march on to Concord.

In Concord, the minutemen who had arrived from nearby villages observed from a hilltop as British soldiers began to search for the supplies. Aware that fires were burning in the town below, and fearful that the British would raze Concord, the patriots descended to the **Old North Bridge**, where they found themselves confronted by the enemy. There, a battle ensued until the British, weary and reduced in numbers, began their retreat to Boston along Battle Road. Snipers firing from the woods added to the day's British casualties; before nightfall another skirmish between the two forces took place at **Meriam's Corner**.

SIGHTS *4hrs*

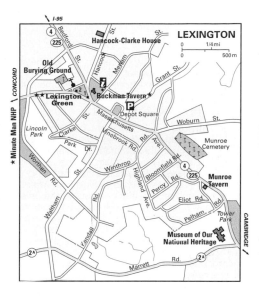

★★ **Lexington Green** – The first confrontation between the British soldiers and the minutemen on April 19 took place in this triangular park. Henry Kitson's statue **The Minuteman** (**1**) represents the leader of the Lexington militia, Captain Parker. Seven of the colonists killed here that day are buried beneath the **Revolutionary Monument** (**2**).

★ **Buckman Tavern** – *1 Bedford St. Visit by guided tour (30min) only, Apr– Oct Mon–Sat 10am–5pm, Sun 1pm–5pm. $4. Combination ticket ($10) available for Buckman Tavern, Hancock-Clarke House & Munroe Tavern.* ☎ *781-862-5598.* The minutemen gathered here on the evening of April 18 to await the arrival of the British troops. Following the battle between the British and the militia on the green, the minutemen who had been wounded were carried to Buckman Tavern, where they were given medical care. Restored to its original 18C appearance, the tavern comprises a bar, bedchambers, a ballroom, separate rooms set aside for women, and an attic where, for a few pennies a night, drovers were permitted to sleep.

★ **Minute Man National Historical Park** – *Off Rte. 2A west of Lexington Green. See Entry Heading Concord.*

Old Burying Ground – In the old cemetery behind the church there are well-preserved examples of grave markers dating from the 17C.

Hancock-Clarke House – *36 Hancock St. Visit by guided tour (30min) only, Apr–Oct Mon–Sat 10am–5pm, Sun 1pm–5pm. $4.* ☎ *781-861-0928.* Samuel Adams and John Hancock were at this house (1698) the evening of April 18, 1775, when Paul Revere rode into Lexington to warn them to flee.

■ Freemasonry

Reputedly the world's largest and oldest global fraternal order, Freemasonry had its origins in the stonemason guilds of the late Middle Ages. Its official founding, however, was in England in 1717. Established in the American colonies in the late 1720s, it was embraced by prominent leaders of the Revolutionary period. George Washington is perhaps the best-known member of this society. In fact, 14 US presidents have been Masons. Though Freemasonry is not a secret society, as is often believed, it does maintain secrecy concerning its ritual practices, which include the symbolic use of architectural concepts and implements to recall stonemasonry.

Munroe Tavern – *1332 Massachusetts Ave. Visit by guided tour (30min) only, Apr–Oct Mon–Sat 10am–5pm, Sun 1pm–5pm. $4.* ☎ *781-674-9238.* This 17C tavern served as the headquarters and hospital for the British troops during their retreat from Concord to Boston on April 19.

Museum of Our National Heritage – *Rte. 2A and Massachusetts Ave. Open year-round Mon–Sat 10am–5pm, Sun noon–5pm. Closed Jan 1, Thanksgiving Day, Dec 24, 25, 31.* ♿ ☎ *781-861-6559.* This contemporary brick and glass building contains a museum and library of American history. Two large permanent displays—a retelling of the story of the skirmish at Lexington and an interesting exhibit on the Freemasons and other such organizations—are supplemented with changing exhibits that feature the growth and development of the nation from its founding to the present. The content of these temporary shows ranges from summer camps to interiors designed by Frank Lloyd Wright. Weekend programs feature lectures, concerts and special events.

LOWELL

Population 103,439
Map of Principal Sights
Tourist Office ☎ 978-459-6150

This sizable manufacturing center, one of the state's largest cities, originated as the earliest planned industrial city in the country. Proximity to the Merrimack River was a key factor in its development as a leading 19C producer of textiles.

Historical Notes

First Mill Town – In the early 19C New England merchant Francis Cabot Lowell (1775-1817) developed a modified version of the English power loom with a view toward improving the manufacture of American textiles. He and a group of investors built their first mill in Waltham on the banks of the Charles River west of Boston. There Lowell revolutionized the manufacturing process by successfully integrating all aspects of production within a single mill. After Lowell's death, the investors, desirous of expanding their operations, selected the present site because of its proximity to a larger power source: **Pawtucket Falls**, a 1mi stretch of the Merrimack River that drops some 32ft in elevation. The new mill town, appropriately named Lowell, was planned by Kirk Boott, a former British army officer. Soon blocks of brick factories, company-owned dwellings, warehouses, stores, a church, and 5.6mi of canals (required to transport the water from the falls to the turbines) had been constructed.
Incorporated as a town in 1826, Lowell quickly rose to prominence as the nation's largest cotton textile producer. Initially the city's labor force consisted of young Yankee women from the farms of New England, but by the mid-19C, the so-called "mill girls" were replaced by Irish and French-Canadian immigrants willing to accept lower wages. Successive waves of newcomers from other European countries followed. The early chapters of America's labor history unfolded in the mills of Lowell, where strikes and social unrest periodically disrupted production.

Exemplary Rehabilitation – A number of factors, including increased competition from Southern mills, and the development of steam as an alternative energy source, contributed to the city's decline in the late 19C. The crash of 1929 sounded the death knell for Lowell.
The revitalization of Lowell's economy in the late 1970s is attributed to the concerted efforts of preservationists and the influx of modern industries, such as Wang Labs, Raytheon and other major employers. Local and state bodies, in collaboration with the federal government, restored many of Lowell's 19C buildings and its canal system to preserve the city's unique industrial heritage. This successful restoration project has served as a model for similar sights around the US.

Art-World Celebrities – Lowell is the birthplace of three famous personalities in the arts: painter **James Abbott McNeill Whistler** *(birthplace/museum at 243 Worthen St., one block from visitor center)*, writer Jack Kerouac and screen star Bette Davis.

SIGHTS

★★**Lowell National Historical Park** – *Begin your visit at the visitor center to obtain a free map, daily schedule of tours and opening hours of sights mentioned below.* ☎ *978-970-5000.* Established in 1978, the park comprises a group of buildings, canals and walkways scattered throughout Lowell's downtown district. The **visitor center**, located in a renovated mill complex, offers an introduction to Lowell's history through an award-winning video *(20min)* and display panels *(246 Market St.; open year-round daily 9am–5pm; closed Jan 1, Thanksgiving Day, Dec 25;* ⚮ ♿ *).* Restored vintage **trolleys** *(free boarding)* run continuously around the downtown area and allow visitors to tour the attractions at leisure.

Canal tours explore the remarkable man-made water network that channeled the waters of the Pawtucket Falls to the mill turbines *(depart from the visitor center Jul–Sept Mon–Thu 10:30am–4pm, Fri, Sat, Sun 10:30am–5:30pm; $6; advance reservations required)*.

★★ **Boott Cotton Mills** – *Open year-round daily 9:30am–5pm. $4.* &. Wedged between the Eastern Canal and the Merrimack River, this imposing industrial complex (1873) graced by a central bell tower houses the park's main exhibit. The first floor **weave room**, equipped with 88 operating power looms *(earplugs provided at entrance)*, re-creates the jarring atmosphere of a 1920s textile mill. The second floor features a series of exhibits focused on America's Industrial Revolution, Lowell's history, textile production and technology and labor relations, including a riveting labor-oriented film *(24min)* entitled *Wheels of Change: The First Century of American Industry*. Recorded oral histories of former mill workers provide poignant testimony to the grim realities of mill life.

Additional Sights – Located in an authentic boardinghouse across the street from the Boott mills, the Working People Exhibit offers insight into the lives of factory workers from the "mill girls" to 20C immigrants. St. Anne's Church (1825), the Gothic Revival structure fronting Merrimack Street near the Merrimack Canal, was conceived as a religious center for the mill community. The enlightening tour of the Suffolk Mill *(visit by guided tour only)* includes a close look at an operating 19C turbine and a power loom.

Fronting the long facade of the Massachusetts Mills, Eastern Canal Park contains an elegant group of marble monoliths inscribed with quotations from the works of native son and Beat generation writer **Jack Kerouac** (1922-69). *A handout locating sights associated with Kerouac is available at the visitor center.*

★ **American Textile History Museum** – *491 Dutton St. Open year-round Tue–Fri 9am–4pm, weekends & holidays 10am–4pm. Closed Jan 1, Thanksgiving Day, Dec 25. $5.* ✗ & ☎ *978-441-0400. www.athm.org.* Established in North Andover in 1960, this museum is now housed in a renovated 160,000sq ft brick warehouse in Lowell. Opened in 1997 in its new home, the museum serves as a testament to the nation's textile production and covers 300 years of American textile history, from dependence on foreign imports through industrialization. The core exhibit includes a wide array of clothing, tools, illustrations and machines that trace changes occurring as automation replaced traditional methods of cloth making. Exhibits proceed chronologically through early fabrics, spinning wheels, hand looms and dyes to the 20C weave shed, where visitors can see and hear cloth being made. Re-created interiors, such as an 18C weaver's log cabin, 1820s general store and 1870s woolen mill, illustrate the impact of textiles on daily life. A special exhibit gallery features textile-related shows throughout the year.

New England Quilt Museum – *18 Shattuck St. Open May–Nov Tue–Sat 10am–4pm, Sun noon–4pm. Rest of the year Tue–Sat 10am–4pm. Closed major holidays. $4.* & ☎ *978-452-4207. www.nequiltmuseum.org.* This two-level, sunlit gallery showcases traditional and contemporary quilts—some hung like paintings, some thrown over beds—on a rotating basis. Informative placards explain the history of certain designs and quilting's ongoing appeal as a cherished part of Americana.

EXCURSION

Andover – *11mi northeast of Lowell by Rte. 495 (Exit 41), then Rte. 28.* This small colonial village is home to the select preparatory school **Phillips Academy** (1778). The focal point of the village is the academy's spacious green and attractively designed buildings: Bulfinch Hall, the Andover Inn, the Archaeological Museum and the **Addison Gallery of American Art**, which has a noteworthy collection of American paintings and sculpture *(open year-round Tue–Sat 10am–5pm, Sun 1pm–5pm; closed Aug & major holidays;* & ☎ *978-749-4015. www.andover.edu/addison.*

MARBLEHEAD★

Population 19,971
Map p 151
Tourist Office ☎ 978-356-8540

Marblehead is a prosperous resort and boating center largely because of its magnificent harbor. The community continues to be one of the East Coast's major yachting capitals.

Historical Notes – Prior to the Revolution, this small fishing port had grown into a flourishing trade center. Marblehead vessels returned home with great wealth, and their owners and captains spent freely in building the Colonial and Georgian homes that line the narrow, winding streets of Old Marblehead. Losses suffered during the war, competition from other ports and the gale of 1846, which destroyed 10 Marblehead ships and killed 65 men, caused the inhabitants to turn to industry, such as shoe manufacturing, to earn their living.

The sea again became the source of prosperity for Marblehead when, in the late 19C and early 20C, the town developed into a resort, with boating as a major attraction. The sail and motor pleasure craft that crowd the harbor in season today are especially impressive when viewed from **Fort Sewall** *(at the end of Front St.)*, **Crocker Park★** *(off Front St.)* or the lighthouse on **Marblehead Neck**, a select residential area. Meticulously preserved 18C and 19C structures along **Atlantic Avenue★** and surrounding side streets are crammed with both tony antique shops and laid-back bars and coffee houses.

SIGHTS

★**Jeremiah Lee Mansion** – *161 Washington St. Visit by guided tour (50min) only, mid-May–Oct Mon–Sat 10am–4pm, Sun 1pm–4pm. $5.* ☎ *781-631-1768.* The wood blocks composing the exterior of this dignified 16-room Georgian dwelling, built in 1768 for the successful merchant Col. Jeremiah Lee, have been refinished with a mixture of paint and sand to resemble stone.

Inside, the immense **entrance hall**, with its grandiose proportions, highly polished mahogany woodwork and English mural wallpapers, makes this house one of the most memorable of the period in New England. Reproductions of two full-length portraits of the Lees by John Singleton Copley are hung in the hall. In several rooms, wallpaper hand-painted in the style of the 18C Italian artist Giovanni Pannini depicts classical ruins and fishing scenes. The house contains 18C and 19C furniture, silver, ceramics and textiles.

Across the street, a newly refurbished **gallery** (no. 170) displays sculpture and a group of brightly colored primitive seascapes by self-taught Marblehead artist John Frost, formerly a Grand Banks fisherman.

Abbot Hall – *Town Hall. Open Jun–Oct Mon–Fri 8am–5pm, Sat 9am–6pm, Sun 11am–6pm. Rest of the year Mon–Thu 8am–5pm, Fri 8am–1pm. Closed major holidays. Contribution requested.* ♿ ☎ *781-631-0000.* The familiar patriotic canvas **The Spirit of '76**, painted by A.M. Willard to celebrate the nation's centennial, hangs in the Selectman's Room. The picture was given to the town by Gen. John Devereux, whose son was the model for the drummer boy in the painting.

MARTHA'S VINEYARD★★

Map of Principal Sights
Tourist Office ☎ 508-693-0085

This triangular-shaped island, 5mi south of CAPE COD, is blessed with a landscape that resembles the cape. Here, rolling heaths spotted with ponds and lakes give way to forests of oak and pine, seaside cliffs and broad beaches (both pebble and sand). The towns on the Vineyard are small fishing villages and summer resorts, each with its own history and character.

When Bartholomew Gosnold landed on this island in 1602, he found an abundance of wild grapes growing here. He thus named this land Martha's Vineyard, in honor of his daughter Martha. Today, however, wild grapes no longer cover the island.

As with the cape and Nantucket, the population of Martha's Vineyard skyrockets in the summer, bringing a mix of day-trippers and wealthy second-home owners and making off-season visits particularly appealing.

SIGHTS *1 day. Map p 186.*

Vineyard Haven – Ferries arrive at and depart from this upscale community. Shops and eateries border Main Street.

★**Oak Bluffs** – In the 1830s, the Methodists of Edgartown began to meet regularly in an oak grove at the northern end of town. Each summer the group attracted a larger number of followers who spent three months in a tent camp situated a short distance from the place where religious services were held.

By the 1850s more than 12,000 persons were attending the annual services at Cottage City (as the encampment came to be known), and by the end of the 19C the city had been renamed Oak Bluffs for the oak grove where the first revival meetings were held. At about the same time, small wooden cottages were built to replace the tents that stood near the tabernacle, the center of religious worship.

★**Trinity Park and Gingerbread Cottages** – *Leave the car near the harbor and follow Central Ave. to Cottage City.* Small ornate Victorian "gingerbread" houses, colorfully painted and decorated with lacy wooden trim resembling cake frosting, ring the tabernacle, a beautiful example of ironwork architecture.

★**Edgartown** – Most of tony Edgartown's large, handsome dwellings were built in the 1820s and 1830s when the town was an important whaling center. A number of these homes line North Water Street and face Edgartown Harbor, once dominated by a fleet of whaling vessels and now filled with modern pleasure craft. Two

PRACTICAL INFORMATION .... Area Code: 508

Getting There – From **Boston** to **New Bedford** (64mi): I-93 south to Rte. 24 west to Rte. 140 east. From **Boston** to Sagamore Bridge, **Cape Cod** (56mi): I-93 south to Rte. 3 south; to **Hyannis** (17mi): Rte. 6 west to Rte. 132 west; to **Falmouth** (20mi) Rte. 6 west to Rte. 28 east (continue on Woods Hole Rd. to Woods Hole).

International and domestic flights to **Logan International Airport** (Boston) ☎ 617-561-1800 or **T.F. Green State Airport** (Providence) ☎ 401-737-4000. Major rental car agencies *(p 306)*. Closest Amtrak **train** station: Providence, RI ☎ 800-872-7245. **Bus** stations: Hyannis – Plymouth & Brockton Bus Lines ☎ 778-9767; Woods Hole – Bonanza Bus Lines ☎ 800-556-3815.

Ferry Schedule

Departure/ Destination	Schedule (one-way)	Duration (round-trip)	Adult Fare	Company
Falmouth to **Oak Bluffs**	late May–mid Oct, daily	35min	$10	Island Commuter Corp. ☎ 548-4800
Falmouth to **Edgartown**	mid-Jun–Labor Day, daily; Memorial Day– Jun & early Sept– Columbus Day, weekends only	1hr	$22	**Falmouth Ferry** ☎548-9400
Hyannis to **Oak Bluffs**	early May–Oct, daily	1hr 45min	$24	**Hy-Line** ☎ 778-2600
Woods Hole to **Vineyard Haven**	year-round, daily	45min	$10	**Steamship** **Authority** ☎ 477-8600
Woods Hole to **Oak Bluffs**	year-round, daily	45min	$10	**Steamship** **Authority** ☎ 477-8600
Nantucket to **Oak Bluffs**	Jun–mid-Sept, daily	2hr 15min	$24	**Hy-Line** ☎ 693-0112
New Bedford to **Vineyard Haven**	mid-May–mid-Oct, daily	1hr 30min	$17	**Martha's Vineyard** **Ferry** ☎ 997-1688

Getting Around – Streets in Martha's Vineyard are often congested and parking may be difficult (especially in July and August); bicycle or public transportation recommended. Shuttle service between main island towns of Vineyard Haven, Oak Bluffs and Edgartown Apr–Oct, Island Transport ☎ 693-0058. Bicycle and car rentals available in main island towns.

Visitor Information – **Martha's Vineyard Chamber of Commerce** is located on Beach Rd., mailing address: PO Box 1698, Vineyard Haven MA 02568 ☎ 693-0085. www.mvy.com.

Accommodations – Reservation services: **About the Beach** PO Box 269, Oak Bluffs MA 02557 ☎ 693-1718, **Destinnations** 572 Rte. 28, W. Yarmouth MA 02673 ☎ 800-333-4667, **Martha's Vineyard & Nantucket Reservations** PO Box 1322, Vineyard Haven MA 02568 ☎ 693-7200. Lodging directory available from Chamber of Commerce *(above)*. Accommodations include economy and moderate hotels, bed and breakfasts and rental cottages. **Camping:** Vineyard Haven. **American Youth Hostel:** Edgartown-West Tisbury Rd. Mailing address: PO Box 3158, West Tisbury MA 02575 ☎ 693-2665.

Recreation – Southern **beaches** offer heavy surf; northern and eastern beaches are more protected. **Boat rentals** in main island towns; windsurfing equipment rentals in Vineyard Haven. Paved **biking** trails are located throughout island. Most specialty **shopping** and supplies can be found in main island towns. *Contact chamber of commerce for more information regarding shopping and recreation on Martha's Vineyard.*

historic houses interpret island life and history: the 1672 **Vincent House** *(Main St.; open May–Oct Mon–Sat noon–3pm; $3;* ☎ *508-627-8619)* and the 1765 **Thomas Cooke House** *(Cooke and Schools Sts; open mid-Jun–mid-Oct Tue–Sat 10am–5pm; $6;* ☎ *508-627-4441; www.vineyard.net/org/mnhs).*

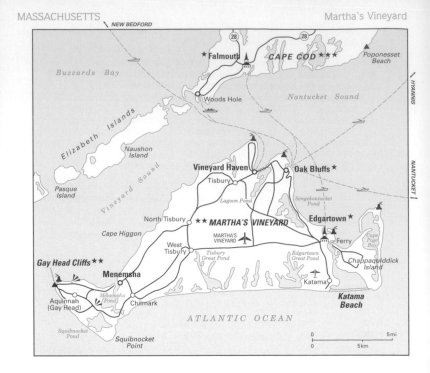

Vineyard Museum – *59 School St. Open mid-Jun–mid-Oct Tue–Sat 10am–5pm. Rest of the year Wed–Fri 1pm–4pm, Sat 10am–4pm. $6. ☎ 508-627-4441. www. vineyard.net/org/mvhs.* The skill of the ships' carpenters who built the Thomas Cooke House is reflected in its fine interior wood paneling and trim. Artifacts related to whaling, including a picture of Capt. Valentine Pease (master of the *Acushnet*, on which Herman Melville sailed), on whom Melville based his character of Captain Ahab in *Moby Dick*, offer glimpses of the era of whaling.

Opposite Edgartown is **Chappaquiddick Island**, where private homes and unspoiled natural areas are sheltered by thick woodlands. The ferry whose name is *On Time*, so-called as an ironic reference to its irregular schedule, provides service between Edgartown and Chappaquiddick.

Gay Head Cliffs

Katama Beach – This sandy stretch of beach linking Chappaquiddick to the main island extends the entire length of the south shore.

As the road approaches Gay Head, it climbs above Menemsha and Squibnocket Ponds, where alewives spawn in the spring, permitting a **view** of Menemsha.

★★Gay Head Cliffs – Located at the western tip of the Vineyard, these 60ft cliffs, composed of striated layers of clay, display a rainbow of color: blue, tan, gray, red, white and orange. Dating back 100 million years, the cliffs contain fossils of prehistoric camels, wild horses and ancient whales. Erosion of the cliffs often causes the inshore waters to turn a reddish color. Today Gay Head's Native American residents use the clay to make decorative pottery.

Menemsha – With its picturesque lobster traps and weathered fishing sheds, this tiny waterfront village is a favorite subject of photographers.

MOHAWK TRAIL★★

Map of Principal Sights
Tourist Office ☏ 413-664-6256

The scenic 63mi stretch of Route 2 through northwestern Massachusetts, running from Millers Falls to the New York border, is known as the Mohawk Trail. Following an old Indian path along the banks of the Deerfield and Cold Rivers, through the Connecticut Valley and into the Berkshire Hills, this trail was used by the Mohawks as an invasion route during the French and Indian War. It passes through tiny mountaintop hamlets, sheer river gorges and dense forests. Views from the highway and off-road overlooks are spectacular in foliage season. The latest addition to the trail is the **Massachusetts Museum of Contemporary Art** in North Adams.

DRIVING TOUR *3hrs. 67mi.*

Greenfield – This agricultural town at the eastern end of the Mohawk Trail is named for its fertile green valley. The revitalized Main Street sports a tiny triangular common and handsome brick buildings housing a variety of shops and restaurants.

Follow Rte. 2. After 6mi the road rises, affording views into the valley. Continue to the intersection of the road to Shelburne Falls (13.5mi after Greenfield).

Trail Trinkets

Like bookends for the Mohawk Trail, two large souvenir stores flank each end of Route 2. Distinguished by a huge statue (28ft) of a Native American at the entrance, the **Big Indian Shop** 🅺🅸🅳 *(2217 Mohawk Trail, ☏ 413-625-6817)*, on the Shelburne Falls side, has toys and trinkets for the whole family. Jewelry, moccasins, t-shirts, prints, postcards, candy and much more are affordably priced, allowing kids in particular to stretch their spending money. Children will enjoy the tiny petting zoo outside. Near the North Adams side, the **Wigwam and Western Summit Giftshop** 🅺🅸🅳 *(☏ 413-663-3205)* features rocks and minerals, native garb and jewelry, maple products and fudge, t-shirts, toys, mugs and dozens of Mohawk Trail and Massachusetts souvenirs. Make a small purchase as a memento of this memorable trip.

★ Shelburne Falls – This quiet mountain village is located beside the falls of the Deerfield River. Glacial potholes, ground out of granite during the last Ice Age, can be seen on the riverbank near Salmon Falls *(Deerfield Ave.).*

Bridge of Flowers – *On the south side of the bridge over the Deerfield River.* Originally used by trolleys, this bridge has been transformed into a 400ft-long path of flower beds above the Deerfield River.

Return to Rte. 2.

Two miles past Charlemont the road enters **Mohawk Trail State Forest**. At the entrance to the forest stands a statue of an Indian brave titled **Hail to the Sunrise**. This bronze sculpture was created as a memorial to the five Indian tribes that once lived along the Mohawk Trail.

The road continues through a mountainous and rugged section of Route 2. Between Florida and North Adams there are good views to the north of Mt. Monadnock and Mt. Greylock.

From **Whitcomb Summit** (the highest peak on the trail at 2,240ft), the Green Mountains stretch into the distance; from **Western Summit** the Hoosac Valley is visible. **Hairpin Curve** offers broad **views★★** across the Hoosac and Berkshire Valleys to the Taconic Range. *Scenic flights (25min) available at the Harriman-West Airport in North Adams (below). $20 each/2 persons; $18 each/3 persons. Esposito Flying Service, Inc. ☏ 413-663-3330.*

Just before North Adams turn right onto Rte. 8 north, then turn left after .5mi.

★**Natural Bridge State Park** – *Open late May–early Oct daily 9am–5pm, holidays 10am–6pm. $2/car.* ☎ *413-663-6392.* The white marble natural bridge that gives the park its name rises 60ft above the churning waters of a narrow 475ft-long chasm. Glaciers sculpted and polished this marble, which was formed primarily from seashells deposited about 550 million years ago.

North Adams – North Adams' large brick mill buildings provide wistful reminders of the city's past as a leading industrial center in western Massachusetts. The mills attracted thousands of Canadians and Italians to settle in the area. In 1875, with the opening of the **Hoosac Tunnel** linking Massachusetts to the West, North Adams also grew into a bustling railroad center. Manufacturing and light industry continue to support the economy today, but the town has undergone tough times over the years as cloth and electronic components manufacturers have closed down. A bright spot, however, is the recent conversion of a vacant manufacturing complex into an art museum.

★★**Massachusetts Museum of Contemporary Art (MASS MoCA)** – *87 Marshall St. On Rte. 8, just north of Rte. 2. Open Jun–Oct daily 10am–5pm (Fri & Sat 7pm). Rest of the year Tue–Sun 10am–4pm. Closed Jan 1, Thanksgiving Day, Dec 25. $8.* ✕ ⅋ ☎ *413-664-4481. www.massmoca.org.* Spread out within the spacious, renovated interiors of a former factory, complete with clocktower, this sprawling new modern art campus (1999) is poised to fill the need for ever larger exhibit spaces for increasingly larger installations of contemporary art. The museum takes advantage of the intimate courtyards and vast wood-floored rooms of the 19C brick buildings to display works that have gone largely unseen because their size and weight had heretofore made exhibition impossible. The 27-structure complex, which goes by the acronym **MASS MoCA**, occupies a 13-acre site in downtown North Adams, making it the biggest center for contemporary visual and performing arts in the US to date—indeed one of the 19 galleries measures the length of a football field *(Building 5)*; another rises 40ft in height *(Building 4)*.

The idea to convert an empty electronics plant into an art gallery was born in 1987. As a result of a study by a team of architectural heavyweights, including Frank Gehry and Robert Venturi, the state legislature authorized matching grant funds to the city of North Adams. However, the troubled state economy stalled progress. By 1995 needed financing was in place, nonetheless, and rehabilitation began in phases under the direction of architects Bruner/Cott & Assocs. of Cambridge, MA. Festivities for the official opening in May 1999 were sold out, attracting attendees from other states as well as area residents.

The museum contains 120,000sq ft of exhibit area, but since the idea is to show gigantic works, only 25 to 30 pieces are on view at any one time. Works by such artists as Robert Rauschenberg, Mario Merz, Joseph Bueys and video artist Tony Oursler come from studios and museums around the world and change on a regular basis. Additionally MASS MoCA mounts sound-art installations, "environments," conceptual pieces, multimedia theatrical performances, and dance and music concerts—all made possible by the commodious theaters, rehearsal studios, outdoor stages and art-fabrication spaces that have found homes in this recycled industrial plant. Visitors are also invited to view works and installations in progress.

Western Gateway Heritage State Park – *Rte. 8 south.* Occupying the restored buildings of the city's old freight yard, this urban park preserves the history of North Adams' heyday as a manufacturing and railroad boomtown. In the **visitor center**, displays tell the story of the Hoosac Tunnel, one of the major engineering feats of the 19C *(open year-round daily 10am–5pm; closed Jan 1, Thanksgiving Day, Dec 25; contribution suggested;* ✕ ⅋ ☎ *413-663-6312).*

Built over a period of 25 years (1851-75), the 4.8mi tunnel through Hoosac Mountain marked the first use of nitroglycerin as a blasting agent and was the longest tunnel in the nation when it was completed. Its glory has always been overshadowed by the fact that almost 200 workers lost their lives during its construction.

Return to Rte. 2 west, then 1mi after North Adams center turn left onto Notch Rd. Follow the sign for Mt. Greylock Reservation. The road rises through wooded areas to the summit.

★★**Mt. Greylock** – *9mi ascent by car.* Located between the Taconic and Hoosac Ranges, Mt. Greylock (3,491ft) is the highest point in Massachusetts. The mountain was named for chief Grey Lock, whose tribe once hunted on these lands. Near the top, the rustic **Bascom Lodge**, a haven for hikers and nature lovers, offers overnight accommodations, meals *(reservations required)*, workshops, snacks, trail guides and maps *(AMC Mountain Club* ☎ *413-443-0011. www.ooutdoors.org).* From the War Memorial Tower at the summit there is are magnificent **views**★★★ of the entire region, including the Berkshire Valley, the Taconic Range and nearby Vermont and New York.

Descend to North Adams and continue on Rte. 2 west.

★★**Williamstown** – *See Entry Heading.*

NANTUCKET★★★

Population 3,069
Map of Principal Sights
Tourist Office ☎ 508-228-1700

Lying 30mi south of CAPE COD, Nantucket is a triangular patch of land 14mi long and 3.5mi wide that Herman Melville described in *Moby Dick* as "a mere hillock and elbow of sand." The flat relief, sandy soil, rounded ponds and tree-studded moors are evidence of the island's glacial origins and underlying moraine. The island of Nantucket—an Indian word meaning "distant land"—includes the village of the same name, situated on a magnificent harbor protected by a long, narrow barrier of sandy beach.

Historical Notes

The Rise and Fall of Whaling – The history of the island is interwoven with that of its famous port, which was the world capital of the whaling industry in the early 19C. In the 17C the Indians taught the settlers how to harpoon whales that passed close to shore. As hunting depleted the whale population in the Atlantic Ocean, Nantucketers sought their prey in the unexploited waters of the Pacific. For almost 100 years, between 1740 and the 1830s, Nantucket reigned as the preeminent whaling port. Merchants and shipowners grew rich by selling as many as 30,000 barrels a year of precious whale oil in London and other major cities. With their wealth whalers built the magnificent homes that stand on Main Street near the wharves.

Then came the decline. A sandbar stretching across the mouth of Nantucket harbor prohibited the entrance of the large whale ships that were being constructed in the early 19C, and the island's whaling industry gradually migrated to

A Nantucket Cottage

Carolyn L. Bates/f/STOP PICTURES

the deepwater port of New Bedford. During that period the island tragically lost much of its population to a great fire in 1846, to the California Gold Rush and to the discovery of oil in Pennsylvania, events that ultimately brought Nantucket's golden era to a close.

Nicknamed "the little gray lady in the sea" by early sailors because of its weathered gray cottages covered with pink roses in the summer, Nantucket was spared the industrialization of the 19C. With its comfortable old homes, wharfside structures and cobblestone streets, Nantucket today reigns as one of the most charming, well-preserved towns on the East Coast.

Nantucketers – The difficult life led by seamen and their wives, and the Quaker religion many of them practiced, contributed to the simple, austere and strong character for which Nantucketers are known. **Peter Foulger**, the grandfather of Benjamin Franklin, and **Maria Mitchell**, the first American woman astronomer, were both from Nantucket. A less well-known, yet splendid example of the determination of Nantucketers was the wife of Capt. Charles Grant. Tired of spending years alone at home while Grant was at sea, Nancy Grant joined her husband on a whaling voyage in 1849, and spent the better part of the next 32 years sailing with him.

★★★THE CENTER *1 day. Map p 191.*

The Nantucket Historical Association sells a combination ticket ($10) to the historic houses and museums it administers: the Hadwen House, Whaling Museum, Oldest House, Old Gaol, and Old Mill. The ticket may be purchased at any of these sights. ☎ 508-228-1894. www.nha.org.

★★★**Main Street** – Shaded by venerable elms, paved with cobblestones and lined with captains' homes and shops, Main Street has preserved its colonial atmosphere despite the upscale boutiques and galleries that fill the storefronts. During the summer it is a delightful place for a leisurely stroll.

★**Straight Wharf** – This wharf at the eastern end of Main Street and its old fishing sheds have been transformed into modern marinas and shops, art galleries and restaurants. Yachts and other pleasure craft tie up here in summer.

189

PRACTICAL INFORMATION .... Area Code: 508

Getting There – From **Boston** to **Hyannis** (74mi): I-93 south to Rtes. 3 and 6 south to Rte. 132 east. International and domestic flights to **Logan International Airport** (Boston) ☎ 617-561-1800 or **T.F. Green State Airport** (Providence) ☎ 401-737-4000. Major rental car agencies *(p 306)*. Closest Amtrak **train** station: Providence, RI ☎ 800-872-7245. Greyhound **bus** station: Hyannis ☎ 800-231-2222.

Ferry Schedule

Departure	Schedule	Duration (one-way)	Adult Fare (round-trip)	Company
Hyannis	year-round, daily	2hrs 15min	$24	Steamship Authority ☎ 477-8600
Harwich Port	mid-May–mid-Oct	1hr 45min	$35	Freedom Cruise Line ☎ 432-8999
Hyannis	May–Oct, daily	1hr 50min	$24	Hy-Line ☎ 778-2600
Martha's Vineyard	Jun–mid-Sept, daily	2hrs 15min	$24	Hy-Line

Getting Around – Nantucket is best visited on foot or bicycle as streets are often congested and parking may be difficult *(especially May–Sept)*. Bicycle and moped rentals available. Steamship Authority ferries offer automotive transport *($230 car & driver round-trip, reservations suggested)*.

Visitor Information – **Nantucket Island Chamber of Commerce** visitor center: 48 Main St., Nantucket MA 02554-3595 ☎ 228-1700, www.nantucketchamber.org. **Nantucket Visitor Services:** 25 Federal St., Nantucket MA 02554; kiosks throughout island operate seasonally ☎ 228-0925. www.nantucket.net.

Accommodations – Reservation services: **Nantucket Accommodations** PO Box 217, Nantucket MA 02554 ☎ 228-9559; **Destinnations** ☎ 800-333-4667; **Nantucket & Martha's Vineyard Reservations** PO Box 1322, Vineyard Haven MA 02568 ☎ 693-7200. Accommodations directory available from Nantucket Island Chamber of Commerce *(above)*. Accommodations range from hotels and inns *($85–$300/day)* to bed and breakfasts *($90–$150/day)*. *Average prices for a double room.* **American Youth Hostel** 31 Western Ave., Nantucket MA 02554 ☎ 228-0433. Camping is prohibited on island.

Recreation – **Swimming** at all island beaches, **surfing** at South Shore beaches. **Bicycle** and **hiking** paths throughout island. Most specialty **shopping** and supplies can be found in downtown Nantucket.

★**Hadwen House-Satler Memorial** – *Main and Pleasant Sts. Visit by guided tour (30min) only, Jun–mid-Oct daily 10am–5pm. $3. ☎ 508-228-1894. www.nha.org.* This impressive dwelling, with its Neoclassical pediment and columns, was built in 1845 for the whale oil merchant William Hadwen. The house and its rich decor bear witness to the life of luxury led by its owner. Large, well-lit rooms contain beautiful furnishings and numerous other treasures.

Opposite the Hadwen House stand the identical **Three Bricks**, dwellings built by a wealthy merchant for his three sons.

★**Whaling Museum** – 🏛 *Broad St. Open Jun–mid-Oct daily 10am–5pm. May & late Oct–Dec weekends only 11am–3pm. $5. ☎ 508-228-1894. www.nha.org.* The building, once a factory where candles were made from whale oil, contains fine collections of scrimshaw, harpoons, models and paintings. Workshops have been reproduced, illustrating the trades and crafts related to the whaling industry: a blacksmith shop, sail loft and cooper's shop. There is an interesting model of the **Camel**, a type of floating dry dock that was used from 1840 to 1850 to help the new and larger vessels enter the shallow waters of Nantucket Harbor.

Congregational Church – *Centre St. Open mid-Jun–mid-Oct Mon–Sat 10am–4pm. $2. ☎ 508-228-0950.* The original Old Vestry (1725) now functions as a rear chapel to the present structure (1834). The interior seems larger than it is because of the trompe l'œil paintings on the front wall and ceiling. Nantucket history is presented in displays on the tower landing. The tower itself affords a **panorama★** of the town and island.

The Oldest House – *Sunset Hill. Visit by guided tour (20min) only, Jun–mid-Oct daily 10am–5pm. $3. ☎ 508-228-1894. www.nha.org.* A narrow gravel road outside town leads to the oldest house on the island, the **Jethro Coffin House**. Built in 1686 for Jethro Coffin and his wife, this wooden saltbox house, with its casement windows and large central chimney, typifies 17C Colonial architecture. The horseshoe design, fashioned in brick on the chimney, was intended as a special charm to protect the residents from witches.

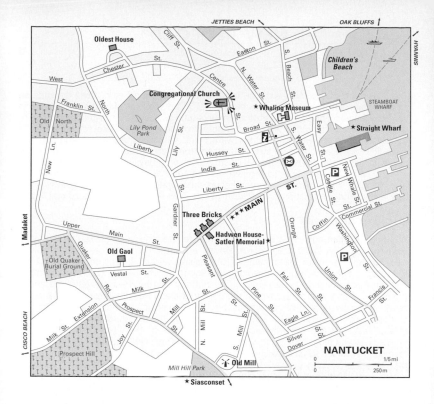

Old Gaol – *Vestal St. Open Jun–mid-Oct daily 10am–5pm.* ☎ *508-228-1894. www.nha.org.* One of the oldest surviving prison buildings in the country, this jail was used for over 125 years. Inside, the four stone prison cells appear as they did in the early 19C.

Old Mill – *Mill Hill. Visit by guided tour (20min) only, Jun–mid-Oct daily 10am–5pm. $2.* ☎ *508-228-1894. www.nha.org.* Corn is still ground at this old windmill (1746), which operates with its original handcrafted wooden gears and grinding stones.

ADDITIONAL SIGHTS

★**Siasconset** – Islanders call this village "Sconset." Fishermen who came here during the 17C to fish for cod built the sheds that were later converted into the **gray cottages** of Siasconset. Discovered at the end of the 19C by artists in search of unspoiled natural scenery, the area rapidly grew into a fashionable resort as push estates were built on the land surrounding the small shanties. Between 1881 and 1918 a railroad linked Siasconset to the center of Nantucket. A common pastime in the summer is to bicycle the seven flat miles from Nantucket Village to Siasconset, continuing on to picturesque Sankaty Head Lighthouse, up to Quidnet and returning along Nantucket Harbor to the center of town.

Sankaty Head Lighthouse – The lighthouse is a short walking distance from the shore road, which affords views of the ocean on one side and of cranberry bogs and rolling moors on the other side. The road between Quidnet and Nantucket offers a succession of scenic landscapes.

Surfside Beach – A road *(Surfside Rd.)* and bicycle path lead to the south shore, where visitors can swim at Surfside Beach.

Madaket – A paved road leads through the moors to Madaket Beach on the western end of the island. The afternoon is the best time to enjoy Madaket's white sandy stretches and refreshing surf.

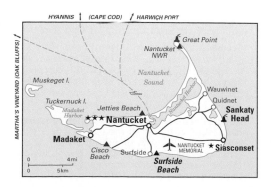

191

NEW BEDFORD★

Population 99,922
Map of Principal Sights
Tourist Office ☎ 508-997-1250

The whaling capital of the world during the mid-19C, New Bedford still depends on income gained from fishing and manufacturing. The smell of saltwater pervades this old New England port city, located an hour south of BOSTON. Once the anchorage of majestic whaling ships, the wharves are now crowded with modern fishing craft. Cobblestone streets lead down to the waterfront, where ships' supplies and antiques are sold. Follow one of these streets up from the waterfront to Johnny Cake Hill to discover memories of New Bedford's illustrious whaling days, which are well preserved in the Whaling Museum and the Seamen's Bethel, or mariner's chapel. These and other New Bedford sights were linked together as a national park in 1996; a visitor center has guides and information *(33 William St. ☎ 508-996-4095. www.nps.gov/nebe)*.

Historical Notes

Whaling's Golden Age – New Bedford's 30-year reign as the world capital of the whaling industry began in 1765 when Joseph Rotch, a Nantucketer who had established the whaling industry on his island, came to this fishing village. Rotch's efforts formed the foundation of New Bedford's burgeoning whaling trade. By the late 1830s New Bedford had surpassed NANTUCKET as the center of the industry. In 1840 Herman Melville described the influence that whaling exerted on the quality of life in New Bedford: "All these brave houses and flowery gardens came from the Atlantic, Pacific and Indian Oceans, one and all they were harpooned and dragged up hither from the bottom of the sea."
Sperm whale oil and bone indeed formed the basis of the city's wealth. Factories worked day and night converting the oil into candles; whalebone, destined to be transformed into corset stays, umbrellas and walking sticks, was set out along the piers to dry. New Bedford's glory days peaked in the 1850s, when 80 percent of America's whale ships sailed from this town, and more than 10,000 men—about half the town's population—participated in whaling.

The Decline – Although the discovery of petroleum in Pennsylvania brought about a decline in the demand for whale oil, the fatal blow to New Bedford's principal industry was also due, in large part, to the reduction in the size of its fleet: 39 vessels were lost in the Stone Fleet episode *(p 28)*, and an additional 32 ships were abandoned after they became icebound in the Arctic Ocean in 1861. Similar disasters diminished the size of the fleet even further until, by the end of the 19C, almost all of New Bedford's capital had shifted from whaling to manufacturing.

SIGHTS *3hrs*

★★ **New Bedford Whaling Museum** – 🆂 *18 Johnny Cake Hill. From I-95 Exit 15, follow the signs to downtown New Bedford. Turn right on Elm St., then left on Bethel St. Open Memorial Day–Labor Day daily 9am–5pm (Thu 8pm). Rest of the year daily 9am–5pm. Closed Jan 1, Thanksgiving Day, Dec 25. $4.50. ♿ ☎ 508-997-0046. www.whalingmuseum.org.* The museum's collections, which relate to the history of whaling, are among the finest in the world. On the ground floor, there is the section devoted to **scrimshaw**. A large hall contains the 89ft half-scale model of the fully rigged whaling bark **Lagoda**. Formerly a trade ship, the *Lagoda* made 12 whaling voyages out of New Bedford in the 1800s. Visitors may climb aboard the replica, which is the largest of its kind in the world, to examine the elaborate rigging and the tryworks.
The collection of marine engravings, whale hunt illustrations, oils and watercolors includes ship portraits and seascapes by 19C artists Benjamin Russell and **William Bradford**, as well as a series of panels painted by Charles Raleigh in the 1870s. A separate gallery displays sections from the vast **panorama★** by **Benjamin Russell** and **Caleb Purrington**, entitled *Whaling Voyage 'Round the World*.
More than 1,000 logbooks, with their simple and often humorous illustrations, give vivid accounts of life aboard a whaling ship.

Seamen's Bethel – *15 Johnny Cake Hill. Open late May–early Sept Mon–Sat 10am–4pm, Sun 1pm–4pm. Rest of the year call for hours. Contribution requested. ☎ 508-992-3295.* This chapel (1832), described in Herman Melville's classic novel *Moby Dick*, was a necessary stop for the mariner who was about to embark on a perilous whaling voyage. Still used for services today, the chapel contains a pulpit shaped to resemble the hull of a whaleship.

★ **Rotch-Jones-Duff House and Garden Museum** – *396 Country St. Open Jul–Dec daily 10am–4pm. Rest of the year Tue–Sun 10am–4pm. Closed Thanksgiving Day & Dec 25–Jan 1. $4. ♿ ☎ 508-997-1401.* Located within walking distance of the Whaling Museum and the historic downtown district, this Greek Revival mansion (1834, Richard Upjohn) and its sylvan grounds typify the "brave houses and flowery gardens" of New Bedford that Herman Melville immortalized in *Moby Dick*.

Sumptuous period rooms and historical exhibits chronicle 150 years of the economic and social evolution of the city as it was experience by the New Bedford whaling elite.

Lightship New Bedford – *The lightship (not open to the public) is adjacent to, and part of, the Coast Guard Exhibit at the State Pier.* This vessel was one of the dozens of lightships that once guarded the waters near which it was considered too dangerous to erect lighthouses.

NEWBURYPORT★

Population 16,317
Map of Principal Sights
Tourist Office ☎ 800-742-5306

This small city at the mouth of the Merrimack River was the home of a large fleet of merchant vessels in the 18C and 19C. The dignified Federal mansions built on **High Street** by sea captains, and the charming lanes reaching from Bartlett Mall to the restored **Market Square District★** evoke Newburyport's heyday as a bustling shipbuilding port and trading center. Down by the waterfront, historic structures mark the site of the 19C boatyards that produced some of the finest clippers ever to sail the seas.

SIGHTS

★**High Street** – Ornamented with carved porches and columns, the houses represent the major styles of early American architecture: late Georgian, Federal and Greek Revival. **Frog Pond** and **Bartlett Mall**, fronting High Street, provide the setting for the **Court House** (1800) designed by Charles Bulfinch and remodeled 53 years later.

Cushing House – *No. 98. Visit by guided tour (1hr) only, May–Oct Tue–Fri 10am–4pm, Sat 11am–2pm. $4. ☎ 978-462-2681.* The brick mansion (c.1808) was home to three generations of the Cushing family. The dwelling's most famous occupant, Caleb Cushing, was the first US envoy to China in 1842. Furnishings that Cushing acquired in the Orient, a small group of early American folk paintings and a collection of silver, clocks and needlework are among the exhibits.

Custom House – *25 Water St. Open Apr–Dec Mon–Sat 10am–4pm, Sun 1pm–4pm. $3. ☎ 978-462-8681.* Designed by Robert Mills, architect of the Washington Monument in the nation's capital, this granite structure once welcomed mariners returning from long sea voyages. Today it contains the **Museum of the Newburyport Maritime Society**, featuring exhibits on shipbuilding, the Coast Guard and foreign imports.

David's

11 Brown Square. ☎ 978-462-8077. This large restaurant on the square that borders Pleasant and Titcomb Streets offers dining on two floors. Upstairs (entrance level) is the pleasant, formal dining room with cloth-covered tables and attentive service. Dinners here *(served daily)* can be ordered from an extensive menu that includes steak, lobster, veal, chicken and duck. If you're a twosome, ask if the prix-fixe, four-course dinner for two is available. David's Downstairs is a less pricy, casual eatery with a full dinner menu of beef, fish, fowl and pasta. Lunch is served here weekdays.

EXCURSIONS

★★**Plum Island-Parker River National Wildlife Refuge** – *3mi from Newburyport by Water St., then Plum Island Tpk. Open year-round daily dawn–dusk. Refuge Beach closed Apr–Jun. $2 ($5/car). Refuge closes when parking capacity is reached. Parking available in the small lots off the road that leads through the refuge. Certain lots provide access to observation towers, trails & beach. Camping prohibited. ♿ ☎ 978-465-5753.* The southern two-thirds of this island has been designated as a haven for waterfowl in the Atlantic Flyway. Opportunities for birdwatching abound (more than 270 species have been sighted), especially during the spring and fall migrations. The observation towers offer **panoramas** of the island's 4,650 acres of dunes, marshlands and oceanfront beach. From Hellcat Trail and Pines Trail, you can see the marshes.

Haverhill – Industry continues to be important to this community, a major center for the production of shoes in the 19C.

John Greenleaf Whittier Birthplace – *305 Whittier Rd. 13mi from Newburyport by Rte. 1 north, then Rte. 110 west. Visit by guided tour (45min) only, May–Oct Tue–Sat 10am–5pm, Sun 1pm–5pm. Rest of the year Tue–Sun 1pm–5pm. Closed major holidays. $2. ☎ 978-373-3979.* The 19C Quaker poet and abolitionist John Greenleaf Whittier was born in this rustic farmhouse. Whittier's poem *Snow-bound* describes the writing desk and fireplace in this restored dwelling.

A stopping place for travelers since the colonial days, the town of Sturbridge provides an ideal site for Old Sturbridge Village, one of the region's best-known attractions. Old Sturbridge is a living history museum that re-creates life between 1790 and 1840 in a rural New England community.

The village was initiated by Albert and Joel Cheney Wells and their families to exhibit their collections of American antiques. When the museum was opened to the public in 1946, historic houses, farm buildings and shops had been moved to and reconstructed on the Sturbridge site.

Remarkable for the beauty of its woodsy site and the authenticity of its buildings and atmosphere, the village is the result of extensive research. Interpreters wearing 19C dress farm the land, cook and make tools and implements according to traditional methods.

Publick House

Rte. 131 in the town of Sturbridge. ☎ *508-347-3313.* You can't go to Sturbridge and miss this large, historic inn. It's a local institution, established way back in 1771. Although there are other restaurants and a tavern on the premises where meals are served, reserve a table in one of the dining rooms (preferably with candlelight) in the Publick House itself for truly New England fare in a colonial setting. Wait staff are attired in period dress and many dishes are based on 18C recipes. Try the award-winning clam chowder or the wild mushroom stifle as an appetizer. The house specialty baked lobster pie; the roast duckling with apples, cabbage and cider sauce; or the roast native turkey with country stuffing and pan gravy are great choices for the main course. Since the on-site Bake Shoppe makes sweets (breads and relishes too), you know the desserts will be special. Save time to look at the Bake Shoppe and other rooms of the inn and take a stroll on the grounds.

VISIT *1 day*

Kids *In Sturbridge, at the intersection of Mass. Tpk. and I-84. Open Apr–Oct daily 9am–5pm. Nov–Dec & Mar daily 10am–4pm. Jan–mid-Feb weekends only 10am–4pm. Closed Dec 25. $16 (2nd consecutive day free).* ✕ ♿ ☎ *508-347-3362. www.osv.org.*

Visitor Center – *Map guide/schedule of events and demonstrations available.* Exhibits and a slide presentation *(15min)* introduce the visitor to farm and community life in 19C New England. Following the path to the common, you will pass the small clapboard **Friends Meetinghouse** (1796), which typifies the simplicity that reflects the austere piety associated with the Quakers.

The Common – At the west end of the common is a white Greek Revival **Center Meetinghouse**, its spire rising gracefully above the other village structures. Daylight, streaming in through large windows, illuminates the building's simple interior.

Houses on the common reflect a diversity of architectural styles. The **Fenno House** (1704), covered with wide rustic clapboards, is the oldest. Inside, the rooms are appointed with New England furnishings and the walls are covered with sheathing typical of the 18C. The more refined **Fitch House** (1737), furnished as the home of a prospering printer, contains double-hung sash windows. The **Richardson Parsonage** (1748), a white "saltbox," is the home of the village minister. The Parsonage Barn is used seasonally for storytelling, music and other early 19C entertainment *(check the map guide for the day's schedule).* In the **Tin Shop** next to the parsonage, a smith turns out utilitarian wares like those used in early-19C households. On the other side of the parsonage sits a tiny **Law Office** originally used by Connecticut lawyer John McClellan. Nearby is the well-stocked **Knight Store**, typical of the country store that was often the sole supplier of the farmer's needs and was indispensable in selling his surplus produce to urban consumers.

Towne House – Opposite the Center Meetinghouse and facing the common, this attractively proportioned Federal-style house (1796) is similar to those dwellings built by the most prosperous rural families. Unusually comfortable and luxurious for residences in this community, the house contains period furnishings, delicately carved woodwork, English porcelain, a hand-painted floor cloth and woven carpets. The large meeting room/ballroom on the second floor is embellished with scenes painted directly on the plaster.

Thompson Bank – This modest Greek Revival building exemplifies the architectural style commonly used by financial institutions established throughout the region in the 19C.

Thomas Neill/Old Sturbridge Village

The Gristmill

Printing Office – The yellow wooden building beyond the bank is an early 19C printing office. Such offices usually printed books for urban publishers, as well as pamphlets and broadsides.

Cross the common and follow the road that leads to the Pliny Freeman farm. You will pass the **Town Pound**, where stray animals were kept, the **Shoe Shop**, **the District School** and the **Pottery Shop**.

Freeman Farm – This farm, with its livestock fields and farmhouse, is one of the liveliest areas in the village. Men and women in period dress cook, work in the fields and care for the animals as they did more than 150 years ago. Depending on the season, the activities performed include plowing, cultivating and harvesting field crops, milking cows, shearing sheep, preserving food, building fences and making butter and cheese.

Bixby House – This dwelling is the former home of a 19C blacksmith, moved from its original site in Barre, Massachusetts, in 1986. Archaeological discoveries made during recovery and restoration provide an accurate picture of a craftsman's family in 1830s rural America.

Across the road, in a stone building, is the **Blacksmith Shop**; farther on are the **carding mill**, **gristmill** and an 1820 water-powered **sawmill** located beside streams fed from the Mill Pond. Seasonal boat rides on the Quinebaug River depart near the covered bridge *(daily 9:30am–4:30pm; round-trip 15min; commentary; $3)*. Meals are served in the **Bullard Tavern** beyond the covered bridge.

To reach the J. Cheney Wells Clock Gallery *(adjacent to the visitor center)*, the Formal Exhibits Area and the herb garden, cross the common and continue past the Printing Office.

Exhibits – In one area of the village, small museums contain formal displays of traditional crafts and artifacts.

Glass Exhibit – Glassmaking was an important industry in New England in the 19C *(p 38)*. The collection at Sturbridge includes a wide variety of forms ranging from window glass to decorative paperweights. An interesting assortment of flasks features political, social and patriotic subjects as decorative motifs.

Firearms, Fibers and Fashion Exhibit – Exhibits illustrate 19C textile and manufacturing in the home and the influence of fashion. A fine collection of guns and military equipment is accompanied by informative panels that present a detailed history of the New England militia.
Nearby, Samson's Children's Museum is a space for family activities, with an emphasis on younger children.

Lighting Exhibit – The exhibit presents lighting devices from prehistoric times to the 19C. Roman and Greek oil lamps, Betty Lamps (popular in early New England), whale-oil lamps and kerosene lamps are among the interesting devices displayed.

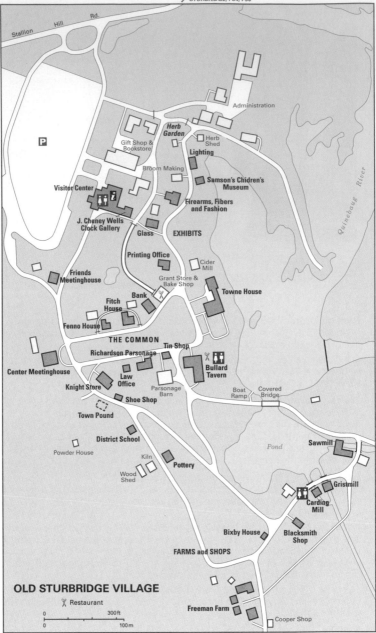

OLD STURBRIDGE VILLAGE

✗ Restaurant

0 ———— 300ft
0 ———— 100m

Across the path, in the shop adjoining the herb garden, brooms are made from broom corn *(seasonally)*. The **herb garden**, a popular attraction of the village, consists of over 400 varieties of herbs grown seasonally in terraced beds and grouped according to their traditional 19C uses: household, medicinal, culinary and commercial.

J. Cheney Wells Clock Gallery – This gallery, adjoining the visitor center, contains a collection of more than 100 New England clocks, many in working order, produced between 1725 and 1850 by regional clock makers. Thomas Claggett, Caleb Wheaton, Simon and Aaron Willard, Seth Thomas and Eli Terry are among the craftsmen represented.

Consult the practical information section at the end of the guide for details on annual events, sports, recreation, restaurants, shopping and entertainment.

PIONEER VALLEY★

The fertile Connecticut River Valley, extending north to south through the center of Massachusetts, was once the haunt of dinosaurs. Today the area is known particularly for its concentration of institutions of higher education.

Geological Notes

Unusual Relief of a Fertile Valley – The broad, gentle farmlands that reach from one end of the valley to the other are framed against a backdrop of dramatic rocky ledges and craggy, volcanic **basalt ridges**. These asymmetrical ridges rise abruptly from the valley floor, forming sheer, steep drops on the west side and gentle slopes on the east, because of the way the basalt split. Vantage points along these ridges command beautiful views of the valley and the Connecticut River. Vegetables and tobacco are raised in the valley's fertile soil; netted coverings distinguish the fields where tobacco grows.

Valley of the Dinosaurs – Less dramatic in appearance than the basalt ridges, but of great geological interest, are the finer-grained sedimentary rocks containing the tracks of dinosaurs that roamed the Connecticut Valley approximately 200 million years ago. These footprints, pressed into the mud on the valley floor and baked by the sun, were later covered and preserved by additional layers of mud. Eventually, they became layers of sedimentary rocks, primarily sandstone and shale. Today these rocks reveal the fascinating story of the region's prehistoric past. The creatures that once roamed this area were small, about the size of a man, according to the size of their footprints. Dinosaurs did not attain their mammoth size until about 100 million years later.
Dinosaur tracks can be seen at the **Pratt Museum** at Amherst College, in their original formation in Rocky Hill and at various other locations.

Historical Notes

Western Boundary – During the 17C the valley was one of the major axes settled by pioneers, who were attracted by its rich soil and plentiful water resources. It remained the western frontier of New England until the 18C, as the colonists did not dare risk crossing the Berkshire Hills and venturing into the Hudson Valley, the domain of the Dutch.

A Center of Education – More than 60,000 students attend the numerous schools, colleges and the university in the Pioneer Valley. Five of these institutions have joined together to form a consortium, sharing such projects as a radio station and a bus system, as well as departments and courses.
The consortium includes the **University of Massachusetts** at Amherst, a sprawling campus with tall modern towers, where 26,000 students attend classes; **Amherst College**, established in 1821; innovative **Hampshire College**, established in 1971 by the other members of the consortium; **Smith College** at Northampton, one of the most select colleges in the nation for women, founded in 1875 by Sophia Smith; and **Mt. Holyoke College**, across the river in South Hadley, established in 1837 as the first women's college in the US. The poet **Emily Dickinson** was a student at Mt. Holyoke before she settled in Amherst, where she lived the remainder of her reclusive life.

SIGHTS

★★**Deerfield** – *See Entry Heading.*

★**Quabbin Reservoir** – *Access from Rte. 9; 2mi from Belchertown. Drive on Windsor Dam then follow the signs for Quabbin Hill Tower.* Construction of the 28sq mi reservoir (storage capacity: 412 billion gallons) that serves the Boston region was accomplished by damming the Swift River and flooding four of the valley towns. The many islands that stud Quabbin's vast water reserves (*quabbin* in the Nipmuck language means "a lot of water") were created by hilltops jutting out of the submerged area. Impressive **views**★★ are available from **Enfield Lookout** and from the **observation tower** on Quabbin Hill. The reservoir offers opportunities for fishing, hiking, picnicking and scenic shore drives *(swimming and hunting prohibited)*.

Mt. Sugarloaf State Reservation – *Follow the signs from Rte. 116.* From the top of this basalt ridge there is an expansive **view**★★ of the Connecticut River as it meanders through open farmlands. Small towns fleck the valley landscape.

Mt. Tom State Reservation – *From Holyoke take Rte. 141 north 3mi. Open Memorial Day–Columbus Day Mon–Fri 8am–8pm, weekends 9am–8pm. Rest of the year daily 8am–4pm. Closed Jan 1, Thanksgiving Day, Dec 25. $2/car (Memorial Day–Columbus Day only).* ♿ ☎ *413-527-4805 or 413-534-1186 (off season).* Easthampton and Northampton can be seen in the valley below the access road to this 1,800-acre recreation area, which includes some 30mi of hiking trails.

■ **Pioneer Valley Picks**

Here are some popular places in the valley to take a break from sightseeing:
In Amherst:

Judie's Restaurant, *51 N. Pleasant St.* ☎ *413-253-3491*. A favored student spot in the heart of the village, known for its giant popovers, burgers and big portions.

Atticus Bookstore, *8 Main St.* ☎ *413-256-1547*. A well-stocked repository with an intellectual feel and friendly, helpful staff.

Atkins Farms Country Market, *1150 West St.* ☎ *413-253-9528*. A complete produce store with a bakery (known for its cider donuts) and deli that draws repeat customers from far and wide.

In Northhampton:

Green Street Café, *64 Green St.* ☎ *413-586-5650*. Creative cuisine served in a sparse, sophisticated interior. *Reservations advised.*

Del Raye Bar & Grill, *1 Bridge St.* ☎ *413-586-2664*. A crowded upscale dining spot cum bar for dinner, after-theater drink or gourmet dessert and coffee. *Reservations advised.*

In Holyoke:

Yankee Pedlar Inn, *1866 Northampton St.* ☎ *413-532-9494*. A cozy 19C wayside inn with downhome cooking at affordable prices.

The summit of Mt. Tom commands a view of the curved arm of the Connecticut River, made famous by Thomas Cole's painting *The Oxbow* (Metropolitan Museum of Art), as well as Northampton and the Berkshire Hills beyond. The slopes of Mt. Tom provide a venue for skiing in winter.

Northampton – Northampton has grown from a remote frontier town into a bustling commercial center. The **Smith College Museum of Art**, on Elm Street, owns a collection noted for its American and French works of the 19C and 20C *(open Jul–Aug Tues–Sun noon–4pm; rest of the year Tue, Fri, Sat 9:30am–4pm, Wed & Sun noon–4pm, Thu noon–8pm; closed Jan 1, Jul 4, Thanksgiving Day, Dec 25;* ♿ ☎ *413-585-2760).*

Skinner State Park – *From Rte. 47 follow the signs for the Summit House. Open Memorial Day–Labor Day Mon–Fri 8am–8pm, weekends 10am–8pm. Mid-Apr–mid-May & rest of Sept–Oct daily 10am–6pm. $2/car (weekends & holidays May–Oct).* ☎ *413-586-0350.* The old summit hotel *(open Memorial Day–Columbus Day weekends & holidays only 11:30am–5:30pm),* built on a basalt ridge, offers a **view**★ of the valley. The towers of the University of Massachusetts at Amherst are visible in the distances.

PLYMOUTH★★

Population 45,608
Map of Principal Sights
Tourist Office ☎ 800-872-1620

This modern and attractive town is a residential and industrial community with hilly streets sloping down to the harbor as well as the site of the first permanent settlement in New England. The long voyage of the *Mayflower*, the hardships the Pilgrims endured and the eventual success of Plymouth Colony form part of the cherished story related in Plymouth's historic monuments and sites.

Historical Notes

A Colony Off Course – During the 16C a group of Puritans known as **Separatists** attempted to reform the Church of England. In 1607, to avoid persecution by the authorities, members of the group emigrated from Scrooby, England, to Holland. They remained there until, impressed by favorable accounts of the New World, they decided to emigrate to America. Early in September 1620, 102 passengers, including 35 Separatists, boarded the *Mayflower* at Plymouth, England, and set sail for the Virginia Colony in North America. Diverted north by a storm, the settlers landed two months later on the shores of CAPE COD. They spent five weeks in the region before again setting sail for Virginia. Detoured a second time by strong winds, the Pilgrims headed for the bay that had been charted six years earlier by Capt. John Smith; on the shores of this bay they established Plymouth Colony.

The First Winter – The harsh weather and a scarcity of food left almost half the colony dead by the end of the first winter. Burials were held at night on **Cole's Hill**, and graves were left unmarked to conceal the settlers' dwindling numbers from the neighboring

Wampanoag tribe. The spring brought hope to the settlement along with a group of Indians who befriended the Pilgrims and taught them how to raise crops and to hunt and fish. After the harvest that fall, members of Plymouth Colony joined with the Indians in a three-day feast, the first American **Thanksgiving celebration**, in gratitude for their blessings.

From **Burial Hill**, where an old cemetery contains gravestones dating back to the Plymouth Colony, there are views that reach beyond the town and out to sea. The **Town Brook**, close to the place where the Pilgrims built their first homes, runs through a lovely public park, **Brewster Gardens**.

> "To think of landing here (at Plymouth) on the 22nd of December without a shelter and 3,000 miles from what once was a beloved home. The idea as I stood upon the burying place which is high and overlooks the harbour made me shiver."
>
> Charles Francis Adams,
> *Diary*, 14 September 1835

Pilgrims' Progress – Every Friday in August and on Thanksgiving Day, modern Plymouth residents dress as Pilgrims and take part in a Sabbath procession up Leyden Street to Burial Hill, where a religious service is held.

HISTORIC DISTRICT *1 day. Map p 200.*

Begin at the visitor center at 225 Water St. (open Apr–Nov daily 9am–9pm; rest of the year daily 9am–4pm; ☎ *800-872-1620; www.visit-plymouth.com).*

★★**Mayflower II** – 🅺🅸🅳🆂 *Berthed at the State Pier. Open Apr–Nov daily 9am–5pm. $6.50 (combination ticket with Plimoth Plantation $19).* ☎ *508-746-1622.* The *Mayflower II*, built in England (1955-57), is a full-scale replica of the type of ship that brought the Pilgrims to Plymouth in 1620.

★**Plymouth Rock** – 🅺🅸🅳🆂 *On the beach at Water St.* This boulder set at the harbor's edge has traditionally been regarded as the stepping stone used by the *Mayflower* passengers when they disembarked at Plymouth. The boulder is sheltered by a multicolumned granite structure. Opposite is **The Pilgrim Mother** (**1**), a fountain honoring the women of the *Mayflower*.

Plymouth National Wax Museum (**M¹**) – 🅺🅸🅳🆂 *16 Carver St. Open Jul–Aug daily 9am–9pm. Jun, Sept & Oct 9am–7pm. Mar–May & Nov 9am–5pm. $5.50.* ☎ *508-746-6468.* Located on **Cole's Hill**, the museum contains 26 life-size dioramas which, enhanced by realistic soundtracks, depict the Pilgrim story from the emigration of the Separatists to Holland in 1607 to the first Thanksgiving celebration in 1621. In front of the museum stands a statue of **Massasoit** (**2**), chief of the Indians who helped the Pilgrims survive that first spring.

★**Mayflower Society Museum** (**M²**) – *4 Winslow St. Visit by guided tour (30min) only, Jul–Aug daily 10am–4:15pm; end of May–Jun & Sept–mid-Oct Fri–Sun only 10am–4:15pm (& Wed in Sept); closed Jul 4; $3.* ☎ *508-746-2590.* Built during the colonial period and enlarged in the 19C, the house is a graceful blend of Colonial and Victorian architectural features. Attractive roof railings and the multipaned cupola add harmonious relief to the white brick exterior.

Inside, a flying stairway joins the original rooms with later sections of the house. Among the antiques found throughout the house is a rare set of biblical fireplace tiles in the drawing room.

Spooner House – *26 Water St. Visit by guided tour (30min) only, Jun–mid-Oct Thu–Sat 10am–4pm. $3.* ☎ *508-746-0012.* This quaint mid-18C dwelling preserves many of the furnishings belonging to members of the Spooner family, who owned the house for over 200 years.

Richard Sparrow House (**A**) – *42 Summer St. Open Apr–Dec Thu–Tue, 10am–5pm (summer Fri, Sat 8pm). $2.* ☎ *508-747-1240. www.sparrowhouse.com.* The oldest dwelling (1640) in Plymouth contains 18C furnishings.

Jabez Howland House (**B**) – *33 Sandwich St. Visit by guided tour (1hr) only, late May–mid-Oct daily 10am–4:30pm. $ 3.50.* ☎ *508-746-9590.* This is the only house remaining in Plymouth where Pilgrims are known to have lived.

★**Pilgrim Hall Museum** – *75 Court St. Open Feb–Dec daily 9:30am–4:30pm (closes at noon Dec 24 & Dec 31). Closed Jan 1, Dec 25. $5.* ☎ *508-746-1620. www.pilgrimhall.org.* Built as a memorial to the Pilgrims and Plymouth Colony, this austere granite structure (1824), designed by Alexander Parris, contains original Pilgrim furnishings and artifacts, including chairs owned by Governors Bradford and Carver; the cradle of Peregrine White, who was born on the *Mayflower*; Bibles belonging to John Alden and Governor Bradford; and a sampler made by Lora Standish, daughter of Myles Standish.

National Forefathers' Monument – *Allerton St. off Rte. 44.* Representing the virtue Faith, this large monument (36ft) honors the Pilgrims and their small colony.

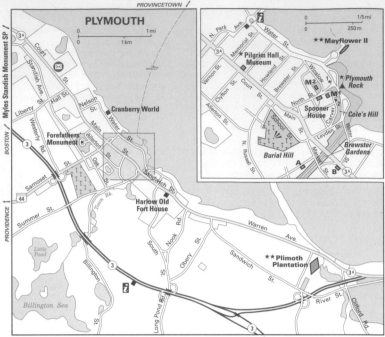

PLYMOUTH

ADDITIONAL SIGHTS *Map above*

★★**Plimoth Plantation** – Kids *3mi south on Rte. 3 from the center of Plymouth, Exit 4. Open Apr–late-Nov daily 9am–5pm. $16. ✗ ☎ 508-746-1622. www. plimoth. org.* The plantation is a reproduction of the Pilgrims' village as it appeared in 1627. (The spelling "Plimoth" was adopted from Governor Bradford's early journals by the museum curators.) Buildings, paths and gardens have been constructed to resemble those that once stood on the site of modern Plymouth's business district.

The **Fort/Meetinghouse**, at the entrance to the plantation, offers a good vantage point from which to view the entire village, with its neat rows of thatched-roof cottages similar to those inhabited by the Alden, Carver, Bradford and Standish families. Rooms inside the houses are decorated with reproductions of 17C English furnishings. Throughout the village, costumed guides portray specific Pilgrim settlers, sharing experiences with visitors while performing tasks such as gardening, cooking and harvesting crops according to the methods used in the early colony.

Plimoth Plantation

A path leads to **Hobbamock's Wampanoag Indian Homesite**, where the culture of this Native American group is interpreted by staff members engaged in raising crops, drying food, weaving and other chores traditionally performed by the Wampanoag people. The campsite includes examples of the *wetus*, a domed dwelling once built as shelter by the Wampanoag. Visitors can watch as workers use 17C methods to make handicrafts in the modern **Carriage House Crafts Center**. The walk-through exhibit **Irreconcilable Differences** tells the story of the colony through the perspectives of a *Mayflower* passenger and a female Wampanoag sachem.

Harlow Old Fort House – *119 Sandwich St. Visit by guided tour (30min) only, Jun–mid-Oct Thu–Sat 10am–4pm. $3.* ☎ *508-746-0012.* The framework of this house (1677) contains timbers of a 17C fort that originally stood on Burial Hill.

Cranberry World Visitor Center – 🔣 *From Rte. 3, take Rte. 44 east .75mi. Cross Rte. 3A and continue on Rte. 44 to the waterfront rotary, then bear left. Open May–Nov daily 9:30am–5pm.* ♿ ☎ *508-747-2350.* A leading producer of cranberries, the Ocean Spray cranberry cooperative sponsors this historical and educational exhibit in Plymouth. The visitor center features exhibits, antiques and outdoor bogs.

EXCURSION

Myles Standish Monument State Park – *In Duxbury, 8mi from Plymouth by Rte. 3A to Crescent St. Turn right and enter through the gate at left. Open Memorial Day–Labor Day daily 8am–8pm. Rest of the year daily 8am–4pm. Closed Jan 1, Thanksgiving Day, Dec 25.* ♿ ☎ *508-866-2526.* The Standish monument, a gigantic figure of Pilgrim leader Myles Standish, overlooks the bay and offers a **view★★** of Plymouth, Cape Cod Bay and Provincetown.

PROVINCETOWN★★

Population 3,561
Map of Principal Sights
Tourist Office ☎ 508-362-3225

Extending to the tip of Cape Cod, Provincetown, or "P-town," as it is called, combines elements of a fishing village, artists' colony and resort. During the summer, the arrival of large numbers of tourists, many gay and lesbian, swell the population of the town from 3,500 to 75,000.
As Route 6 heads north through the Province Lands sector of the Cape Cod National Seashore (CCNS), Provincetown Harbor is visible to the left; in the distance a tall, solitary monument resembling an Italian campanile appears. Motels and bungalows stand like sentries along the road, guarding the sandy stretches that lead into the town.

Historical Notes

Pilgrims and Mooncussers – When the *Mayflower* was blown off course and arrived at this end of the cape in November 1620, the Pilgrims saw only stark, endless stretches of sand. The settlers spent five weeks exploring this region and, aware that this area was not within the bounds of their charter, drew up the **Mayflower Compact** to serve as their instrument of government. Then they reset their sails for a voyage that ended a few days later at Plymouth.
By the 18C, less than 100 years after the Pilgrims landed on the cape, Provincetown had grown into the third-largest whaling center after Nantucket and New Bedford. In the mid-19C, 75 wharves could be counted along its shores, and the beaches were covered with fish flakes, or racks for drying fish, and saltworks, wooden structures used to filter salt from seawater. Provincetown vessels recruited seamen in the Azores and Cape Verde Islands, a factor that accounts for the town's large Portuguese population and the traditions they have preserved.
Other Provincetowners found fortune closer to home. Villains known as mooncussers erected lights along the shore to lure unwitting ships into dangerous shoals where they ran aground. They then boarded the vessels, killed the crew and stole the valuable cargo. The place where these rogues gathered was nicknamed "Helltown" and was cautiously avoided by the village's more respectable citizens.

Provincetown of the Artists – At the beginning of the 20C, Provincetown's wild natural beauty attracted artists and writers to its shores. In 1901 Charles W. Hawthorne founded the **Cape Cod School of Art** here, followed 15 years later by the establishment of the **Provincetown Players**, a group of playwrights and actors rebelling against the rigid criteria of the Broadway stage. Eugene O'Neill's career as a playwright was launched at Provincetown in 1916 when his first play, *Bound East for Cardiff*, was produced at the Wharf Theatre. At about the same time, the town became a prestigious artists' colony, where writers and dramatists such as O'Neill, John Dos Passos, Sinclair Lewis and Tennessee Williams gathered. Over the ensuing decades, the town has hosted art-world celebrities such as Robert Motherwell and Mark Rothko. Today the numerous galleries along Commercial Street, the **Provincetown Art Assn.** and the **Provincetown Theater Company** carry out the cultural and artistic traditions so closely associated with the town's character. *For a listing of current art shows, consult the free gallery guide available from the visitor center at MacMillan Wharf and from major galleries.*

Tourist Mecca – In the summer, crowds weave in and out of the shops, galleries and eating places that line the narrow streets, and **Commercial Street★**, the main thoroughfare in town, becomes almost impassable. Visitors and residents alike find the nearby beaches of the CCNS—including **Herring Cove Beach** and **Race Point Beach** *(map p 167)*—a refreshing contrast to the hustle and bustle that characterizes the center of town at this time of year *(in summer, shuttle buses run hourly along Bradford St. and to Herring Cove Beach)*. The **Province Lands Trail★★** *(7mi)* offers cyclists a challenging, but spectacular ride through forests and dunes with expansive views of the water *(for details, contact CCNS ☎ 508-349-3785)*. Nature lovers will appreciate the nature walks and lectures organized by the **Center for Coastal Studies (CCS)**, a research organization devoted to conservation of the marine habitat *(☎ 508-487-3622)*.

SIGHTS *4hrs. Map below.*

MacMillan Wharf – *At the end of Standish St. Public parking lot on the wharf.* Late in the afternoon, fishing boats, announced by the procession of seagulls that greets them, return to the wharf, where their fresh catches are unloaded and shipped to markets in BOSTON and New York. On the last Sunday in June, the **Blessing of the Fleet**, a colorful and impressive Portuguese celebration, takes place in the harbor. This lively pier is also the departure point for ever-popular **whale-watching cruises** *(p 312) (obtain schedules from the visitor center)*.

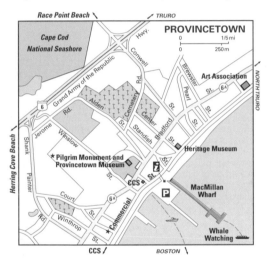

Provincetown Heritage Museum – *Commercial & Center Sts. Open late May–Columbus Day daily 10am– 5:30pm. $3. ☎ 508-487-7098.* Housed in a gleaming white Neoclassical edifice (1860) originally built as a Methodist church, the town's eclectic history museum presents multiple aspects of Provincetown's past through artifacts, photos and re-created 19C interiors. The second floor is dominated by the 66ft *Rose Dorothea*, a half-scale model of a fishing schooner that plied the Grand Banks in the early 20C.

★Pilgrim Monument and Provincetown Museum – *Winslow St. Open Jul–Aug daily 9am–7pm. Apr–Jun & Sept–Nov daily 9am–5pm. Last admission 45min before closing. $5. ☎ 508-487-1310. www.pilgrim-monument.org.* The small museum is located near the base of the tower. The permanent collection of documents and objects, including a model of the *Mayflower*, illustrates the town's rich history.
The monument, inspired by the 14C bell tower in the Tuscan hill town of Siena, was erected in 1910 to commemorate the 1620 landing of the Pilgrims at Provincetown. The observation deck atop this 252ft granite structure affords sweeping **views★★** of the entire cape *(116 steps and 60 ramps)*.

★★Dunes Tour – *May–Oct daily 10am–dusk. 1hr. Commentary. $12. Art's Dune Tours. ☎ 508-487-1950.* This tour by vehicle is a magnificent way to explore the spectacular Provincetown Dunes of the Cape Cod National Seashore, both of which are constantly being reshaped by the winds.

Before planning your trip to New England, be sure to consult:
  • *the Map of Principal Sights and*
  • *the Recommended Driving Tours, both found at the front of this guide and*
  • *the Practical Information section (the blue pages at the back of this guide)*
for travel tips, useful addresses and phone numbers, and information on sports, recreation and annual events.

QUINCY

Population 84,985
Map of Principal Sights
Tourist Office ☎ 617-847-1454

This large community on the state's south shore was prominent during its early days as the home of the Adams family, which gave the nation its second and sixth presidents: **John Adams** and **John Quincy Adams**. Today the Boston suburb is a hub of industrial and commercial activity.

Historical Notes

Mining and Shipbuilding – In the 19C Quincy's granite quarries and shipyards attracted laborers from Finland, Greece, Ireland, Italy and Eastern Europe. Their descendants form the basis of the town's ethnically diverse population. Quincy shipyards produced the only seven-masted schooner *(Thomas W. Lawson)* ever built, as well as the first atomic-powered surface ship.

Father and Son – John Adams (1735-1826), a spokesman for the revolution against England's colonial policies, was among the men who drafted the Declaration of Independence. Beginning in 1778, his diplomatic posts took him to France, Scotland and England, where he was instrumental in negotiating the Treaty of Paris (1783) to end the Revolution. He served as vice president under George Washington, then as president from 1797 to 1801. After his defeat in 1801, John Adams retired to his home in Quincy. By incredible coincidence, John Adams and Thomas Jefferson, who also helped draft the Declaration of Independence, died on the same day—July 4, 1826—50 years to the day after the historic document was signed.

John Quincy Adams (1767-1848), who followed in the steps of his father, studied law before beginning a diplomatic career, serving at various times as ambassador to Prussia, the Netherlands, Russia and Great Britain. In 1824 he was elected president of the US, an office he held until 1829. Having lost the election in 1828, Adams retired to his hometown. His election to Congress two years later began a 17-year career in the legislature for this devoted statesman.

SIGHTS *3hrs. Map p 151.*

★**Adams National Historic Park** – *Visit by guided tour (2hrs 30min) only, mid-Apr–early Nov daily 9am (last tour 3pm). Tours depart from the visitor center, 1250 Hancock St. $2. ☎ 617-770-1175. www.nps.gov/adam.* Administered by the National Park Service, this 13-acre site contains the birthplaces of two US presidents, the homestead of the Adams family and a visitor center.

John Adams and John Quincy Adams Birthplaces – *133-141 Franklin St.* These modest Colonial saltbox houses, where John Adams and John Quincy Adams were born, contain memorabilia and period furnishings.

The Old House – *135 Adams St.* In 1787 John Adams and his wife, Abigail, bought this house, referred to by the Adams family as the "Old House." Each of the four successive generations of Adamses who lived here added their own mementos and furnishings to the house, which explains the diversity of styles. Especially noteworthy is the study where John Adams died, the rich mahogany in the Panelled Room, and the Long Room, which is furnished with elegant French pieces. The Stone Library contains the Adams family collection of 14,000 volumes.

United First Parish Church – *1306 Hancock St. Visit by guided tour (40min) only, Jul–Aug daily 9am–5pm. Mid-Apr–Jun & Sept–early Nov Mon–Sat 9am–5pm, Sun 1pm–5pm. $2. ☎ 617-773-0062.* This granite Greek Revival structure, known as the "Church of the Presidents," is the final resting place of both John Adams and John Quincy Adams and their wives.

SALEM★★

Population 38,091
Map of Principal Sights
Tourist Office ☎ 877-725-3662

Salem, a town tormented by its fear of witchcraft in the 17C, and a seaport that launched nearly 1,000 ships in the following centuries, is a bustling and pleasant city where historic districts adjoin industrial sites. Today the city makes its living from revenues generated by tourism, manufacturing, the North Shore Medical Center and Salem State College.

Historical Notes

A City of Peace – Founded in 1626 by Roger Conant, Salem derives its name from the Hebrew word *Shalom*, meaning peace. Ironically, intolerance and violence dominated the early days of this Puritan city. Roger Williams, persecuted by the authorities, fled to Rhode Island in 1636, and thereafter zealous Salemites devoted their energies to driving the "evil ones" from the colony. Intended to rid the colony once and for all of evildoers, the notorious witch-hunts began in the early 1690s.

The Witchcraft Hysteria – In 1692 several young girls, whose imaginations had been stirred by tales of voodoo told to them by the West Indian slave Tituba, began to have visions and convulsive fits. After examining the girls, a doctor declared them to be victims of "the evil hand." Impressionable and frightened, the youngsters accused Tituba and two other women of having bewitched them, and the women were immediately arrested and put into prison. From that point on, fear and panic spread through Salem, leaving no one free of suspicion. More than 200 persons were accused of witchcraft, 150 of whom were imprisoned and 19 found guilty and hanged. The hysteria, credited in retrospect to rivalries between several prominent Salem families, came to an abrupt end about a year later when Gov. William Phips' wife was accused of witchcraft.

An Era of Maritime Glory – Salem's sizable fleet of vessels, important to colonial trade in the 17C, won special recognition during the Revolution. When the ports of BOSTON and New York were occupied by the British, it was Salem's ships that carried arms and supplies to the colonial troops. Operating as privateers, the town's vessels also weakened the enemy by raiding and capturing about 400 British ships before the war ended. After the Revolution, Salem's merchant craft were prominent in worldwide trade. In 1786 the *Grand Turk*, sailing out of Salem to China, returned home to New England laden with luxury goods. To the many ships that followed the *Grand Turk*, the route to the Far East *(p 28)* became a familiar one; "To the farthest port of the rich East!" became Salem's motto. The Chinese, who saw great numbers of vessels arriving in their ports bearing Salem's name, imagined Salem was a vast and magnificent country. Two years after the *Grand Turk* set sail for China, trade between Salem and India was opened by another Salem ship, the *Peggy*, owned by Elias Hasket Derby. The China trade brought such enormous wealth to Salem that taxes paid in the town on imported goods alone provided eight percent of the nation's revenues. Salem merchants, including the Derbys, Peabodys and Crowninshields, were among the richest men in America; their mansions were filled with treasures retrieved from the Orient aboard their ships.

The decline of the port of Salem, due in part to the embargo on foreign trade enforced by President Jefferson in 1807, was hastened by the development of new, deep-draft clipper ships that could only be outfitted in deepwater ports such as those of Boston and New York.

Salem Today – Renewal programs in the heart of the downtown area, around **Essex Street**, have created the look of the colonial era with brick walkways and a pedestrian mall. A number of shops devoted to the occult offer tarot and psychic readings and sell witchcraft and New Age items. Operated by the National Park Service, the **visitor center**, housed in the town's renovated, turn-of-the-century armory, just off Essex Street, features a film *(27min)* on the history of Essex County *(2 New Liberty St.; open Jun–Labor Day daily 9am–6pm; rest of the year daily 9am–5pm; closed Jan 1, Thanksgiving Day, Dec 25;* ఉ ☎ *978-740-1650; www.nps.gov/sama).*

■ Two Famous Men of Salem

Samuel McIntire (1757-1811), carpenter, wood carver, sculptor, builder and architect, influenced much of Salem's architecture. His solid, four-square wood and brick mansions, such as the Peirce-Nichols House (1782) on Federal Street *(not open to the public)*, ornamented with handsome porches and balustrades, are among the finest examples of American Federal architecture. The masterfully carved doorways, ceilings, cornices and fireplaces for which McIntire is known, are adorned with a variety of classical motifs (garlands, rosettes, fruit baskets) that reflect his refined taste and attention to detail.

Nathaniel Hawthorne (1804-64), a leading 19C American literary figure, was born in Salem, where he wrote his earliest stories. Salem provided the inspiration or setting for many of Hawthorne's works, including *The House of the Seven Gables*. Much of the description in his novel *The Scarlet Letter*, especially that of the Custom House *(below)*, was influenced by the years he spent as surveyor of the port.

SEASIDE SALEM *3hrs. Map p 206.*

The historic waterfront district may be visited on foot; begin at the visitor center (below) on Central Wharf.

After more than a century, Salem is once again alive with a vitality reminiscent of its days of maritime supremacy. **Pickering Wharf** boasts a concentration of restaurants and specialty shops; just beyond it, on Derby Street, is the Salem Maritime National Historic Site.

★**Salem Maritime National Historic Site** – 🄺 *Open Jun–Labor Day daily 9am–6pm. Rest of the year daily 9am–5pm. Closed Jan 1, Thanksgiving Day, Dec 25.* ☎ *978-740-1650. www.nps.gov/sama.* The city's historic waterfront site is administered by the National Park Service. The **visitor center** features a film *(18min)* on the seafaring history of Salem. At one time more than 40 wharves reached out into the harbor from the town's shoreline. **Derby Wharf**, the longest (2,100ft), and for many years a busy mercantile center, still remains.

★**Custom House** (**A**) – *Visit by guided tour only.* This Federal-style building with its symbolic eagle was constructed in 1819 to house the customs offices of Salem. Inside, several of the offices, including the one used by Nathaniel Hawthorne when he was an officer of the port, have been restored.

At the rear of the Custom House, the **Bonded Warehouse** (**B**) contains samples of cargoes carried by Salem vessels, cargo handling equipment and weighing devices.

Derby House (**C**) – *Visit by guided tour only.* This brick mansion was built in 1762 for merchant Elias Hasket Derby, whose ships opened trade with India and the Orient, making him very rich. From the waterfront location of this house, Derby could see his ships as they docked at or near Derby Wharf. Inside, the wave motif ornamenting the stairway and the staircase balusters, carved to resemble twisted rope, is an appropriate feature for the home of a man who earned his living from the sea.

House of the Seven Gables

★**House of the Seven Gables** – 📷 *54 Turner St. Visit by guided tour (45min) only, May–Nov daily 10am–5pm. Rest of the year Mon–Sat 10am–5pm, Sun noon 5pm. Closed first two weeks of Jan, Thanksgiving Day, Dec 25. $7.* ✕ ☎ *978-744-0991. www.7gables.org.* A rambling three-story Colonial with steeply pitched roofs, this house was immortalized by Hawthorne's novel of the same name. Built in 1668, the house was completely restored in 1968. Inside, scenes from Hawthorne's novel come alive as visitors pass from Hepzibah's Cent Shop to the parlor where the judge was found, and into Clifford's room, under the eaves, at the top of a secret staircase. Tours cover 6 of the 16 rooms, as well as Hawthorne's birthplace (c.1750, moved from its original location on Union Street).

Other buildings in this garden setting include the Retire Becket House (1655, which contains the museum shop), the Hooper-Hathaway House (1682) and a counting house (c.1830).

★★★PEABODY ESSEX MUSEUM   *1 1/2 days*

This illustrious museum focuses on America's maritime history from the 17C to the present, and on the historical significance of the city of Salem and Essex County. It pays special tribute to Salem's great 18C and 19C maritime era, during which the town flourished as a major American port. Most of the nearly 400,000 pieces in the collections reflect the global range of Salem's ship captains, who returned from their travels with porcelain, carvings and other artifacts from the Far East, India, Africa and the Pacific Islands. Several historic houses and an extensive research library are part of the museum complex.

In 1799 a group of local ship captains organized the **Salem East India Marine Society** and eventually built the East India Marine Hall. Still located on Essex Street, it originally housed a meeting hall, bank, insurance company and museum of "natural and artificial" curiosities from around the world. When the port declined, leaving

Salem with serious economic problems, philanthropist George Peabody offered financial assistance. The society's museum was renamed for him in the early 20C, and in the latter half of the century, spacious modern galleries were added to the original hall. Two additions to the museum—a smooth-surfaced structure completed in 1976, and the Asian Export Wing, dedicated in 1988—have greatly increased exhibition space. In spring 1992, as part of the revitalization of historic Salem, the Peabody Museum was joined with the nearby Essex Institute, originally founded in 1821 to serve as the Essex County Historical Society. That society's holdings encompassed a museum of decorative arts, nine historic structures and a research library.

The combined museum displays art and artifacts from six curatorial departments. What is now the **Phillips Library**, located in Plummer Hall, preserves some 400,000 rare books, 1,000,000 photographs, and manuscripts, log books, letters and diaries detailing life in early Salem. In 1998 the library opened a permanent exhibit titled "The Real Witchcraft Papers," showcasing some of the 500 documents from the court that tried the accused. In celebration of its bicentennial, the museum will initiate a major, $100 million expansion. Designed by renowned architect Moshe Safdie, six new galleries, an auditorium and family center are to be created *(constructed projected to begin fall, 2000)*.

Visit

🄺🄸🄳 *East India Square. Open Memorial Day–Oct Mon–Sat 10am–5pm, Sun noon–5pm. Rest of the year Tue–Sat 10am–5pm, Sun noon–5pm. Closed Jan 1, Thanksgiving Day, Dec 25. $8.50 (includes admission to on-site historic houses). ✗ ♿. The historic houses can be visited by guided tour (30min) only. ☎ 800-745-4054. www.pem.org.*

Museum – The collections are organized into six categories: Maritime Art and History; Asian Export Art; Asian, African and Pacific Islands Art; Native American Arts and Archaeology; Natural History; and American Decorative Arts.

Maritime Art and History – The collection of marine paintings includes works by major artists, such as Fitz Hugh Lane and Antoine Roux; port scenes illustrating commerce with the Orient; and ships' portraits commissioned by the vessels' owners. Portraiture and other paintings by such famed artists as John Singleton Copley and Gilbert Stuart are also featured, as are rare nautical instruments and charts and a dramatic collection of carved ships' figureheads.

Asian Export Art – Considered one of the most complete collections of its kind in the world, the collection features 19C and early-20C decorative and utilitarian porcelain, silver, furniture, textiles and precious objects. Created in China, Japan, India, the Philippines and Ceylon (now Sri Lanka), the pieces were intended for export to England and America and therefore reflect a melding of Eastern artistry and Western tastes. The lacquer, ivory and mother-of-pearl pieces, as well as the items fashioned in gold and silver, are particularly impressive for their refined style and exquisite detail.

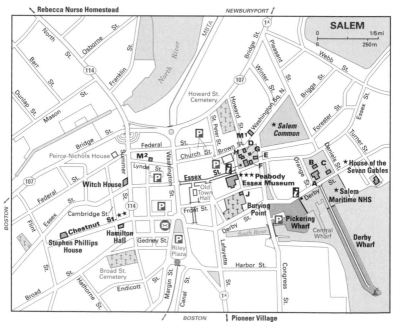

Asian, African and Pacific Islands Art – This section encompasses textiles, shields, ritual costumes, masks and pottery from the tropical Pacific Islands, Indonesia, Japan and Africa. The Edward S. Morse Collection of 19C Meiji costumes and crafts is reputedly the largest of its kind outside Japan.

Native American Arts and Archaeology – The collection includes artifacts from the Indian cultures of the Eastern seaboard, Great Lakes, Great Plains, Northwest Coast and South America.

Natural History – This section contains specimens of flora and fauna, predominantly from eastern America.

American Decorative Arts – The collection consists of furnishings, paintings, textiles, toys and costumes from the colonial period through the early 20C.

Historic Houses – The following historic houses, located near the museum, are open to the public *(visit by 30min guided tour only; entry fee included in museum admission).*

★ **John Ward House (D)** – The Ward House (1684) is a good example of 17C American Colonial architecture, with its steep gables, clapboard exterior and small casement windows. The furnishings are of the same period.

Crowninshield-Bentley House (E) – The hipped roof, symmetrical windows and pedimented doorway of this 1730 dwelling are typical of mid-18C New England architecture. The furnishings represent several different periods.

★★ **Gardner-Pingree House (F)** – The solid four-square silhouette of this handsome brick mansion (1805)—another of Samuel McIntire's designs—is lightened by its balustraded roof, numerous windows and curved entry porch supported by Corinthian columns.
Inside, the furnishings and decor create a mood of elegant refinement. In the front entrance hall, wave and rope motifs ornament the staircase. In the parlor, decorative motifs, including sheaves of wheat and baskets of fruit on the fireplaces and above the doorways, reflect the work of master-carver McIntire. The bedchambers reveal the same refinement of taste. Most of the furniture was made in Salem.
The grounds also include the **Derby-Beebe Summer House (G)** (1799), designed by Samuel McIntire as a garden tea house, and the **Lyle-Tapley Shoe Shop (H)** (1830).

ADDITIONAL SIGHTS 5hrs

★ **Salem Common** – In the 19C a number of Federal mansions were built bordering the common of colonial Salem, called Washington Square. A notable group of these residences stands on Washington Square North.

★★ **Chestnut Street** – This broad street lined with Federal-style mansions illustrates the wealth of 19C Salem. The majority of the dwellings on Chestnut Street were built between 1800 and 1820; their size and richly adorned facades are unrivaled. **Hamilton Hall** *(no. 9)* was designed by Samuel McIntire. The **Stephen Phillips Memorial Trust House** *(no. 34)*, decorated with furnishings from around the world, is open to the public *(visit by 40min guided tour only, late May–late Oct Mon–Sat 10am–4:30pm; $3; ☎ 978-744-0440; www.salemweb.com/org/phillipshouse).*

Gourt-Pickman House (J) – *Charter St. Not open to the public.* This Colonial dwelling (c.1680) is adjacent to Salem's old cemetery, the **Burying Point**, which contains interesting examples of early tombstones.

Salem 1630: Pioneer Village – 🅺🅸🅳🆂 *Forest River Park, east of Salem State College, at the junction of Rtes. 1A & 129. Open mid-Apr–late Nov Mon–Sat 10am–5pm, Sun noon–5pm. $5. ☎ 978-744-0991. www.7gables.org.* This site features replicas of the diverse kinds of dwellings built by Salem's early settlers: thatched cottages, dugouts of mud and straw, and a wigwam that highlights the influence of the Indians on the first settlers. Costumed interpreters demonstrate the activities of 17C domestic life.

■ Salem Bewitched

In recent years Salem has become a center for adherents of the ancient religion of Wicca, a belief system based on goddesses and nature. Several thousand witches, as followers of Wicca call themselves, currently live in the area, quietly practicing their religion and attempting to dispel long-held public opinions concerning witchcraft. To that end a Witches' League for Public Awareness was founded in 1986 by Laurie Cabot, who was named by former Gov. Michael Dukakis as the "official Witch of Salem."
Several points of interest in or near Salem individually re-create the tale of the witch-hunts and the story of their unfortunate victims. In 1992 the city celebrated the tercentenary of the witch trials. Each year at Halloween, Salem hosts Haunted Happenings, a 10-day festival that recalls the city's past.

Salem Witch Museum (**M¹**) – *19 1/2 Washington Square. Open Jul–Aug daily 10am–7pm. Rest of the year daily 10am–5pm. Closed Jan 1, Thanksgiving Day, Dec 25. $6.* & ☎ *978-744-1692. www.salemwitchmuseum.com.* The museum presents a multimedia program *(30min)* of 13 life-size scenes that sensationalize the major events of the witchcraft hysteria from 1692 to its final days in 1693. A new permanent exhibit (1999) titled "Witches: Evolving Perceptions" traces the meaning of the word *witch* up to current times and includes a look at the Wicca movement.

Across from the museum stands Henry H. Kitson's statue of Salem's founder, **Roger Conant**.

Witch House – *310 1/2 Essex St. Visit by guided tour (40min) only. Jul–Labor Day daily 10am–6pm. Mid-Mar.–Jun & rest of Sept–Nov daily 10am–4:30pm. Closed Easter Sunday & Thanksgiving Day. $5.* ☎ *978-744-0180.* This large dwelling (1642) was the home of Judge Corwin, one of the men who presided over the witch trials. The interior appears much as it did in the late 17C, when more than 200 persons accused of witchcraft were brought to the judge's chamber for preliminary hearings.

Witch Dungeon Museum (**M²**) – *16 Lynde St. Visit by guided tour (25min) only, Apr–Nov daily 10am–5pm. $5.* ☎ *978-741-3570. www.witchdungeon.com.* A live stage presentation, based on historic transcripts of a 1692 witch trial, captures the hysteria that swept Salem in the late 17C. Following the presentation, visitors tour a re-creation of the dank dungeon where local "witches" were jailed in tiny, unlit cells.

Rebecca Nurse Homestead – *149 Pine St., in Danvers, 4mi north of Salem. Visit by guided tour (1hr) only, mid-Jun–Labor Day Tue–Sun 1pm–4:30pm. Mid-Sept–Oct weekends only 1pm–4:30pm. $4.* ☎ *978-774-8799. www.rebeccanurse.org.* Rebecca Nurse, a victim of the Salem witch-hunts, lived in this saltbox house (c.1678). Accused of being a witch, Rebecca was tried, convicted and hanged, despite a petition in her favor that had been signed by many of the townspeople. A short walk from the house leads to the Nurse Burial Ground, where a monument marks Rebecca's presumed grave.

SANDWICH★

Population 15,489
Map p 166
Tourist Office ☎ 508-362-3225

On the shores of Shawme Pond, tranquil and shaded by willow trees, are the Dexter Mill and the Hoxie House. Built in the 17C, the mill, which is still in use, and the house evoke the colonial charm of Sandwich—the first settlement on Cape Cod, founded in 1637. Across from the village green stands the Sandwich Glass Museum.

Historical Notes – In 1825 Deming Jarves chose Sandwich as the site of his Boston and Sandwich Glass Co. because of the region's vast forests, which provided the wood needed to fuel the furnaces in which he fired glass. An efficient administrator, Jarves brought skilled craftsmen from Europe to work in the factory, and built homes and company stores for them. He reintroduced the use of the three-part mold that had been used centuries before by the Romans, and developed a process to mass-produce clear, cut glass in a variety of shapes, forms and patterns. The delicate lacy pattern of the glass Jarves made became known as Sandwich glass *(p 38)* and brought fame to the factory and the town. By 1850, 500 workers were employed at the factory, but labor disputes in 1888 eventually forced the company to shut its doors permanently.

SIGHTS

★**Sandwich Glass Museum** – *129 Main St. Open Apr–Oct daily 9:30am–5pm. Rest of the year Wed–Sun 9:30am–5pm. Closed the month of Jan, Thanksgiving Day & Dec 25. $3.50.* & ☎ *508-888-0251.* Founded in 1907, the museum owns an extensive collection of the glass made in Sandwich between 1825 and 1888. Moderately priced when it was produced in the 19C, Sandwich glass is today highly valued by collectors.

Before visiting the general exhibit rooms, pause at the diorama that illustrates the Sandwich factory and its craftsmen at work. Various stages of glassmaking are portrayed: sand is mixed with potash, carbonate of soda, or lime, heated in the furnace (at 2,500° F) and then blown, molded or pressed.

Exhibits display a variety of patterns in a wide range of Sandwich glass items, such as candlesticks, tableware, vases, furniture knobs and tiebacks. Examples of early pressed lacy glass, the colorful (canary, blue, green, opalescent) mid-period pattern glass, and the lesser-recognized blown, cut and engraved glassware are included. Note in particular the collections of decorative Sandwich paperweights and the one-of-a-kind presentation pieces made to commemorate special occasions or events.

★**Heritage Plantation of Sandwich** – [Kids] *76 Grove St. From the Sandwich town hall (Rte. 130), turn left onto Grove St. Open mid-May–mid-Oct daily 9am–5pm. $9.* ✗ ♿ ☏ *508-888-3300. www.heritageplantation.org.* This impeccably maintained, 76-acre park setting includes three museums as well as an expansive rhododendron garden. The museum's collections of early-American historical artifacts and folk art are arranged in several buildings designed to harmonize with the landscape. Formerly the estate of horticulturist Charles Dexter, who performed extensive research on rhododendrons in the 1920s and 1930s, the plantation is especially lovely from mid-May through mid-June, when the plants are in bloom.

Automobile Museum – This replica of the Round Stone Barn, constructed by the Shakers at Hancock, contains antique automobiles in mint condition dating from 1899 to the 1930s, and includes the 1931 Duesenberg owned by Gary Cooper. Silent movies *(10min)* of the early days of the automobile are shown. The **Old East Mill** was built in Orleans about 1800.

Military Museum – This reproduction of the Publick House, a recreation hall built by the Continental Army (1783) in New Windsor, New York, contains antique firearms (including a rifle owned by Buffalo Bill Cody), flags and 2,000 hand-painted miniatures representing American military units from 1621 to 1900.

Art Museum – The superb collection of folk art comprises primitive portraits, wood carvings, metalwork, glass, scrimshaw, birds carved by A. Elmer Crowell and some 150 Currier and Ives prints. Children will enjoy riding on the carousel (1912).

SPRINGFIELD
Population 156,983
Map of Principal Sights
Tourist Office ☏ 413-787-1548

A rich industrial past has contributed to making Springfield the hub of business, finance and industry in the PIONEER VALLEY and the third largest city in Massachusetts, with tools and plastics among its leading products.

Established on the banks of the Connecticut River in 1636 as a trading post, Springfield grew into an industrial center by the 19C. For over 200 years the city was known for the **Springfield Armory**, the government arsenal that turned out the first American musket (1795) and weapons used by the Union troops in the Civil War.

Every September the Springfield area hosts the **Eastern States Exposition**, the largest fair in the Northeast. Located on the 175-acre fairgrounds in West Springfield *(2mi west of the center of Springfield on Rte. 147)*, the "Big E," as the annual fair is called, features exhibits, entertainment, the Eastern States Horse Show and a tour of **Old Storrowtown Village**, a restored colonial village on the grounds. In June the fairground is also the site of the annual **American CraftFair**, formerly held in New York.

SIGHTS *4hrs*

★**Basketball Hall of Fame** – [Kids] *1150 W. Columbus Ave. Open year-round daily 9:30am–5:30pm. Closed Jan 1, Thanksgiving Day, Dec 25. $8.* ♿ ☏ *413-781-6500. www.hoophall.com.* Basketball was originated by Dr. James Naismith, whose Springfield College team played the first game in 1891. Dr. Naismith developed the sport to provide students with an alternative to the monotonous exercise program practiced in physical education classes during the winter months. Equipment consisted of a ball and a peach basket; each time a team scored, someone had to climb a ladder to remove the ball from the basket. The game was adopted by the YMCA three years later, and by 1936 it had gained international recognition and acceptance as an Olympic sport.

Exhibits trace the development of the sport from amateur to professional and international status. Life-size action photos of such basketball greats as Wilt Chamberlain and Bob Cousy, videotapes of unforgettable coaches in action on the sidelines, film clips of the celebrated Harlem Globetrotters, and a selection of uniforms, equipment and memorabilia constitute the displays. The Honors Court commemorates outstanding players, coaches, and contributors to the sport in a series of portrait medallions. Visitors may test their skill at the Shoot Out on the ground floor or play one-on-one against former stars in the virtual reality exhibit.

Court Square – This pleasant park in the heart of downtown Springfield is bordered by buildings representing a variety of styles. Diagonally opposite the square rises the **Municipal Group**★ (1913), a complex consisting of a pair of classically inspired structures: City Hall and Symphony Hall, with identical columned porticoes, and an Italian Renaissance bell tower. The **First Church of Christ** (1819), at the west end of the square, is a two-story wood-frame meetinghouse surmounted by a gilded cock brought to America about 1750. Just beyond stands the **Hampden County Courthouse** (1871), a granite structure that has been substantially altered, yet retains the late-Gothic character of its original H.H. Richardson design.

The Quadrangle – *Open Jul–Aug Tues–Sun noon–4pm. Rest of the year Wed–Sun noon–4pm. Closed major holidays. $4.* ✗ & ☎ *413-263-6800. www.quadrangle.org.* The Museum of Fine Arts, the George Walter Vincent Smith Art Museum, the Connecticut Valley Historical Museum, the Springfield Science Museum and the city library are grouped together on the Quadrangle bounded by Chestnut and State Streets.

Museum of Fine Arts – Holdings include European paintings of the 17C Dutch, 18C Italian, and 18C and 19C French schools. The American section contains canvases by eminent 19C painters, such as Winslow Homer and Frederic Edwin Church, and the finely detailed *Historical Monument of the American Republic*, painted by Erastus Salisbury Field to commemorate the nation's Centennial.

★ **George Walter Vincent Smith Art Museum** – This building, designed to suggest an Italian Renaissance villa, contains a collection of Oriental and American art and furnishings, and casts of ancient Greek and Roman statues.
The collection includes American paintings, interesting examples of Japanese armor, screens, lacquers and ceramics and **Chinese cloisonné** (enamel poured into raised compartments).

Connecticut Valley Historical Museum – This building boasts a doorway similar to the type found throughout the Connecticut Valley. Inside, changing exhibits of the museum's collection of furniture, pewter, silver and portraits depict the social and cultural development of the Connecticut Valley from the 17C. The museum also contains a genealogy and local history library.

Springfield Science Museum – 🄺🄸🄳🅂 The museum contains a planetarium and a hands-on exploration center, as well as displays devoted to plant and animal life, geology and dinosaurs.

Springfield Armory National Historic Site – *1 Armory Sq. Open year-round Wed–Sun 10am–4:30pm. Closed Jan 1, Thanksgiving Day, Dec 25.* & ☎ *413-734-8551. www.nps.gov/spar.* The main arsenal building of the defunct Springfield Armory—home of the Springfield rifle—contains a collection of small arms, edged weapons and related military items dating from the 15C to the present, including examples of some of the guns manufactured here.

EXCURSION

Stanley Park – *400 Western Ave. in Westfield. 15mi west of Springfield by Rte. 20, then turn left onto Elm St., left onto Court St., and bear left onto Granville Rd. Open year-round daily 8am–dusk.* & ☎ *413-568-9312.* A 61-bell Flemish carillon, an English herb garden and a rose garden are among the many attractions in this 275-acre park, an expansive recreational space for the surrounding communities. Located in the pond area are a covered bridge, an old mill and a blacksmith's shop.

STOCKBRIDGE★★

Population 2,408
Map of Principal Sights
Tourist Office ☎ 413-443-9186

Founded in the early 18C as an Indian mission, this quintessential New England town nestled in the heart of the Berkshires exudes a grace and charm that has traditionally endeared it to well-heeled Bostonians and New Yorkers as well as to artists and writers. The town's **Main Street★** is lined with a picturesque row of pedimented buildings bounded to the west by the sprawling white facade of the **Red Lion Inn**, a cozy country hostelry dating from colonial times. Beyond the inn, Main Street gives way to large clapboard dwellings rimmed by broad landscaped lawns.
Owing to its prime location equidistant from BOSTON and New York *(both are accessible by car in 2hrs 30min)*, Stockbridge welcomes a steady stream of visitors throughout the year. In the summer, performances of classic American drama are presented at the Berkshire Theater Festival housed in the Berkshire Playhouse, a 19C casino on Main Street designed by McKim, Mead and White.

SIGHTS *1 day. Map p 115.*

Mission House – *Rte. 102 (Main St.). Visit by guided tour (45min) only, late May–Columbus Day daily 10am–5pm. $5.* ☎ *413-298-3239. www.thetrustees.org.* John Sergeant, the first missionary sent to educate and convert the local Indians to Christianity, arrived in Stockbridge in 1734. This house, which Sergeant built five years later (1739) as a wedding present for his wealthy wife, Abigail, was extremely luxurious for its day. The elaborate front door made in the Connecticut Valley was hauled across the high mountains in an oxcart to adorn the entranceway of the

Mission House. A tour of the interior, semi-dark due to the lack of electricity, suggests the conditions under which the pastor and his young bride lived in the early 18C. Most of the furnishings date from this period.

★★Norman Rockwell Museum – Kids *2.5mi from Stockbridge center. Take Rte. 102 west (Main St., then Church St.). After 2mi turn left onto Rte. 183 and continue .6mi to museum entrance on left. Open May–Oct daily 10am–5pm. Rest of the year Mon–Fri 10am–4pm, weekends 10am–5pm. Closed Thanksgiving Day & Dec 25. $9.* ☎ *413-298-4100.*

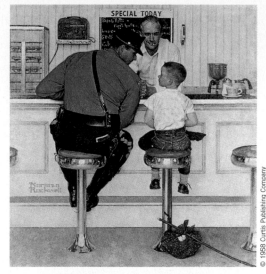

The Runaway by Norman Rockwell

© 1958 Curtis Publishing Company

www.nrm.org. Occupying a 36-acre estate overlooking the Housatonic River Valley, this immensely popular museum is the repository of the largest collection of original works by America's premier 20C illustrator.

Visit – The core collection comprises Rockwell's personal holdings along with his studio and personal library and archives. In addition, the museum has acquired works through gifts or purchases, bringing the total holdings to more than 500 paintings and drawings, including 172 large-scale works. From 1969 until 1993, highlights from the collection were displayed in the small rooms of the Old Corner House on Stockbridge's Main Street.

The main building, containing nine galleries, was designed by the eminent Postmodern architect **Robert Stern** to provide a more spacious setting for the collection. Clearly inspired by local Neoclassical architecture, and in particular the New England town hall, the low-lying clapboard and fieldstone structure is fronted by a pedimented entrance facade surmounted by a miniature "temple."

On display inside is a sizable sampling of Rockwell's works, including *Stockbridge Main Street at Christmas, Triple Self-Portrait* and *The Problem We All Live With.* The central octagonal gallery was specially designed as a sanctuary for the celebrated **Four Freedoms Series** (1943) inspired by President Franklin Delano Roosevelt's 1941 landmark speech rallying the nation to defend the rights of all people menaced by the Axis powers: freedom of speech, freedom of worship, freedom from want and freedom from fear. During World War II, these poignant images toured the nation on posters that formed the centerpiece of a fund-raising drive that yielded over $130 million in government bonds to support the war.

The museum also features temporary exhibits focusing on the work and life of Rockwell and, more broadly, on the art of illustration.

■ Norman Rockwell: Illustrator of American Life

Trained at the Art Student's League and the National Academy of Design in New York, Norman Rockwell (1894-1978) began his long and prolific career in his teens. At age 22 the artist drew his first cover for the *Saturday Evening Post,* thereby beginning a collaboration that would result in a total of 321 covers for the prestigious magazine over the next 47 years.

Rockwell's realistic paintings chronicle the changing times in America, while capturing the timeless essence of humanity—mankind's comic foibles, noble aspirations and wrenching tragedies. His homespun scenes, often depicting the routines of day-to-day living, are seasoned with a sense of humor and wonder. A hallmark of Rockwell's works is the attention to detail: every wink of the eye, gesture and accessory reveals a meticulously conceived scheme. Rockwell often depicted children, and in many cases his subjects were modeled on family, friends or neighbors. When Rockwell embarked upon a 10-year association with *Look* magazine in the 1960s, he focused on contemporary political figures and American social issues, such as the civil rights movement and poverty. In 1978 Rockwell died in Stockbridge, his home since 1953.

Just a short stroll from the museum, on a rise overlooking the valley, stands **Rockwell's studio** *(open May–Oct)*, a simple red wooden building relocated from its original site in downtown Stockbridge.

★**Chesterwood** – *3mi from Stockbridge center. Take Rte. 102 west and turn left onto Rte. 183. Continue .8mi and turn right onto Mohawk Lake Rd., then left on Willow St. and continue .5mi to Chesterwood. Open May–Oct daily 10am–5pm. $7.50.* ☐ ☎ *413-298-3579.* This large estate, formerly a farm, was acquired in the late 19C by the American sculptor **Daniel Chester French** (1850-1931). Although French achieved his first major success at the age of 25 with his *Minute Man* statue at Concord, he is probably best remembered for the impressive seated *Abraham Lincoln* he sculpted for the Lincoln Memorial in the nation's capital *(see Michelin Green Guide Washington DC)*. French executed more than 100 public monuments during his lifetime.

Models and casts of French's works, including the Dupont Circle Fountain he sculpted for Washington, DC, occupy the **Barn Gallery**. The large Colonial Revival **house** (designed by Henry Bacon) replaced the farmhouse originally on the property. The house is furnished as it was when the artist lived here. Also on the grounds is French's spacious, well-lit **studio** (another Henry Bacon design), with its tall double doors and railroad tracks that allowed French to move large works outdoors, where he could work in the natural light. The studio is appointed with interesting objets d'art and handsome furnishings, since French frequently entertained houseguests here.

A woodland walk *(20 min)* affords views of the hilly countryside.

Naumkeag – *2mi from Stockbridge center. From Main St. turn right onto Pine St., then bear left at Shamrock St. and continue on Prospect St. Visit by guided tour (45min) only, late May–Columbus Day daily 10am–5pm. $7.* ☎ *413-298-3239. www.thetrustees.org.* This Norman-style mansion (1886, Stanford White) and its terraced hillside gardens were built for Joseph Choate (1832-1917), US ambassador to England. The unusual design of the entrance to the Chinese garden was intended to keep the devil out.

WILLIAMSTOWN★★

Population 8,220
Map of Principal Sights
Tourist Office ☎ 413-664-6256

This beautiful colonial village nestles snugly in the northwest corner of Massachusetts, at the place where the MOHAWK TRAIL enters THE BERKSHIRES. The Berkshires' verdant rolling hills provide a lovely setting for Williams College, as well as for the Sterling and Francine Clark Art Institute and the Williamstown Theater Festival, which is held each summer. In 1753 the early settlement of West Hoosuck was established here by soldiers from Fort Massachusetts. Later, one of the soldiers, Col. Ephraim Williams Jr., bequeathed part of his estate for the founding of a free school in West Hoosuck—provided the town be renamed in his honor. Soon after the colonel's death, West Hoosuck was renamed Williamstown.

★★★CLARK ART INSTITUTE

The paintings, sculpture and decorative arts of the illustrious **Sterling and Francine Clark Art Institute** were gathered by Robert Sterling Clark and his wife, Francine, during the years between World War I and 1956. The collection, worthy of being compared with those of some of the world's finest museums, reflects the Clarks' early taste for classical art and, later, 19C paintings. The couple chose Williamstown as the site of their institute for its idyllic natural setting and its location far from urban centers (most likely to be threatened during wartime). The white marble building (1956), designed to house the collection, suggests a private residence and provides a splendid setting for the works. The red granite annex (1973, Pietro Belluschi) houses additional gallery space as well as the museum's auditorium. The museum shop in the entrance court stocks an extensive selection of books on art, architecture, photography, art history and art criticism.

Visit *2hrs*

225 South St. Open Jul–Aug daily 10am–5pm. Rest of the year Tue–Sun 10am–5pm. Closed Jan 1, Thanksgiving Day, Dec 25. $5 (Jul–Oct, free Tue). ☒ ☐ ☎ *413-458-2303. www.clark.williams.edu. Gallery guide (floor plan) available.*

In a room off the entrance court dedicated to the works of Remington, Homer and Sargent, it is interesting to note the different personalities of these three American artists who lived in the late 19C. **Frederic Remington** was the painter of the American West. During his lifetime he created several thousand paintings and pieces of sculpture that portrayed his favorite subjects: cowboys, Indians and the cavalry, and their heroic way of life. **Winslow Homer**, also a student of the American scene, chose to depict the rugged New England landscape—the White Mountains of New Hampshire and the rocky Maine coast—in his paintings. In contrast to Remington and Homer, **John Singer Sargent** was a modern portraitist whose subjects, generally members of high society, were rendered with the artist's flair for sophistication. Sargent painted his famous *Fumée d'Ambre Gris* while on a voyage to Tangiers.

Housed in the marble building, the earliest works are from the Renaissance period. Highlighting this section are the Italian paintings, including a seven-part panel altarpiece by Ugolino da Siena, *Virgin and Child Enthroned with Four Angels* by **Piero della Francesca**, and Netherlandish portraits (*Portrait of a Man* by Jan Gossaert). The 17C and 18C are represented by masters of the European schools: the Spanish school by **Murillo** and **Goya**; the English school by **Gainsborough**, **Turner** and **Lawrence**; the Dutch and Flemish schools by **Ruisdael and Pynacker**; the French school by **Lorrain** and **Fragonard**; and the Italian school by **Tiepolo**.

However, it is in the realm of 19C French and American art that the collection excels. In the section devoted to the French school, the group of paintings by **Corot** shows the artist's skill in executing landscapes as well as figures. *The Trumpeter of the Hussars* by **Gericault**, the Romantic painter, typifies his masterful style and contrasts with the muted tones used by **Millet**. Among the Impressionist canvases are more than 30 works by **Renoir**, including *Sleeping Girl with a Cat, The Blonde Bather, The Onions* and others painted between 1870 and 1890. **Degas'** treatment of his favorite subjects, dancers and horses, shows his extraordinary sense of movement. Shimmering with color, the paintings by **Monet** include one from his *Rouen Cathedral* series, and *The Cliffs at Étretat*. The Postimpressionist **Toulouse-Lautrec** is represented by several works, including his *Dr. Péan Operating*.

Displays of porcelain, furniture and silver accompany the paintings and sculpture. The Clark collection of American and European silver, one of the finest in the world, includes pieces made by the 18C English silversmith **Paul de Lamerie**.

On the upper level of the granite building, recent acquisitions of early photography, from the invention of the medium in 1839 to the threshold of Modernism around 1910, invite the viewer to ponder the rich and varied currents of 19C art. A selection of works by French, English and American photographers inaugurates the museum's first new medium of collecting since the Clark Institute opened to the public in 1956.

ADDITIONAL SIGHTS

Williams College – Chartered in 1793 and named for Ephraim Williams, the college has more than 50 buildings from different periods, beginning in the late 18C. Set on the wide, luxuriant campus lawns on Main and nearby streets are good examples of the Georgian, Federal, Gothic Revival (Thompson Memorial Chapel) and Greek Revival (Chapin Hall and Williams College Museum of Art) styles. On Main Street, note the president's house (Sloane House, 1801), an attractive, well-proportioned Federal-style dwelling. Opposite is West College (1790), the free school that became Williams College.

★ **Williams College Museum of Art** – *On Main St. between Spring & Water Sts. Open year-round Tue–Sat 10am–5pm, Sun 1pm–5pm. Closed Jan 1, Thanksgiving Day, Dec 25. & point; ☎ 413-597-2429. www.williams.edu/WCMA.* This building, one of the finest

---

■ Spring Street Treats

At the end of Spring Street, the retail center of Williamstown, sits an artsy restaurant, comfortable and eclectic, called **Robin's** (☎ *413-458-4489*), which serves lunch, dinner and Sunday brunch. Boldly colored walls awash with bright paintings embrace diners in two small rooms. Tiny lights illumine the delightful outdoor deck, adding a romantic glow. The cuisine is just as pleasing to the palate: lobster ravioli with pesto, smoked salmon fettucine or mixed sausage grill (lamb rosemary and wild boar) as entrées, for example. Appetizers include Italian spinach soup and white bean/roasted garlic paté. Desserts range from raspberry sorbet to Chocolate Torte Colin. After dinner, walk up the street to a popular student hangout for an ice-cream cone. **Lickety-Split** (☎ *413-458-1818*) serves many flavors, plus salads, sandwiches and quiche for lunch. Then cross the street and duck into the intimate **Images Cinema** (☎ *413-458-5612*) to see a foreign film. Housed in a historic brick building, this independent filmhouse has evolved from the Walden Theatre, which opened on this spot in 1916. Subscription memberships and creative events such as a film discussion series over Sunday brunch, family films and late-night bites have enabled the community institution to survive in an era of mall-anchored mega-cinemas.

on campus, has evolved over the years from a brick Greek Revival octagon (1846) to its present size, which includes additions in 1983 and 1986 by renowned architect Charles Moore. The building's unassuming exterior belies the dramatic atrium and neatly sculpted, well-lit gallery spaces within.

The collection includes examples of European, non-Western and ancient art, but its strength lies in American art: Copley, Homer, Eakins, Hopper, Inness, O'Keeffe and Wood are all represented. Changing exhibits of modern and contemporary art are also presented.

WORCESTER

Population 169,759
Map of Principal Sights
Tourist Office ☎ 508-753-2920

Worcester, the second largest city in New England, is a commercial and industrial center brimming with manufacturing plants. Its central location within the state has promoted the growth of a diverse economy, which includes retail and medical services.

Historical Notes – Between 1770 and 1776 the fiery anti-British newspaper the *Massachusetts Spy* was printed in Worcester by patriot editor Isaiah Thomas. Following the Revolution, Thomas helped establish the **American Antiquarian Society** (1812), which today owns an important collection of early-American source material. Printing and publishing continue to contribute to the city's economy.

The opening of a canal on the Blackstone River in 1828 sparked the city's rapid industrial growth. Today electrical equipment, machinery, plastics, chemicals, pharmaceuticals and other products are manufactured in the Worcester area.

Playing an important role in the rejuvenation of downtown are Centrum, the city's civic center, with its facilities for trade shows and concerts, and preservation projects such as the renovation of **Mechanics Hall** (1857), a 19C architectural gem now used as a concert hall and the conversion of Union Station into an intermodal transportation facility. Educational institutions in the Worcester area include **Holy Cross College** and **Clark University**. The modernistic library on the Clark campus is named for physicist **Dr. Robert Goddard** (1882-1945), a native of Worcester and former professor at Clark, who built and successfully fired the world's first liquid-fuel rocket.

SIGHTS 3hrs

★★**Worcester Art Museum** – *55 Salisbury St. Open year-round Wed–Fri & Sun 11am–5pm, Sat 10am–5pm. Closed Jul 4, Thanksgiving Day, Dec 25. $8. ✗ ☎ 508-799-4406. www.worcesterart.org.* The museum owns collections of paintings, sculpture and decorative arts spanning 50 centuries from antiquity to the present. Displayed in a building inspired by Italian Renaissance architecture, the collections are arranged in galleries that surround an arcaded central court. The museum also provides gallery space for prints and drawings, 20C and Contemporary art and changing exhibits, and retains an outdoor sculpture garden.

The **first floor** is devoted to ancient art, the art of the Middle Ages, and Asian art, including extensive holdings of Japanese prints from the Edo period. Highlights include the 11-headed Japanese Kannon (9-10C AD); the 12C **Chapter House**, formerly part of a Benedictine priory in France; and *The Last Supper*, one of a group of c.1300 frescoes from Spoleto, Italy. The central court contains the large floor mosaic, *Hunting Scenes* (6C), from Antioch. Worcester's sculpture collection includes an Egyptian female torso dating from Dynasty IV.

On the second floor the European schools of painting from the Middle Ages through the 20C are represented. Highlights include El Greco's intense *Repentant Magdalene; The Flight into Egypt* by Nicolas Poussin; a portrait by Gainsborough of his daughters; Gauguin's *Brooding Woman;* and in the Italian section, the dramatic *Calling of St. Matthew* by Strozzi.

The third-floor **American wing** features the American school of painting with works by John Copley, Worcester native Ralph Earl, James McNeill Whistler, Winslow Homer, John Singer Sargent, Mary Cassatt, Childe Hassam and the landscapists George Inness, Albert Ryder and Samuel Morse. The portrait of **Mrs. Elizabeth Freake and Baby Mary**, by an anonymous 17C artist, is considered one of the finest portraits of the colonial period. An unusual feature of the self-portrait by Thomas Smith (c.1680) is the naval battle scene that replaces the traditional landscape in the background. Another early work, *The Peaceable Kingdom* by Quaker Edward Hicks, is noteworthy for its simple, unsophisticated theme and treatment.

Located on the fourth floor, a more contemporary work, *The Wave*, was painted by Marsden Hartley (1877-1943), an organizer of the 1913 New York Armory Show, which introduced the American public to trends in modern European painting, particularly Cubism. The museum's distinguished **pre-Columbian collection** *(4th floor)* is also worth viewing. Works in gold, jade, clay, stone and ceramics represent various pre-Columbian cultures, such as Zapotec and Chimu.

*★**Higgins Armory Museum** – 🆚 *100 Barber Ave. Open year-round Tue–Sat 10am–4pm, Sun noon–4pm. Closed major holidays. $5.75.* ♿ ☎ *508-853-6015. www.higgins.org.* This multistoried steel and glass building (1931) constructed by John W. Higgins, Worcester native and former president of the Worcester Pressed Steel Co., houses a prized collection of armor as well as early tools and weapons that Higgins gathered during his travels abroad and across the US. Presented in multimedia shows, live demonstrations and historical exhibits, these objects provide a unique perspective on knightly culture.

Principal displays are arranged in an enormous exhibit gallery, modeled after the Great Hall of an 11C Austrian castle. Paintings, furnishings, tapestries, banners and stained glass in the gallery add to the illusion of being in a Medieval castle. Along the walls stand some 100 suits of parade, combat and jousting armor dating from the 14C to the 16C. Produced by highly skilled craftsmen, some of these suits are truly works of art, such as the suit of Maximilian armor named for **Emperor Maximilian**, who preferred fluted armor, and the **Franz von Teuffenbach** armor, with its elaborate decorative etching. Tools and weapons of the Stone and Bronze Ages and a rare gladiator's helmet (1C AD) are included in the other exhibits. The fourth floor features a time line showing the evolution of armor and on the second floor, children can don Medieval dress and a variety of helmets as well as participate in period board games.

EXCURSION

Willard House and Clock Museum – *11mi southeast of Worcester, in Grafton. 11 Willard St. Take Rte. 122, then Rte. 140 to the center of Grafton. From there follow the signs 1.5mi. Visit by guided tour (1hr 15min) only, year-round Tue–Sat 10am–4pm, Sun 1pm–5pm. Closed major holidays. $5. Reservations suggested.* ☎ *508-839-3500.* Situated in a lovely rural **setting** along a country road is a group of red wooden buildings, including a barn. In this complex, a collection of more than 70 clocks made by the **Willard brothers** (Simon, Benjamin, Aaron and Ephraim) is on view. The 1718 Willard House and clock shop, where the Willards lived and worked in the 18C, is now a museum. Simon became famous for his improved timepiece, the **banjo clock**, which resembles the musical instrument in shape. Willard clocks were produced in a variety of styles (wall, shelf and tall case clocks). Today these valuable clocks are sought by collectors and antique dealers.

New Hampshire

Area: 9,304sq mi
Population: 1,109,252
Capital: Concord
Nickname: Granite State
State Flower: Purple lilac

Forests cover 80 percent of the land in this triangle, 168 miles long and 90 miles at its widest point. The mountainous relief of the Appalachian ridges to the west and north contrasts with the hilly coastal region that slopes gently down to the Atlantic Ocean. The southern section of the state, benefiting in recent decades from the overflow of business from the Boston area, is heavily industrialized and more densely populated than the rest of the state. Located here are New Hampshire's largest cities—**Concord, Manchester, Nashua, Keene**—as well as its only seaport, **Portsmouth**.

"Live Free or Die" – "Here no landlords rack us with high rents. Here every man may be master of his land in a short time," wrote Capt. John Smith about New Hampshire in 1614. Despite Smith's tribute, the colonization of New Hampshire proceeded slowly. The first settlement, established in 1623 on the coast, was followed by several other small settlements. New Hampshire was administered as a part of Massachusetts until 1679, when the region became a royal colony.
Its people, self-reliant, taciturn, industrious and independent, were staunch supporters of the Revolution. The New Hampshire colony declared its independence from Great Britain and set up its own government seven months before the Declaration of Independence was signed. The heroic words of Revolutionary War colonel John Stark, "Live free or die," are immortalized in the state motto.
The character of New Hampshire's early population, primarily of Anglo-Saxon stock, was altered in the 19C and 20C by an influx of French Canadians and Europeans to the region.

Economy – In the 19C factory complexes such as the **Amoskeag Mills** *(p 223)*, once the world's largest textile manufacturer, were built on the banks of the Merrimack River. Textiles are still produced but have been surpassed by machinery, electronic and computer equipment, and business and financial services as principal sources of income. Since the 1960s many companies have established

branches in New Hampshire, attracted to the state's favorable tax structure and proximity to Boston. Today tourism and industrial development share equal importance in New Hampshire's economy. Lacking a state income tax or sales tax, New Hampshire obtains revenues from alternate sources, notably the state-operated liquor monopoly, pari-mutuel betting, and taxes on business profits, meals and rooms.

Bob Grant

Farming is oriented chiefly toward dairy products, Christmas trees, specialty products such as apples and maple sugar, and vegetables, livestock and poultry. Sand, gravel and feldspar are among New Hampshire's most important minerals, and building granite is quarried on a limited scale. The introduction of concrete and steel construction has resulted in a decline of the granite industry that gave the state its nickname.

CANTERBURY SHAKER VILLAGE★★

Map of Principal Sights

In the rural woods of southern New Hampshire, just north of Concord, this Shaker village, now a nonprofit, privately-held living museum open to the public, occupies a beautiful hilltop **site** overlooking the foothills. The only reminder of modern civilization is the paved public road that bisects the community.

Historical Notes – Attracted by the serene countryside and the gift of a large tract of land in Canterbury, the Shakers established a community near the small village of **Canterbury Center**. Founded in the 1780s, the village was formally organized in 1792, the year the Meeting House was built, and grew to include some 300 residents and 100 buildings on 4,000 acres at the height of the community in the mid-19C. Today 24 original buildings still stand on 694 acres.

Like other Shaker communities, the **Canterbury Shakers** farmed and made their own clothing, tools, furniture and machinery. To obtain goods they were not able to produce, they specialized in the preparation of medicines, seeds and herbs that they sold throughout the US and abroad. In addition to daily demonstrations of these crafts and skills at the village, the museum annually mounts a program of public workshops and special events, such as Wood Day in May, Harvest Day in October and a Canterbury Christmas in November.

The Creamery Restaurant

Truly an unforgetable repast, dining by candlelight at The Creamery is a treat not to be missed. Entrées based on Shaker recipes, fresh baked goods and vegetables from the on-site gardens are served family style under the direction of the restaurant's chef, who often introduces the meal with an explanation of the dishes and their ingredients. A typical prix-fixe dinner consists of a delicious grape punch, cream of asparagus soup, D'Anjou pear and blue cheese salad with toasted walnuts, a choice of tarragon-lemon chicken or loin of pork with oyster mushrooms or Atlantic salmon with minted sweet pea cream, and cheesecake with fresh strawberries and cream for dessert. Merlot, beer and ale are available *(extra charge). Fri and Sat only. Dinner price includes tour of the village. Reservations essential* ☎ *603-783-9511. The Creamery serves lunch daily.*

VISIT *2hrs*

15mi north of Concord. From I-93 take Exit 18, follow signs (7mi) to Shaker Village. Open May–Oct daily 10am–4pm. Apr, Nov & Dec weekends only 10am–4pm. $9.50. 🍴 ☎ *603-783-9511. www.shakers.org. Begin your visit at the visitor center, where a site plan of the village and schedule of craft demonstrations are available.*

An idyllic atmosphere pervades the orchards, meadows, vegetable gardens and grassy yards that surround the dwellings and farm buildings. Bordered by nature trails, several manmade ponds dot the distant acreage, attracting waterfowl and deer. After your tour of the village, sit by the ponds or walk a trail as a way of extending your stay in this peaceful area of New Hampshire.

Meeting House – Magnificent maple trees line Meeting House Lane as one acends the grassy slope to the Shakers' house of worship, which has separate entrances for men and women. The 1792 structure, where the Shakers gathered for religious services, contains exhibits of their products: furniture, tools, wooden boxes and such Shaker inventions as the flat broom and the threshing machine.

Dwelling House – The simplicity of the Meeting House contrasts with the subtle ornamentation of the large house with its pedimented porch and cupola. Here the Brothers and Sisters resided in segregated quarters, dormitory style. The dining room on the first floor serves as the Summer Kitchen and is open to the public seasonally for light fare.

Schoolhouse – The well-equipped schoolhouse reflects the Shakers' commitment to educating the young people in their community. Originally a one-room school, the facility accommodated boys in the winter and girls during the summer.

Laundry – This sizable building was the domain of the women of the village. Visitors can see the evolution of equipment and machinery, since the Shakers readily adopted the latest methods of laundering as they became available. The Shakers also made improvements of their own, such as the tall, pullout drying racks.

Other buildings – The residence of the ministry, an infirmary, a Sisters' workshop and the syrup shop *(demonstrations)* are a few of the other structures of interest to visitors. An 1837 bee house skirts the premises. Housed in the 1910 power house is the village bakery and a large gift shop is contained within the 1825 carriage house, where broom-making demonstrations and exhibits *(upstairs)* are held. The area renowned **Creamery Restaurant** occupies the 1905 creamery building.

CONCORD

Population 36,006
Map of Principal Sights
Tourist Office ☎ 603-224-2508

The capital of New Hampshire since 1808, Concord boasts the largest state legislature in the nation, with 424 representatives. The gilded dome of the State House dominates the cluster of buildings that rise alongside the Merrimack River. A modern center of government and commerce, the city is also a hub of railway and road systems linking all corners of the state.

Originally called Rumford, this town was claimed by both the colonies of New Hampshire and Massachusetts. Following a royal declaration that settled the dispute by granting Rumford to New Hampshire in 1741, the town was appropriately renamed Concord. In the 19C Concord became known for its granite and for the **Concord coaches** that were built here from 1813 to 1900 by the Abbot-Downing Co. Offering increased riding comfort, the Concord coach encouraged passenger travel and was later credited with having helped settle the West.

SIGHTS

State House – *107 N. Main St. Open year-round Mon–Fri 8am–4:30pm. Closed major holidays.* ✗ ♿ ☎ *603-271-2154. www.state.nh.us.* Completed in 1819, the New Hampshire State House is the oldest state capitol where the legislature still meets in its original chambers. A visitor center contains exhibits and dioramas of historic events. Regimental colors hang in the Hall of Flags *(ground floor)*, while Barry Faulkner murals in the Senate Chamber *(second floor)* depict scenes from the state's history. The House Chamber may also be viewed from off the third floor. Statues of New Hampshire sons John Stark, Daniel Webster and Franklin Pierce (14th president of the US) stand on the grounds.

Museum of New Hampshire History – **Kids** *Eagle Sq. Open Jul–mid-Oct Mon–Sat 9:30am–5pm (Thu & Fri 8:30pm), Sun noon–5pm. Rest of the year Tue–Sat 9:30am–5pm (Thu & Fri 8:30pm), Sun noon–5pm. Closed major holidays $5.* ♿ ☎ *603-226-3189. www.nhhistory.org.* More than five centuries of the Granite State's history are depicted by the museum's exhibits, which include a Concord coach made in the 19C by the Abbot-Downing Co. A stairwell reminiscent of a White Mountains fire tower elevates visitors to a fifth-floor view of the city's rooftops.

League of New Hampshire Craftsmen – *205 N. Main St. Open year-round Mon–Fri 8:30am–4:30pm. Closed major holidays. The retail shop is located at 36 N. Main St.* ♿ ☎ *603-224-3375. www.nhcrafts.org.* The League of New Hampshire Craftsmen maintains its headquarters in Concord. Handcrafted textiles, jewelry, glass and silver number among the items sold. The League Gallery features changing exhibits of handicrafts.

Concord Comestibles

The imposing, turreted brick **Centennial Inn** *(96 Pleasant St.* ☎ *603-225-7102),* built at the end of the 19C, is hard to miss as one approaches downtown Concord. Its small, wood-panelled Franklin Pierce Dining Room serves a satisfying lunch of soups, salads, wraps, sandwiches and the like. The nearby lounge is known locally for its "staircase bar." Dinner and Sunday brunch are served at the inn as well.

For a light bite downtown, look for **Bread & Chocolate** *(29 S. Main St.* ☎ *603-228-3330),* a European bistro-bakery with lace curtains and big bouquets of flowers. The array of cakes, tarts, breads, cookies and sandwiches is formidable. Coffees and other beverages are available too. Before or after eating, step into the adjoining **Gibson's Bookstore** *(29 S. Main St.* ☎ *603-224-0562)* for a browse. This well-stocked, friendly staffed, century-old repository stages events like Dress as a Book Title Party, with finger food for all and a gift certificate for the winner.

EXCURSIONS

Hopkinton – *8mi west of Concord by Rte. 9.* Antique hunters haunt this appealing Concord suburb. The town's wide main street is lined with attractive dwellings and shops, the town hall and St. Andrew's Church.

Henniker – *15mi west of Concord by Rte. 9.* This lively college town is home to New England College. From Route 114 between the college and the village center, the Henniker covered bridge can be seen, and maybe a kid or two swimming in the Contoocook River.

Hillsborough – *22mi west of Concord by Rte. 9.* A small commercial center, Hillsborough has structures dating from the last century. From Route 9, a back road leads through **Hillsborough Center★** *(turn west onto School St.),* a country hamlet with white buildings and rambling stone walls tucked among the trees.

■ Hillsborough Trout Farm

Kids *Old Henniker Road (opposite the Agway store) off Rte. 202 East. Then bear right at the fork. Small fish sign marks the entrance to the farm.* ☎ *603-464-3026.* Out in the countryside just past Hillsborough center, and set within a green expanse bordered by woods, lie three tranquil fishing ponds, stocked with rainbow trout. At the small shack on the grounds, you can rent a pole and fish til your heart's content. There's no limit; you simply pay for what you catch by the inch or, from the northern pond, by the pound. Or you can catch-and-release fly fish for a small hourly fee. No license is required. Picnic tables and Port-o-lets are on the premises. Bait is also for sale. *Open at noon Wed–Fri and at 8am on weekends from May to October.*

CONNECTICUT LAKES REGION

Map of Principal Sights
Tourist Office ☎ 603-538-7405

The narrow section of New Hampshire near the Canadian border is a densely wooded lake region, a haven for hunters and fishermen because of its wide variety of animal life. South of the Canadian border, the **Third**, **Second** and **First Connecticut Lakes** give rise to the Connecticut River, which continues southwest, forming the Vermont–New Hampshire border. From Route 3, between Pittsburg and the Canadian border, there are glimpses of the lakes through the trees.

SIGHT

Lake Francis State Park – *7mi northeast of Pittsburg by Rte. 3. Turn right onto River Rd. Park entrance is 2mi after passing the covered bridge. Open mid-May–mid-Dec daily dawn–dusk.* △ ☎ *603-538–6965. www.nhparks.state.nh.us.* The scenic shores of Lake Francis in New Hampshire's northern wilderness provide an ideal spot to camp, picnic or fish.

DIXVILLE NOTCH

Map of Principal Sights
Tourist Office ☎ 603-237-8939

In northern New Hampshire, Route 26, between Colebrook and Errol, passes through Dixville Notch, an area of rugged cliffs and thick stands of evergreens. Here on the shores of Lake Gloriette, near the highest point (1,871ft) in the notch, stands the grand resort hotel, the **Balsams**, built in the 19C.

VISIT

Hiking Trails – Several trails compose the Dixville Notch Heritage Trail, which, when connected, encompass Dixville Notch State Park in a 51mi loop. Two of these trails are located east of the Balsams Hotel and lead to waterfalls. The first is an easy .3mi walk that begins at the **Flume Brook Parking Area** on Route 26. The second, the **Cascades-Waterfalls Trail** (.5mi) to **Huntingdon Falls**, begins 1mi east of the Flume Brook Parking Area at the Dixville Notch State Park wayside. You may want to stop for refreshment at the Balsams Hotel's spring house, located on the hotel's entrance road, were cold, spring water flows continuously from a drinking fountain during the summer months.

■ Rafting, Kayak and Canoe Trips

The small village of Errol is becoming an outdoor center for wildnerness camps and water trips, given its proximity to the broad, beautiful Androscoggin River, a popular white-water passage best suited to experienced paddlers. **Northern Waters Outfitters** (☎ *603-447-2177)* and **Downeast Rafting Co.** (☎ *603-447-3002)* offer a host of water treks and camping trips, paddling and kayaking classes and pontoon boat cruises in the region. Touring kayaks and canoes can be rented as well as camping equipment. These outfitters can also help you find rental cabins and campsites in the area.

GRAFTON CENTER

Population 923
Map of Principal Sights

South of the White Mountains, several areas have been exploited for their mineral resources. Among the mines no longer worked is the Ruggles Mine, on Isinglass Mountain outside the hamlet of Grafton Center.

SIGHT

★**Ruggles Mine** – *2mi from the village green at Grafton Center; follow signs. Open Jul–Aug daily 9am–6pm. Mid-Jun–end of Jun & Sept–mid-Oct daily 9am–5pm (Jul–Aug 6pm). Last admission 1hr before closing. $15. ☎ 603-523-4275. Insect spray advisable.* The mammoth abandoned pegmatite mine on Isinglass Mountain is an eerie and curious place to explore, with its huge arched stone tunnels, winding passageways, large open pits and mine dumps. Sam Ruggles, a 19C Yankee farmer who discovered mica deposits on his property, worked the mine only at night and sold the mica outside the US to prevent local landowners from learning his secret. The Ruggles Mine remained New Hampshire's first and only commercial mine until 1868. Private companies worked the mine in more recent years for mica and feldspar.

Amateur rock hounds may wish to rent equipment and dig for mica, feldspar or one of the other 150 minerals that have been found here.

HANOVER★

Population 9,212
Map of Principal Sights
Tourist Office ☎ 603-643-3115

Dartmouth College, one of the nation's prominent Ivy League schools, occupies this pretty colonial town on the banks of the Connecticut River. Since Hanover is a college community, it is often difficult to separate its buildings and activities from those of Dartmouth. Despite the town's growth into a regional center, Hanover's colonial charm and pleasant tree-lined streets remain essentially unspoiled.

Fred Sieb Photography

Dartmouth Hall, Dartmouth College

★DARTMOUTH COLLEGE

Established in 1769 by the Reverend Eleazar Wheelock "for the education of Youth of the Indian Tribes" and "English Youth and any others," Dartmouth today offers its 4,500 students undergraduate programs in the liberal arts and sciences, as well as graduate studies in medicine, engineering, sciences and business administration. Dartmouth's list of illustrious alumni includes the lawyer and orator Daniel Webster

(1782-1852) and Nelson A. Rockefeller (1908-79), the former governor of New York and US vice president. The popular Dartmouth **Winter Carnival**, held each February, features skiing, skating, art shows and other special events.

★**The Green** – The spacious green is bordered by the **Hanover Inn** and a number of college buildings. The corner of Main and Wheelock Streets commands a good view of Dartmouth Row, which is flanked by Hopkins Center *(right)* and Webster Hall *(left)*, originally built as an auditorium. Beyond Webster Hall is Baker Library.

Hopkins Center – Recognizable by its multistoried windows, the performing arts center (1962) houses theaters and two concert halls. The center provides the college and the entire Hanover region with a year-round program of cultural events.

Hood Art Museum – *Open year-round Tue–Sat 10am–5pm, Sun noon–5pm. Closed major holidays.* ✕ ᕼ ☎ *603-646-2808. www.dartmouth.edu/~hood.* Dartmouth's art museum connects the Romanesque Wilson Hall (1885) and the modern Hopkins Center. Opened in 1985, the Hood galleries contain works from the permanent collection, which features Native American, American, European, African and ancient art. On the lower level, a special area displays a group of 9C BC Assyrian reliefs; on the upper level, Contemporary art occupies a spacious loft gallery.

Dartmouth Row – This group of four Colonial buildings includes **Dartmouth Hall** *(center)*, a replica of the original building (1784) that was destroyed by fire in 1904.

Baker Memorial Library – *North end of the Green. Open year-round daily 8am–midnight. Closed major holidays.* ᕼ ☎ *603-646-2560.* On its lower level, the building houses **Epic of American Civilization**★, a series of wall murals painted by the Mexican artist José Clemente Orozco (1883-1949) between 1932 and 1934. Powerful and often brutal in their expression of the forces of good and evil, the murals are Orozco's interpretation of the 5,000-year history of the Americas. *Interpretation pamphlet available at the information desk.*

■ Hanover Hot Spots

The upscale, venerable 1780 **Hanover Inn** *(Wheelock and Main Sts. ☎ 800-443-7024)* presents sumptuous meals in the Daniel Webster Room. In summer alfresco dining is popular on the flower-bedecked terrace, which overlooks the college green. A wine bar and a lounge are also located in the inn. Breakfast, lunch and dinner are served to the public at the inn.

A favorite with students and young profressionals, **Rosey's Cafe** *(15 Lebanon St. ☎ 603-643-6339)*, ensconced at the rear of a clothing store, is a tiny cafe-deli that makes terrific sandwiches to go or eat there. Try the Norma (eggplant, feta, tomatoes and pesto on farm bread), the Saucisson (herbed salami and provolone with dijon on a baguette) or the Tuna Panini (white albacore with capers, dill and watercress on semolina bread). Italian soda, apple cider, lemonade, root beer, coffees, teas and other beverages are on hand to complement your sandwich choice.

Another popular spot, particularly for visitors to town, is the **Dartmouth Co-op** on South Main Street, where logo-laden college souvenirs come in all forms, shapes and sizes, from mats to memo pads, key chains to coffee mugs, sweatshirts, ball caps, socks, pens—you name it, the Co-op's got it in Dartmouth's school colors. There's a sizable selection of apparel and sporting goods as well.

KEENE

Population 22,430
Map of Principal Sights
Tourist Office ☎ 603-352-1303

This commercial and manufacturing center has grown rapidly during the past several decades, largely because of its location near the industrialized areas of Massachusetts that have spilled over the border into New Hampshire. Keene's pottery and glassworks, which were major New Hampshire industries in the 19C and early 20C, have been replaced by the city's more than 50 manufacturing facilities, which produce tools, machine parts, textiles and medical products.

A pleasant tree-lined Main Street sports gift shops, restaurants and many other retail businesses. It also boasts several historic, predominately Georgian, Federal, Italianate and Second Empire, structures dating from 1762. *A walking tour guide is available from the Historical Society (below).* The thoroughfare divides at **Central Square**, which is dominated at the north end by the stately United Church of Christ (1788). Opposite stands the community gazebo on the small common. West of the downtown core lies the Ashuelot River, where 46 acres of riverfront were donated to the city in 1960 for recreation. The gardens and woods of **Ashuelot River Park** offer opportunities to cycle, walk or jog.

SIGHT

Historical Society of Cheshire County Museum – *246 Main St. Open year-round Mon–Fri 9am–4pm (Wed 9pm), Sat 9am–noon.* & ☎ *603-352-1895.* Glass and pottery made in Keene and the nearby village of Stoddard are on exhibit in this Italianate mansion (1870). Among the many pieces of locally made glass on display are the pictorial flasks embossed with patriotic themes, and one-of-a-kind pieces including walking sticks and miniatures. Light green or aqua color distinguishes the glass inks, bottles and flasks produced in Keene. Stoddard glass characteristically exhibits a deep shade of amber.

> ### Hannah Grimes Marketplace
> *46 Main St.* ☎ *603-352-6862.* If you're looking for New Hampshire made products, this well-stocked store, named after a Keene woman born in 1776, is brimming with locally and regionally made crafts, furnishings and foodstuffs. Wooden whirligigs and jigsaw puzzles, woven scarves and handmade quilts, packaged herbs and baked goods, paintings and pottery, baskets and banners are offered, along with antiques and other household items, as evidence of the creativity and productivity of Granite State artists and crafters. Flavored teas and coffees are served on the premises with a selection of locally baked cookies and pastries.

EXCURSION

Covered Bridges on the Ashuelot River – Covered bridge enthusiasts will enjoy a side trip on Route 10 south to covered bridges **Nos. 2**, **4** and **5**. *Roadside markers indicate directions to the bridges.*

MANCHESTER

Population 99, 567
Map of Principal Sights
Tourist Office ☎ 603-666-6600

In the 19C the largest textile factory in the world, the **Amoskeag Mills**, was built here beside the Merrimack River. The mile-long stretch of brick buildings still standing along the river proves an awesome sight. The city's clothing and shoe outlets are attractions in themselves.

The factory was the major employer in Manchester, and when the mills closed down permanently in 1935, the city was left financially destitute. The future appeared bleak until a group of investors, determined to revive the city, bought the mills with the idea of selling or leasing space to various businesses. Within 10 years, dozens of industries relocated in the mill complex, putting Manchester on the road to economic recovery. Financial services have replaced manufacturing as Manchester's main industry.

SIGHTS

★Currier Gallery of Art – *201 Myrtle Way. Open year-round Mon, Wed, Thu, Sun 11am–5pm, Fri 11am–8pm, Sat 10am–5pm. Closed major holidays. $5.* ✗ & ☎ *603-669-6144. www.currier.org.* The north entry fronting a granite-paved courtyard (tent-covered in summer) provides access to this museum, known for its fine collection of paintings, sculpture and decorative arts. The former south entrance is flanked by tall mosaic panels.

The main level is devoted largely to temporary exhibits (including the remarkable work of children attending the gallery's art classes) and, in the Henry Melville Fuller Gallery, Contemporary and 20C art. On the second floor, the east gallery contains the **European collection:** early Italian paintings; drawings by **Tiepolo;** Jan Gossaert's superb self-portrait, *Portrait of a Man;* and canvases from the French,

Chez-Vachon
136 Kelley St. ☎ *603-625-9660.* The mills of Manchester attracted foreign workers, and in particular, French Canadians from Quebec. The French influence is still evident today in the city's Franco-American Centre, with its public art gallery, and in this restaurant, which caters to the big appetites of locals and laborers alike. Its popular attraction is the all-you-can-eat-buffet midweek through Sunday *(4pm–8pm)* consisting of haddock, chicken, baked ham, pot roast, pork and turkey, pork and salmon pies, spaghetti, meatloaf, salad bar and 11 varieties of *poutine* (french fries in Canadian curd cheese with chicken gravy).

Spanish, English and Dutch schools. The west gallery showcases American paint-ings, and **American decorative art** from the 17-19C, with emphasis on New Hampshire pieces. Among the paintings are portraits by Copley and Trumbull and landscapes by Cole, Bierstadt and Church. Early portraits such as *Abraham Sleight and Ruth Rose Sleight* (1820-25) by Ammi Phillips and Samuel Miller's *Emily Mouton* (1852) charm the viewer with their simplicity. Works by **Andrew Wyeth**, **Edward Hopper**, O'Keeffe, Nevelson, Calder and others represent 20C American painting. A collec-tion of American silver and pewter is also housed on this floor.

★**Zimmerman House** – *Visit by guided tour (2hrs) only, Mar–Nov, Fri & Mon 2pm, weekends 1pm & 2:30pm. $7. 5-day advance reservations suggested.* ☎ *603-626-4156. www.currier.org.* Designed by Frank Lloyd Wright in 1950 and bequeathed to the Currier Gallery in 1988, this low-roofed, single-story house made of brick, concrete and cypress typifies the famed architect's "Usonian" style. Wright's own term for the small, utilitarian, yet elegant houses he created late in his career to counter the housing shortage of the Great Depression. The interior contains Wright-designed textiles, and his built-in and freestanding furniture.

EXCURSION

"America's Stonehenge" – *19mi from Manchester by I-93 south to Exit 3, then follow Rte. 111 east 5mi; turn right onto Island Pond Rd to Haverhill Rd. Open late Jun–Labor Day daily 9am–7pm. Mar–mid-Jun & rest of Sept–Dec daily 10am–5pm. Rest of the year weekends only. $7.95.* ☎ *603-893-8300. www.stonehengeusa.com.* The standing granite slabs of this stone complex give the site its name, although these stones are much shorter than their counterparts in England. Many theories exist concerning the site's origin and function; the aligned slabs led scientists to speculate that this may be the remnant of a calendar laid out 4,000 years ago by an advanced civilization with a knowledge of the move-ment of the stars, moon and sun. Carbon datings were first conducted here in 1967 and, most recently, in 1989.

Names of the stone structures, such as the Oracle Chamber and the Sacrificial Table, suggest their possible use. It is especially interesting to follow the astro-nomical alignment trail on June 21 and September 22 to see the slabs that accurately indicate the summer solstice and the fall equinox.

MOUNT MONADNOCK REGION★

Map of Principal Sights
Tourist Office ☎ 603-352-1308

The centerpiece of Monadnock State Park, Mt. Monadnock (3,165ft), the isolated remnant of a range formed eons ago, looms above the surrounding tiny colonial vil-lages with their white, steepled churches and the farmlands of southwestern New Hampshire. The word **monadnock**, derived from an Algonquian word meaning "a moun-tain that stands alone," has entered the vocabulary of geographers to describe the residual relief of a landscape that has passed through various stages of evolution. Hiking to the top of Mt. Monadnock for its spectacular view became popular in the 19C, and today it is one of the most frequently climbed peaks in the world. Each year some 125,000 persons scale its summit to enjoy the exhilarating view.

DRIVING TOUR *1 day. 47mi. Map p 225.*

Fitzwilliam – Large clapboard structures, an old meetinghouse, an inn and a Congregational church, which is crowned by a wedding-cake steeple, face the green. To the west *(2.5mi off Rte. 119)*, **Rhododendron State Park** encompasses 16 acres of wild rhododendrons that provide a colorful spectacle when they burst into bloom in July.

Take Rte. 119 east; after the intersection with Rte. 202, follow the signs for the cathedral.

★**Cathedral of the Pines** – *Open May–Oct daily 9am–5pm. Contribution requested.* よ ☎ *603-899-3300. www.cathedralpines.com.* Situated on the crest of a pine-car-peted hill, this outdoor cathedral, the work of a couple who lost their son in World War II, commemorates all Americans who were killed in battle. The place of worship welcomes persons of all faiths. Services are held at the **Altar of the Nation**, which faces Mt. Monadnock; stones set into the altar were tributes from US presidents, military leaders and the 50 states and four territories. The **Memorial Bell Tower**, rising in a clearing, is dedicated to American women who served their country in wartime; Norman Rockwell designed the plaques above the tower arches. The **museum** con-tains artifacts from around the world, including medals from World War I.

Turn left when leaving the Cathedral of the Pines; 1.5mi farther, at the fork, bear right onto Rte. 124.

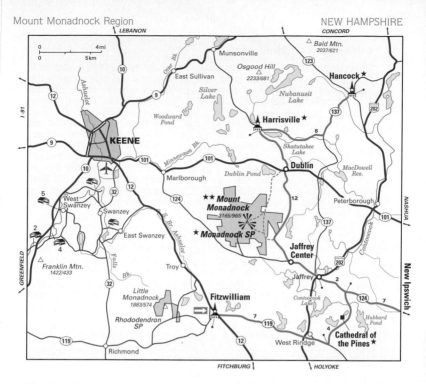

New Ipswich – The **Barrett House**, a handsome Federal mansion on Main Street, and its sedate rustic surroundings have changed little over the years. Built in 1800 by wealthy mill owner Charles Barrett as a wedding gift for his son, the house is furnished with family pieces and features two late-19C bathrooms *(visit by 45min guided tour only, Jun–mid-Oct weekends only 11am–5pm; $4; ☎ 603-878-2517; www.spnea.org).*

Follow Rte. 124 west to Jaffrey. Located at the foot of Mt. Monadnock, Jaffrey provides easy access to Monadnock State Park. Continue on Rte. 124.

Jaffrey Center – A series of lectures held each year *(Jul–Aug Fri 7:30pm)* at the old meetinghouse (Rte. 124) honors **Amos Fortune**, a former slave who bequeathed a sum of money to the Jaffrey School when he died. The tombstones of Fortune and his wife stand in the cemetery behind the meetinghouse. The inscription on Amos' tombstone reads: "To the memory of Amos Fortune who was born free in Africa, a slave in America, he purchased liberty, professed Christianity, lived reputably, and died hopefully."

Take Rte. 124 west and .5mi after the meetinghouse turn right.

★**Monadnock State Park** – *Open year-round daily 8am–dusk. $2.50. ⚠ ☎ 603-532-8862.* Trails to the summit of Mt. Monadnock begin at the end of the tar road beyond the toll booth.

★★**Mt. Monadnock** – Of the 40 trails leading to this peak, the trail most frequently taken is the **White Dot Trail** *(several steep sections, round-trip 3-4hrs).* A similar route, the **White Cross Trail** is somewhat more difficult. **Pumpelly Trail** is the longest, but easiest, path to the top. Longer and less popular connecting trails include **Cascade Link**, **Red Spot** and **Spellman** *(steepest trail).* The far-reaching **view**★★ from the summit on a clear day includes Mt. Washington *(north)* and the Boston skyline *(southeast).* The summit is the only place in New England from which parts of all six of the region's states can be seen.

As you leave the park, turn left onto Upper Jaffrey Rd.

Dublin – Mark Twain summered in this hillside hamlet, today the home of *Yankee Magazine* and *The Old Farmers Almanac.*

Continue north on Upper Jaffrey Rd., turn right on Rte. 101, then left onto New Harrisonville Rd.

★**Harrisville** – The handsome ensemble of modest brick buildings, dwellings, mills and Congregational church reflected in the village pond creates a pleasing tableau of an early rural mill town. To preserve the character of the village, residents of Harrisville restored these structures themselves. In 1970, when the textile industry that operated here for two centuries closed down, the town's residents succeeded in attracting several small companies to relocate in Harrisville.

Follow the unmarked road east along the lakes, then turn left onto Rte. 137.

■ **Monadnock Memories**

Sometimes it's the little things that make a trip memorable: a stop at a farm, a roadside ice-cream cone on a hot day or a trail ride through the woods. Two miles west of Dublin, not far from Dublin Lake, sits the 5-acre **Friendly Farm** 🅺 *(Rte. 101 ☎ 603-563-8444; closed in winter)* filled with pigs, goats, sheep, ducks, chickens, rabbits and the like, many of them babies. Visitors, especially children, are encouraged to feed and pet the animals, as well as watch eggs hatch. Just about a mile from Jaffrey, along Route 124, is a popular stop for ice cream or cold drinks. **Kimball Farm Restaurant** 🅺 *(Rte. 124 ☎ 603-532-5765)* has a walk-up window for quick orders and the place is often packed. It's only open seasonally though *(Memorial Day–Columbus Day)*. Across the road from Kimball's is the **Silver Ranch** 🅺 *(Rte. 124 ☎ 603-532-7363)*, a livery stable that offers trail, hay and sleigh rides, as well as scenic carriage tours. Take your pick and begin your memory-making today.

★**Hancock** – The tranquillity of this colonial village is disturbed only once a year, on July 4th, when the bells of the meetinghouse peal from midnight to one o'clock in the morning to celebrate the anniversary of America's independence. The **John Hancock Inn** sits in the center of the village, opposite the general store. Headstones in the old **cemetery** at the end of the street provide good examples of the skill of early stonecutters.

NASHUA

Population 79,662
Map of Principal Sights
Tourist Office ☎ 603-881-8333

Located 39mi northwest of BOSTON, Nashua has experienced a surge of industrial growth since the 1960s, making it the second largest city in New Hampshire. The Nashua River lies perpendicular to the city's Main Street, which sports a variety of retail shops, eateries and other establishments.

EXCURSION

Anheuser-Busch Hamlet – *221 Daniel Webster Hwy. 7mi from Nashua in Merrimack. Take Rte. 3 to Exit 10, bear right, then turn left and continue to Hamlet (on the grounds of the Anheuser-Busch brewery). Visit by guided tour (1hr 15min) only, Jun–Aug daily 9:30am–5pm. May & Sept–Dec daily 10am–5pm. Rest of the year Thu–Mon 10am–5pm. Closed major holidays. ⅙ ☎ 603-595-1202. www.budweisertours.com.* Budweiser Clydesdales clip-clop through the picturesque hamlet where they are raised and trained. The "white-stockinged" horses have been the symbol of Anheuser-Busch since 1933, when the company acquired its first team to celebrate the repeal of prohibition. Today teams of Clydesdales tour the country, appearing in parades and at fairs and other events.

Nashua Noshings

Nashua's restaurants offer a range of good eating from Italian and Continental to Mexican and Southwest. Several fine dining establishments are located in the downtown core. Classy **Michael Timothy's** *(212 Main St. ☎ 603-595-9334)* is a chef-owned "urban bistro" serving up sophisticated entrées in an upscale milieu. Tournedos Napoleon, Five-spice Rubbed Pork Loin, Atlantic Striped Bass and Veal Medallions, among other dishes, are served with flare. Wood-grilled pizzas are a house specialty for lunch or dinner. Weekends bring live jazz in the Wine and Jazz Bar and a jazz brunch is served on Sundays. Housed in a former bank, **Villa Banca Cafe and Grill** *(194 Main St. ☎ 603-598-0500)*, open for lunch and dinner, specializes in freshly made pastas and ravioli. Secondi such as Salmon Pistachio, Porterhouse Florentina and Chicken Pomodoro follow tempting antipasti, zuppe and *insalate* at dinnertime. Just off Main Street **Margarita's** *(1 Nashua Dr. ☎ 603-883-0996)*, part of a regional chain of restaurants under the same name, occupies a great spot over the canal. This festive Mexican eatery boasts two floors of dining/drinking space—their walls flamboyantly attired with sombreros and serapes—and caters to customers seeking spicy enchiladas, burritos, fajitas, chimichangas and quesadillas. And, yes, there's a variety of fruit margaritas, cerveza and tequila to wash them down.

NEW HAMPSHIRE COAST

Sandy beaches, rocky ledges and state parks alternate along New Hampshire's 18mi coastline. Coastal Route 1A from Seabrook to PORTSMOUTH winds past resort areas and elegant estates, affording views of the ocean.

SIGHTS

Hampton Beach – *On Rte. 1A, 1mi north of Seabrook.* This lively resort center claims a casino, large clusters of ocean-front hotels, motels and eating places, as well as a 3.5mi sandy beach. The **New Hampshire Marine War Memorial**, a granite statue of a seated maiden looking out to sea, borders Route 1A in the center of Hampton Beach. North of Hampton Beach the road skirts the waterfront estates of **Little Boars Head**.

Fuller Gardens – *On Rte. 1A, just north of Rte. 111 junction at Little Boars Head. Open mid-May–Oct daily 10am–6pm. $5.* ♿ ☎ *603-964-5414.* Redesigned by Olmsted Assocs. in the 1930s, this formal garden occupies the summer estate of Al-van T. Fuller, a former governor of Mass-achusetts. A stroll through the formal rosebeds containing over 2,000 rose bushes, Japanese gardens, greenhouses and beds of annuals and perennials is punctuated with glimpses of the sea beyond.

> **Ron's Landing**
> *379 Ocean Blvd., Hampton Beach.* ☎ *603-929-2122.* Situated in the thick of the beachfront commercial strip, the restaurant features two floors of dining, including a second-story deck overlooking the ocean (heavy winds off the sea may necessitate deck protection by a thick plastic covering, which can block the view, however). A wide selection of seafood, steaks and pastas is offered at this casual, full-service, family-friendly restaurant.

Rye Harbor State Park – *On Rte. 1A in Rye. Open year-round daily 8am–8pm. $2.50 (mid-Jun–early Sept).* ♿ ☎ *603-436-1552. www.nhparks.state.nh.us.* This rocky headland overlooking the Atlantic Ocean provides good picnic and fishing grounds.

Wallis Sands State Park – *On Rte. 1A in Rye. Open year-round daily 8am–8pm. $5/car Mon–Fri, $8/car weekends (mid-Jun–mid-Sept).* ♿ ☎ *603-436-9404. www.nhparks.state.nh.us.* A gentle surf breaks onto the park's quarter mile-long beach, which is thronged in summer.

Odiorne Point – *On Rte. 1A in Rye.* This location was the site of Pannaway Plantation, the first settlement in New Hampshire, established in 1623.

NEW LONDON⋆

New London's hilltop setting overlooks neighboring and far-reaching ridges and wood-lands that flame with color during Indian summer. On the main thoroughfare, Route 114, there is a comfortable old inn, the expansive campus of **Colby-Sawyer College** (1837) and a Baptist meetinghouse. Travelers are easily tempted to stop and spend a few days in this small, unspoiled New England village.
The **Barn Playhouse**, identifiable by its bright red exterior along the main street, has been entertaining summer audiences since 1933; an annual Straw Hat Revue kicks off the season and there's a weekly children's theater series in addition to evening performances ☎ *603-526-4631.* Lovely Pleasant Lake, accessible via North Pleasant Street, provides a good view of Mt. Kearsarge. *A map of the town and environs is available from the visitor information booth on Route 114.*

EXCURSIONS

⋆**Sunapee Harbor** – *8mi from New London by Rte. 11 south.* This diminutive, col-orful resort community is dominated by lovely Lake Sunapee. Shops, restaurants and residential homes crowd its shore. The tiny hillside common sports a bandstand and the busy harbor teems with small pleasure craft, cruise boats and fishing vessels.

Lake Cruise – Open top-deck seating or indoor seating with a window view are avail-able on this narrated excursion of Lake Sunapee aboard the *M.V. Sunapee II (departs late Jun–Labor Day daily 10am & 2:30pm; mid-May–mid-Jun & rest of Sept–mid-Oct weekends only 2:30pm; 1hr 30min; commentary; $10;* ♿; *M.V. Sunapee II Excursions* ☎ *603-763-4030).*

■ **Sunapee Sundries**

The community of Sunapee Harbor offers a variety of shops and eateries for its small size, all clustered within walking distance of each other along the short main street. After a relaxing afternoon of boating and sunning, browse in the **Wild Goose Country Store** for collectibles, gift items or penny candy. Then pull up a chair at **The Anchorage** restaurant *(Garnet St. ☎ 603-763-3334)* for lakeside dining, dancing and live entertainment in the summer. Top off the evening with a peppermint ice-cream cone, just one of the many flavors available from **Harbor Falls Deli** across the street.

For countryside dining, turn right after the bandstand onto Burkehaven Hill Road and proceed half a mile to **The Inn at Sunapee** *(☎ 603-763-4444)*. Here guests enjoy such entrées as peppered salmon, shrimp in lemon thyme sauce, chicken marsala or veal scaloppine in a dining room that provides year-round views of Mount Sunapee. A spacious, comfortable lounge with a fieldstone fireplace adjoins the dining area.

Mt. Sunapee State Park – *13mi from New London by Rte. 11 south. After crossing I-89, turn left onto Rte. 103A south, then turn onto Rte. 103 west. Open daily year-round.* ♿ ☎ *603-763-5561. nhparks.state.nh.us.* Lake Sunapee and the mountain of the same name form the center of a year-round vacation resort. Opposite the entrance to the park is the entrance to the **State Beach** on the shores of Lake Sunapee *(open Jun–Labor Day daily 9am–6pm; $2.50)*. The League of New Hampshire Craftsmen holds its annual Craftsmen's Fair at the park in early August. The **chairlift** to the summit of Mt. Sunapee (2,700ft) operates from North Peak Lodge during the summer and early fall, offering good **views**★ of the region *(late Jun–Labor Day daily 10am–5pm; Oct weekends only 10am–5pm; Nov–Apr Mon–Fri 9am–4pm, weekends 8am–4pm; $7; Mount Sunapee Resort ☎ 603-763-2356; www. mtsunapee.com)*.

PLYMOUTH

Population 5,811
Map of Principal Sights
Tourist Office ☎ 603-536-1001

Lying just outside the White Mountain National Forest is Plymouth, a small resort town that is home to Plymouth State College.

SIGHT

Polar Caves Park – *On Rte. 25, 5mi west of Plymouth. Open mid-May–early Oct daily 9am–5pm. $9.50.* ✗ ☎ *603-536-1888. www.polarcaves.com.* The Polar Caves consist of a series of caves and stone passageways that were formed during the last Ice Age, as freezing temperatures and ice caused gigantic boulders to break loose from the mountain. Five conveniently placed stations with taped commentaries allow visitors to tour the caves at their own pace.

Wooden walkways lead to the first cave, the Ice Cave, named for the cool air that rises from within to fill it. The walkways continue over, around and through four more caves to the last, Smugglers Cave, which is entered by the narrow Lemon Squeezer passage or the more comfortable corridor called Orange Crush. The Cave of Total Darkness contains an exhibit of fluorescent minerals.

EXCURSION

★**Hebron** – *14mi from Plymouth by Rte. 25 west, then Rte. 3A.* Hebron possesses all the elements of a New England village: an emerald green, a church with a pointed steeple, a general store, a post office and, nearby, a handful of attractive dwellings. Together, they form a harmonious and charming ensemble.

Newfound Lake – The tranquil setting of this spring-fed lake, nestled between two mountains, is best viewed from its western shore, the site of **Wellington State Beach**, south of Hebron.

Respect the life of the countryside.
Go carefully on country roads.
Protect wildlife, plants and trees.

PORTSMOUTH★★

Population 25,925
Map of Principal Sights
Tourist Office ☎ 603-436-1118

New Hampshire's only seaport and the colonial capital until 1808, when the seat of government was moved to Concord, Portsmouth is a small, quiet city on the banks of the Piscataqua River, except in summer when tourists flock to its waterfront, historic houses and numerous shops and restaurants. Since the 1950s, renewal projects aimed at preserving Portsmouth's colonial structures and character have been implemented in the older sections of the city, and a number of these historic houses are open to the public as museums. The most interesting of these projects is the transformation of **Strawbery Banke**, the city's early waterfront community, into a museum.

Historical Notes

In 1623 a group of English settlers arrived on the banks of the Piscataqua River. Noting that the riverbanks were covered with wild strawberries, they named their community "Strawbery Banke." Not until three decades later was the "port at the mouth of the river" renamed Portsmouth.

Fred Sieb Photography

Portsmouth Harbor

Fishing, shipbuilding and the region's many sawmills, which transformed New Hampshire's largest trees into timber for the British Navy, provided settlers with their livelihood. After the Revolution, maritime commerce brought increased prosperity to the city. Beginning in the 18C and continuing into the 19C, merchants and ship captains built dwellings that reflected their wealth. These residences were among the finest Georgian and Federal houses in the country.

In 1800 Portsmouth lent its name to the new naval base constructed in KITTERY, Maine. The Treaty of Portsmouth, which ended the Russo-Japanese War, was signed at this base in 1905.

Vintage Georgian mansions, reminiscent of Portsmouth's past as a lumber and seafaring center, line the streets leading to the waterfront. In the **Old Harbor District—Bow, Market and Ceres Streets**—restored and freshly painted restaurants, craft studios and antique shops, as well as the tugboats tied up at the Ceres Street cove, remind visitors of a time when commerce was the mainstay of Portsmouth's economy. Although commerce still reigns as one of the city's most important industries, the **Portsmouth Naval Shipyard** (located in Kittery, Maine) is among the area's largest employers. **Harbor cruises** on the Piscataqua River offer a pleasant way to view the city and its environs *(depart from Ceres Street Dock mid-Jun–mid-Sept daily 10am, noon, 3pm, 5:45pm & 7pm with an additional 4:30pm departure Fri, Sat & Sun; late Sept–Oct call for schedule; 1hr 30min; commentary; reservations suggested; $8.50-$12; ✗; Portsmouth Harbor Cruises ☎ 603-436-8084; www. portsmouthharbor.com).*

★★STRABERY BANKE MUSEUM *3hrs. Map p 231.*

Overlooking lovely Prescott Park and the broad Piscataqua River beyond, this village-museum is a pleasant assembly of tree-shaded paths, historic houses and period gardens that border an expansive green. The slower pace of bygone eras envelopes visitors as they enter this remnant of yesteryear, which traces over 300 years of American architectural styles.

In the 1670s the 10-acre site near the cove of the river held a working farm that was divided into smaller plots 20 years later. By the mid-18C Portsmouth's waterfront had become the economic center of town. In the early 1900s, the cove and the neighborhood that had grown up around it were known as **Puddle Dock**; the open waterway was filled in and replaced with a street. The idea of preserving the historic south end of the city, including Puddle Dock, was proposed during the 1930s, but was overshadowed by World War II. Advised in the 1950s that renewal plans for the city included demolition of the Puddle Dock neighborhood, citizens urged that funds be made available to restore the district's old shops and dwellings. Their strong support never waned, and in 1957 they began the overhaul of the dock. In 1965 the neighborhood was opened to the public as a museum. Today the site of Portsmouth's Strawbery Banke settlement (1630) remains a living model of the techniques used to rehabilitate an entire district.

Nineteen of the thirty-six structures at Strawbery Banke have been restored and are open to the public; others can be viewed in varying stages of restoration. The most recent addition is the **Shapiro House**, restored to its 1943 appearance and illustrative of the home life of a Jewish family from the Ukraine. A new, multimillion dollar visitor facility, the Tyco Museum Center, is to be built on the premises. In late 1997 the unearthing of a historic wharf on the building site has postponed the center's construction, while archaeologists uncover relics from the 1700s.

Visit

Open Apr–Sept daily 10am–5pm. $12 (valid for 2 consecutive days). Site plan available at entrance (Marcy St.). ✗ ☎ *603-433-1106. www.strawberybanke.org.*

Helpful Hints

The admission ticket is valid for two consecutive days. To fully enjoy this museum, plan to visit over a two-day period. The tour of Strawbery Banke is self-guided. You may want to follow the sequence in which the buildings are numbered on the museum's site plan. Interpreters in period dress staff several of the structures and are available to answer questions. Conant House (c.1791), on the Washington Street side of the museum, serves lunch and light refreshment during the day. On the opposite end, bordering Marcy Street, the Dunaway Store houses the main museum shop, which is stocked with souvenirs, reproductions, books, stationery, toys, jewelry and other merchandise. A satellite store carrying specialized items can be found in the Peacock House off Jefferson Street. Throughout the site, benches are placed at intervals, usually in shaded spots, for visitors to take a break from touring. In addition, some eight period gardens grace the grounds (a kitchen garden, Victorian and Victory gardens, cutting and herb gardens for example); the outdoor seating in the Colonial Revival garden at the Aldrich House offers visitors rest and refreshment.

Described below are highlights of the museum.

Sherburne House (1) – This Medieval-looking timber structure with twin gables and small casement windows is the only remaining building (c.1695) in Strawbery Banke dating from the 1600s. The interior holds an interesting exhibit on 17C construction methods.

Lowd House (2) – This plain Federal house (1810) features a fine exhibit on craftsmen's tools of the 18-19C.

Joshua Jackson House (3) – This unrestored house (c.1750) reveals the structural changes undertaken by its occupants over the last two centuries.

Wheelwright House (4) – The paneling in this middle-class 18C dwelling is noteworthy.

William Pitt Tavern (5) – This three-story structure (1766) functioned as the center of the community's social life, providing food, lodging and a gathering place for groups such as the Masons.

Aldrich House (6) – Fronted by a lovely flower garden, this house (late 18C) preserves the domestic atmosphere captured in the autobiography of Thomas Bailey Aldrich, who dwelled here in the mid-19C.

Chase House (7) – This handsome Georgian residence (c.1762), owned by a prosperous merchant family, is appointed with fine period furniture and elaborately carved woodwork.

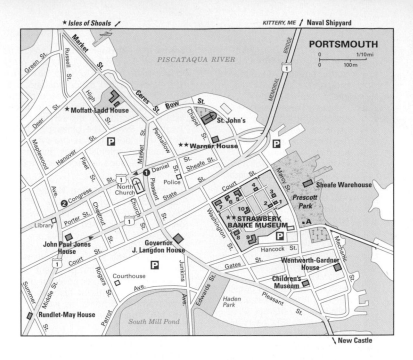

Walsh House (8) – This late-18C house is graced with a handsome curved staircase, period furniture and several examples of faux grain and marble.

Goodwin Mansion (9) – Behind a lovely garden rises the elegant three-story residence (1811) of a former state governor. Victorian furnishings grace the interior.

Jones House (10) – The interior of this modest late-18C house features artifacts excavated on-site and a small archaeological lab.

Between Strawbery Banke and the river lies **Prescott Park**, which is planted with lush flower gardens during the summer and filled with weekend picnickers, sunbathers, volleyball players and flying kites. Opposite the entrance to Strawbery Banke is a **liberty pole (A)**, similar to those raised by the patriots during Revolutionary days to signify their opposition to the Crown. The old **Sheafe Warehouse**, located at the water's edge, contains temporary exhibits.

Just up the hill from Strawbery Banke, on Marcy Street, is the **Children's Museum of Portsmouth** 🧒. Housed in a former meetinghouse, this funhouse for children and adults features 19 educational and entertaining hands-on exhibits. The popular submarine and space shuttle allow kids to take the controls. Youngsters can brush a set of giant teeth, send an electronic message, don a mask from a foreign country or create a sculpture of their own *(280 Marcy St.; open year-round Mon–Sat 10am–5pm, Sun 1pm–5pm; closed Thanksgiving Day, Dec 25 & 2 weeks in Sept; $4;* ☎ *603-436-3853; www.childrens-museum.org).*

HISTORIC HOUSES *Map above*

★★**Warner House** – *150 Daniel St. Visit by guided tour (45min) only, Jun–Oct Mon–Sat 10am–4pm, Sun 1pm–4pm. Closed major holidays. $5.* ☎ *603-436-5909. http://our world.compuserve.com.* This brick Georgian mansion was built in 1716 for the Scottish sea captain Archibald MacPheadris. Decorated with European- and New England-made furnishings, the house contains a group of Warner family portraits by Joseph Blackburn. The series of 18C murals adorning the walls of the stairwell includes life-size portraits of two Mohawk sachems who journeyed to London with Peter Schuyler in 1710.
Behind the house stands **St. John's Church**.

★**Moffatt-Ladd House** – *154 Market St. Visit by guided tour (1hr) only, mid-Jun–mid-Oct Mon–Sat 11am–5pm, Sun 1pm–5pm. $5.* ☎ *603-436-8221.* This elegant three-story Georgian mansion, built in 1763 for local shipbuilder Samuel Moffatt, remained in the same family until 1913, when it was opened to the public as a house museum. Portsmouth furniture and family portraits grace the interior. Highlights include the grand entrance hall with its period wallpaper and elaborate wood paneling. A pleasant terraced garden (mid-19C) adjoins the house.

231

1 Market Square Munchies

Bordering North Church, the popular square at the intersection of Market, Pleasant, Daniel and Congress Streets, is a great place for people-watching, relaxing and eating. There are many restaurants to choose from downtown. European styled **Cafe Brioche** *(14 Market Square ☎ 603-430-9225)* sits at the heart of the square, its outdoor tables and chairs populated with townspeople and tourists alike. This sidewalk cafe/bakery offers croissants, soups, salads, sandwiches, quiches, pastries, breads and boxed lunches. Adjacent restaurant **Bella Luna** *(10 Market St. ☎ 603-436-9800)* serves up international cuisine in the evenings in its attractive, but small dining space just off the square. *Reservations advised.*

2 The Friendly Toast

121 Congress St. ☎ 603-430-2154. This 1950s style eatery is popular for its funky garage-sale interior, creative menu and hours of operation *(open 24hrs. a day)*. Start the day with Almond Joy cakes (buttermilk pancakes, chocolate chips, coconut and almonds), Orange French Toast (seasoned with grand marnier and marmelade) or The Peasant (egg whites scrambled with Cuban brown rice, corn and carrots plus fresh spinach mixed with black beans and feta). Lunch brings a variety of salads, burgers and clubs, but try one of the special sandwiches such as the Hummingbird (homemade hummus with cukes, black olives, sprouts, tomatoes and feta on toasted oatmeal bread), Matt #2 (grilled anadama bread with black beans, salsa, cream cheese, cheddar and avocado) or the Falafel (classic Middle Eastern sandwich of chick pea nuggets served with lettuce, tomato, cukes and Tahini dressing in a flour tortilla).

Wentworth-Gardner House – *Mechanic & Gardner Sts. Visit by guided tour (1hr) only, mid-Jun–mid-Oct Tue–Sun 1pm–4pm. Closed major holidays. $5. ☎ 603-436-4406.* The facade of this lovely Georgian mansion, built in 1760, casts its reflection on the surface of the Piscataqua River. The pineapple carved above the doorway was the symbol of hospitality in colonial times. Inside, the paneling, balusters and cornices are flawlessly carved.

Governor John Langdon House – *143 Pleasant St. Visit by guided tour (45min) only, Jun–mid-Oct Wed–Sun 11am–5pm (on the hour). Closed Labor Day. $5. ☎ 603-436-3205. www.spnea.org.* This handsome Georgian mansion (1784) is known primarily for its original owner John Langdon, the first president of the US Senate and a former governor of New Hampshire. The interior features wood-carved embellishments, as well as 18C and 19C furniture that was made in Portsmouth.

John Paul Jones House – *43 Middle St. Vist by guided tour (30min) only, Jun–mid-Oct Mon–Sat 10am–4pm, Sun noon–4pm. $5. ☎ 603-436-8420. www.nhseacoast.com.* The American naval hero John Paul Jones stayed in this Colonial-style home on two occasions during the Revolution. Early furnishings, china, clothing and historical memorabilia owned by the Portsmouth Historical Society are on display.

Rundlet-May House – *364 Middle St. Visit by guided tour (45min) only, Jun–mid-Oct weekends only 11am–5pm (on the hour). Closed Labor Day. $5. www.spnea.org. ☎ 603-436-3205.* This elegant three-story Federal residence, perched on an artificial rise, reflects the taste and lifestyle of the merchant family who owned the property from its construction in 1807 until the 1970s. The interior is appointed with many of the original embellishments and amenities, such as fine pieces of Portsmouth furniture, English wallpaper and innovative early-19C kitchen conveniences. The attached outbuildings and garden further enhance the dwelling's charm.

EXCURSIONS

★ **Cruise to Isles of Shoals** – *Departs from Market St. dock mid-Jun–Labor Day daily 11am & 2pm. Limited schedule spring & fall. Round-trip 2hr 30min. Commentary. Reservations suggested. $16. ✗ & Isles of Shoals Steamship Co. ☎ 603-431-5500.* The 10mi boat trip to this group of nine islands follows the banks of the Piscataqua for 5mi before heading out to sea. There are good views of sights along the river: the dry docks of the Portsmouth Naval Shipyard, the castle-like former maximum security prison that once held 3,500 inmates, **Fort McClary** (Kittery, Maine), **Fort Constitution**, and the lovely homes in the island town of New Castle.

Discovered by Capt. John Smith in 1614, the Isles of Shoals we... Smith's Isles until they were renamed by fishermen for the vast... of fish found in the offshore waters. When the boundary line... 1635 between Maine and New Hampshire, the islands were d... two states. In the 19C their stark beauty was popularized by at... and other writers who gathered at her home on Appledore Isla... The most important islands are: **Appledore**, site of the marine labs of the University of New Hampshire and Cornell; **Smuttynose**, a private island linked by a breakwater to **Cedar Island**; **Star Island**, dominated by a rambling old hotel operated by the Unitarian and Congregational churches as a summer religious conference center; and **White Island**, with its solitary setting and lighthouse, which delights photographers.

New Castle – *Take Pleasant St. south to New Castle Ave. (Rte. 1B).* Built on an island linked to the mainland by a bridge and causeway, New Castle is a residential town known for its large number of Colonial dwellings. Along the waterfront rises the sprawling white clapboard **Wentworth-by-the-Sea**, a 19C hotel complex that continued to draw visitors for almost a century until it closed its doors in the 1970s. The walls of **Fort Constitution**, one of the oldest forts on the coast, overlook the point where the Piscataqua River enters the Atlantic Ocean.

Wentworth-Coolidge Mansion – *On Little Harbor Rd. off Rte. 1A, 2mi south from downtown Portsmouth. After crossing the Portsmouth city line (.25mi, sign says "Welcome to Portsmouth") turn right just before the cemetery onto Little Harbor Rd. After 1mi, look for sign to mansion. Visit by guided tour (1hr) only, May–Oct Tue & Thu–Sat 10am–3pm, Sun noon–5pm. $2.50. ☎ 603-436-6607.* This 18C mansion on the banks of the Piscataqua River was the home of Benning Wentworth, the son of John Wentworth, New Hampshire's first colonial governor. Although only partially furnished today, the house remains an elegant example of the sophisticated early-American architecture of the Portsmouth region.

Exeter – *13mi southwest of Portsmouth by Rtes. 101 and 108.* The townspeople of Exeter were regarded as rebels against the Crown as early as 1734, when they stood their ground and prevented the king's agents from appropriating the tallest trees in the region for the British Navy. Exeter remained a patriot stronghold throughout the Revolution and served as the wartime capital of provincial New Hampshire in the 1770s. Tranquil and reserved today, the town is graced with wide, shaded streets and Colonial dwellings, which identify Exeter as one of New Hampshire's earliest settlements.

The community is the home of **Phillips Exeter Academy**, a renowned preparatory school founded in 1781. The school's more than 100 buildings, many in the Georgian style, stand on the academy's broad, emerald-green campus. The Academy Building, a large Georgian structure set back on the lawn facing Front Street, is the main classroom building for the school's 990 students. The nine-level library was designed by Louis Kahn in 1965.

SAINT-GAUDENS NATIONAL HISTORIC SITE★

Map of Principal Sights

Augustus Saint-Gaudens (1848-1907) was America's foremost sculptor in the 19C. During the two decades he lived in Cornish, Saint-Gaudens produced about 150 sculptures. His home, studios and extensive gardens are maintained as a museum by the National Park Service.

Born in Dublin, Saint-Gaudens was the offspring of a French cobbler and his Irish wife. The family emigrated to New York City, where Augustus spent his childhood. Apprenticed to a cameo cutter as a boy, he later worked in Rome and studied at the École des Beaux-Arts in Paris before establishing himself in New York, where he quickly became famous. He is remembered for the monumental Civil War memorials he created, such as the Shaw Memorial in Boston, and for his portrait reliefs, which brought him membership in the French Legion of Honor and the Royal Academy.

He first visited Cornish, New Hampshire, in 1885 to spend the summer months. In 1892 he bought the old inn he had rented over the years and converted it into a summer residence. After Saint-Gaudens was diagnosed with terminal illness in 1900, he and his family moved to the home permanently. His wife and son founded the Saint-Gaudens Memorial to preserve the sculptor's home and studio for posterity. In 1965 it became a National Historic Site.

VISIT *1hr 30min*

In Cornish, 20mi south of Hanover. From Hanover, take Rte. 10 south to Rte. 12A. Travel approximately 15mi on Rte. 12A and follow signs to site. Open Memorial Day–Oct daily 9am–4:30pm. The house can be visited by guided tour only; make your reservation upon arrival. $4. Summer concerts Jul–Aug Sun 2pm. ♿ ☎ 603-675-2175. www.sgnhs.org.

...n a secluded site in an expansive opening in the woods bordering the ...nnecticut River, five buildings are open to the public. In addition, flower and cutting gardens, a bowling green and trails through the Blow-Me-Down Natural Area, an 80-acre woodland of primarily white pines, may be visited.

House – *Visit by guided tour (30min) only, 9am–4pm.* Formerly a tavern before Saint-Gaudens bought and renovated it, the house (c.1800) was named "Aspet" after his father's birthplace in France. From the side porch there are expansive views of Mt. Ascutney in neighboring Vermont.

Studios and Galleries – The Little Studio was Saint-Gaudens' workshop. A selection of his bas-relief portrait plaques and the *Diana* he sculpted for the tower of the former Madison Square Garden are here. A cast of his formidable statue *The Puritan* (Springfield, Massachusetts) stands among the other works in the gallery. A cast of the enigmatic **Adams Memorial** (commissioned by Henry Adams for the grave of his wife, Marian, in 1885), regarded as an expression of the artist's interpretation of death, grief and divine peace, graces the grounds. The New Gallery features a Roman-style atrium and reflecting pool, the highlight of which is the bronze bas-relief *Amor Caritas*, a winged and draped female figure, symbolic of ideal love.

THE WHITE MOUNTAINS★★★

Map of Principal Sights
Tourist Office ☎ 603-745-8720

Spreading across northern New Hampshire and into Maine, the White Mountains make this region the most mountainous in New England. Renowned for its spectacular natural attractions, picnic areas, campgrounds and more than 1,200mi of hiking trails, the federally managed White Mountain National Forest encompasses 772,000 acres. The region's long winter offers numerous opportunities for skiing in the National Forest and in the valleys close by. Throughout the summer, hikers and motorists enjoy the cool woods and waterfalls and the views from the mountain summits; in the fall, nature transforms the White Mountains into a leaf-looker's paradise.

Geological Notes – Named for the snow that blankets the area during most of the year, these mountains, dominated by Mt. Washington (6,288ft), are characterized by their rounded summits and deep, broad, U-shaped valleys known as **notches**.

The mountains are remnants of ancient, primarily granite, mountain ranges. During the last Ice Age, they were covered by an immense ice sheet, which ground and carved the summits until they were rounded. As the ice sheet retreated, glaciers created steep-walled valleys, polishing them to smooth U-shaped notches, while the swirling action of melting glacial water sculpted giant potholes, such as the basin found in Franconia Notch. The climatic regime that dominates the upper slopes of Mt. Washington is severe for mountains of this relatively low altitude. The harsh, subarctic climate is responsible for the 4,000-5,000ft timberline of the White Mountains, which is low compared to the 8,000-9,000ft timberline of the Colorado Rockies. At the summit, the alpine vegetation resembles the flora of the arctic tundra and includes species found nowhere else in the Northeast.

■ Why "Notch"?

When you visit the Old Man of the Mountains viewing area, you'll come upon a panel near Profile Lake that explains the origin of the word *notch*. Here's a summary. The pioneer settlers built their houses from logs. When felling a tree, they made V- or U-shaped cuts at its base to make it fall away from those doing the chopping. They made similar cuts in the logs themselves to hold the resulting cabin together. The settlers called these cuts "notches." Because they felt the openings or narrow passages between the mountains resembled the notches on their logs, they applied the term to nature's handiwork too.

Historical Notes – Giovanni da Verrazzano sighted the White Mountains from the coast in 1524, and as early as 1642 a settler scaled the peak we now call Mt. Washington. The artists and writers who visited the region in the early 19C depicted the rugged beauty of the White Mountains in their paintings, novels, short stories and poetry. During the same period, New Hampshire residents named Mt. Washington and the other peaks in the Presidential Range after former US presidents. Shortly thereafter, tourists began to arrive. By the end of the century, with the construction of the railroad and the abundance of Victorian hotels that had sprung up in the valley, tourism was established on a grand scale in the White Mountains. Many of the fine old hotels have since been destroyed by fire and replaced by clusters of motels and cottages.

★★★MOUNT WASHINGTON *Map p 239*

Mt. Washington is the highest point in New England (6,288ft) and the principal peak in the Presidential Range, which includes Mts. Adams, Clay, Jefferson, Madison, Monroe and, most recently, Mt. Eisenhower. A subarctic climate, similar to that of northern Labrador—characterized by bitter cold, wind and ice—predominates in the higher altitudes of this peak, influencing the plant and animal life near the summit. Tiny plants and dwarfed fir and spruce trees have adapted to this harsh environment and thrive in mountain crevices and amid the chaotic jumble of boulders that lie in the region above the timberline. The strongest winds ever recorded (231mph) swept across Mt. Washington's summit on April 12, 1934. Snow has fallen on this peak during every month of the year. Fogbound at least 300 days each year, the summit of Mt. Washington, with its group of mountaintop buildings, has been dubbed the "City Among the Clouds."

The Summit – *The Mt. Washington Cog Railway and the Auto Road (below) (closed during severe weather) are the quickest means of reaching the summit. Hikers in good condition with the proper equipment will want to try taking one of the four strenuous trails to the top.* Among the half-dozen structures that cap Mt. Washington are the stone-walled Tip Top House (1853), radio and TV broadcasting facilities, and the Summit Building. The summit and its facilities have served as testing grounds for items ranging from cold-weather clothing to equipment used to control icing on aircraft engines.

PRACTICAL INFORMATION .... Area Code: 603

Getting There – From the south take (**Boston** to **Lincoln** 136mi) I-93 north; from the west (**New York City** to **Warren/western White Mountains** 309mi) take I-91 north to Rte. 25A or (**New York City** to **Bretton Woods/Crawford Notch** 331mi) I-91 north to Rte. 302 east; from the north (**Montreal** to **Franconia Notch** 233mi) Rte. 10 west to Rte. 55/I-91 south to I-93 south. International and domestic flights to **Portland International Airport** (Portland, ME) ☎ 207-774-7301. Major rental car agencies *(p 306)*. Closest Amtrak **train** station: South Station, Boston MA ☎ 800-872-7245. Greyhound **bus** station: Stickney Ave., Concord ☎ 800-231-2222.

Getting Around – Many scenic routes traverse the National Forest, including I-93 from **Plymouth** to exit 35 (30mi); Rte. 112 from **Lincoln** to **Conway** (37mi); and Rte. 15 from **Milton Mills** (south of the National Forest) to **Gorham** (86mi). Off-road vehicles prohibited. Some sights accessible only on foot.

Visitor Information – **White Mountain National Forest** visitor centers: **headquarters** 719 Main St., Laconia 03426 ☎ 528-8721; **Saco Ranger Station** 33 Kancamagus Hwy., Conway 03818 ☎ 447-5448; **Androscoggin Ranger Station** 300 Glen Rd. (Rte. 16), Gorham 03581 ☎ 466-2713; **Ammonoosuc Ranger Station** 660 Trudeau Rd., Bethelem 03574 ☎ 869-2626; **Evans Notch Ranger Station** 18 Mayville Rd., Bethel, ME 04219 ☎ 207-824-2134. National Forest mailing address: 719 N. Main St., Laconia NH 03246. **Appalachian Mountain Club (AMC)** visitor center: Pinkham Notch Camp, Gorham 03581 ☎ 466-2725; *Appalachian Mountain Club White Mountain Guide* available from AMC Books, PO Box 298, Gorham 03581 ☎ 800-262-4455. **Mt. Washington Valley Chamber of Commerce** visitor center Main St., North Conway *(open Memorial Day–Nov daily Mon–Sat 9:am–6pm, Sun 9am–2pm)*. Mailing address: PO Box 2300, North Conway NH 03860 ☎ 356-3171. www.4seasonresort.com.

Accommodations – Reservation service: **Country Inns in the White Mountains** PO Box 2025, North Conway NH 03860 ☎ 356-9460. **Mt. Washington Valley Chamber of Commerce** *(above)* offers reservation assistance for towns located near the southeastern edge of the National Forest. **Appalachian Mountain Club** *(above)* administers a system of huts and shelters, a lodge at the base of Mt. Washington and the **Crawford Notch Hostel** ☎ 466-2727. Year-round **camping** (advance reservations available for many campsites through the National Park Service ☎ 800-365-2267). Permits not required for **backcountry camping**; information at ranger stations.

Recreation – Over 1,100mi of **hiking** trails: trail maps available at ranger stations and AMC visitor center. **Hunting** and **fishing** permitted; licenses and rental equipment available in neighboring towns. **Swimming, canoeing** and **kayaking** allowed on many lakes and rivers; contact ranger stations for more information. **Cross-country skiing** trails throughout the area; **downhill skiing** primarily in Mt. Washington Valley, Waterville Valley and Franconia Notch. **Horse-drawn carriage** trips depart from North Conway area. Specialty **shopping** and supplies in North Conway. Outlet stores in Mt. Washington Valley. *Contact organizations listed above for more information regarding recreation in the area.*

Sudden and extreme changes in weather are not uncommon throughout the year; it is advisable to obtain current local weather forecast before departing. Hikers should heed warning signs and exercise extreme caution when hiking on Mt. Washington.

The **Sherman Adams Summit Building**, a modern structure set into the mountain, is the home of the Mt. Washington Weather Observatory *(open May–Oct daily 9am–4pm; ✕ ♿ ☎ 603-466-3347; www.nhparks.state.nh.us)*. The observatory operates a small museum, located within the Summit Building, containing exhibits related to the weather, geology and history of the mountain *($2)*.
On a clear day, the rooftop deck of the building offers an impressive **panorama★★★** from the summit of Mt. Washington. This 240mi vista, which encompasses the entire region, stretches north to Montreal.

★★**Mt. Washington Cog Railway** – *6mi east of Fabyan. Description p 240.*

★★PINKHAM NOTCH – North Conway to Glen House
4hrs. 26mi via Rtes. 302 and 16. Map p 239.

★**North Conway** – Situated on the edge of the White Mountain National Forest, this town serves as a gateway to the White Mountains. The town, located near Attitash, Mt. Cranmore, Black Mountain and Wildcat Mountain ski areas, offers many facilities for tourists.
The Roman-style railroad station (1874) has been transformed into a museum and ticket office *(Rte. 16)* for the **Conway Scenic Railroad** 🅺, which operates an 11mi ride on an antique train through the Saco Valley *(departs from North Conway depot*

mid-May–late Oct daily, call for departure times; spring & Nov–Dec hours vary; round-trip 1hr; commentary; $8.50; ✕ Conway Scenic Railroad ☎ 603-356-5251; www.conwayscenic.com).

Cathedral Ledge – *Traveling north, turn left at 2nd traffic light after the Scenic Railroad and continue 1mi to the sign for Cathedral Ledge.* Towering 1,000ft above the valley, this ledge commands a good **view★** of Echo Lake and the ruggedly beautiful Mt. Washington Valley that surrounds it.

■ Scenic Shopping and Miniature Golfing...

Surrounded by the White Mountains, North Conway holds a shopper's haven along its main thoroughfare (Route 16), especially opposite Schouler Park. The **North Conway 5¢ and 10¢** on the corner dubs itself "purveyors of worthwhile goods" like penny candy and homemade fudge, souvenirs, t-shirts, jewelry, stationery, kitchen items and hats. Nearby **Zeb's General Store** is a handsome emporium filled with maple syrup, jams, candy, books, puzzles and many other 100% New England-made products. Just doors away **The Penguin Gallery** stocks pet-related items as well as bird seed and feeders, wind chimes, banners, rocking chairs, hammocks, books and other merchandise. After your shopping spree, head for a round of miniature golf at **Banana Village** 🄺 *(☎ 603-356-2899)* or **Pirate's Cove** 🄺 *(☎ 603-356-8807),* both on Route 16.

■ And Dining with a View

Located near the Scenic Vista on Route 16 in North Conway is a hostelry known for its award-winning cuisine and fine views of Mt. Washington from the dining room. **The 1785 Inn** *(☎ 603-356-9025)* presents an ambitious menu of raspberry duckling, sherried rabbit, a veal & lobster combination, sea scallops, and shrimp as well as steak, lamb and chicken entrées, all served with panache. Appetizers and desserts are equally impressive and the wine list is extensive. Breakfast is also available to the public. *Dinner reservations advised.*

Return to Rte. 302/16 north. Mt. Washington is visible from the road.

Glen – Located at the intersection of Routes 16 and 302 (Crawford Notch), Glen has two popular attractions: Story Land and Heritage-New Hampshire.

Story Land – 🄺 *Open mid-Jun–Labor Day daily 9am 6pm. Mid-Sept–Columbus Day weekends only 10am–5pm. $18. ✕ ಕ ☎ 603-383-4186. www.storyland.com.* This theme park features life-size characters and settings from children's stories and nursery rhymes, along with rides, a picnic grove and snack bars.

Heritage-New Hampshire – *Visit by guided tour (1hr 30min) only, mid-Jun–Columbus Day daily 9am–5pm. Last tickets sold 1hr before closing. $10. ಕ ☎ 603-383-4186. www.heritagenh.com.* Costumed guides and interpreters plus lifelike scenes enhanced by special techniques allow visitors to experience significant events in New Hampshire's past. Beyond the building's classic white exterior, you will discover the state's mountainous landscape, walk through the grim interior of the Amoskeag Mills in 19C Manchester, and see Daniel Webster age as he tells the story of his life. The visit concludes with a simulated train ride through Crawford Notch.

Continue north on Rte. 16 through the village of Jackson. Cross over the Jackson covered bridge to glimpse the village's old resort hotels, such as the grand Wentworth Inn. Follow Rte. 16A to return to Rte. 16.

★★ Pinkham Notch – (2,032ft) The valley narrows in this gap between Mt. Washington and Wildcat Mountain.

★ Glen Ellis Falls – *Parking lot on left side of the road.* The falls and its pools, located on the east side of the road *(take the underpass),* are formed by the Ellis River.

Wildcat Mountain – *Parking area off Rte. 16.* Ski trails that look across Pinkham Notch to Mt. Washington have been cut on the slopes of Wildcat Mountain (4,397ft). An aerial gondola provides access to the summit, which offers **views★★** of Mt. Washington and the northern peaks of the

Wentworth Inn

Jackson Village. ☎ 603-383-9700. For country dining in the grand manner, stop in at this well-appointed resort hotel, established in 1869. In the formal dining room, chef-prepared entrées such as New Zealand lamb, Galacian style halibut or sesame crusted salmon follow an appetizer of lobster bread pudding, seared ostrich carpaccio or Tuscan raviolis. After dessert and coffee, linger beside the lobby fireplace or stroll the extensive grounds, which contain cottages and condominiums, a swimming pool, tennis court and 18-hole golf course.

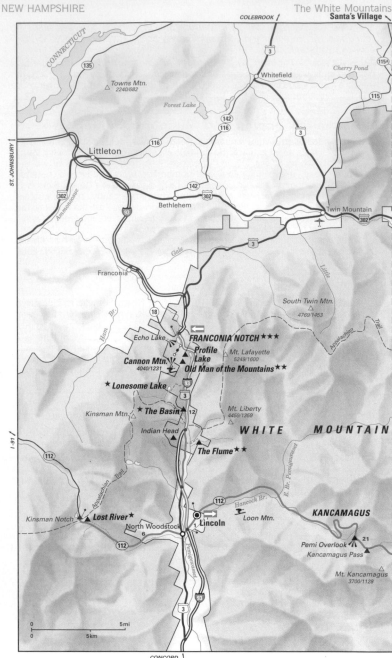

Presidential Range *(gondola operates mid-Jun–mid-Oct daily 9am–4:30pm; mid-May–early Jun weekends only 9am–4:30pm; $9; ⚒ ♿ ☎ 603-466-5152 or 800-255-6439; www.skiwildcat.com).*

Auto Road – The 8mi trek to the summit of Mt. Washington begins at **Glen House**. You can drive your car or take a guided tour *(below)*. From the summit and scenic outlooks there are spectacular views of the Great Gulf Wilderness Area and the Presidential Range. *Open to private vehicles mid-May–mid-Oct daily 7:30am–6pm (weather permitting). $16/car & driver; $6/adult passenger. Motorists planning to drive to the summit should be sure their car is in good condition before starting (check gas, brakes, water). The road, partially unpaved, can be narrow and steep in places. For safety reasons, mobile campers and overloaded vehicles not allowed. Guided tours (1hr 30min) depart from Glen House. $20. ⚒ ♿ ☎ 603-466-3988. www.mt-washington.com.*

Shelburne Birches – *14mi from Glen House. Take Rte. 16, then Rte. 2 through Gorham.* This is a picturesque roadside stand of tall, slender white birch trees.

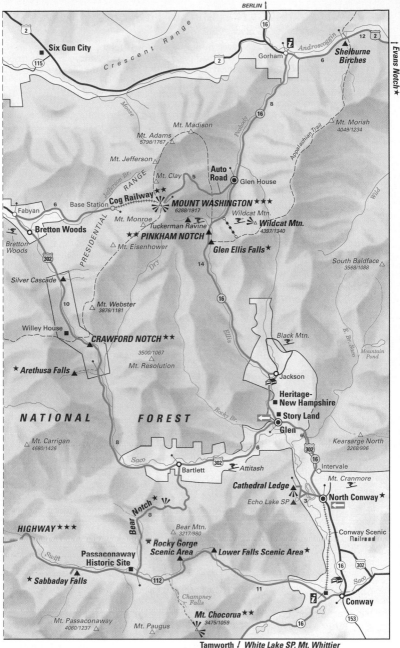

Tamworth / White Lake SP, Mt. Whittier

★**Evans Notch** – *12mi by Rte. 2 from Shelburne Birches. See Entry Heading Bethel (in Maine).*

Strictly Moose

Kids *Rte. 2/16 in Gorham.* ☎ *603-466-9417.* It's hard to miss a large, colorful wooden house on the main thoroughfare in Gorham, since there are all types and sizes of moose in the front yard (stuffed and wooden, that is). This unusual store concentrates on stocking every imaginable product that could possibly be shaped like, or decorated with, the ruminant mammal: pens, pencils, lapel pins, key chains, mugs, hats, baseball caps, napkins and placemats, towels, handkerchiefs, t-shirts and sweatshirts, banners, and all sizes of toy moose (in wood, plastic and fabric). Someone must be buying them, because the popular, filled-to-the-corners shop is expanding, and more moose merchandise is moving in.

★★CRAWFORD NOTCH – Glen to Fabyan
3hrs. 24mi via Rte. 302. Map p 239.

Route 302 follows the Saco River through Crawford Notch, a broad valley in the heart of the White Mountains. The road passes the **Attitash Ski Area**, a popular resort, and continues to Bartlett. In **Bartlett** a road located just past the library leads south through Bear Notch.

★**Bear Notch** – *An additional 8mi between Bartlett and the Kancamagus Hwy.* This drive is especially scenic during the foliage season. At the point where the road leaves Crawford Notch *(3.5mi after Bartlett)*, there is a beautiful **view** of the valley.

★★**Crawford Notch** – (1,773ft) This pass was named for the Crawford family, White Mountain pioneers who cut the first trail to the summit of Mt. Washington in the 19C, and whose home in the notch served as a shelter for hikers.

★**Arethusa Falls** – *Parking lot on the left side of the road. Cross the railroad tracks, then fol-low the path (right) into the woods.* The trail *(round-trip 2hrs)* follows a brook, then crosses it just before reaching the falls, situated in a refreshing forest setting.

Route 302 passes in front of the rustic **Willey House** and **Mt. Webster**, its slopes covered in places with the rocky debris of recent landslides. Farther on you will pass the **Silver Cascade**, a roadside waterfall tumbling from a high ledge.

Bretton Woods – The slopes of the Presidential Range form the backdrop for the **Mount Washington Resort**, a sprawling complex that is one of the few 19C hosteleries still in existence. In 1944 the hotel was the site of the United Nations Monetary and Financial Conference (Bretton Woods Conference), which established the American dollar as the medium of international exchange and developed plans to establish the World Bank.

Continue north on Rte. 302. At Fabyan, turn right onto the road leading to the Cog Railway.

Mt. Washington Cog Railway

★★**Mt. Washington Cog Railway** – 🚸 *Departs from Marshfield Base Station 6mi east of Rte. 302 mid-Jul–Labor Day daily 8am–5pm (hourly). Rest of the season (May–Oct) departure times vary; call for hours. Round-trip 3hrs (includes 20min stop at summit). Commentary. Reservations suggested. $44. Mt. Washington Cog Railway* ☎ *603-278-5404 or 800-922-8825. www.thecog.com.* This small steam train is almost as famous as the mountain itself. Built in 1869, the 3.5mi railway represents an outstanding technological achievement for its day, and still offers passengers a thrilling ride to the summit of the mountain, especially as the train ascends **Jacob's Ladder**, the steepest grade (37 percent) on the trestle.

During the leisurely ride *(1hr 30min)* to the top, note how the vegetation and land-scape change with increasing altitude.

★★★FRANCONIA NOTCH   *1/2 day. 13mi via Rte. 3. Map p 238.*

Running along the floor of this scenic notch cradled between the Franconia and Kinsman Ranges, Route 3 offers easy access to **Echo Lake** (Rte. 18) and to many of the area's natural attractions.

Cannon Mountain – Cannon Mountain is one of New Hampshire's finest ski areas. An **aerial tramway** travels to the summit (4,040ft), which overlooks Echo Lake and affords a **view★★** of the notch *(tramway operates mid-Jul–Labor Day daily*

9am–5:30pm; mid-May–early Jul & rest of Sept–mid-Oct daily 9am–4:30pm; round-trip 15min; commentary; $9; ♿ ☎ *603-823-8800; www.cannonmt.com).* Located next to the tramway station, the **New England Ski Museum** illustrates skiing history with audiovisual presentations, photographs, equipment and memorabilia *(open Memorial Day–Columbus Day daily noon–5pm; Dec–Mar Fri–Mon noon–5pm;* ✕ ♿ ☎ *603-823-7177 or 800-639-4181).*

★★ **Old Man of the Mountains and Profile Lake** – A rocky formation that resembles a man's profile (40ft from chin to forehead) juts out from a mountainside above Profile Lake. The profile was discovered in 1805 by two men who compared it to a likeness of President Jefferson. Nathaniel Hawthorne described the profile in his short story *The Great Stone Face,* and when P.T. Barnum toured the notch almost 20 years later, he was so impressed that he wanted to purchase the attraction for his circus. The Old Man of the Mountains is best viewed from a vantage point on the lakeshore.

> **"Men hang out their signs indicative of their respective trades; shoemakers hang out a gigantic shoe; jewelers a monster watch; and the dentist hangs out a gold tooth; but up in the mountains of New Hampshire, God Almighty has hung out a sign to show that there he makes men."**
>
> Attributed to Daniel Webster

Lovett's Inn

Rte. 18 in Franconia. ☎ *603-823-7761.* For superb dining in Franconia, look for Lovett's on the left before you reach the village proper. The rambling, roadside complex of white cottages, swimming pool and grassy expanses surrounding the main building is set on a broad plain at the base of the mountains. Have a libation in the lounge, with its marble bar. Then move to the spacious dining room for chilled blueberry soup and spinach salad with dried fruits and sherry hazelnut vinaigrette. For the main course, among other entrées, choose roast duck, poached salmon or pork tenderloin, prepared to perfection. A selection from the array of homemade desserts brings the meal to a satisfying conclusion. Afterward, take an evening stroll on the property, being sure to cross the road to visit the small pond. *Reservations advised. Brunch served on Sundays.*

The Flume

Bob Grant

★ **Lonesome Lake** – *Trail (3hrs) leaves from the parking lot at Lafayette Campground. Follow the yellow markers.* This lake occupies a clearing 1,000ft above Franconia Notch. A trail around the lake leads to the Appalachian Mountain Club Hut, which accommodates hikers in the summer.

★ **The Basin** – The action of churning waters rushing down from the falls above has formed this 30ft granite pothole.

★★ **The Flume** – *Open May–Oct daily 9am–5:30pm. $7. Bus transportation to Boulder Cabin (.5mi walk to Flume) is available from the visitor center.* ✕ ☎ *603-745-8391. www.nhparks.state.nh.us.* A series of connecting paths forms a 2mi loop trail beginning at the visitor center. **Flume Path,** a system of boardwalks and stairways, guides visitors through the Flume, a deep, narrow granite chasm through which Flume Brook

North Woodstock Notables

Stop for lunch at the **Woodstock Inn** (☎ *603-745-3951*) on Main Street in North Woodstock. There's indoor dining in the Clement Room and its glass-enclosed "petticoat porch" or an outdoor umbrella-covered patio for warmer weather. Sandwiches and dinner are also served evenings in the informal Woodstock Station. One of the inn's big attractions is its brewpub, since the beer served is made on the premises in the Woodstock Inn Brewery, a microbrewery that uses the traditional seven-barrel system. *Breakfast and lunch service. Dinner reservations suggested.*

On the other side of the street is **Truants Taverne and Restaurant** (☎ *603-745-2239*), open for lunch and dinner daily. The dark wooded interior is dressed with black and white photos of old schoolhouses and class pictures, musty books and free-standing globes. Sandwiches such as The Salutatorian, Class Bully and Teacher's Pet come with fries and can be complemented with home-made root beer. The Dean's List, the after 5pm menu, features Truant Steak, Taverne Scallops and other seafood, chicken entrées, plus pasta and vegetarian dishes. Detention Delights is a listing of the evening's desserts. *Outdoor deck seating available.*

flows. **Ridge Path** leads to Liberty Cascade and then passes the **Sentinal Pine-Covered Bridge**, which overlooks a clear natural pool. **Wildwood Path** completes the circuit, winding past mammoth boulders that were deposited here by glaciers thousands of years ago.

Upon leaving the Flume, look across Route 3 for a rocky formation that resembles the profile of a human head. This rock is called **Indian Head**. Route 3 continues south toward the village of Lincoln.

Lincoln – Located at the southern entrance to Franconia Notch, Lincoln is a center for neighboring resorts, boasting a plentiful assortment of motels, restaurants, shops and commercial attractions.

En route to Lost River, travelers pass the colorful mountain community of **North Woodstock**, whose main street brims with shops and eateries.

★ **Lost River** – *7mi from Lincoln by Rte. 112 west. Open Jul & Aug 9am–6pm. Early May–Jun & Sept–late Oct daily 9am–5pm. $8.* ☎ *603-745-8031. www.findlostriver.com.* Located in Kinsman Notch, between the Connecticut and Pemigewasset Valleys, the Lost River Gorge is a steep-walled glacial ravine filled with enormous boulders that have been sculpted into potholes by the river. A system of boardwalks and staircases allows visitors to tour the caves, potholes and waterfalls in the gorge.

★★★ THE KANCAMAGUS HIGHWAY – Lincoln to Conway
3hrs. 32mi. Map pp 238-239.

This road through the White Mountain National Forest follows the **Hancock Branch** of the Pemigewasset River and the **Swift River**. It is one of the most spectacular drives in New England during the foliage season, when the maples and birch trees take on their fall colors. Picnic areas and campgrounds along the highways invite visitors to relax by the clear mountain streams and scenic rapids.

The mountains south of the highway are named for some of New Hampshire's famous Indians: the Passaconaway, Kancamagus ("a friend of the settlers") and Chocorua.

The road passes in front of **Loon Mountain Recreation Area**, a year-round resort, then begins to climb to Kancamagus Pass. During the ascent, there is an exceptionally scenic **view**★ from the **Pemi Overlook**. The road then dips into the Saco Valley.

★ **Sabbaday Falls** – *Parking area on south side of the road. Take the Sabbaday Brook Trail (round-trip 30min), an easy trail to follow.* The falls tumble over a series of ledges into two giant potholes, then through a flume.

Passaconaway Historic Site – The **Russell Colbath Historic Homestead** houses an information and nature center for the White Mountain National Forest *(open Jul–Columbus Day Wed–Mon 9am–4:30pm; Jun weekends only, 9am–4:30pm;* ☎ *603-447-5448).* The short, self-guided **Rail 'N' River Trail** *(.75mi)* begins here. Nicknamed for the former railroad bed it follows, the trail provides an introduction to the trees and shrubs in this part of the forest.

The highway passes the road (on the left) to Bear Notch.

★★ **Mt. Chocorua** – *Round-trip 5hr hike to the summit from Champney Falls Trail parking area.* Follow the **Champney Falls Trail–Piper Trail**, which ascends gently the first 1.5mi and leads to a bypass *(on the left)* to Champney Falls. Return to the main trail, which becomes moderately difficult as it climbs rapidly through various stages of forest vegetation to the rocky summit of Mt. Chocorua. From the summit, there are **views★★★** of the White Mountains on one side and of Chocorua Lake on the other. Both the lake and the mountain are named in honor of the Indian chief who, according to legend, avenged the death of his son by killing the family of the man suspected of accidentally poisoning the boy. A group of angry settlers pursued the chief to the upper ledge of the mountain that today bears his name. Cornered, Chocorua uttered a curse on all white men, then jumped to his death. Settlers recalled the Indian's curse when an epidemic killed many of their cattle; the cause was eventually traced to polluted drinking water.

To return to the parking lot, follow the signs for Champney Falls Trail; there are many paths on Mt. Chocorua, so it is easy to stray from the main trail.

★**Rocky Gorge Scenic Area** – The Swift River forms rapids at this point, where the valley narrows.

★**Lower Falls Scenic Area** – The eastern end of the site affords the best view of the falls formed by the Swift River.

Conway – Conway is a resort for all seasons. Ski shops, motels and restaurants border Route 16, outside the town. The covered bridge spanning the Saco River can be seen from Route 16, about .5mi north of Conway.

Tamworth – *13mi from Conway. Take Rte. 16 south.* After 10mi, there's a picture-postcard **view★★** of Mt. Chocorua, reflected in the lake of the same name. A little farther south, pass through the tiny village of Chocorua. Route 113 west leads to the tranquil village of Tamworth, with its white houses and cozy inn. The **Barnstormers**, a local theater group, perform here during the summer.

ADDITIONAL SIGHTS

White Lake State Park – *14mi south of Conway, .5mi north of West Ossipee on Rte. 16. Open daily mid-May–Columbus Day 8am–dusk. $2.50.* ⚠ ♿ ☏ *603-323-7350.* Located south of the White Mountains, this park attracts swimmers and fishermen to its sandy beach.

Mt. Whittier – *Rte. 25 from West Ossipee.* From the summit (2,205ft) of this mountain, named for the poet John Greenleaf Whittier, who summered nearby, there is a view that includes the White Mountains and Mt. Chocorua.

Santa's Village – 🧒 *Rte. 2 in Jefferson. Open mid-Jun–Labor Day daily 9:30am–6:30pm. Memorial Day–early Jun & rest of Sept–mid-Oct weekends only, 9:30am–5pm. $16.* ✗ ☏ *603-586-4445. www.santasvillage.com.* The village claims to be the summer home of Santa Claus, his reindeer and his helpers. Its 40 colorfully painted and decorated buildings are set in a grove of tall evergreens.

Six Gun City – 🧒 *South of junction Rtes. 2 and 115A, near Jefferson. Open May–Sept daily 9am–6pm. Memorial Day–early Jun weekends only 10am–4:30pm. $12.95.* ✗ ☏ *603-586-4592. www.sixguncity.com.* This replica of a small western town includes a blockhouse, jail, saloon and 35 other buildings. Visitors can enjoy the waterslide and ride logs through a mill.

Lake WINNIPESAUKEE REGION★

Map of Principal Sights
Tourist Office ☏ 603-774-8664

New Hampshire's largest lake covers an area of 72sq mi, has a shoreline of 300mi, and is dotted with more than 200 tiny islands. On a clear day, the lake, set against the backdrop of the White Mountains, is a magnificent sight. The best way to view it is by taking a cruise *(below)*.

The lake's name originated with an Indian legend about a brave who was canoeing on the lake one night. The sky suddenly darkened. Without warning, a brilliant ray of light shone on the water, guiding his boat safely to shore. He interpreted this light as a divine miracle, and named the lake Winnipesaukee, meaning "the smile of the Great Spirit."

Lakeside Villages – Each of the villages on the lake possesses its own character. **Laconia** is the industrial and commercial center of the region. The small charming village of **Wolfeboro★**, with its large homes overlooking the lake, has attracted summer vacationers for centuries. Unspoiled by industry, it is one of the prettiest communities on the shores of Lake Winnipesaukee. **Weirs Beach**, with its amusement arcade, souvenir shops and lakefront Victorian dwellings, is a lively resort; attractive **Center Harbor**, as well as Meredith, on bays at the northern end of the lake, serve as shopping centers for the resort cottages and campgrounds nearby.

Every summer thousands of vacationers enjoy boating on Winnipesaukee's waters. Public docks, marinas and launching ramps abound. Popular beaches include Weirs Beach and **Ellacoya State Beach**. For hikers, walking trails in the hills encircle the area. During the winter, **Gunstock Ski Area** and **Ragged Mountain Ski Area** teem with activity. Ice fishing, snowmobiling and the dogsled championships held each February in Laconia provide additional winter attractions.

Browsing ...

In Moultonboro **Carriage House Crafters** *(Rte. 25* ☎ *603-253-9724)* tempts browsers with New England-made wooden toys and wall hangings, pillows and pin cushions, dried flower arrangements, baskets, Christmas ornaments, mugs, clothing and a host of other handcrafted items all housed within a bright fushia-colored roadside carriage house. There's even a bench outside labeled "Husbands' waiting area." The **Old Country Store** *(Rtes. 25 & 109* ☎ *603-476-5750)* delights those who venture in with its bygone-era charm and cluttered array of penny candy, pickles in crocks, aged cheddar cheese, New Hampshire maple syrup and a myriad of other products of interest to those just looking.

And Dining

For a fancy meal near Meredith, locate the **Red Hill Inn** *(off Rte. 3 at Rte. 25B* ☎ *603-279-7001; best to phone for directions)*, housed in a hilltop mansion on expansive grounds overlooking Squam Lake and Squam Mountain. Both dining rooms have a view of the mountain. Have a drink in the Runabout Lounge followed by a dinner of delicious pork tenderloin, lamb or shrimp scampi, among other choices. (Lunches and Sunday brunch are equally pleasing.) After a scrumptious dessert, assuage your guilty conscience with a stroll along the herb path, or better yet, a strenuous walk down to the gazebo-encased hot tub and back up the hill.

SIGHTS

★★**Sightseeing Cruises** – *The following excursion boats are operated on the lake by Winnipesaukee Flagship Corp. (dinner cruises also available).* ☎ *888-843-6686. www.info@msmountwashington.com.*

★★**M/S Mount Washington** – *Departs mid-May–mid-Oct from: Weirs Beach daily 10am & 12:30pm (Jul–Aug additional 2hr cruise 3pm; $14); Center Harbor Mon 11am; Alton Bay Thu 11:15am; Wolfeboro Tue, Wed, Fri–Sun 11:15am. Round-trip 2hrs 30min. Commentary. $16.* ✗ &.

M/V Doris E. – *Departs late Jun–Labor Day daily from: Meredith 10am–8:30pm & Weirs Beach 10:30am–8pm. Round-trip 1–2 hrs. Commentary. $8–$13.*

M/V Sophie C. – *The Sophie C. is a mail boat that travels to the lake's upper islands. Departs from Weirs Beach mid-Jun–early Sept Mon–Sat 11am & 3:30pm. Round-trip 2hrs. Commentary. $13.*

★**Castle in the Clouds** – *In Moultonborough via Rte. 109 then Rte. 171. Open late Jun–Labor Day daily 9am–5pm. Rest of Sept–late Oct daily 9am–4pm. May weekends only. $11.* & ☎ *603-476-2352 or 800-729-2468. www.castlesprings.com.* This 6,000-acre estate was acquired in 1910 by the millionaire Thomas Plant, who made his fortune by developing machinery for use in the shoe industry. The residence Plant commissioned high on the slopes of the Ossipee Mountains overlooks the forests and lakes below. From the terrace, there is a **view**★★ of Lake Winnipesaukee with its myriad tree-clad islands. Miles of foot and horse trails thread through the property *(horse rental $25/hr)*. A path *(.25mi)* beginning about 1mi from the entrance gate leads to two waterfalls, the **Fall of Song** and **Bridal Veil Falls**.

Loon Center and Markus Wildlife Sanctuary – *In Moultonborough. From Rte. 25 turn onto Blake Rd. (look for Loon Center sign) and continue 1mi to the end, then turn right onto Lee's Mills Rd. Trails open year-round daily dawn–dusk. Center open Jul–Columbus Day daily 9am–5pm; rest of the year Mon–Sat 9am–5pm.* ☎ *603-476-5666. Inspect repellant and binoculars are advised. Trail map available.* Begin your visit inside, viewing the various exhibits on this threatened species and other birds, funded by the Audubon Society of New Hampshire. A small gift shop features loon-emblazoned items, nature books and bird-call recordings. In the 200-acre wildlife sanctuary, there's a 10min **Forest Walk** through mixed woods and wildflowers, but opt for the longer **Loon Nest Trail** *(allow a minimum 1hr)* through marshland, streams and upland forests bordering Lake Winnipesaukee. At about a third of the distance, a lookout permits a view of a nesting site, and if your timing is right, a loon or two.

★**Center Sandwich** – *5mi north of Moultonborough by Rte. 109.* Situated at the foot of the White Mountains, Center Sandwich is one of New England's prettiest villages. In the fall a tapestry of brilliant autumn color frames its simple white clapboard structures. On the green sits the sales shop (nearly hidden by trees) of the **Sandwich Home Industries**, the founding member of the statewide guild of the League of New Hampshire Craftsmens.

Where to Find Native American Art and Culture in New England

Rhode Island

Area: 1,214sq mi
Population: 1,003,464
Capital: Providence
Nickname: Ocean State
State Flower: Violet

The smallest state in the nation, Rhode Island measures only 48 miles long and 37 miles wide. In 1524 Italian navigator Giovanni da Verrazzano sailed into Narragansett Bay and along the coast of the island known to the Indians as Aquidneck. Impressed by the brilliance of the natural light here, Verrazzano noted the similarity in appearance between Aquidneck and the Greek isle of Rhodes. More than a century later, Aquidneck was renamed Rhode Island. Its official name, the State of Rhode Island and Providence Plantations, reflects the state's origin as a series of independent settlements. The Royal Charter of 1644 united "Providence Plantations" at the head of the Narragansett Bay with settlements at Newport and Portsmouth on Aquidneck Island. Today the state ranks as the third most densely populated state in the US. Narragansett Bay, Rhode Island's dominant natural feature, extends 28 miles inland, nearly bisecting the state. The bay fostered the early commercial trade that contributed to the wealth of Newport, Providence and Bristol. Sprawling inland from the bay, the Providence metropolitan area remains the only large urban center in the state.

A Land of Tolerance The earliest colonists came to Rhode Island in search of religious freedom they could not find in Massachusetts. The first to arrive, in 1630, was the **Reverend Blackstone** *(p 116)*, fleeing the Puritans' invasion of his privacy on the Shawmut Peninsula. He was followed by the minister **Roger Williams**, who founded Providence in 1636. Exiled from Massachusetts for his "new and dangerous opinions," Williams established Providence Plantations, a farming community, on lands that he purchased from the Narragansett Indians. Two years later a group of disgruntled Bostonians bought the island of Aquidneck and started the colony of Portsmouth (north of present-day Newport). The religious leader **Anne Hutchinson** soon joined them, with her own adherents in tow. Newport was founded in 1639 by 11 former Portsmouth colonists who left after a factional dispute. Relations between the colonists and the Indians remained friendly until 1675 when Philip, chief of the Wampanoags, led his tribe, along with the Narragansetts and Nipmucks, in raids against the settlers in **King Philip's War** (1675-76). During the Great Swamp Fight (in Mt. Hope, Rhode Island) on December 19, 1675, colonists launched a surprise attack on the Narragansetts, Rhode Island's most powerful tribe. The war dissipated the tribe's strength and greatly reduced the local Indian population.

Economy – Rhode Island's economy was at first based on the sea, with Newport and Providence vying for positions as the nation's leading seaports. By the 1650s Rhode Island had gained a portion of the trade between New England and the West Indies. The great fortunes made from trade provided capital for the textile industry, which had its beginnings at Pawtucket in 1793. One of the country's leading textile producers throughout the 19C, Rhode Island soon became the most heavily industrialized state in the US. The exodus of the textile factories to the South after World War II led to an emphasis on diversified manufacturing, which today ranks as the state's leading source of income and its largest employer. Rhode Island's early manufacture of machine tools gave rise in 1796 to the production of jewelry and silverware, now a major industry. Tourism generates over a billion dollars a year in revenues for the state. Government jobs, wholesale and retail trade and health care provide additional sources of income.

BLOCK ISLAND★

This unspoiled island, 10mi south of the mainland, is covered with cliffs, sand dunes and grassy moors. Visitors enjoy the quiet island for its good beaches, deep-sea fishing and boating.

Probably discovered in the 16C by Verrazzano, Block Island was named for **Adrian Block**, the Dutch navigator who explored the region in 1614. The first permanent colonists to settle here arrived at the end of the 17C. They were followed by smugglers, pirates and most likely those shipwrecked off the frequently fogbound coast of Block Island. In the late 19C the island developed into a summer resort with large, prim Victorian hotels, such as those that front **Old Harbor**. Tourists were attracted by the mild sea breezes and refreshing climate. Today **New Harbor** serves as a superb haven for boats and a playground for water sports enthusiasts.

SIGHTS *4hrs*

★★**Mohegan Bluffs** – The island's south shore is formed by a series of spectacular multicolored cliffs. Steep paths descend to the beach at the base of the cliffs.

★**Sandy Point** – The northern end of the island has been set aside as a bird and wildlife preserve. A sandy path leads to the stone lighthouse. No longer in use, the old lighthouse, with its 18in-thick walls, has managed to withstand the force of shifting sands and powerful gales over the years.

Crescent Beach – *Entrance off Corn Neck Rd. From Water St., turn left on Dodge St. and right on Corn Neck Rd. at four-way stop.* Dressing rooms, showers and eating facilities are available at the locally owned, guarded section of Crescent Beach. *Swimming is advised at guarded beaches only because of the strong undertow and rough surf at some of the beaches.*

PRACTICAL INFORMATION .... Area Code: 401

Getting There – From **Providence** to **Point Judith** (33 mi): I-95 south to Hwy. 4 west to Hwy. 1 south to Hwy. 108; from **Newport** to **Point Judith** (20 mi): Hwy. 138 west to Hwy. 1 south to Hwy. 108. International and domestic flights to **T.F. Green State Airport**, Providence ☎ 737-4000; bus service to Point Judith available ☎ 781-9400. Major rental car agencies *p 306*. Nearest Amtrak **train** station: New London CT ☎ 800-872-7245. Closest Greyhound **bus** station: Newport ☎ 800-231-2222.

Ferry Schedule *(advance reservations for vehicles strongly suggested)*

Departure	Schedule	Duration (one-way)	Adult Fare (round-trip)	Company
Point Judith	year-round, daily	1hr 10min	$13.50	Interstate Navigation ☎ 401-783-4613
Newport	late Jun–Labor Day, daily	2hrs	$11.85	
Providence	late Jun–Labor Day, daily	4hrs	$13.70	
New London, CT	mid-Jun–early Sept., daily	2hrs	$19.00	
Montauk, NY	late May–early Sept., weekends only	1hr 45min	$35.00	Viking Ferry ☎ 516-668-5709

Getting Around – Block Island is best visited by bicycle, as streets are often congested and parking may be difficult (especially in July and August). Bicycle and car rentals in Old and New Harbor.

Visitor Information – **Block Island Chamber of Commerce** visitor center: Old Harbor. Mailing address: Drawer D, Block Island RI 02807 ☎ 800-383-2474.

Accommodations – Information available from **Chamber of Commerce** *(above)*. Accommodations include historic hotels and bed and breakfasts *($85–$125/day)*. Camping is prohibited. *Average prices for a double room.*

Recreation – Swimming **beaches** stretch from Old Harbor to the north end of the island. **Hiking** trails are located throughout the island, including The Maze, a 128-acre preserve. **Fishing**: licenses from town hall; rental equipment available in New Harbor. Most specialty **shopping** and supplies in Old Harbor. *Contact the Chamber of Commerce for more information regarding shopping and recreation on Block Island.*

Block Island/Jonathan Wallen

BRISTOL★

Population 21,625
Map of Principal Sights
Tourist Office ☎ 401-245-0750

Bristol survived the Revolution to become a leading seaport and shipbuilding center. Some of its wealthy citizens, who prospered from trade with Africa, the West Indies and the Orient, built mansions throughout the waterfront district.

For over 80 years the **Herreshoff** boatyards turned out steam and sailing yachts, among which were several successful America's Cup *(p 252)* defenders. A drive through **Colt State Park** *(off Rte. 114)* affords views of Narragansett Bay. Today Bristol is known for its Fourth of July parade, first held in 1785 and said to be the oldest in the country.

SIGHTS

★**Linden Place** – *500 Hope St. Visit by guided tour (45min) only, May–Columbus Day Thu–Sat 10am–4pm, Sun noon–4pm. $5. &. ☎ 401-253-0390.* Notorious Rhode Island slave trader George DeWolf spent $60,000 to build this splendid three-story clapboard mansion. Designed by Russell Warren, the Federal-style house, with its Corinthian columns and leaded fanlights, was completed in 1810. It contains DeWolf family furnishings.

Blithewold Mansion and Gardens – *101 Ferry Rd (Rte. 114). Grounds open year-round daily 10am–5pm. $5 (grounds only). Mansion visit by guided tour (1hr 30min) only, mid-Apr Oct Wed–Sun 11am–3:30pm. Mansion closed major holidays. $8 (house & grounds). ☎ 401-253-2707. www.blithewold.org.* Flower gardens *(in season),* as well as trees and shrubs from Europe and the Orient, adorn the grounds of this former estate, built in 1907 for Augustus Van Wickle, a coal magnate. Even during the off-season, this is a delightful place for a stroll, with its spacious surroundings, harborside setting and expansive views of Narragansett Bay. A rock garden and water garden occupy clearings a short distance from the water's edge; near the mansion stands a 90ft-tall giant sequoia.

The mansion, a stone and stucco residence designed as an English manor house, is furnished with objects and artifacts acquired by the Van Wickles on their trips abroad. Twelve of the rooms in the house are open to the public.

Haffenreffer Museum of Anthropology – *Tower St. From Rte. 136 take Tower St. east and follow the signs. Open Jun–Aug Tue–Sun 11am–5pm. Rest of the year weekends only 11am–5pm. $3. &. ☎ 401-253-8388. www.brown.edu/facilities/haffenreffer.* This small museum is affiliated with Brown University's *(p 264)* Department of Anthropology. Exhibits are from Brown's rich collection of artifacts related to the cultures of aboriginal peoples of Africa, Asia, the Pacific and the Americas.

Herreshoff Marine Museum – 🅺🅸🅳🅸 *1 Burnside St., .5mi south of downtown. Open May–early Oct Mon–Sat 10am–4pm, Sun 11am–4pm. $3. ☎ 401-253-5001.* From 1863 to 1946 the waterside boatyards along Route 114 here were the site of the Herreshoff Manufacturing Co., designer of naval torpedo boats, acclaimed wooden sailing and motor yachts, and seven America's Cup defenders (1893-1934).

Located in a one-story warehouse, the museum offers an in-depth tribute to the company's glory days through photos, film, models and some 40 craft in various stages of restoration. The **America's Cup Hall of Fame** is also housed in the museum.

LITTLE COMPTON

Population 3,339
Map of Principal Sights
Tourist Office ☎ 401-849-8048

Located in the southeastern portion of the state known for its production of "Rhode Island Red" chickens, Little Compton is one of Rhode Island's prettiest villages, with its village green, white Congregational church and old cemetery.

VISIT

In the burial ground stands a monument honoring Benjamin Church, a colonist who took part in the Great Swamp Fight and the capture and execution of King Philip. Marshes fringe the narrow roads (such as Route 77) that wind through the rural countryside and down to the coast.

NARRAGANSETT PIER

Population 14,985
Map of Principal Sights
Tourist Office ☎ 401-789-4422

Narragansett Pier and the coastal region extending south to Point Judith and Jerusalem possess some of the finest beaches in New England. The lively atmosphere of **Scarborough Beach** draws a young crowd, while surfers prefer **East Matunuck State Beach**. Families with young children are drawn to the calm waters at **Galilee Beach**.
Narragansett Pier began to develop into a fashionable seaside resort in the 19C, after Rhode Island governor William Sprague and his wife built their summer mansion in the area. All activity centered on the pier (only the name survives), which extended from the southern end of Town Beach into the ocean. Beyond the beachfront Victorian hotels stood the vacation homes of American businessmen and political figures. The **Towers**, two stone structures joined by an arch extending across Ocean Road, are all that remain of the lavish Narragansett Casino, designed by McKim, Mead and White in 1884. The main section of the casino and many of Narragansett's grand hotels were destroyed by fire in 1900.

DRIVING TOUR *30min. 6mi.*

Drive south on Ocean Rd. (Rte. 1A), which passes under the Towers and skirts shorefront mansions that overlook the pounding surf. About 2mi after Scarborough Beach, you will enter Galilee.

Galilee – In September this fishing village hosts the annual **Rhode Island Tuna Tournament**, a major sporting event. The Point Judith ferry to BLOCK ISLAND leaves from the State Pier at Galilee year-round *(p 248)*. On the opposite shore of Point Judith Pond is **Jerusalem**, another tiny fishing village.

Point Judith – The rocky headland with its octagonal-shaped lighthouse is a familiar landmark to mariners who sail these waters.

Addresses, telephone numbers, opening hours and prices published in this guide are accurate at press time. We apologize for any inconvenience resulting from outdated information. Please send us your comments:

*Michelin Travel Publications
Editorial Department
P. O. Box 19001
Greenville, SC 29602-9001*

Population 28,227
Map of Principal Sights
Tourist Office ☎ 401-849-8048

An all-encompassing view of the city's beautiful setting in the midst of Narragansett Bay greets motorists arriving from the west by Newport Bridge *(passenger vehicles $2 one-way)*. A resort once devoted exclusively to the wealthy, Newport, today a major sailing center and home of the **Newport Music Festival**, is fascinating for its history and architecture.

Historical Notes

A Harbor of Refuge – In the wake of a political dispute with Anne Hutchinson in Portsmouth, **William Coddington**, another Boston exile, led a group of settlers to the southern part of Aquidneck Island in 1639. There, on the shore of a large harbor, they founded Newport. Other religious minorities—Quakers, Baptists and Jews—soon followed, seeking the religious tolerance for which the Rhode Island settlements were known. These settlers were talented entrepreneurs, and with their help the colony rapidly developed.

The Breakers

Newport's Golden Age – By 1761 Newport had grown into a bustling port center second only to BOSTON. The colony's prosperity was due largely to the **triangular trade**. Vessels bearing cargoes of rum sailed to Africa, where the rum was exchanged for slaves. Merchants then transported the slaves to the West Indies and traded them for molasses used to produce rum. The slave market represented an important source of income to Newport. An import tax levied on each slave brought into the colony yielded sufficient revenue to build the roads and bridges needed to link the growing settlements. Rum was also exported to Europe, where it was exchanged for goods not available in the colonies.

The Revolution – Newport's fortunes were abruptly reversed with the outbreak of the American Revolution. Marked by the British for destruction, Newport was occupied from 1776 to 1779. Inhabitants were forced to house English soldiers, and looting and burning were widespread. Following the British defeat, French troops, allies of the Americans, occupied Newport. It was here that meetings between General Washington and Count Rochambeau took place.
By the end of the war, Newport lay in ruins. Most of its merchants had fled to Providence, and the colony would never again regain its commercial splendor.

Summer Resort of the Wealthy – During the years before the Revolution, planters from Georgia and the Carolinas escaped the heat of the southern summer by vacationing in Newport. In the mid-19C, with the introduction of steamboat travel between New York and Newport, an increasing number of visitors arrived each year. Following the Civil War, America's wealthiest families—including the Astors, Belmonts and Vanderbilts—began to summer here. Impressed by the magnificence of the palaces and chateaus they had seen while touring Europe, they commissioned America's finest architects to design the enormous "cottages" that grace Ocean Drive and Bellevue Avenue. In summer Newport's rich, part-time residents held fabulous picnics, dinner parties and balls, famed for their extravagance. Presiding over these events were Mrs. William Astor, Mrs. O.H. Belmont, Mrs. Hermann Oelrichs and other high-society matriarchs. The search for unusual diversions led to such eccentricities as the champagne and

caviar dinner given by Harry Lehr for his friends and their pets, during which masters and pets ate and drank at the same table; and the fleet of full-size model ships made for Mrs. Oelrichs and placed on the ocean to convey the impression of a harbor.
Attracted by the latest fads and inventions, the affluent residents of Newport drove the first motor cars, built the first roads, filled the harbor with princely mahogany and brass-trimmed yachts, and introduced boat racing to the town.

■ Newport and Sports

Several sports owe their development and popularity to Newport society, whose favorite pastimes included tennis, golf and boating. In 1881 the first US tennis championships were held on the courts of the Newport Casino; annual tennis tournaments, including the **International Tennis Hall of Fame Grass Court Championships** *(held in early July)*, are still played here. The first US amateur and open golf championships took place on a nine-hole course laid out on Brenton Point in 1894 by members of the "400" *(p 256)*.
It was, however, in the realm of sailing—especially yachting—that Newport became internationally famous. By the late 19C several yachting clubs had been established in Newport, and from 1930 to 1983 the city hosted the celebrated **America's Cup** races. These races, an international competition among the most sophisticated sailing yachts in the world, date from 1851, when the New York Yacht Club sent the schooner *America* across the Atlantic to compete against the British for the prestigious Hundred Guinea Cup. The *America* won the race and returned home with the cup—actually an ornate silver pitcher thereafter known as the America's Cup. Held only 28 times since 1851 because of the tremendous expense involved, the race was won consistently by the US until 1983, when the trophy passed into the hands of Australia. An American victory in 1987 by the challenger *Stars and Stripes* once again brought the cup home to the US, where it remained until New Zealand's win in 1995. The next America's Cup race is scheduled for 2000 in New Zealand.
Newport is the starting point of the biennial 685mi **Newport-Bermuda Race** and the destination of the **Single-Handed Transatlantic Race** that begins at Plymouth, England.

Newport Today

Newport Music Festival – The Newport Music Festival is a 10-day series of musical programs presented in the mansions (Rosecliff, Beechwood, The Elms and The Breakers) during the month of July. The **Newport Jazz Festival**, a celebrated annual event in the music world, first took place in Newport in 1954. Moved to New York during the 1970s, the festival has since returned to Newport and is currently known as the **JVC Jazz Festival**. Performances are held at Fort Adams State Park, which is also the site of the **Ben & Jerry's Folk Festival**, held in mid-August.

Newport Architecture – Newport provides an architectural sampler of the nation's most aesthetically pleasing building styles from the 17C to the 19C. The city's large group of Colonial structures range from the simple and austere Quaker meetinghouse to Trinity Church, inspired by the work of Christopher Wren. They also include Georgian structures designed by **Peter Harrison**: the Redwood Library, the Touro Synagogue and the Brick Market. Approximately 60 restored dwellings stand in the Easton's Point and Historic Hill (in the vicinity of Trinity Church) sections of town. The sumptuous mansions on Bellevue Avenue and Ocean Drive are among the most impressive private residences in the US. The evolution in the style of these mansions begins with the eclecticism of the mid-19C Victorian period, as illustrated by Kingscote (1839) and Château-sur-Mer (1852). Displaying a splendor and magnificence never before expressed in American architecture, Marble House (1892), the Breakers (1895), The Elms (1901) and Rosecliff (1902) represent elaborate imitations of the chateaus of France and the palaces of Italy.

★★★THE MANSIONS *Map p 253*

The mansions can be visited by guided tour (1hr each) only. Combination tickets are available for two to eight houses. ☎ 401-847-1000. www.newportmansions.org.

A number of the mansions can be seen by driving along **Bellevue Avenue★★★** and **Ocean Drive★★** *(10mi)*. Ocean Drive follows the coast to the southern end of the island and at sunset offers beautiful **views**, especially from **Brenton Point State Park**. The **Cliff Walk★★** is a 3mi coastal path straddling the rocky shoreline that separates The Breakers, Rosecliff, Marble House and Salve Regina College from the sea. In the 19C, when fishermen protested against estate owners who attempted to close off the path, the state ruled in favor of the "toilers of the sea," and the walk has

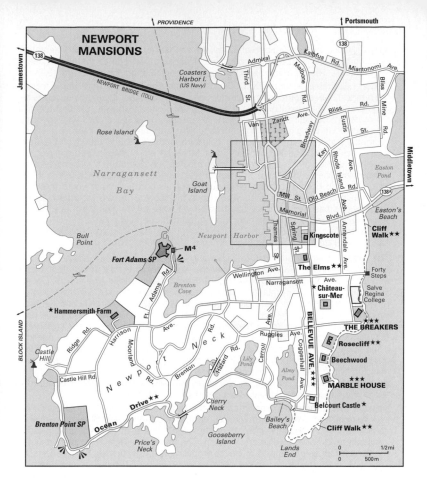

remained a public way ever since. Cliff Walk extends from Memorial Boulevard *(near Easton's Beach)* to Bailey's Beach *(private)*, with an additional access at the Forty Steps. *It is advisable to wear sturdy, rubber-soled shoes on this path, especially after a rainstorm.*

★★★ **The Breakers** – *Visit by guided tour (1hr) only, late Mar–Oct daily 10am–5pm (Jul & Aug Fri Sat 6pm). Nov weekends only 10am–4pm. Call for Dec hours. $12.* ⚅ 🅿 ☎ *401-847-1000.* In 1885 **Cornelius Vanderbilt II**, the grandson of the "Commodore," who had made his fortune in steamships and railroads, purchased the Ochre Point property and hired **Richard Morris Hunt** to design a summer residence on the site. Selecting a High Renaissance Italian palace as his model, Hunt created this opulent 70-room mansion, which was completed in 1895. The palatial design, with its elaborate use of French and Italian stone, marble and alabaster, reflected the Vanderbilts' great wealth. The exterior, heavily ornamented with arcades, columns and cornices, reveals the Italian influence. Within, the Breakers blends rich marbles and wooden trim with gilded plaster, mosaics and ceiling painting.

Interior – The **Great Hall**, more than two stories high, is a spectacular array of columns and pilasters, marble plaques and ornate cornices. In the Grand Salon (Music Room) the coffered ceiling bears a painting with figures representing Music, Harmony, Song and Melody. The **Morning Room** contains four corner panels painted in oil on silver leaf representing the Muses; the room looks out onto the loggia, where there is a beautiful Italian mosaic. Most impressive of all the rooms is the **Dining Room** where the Vanderbilts entertained their guests amid a setting of warm red alabaster, bronze and gilt. On the floor above lies Mrs. Vanderbilt's spacious oval bedroom, one of a series of rooms on this floor decorated by Ogden Codman.

★★★ **Marble House** – *Visit by guided tour (1hr) only, late Mar–Oct daily 10am–5pm (Jul & Aug Fri–Sat 6pm). Early Jan–mid-Mar weekends only 10am–4pm. Call for Dec hours. $9.* ⚅ 🅿 ☎ *401-847-1000.* A gracefully curved, balustraded drive leads to the columned facade of Marble House, one of several Newport mansions designed by **Richard Morris Hunt**. Built for millionaire yachtsman **William K. Vanderbilt**, Marble House is thought to have been inspired by the White House in Washington, DC, or by the Petit Trianon at Versailles. Among the most lavish dinner parties and balls held at

Marble House was the debut of Consuelo Vanderbilt, who, after the celebration, locked herself in her room to protest her upcoming marriage to the ninth Duke of Marlborough. The marriage nevertheless took place a short time later, in 1895.

Interior – Containing some 500,000cu ft of American, African and Italian marble, the interior is as elegant as the exterior suggests. Gobelins' tapestries decorate the huge entrance hall, which is faced with yellow Siena marble. In the **Gold Ballroom**, the most ornate ballroom in Newport, gilt panels, pilasters, arches and doorways are reflected in the glittering crystal chandeliers and mirrors that capture every ray of light. In striking contrast to the ballroom is the subdued mood of the **Gothic Room**, where the Vanderbilt collection of Medieval art objects was displayed. The elaborate use of pink Numidian marble creates the luxuriant atmosphere of the **Dining Room**. The bronze Louis XIV chairs, weighing about 70lbs each, made it necessary for the host to provide each guest with a footman, who would move the chair when the guest wished to sit or leave the table. The tour includes a visit to the spacious basement **kitchen**, boasting an elegance all its own with its 25ft-long stove, built-in iceboxes, and shiny monogrammed cookware.

The **Chinese Teahouse** *(open May–Oct)*, designed by Hunt's sons, contains 8ft wooden panels decorated with scenes inspired by a 15C Chinese court painter.

★★ **The Elms** – *Visit by guided tour (1hr) only, May–mid-Nov daily 10am–5pm. Late Nov–early Jan daily 10am–4pm. Rest of the year weekends only 10am–4pm. Closed Dec 24 & 25. $9.* 🅿 ✉ *401-847-1000.* Edward Julius Berwind, the son of German immigrants, rose to prominence in the second half of the 19C as the "king" of America's coal industry. His coalfields in Pennsylvania, West Virginia and Kentucky supplied most of the coal for the US and other nations. In 1899, wealthy and powerful, he commissioned **Horace Trumbauer** to build a residence to rival the cottages of Newport's established millionaires, who regarded him as a nouveau riche outsider. Inspired by the 18C Château d'Asnieres near Paris, Trumbauer created the Elms, a reserved and dignified country-style residence on the outside, a grandiose mansion within. The housewarming given by the Berwinds in August 1901 was the social highlight of the season; countless varieties of exotic plants were used to adorn the house, and monkeys scampered about the grounds.

Interior – The large-scale proportions of the rooms, especially of the entrance hall and **ballroom**, are awesome. In the ballroom, smoothly curved corners, restrained decoration, and an abundance of natural light create an inviting and pleasant atmosphere, despite the size of the room. The French Classical style predominates: the **Conservatory** was intended to house tropical flora, the **Drawing Room** reflects the Louis XVI style, the stucco reliefs and fine woodwork of the ballroom suggest the earlier style of Louis XV. The four black and gold lacquer panels ornamenting the **Breakfast Room** date from China's K'ang-hsi period (17C).

★★ **Rosecliff** – *Visit by guided tour (1hr) only, late Mar–Oct daily 10am–5pm. $9.* ♿ 🅿 ✉ *401-847-1000.* In 1891 **Mrs. Hermann Oelrichs**, the daughter of a wealthy Irish immigrant who had discovered the Comstock Lode in Nevada, and her husband moved to Newport. They purchased the Rosecliff estate, named for its many rosebeds and, finding the house on the property too modest for their taste, engaged **Stanford White** to design a more elaborate residence. The result was a graceful imitation of the Grand Trianon at Versailles.

Mrs. Oelrichs was one of society's most celebrated hostesses. Among the most spectacular events ever held in Newport were the official opening of Rosecliff in 1902; Mrs. Oelrichs' famous Bal Blanc, where everyone was required to wear white; and the "Mother Goose" Ball, where guests dressed as fairy tale characters. The off-white, glazed terra-cotta exterior walls are finished to imitate stone. Inside the mansion, a heart-shaped staircase leads upstairs to the sleeping quarters. Designed primarily for entertaining, Rosecliff boasts the largest **ballroom** (80ft by 40ft) in Newport. Windows open onto the terraces, allowing the outdoors to become an extension of the ballroom. Scenes from *The Great Gatsby* (1974) were filmed here.

★ **Château-sur-Mer** – *Visit by guided tour (1hr) only, late Mar–Sept daily 10am–5pm. Late Nov–early Jan daily 10am–4pm. Rest of the year weekends only 10am–4pm. $9.* 🅿 ✉ *401-847-1000.* In 1877 Château-sur-Mer was considered the most "substantial and expensive residence in Newport." Constructed in the Second Empire style, this "Castle by the Sea," with its massive asymmetrical silhouette, was built in 1852 for **William S. Wetmore**, who earned his wealth in the China trade. Extremely spacious and luxurious for its day, Château-sur-Mer was later enlarged in 1872 **by Richard Morris Hunt**.

Interior – Several interesting decorative effects have been created. Light streams into the elaborately carved entrance hall through a colored-glass ceiling panel 45ft above its floor; the ballroom is embellished with decorative stucco moldings and trim fashioned to resemble wood. Illuminated by stained-glass windows, the stairwell is lined with canvas painted to resemble tapestries. In the Turkish sitting room, the blend of Oriental, European and American design elements and furnishings creates a style that is distinctly Victorian in character. The library and dining room were decorated in the Renaissance style by the Florentine artist Luigi Frullini.

Rosecliff Ballroom

★**Belcourt Castle** – *Visit by guided tour (1hr) only, late-May–mid-Oct Mon–Sat 9am–5pm, Sun 10am–5pm. Rest of the year Mon–Sat 10am–4pm, Sun 10am–4pm. Call for Jan hours. Closed Thanksgiving Day, Dec 25. $8.* 🅿 ☏ *401-846-0669.* Richard Morris Hunt chose one of Louis XIII's hunting lodges as the model for this castle (1896) designed for the 35-year-old bachelor **Oliver Hazard Perry Belmont**. In 1898, Belmont married Alva Smith Vanderbilt, formerly the wife of William K. Vanderbilt. The castle, owned since 1959 by the Tinney family, contains an outstanding collection of European furnishings.

The interior is inspired by different periods of French, Italian and English design. Decorated with plush red upholsteries and stained-glass windows, the vast **Banquet Hall** can comfortably accommodate 250 dinner guests. A huge crystal chandelier, which formerly graced a Russian palace, dominates the room.

From the oval Family Dining Room on the second floor there is a view out to the ocean. The spacious **French Gothic Ballroom**, also on this floor, contains stained-glass windows (13C), Oriental carpets, tapestries, distended vaults and the enormous castle-shaped fireplace.

★**Hammersmith Farm** – *Visit by guided tour (40min) only, Apr–early Nov, daily 10am–5pm. Late Nov–mid-Dec weekends only 10am–4pm. $8.50.* 🅿 ☏ *401-846-7346. www.hammersmithfarm.com.* This estate was formerly owned by **Mrs. Hugh Auchincloss**, whose daughter Jacqueline married John F. Kennedy here in 1953. The Kennedys returned to Hammersmith on numerous occasions after their wedding; following John Kennedy's election as president of the US, the farm served on occasion as the summer White House.

The mansion (1887) takes its name from the farm that has operated on the property since 1640. The modest exterior, covered uniformly with wooden shingles, exemplifies the Shingle style that was popular during the last several decades of the 19C. The bayside setting, enhanced with gardens designed by **Frederick Law Olmsted**, is especially scenic.

The interior is simple, yet comfortably furnished. Highlights of the tour include Hammersmith's many mementos relating to the years Jacqueline spent here, first as a young girl, then with her husband and children.

Kingscote – *Visit by guided tour (1hr) only, May–Sept daily 10am–5pm. Oct & late Mar–Apr weekends only 10am–5pm. $9.* 🅿 ☏ *401-847-1000.* Designed in 1839 by **Richard Upjohn**, Kingscote was one of the earliest examples of a new trend in American architecture: the adaptation of Gothic Revival motifs and effects to private residences. Kingscote's irregular shape, expressed in wood rather than stone, and emphasized by gables, arches, eaves and varied rooflines, form a striking contrast to the symmetrical, solid shape of earlier dwellings.

This mansion was built for the southern planter **George Noble Jones**, then sold in the 1860s to **William H. King** after whom it (King's Cottage) was named.

The Victorian interior contains Tiffany windows, heavy furniture and somber rooms. Among the furnishings is a prized collection of Oriental paintings, rugs, porcelain and furniture attributed to Newport cabinetmakers Goddard and Townsend.

Beechwood – *580 Bellevue Ave. Open mid-May–early Nov daily 10am–5pm. Feb–early May Thu–Sun only 10am–4pm. $8.75.* 🅿 ☏ *401-846-3772. www. astors-beechwood.com.* A tour of this Mediterranean-style villa, acquired in 1880 by **William** and **Caroline Astor**, is unlike that offered by its palatial neighbors. From the moment visitors are greeted at the door by the "butler," they are transported back to the 1890s by "servants" and "house guests" (portrayed by members of a theater group) who accompany callers throughout the house.

Named for the beech trees on the grounds, Beechwood was originally built by Andrew Jackson Downing for the merchant Daniel Parrish. Destroyed by fire in 1855, the mansion was rebuilt by Calvert Vaux for Parrish, and was later redecorated and refurnished by the Astors. The ballroom added at that time by Richard Morris Hunt was the largest in Newport when it was completed. Beechwood is famous as the home of Caroline Astor—*the* Mrs. Astor as she insisted upon being called—whose husband was the grandson of John Jacob Astor. Mrs. Astor, the grande dame of New York as well as Newport society, compiled the list of society's elite "400," the number of persons her ballroom could accommodate.

A copy of Duran's portrait of Caroline Astor hangs in the entrance hall. Among the public rooms on the main floor is the light-filled **ballroom**, ornamented with gesso relief, and containing more than 800 mirrors.

On the floor above, Mrs. Astor's Victorian bedroom overlooks the ocean. She is reputed to have ordered the window that formerly looked out on Rosecliff sealed off, after she learned that Rosecliff's ballroom was larger than Beechwood's.

★★COLONIAL NEWPORT *4hrs. Map below.*

Newport's extraordinarily large group of Colonial structures constitutes one of the nation's great architectural treasures. The itinerary below represents a selection of these dwellings and public buildings.

From the Gateway Visitors Center, head south on America's Cup Ave. and turn left on Marlborough St. Turn right on Thames St. and walk one block south to the Brick Market.

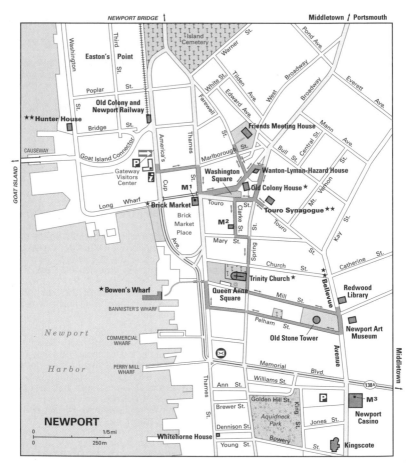

★**Brick Market** – *127 Thames St.* Designed in 1762 by **Peter Harrison**, this handsome three-story building with its arcaded base and massive pilasters above provides a fine example of the Palladian style's influence on Georgian architecture. The market was the commercial center of Newport; open market stalls were located on the ground floor, while the upper floors were reserved for offices and storage.

Today two floors are occupied by the **Museum of Newport History (M¹)**, which includes displays on Newport's early colonial life, maritime commerce and naval history *(open Apr–Dec Mon, Wed–Sat 10am–5pm, Sun 1pm–5pm; rest of the year Fri, Sat 11am–4pm, Sun 1pm–4pm; $5; ▣ ☎ 401-846-0813)*.

Washington Square – Adjoining Brick Market Place, Washington Square was the crossroads of colonial Newport. At one end of the square stood the Old Colony House, at the other end was the marketplace. The homes, shops and warehouses of Newport's merchants were clustered nearby.

★**Old Colony House** – *Washington Square. Visit by guided tour (30) only. Jun–Sept Thu–Sat 10am–4pm. $3. ☎ 401-846-0813.* This building, designed by **Richard Munday**, was the seat of Rhode Island's government from the colonial period through the early 19C. In 1781 General Washington and Count Rochambeau, the leader of the French troops, met here to discuss plans for the battle of Yorktown. Furniture made by Goddard and Townsend, and one of Gilbert Stuart's full-length portraits of George Washington decorate the interior.

Turn left on Farewell St. and continue to Marlborough St.

Friends Meeting House – *Marlborough St. Open by appointment only, one week advance reservations required. $3. ☎ 401-846-0813.* By the end of the 17C, Newport supported a large population of Quakers. This meetinghouse, constructed by the Society of Friends in 1699 and enlarged as the society grew, was the regional center for New England's Quakers. The building is architecturally interesting for its pulley-operated walls, large stone supports, which prevent the lower floor from resting directly on the ground, and remarkable vault.

Walk back to Broadway and turn left.

Wanton-Lyman-Hazard House – *17 Broadway. Closed until mid-2000 for renovation. Otherwise call for hours. ☎ 401-846-0813.* Prior to the Revolution, this house was the residence of Martin Howard, a tax collector whose official duties made him an unpopular person in town. During the Stamp Act riots, while the patriots ransacked his house, Howard fled Newport. Considering himself fortunate to have escaped, he eventually settled in England, never to see Newport again.

Walk around the house to Spring St. Turn right and follow Spring St. to Touro St. Turn left onto Touro St.

★★**Touro Synagogue** – *85 Touro St. Visit by guided tour (25min) only. Jul–Labor Day Sun–Fri 10am–5pm. Rest of the year Mon–Fri 1pm–3pm, Sun 11am–3pm. ☎ 401-847-4794. Closed Jewish holidays. www.tourosynagogue.org.* The earliest members of Newport's Jewish community arrived from the Carribean in 1658. However, it was not until a century later (1759), under the guidance of their leader, Isaac de Touro, that a synagogue—one of the earliest constructed in the US—was built, and dedicated in 1763.

The building, designed by architect **Peter Harrison**, successfully adapts the Georgian style to Sephardic Jewish tradition. Situated on a quiet street and set on a diagonal with the east wall facing the direction of Jerusalem, the exterior of the synagogue is almost stark in appearance. The interior is richly adorned with hand-carved paneling, balustrades and columns. Twelve columns support the galleries, and twelve columns support the ceiling, symbolizing the twelve tribes of Israel. The Scrolls of the Law, the Torah, are preciously guarded in the Holy Ark.

Cross Spring St. to Clarke St. and turn left.

Armory of the Artillery Company of Newport (M²) – *23 Clarke St. Open Jun–Oct Sat only 10am–4pm. Rest of the year by appointment only. $3. ♿ ☎ 401-846-8488.* The Newport Artillery Co. participated in every major American military campaign from the colonial period through World War I. This granite-walled Greek Revival building, constructed in 1836 as the company's armory, now houses American and foreign military weapons, uniforms and flags, as well as personal mementos of well-known military figures.

At the end of Clarke St., turn left on Mary St. and right onto Spring St.

★**Trinity Church** – *Queen Anne Sq. Open Jul–Aug daily 10am–4pm. Rest of the year call for hours. $2 contribution suggested. ♿ ☎ 401-846-0660. www.trinitynewport. org.* This white clapboard church (1726) rising above **Queen Anne Square** was designed by Richard Munday and is contemporary with Boston's Old North Church *(p 133)*. Both were influenced by the designs of Christopher Wren. Trinity's arcaded belfry, surmounted by a tall Colonial spire, is a distinct landmark. Inside, the original three-tiered pulpit remains the only one of its kind in the country. The left wall of the nave features two stained-glass windows by Tiffany, one of which commemorates Cornelius Vanderbilt; the face is said to be that of Vanderbilt himself.

The Colonial dwellings bordering the square were moved to this location by the **Newport Restoration Foundation**, an organization established in 1968 to preserve Newport's early architecture.

Continue south on Spring St. and turn left on Mill St.

Old Stone Tower – Nicknamed the Mystery Tower because of the various legends surrounding its origin, this stone structure has been attributed to the Vikings, the Portuguese, the Indians and the Irish. Less romantic, but perhaps a bit more realistic, is the theory that the tower is the remnant of a 17C mill.

Continue east on Mill St. and turn left on Bellevue Ave.

Redwood Library – *50 Bellevue Ave.* Architect **Peter Harrison** selected a Roman temple as his inspiration for the library, his first important architectural achievement. The building's classical design, which includes a columned entranceway, seems out of proportion to its modest size, and the wooden exterior, painted and sanded to imitate stone, appears artificial. Yet in its day, the library—the first structure in the US to employ a freestanding portico—illustrated an impressive innovation in American architecture.

Newport Art Museum – *76 Bellevue Ave. Open Jun–mid-Oct Mon–Sat 10am–5pm, Sun noon–5pm. Rest of the year Mon–Sat 10am–4pm, Sun noon–4pm. Closed Jan 1, Jul 4, Thanksgiving Day, Dec 25. $4. ⬤ ⬛ ☎ 401-848-8200.* Designed by **Richard Morris Hunt**, the Griswold House provides an example of Stick-style architecture: sticks expressing the framing elements are used as exterior decoration. The house is reserved for changing exhibits. The adjacent building, Cushing Memorial Gallery, houses the museum's collection of American art, mainly 19C oil paintings, including works by Winslow Homer, George Inness, Fitz Hugh Lane and William Trost Richards.

Continue on Bellevue Ave. Turn right on Pelham St., which is lined with Colonial dwellings. Turn right on Thames St., then left on Mill St. to the waterfront.

★**Bowen's Wharf** – Salty old dockside structures have been transformed into indoor and outdoor eateries. Along with neighboring craft shops and boutiques, they form the heart of this waterfront square.

ADDITIONAL SIGHTS *Map p 256*

★★**Hunter House** – *54 Washington St. Visit by guided tour (1hr) only, May–Sept daily 10am–5pm. Late Mar–Apr & Oct weekends only 10am–5pm. $9. Combination ticket available for public historic homes (p 252). ☎ 401-847-1000.* This elegant dwelling, built in 1748 by a prosperous merchant, was purchased by ambassador William Hunter and subsequently served as the home of two governors and as the headquarters of Adm. Charles de Ternay, commander of the French fleet during the Revolution.

The house is a beautiful example of the 18C Colonial style. The carved pineapple ornamenting the doorway is a symbol of hospitality that originated during the

colonial period when a sea captain, returning home from a voyage, placed a pineapple outside his home to announce his safe arrival and to invite everyone to share the refreshments that were waiting inside. The interior contains an exceptional collection of **Goddard and Townsend** furniture and skillfully carved woodwork.

Easton's Point – Most of the restored homes in this quiet residential neighborhood date from the 18C, when the point prospered as a mercantile community. Quakers, who lived in the area, named the streets after trees or numbered them to avoid "manworship." Washington Street was later renamed for George Washington.

Preservation Society of Newport County

Hunter House

Old Colony and Newport Railway – 📷 *Departs from depot at 19 A[...]*
Ave. Jul–early Sept Tue–Thu & Sat 11am, 12:35pm, 2:05pm
1hr 10min), Sun 12:35pm (round-trip 3hrs). May–late Jun & mid-Sep[...]
weekends only. Late Oct–mid-Nov Sun only. $5.50–$10. Old Colony & [...]
Railway ☎ 401-624-6951. Chartered in the 19C, the railway experienc[...]
busiest year in 1913 when 24 trains daily, including the Boston "Dandy Expr[...]
arrived and departed from Newport.
Today the railway operates along the eastern shore of Narragansett Bay betwee[...]
Newport and Portsmouth. Round-trip excursions from Newport *(3hrs)* stop at the
Navy base, the Bend Boat Basin at Melville, and Portsmouth. At Portsmouth a
stopover *(1hr)* allows passengers to visit the Green Animals *(see Excursions below).*

Samuel Whitehorne House – *416 Thames St. Visit by guided tour (1hr) only,*
May–Oct Mon, Thu–Fri 11am–4pm, weekends 10am–4pm or by advance appoint-
ment. $8. ☎ 401-847-2448. The four-square brick Federal dwelling, topped by a
square cupola, was built (1811) for Samuel Whitehorne Sr., a sea captain. Later
subdivided into apartments, the building eventually deteriorated until the Newport
Restoration Foundation acquired and restored it. The interior is refurbished with
a **collection of 18C furniture★**, many pieces of which were crafted in the workshops
of Goddard and Townsend.

Newport Casino – *194 Bellevue Ave.* Facing Bellevue Avenue, this complex with
its ground-floor shops gives the impression of a commercial block. The casino was
the most exclusive country club in the East when it was built in 1880, during the
height of Newport's "gilded age." Pass through the deeply arched entranceway to
discover the casino's tennis courts and the Shingle-style buildings designed by
McKim, Mead and White. The casino's grass courts hosted the first Men's US Lawn
Tennis Assn. tournament (now the US Open) in 1881, which later moved to Forest
Hills, New York. Tournaments are still held here in July.

International Tennis Hall of Fame (M³) – *In the casino. Open year-round daily*
9:30am–5pm. $8. Closed Thanksgiving Day, Dec 25. ☎ 401-849-3990. www.
tennisfame.org. Exhibits of tennis memorabilia, one of the largest collections in the
country, focus on the history of the sport. Among the artifacts on display is the
sterling silver punch bowl awarded to Bostonian Richard Sears, the first US men's
singles champion in lawn tennis.

Fort Adams State Park – *Map p 253. Fort Adams Rd., off Harrison Ave. Park*
open year-round daily dawn–dusk. The fort is open by guided tour (45) only,
Jun–Sept daily 10am, 1pm & 3pm; $5. ♿ 🅿 ☎ *401-847-2400.* Fort Adams, its
walls constructed of granite hauled from Maine by schooner, was originally built
to guard the entrance to Narragansett Bay. The fort ultimately developed into the
command post for the coastal batteries in the Northeast; until 1945 it was the
center of a system of defenses to protect the bay and Long Island Sound.
Today the fort is a state park where the JVC Jazz Festival is held each summer.
From the park's roadways there is a sweeping **view★★** of the harbor, Newport
Bridge and Newport, including the downtown area.
The small, two-story **Museum of Yachting (M⁴)** 📷 houses classic small craft and displays on Newport yachting history. Videos focusing on 12-meter yachts are shown
continuously and the museum's two-time America's Cup winner *Courageous* is
moored offshore *(no boarding permitted). Open mid-May–early Oct daily 10am–5pm;*
rest of the year by appointment; $4; 🅿 ☎ *401-847-1018; www.moy.org.*

EXCURSIONS

Jamestown – *3mi west of Newport via Newport Bridge (toll). On Conanicut Island
in Narragansett Bay.* At the island's center, on North Road, is the 1787 **Jamestown
Windmill** *(open mid-Jun–Labor Day weekends 1pm–4pm; contribution requested).*
From **Beaver Tail Lighthouse** *(at the end of Beaver Tail Rd.)* there is a view along the
south shore. An expansive vista across the bay to Newport can be admired from
Fort Wetherill *(off of Rte. 138 and Walcott Ave.).* The fort's ramparts are built on
granite cliffs that rise up to 100ft. The shores of picturesque **Mackerel Cove** are
flecked with summer homes.

★ **Watson Farm** – 📷 *455 North Rd. Open Jun–mid-Oct Tue, Thu, Sun 1pm–5pm. $3.*
🅿 ☎ *401-423-0005. www.spnea.org.* Job Watson purchased this farm in 1789;
it was operated by five successive generations of his family until 1979. Still a
working farm, devoted to sheep and beef cattle, the property comprises some
230 acres of barnyard, hay fields, orchards and meadows. The site affords sublime
views★ of Narragansett Bay.

Middletown – *North of Newport by Memorial Blvd.* This small community is a
blend of long sandy beaches and rural countryside.

Whitehall Museum House – *311 Berkeley Ave. From Memorial Blvd., take Aquidneck
Ave. to Green End Ave. Travel east to Berkeley Ave. and follow signs to the house.
Open Jul–Aug Tue–Sun 10am–5pm. Rest of the year by appointment only. $3.* 🅿

This red clapboard Georgian-period farmhouse was built in bishop and philosopher George Berkeley, who hoped the farm school he planned to establish in Bermuda. When his plans failed, ...ed to Ireland in 1731 and deeded the farm to Yale University; the ... of America took it over in 1902. The interior contains furnishings ... of Berkeley's residence.

– **Kids** *2009 W. Main Rd. (Rte. 114). Open Apr–Nov Mon–Sat ... $2.* ☎ *401-847-6230.* This pastoral setting features an herb garden ... assemblage of historic buildings (some moved here from other locations), including British general Richard Prescott's guardhouse (c.1730), a 19C wood-shingled windmill still used to grind cornmeal and a former ferry master's dwelling (c.1715), which now houses a country store.

Portsmouth – *North of Newport by Rte. 114.* Settlers from Portsmouth moved south and founded Newport in 1639. Today this hilly township is a popular summer resort.

★ **Green Animals Topiary Gardens** – **Kids** *From Rte. 114, turn left onto Cory's Lane. Open May–Oct daily 10am–5pm. $9. Combination ticket available for public historic homes.* ▣ ☎ *401-847-1000.* Colorful flower beds punctuate this group of 80 tree and shrub sculptures, which includes representations of a giraffe, a lion and an elephant. The country house features a toy museum, dolls and dollhouses.

PAWTUCKET

Population 72,644
Map of Principal Sights
Tourist Office ☎ 401-724-2200

This bustling city just north of Providence gave birth to the Industrial Revolution in America. It was here, at the falls of Blackstone River in 1793, that the **Slater Mill**, the first US water-powered textile mill to successfully produce cotton yarn, was built.

Historical Notes – Construction of the mill resulted from an association between **Samuel Slater**, who had been employed in a textile factory in England, and **Moses Brown**, a wealthy Providence Quaker. Combining their resources—Slater's technical knowledge and the Brown family capital—the two men laid the groundwork for the transition from manual to machine production. The mill they built pioneered the way for this change, as well as for the growth of the textile industry throughout New England.

Several years later, in 1810, another factory, the Wilkinson Mill, specializing in the production of machine parts and tools, was built nearby. The two factories and a dwelling of the same period have been restored, forming a part of the 5-acre Slater Mill Historic Site devoted to the origins of the industrial age in America.

Slater Mill

Fred Sieb Photography

VISIT

★Slater Mill Historic Site – 🔲 *From I-95 south take Exit 29 (downtown Pawtucket); proceed straight ahead onto Broadway, cross Main St. Bridge, then turn right on Roosevelt Ave. Open Jun–Nov Mon–Sat 10am–5pm, Sun 1pm–5pm. Mid-Dec–May Sat 10:30am–5pm, Sun 1pm–5pm. Christmas week open daily 1pm–5pm. Closed major holidays. $6.50.* ♿ ☎ *401-725-8638.*

Slater Mill – Here operating textile equipment (including a carding device, spinning frame and mule, power looms, and knitting and braiding machines) demonstrates the processes involved in transforming cotton from raw fiber to finished goods.

Wilkinson Mill – This mill contains a 19C machine shop with belt-driven machine tools: a jigsaw, lathes, drill pressers, planers and shapers. An eight-ton breast wheel has been reconstructed in the basement. Water from the Blackstone River is admitted to the wheel through restored raceways; the wheel drives the machine tools on the floor above. The mill originally housed a machine shop where textile machinery was built and repaired. Cotton and woolen thread were produced on the floor above.

Sylvanus Brown House – Furnished as it was in the early 1800s, this dwelling (1758) was the home of a millwright and pattern-maker. Demonstrations of hand spinning and weaving illustrate the tasks performed by household members.

PROVIDENCE★★

Population 160,728
Map of Principal Sights
Tourist Office ☎ 401-274-1636

The capital of Rhode Island, a center of business and industry, and the third largest city in New England, Providence occupies the hub of a metropolitan region that has more than 900,000 inhabitants.

The city's location on a natural harbor at the head of Narragansett Bay offered special advantages for the shipping and commercial activity that allowed Providence to prosper and expand. A result of this expansion was the development of the College Hill district with its lovely 18C and 19C structures. Today this tree-shaded residential neighborhood is the home of Brown University and the Rhode Island School of Design. Across the city from College Hill, the majestic capitol building rises above the growing business area below.

> **① Fine Dining in Federal Hill**
> You're in the area known as Federal Hill when you pass under the huge *pigna* (pine cone), the Italian symbol for abundance that graces the arch spanning the eastern end of **Atwells Avenue**, located west of Empire Street. Never mind that some locals claim it's a pineapple or even an artichoke. Atwells is *the* street for Italian food, no matter what your budget. Newcomers **Mediterraneo** *(no. 134)* and the Eclectic Grill *(no. 245)* draw younger crowds with their arty decor, alfresco seating and nouveau cuisine, while the formal **Blue Grotto** *(no. 210)* and **L'Epicureo** *(no. 238)* have become traditions among Providence's upper crust for exquisitely prepared Old World food and impeccable service. A nice middle ground is struct by **Camille's Roman Garden** *(71 Bradford St.),* where the food is always superb and white-linen ambience is offset by friendly waiters. Have your after dinner espresso at **Caffe Dolce Vita** *(59 De Pasquale Plaza)* along with luscious tiramisu, zuppa inglese or sweet-and-tangy gelato.

Historical Notes

Providence Plantations – After **Roger Williams** was banished from his pastorate in Salem, Massachusetts, he traveled south with a group of his followers until they arrived on the banks of the Moshassuck (later the Providence) River in June 1636. Having decided to settle here, they bought land from the Narragansett Indians and named it Providence, in honor of the divine Providence that they believed had led them to this place. Williams declared that the new colony would be a safe and sure refuge for all persons seeking freedom of worship.

In 1644 he journeyed to England to obtain a charter for Providence and the Rhode Island (Newport) colony. The charter united the two colonies but was declared void in 1660 following the restoration of the monarchy to the throne. Three years later, Charles II issued a royal charter granting "full liberty in religious concernments" to all Rhode Island inhabitants.

The Development of Providence – Originally a farming settlement, Providence rapidly developed into a commercial center as its inhabitants turned to shipping and trade. By the mid-18C Providence vessels were engaged in the triangular trade, and in 1772, when the British parliament passed legislation that threatened to limit American shipping, citizens were quick to react. One evening in June, they forced the British revenue schooner *Gaspee* aground at Warwick, burned the vessel and captured its crew. Despite a generous reward offered by the Crown, the culprits were never captured. Strongly defended as the "backdoor to Boston" during the Revolution, Providence prospered as a privateering and supply depot. Following the war, the city emerged as Rhode Island's leading port. In 1787 Providence resident **John Brown** *(below)* sent his first ship to China. Other merchants followed his lead and amassed great fortunes in the China trade.

As maritime trade declined, capital investment shifted toward industry. Providence developed into a center for the manufacture of textiles, tools, files and steam engines, attracting thousands of immigrants to work at its many factories. The city underwent an economic crisis after World War II, when a number of factories moved to the South. Today Providence again enjoys an active business life as a manufacturer of a variety of products, including jewelry and silverware. The city is becoming recognized for its urban revitalization in recent years, notably terraced **Waterplace Park★**, site of summer concerts, near Exchange Street. Downtown features the landmark Art Deco **Fleet Building** *(Fulton St.)* and the 1828 Arcade *(below)*. Completed in 1999 and located near the State House, block-long Providence Place Mall dominates the downtown, offering the latest in big brand-name and local retail stores as well as myriad eateries and entertainment venues. The famed **Trinity Repertory Company** holds performances from September through June *(Lederer Theater, 201 Washington St., ☎ 401-351-4242; www.trinityrep.com)*. Summer and early fall herald multiple stagings of the popular public art event **WaterFire**, wherein fires, accompanied by music, are lit after dark in iron baskets placed in and along the river fronting Waterplace Park and Riverwalk *(for schedule ☎ 401-272-3111)*.

■ The Brown Brothers

The Brown name, closely associated with the industrial, cultural, political and commercial growth of Providence, identifies one of the city's oldest and most illustrious families. At the end of the 18C, the four Brown brothers were prominent among the leaders of Providence. Bold and adventurous, **John**, a leader of the attack on the *Gaspee*, was a prosperous merchant. His was the first ship from Providence to reach China. **Joseph**, an architect, designed the Market House, the First Baptist Church and the John Brown House, among other buildings. **Moses**, a prosperous Quaker who established the Providence Bank, was the first to finance the development of the textile industry in the US at Pawtucket. Finally, there was **Nicholas**, a successful businessman whose mercantile enterprise was internationally known.

★★**COLLEGE HILL** *4hrs. Map p 263.*

In the early 18C the city's main thoroughfare—present-day **North** and **South Main Street**—bordered the waterfront and was crowded with warehouses, wharves and shops. To relieve the congestion, a dirt path running along the crest of the hill that rose behind the main street was widened for the "common benefit of all," thus creating Benefit Street. Wealthy merchants built their homes on Benefit Street, high above the waterfront, and by the beginning of the 19C the hill had developed into a fashionable residential enclave. Chosen as the site of Rhode Island College (now Brown University) in 1770, the district came to be known as College Hill.

This area's charming, tree-shaded streets, lined with architecture ranging from Colonial to Italianate, represents one of the most beautifully preserved historic districts in the nation. High on the hill sits **Thayer Street**, the shopping center of the university community, with its bookstores, coffee houses, restaurants and many stores. Former warehouses and shops below the hill on South Main Street have been converted into boutiques and restaurants, adding to the aura of the past that pervades this section of the city.

Walking Tour

From the intersection of College and Main St., continue north on Main St.

Market House – *4 S. Main St.* This was the commercial center of early Providence. Because of the building's location beside the river, boats could easily load and unload their cargoes here. Market House now belongs to the Rhode Island School of Design.

Continue on Main St. past Waterman St.

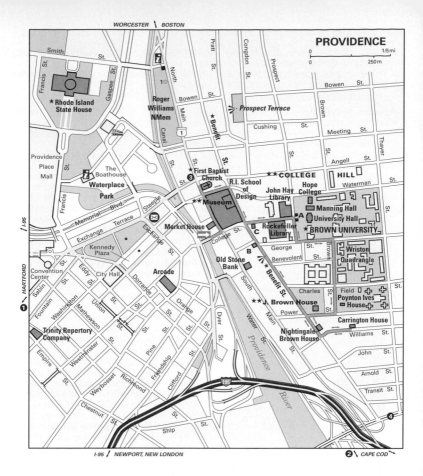

PROVIDENCE

*First Baptist Church in America – *75 N. Main St. Open year-round Mon–Fri 10am–noon & 1pm–3pm, Sat 10am–noon. Sunday tour at 12:15pm. Closed major holidays. Contribution suggested. & ☎ 401-454-3418.* The Baptist Church, founded by Roger Williams, dates back to 1638. The first house of worship built by the Baptists in America stood on North Main Street, a short distance from the present site of the wooden clapboard church (1775) designed by Joseph Brown. The handsome steeple rises 185ft. Inside, the paneling, scrolled pediments, lighted urns and arches are painted in soft tones of green and white. Enormous columns support the galleries and roof, leading the eye upward to the carved ceiling.

Return to Waterman St. and turn left. After one block, turn right on Benefit St.

*Benefit Street – At Benefit Street, pause to admire the graceful profile of the restored dwellings to the right and to the left. More than 100 homes, ranging from Colonial to Victorian in style, line the narrow streets and brick walks leading to the Rhode Island School of Design and to Brown University.

Rhode Island School of Design – Established in the 19C to train artisans for industry, RISD (RIZ-dee) is renowned as a teaching institution for design, architecture and the visual arts. Facilities available to the school's 1,990 students include sculpture, wood and metal labs; apparel design studios; and textile workshops.

RISD Museum – *224 Benefit St. Open year-round Tue–Sun 10am–5pm (Fri 8pm). Closed Jan 1, Thanksgiving Day, Dec 25. $5. & ☎ 401-454-6500. www.risd.edu.* The museum presents, in an engaging manner, collections of art from various periods and civilizations: Egyptian, Greek, Roman, Asian, European, African and American. Many exhibits are arranged in chronological order, but they often cross period boundaries to illustrate common trends in contemporary sculpture, painting and textiles. The fourth level *(entrance)* is devoted to Medieval carvings, 19C American and French paintings, and Greek bronzes. On the fifth level is Oriental, Eastern, aboriginal and Egyptian art. The **Dainichi Buddha (10C Japan), a wooden temple figure discovered in 1933 in the attic of a farmhouse, dominates one of the galleries. Adjoining the museum is **Pendleton House**, built in 1904 to display the **Charles Pendleton collection** of 18C American furnishings and decorative arts, the highlight of the museum. The elegant interior with its rich mahogany woodwork features a large central hall and several luxurious rooms.

Constructed in 1993, the three-level Daphne Farago Wing features changing exhibits of Contemporary art in all media.

In the museum courtyard there are several contemporary sculptures, including works by George Rickey and Clement Meadmore.

Turn left on College St.

★**Brown University** – The seventh college established in the US (1764), this Ivy League school was founded at Warren as Rhode Island College and renamed in 1804 for its principal benefactor, Nicholas Brown II. The university is known for its liberal education philosophy, implemented in 1969.

Approximately 5,600 undergraduate and 1,700 graduate students are enrolled at Brown's 145-acre College Hill campus, which consists of some 245 buildings: large halls housing classrooms and administrative offices, student and faculty residences, libraries, and a sports complex that includes a 20,400-seat football stadium. The five university libraries contain more than 4.7 million volumes and related items, including distinguished collections of material printed prior to 1500 and sources related to colonial America. Pembroke College (1891), founded by the university as a separate school for women, merged with Brown in 1971.

At the main entrance to the university, on Prospect Street, are the **Van Wickle Gates** (**A**), which are opened twice a year: inward on the first day of classes for freshmen, and outward on commencement day. From within the gates *(note campus map table to the left)*, Brown's oldest buildings are visible: **University Hall** (1771), a stately brick building known as the College Edifice, was the sole university structure until 1822; the building with the four granite columns is **Manning Hall** (1835), a Greek Revival structure that houses the University chapel; and **Hope College** (1822), which serves as a dormitory. On the west side of Prospect Street, opposite the gates, are the **John Hay Library** (1910) and the **Rockefeller Library** (1964). The "Rock" houses the university's general collection in the humanities and social sciences.

Continue south one block on Prospect St. and turn left on George St. After one block, turn right on Brown St.

On Brown Street you will pass **Wriston Quadrangle** (1952), the campus residence of approximately 1,000 students.

Continue south on Brown St. to Power St.

Power Street – At the corner of Brown and Power Streets stands **Poynton Ives House** (*no. 66*), a classic example of Federal architecture.

★★**John Brown House** – *52 Power St. Visit by guided tour (50min) only, Mar–Dec Tue–Sat 10am–5pm, Sun noon–4pm. Rest of the year by appointment Mon–Fri. $6.* ☎ *401-331-8575.* The three-story brick mansion (1788), designed for John Brown by his brother Joseph, impressed many who came to see it. John Quincy Adams, who visited the house, proclaimed it to be "the most magnificent and elegant private mansion that I have ever seen on this continent." Inside, the carved doorways, columns,

2 Al Forno

57 S. Main St. ☎ *401-273-9760.* The former city stables house this popular wisteria-covered restaurant, which faces the river. Downstairs and upstairs dining rooms serve house classics: clams Al Forno, roasted asparagus under a blanket with reggiano parmigiano, and grilled pork chops with roasted celery root. Squid, salmon, catfish, wood-grilled sausage and lamb steaks are other inviting menu items. Made-to-order desserts must be requested ahead of time: try the Baby Baci with cinnamon ice cream for a sweet you'll never forget.

3 New Rivers

7 Steeple St. ☎ *401-751-0350.* The highly favored American bistro has a steady clientele of discerning diners, who nightly enjoy the intimate rooms and upscale ambience of this small restaurant. In addition to à la carte choices, an affordable prix-fixe dinner is offered. Try the peanut soup for starters, then grilled quail with artichokes and sweet potatoes, and end with the pineapple truffle. A brimming bread basket, with olive paté or some other delicacy, accompanies the meal.

fireplaces, cornices, highly polished natural wood trim, and lavish plaster ornamented ceilings provide an appropriate setting for the treasured collection of Rhode Island furnishings, most of which are Brown family pieces. The unique **blockfront secretary** boasts nine shells carved into its front (shell secretaries normally have only six carved shells). Attributed to Rhode Island cabinetmaker John Goddard, this piece is one of the finest existing examples of American Colonial furniture.

Continue west on Power St. and turn left on Benefit St.

Note at no. 357 Benefit Street an attractive Federal dwelling, the **Nightingale-Brown House**, set amid pleasants grounds *(visit by 30min guided tour only, year-round Fri 1pm–4pm; closed Fri holidays; $3;* ☎ *401-272-0357; www.brown.edu)*. The structure houses a Brown University study center devoted to American civilization.

Continue south on Benefit St. and then turn left on Williams St. At no. 66 stands another Federal-style mansion, the Carrington House. Return to Benefit St. and continue north.

Just beyond Benevolent Street, there is a good **view** of the gilded ribbed dome of the **Old Stone Bank**. A little farther, on the left, is an 18C red clapboard dwelling, the **Stephen Hopkins House** *(no. 43)* (**B**), formerly the home of Quaker governor Stephen Hopkins, signer of the Declaration of Independence and 10-time governor of Rhode Island. The Greek Revival style is represented by the **Providence Athenaeum** (**C**) (1838, William Strickland) where, after the death of his wife in 1847, Edgar Allen Poe courted poet Sarah Whitman, a resident of Benefit Street.

ADDITIONAL SIGHTS *Map p 263*

★**Rhode Island State House** – *Smith St. Open year-round Mon–Fri 8:30am–4:30pm. Closed major holidays.* ♿ ☎ *401-222-2357.* From its position on Smith Hill, the capitol building (1901), by McKim, Mead and White, commands a good view of downtown Providence. On a clear day the white marble exterior is especially impressive, set against the deep blue sky.

Rhode Island Historical Society

Blockfront Secretary (c.1760)

★**The Dome** – The central section of the building is topped with the second largest freestanding dome in the world (the dome of St. Peter's in Rome is the largest) and surmounted by a statue of the **Independent Man**, a symbol of Rhode Island's long-standing spirit of liberty and tolerance. From the first floor, there is a good view of the dome mural portraying the history of Rhode Island and of the Latin inscription inside the dome: "Rare felicity of times when it is possible to think as you like and to say what you think."

Legislative Chambers and Governor's Office – *Second floor.* A full-length portrait of George Washington, painted by Gilbert Stuart, hangs in the Governor's Reception Room. The Royal Charter of 1663 is among the historical documents on display.

Roger Williams National Memorial – *Between Smith St. and Park Row. Visitor center (282 N. Main St.) open year-round daily 9am–4:30pm. Closed Jan 1, Thanksgiving Day, Dec 25.* ♿ ☎ *401-521-7266. www.nps.gov/rowi.* A 4.5-acre landscaped memorial park surrounds the site of the **spring** (**1**) around which, according to tradition, Roger Williams founded the Providence colony. The place where the spring once flowed to the surface is marked by a stone well curb.

Prospect Terrace – From this small park on Congdon Street, high on the slopes of College Hill, there is a **view**★ across the city to the State House.

Providence Arcade – Extending from Weybosset Street through to Westminster Street, this Greek Revival "temple of trade," designed by Russell Warren and James Bucklin in 1828, is one of the few surviving 19C shopping malls in the US.

④ Wickenden Street Wares

Marking the southern edge of Providence's East Side, this road between Benefit and Governor Streets has long been a hangout for RISD and Brown students willing to walk a few blocks from campus for sushi, gourmet pizza or Guinnes on tap. But in recent years a handful of funky new antique shops, art galleries and gift stores have made it a destination for collectors and browsers as well. **Doyle's Antiques** *(no. 197)* is an upscale purveyor of fine furniture, chandeliers and silver, while the **This and That Shoppe** *(no. 236)* provides floor space to some 50 vendors hawking kitschy knickknacks like vintage lunch boxes and rotary phones. **Friendly Round Again Records** *(no. 278)* has been selling records (which are increasingly considered antiques) to the low-fi crowd for 20 years. **Providence Antique Center** *(no. 442)* often has a great selection of mission-style furniture, Fiestaware and stained-glass lamps. Anchoring the east end is **Acme** *(no. 460)*, whose arty showroom mixes Heywood-Wakefield elegance with space-age chic. When you're finished, backtrack to the always bustling **Coffee Exchange** *(no. 207)* for a Narragansett mogambo (a big coffee).

SAUNDERSTOWN

Map of Principal Sights
Tourist Office ☎ 401-789-4422

Gilbert Stuart, the celebrated early American portrait artist, was born in this village, located within the town of North Kingstown.

SIGHTS

Gilbert Stuart Birthplace – *From Rte. 1A, exit onto Gilbert Stuart Rd. and continue 1.5mi. Visit by guided tour (45min) only, Apr–Oct Thu–Mon 11am–4pm. Last tour 45min before closing. $3. ✗ ☎ 401-294-3001.* Born in the American colonies in 1755, Gilbert Stuart later studied in London and Dublin before he returned to the US, where he painted his most famous works. Stuart is best known for his portraits of George Washington: a full-length portrait now hanging in the Rhode Island State House and the Athenaeum Portrait, a likeness of which appears on the one-dollar bill.
Gilbert Stuart lived in this small frame dwelling until he was seven years old. Located in a wooded setting, the house contains period furnishings and an old snuff mill formerly worked by the artist's father.

Casey Farm – *Rte. 1A, 2mi south of Jamestown Bridge. Open Jun–mid-Oct Tue, Thu, Sat 1pm–5pm. $3. ☎ 401-295-1030.* A spartan but elegant mid-18C farmhouse *(visit by 30min guided tour only)* dominates this 300-acre farm, established in 1702 on the Narragansett Bay shore. The former dairy enterprise is now a community-supported farm where some 100 subscribing households raise organically grown produce and eggs. A stone-walled garden, the family cemetery and wooded trails enrich the visit.

WATCH HILL

Map of Principal Sights
Tourist Office ☎ 401-789-4422

Located at the southwesternmost point on the mainland of Rhode Island, Watch Hill is a fashionable seaside community with elegant summer houses, including several in late-19C Shingle style. Swimming, boating, golf and browsing in the fine shops are popular pastimes here.

VISIT

From the **Watch Hill Lighthouse** *(south on Watch Hill Rd)*, you can see **Fishers Island**, a private island off the coast of Connecticut. A short distance from Watch Hill, in Westerly, is **Misquamicut State Beach**, where swimming, sunning and surfing are the order of the day.

■ Flying Horse Carousel

Kids *Bay St. and Larkin Rd. Open Jun–Labor Day. 50¢.* Kids can take a spin on what is reputedly the oldest continually operating flying horse carousel (c.1883) in the country. The 20 hand-carved wooden horses feature leather saddles, agate eyes, and manes and tails made of real horsehair. And "fly" they do, since they hang from a central unit that enables them to swing outward as the carousel turns. The child who can grab the traditional brass ring wins a second ride—free. Accompanying each round is the customary caliope music. *The carousel is open only to children.*

WICKFORD

Map of Principal Sights
Tourist Office ☎ 401-789-4422

This colonial village on the shores of Narragansett Bay developed in the 18C as a center for goods shipped to Newport from plantations on the mainland. Fishing and shipbuilding became principal activities after the Revolution, as Wickford grew into a bustling, prosperous shipping port. The large concentration of 18C and 19C white clapboard dwellings that distinguish Wickford date from this period.

SIGHT

Smith's Castle – *1.5mi north of Wickford by Rte. 1. Grounds open daily year-round. Castle open by guided tour (45min) only, Jun–Aug Thu–Mon noon–4pm; May & Sept Fri–Sun noon–4pm; $3. ⚅ ☎ 401-294-3521.* In 1638 a blockhouse stood on this site, a short distance from the trading post established by Roger Williams. The Indians destroyed the blockhouse during King Philip's War, and three years later, in 1678, a small dwelling, later enlarged to its present two-and-a-half-story size, was constructed here. The house contains 18C and 19C furnishings.

A Sampling of the Cities and Museums of New England

The villages and cities that developed along the coast looked out toward the sea and the rest of the world. This wider point of view contributed to the richness of the architecture and decoration of their houses, particularly in the following locations:

Nantucket★★★ (Massachusetts)

Newburyport★ (Massachusetts)

Newport★★★ (Rhode Island)

Plymouth★★ (Massachusetts)

Portsmouth★★ (New Hampshire)

Salem★★ (Massachusetts)

Wiscasset★ (Maine)

A great impetus toward renovation and restoration resulted in new life for old districts. Arts and crafts stalls, shops and restaurants soon appeared and today visitors can enjoy a leisurely stroll or meal in the following colorful places:

Bowen's Wharf★ (Newport)

Market Square District★ (Newburyport)

Old Port Exchange★★ (Portland)

Quincy Market★★ (Boston)

The museums of New England vary widely in their conception and in their collections. A listing of must-see art museums and marine museums follows:

Art Museums

Sterling and Francine Clark Art Institute★★★
(Williamstown)

Isabella Stewart Gardner Museum★★★ (Boston)

Museum of Fine Arts★★★ (Boston)

Rhode Island School of Design Museum★★
(Providence)

Wadsworth Atheneum★★ (Hartford)

Worcester Art Museum★★ (Worcester)

Yale University Art Gallery★★ (New Haven)

Marine Museums

Maine Maritime Museum★★ (Bath)

Mystic Seaport★★★ (Mystic)

Peabody Essex Museum★★★ (Salem)

Penobscot Marine Museum★ (Searsport)

Whaling Museum★ (Nantucket)

Whaling Museum★★ (New Bedford)

Peacham/© Dick Dietrich

Vermont

Area: 9,609sq mi
Population: 562,758
Capital: Montpelier
Nickname: Green Mountain State
State Flower: Red clover

In 1609, when the French explorer Samuel de Champlain first set eyes on the forested mountains extending southward from the lake that now bears his name, he reportedly exclaimed, *"Les verts monts!"* ("The green mountains!"). More than a century later, Champlain's description of these peaks was adopted as the state's official name.

Rural and uncluttered, Vermont has no large cities or industrial centers (the largest city is Burlington with 39,127 inhabitants). Miles of back roads skirt rocky streams and cross the wooden covered bridges scattered throughout the open countryside. Dormant under a heavy cover of glistening white snow in winter, the region becomes a palette of rich greens in the spring and summer and blazes with color in autumn.

An Independent State – After many other parts of New England had been settled, Vermont remained virtually uninhabited and served as a battleground among the English, the French and the Indians. Not until the British defeated the French at Quebec in 1759 did colonists begin to arrive in large numbers. Prior to the outbreak of the Revolution, **Ethan Allen** and the Green Mountain Boys *(p 270)* (also known as the Bennington Mob), together with Benedict Arnold and his men, captured Fort Ticonderoga *(p 273)* from the British. The artillery and supplies they seized at the fort were used by the Continental Army the following spring in the siege of Boston *(p 117)*. In 1777 Vermont declared itself independent, and a constitution was drawn up outlawing slavery and eliminating property ownership and personal wealth as voting requirements. Denied admission to the Union because of land claims by New York, Vermont remained independent for 14 years, coining its own money, operating its own post office and negotiating with foreign powers. After the dispute with New York was settled, Vermont joined the Union in 1791 as the 14th state. For generations since, Vermonters have guarded their spirit of independence and the principle of strong local government.

Economy – Although forests cover 80 percent of the land, agriculture, primarily dairy farming, fuels the state's economy, as do manufacturing and tourism. Vermont's farms supply milk and dairy products, including the famous **cheddar cheese**, to the Boston region and to southern New England. **Maple syrup** is the state's other important agricultural product. In early spring, steam rises from small wooden sugarhouses, where farmers use evaporators to boil down the maple-tree sap into rich, amber syrup. **Granite** quarried near barre and **marble** quarried in the Green Mountains near Danby are leading state exports. Industrially Vermont is a producer of electrical equipment, fabricated metal products and paper. Year-round tourism is the second largest industry (skiing alone generates over $200 million annually). Outdoor advertising is prohibited by law; a uniform state-wide sign system indicates lodging and services.

BARRE

Population 9,482
Map of Principal Sights
Tourist Office ☎ 802-229-5711

Situated on the hilly eastern flank of the Green Mountains, Barre (BER-rie) is the center of the largest granite industry in the nation. It is home to two quarries on Millstone Hill and a nearby manufacturing plant operated by the Rock of Ages Co. For over 150 years, this city's superior quality granite has been shipped to states across America, formerly to be used in the construction of public buildings, and today to produce memorials, tombstones and industrial equipment. Dozens of quarries have been worked here since 1812; in 1833 the capitol in Montpelier was the first public building in the US to be constructed of Barre granite.

SIGHTS

★**Rock of Ages Quarry** – *4mi from the Barre Information Center (Main St.) by Rte. 14 south. Turn left after 2mi onto Middle Rd. and follow the signs for the Rock of Ages Visitor Center and Quarries (located in Graniteville). Open May–Oct Mon–Sat 8:30am–5pm, Sun noon–5pm. Closed Jul 4. Bus tours (30min) of the quarry available Jun–mid-Oct Mon–Fri 9:15am–3pm; $4.* ☎ *802-476-3119. www.rockofages.com.*

The Quarries – At the two gigantic quarries—one still in use, the other 475ft deep and half-filled with green water—visitors are shown how granite is wrested from the earth. From the edge of the active quarry, the view 600ft down to the bottom is awesome. Enormous derricks, capable of hauling stone blocks weighing up to 250 tons, are used to lift massive granite slabs out of the quarry. Use of modern machinery, such as jet-channeling flame machines and pneumatic drills, has increased efficiency; yet quarrying remains a formidable task.

Manufacturing Facility – *Open year-round Mon–Fri 8am–3:30pm. Closed major holidays.* Visitors may observe the workers at this manufacturing plant as they skillfully cut, polish and carve the granite with gyrating power tools, transforming it from rough stone into finished monuments and statues.

★**Hope Cemetery** – *On Rte. 14 north of Barre center. Open year-round daily 7am–dusk.* ☎ *802-476-6245.* The cemetery has come to be regarded as an outdoor museum of granite memorial sculpture. Gravestones carved by craftsmen for departed members of their families reflect their sculptors' artistry and originality. Note in particular the memorials adorned with scenes depicting rural landscapes.

EXCURSION

Brookfield – *15mi south of Barre by Rte. 14, then Rte. 65 west.* Lying off the beaten path, this tiny picturesque community on the shores of Sunset Lake is sought out primarily for its inn, lakeside restaurant (formerly a pitchfork factory) and **floating bridge**, which carries traffic across the lake. The bridge is buoyed by a network of 380 barrels that rise and fall with the water level. The present bridge, completed in 1973, is the latest replacement for the original floating structure constructed in 1832.

BENNINGTON★

Population 16,451
Map of Principal Sights
Tourist Office ☎ 802-447-3311

Surrounded by the Taconic Range and the Green Mountains, this southern Vermont community includes commercial North Bennington; the historic district known as Old Bennington; Bennington Center, the business district; and Bennington College. During the early days of the nation, Bennington was the home of Revolutionary War hero Ethan Allen and his Green Mountain Boys.

Historical Notes

The Battle of Bennington – Bennington was an important rallying point and supply depot for colonial troops even before the outbreak of the Revolution. In May 1775 **Ethan Allen** and the Green Mountain Boys gathered here before they marched north to attack Fort Ticonderoga.

Two years later, in August 1777, Bennington was once again associated with an important military victory for the patriots: the Battle of Bennington. On August 11, desperately in need of supplies for his army, British general John Burgoyne dispatched Lt. Col. Friederich Baum and his troops to Bennington to seize the arms and munitions stored there. Forewarned of the British plan, New Hampshire's Gen. **John Stark** led the colonial militia from Vermont into New York to head off the enemy. There they

■ Potters Yard

324 Country St. ☎ *802-447-7531.* Recognizable by its metal tower, this complex—the site of the Bennington Potters—contains a gallery shop, a factory outlet store and The Brasserie restaurant *(currently closed for renovation).* Kitchen and other household accessories such as candles, linens and glassware are artistically arrayed and for sale in the gallery shop. A wide range of Bennington dinnerware, with its distinctive dark, mottled appearance, and serving utensils is offered at reduced prices. If you're patient you may find a real bargain in the bins containing "seconds." *Tours of the production process daily 10am and 2pm.*

encountered Baum and his men at the present-day site of Wallomsac Heights, New York. General Stark led his men into battle with the shout: "There are the Red Coats and they are ours, or Molly Stark sleeps a widow tonight!"
The fight was a disaster for the British. For the Americans, the battle served as a prelude to the defeat of General Burgoyne's army at the Battle of Saratoga (October 17) that same year.

Bennington Today – Located as it is near the states of New York and Massachusetts, Bennington is a crossroads community, divided by several US and local routes. Known primarily for its pottery, the town supports gift shops and craft centers that sell a variety of ceramics and glassware made by local artisans. Chief among these is the Potters Yard, where the Bennington Potters was founded in 1948, although the craft had its beginnings in Bennington in the 1820s. Tourism and **Bennington College**, a liberal-arts school distinguished for its progressive ideas and programs, are other draws for the town.

Rattlesnake Cafe

230 North St. ☎ *802-447-7018.* Awash in eye-catching colors, this small house in Bennington Center is home to fine and festive Mexican cuisine, popular with the local dining crowd. For appetizers, try the House Quesadilla (jack cheese, guacamole, sour cream and smoked trout topped with salsa cruda) or the Queso Fundido (a crock of spiced cheese, chorizo, mushrooms, onions and bell peppers). Entrées such as Aztec shrimp or steak Roja come with mango salsa and other tiny treats. Desserts are equally creative.

Bennington Station

150 Depot St. ☎ *802-447-1080.* Housed in a century-old railroad depot in downtown Bennington, this favored restaurant serves lunch and dinner daily plus a Sunday brunch. Try the Chilean Sea Bass (pan-seared with shrimp sauce) or Sam Adams Pie (angus beef roasted with vegetables, Sam's beer and burgundy) All entrées include a trip to the bounteous salad bar. The Deli Depot's offerings include the Cattle Car, Rail Splitter and Southbound sandwiches.

★ OLD BENNINGTON *2hrs*

Blessed with a rich ensemble of early American architecture, this historic section of Bennington, situated largely between the Old First Church and the Battle Monument, is a peaceful reminder of unhurried times. More than 80 primarily Georgian and Federal houses, the earliest dating from c.1761, have been preserved amid shade trees and expansive grounds. *A walking-tour brochure is available from the Chamber of Commerce, Veterans Memorial Dr.* ☎ *802-447-3311.*

Vermont Dept. of Tourism & Marketing

Old First Church

271

★Old First Church – *Monument Ave. From the junction of Rtes. 9 and 7, take Rte. 9 west and turn left onto Monument Ave. Open Jul–Columbus Day Mon–Sat 10am–4pm, Sun 1pm–4pm. Memorial Day–Jun Sat 10am–4pm, Sun 1pm–4pm. Contribution suggested.* ☎ *413-738-5420.* This white clapboard church (1805), with its graceful lines and three-tiered steeple, has been the subject of numerous paintings and photographs. The interior, including box pews and six tall columns, each fashioned from a single pine tree, has been restored to its 19C appearance. The old cemetery in the rear is the resting place of Revolutionary War soldiers and early founders of Vermont. One white marble tombstone marks the grave of poet **Robert Frost** (1874-1963), who penned his own epitaph: "I had a lover's quarrel with the world."

Bennington Battle Monument – *From Rte. 9 west turn right onto Monument Ave. Open mid-Apr–Oct daily 9am–5pm. $1.* ☎ *802-447-0550. www.cit. state.vt.us/dca/historic/hpsites.htm.* This 306ft obelisk was erected in 1891 to commemorate the Battle of Bennington. The **view★★** from the observation deck *(accessible by elevator)* includes the Berkshires, the Green Mountains and New York State.

★Bennington Museum – *1mi west of Bennington center on Main St. (Rte. 9). Open Jun–Oct daily 9am–6pm. Rest of the year daily 9am–5pm. Closed Jan 1, Thanksgiving Day, Dec 25. $6.* ☎ *802-447-1571. www.benningtonmuseum. com.* The museum's diverse collections are related to Vermont and New England history and life. Highlights include choice examples of fine American glassware, furniture, 19C Bennington pottery and the Bennington Flag, one of the oldest Stars and Stripes in existence. A large group of paintings by **Grandma Moses** hangs in a ground-floor gallery.

Grandma Moses Schoolhouse – *Adjacent to and part of the Bennington Museum.* Several paintings by Grandma Moses and memorabilia of her life are exhibited in this schoolhouse, where she attended classes as a young girl.

■ Grandma Moses

The story of **Anna Mary Robertson Moses**' career as a painter is as memorable as her paintings. Grandma Moses (1860-1961), as she became known, lacked formal training. After years of life as a farm wife, she began to paint at the age of 70. Her simple scenes of the countryside and farm life appealed to the public, and her first show, in 1940, won her immediate fame. Grandma Moses was received by President Harry Truman when she was 90, and she continued to paint until her death at 101. Her works have been shown throughout the US and Europe and are familiar subjects of prints and greeting cards.

EXCURSIONS

★Park-McCullough House – *North Bennington. From Bennington center, take Rte. 7 north to Rte. 7A. Continue on Rte. 67A 3mi. Turn left on West St. Visit by guided tour (1hr) only, late May–late Oct Thu–Mon 10am–3pm. $5.* ☎ *802-442-5441.* Situated on six pleasantly wooded acres, this 35-room Second Empire mansion was home to the respected Vermont families of Hall, Park and McCullough, whose members were governors, Bennington College founders and recognized corporate figures. Built by Trenor Park as a summer home in 1865, the richly panelled house contains art glass, European and American paintings, decorative arts and family heirlooms.

Molly Stark Trail – Route 9 between Bennington and BRATTLEBORO *(40mi)* is named for the wife of Gen. John Stark. Scores of area businesses trade under her name. The roadside village of Wilmington makes a good midway stopping point with its attractive shops and eateries. From the turnout on Hogback Mountain (2,410ft), there are views east to Mt. Monadnock (3,165ft) in New Hampshire and south to the BerkshireHills and the Holyoke Range in Massachusetts.

Woodford State Park – *10mi east of Bennington on Rte. 9. Open mid-May–Columbus Day daily 9am–9pm. $2/day.* ☎ *802-241-3655. www.vtstateparks. com.* The 400-acre park hugs the shores of Adams Reservoir, a peaceful site encircled by trees.

Planning a trip to the United States?
Don't forget to take along the Michelin Road Map (No. 930).

BRANDON and MIDDLEBURY GAPS★

Map of Principal Sights
Tourist Office ☎ 802-247-6401

Broad vistas unfold as you follow this itinerary through mountain gaps and past the open farmlands of the Lake Champlain Valley.

DRIVING TOUR *1 day. 81mi. Map below.*

From Rte. 100 in Rochester take Rte. 73 through Brandon Gap.

Route 73 passes tidy houses and tranquil meadows along the White River Valley as it enters the Green Mountain National Forest and skirts the base of **Mt. Horrid** (3,216ft), with its rocky face, before reaching **Brandon Gap★** (2,170ft). From this point there is a **view★** of the Lake Champlain Valley, with the Adirondacks as a backdrop. Descending west through the gap, the road continues to the village of **Brandon**, anchored by its historic inn. Begun as a one-room tavern in 1786, the current stone and wood hostelry features a late-19C Dutch Colonial interior. After Brandon Route 73 continues west to LAKE CHAMPLAIN, yielding vistas of rock-studded pasturelands, dairy farms and the Adirondack Mountains to the west.

The ferry *(schedule p 277)* from **Larrabees Point** crosses Lake Champlain, which is very narrow at this point, and provides access to Fort Ticonderoga in New York.

★★**Fort Ticonderoga** – 🔢 *Rte. 74 in Ticonderoga, New York. Open Jul–Aug daily 9am–6pm. Early May–Jun & Sept–late Oct daily 9am–5pm. $10. Fife & drum corps performances Jul & Aug daily.* ✕ ☎ *518-585-2821. www.fort-ticonderoga.org.* Built in 1755 by the French, Fort Ticonderoga was captured by the British in 1759. The fort is famous for the surprise attack launched here against the British on May 10, 1775 by **Ethan Allen** and the Green Mountain Boys along with **Benedict Arnold** and his men. The supplies captured were used the following spring by General Washington to drive the British out of Boston.

At Fort Ticonderoga, guides outfitted in French Army uniforms perform artillery drills daily *(Jul & Aug)*. The **Military Museum** houses a fine collection of 18C firearms, pole arms and artifacts from the French and Indian War and the Revolutionary War.

Take the ferry to Vermont, follow Rte. 74 east through Shoreham and West Cornwall to Cornwall, and then take Rte. 30north.

★**Middlebury** – *See Entry Heading.*

From Middlebury take Rte. 125 east, named Robert Frost Memorial Dr. for the well-known New England poet.

On Route 125, 2mi beyond Ripton, the **Robert Frost Interpretive Trail** offers a 1mi loop through scenic marshland and forest, punctuated by markers inscribed with poems by the renowned poet.

Continue east on Rte. 125 for about 1mi.

The crisp buff and green clapboard cottages of Middlebury College's **Bread Loaf** mountain campus, formerly a 19C resort, serve as the setting for the respected Writers' Conference, whose instructors have included Robert Frost, Willa Cather, Sinclair Lewis and other 20C literary figures. The road then continues on through **Middlebury Gap★** (2,149ft).

Texas Falls Recreation Area – *Left from Rte. 125.* A short trail leads to a series of falls that tumble over rocks and giant holes formed by glaciers.

The itinerary ends in the tiny crossroads community of Hancock.

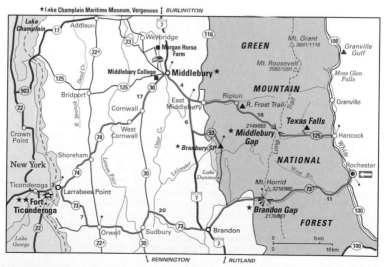

BRATTLEBORO

Population 12,241
Map of Principal Sights
Tourist Office ☎ 802-254-4565

Located at the southeastern tip of Vermont beside the Connecticut River, this commercial and industrial center is the sixth most heavily populated city in the state. Brattleboro is home to wood and paper plants and is a manufacturing center for furniture, leather goods and precision tools.

Brattleboro was the site of the first permanent settlement in Vermont (1724); during the following century the town grew largely because of industry and tourism. In the mid-19C, Jacob Esty founded a company that manufactured parlor organs here. Another Brattleboro resident, albeit briefly, was Rudyard Kipling, who built a mansion here, which he named Naulakha *(not open to the public)* and there penned *Captains Courageous* and *The Jungle Book*.

Handsome 19C brick structures form the nucleus of the town center and preserve the atmosphere of that period, when Brattleboro was evolving from a country village into an urban community. Something of a landmark downtown is the restored **Latchis Hotel** on Main Street, owned by the Latchis family since the hostelry's opening in 1938. First-run movies and independent films are shown to the public in the hotel's original main theater, which features panels depicting Greek mythology, a Zodiac ceiling and terrazzo floors.

SIGHTS

Brattleboro Museum and Art Center – *Main and Vernon Sts. Open mid-May–early Nov Tue–Sun noon–6pm. $3.* ♿ ☎ *802-257-0124. www.brattleboromuseum.org.* Changing displays of the work of international and local artists, as well as exhibits on the region's history are shown in this former railroad station. Several locally manufactured Estey organs are also on view.

Living Memorial Park – **Kids** *Guilford St. off Rte. 9 West.* ✗ *(mid-Jun–Labor Day).* Operated by the city, this park is truly a people's park, especially in summer when every facility is filled to capacity. A large swimming pool, baseball diamond, tennis courts, 9-hole golf course, playground and small pond are popular attractions. In winter there's an ice-rink for skaters and a T-bar on the hill for skiers. Those entering the park from Route 9 cross a one-lane covered bridge.

Brattleboro Board

For a superb view of the wide Connecticut River, have breakfast or lunch on the rear deck of the **Riverview Restaurant** *(Bridge St.* ☎ *802-254-9841).* You'll be sitting right over the water. An all-you-can-eat breakfast buffet begins at 5am (6am Sunday) and a variety of tried-and-true sandwiches and burgers are served for lunch. For dinner, try **Peter Haven's** in the downtown area *(32 Elliot St.* ☎ *802-257-3333).* Established in 1989, this intimate restaurant features such entrées as scallops, beef tenderloin, salmon, duck and Pasta del Mar (penne pasta and pesto sauce with scallops, shrimp and artichoke hearts) on its menu. Tempting desserts include chocolate truffle cake or a double-crusted lemon tart. *Open for dinner only.*

BURLINGTON★

Population 39,127
Map of Principal Sights
Tourist Office ☎ 802-863-3489

Located on Lake Champlain, Burlington, the most populous city in the state, reigns as the urban and industrial heart of Vermont. Its successful past as an industrial center and commercial port in the 19C is evidenced in the lovely residences remaining from this period. With the establishment of facilities by IBM, Digital Equipment Corp. and General Electric in the area, the city's industrial sector has been revived. The lively downtown is anchored on the east by the University of Vermont and on the west by the shoreline of Lake Champlain, with the Adirondack Mountains of New York rising in the distance. A colorful, four-block downtown pedestrian mall, **Church Street Marketplace★**, forms the retail heart of the city with its bustling cafes, boutiques and marked student atmosphere *(city & waterfront maps available at visitor information kiosk).* Battery Street, too, is lined with interesting shops, and inviting lakefront restaurants. **Battery Park, Ethan Allen Park** *(North Ave. to Ethan Allen Pkwy)* and boat rides *(see Lake Champlain)* offer opportunities for viewing the lake and its surroundings.

Burlington hosts the annual **Vermont Mozart Festival** in summer and benefits much of the year from the university's programs of art, music and theater.

SIGHTS

University of Vermont – As old as the state itself, the university was chartered in 1791 as the fifth college in New England. Throughout its 200-year history it has pursued a strong commitment to such social concerns as religious freedom and equality for women and minorities. From the campus green *(between S. Prospect St. and University Pl.)*, the grounds rise to a line of buildings that includes the landmark **Ira Allen Chapel** (1925), a Georgian Revival edifice designed by McKim, Mead and White. Arched and ashlar, the adjacent **Billings Center** (1885) reflects the Richardsonian Romanesque style of its designer Henry Hobson Richardson.

Robert Hull Fleming Museum – *Open May–Aug Tue–Fri noon–4pm, weekends 1pm–5pm. Rest of the year Tue–Fri 9am–4pm, weekends 1pm–5pm. Closed major holidays. $3.* & *☎ 802-656-2090. www.uvm.edu/~fleming.* Also designed by McKim, Mead and White, this Colonial Revival building was constructed in 1930 and renovated in 1984. Original funds for its construction were provided by the heir to the estate of Robert Hull Fleming, a Chicago businessman and graduate of the university. The museum's collection includes Egyptian, Asian and Native American artifacts and contemporary Vermont art, as well as **American paintings** and **European works** from the 17C to the 19C. On the grounds, note the abstract, five-figure sculpture entitled *Lamentations Group, 1989*, by Vermont resident Judith Brown (1931-92).

EXCURSIONS

★★**Shelburne Museum** – *12mi south on Rte. 7. See Entry Heading.*

★**Ethan Allen Homestead** – *2mi north on Rte. 127. From Burlington, take Rte. 7 north, turn left on Pearl St., then right on N. Champlain St. to road's end. Turn left, then immediate right onto Rte. 127 north and exit at North Ave. Beaches. Take the first right at the sign for the homestead. Grounds open mid-Jun–mid Oct Mon–Sat 10am–5pm, Sun 1pm–5pm. Mid-May–early–Jun daily 1pm–5pm. Visit of house by guided tour (30min) only, on the half hour. $4.* & *☎ 802-865-4556. www.ethanallentogether.com.* Dedicated to the legendary folk hero, this 5-acre site threaded by the Winooski River includes a reconstructed frame house (c.1785) believed to have been the final home of Ethan Allen. The modern visitor center houses exhibits on regional history and the escapades of Allen and his Green Mountain Boys. A re-created tavern in the center serves as the setting for a multimedia presentation *(15min)* in which Allen is remembered by friends and associates. Trails lead along the river.

Catercorner on Church

Two "cool" eateries in crowded Church Street Marketplace are diagonally across from each other at Church and College. On the east corner is **Sweetwaters** *(120 Church St. ☎ 802-864-9800)*, a popular sidewalk cafe with such menu oddities as Prince Edward Island mussels, bison loaf and grilled flatbread. Burgers, sandwiches, wraps (try The Peep, a house favorite) and quesadillas round out the fare. Its west-corner cousin is **Leunig's Bistro** *(115 Church St. ☎ 802-863-3759)*, an Old World cafe *avec* jazz bar, complete with glass chandeliers, statuary and a tall clock at tableside. Pecan chicken breast, rack of lamb and grilled duck are a few of the temptations on the menu. Both restaurants are open daily for lunch and dinner and serve brunch on Sunday; Leunig's is also open for breakfast.

Off the Marketplace

In a colorfully painted building a block east of Church Street, **The Daily Planet** *(15 Center St. ☎ 802-862-9647)*, topped by a metal sculpture of Saturn, has been serving "globally inspired food" for over 16 years. Creatively combined Greek, Italian, Oriental, Moroccan, Indian, Mexican, Native American and New England dishes are apt to appear on the lunch and dinner menu, while the Sunday brunch features such selections as roast salmon, a breakfast burrito or Eggs Benedict Arnold.

■ Burlington Boathouse

Situated at the foot of College Street, the community's sizable boathouse *(☎ 802-865-3377)* has public phones and restrooms, a cafe, a visitor information booth and sailboat rentals *(☎ 802-863-5090)*. It's also the departure point for some of the scenic cruises on Lake Champlain. Order a morning coffee or afternoon lemonade and take in the lake views, the cool breezes and waterfront activities from the vantage point of this lovable landmark.

JAY PEAK

Located only 8mi from the border crossing into southern Quebec at North Troy, Jay Peak (3,861ft) is an important ski area in northern Vermont and attracts both Americans and Canadians during the winter.

VISIT

The Summit – An **aerial tram** lifts passengers to the peak's summit *(open Jul–Aug weekends only 10am–4pm; round-trip 1hr; commentary; $10;* & *802-988-2611; www.jaypeakresort.com)*. From the top, there are sweeping **views★★** of Lake Champlain, the Adirondacks, the White Mountains and, to the north, Canada.

Scenic Drives – Several drives in the area are especially picturesque during Indian summer; in particular, **Route 242** from Montgomery Center to Route 101, and **Route 58** from Lowell to Irasburg, offer views of northern Vermont against the backdrop of the surrounding mountain ranges.

LAKE CHAMPLAIN

Map of Principal Sights

Tourist Office ☎ 802-863-3489

Cradled in a broad valley between the Adirondacks and the Green Mountains, this immense lake (125mi long) straddles the Vermont–New York border. The lake and its surroundings have become a popular recreation and vacation area. In 1609 the lake was discovered by Samuel de Champlain. Following the last Ice Age, a vast saltwater sea (Champlain Sea) invaded the Champlain Lowlands, separating northern New England from the rest of the continent. As the land began to rise, free from the weight of the glaciers, the sea gradually receded, forming the largest lake in the US after the Great Lakes.

At the northern end of Lake Champlain, bridges provide access to Isle la Motte, North Hero and Grand Isle. In recent years North Hero has become the summer residence of the famed **Royal Lipizzan Stallions** *(below)*.

SIGHTS

Isle la Motte – A **shrine** honoring Saint Anne marks the site of Fort Saint Anne (1666), built by the French as a defense against the Mohawk Indians. The 12ft **statue of Champlain** was sculpted by a Vermonter, Ferdinand Weber, for Expo '67 in Montreal *(open mid-May–mid-Oct daily 9am–7pm;* ✗ & ☎ *802-928-3385; www.sse.org)*.

★**Cruise** – The stern-wheeler *Spirit of Ethan Allen* offers narrated scenic cruises on Lake Champlain with views of the islands and the Adirondacks. *Departs from Burlington Boathouse, College St., Burlington late-May–mid-Oct daily 10am,*

■ **Royal Lipizzan Stallions of Austria**

North Hero, Vermont, serves as the summer residence of these famed horses, who are presented to the public there yearly in July and August, under the direction of Col. Ottomar Herrmann. The stallions take their name from the little village of **Lipizza** (now Lipica), Slovenia (formerly part of Yugoslavia), near Trieste, Italy, where the Archduke Karl of Austria founded a stud farm in 1580. The farm was established to breed and rear stallions for the august **Spanish Riding School of Vienna**, one of the few places in the world where *haute école* dressage, a rigorous equestrian ballet dating from the 16C, can still be seen *(see Michelin Green Guide Vienna)*. Horses are taught a repertoire of exacting movements based on Renaissance military exercises, including trots, jumps, pirouettes (the horse turns on its haunches at the canter) and the extremely demanding *capriole* (the horse rises with all four feet off the ground at the same height and kicks out—the high point of the show).

The present Lipizzaners descend from several great sires, all stemming from an old Spanish strain, famous at the time of Caesar. These magnificent white horses are born grey, bay or chestnut and get their brilliant white coats between 4 and 10 years of age. Characterized by their intelligence, agility and vigor, they are considered the best saddle and parade horses in the world. They begin training when they are 3 years old. (Ten to 15 years are required for a rider to become a master trainer.) Only a few hundred of these horses have existed at a time. They were rescued from imminent extinction in World War II by Herrmann and Gen. George Patton during the Russian advance, an event dramatized in the Disney film *Miracle of the White Stallions* (1963).

noon, 2pm, 4pm (dinner cruises also available). Round-trip 1hr 30min. Commentary. $8.25. ✗ ♿ *Green Mountain Boat Lines Ltd.* ☎ *802-862-8300. www.soea.com.*

Ferries – Ferry services operating on Lake Champlain afford lake crossings between Vermont and New York State. *Rates quoted below are for car and driver, except for Larrabees Point to Fort Ticonderoga Ferry (car and passengers included). Winter service, conditions permitting. Connecting points north to south are:*

Grand Isle to Plattsburgh – *Departs from Gordon Landing (Rte. 314) year-round 24hrs/day. No service Jan 1, Thanksgiving Day, Dec 25. Round-trip 30min. $12.75. Lake Champlain Transportation Co.* ♿ ☎ *802-864-9804. www.ferries.com.*

Burlington to Port Kent – *Departs from King St. dock late Jun–late Aug daily 7:45am–7:30pm. Late May–mid-Jun & late Aug–mid-Oct 8am–6:35pm. Round-trip 2hrs 15min. $23.* ✗ ♿ *Lake Champlain Transportation Co.* ☎ *802-864-9804. www.ferries.com.*

Charlotte to Essex – *Departs from Ferry Rd. late Jun–Labor Day daily 6am–10:30pm, every 30min. Mid-May–mid-Jun & rest of Sept–mid-Oct daily 6am–9pm. Limited service early spring & winter. Round-trip 1hr. $12.75.* ♿ *Lake Champlain Transportation Co.* ☎ *802-864-9804. www.ferries.com.*

Larrabees Point to Fort Ticonderoga – *Departs from Shoreham (Rte. 74) late Jun–Labor Day daily 7am–8pm. May–mid-Jun & rest of Sept–late Oct daily 8am–6pm. One-way 7min. $6/car. Shorewell Ferries, Inc.* ♿ ☎ *802-897-7999.*

MAD RIVER VALLEY★

Map of Principal Sights

Remote, rural, and set in the midst of broad expanses of rolling, mountainous terrain, the Mad River Valley is a premier four-season resort famed for its ski areas, **Sugarbush** and **Mad River Glen**.

The metamorphosis of this once quiet, secluded farm community into a sophisticated vacation getaway followed swiftly after the opening of Mad River Glen in 1947. Sugarbush began operating in the late 1950s, and in the mid-1960s became Sugarbush North. The lovely setting, abundant accommodations and superb downhill and cross-country skiing facilities have contributed to its great success.

Driving north on Route 100 from **Granville**, or along Route 17 through the **Appalachian Gap** (2,356ft), **views**★★ of the region's unspoiled beauty unfold. Especially scenic is the East Warren Road from Warren to Waitsfield.

★DRIVING TOUR *Allow 1hr. 8mi.*

From Rte. 100 turn east onto the road to Warren.

Warren – This small village contains craft shops and a country store frequented for its fresh-baked goods and salads. The Warren covered bridge is reflected in the Mad River, which flows underneath it.

Round Barn near Waitsfield

Leave the village heading east and drive north on East Warren Rd.

The drive along East Warren Road parallels the Mad River and the Green Mountains to the west. After 5mi, you will pass the **Round Barn** (1909), one of several built in the valley, and now part of an inn.

The road continues straight ahead over the Waitsfield covered bridge (1833) crossing the Mad River into Waitsfield.

Waitsfield – The town has been a commercial center since the 19C, when the daily stagecoach from Waitsfield linked the valley with the railroad in nearby Middlesex. Two shopping centers today provide the inhabitants and visitors in the area with a variety of stores and services. Farming continues to be a principal activity in Waitsfield, despite the influx of professionals and artists in recent years.

MANCHESTER★

Population 3,622
Map of Principal Sights
Tourist Office ☎ 802-362-2100

Favored as a summer resort and cultural center for more than a century, Manchester has become popular during the winter as well, with the development of Bromley and Stratton ski areas.

Manchester Center is a busy place year-round, with its rows of restaurants and shops, while farther south off Route 7A, countrified estates nestle among the foothills of the Taconic Range. In **Manchester Village★** the **Equinox Hotel**, a stately 19C hostelry that catered to an elite clientele including Presidents Harrison, Grant, Theodore Roosevelt and Taft, has been renovated to combine modern comforts with the traditions and gracious service reminiscent of an earlier era.

Manchester is the home of the Orvis Co., one of the oldest surviving (1856) fishing tackle manufacturers in the US. In the past two decades it has been joined by numerous clothing outlet stores along Routes 7A and 11.

SIGHTS

★**Hildene** – *Map p 280. On Rte. 7A, 2mi south of the junction of Rtes. 7 and 11/30. Visit by guided tour (1hr 30min) only, mid-May–Oct daily 9:30am–4pm. $8. ☎ 802-362-1788. www.hildene.org.* This 412-acre "hill and valley" estate was the home of **Robert Todd Lincoln** (1843-1926), the eldest of the four children of Abraham and Mary Lincoln. The Lincoln family vacationed in Manchester during Robert's college years. Robert, who eventually became chairman of the board of the Pullman Co., chose this place, tucked between the Taconic and Green Mountains, as the site of his country home. Hildene was occupied by succeeding generations of Lincolns until the 1970s.

In the main house, a 24-room Georgian Revival mansion, an elegant staircase leads from the entrance hall to the floor above. To the left of the entrance, in the dining room, the unusual layered wall covering creates a collage effect; while in the library to the right, the dark, mahogany-stained paneling conveys a subdued atmosphere. The furnishings are family pieces. The tour includes a demonstration of the 1,000-pipe Aeolian organ (1908).

From the gardens there are sweeping **views★★** of the mountains and the valley below.

American Museum of Fly Fishing – *Seminary Ave. North of the Equinox Hotel at Rte. 7A. Open year-round daily 10am–4pm. Closed major holidays. $3. ☎ 802-362-3300.* Novice and serious anglers alike will be interested in this museum devoted to the history and lore of fly-fishing. Early books on the subject, an extensive array of multicolored artificial flies, and fly-fishing tackle belonging to Daniel Webster, Andrew Carnegie, Ernest Hemingway and other well-known Americans are among the artifacts in the collection.

★**Southern Vermont Art Center** – *West Rd. From the village green, take West Rd. 1mi north. Follow winding drive up to the mansion. Open May–Oct Tue–Sat 10am–5pm (Tue 8:30pm), Sun noon–5pm. Dec–Mar Mon–Sat 10am– 5pm. $3. ☎ 802-362-1405. www.svac.org.* Founded in the 1930s to support Vermont artists, the center now makes its home in a 28-room Georgian Revival mansion on the slopes of Mt. Equinox. Galleries on two floors display traveling exhibits in all media, as well as selections from the center's permanent collection, which includes works by Whistler, Grandma Moses, George Inness and others. The addition of a new museum structure on the grounds will nearly double exhibition space *(expected date of completion: May 2000).*

★**Dorset** – *Map p 280. 6mi north of Manchester by Rte. 30.* The abandoned **quarry** on the right, 4.5mi north of Manchester, was one of the first commercially exploited marble quarries in Vermont. It is now a popular swimming hole in the summer. Dorset is an artists' colony of painters and writers attracted by the charm of the village's mountain setting. Summer theater is presented at the **Dorset Playhouse**.

Equinox Skyline Drive – *Map p 280. 5mi south of Manchester by Rte. 7A. Open May–Oct daily 8am–10pm. $6/car. ✗ ☎ 802-362-1114.* The 5.5mi drive leads to the crest of Mt. Equinox (3,816ft), the highest point in the Taconic Range. From the road, the Carthusian monastery *(not open to the public)*, completed in 1970, is visible in the distance. At the summit there are a communications center and an inn. The **view★** reaches from the Hudson River Valley deep into the Green Mountains.

Arlington – *Map p 280. 8mi south of Manchester by Rte. 7A.* This tranquil village and its residents served as models for illustrator **Norman Rockwell**, who lived here at one time. The **Batten Kill River** provides Arlington with some of the best trout fishing in New England. From Route 7A you can admire the St. James Episcopal Church and the gravestones and monuments in its old churchyard.

★★DRIVING TOUR: The Villages of Southern Vermont

1 day. 97mi. Map p 280.

Leave Manchester Village by Rte. 7A. At Manchester Center take Rte. 30 east and continue on Rte. 11.

Bromley Mountain – The Bromley ski area has become popular during the summer season because of its **alpine slide** Kids *(open mid-Jun–Labor Day daily 9:30am–5pm; rest of Sept–mid-Oct Fri–Sun 10am–5pm; $5.50; ✗ ♿ ☎ 802-824-5522).* Bromley's summit (3,260ft) can be reached by hiking trails *(below)* and offers **views** of the Green Mountains. *A chair lift operates mid-Sept–mid-Oct Sat 10am–6pm, Sun 10am–5pm; $5.50; ☎ 802-824-5522; www.bromley.com.*

Long Trail to Bromley Summit – *From the Bromley ski area, follow Rte. 11 approximately 2mi east. A small sign indicates the Long Trail. Parking is on the right. Round-trip 5.6mi.* From the parking lot, a dirt road leads to the trail *(left)*, which is a segment of both the Long Trail and the Appalachian Trail. After gently ascending through forest for 2mi, the trail climbs steeply, then crosses open meadowland. A **panorama★★** of Stratton Mountain (to the south) and the surrounding Green Mountains is afforded from an observation tower.

Two miles after Bromley, take the road on the left through Peru. At the fork bear left and continue through North Landgrove, turning left in front of the town hall. After passing the Village Inn, bear right at the fork and continue to Weston.

★**Weston** – With its attractive village green, craft shops and general stores, Weston is a popular tourist stop on Route 100. Looking out on the green is the **Farrar-Mansur House**, a late-18C tavern that serves as the local history museum *(open late Jun–Labor Day Wed–Sun 1pm–6pm; rest of Sept–Oct weekends only 1pm–6pm; $2).*

■ Appalachian Trail

This famous 2,160 mile interstate footpath in the eastern US traverses 14 states from Maine to Georgia. The hiking trail crosses some 250,000 acres of varied—mostly mountainous—terrain along the Appalachian Mountain chain with its vast river valleys. In 1925 the Appalachian Trail Conference was created as a private nonprofit organization to oversee the trail. A network of volunteers began the work of physically carving out the pathway in 1930. Today, in cooperation with the National Park Service, some 4,500 members in 31 local clubs under the auspices of the Conference maintain the trail, which was completed by 1937. The nation's first official scenic trail is protected by law, the National Trails System Act of 1968, which includes the preservation of natural habitats bordering the trail and the hundreds of species inhabiting them.

The trail's 3 million annual users, on average, are mostly weekend hikers, but the number of through hikers, who usually begin at the southern end (the trail has 500 access points) in spring, is growing. Normally 5 to 6 months are needed to walk the entire length. Permits are not required for hiking, but for overnight camping in Shenandoah National Park, the Great Smoky Mountains National Park and Baxter State Park permits are mandatory. Shelters are situated every 10–12 miles and campsites are numerous; lodges are located in New Hampshire's White Mountains. No bicycles, motorized vehicles or even pack animals are allowed on the trail; dogs must be kept on a leash. There are many books about the trail. A fun read is Bill Bryson's *A Walk in the Woods* about his experiences preparing for and hiking the trail *(see Further Reading). For more information, contact the Appalachian Trail Conference ☎ 304-535-6331. www.atconf.org.*

Vermont Country Store

Rte. 100, Weston Village ☎ *802-824-3184.* Founded in 1946, this popular general merchandiser has expanded over the years from its original home to four buildings (and there's a second store in Rockingham, Vermont). The growth has resulted largely from the firm's mail-order catalog business and its penchant for selling what "must work, be useful, and make sense." Practical and sometimes scarce items such as sleeve garters, drizzle shoes, collar extenders, heel straighteners and metal hairpins can be ordered. The store itself enjoys a statewide reputation for its varied merchandise, from local cheeses to long underwear and is open year-round Monday through Saturday. Take a break from shopping at the **Bryant House Restaurant** *(☎ 802-824-3618)* next door, where homemade soups, smoked ham, chicken pot pies, and freshly baked dessert pies can be ordered for lunch. Afternoon tea is served too.

Behind the house, the **Weston Mill Museum** displays 19C cooperage, milling and tin-smithing tools, weaving and farm implements *(same hours & admission as Far-rar-Mansur House above)*. Nearby is the **Weston Playhouse**, modeled after a church that burned in 1963. *Summer theater is presented at the playhouse.*

From Weston follow Rte. 100 past the green, then bear right at the sign for Chester. Continue through Andover, then east on Rte. 11.

Chester – The wide main street of this community is lined with lodgings and shops, several of which are housed in historic buildings *(walking-tour brochure available from information booth on the village green Jun–Oct)*. The National Survey, a New England cartographic institution, has made its home here since 1912.

From Chester take Rte. 35 to Grafton.

★**Grafton** – In the 19C this village on the old post road between Albany and BOSTON was a prosperous community with sheep farms; woolen, grist- and sawmills; tanneries and a soapstone quarry. By mid-century the town's economic prospects began to fade and continued to decline. In 1963 the Windham Foundation was established by a private benefactor to restore economic vitality in the village. Today more than half the 19C buildings have been renovated by the foundation, which also owns the **Grafton Village Cheese Co.** *(tours on request ☎ 802-843-2221);* the **Red Barns**, housing antique carriages and exhibits on the sheep farming and blacksmithing; and the **Old Tavern** (1801). Once frequented by such luminaries as Ulysses S. Grant, Oliver Wendell Holmes and Rudyard Kipling, the three-story brick tavern, fronted by a two-story porch, has been restored to its innkeeping tradition. The interior is furnished with Federal and country-style antiques and 19C artwork. *Horse-drawn carriage tours of the town available year-round Fri–Mon through Wilbur's Horse Drawn Rides.*

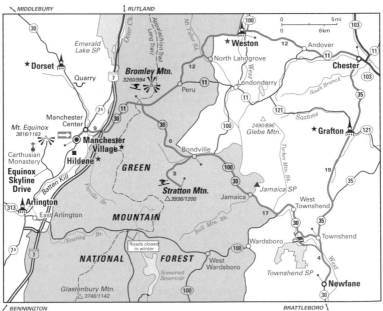

In Grafton turn right, cross the bridge, turn left before the tavern. Follow this road to Rte. 35, which leads to Townshend, then take Rte. 30 south to Newfane.

Newfane – Situated deep in the Green Mountains, this town has grown little since the 18C, when it was selected as the Windham county seat. Newfane's village **green★**, with its white Congregational church, **Windham County Courthouse** and two old inns, is pretty at any time of year, but it becomes a spectacular sight in the fall, when the leaves on the surrounding trees take on hues of red, gold and rust.

Take Rte. 30 back through Townshend. Between Townshend and West Townshend you will pass a covered bridge on the left. Continue through Jamaica into Bondville, where a road to the left leads to the Stratton Mountain Ski Area.

Stratton Mountain – With 92 slopes and trails accessible by a gondola and 14 chairlifts, this mountain (3,936ft) is one of the major ski areas in Vermont. The annual Stratton Arts Festival featuring the work of Vermont artists and craftspeople is held at the base lodge in September and October.

Return to Manchester by Rte. 30.

MIDDLEBURY★

Population 8,034
Map of Principal Sights
Tourist Office ☎ 802-388-7951

Set amid gently sloping hills and rolling countryside, Middlebury is a pleasant town, with its pristine Congregational church, and Victorian-style buildings converted into stores and restaurants. It is the site of stately Middlebury Inn (1827) and Middlebury College.

SIGHTS

Middlebury College – *Map p 273.* Chartered in 1800 and considered a member of the "Little Ivy League," this respected college is well known for its fine liberal-arts curriculum, its foreign language summer schools and its **Bread Loaf Writers' Conference** *(p 273),* which Robert Frost was instrumental in founding. *(Summer visitors are asked to speak quietly if conversing in English; students are pledged to speak only foreign languages on campus.)* The main campus covers some 500 acres and features impressive stone and marble buildings of eclectic architectural styles. Notable are **Painter Hall** (1815), the oldest surviving college building in the state, and **Le Château** (1925), modeled after a pavilion of the French Château de Fontainebleau. The Starr Library contains the **Frost Room**.

Center for the Arts – Incorporating elements of traditional Vermont barns and silos into a bold, modern building of granite and clapboard, this center (1992) houses a dance and studio theater, a concert hall and the college's **museum of art** *(open year-round Tues–Fri 10am–5pm, weekends noon–5pm; closed holidays and latter part of Aug & Dec; ✗ & ☎ 802-443-5007; www.middlebury.edu/~museum).* The museum's permanent collection includes works by such notables as Vermont native Hiram Powers, Gilbert Stuart, Alexander Calder and John Frederick Kensett.

Sheldon Museum – *1 Park St. Open late May–Oct Mon–Sat 10am–5pm. Rest of the year Mon–Fri 10–5pm. $4. & ☎ 802-388-2117. www.middlebury.edu/~shelmus.* In 1884 Henry Sheldon moved into this brick house with his pianos, old clocks and books and hung out a sign that read: "Sheldon Art Museum Archaeological and Historical Society." His museum,

Creekside Cuisine

Just below Frog Hollow, a great little place for lunch, the **Storm Cafe** *(3 Mill St. ☎ 802-388-1063),* occupies the ground floor of Frog Hollow Mill. An outdoor patio overlooking Otter Creek invites alfresco dining and there's indoor seating in the small, attractive dining room. A variety of soups and salads, sandwiches, burgers and light-lunch combos are creatively presented. The House Hummus, Vegetarian Hero on house-made focaccia or the Saltimbocca Sandwich (chicken breast and prosciutto ham with spinach) are good choices. The cafe is open for dinner too.

Woody's *(5 Bakery Lane ☎ 802-388-4182)* is equally compelling for a meal on the creek. Housed in a multistoried structure with a quasi-houseboat look, the restaurant contains a sleek and streamlined interior and an outside deck over the water. There's a full contingent of sandwiches, burgers, salads, burritos and quiches at lunchtime, which can be topped off with a float of rootbeer over Vermont-made ice cream. Weekends bring a popular Saturday and Sunday brunch and dinner is served nightly.

the first of many local museums and historical societies that have since sprung up throughout New England, today includes 19C furnishings, musical instruments, clothing and personal records.

Frog Hollow – This attractive area *(Main & Mill Sts.)* of small boutiques, perched above the cascading waters of Otter Creek, is an appropriate setting for the **Vermont State Craft Center**. Located in a renovated mill, the center displays and sells fine blown glass, metalwork, jewelry, wooden ware and handwoven fabrics made by leading Vermont craftspeople *(open year round daily 10am–6pm;* ⅙ ☎ *802-388-3177; www.froghollow.org).*

EXCURSIONS *Map p 273*

Morgan Horse Farm – 🔳 *In Weybridge, 2.5mi northwest of Middlebury. From the center of Middlebury bear right onto College St. (Rte. 125), then turn right onto Rte. 23 (Weybridge St.). Follow the signs to the farm, bearing left at the fork with the covered bridge. Open May–Oct daily 9am–4pm. $4.* ⅙ ☎ *802-388-2011.* When Vermont schoolmaster **Justin Morgan** obtained a colt in payment for a debt in the 1780s, little did he suspect that the colt would sire the first American breed of horse: the Morgan horse. Strong, thick-muscled and fast, the stallion was capable of out-pulling draft horses in clearing logs and could outrun some of the best thoroughbreds. His descendants have been bred, raised and trained in Vermont ever since the 1790s. An important US export in the 19C, the Morgan was named Vermont's official state animal in 1961.

Owned by the University of Vermont, the farm operates as a breeding, training and instructional facility. Visitors may tour the 19C barn, where descendants of the original Morgan are housed *(20min slide presentation shown hourly).*

★**Branbury State Park** – *Near Brandon, 10mi southeast of Middlebury by Rte. 7 south, then Rte. 53. Open mid-May–Columbus Day daily 9am–9pm. $2/day.* ⚠ ☎ *802-241-3655. www.vtstateparks.com.* This popular warm-weather destination has a large sandy beach on Lake Dunmore *(boat rentals available)* and hiking trails to the **Falls of Llana** *(round-trip 1.1mi, some difficult sections)* and to **Silver Lake** *(round-trip 3mi).*

Vergennes – *13mi northwest of Middlebury by Rte. 7 north.* Vergennes, covering 1.8sq mi, is hailed as the smallest incorporated city in the US.

Whitford House Inn

In Vergennes. 912 Grandey Rd. ☎ *802-758-2704.* Surrounded by the verdant farmlands of peaceful Champlain Valley, this inviting inn, blessed with exquisite views of the Adirondack Mountains, extends a warm welcome to lodgers and diners alike. Come for a lengthy, leisurely evening, beginning with a stroll to the sheep pen and vegetable/herb garden, succeeded by hors d'œuvres and cocktails on the front porch. Fine cuisine and stimulating conversation are inevitable as guests move into the intimate dining room. A sample prix-fixe dinner starts with cold vichyssoise, continues with raspberry vinaigrette-dressed mixed greens, followed by mango sorbet, before an entrée of mahimahi and garden-picked vegetables arrives with home-baked bread. Warm just-out-of-the-oven lemon soufflé and after-dinner coffee complete the repast. *Menu changes nightly. Advance reservations required.*

Button Bay State Park – *6mi west of Vergennes by West Main St. to Panton Rd., turn right onto Basin Harbor Rd., then left on unmarked road. Open mid-May–Columbus Day daily 9am–9pm. $2/day.* ⚠ ☎ *802-241-3655. www.vt-stateparks.com.* Named for the unusual geological formations, resembling buttons, found in the clay banks, the park offers views of LAKE CHAMPLAIN and the Adirondacks. The nature center displays "buttons" of different sizes and has exhibits on local geology.

★**Lake Champlain Maritime Museum** – 🔳 *At Basin Harbor, 21mi northwest of Middlebury by Rte. 7 to Vergennes, then West Main St. to Panton Rd. Turn right onto Basin Harbor Rd. Open May–Oct daily 10am–5pm. Rest of the year Mon–Fri 8am–5pm. $7.* ✗ ☎ *802-475-2022. www.lcmm.org.* Ten exhibit buildings, including a stone schoolhouse (c.1818), trace the history of the lake and its maritime traditions. The grounds showcase a variety of small vessels that have plied the waters of Lake Champlain. Visitors can board the *Philadelphia II*, a replica of a 54ft Revolutionary gunboat, anchored along the museum's lake shoreline. In the Nautical Archaeological Center, a film *(15min)* documents the recent discovery by museum diving teams of 18C and 19C vessels at the bottom of Lake Champlain. Glass display cases enclose artifacts recovered from the lake, including a 1,000 year old Abenaki pot.

MONTPELIER

Population 8,247
Map of Principal Sights
Tourist Office ☎ 802-229-5711

This small city, the capital of Vermont since 1805, sits among the wooded hillsides that rise above the Winooski River. The golden dome of the State House, ablaze in the afternoon sun, dominates the city and is a magnificent sight when the trees change color in autumn. The granite industry, which enabled the city to develop and prosper, has been supplanted in importance by state government and the insurance industry.

SIGHTS *1hr*

★**State House** – *State St. Open Jun–Oct Mon–Fri 8am–4:30pm, Sat 11am–3pm. Rest of the year Mon–Fri 8am–4:30pm. Closed major holidays.* ✗ & ☎ *802-828-2228. www.leg.state.vt.us.* This elegant Classical Revival edifice, built in 1859, is the third state house erected on this site. The first state house (demolished) dated from 1808. The second (1838) was destroyed by fire. The present structure incorporates the Doric columns and portico of the second state house, which was modeled after the Temple of Theseus in Greece. A 14ft statue of Ceres, the Roman goddess of agriculture, rises from the pinnacle of the golden dome.

★**Vermont Museum** – *109 State St., in the Pavilion Office Building. Open mid-Jul–mid-Oct Mon–Fri 9am–4:30pm, Sat 9am–4pm, Sun noon–4pm. Rest of the year Tue–Fri 9am–4:30pm, Sat 9am–4pm, Sun noon–4pm. Closed major holidays. $3.* & ☎ *802-828-2291. www.state.vt.us/vhs.* The Victorian facade of this building was modeled after the Pavilion Hotel, which stood on the site between 1876 and 1965. Inside, the 19C lobby has been reconstructed. Beyond it are the rooms occupied by the Vermont Historical Society. Photographs, documents and artifacts relate the history, economy and traditions of Vermont.

NORTHEAST KINGDOM★★

Map of Principal Sights
Tourist Office ☎ 802-748-3678

This region of forests, lakes, wide-open valleys and back roads that girdle tiny villages includes the three northeastern counties (Caledonia, Essex and Orleans) that surround ST. JOHNSBURY and extend to the Canadian and New Hampshire borders. The region is busiest in the fall, when the countryside is a symphony of color: copper, gold, and everywhere the vibrant reds of the maple trees. During this period, harvest suppers, bazaars, flea markets and auctions are held in many communities.

Seven villages in the region—Barnet, Cabot, Groton, Marshfield, Peacham, Plainfield and Walden—participate in the weeklong **Northeast Kingdom Foliage Festival** during which a different village, each day, hosts activities ranging from church breakfasts to house tours and craft shows *(late Sept–early Oct; reservations recommended)*.

Two other interesting towns are **Craftsbury Common**, with its immense hilltop village green that appears to meet the sky at the horizon, and Danville, home of the American Society of Dowsers.

★LAKE WILLOUGHBY AND BROWNINGTON

Circle tour north of St. Johnsbury – Allow 1 day, if including hike. 87mi.

From St. Johnsbury, take Rte. 5 north through Lyndonville to Rte. 114 and continue north on Rte. 114 to East Burke. From there, follow an unmarked road to Burke Hollow and West Burke.

The Burkes – East Burke, Burke Hollow and West Burke are tiny hamlets at the base of Burke Mountain, a ski area. The gentle mountain landscapes is especially scenic when viewed from the road that leads to the summit of Burke Mountain (3,262ft). In the distance, note Lake Willoughby to the northwest through the gap. *Access to the Burke Mountain Auto Road (toll) is from Rte. 114 in East Burke. From West Burke take Rte. 5A to Lake Willoughby.*

Lake Willoughby – Two mountains rising abruptly opposite each other in a formation resembling the entrance to a mountain pass signal the location of Lake Willoughby *(swimming in season)*. The taller mountain, towering above the southeastern end of the lake, is **Mt. Pisgah** (2,751ft).

South Trail to Mt. Pisgah – *Trailhead parking off Rte. 5A at south end of lake, 5.6mi north of West Burke. Trail begins across the road from the parking area. Round-trip 4mi.* Crossing a picturesque wetland, the trail climbs through a mixed northern forest, with views of Lake Willoughby on the way. Leaving the lake it ascends more steeply through a birch and evergreen forest to the summit, with **views★★** of the surrounding mountains and New Hampshire's Mt. Washington in the distance. A 2mi spur trail leads to a fine overlook of the lake.

Follow Rte. 5A north along the lake shoreline to Rte. 58 west. Continue approximately 4mi on Rte. 58 to Evansville. Turn right on the road marked Brownington Center, which becomes a dirt road. Take the second left and continue to Brownington Center. There, bear right up the hill 1.5mi to Brownington Village Historic District.

* **Brownington Village Historic District** – A once-thriving community, this charming hamlet has changed little since the early 19C, when it was home to the Orleans County Grammar School. The institution was founded in 1823 and was headed for many years by the Rev. Alexander Twilight (1795-1857), an alumnus of Middlebury College who is believed to be the country's first black college graduate. It served as the only secondary school for neighboring communities for 25 years. A four-story granite dormitory building called the **Old Stone House** (1836) now functions as a museum, with period rooms and exhibits on the school *(visit by 1hr guided tour only, Jul–Aug daily 11am–5pm; mid-May–Jun & Sept–mid-Oct Fri–Tue 11am–5pm; $5; ☎ 802-754-2022).* At the north edge of the village, an observatory platform on Prospect Hill affords a **panorama**** of Willoughby Gap *(southeast)*, Mt. Mansfield *(southwest)*, Jay Peak *(west)* and Lake Memphremagog *(north)*.

From Prospect Hill, turn right, continue past the Congregational church and follow the unmarked road 2mi west to the junction with Rte. 58. Turn right and continue through the town of Orleans (1mi). Take Rte. 5 south for 5mi to Rte. 16 south. Take Rte. 16 through the town of Glover, then turn left onto Rte. 122 south and continue for about 1mi to the Bread and Puppet Museum.

Bread and Puppet Museum – *Rte. 122. Open Jun–Oct daily 10am–5pm. Rest of the year by appointment. ☎ 802-525-3031.* In a cavernous barn built in 1863, the socially committed Bread and Puppet Theater Company dramatically displays its larger-than-life puppets. These head masks and mannequin-like creations are the result of almost 30 years of work by founder Peter Schumann, a Silesian-born sculptor and choreographer who established the theater in 1962 in New York City. In 1970 the company moved to Vermont. The puppets and masks have been used in pageants and shows in Europe, Latin America and the US.

Return to St. Johnsbury via Rte. 5 south.

*PEACHAM AND BARNET CENTER

Circle tour south of St. Johnsbury – Allow 3hrs 30min. 65mi.
From St. Johnsbury take Rte. 2 west to Danville.

Danville – Because of its high elevation, this rural agricultural community enjoys refreshing breezes and clear air even on hot summer days. The village is the home of the **American Society of Dowsers**. The society's annual 4-day convention, held in Lyndonville in August, attracts dowsers (dowsers use a forked twig, or divining rod, to search for underground water and minerals) from across the nation.
Continue south on Rte. 2 to Marshfield. Turn right onto Rte. 215 to Cabot.

Cabot – This small community is associated with the production of cheese. The **Cabot Creamery**, in business since 1919, is perhaps the best-known purveyor of Vermont dairy products; it is particularly famous for its variety of cheeses *(free samples avail-*

Peacham

able). A tour *(30min, $1)* of the plant operations, opening with a video presentation *(15min)* explains in detail how cheese, yogurt and butter are made *(open Jun–Oct daily 9am–5pm; rest of the year Mon–Sat 9am–4pm; closed Jan & major holidays;* ♿ ☎ *802-563-2231 or 800-837-4261; www.cabotcheese.com).*

Return to Danville via Rtes. 215 and 2. Take the unmarked road south through Harvey and Ewell Mills to Peacham.

★**Peacham** – Surrounded by a breathtaking hill-and-dale setting, Peacham may be the most photographed of all Vermont's villages during the fall. Lovely white dwellings stand near the church, the general store and Peacham Academy.

Continue to Barnet Center through South Peacham, turning left to West Barnet. At Barnet Center, turn left before the church and continue up the hill.

Barnet Center – From a vantage point past the church near the top of the hill, you can look down on a beautiful pastoral scene of a large barn with its silo. Beyond the barn, there is a **view**★★ of the countryside stretching into the distance.

Return to the foot of the hill and turn left in the direction of Barnet. From there, take Rte. 5 to St. Johnsbury.

PLYMOUTH★

Population 440
Map of Principal Sights

This tiny village abutting the hills of the Green Mountains was the birthplace of **Calvin Coolidge** (1872-1933), the 30th president of the US. The beautiful setting, dotted with a handful of historic buildings, evokes the rural serenity, order and simplcity of earlier times.

It was here, on August 3, 1923, that Vice President Coolidge, upon receiving the news of the death of President Warren Harding, was sworn into office by his father, John Coolidge, a notary public. This was the first and only time in the history of the nation that a president was administered the oath of office by his father.

★CALVIN COOLIDGE STATE HISTORIC SITE *2hrs*

A dozen structures in the hilltop hamlet of Plymouth Notch off Route 100A are part of the Coolidge State Historic Site, including a one-room schoolhouse. The village has changed little since the late 19C, when gasoline was 11¢ and the gas tax 3¢ per the sign on the community gas pump.

Visit

Open late May–mid-Oct daily 9:30am–5pm. $5. ✗ ♿ ☎ *802-672-3773. www.cit.state.vt.us/dca/historic/hpsites.htm. Site plan available at visitor center.*

An exhibit on the life of Calvin Coolidge is featured in the visitor center, housed in a handsome stone building (1972). Coolidge was president from 1923 to 1929. He served out the remainder of Harding's term and was elected to four years of office in 1924.

Coolidge Birthplace – Calvin Coolidge was born in this small, modest dwelling, which has been renovated and restored to its 1872 appearance. The house is attached to the country store once owned by his parents. In 1876 the family moved from this house to the homestead up the road.

Coolidge Homestead – In 1923 Vice President Coolidge, on vacation here at the time, was sworn into the presidency in this house, where the family lived from the time Calvin was a youngster. The ceremony took place in the parlor, lit by kerosene lamps. Furnishings remain largely unchanged from 1923.

Other Buildings – Also in the historic district are a large, weathered barn that has been transformed into a museum of early American tools, and the Coolidge family's **Plymouth Cheese Corp.**, a small operation where visitors can observe the making of traditional granular curd cheese. The church (1840) where Coolidge worshipped stands near his birthplace; a flag marks his pew. Originally a tavern, the mustard-colored Wilder House (c.1830) is now a restaurant, serving breakfast and lunch to the public seasonally.

At the southern end of the village, the Brown Family Farmhouse (1869), with its attached barn, stands as an example of the New England connected farm *(not open to the public).*

Located across Route 100A, opposite the Brown farmhouse, Coolidge's **grave** lies in the village cemetery.

A state forest named in honor of Calvin Coolidge lies to the northeast of the historic district, off Route 100A.

EXCURSION

Woodward Reservoir – *4mi north of Plymouth on Rte. 100.* This state recreation area is a pleasant woodsy oasis amid the high hills of the Green Mountains. Vacationers and local residents launch their boats from the ramp off the paved parking area. The inviting waters of the reservoir offer rest and refreshment in an alpine setting to canoeists, fishermen and swimmers, and picnickers on the shore.
Facilities for a children's summer camp are located nearby.

PROCTOR*

Population 1,979
Map of Principal Sights

With its string of quarries from DORSET to LAKE CHAMPLAIN, Vermont was once the nation's leading producer of marble. The Vermont Marble Co., formerly based in Proctor, operated most of the state's quarries.

SIGHTS

*** Marble Exhibit** – *62 Main St. Open late May–Oct daily 9am–5:30pm $5. ♿ ☎ 802-459-2300.* The exhibit describes the origin, quarrying and finishing of marble. Polished marble slabs from Vermont and around the world are used to illustrate the rich diversity of colors and graining characteristic of this stone. Visitors may view a video about marble *(13min)*, observe a sculptor at work and see marble sculptures. Marble bas-relief portraits of the US presidents occupy a special gallery.

Wilson Castle – *West Proctor Rd., 4mi south of Proctor. Visit by guided tour (45min) only, late May–late Oct daily 9am–6pm. Last tour 5:30pm. $6.50. ☎ 802-773-3284. www.wilsoncastle.com.* This massive brick mansion (1867), built by a Vermont doctor, offers a glimpse of the opulence that characterized the private homes of 19C America's upper classes. Luxurious furnishings and art pieces are complemented by the surrounding heavily carved woodwork, stained-glass windows and hand-painted and polychromed ceilings. Note the Louis XVI crown jewel case.

EXCURSION

New England Maple Museum – *Rte. 7, in Pittsford, 5mi north of Proctor. Open late May–Oct daily 8:30am–5:30pm. Nov–mid-Dec & mid-Mar–mid-May daily 10am–4pm. $2.50. ♿ ☎ 802-483-9414.* Located in the rear of a large retail store, this small museum features homespun exhibits on the history of maple sugaring. An extensive collection of equipment dating from c.1790 to 1938 includes utensils, paddles, scoops, wooden spouts, buckets, kettles, and an oil-fired evaporator capable of producing a gallon of syrup per hour. A slide show *(10min)* illustrating the entire process, plus a display of syrup grades, ends the self-guided tour.

■ Maple Syrup Pie

- 2-1/4 cups Vermont maple syrup
- 1 egg
- 2 egg yolks
- 2 egg whites
- 2/3 cup flour
- 1 teaspoon vinegar
- 1/2 teaspoon salt
- 2 tablespoons butter
- Pecans or walnuts
- 1/2 cup water
- Baked piecrust

Heat syrup in 2-quart pan. Beat egg, yolks, water, flour and salt together. Blend into 2 cups of syrup and cook until boiling, stirring to prevent sticking. Remove from heat, add butter and nuts. Add vinegar to bring out the maple flavor. Pour into piecrust and top with meringue.

Meringue topping: beat 2 egg whites until stiff, add 1/4 cup syrup. Place on top of pie and brown in the oven.

Source: State of Vermont Bulletin #38

RUTLAND

Population 18,230
Map of Principal Sights
Tourist Office ☎ 802-773-2747

Situated at the junction of Otter and East Creeks, Rutland is Vermont's second largest city. The surrounding mountains and lakes make the region a year-round playground for those who love the outdoors. Killington, one of the largest ski resorts in the East, is a popular recreation area nearby.

Settled in the 1770s, the town developed into a railroad center in the 19C and marble quarrying flourished, giving Rutland the nickname "the marble city." Many small industries now thrive, producing a variety of goods.

SIGHT

Norman Rockwell Museum – *2mi east of Rutland on Rte. 4. Open year-round daily 9am–5pm. Closed Jan 1, Easter Sunday, Thanksgiving Day, Dec 25. $3.50.* & ☎ *802-773-6095. www.normanrockwell.vt.com.* The museum contains over 2,500 of examples of the work of Norman Rockwell, illustrator, humorist and chronicler of more than half a century of American life. The series of more than 300 magazine covers that Rockwell created for the *Saturday Evening Post,* and for which he is best remembered, is displayed together with other magazine covers, movie and war posters, advertising work, calendars and greeting cards, which also brought him fame. (Another museum dedicated to the works of Norman Rockwell is located in Massachusetts, in STOCKBRIDGE.)

EXCURSIONS

★Proctor – *6mi from Rutland by West St., then Rte. 3 north. See Entry Heading.*

Hubbardton Battle Site – *18mi northwest of Rutland in East Hubbardton. Take Rte. 4 west to Exit 5. Follow the signs north.* A monument and visitor center commemorate the Revolutionary War battle that occurred at Hubbardton in 1777. American troops, which had held Fort Ticonderoga for two years, were forced by the British to surrender control of the fort early in July 1777. Pursued by the British, the Americans retreated into Vermont, where a small colonial force had been stationed to form a rear guard. When the two armies clashed on July 7 on a hillside in East Hubbardton, the battle left both sides with hundreds of casualties.

Royal's 121 Hearthside
37 N. Main St. (Rtes. 4 & 7). ☎ *802-775-0856.* Serving diners since 1962, this crossroads restaurant is something of an institution. All à la carte entrées come with salad, home-baked popover and tray of carrots, celery and olives along with vegetables, bread and potatoes. Dinner specialties include Royal's supersteak, prime rib, and wiener schnitzel as well as seafood and lamb. Puddings—bread, grapenut and Indian—are served warm for dessert. Lunch is available weekdays and Sunday dinner is served from noon til 9pm.

Bistro Cafe
3 Central St. ☎ *802-747-7199.* Housed in a former bank in downtown Rutland, this handsome bistro presents a varied, affordable menu at lunch and dinnertime. Calamari salad, chilled peanut noodles or a chicken wrap are good noontime choices. For dinner, try the steamed mussels Provençal or brick-fired spanakopita as appetizers; continue with pesto shrimp or chicken *piccata*. You may not have room for the tempting desserts.

After the fight, the British decided to halt their pursuit of the colonists and return to the fort. For the Americans, tired and reduced in number, this was victory enough as they withdrew deeper into Vermont.

Visitor Center – *Open late May–mid-Oct Wed–Sun 9:30am–5pm. $2.* & ☎ *802-828-3051. www.cit.state.vt.us/dca/historic/hpsites.htm.* This building contains a small museum and a diorama of the battle.

Killington – *10mi east of Rutland on Rte. 4; gondola station 15mi east of Rutland on Rte. 4.* Killington, with over 200 trails cut on six interconnecting mountains and on Pico Mountain, is one of New England's most popular ski resorts. The Killington gondola is reputedly the longest *(2.5mi)* ski lift of its kind in the US *(reduced rates for fall foliage viewing mid-Sept–mid-Oct;* ☎ *802-422-6200; www.killington.com).* A ride on the gondola affords **views★★** of the Green Mountains.

Lake St. Catherine State Park – *20mi southwest of Rutland. On Rte. 30 south of Poultney. Take Rte. 4 to Exit 4, then Rte. 30 south. Open Jun–Oct daily 8am–dusk. $2/day.* △ ☎ *802-287-9158.* Cool breezes sweep the calm surface of Lake St. Catherine, making this a popular spot for windsurfing, sailing and fishing for trout and northern pike.

ST. JOHNSBURY

Manufacturing and maple syrup production are major occupations in this small, blue-collar city, gateway to the vast, rural NORTHEAST KINGDOM. The St. Johnsbury Athenaeum and the Fairbanks Museum and Planetarium, both in the downtown area, were established by the Fairbanks family, devoted patrons of their hometown.

St. Johnsbury began to prosper in the 1830s when a grocer named Thaddeus Fairbanks invented and began to manufacture the platform scale here; Fairbanks scales have been produced and shipped around the world ever since.

SIGHTS

★**Athenaeum** – *Main St. Open year-round Mon–Fri 10am–5:30pm (Mon, Wed 8:30pm), Sat 9:30am–4pm. Closed major holidays.* ♿ ☎ *802-748-8291.* Horace Fairbanks built this brick Second Empire building as a public library in 1871, adding an **art gallery** to the rear in 1873. Still hung in the style of a Victorian salon, the gallery is dominated by Albert Bierstadt's monumental *Domes of Yosemite*. Also represented are Asher B. Durand and other painters of the Hudson River school as well as Vermont natives Hiram Powers and Thomas Waterman Wood. The library features ornate woodwork and reading mezzanines.

★**Fairbanks Museum and Planetarium** – 〚Kids〛 *Main and Prospect Sts. Open Jul–Aug Mon–Sat 10am–6pm, Sun 1pm–5pm. Rest of the year Mon–Sat 10am–4pm, Sun 1pm–5pm. Closed Jan 1, Easter Sunday, Thanksgiving Day, Dec 25. $5.* ☎ *802-748-2372. www.fairbanksmuseum.org.* This institution was founded in 1891 by Franklin Fairbanks, who donated his collection of taxidermy wildlife to the museum. Today the museum houses 4,500 mounted birds and mammals, a large collection of antique dolls, and artifacts from many lands.

The ornate Romanesque Revival **building**★, designed by Vermont architect Lambert Packard, is carved of red sandstone, and the interior features a magnificent barrel-vaulted ceiling. A wainscoted circular staircase leads to cultural history exhibits in the second-floor gallery.

Maple Grove Farms – 〚Kids〛 *On Rte. 2 east of the city center. Open year-round Mon–Fri 8am–4:15pm. Sugarhouse open mid-May–mid-Oct daily 8am–5pm. Closed major holidays.* ☎ *802-748-5141.* Exhibits and brief films illustrate how maple syrup is harvested and produced. The factory tour *(20min, $1)* introduces visitors to the step-by-step procedures involved in transforming maple syrup into Maple Grove candies; the sugarhouse contains a continuously operating sap boiler.

■ Maple Sugaring

Vermont is the leading producer of maple syrup in the US (annual average yield 500,000 gallons). From early March to mid-April, when night temperatures drop below freezing but the days get steadily warmer, more than 1,000,000 hard rock or sugar maple trees in the state are tapped with small metal spouts. Under these spouts buckets are hung to collect the 10 to 15 gallons of sap each tree is liable to produce. The sap is then taken to a ventilated sugarhouse to be boiled down to the desired thickness, filtered through layers of cloth, and jarred. The process is quite labor-intensive; each gallon of syrup is the product of about 40 gallons of sap. Some 60 sugaring enterprises throughout the state invite visitors to witness the process during the season, or sample their wares off-season at roadside gift shops. Syrup comes in three grades: delicate light amber, all-purpose medium amber and robust dark amber. Try all three with a side dish of sweet maple-sugar candy.

EXCURSION

★★**Northeast Kingdom** – *See Entry Heading.*

Facility information for many of the state parks mentioned herein may be found in the blue pages at the back of this guide under Sports and Recreation.

For many years a lakeshore resort on LAKE CHAMPLAIN with sweeping vistas of the Adirondacks and the Green Mountains, **Shelburne** today is known primarily for the Shelburne Museum, whose fine collection of American folk art preserves the early spirit of the nation. The museum possesses a preeminent 80,000-piece collection of home crafts, folk arts, trade tools, transportation, fine arts, furnishings and architecture representing three centuries of American life, history and art. These varied collections are well presented in 37 buildings spread across 45 acres on a magnificent **site** overlooking the Lake Champlain Valley.

Historical Notes

During the glory days of steamboat travel, a shipyard on Shelburne Bay turned out vessels that carried passengers and freight on the lake. The SS *Ticonderoga*, the last of these steamers (and a highlight of Shelburne Museum), was launched from a local pier in 1906. The following year New York resident **Electra Havemeyer Webb** (1889-1960) began a lifetime of collecting with an inheritance from her father. In 1910 she married **J. Watson Webb** of Shelburne, Vermont. After his retirement in 1947, the couple made Vermont their primary residence and Mrs. Webb pursued in earnest the creation of a museum for her collections, sparked by the need to find housing for her father-in-law's carriages.

In 1947 the Webbs established the museum. An avid collector of American crafts and folk art, Mrs. Webb had assembled varied collections of Americana over the years, then purchased a number of historic structures and had them moved to Shelburne to house her holdings. Within 10 years, Shelburne had its own church, school, jail, barns, houses, general store, and even a lighthouse, railway depot and steamboat. By 1960 some 23 buildings had been relocated to the museum site. The Webbs' final project was the construction of an art gallery on the property, which opened in 1960.

VISIT *1 day. Map p 291.*

Kids *On Rte. 7. Open late May–mid-Oct daily 10am–5pm. $17.50 (2nd consecutive day free). Late Oct–Dec & Apr–mid-May visit by guided tour only, 1pm–4pm (selected buildings open); $8.75. Closed Easter Sunday, Thanksgiving Day & Dec 25.* ♿ ☏ *802-985-3346. www.shelburnemuseum.org.*

★★**Round Barn** – Built in 1901, this is one of the few remaining round wooden barns in Vermont. The labor-saving design of the three-story barn became popular around the turn of the century, prior to the development of modern technology. Hay was loaded into the huge central silo from the upper level, and the animals, held in stalls surrounding the silo on the middle level, could be easily fed by one person.
The barn, which houses the visitor center, contains agricultural exhibits, equipment and an orientation slide show *(14min, lower level)*.

★**Circus Parade Building** – The semicircular building houses carousel horses, circus posters, and the hand-carved Kirk Bros. 5,000 piece miniature circus.

Beach Gallery and Beach Hunting Lodge – Nature and hunting are the themes of these collections. Western landscape and wildlife paintings, trophies and Plains and Northwest Coast Indian artifacts are shown.

★★**Shelburne Railroad Station** – This structure exemplifies the Victorian-style railroad stations that were built across America in the 19C. The private car *Grand Isle (outside the station)* was owned by former Vermont governor William C. Smith.

★★**The Ticonderoga** – After steaming along on Lake Champlain for almost 50 years hauling passengers, freight and other tourist traffic, this side-wheeler, known as the *"Ti"*—the last vertical-beam, side-wheel steamship left intact in the US—was saved from the scrap heap in the 1950s by Electra Havemeyer Webb.
A specially constructed dike allowed workers to transfer the *Ti* out of the water to a series of tracks that extended several miles overland to Shelburne; a film *(10min)* shown continuously on board illustrates this feat. Inside, exhibits recall the *Ti*'s past as a luxurious steamship.

★**Colchester Reef Lighthouse** – Located at one time off Colchester Point in Lake Champlain, the lighthouse (1871) was moved to Shelburne, where it now serves as a gallery of marine art. Paintings, photos, figureheads, scrimshaw and lithographs depict whaling and the great days of sail.

Prentis House – This 18C house (1733) is impeccably furnished with antiques.

★**Stencil House** – The interior of this dwelling (1790) contains splendid examples of decorative wall stenciling.

Ken Burris/Shelburne Museum

Tuckaway General Store

★★**Tuckaway General Store** – This brick building (1840), which originally stood in Shelburne, houses a general store, post office, barbershop, a dentist's and a doctor's office, a tap room and an apothecary. On the first floor, every imaginable item necessary for daily farm living can be found on the shelves, hanging from the ceiling or tacked onto the timbered posts of the store.

Upstairs in the doctor's and dentist's offices are displays of their instruments. The **apothecary** contains all types of remedies and a sizable collection of razors.

Charlotte Meeting House – The simple brick meetinghouse (1840) has been refurbished with new wooden pews and trompe l'œil wall panels.

Vermont House – Furnished like the home of a New England sea captain, this dwelling (1790) contains colorful hand-painted wallpapers illustrating port scenes.

★★★**Horseshoe Barn** – This barn (1949), in the shape of an enormous horseshoe, contains more than 225 horse-drawn carriages and sleighs. Among the phaetons and coaches on the second floor is a calèche and a luxurious **Berlin** with an exquisite satin interior. Concord coaches, buggies, a Conestoga wagon and brightly painted peddlers' wagons fill the Annex.

★★**Hat and Fragrance Textile Gallery** – This early-19C building contains a superb group of American quilts: appliqué, piecework and reverse appliqué, dating from the 17C through the present. With their intricate patterns and needlework, these quilts are admired as works of art.

Victorian dollhouses, Parisian gowns designed in the 19C for America's richest women, hooked rugs, lace samplers and an assortment of needlecraft are also displayed.

★★**Variety Unit** – This building (c.1835), the only original structure on the site, houses numerous examples of pewter, porcelain, clocks and amusing figure jugs known as Toby mugs. On the second floor there is a multitude of dolls: porcelain, bisque, wax, dried-apple, wood and papier-mâché.

★**Vergennes Schoolhouse** – The books, charts, maps and chalkboard are arranged in this one-room brick schoolhouse (1830) as though students were expected to arrive at any moment.

★★**Stagecoach Inn** – Formerly an inn on the stage route linking southern New England with Canada, the building (1783) contains an outstanding collection of American folk sculpture. An enormous wooden eagle carved for the Marine base at PORTSMOUTH, New Hampshire, numbers among the many other eagles, weather vanes, ships' figureheads, sternboards, trade signs, cigar-store Indians and carousel figures found throughout the inn.

★**Dorset House** – The house (c.1840) contains Shelburne's collection of more than 1,000 decoys, including ducks, geese, swans and shorebirds. The realism and artistry attained by the carvers of some decoys benefited the hunter; other decoys, such as those executed by A. Elmer Crowell, were intended for decorative purposes only.

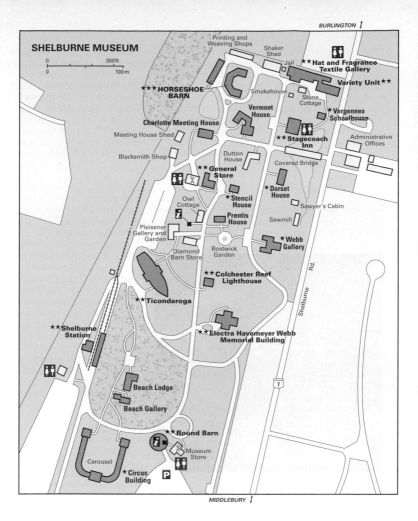

SHELBURNE MUSEUM

BURLINGTON

0   300ft
0   100m

Printing and
Weaving Shops
Shaker
Shed
Jail
★★ Hat and Fragrance
Textile Gallery
Variety Unit ★★

★★★ HORSESHOE
BARN

Smokehouse
Stone
Cottage

Vermont
House
★ Vergennes
Schoolhouse

Charlotte Meeting House

Meeting House Shed

Blacksmith Shop

Dutton
House

★★ Stagecoach
Inn

Administrative
Offices

Covered Bridge

★★ General
Store

★ Dorset
House

Owl
Cottage
★ Stencil
House

Prentis
House

Sawyer's Cabin

Pleissner
Gallery and
Garden

Diamond
Barn Store

Bostwick
Garden

Sawmill

★ Webb
Gallery

★★ Colchester Reef
Lighthouse

★★ Ticonderoga

★★ Shelburne
Station

★★ Electra Havemeyer Webb
Memorial Building

Shelburne Rd.

7

Beach Lodge

Beach Gallery

★★ Round Barn

Museum
Store

Carousel

P

★ Circus
Building

MIDDLEBURY

★ **Webb Gallery** – Three hundred years of American painting are represented in the gallery. Works range from the simple, anonymous, primitive portraits of the colonial period to the classic seascapes (Fitz Hugh Lane) and landscapes (Hudson River school) of the 19C. Canvases by 20C artists, such as Andrew Wyeth and Grandma Moses, are also included.

★★ **Electra Havemeyer Webb Memorial Building** – This imposing Greek Revival mansion dedicated to Mrs. Webb contains works of art acquired by her parents, and six complete rooms from the Webbs' Park Avenue apartment.

Inside, the warm understated elegance is enhanced by the English paneling, European furnishings and the paintings by Rembrandt, Corot, Manet, Degas and Monet that hang in the rooms and hallways.

ADDITIONAL SIGHT

Shelburne Farms – *Follow Harbor Rd. 1.5mi east from traffic light at Shelburne Village. Open mid-May–mid-Oct daily 9am–5pm. $5. ☏ 802-985-8686. www. shelburnefarms.org.* This agricultural estate exemplifying the grand style of the 19C was the country home of railroad tycoon **William Seward Webb** and his wife **Lila Vanderbilt Webb**, granddaughter of Cornelius Vanderbilt (known as the "Commodore"), who founded the Vanderbuilt dynasty. The Webbs were attracted to this beautiful setting on the shore of Lake Champlain.

After acquiring the 30-odd farms that originally stood on the property, they turned to the architect Robert Robertson, the landscape designer Frederick Law Olmsted, and Gifford Pinchot, one of the nation's first conservationists, to plan and build Shelburne Farms. The terrain was leveled, buildings razed, and in their place appeared a new parklike landscape of undulating knolls and forest studded with Queen Anne structures. At its peak the Webb estate, which encompassed some

3,800 acres of fields, pastures and woodlands, was the family residence and a working "model" farm, known for its advanced methods and experimentation in such fields as animal husbandry and crop-raising.

Reduced in size over the years to about 1,400 acres, the farm now operates as an nonprofit environmental education center, with a working dairy on the premises. The **Farm Barn** (1888), an enormous turreted structure enclosing a 2-acre courtyard, and the **Coach Barn** (1901) serve as centers for conservation programs. **Shelburne House★** (1899), a 110-room country manor house with **views★★** of Lake Champlain and the Adirondacks, is completely restored and now operates as an inn. The house also serves as a gracious setting for educational and cultural events and outdoor summer concerts.

EXCURSION

Vermont Wildflower Farm – *On Rte. 7 in Charlotte, 5mi south of Shelburne. Open May–late Oct daily 10am–5pm. $3. ☎ 802-985-9455. An audio-visual presentation (15min) on New England wildflowers is included in the admission fee.* The

many species of wildflowers growing in the farm's six-acre field and woodland habitats transform the landscape into a wonderful display of changing color spring through fall. The familiar Jack-in-the-pulpit, black-eyed Susan, aster and Devil's paintbrush grow here in abundance, together with dozens of lesser-known varieties. Along the paths, descriptive panels accompany the plants, providing facts and anecdotes (the name *daisy* derives from "day's eye," a reference to the flower's golden center believed by the ancients to represent the sun) regarding the history, legends and uses of the flowers. Also on the premises are a seed store, specializing in the farm's wildflower seed mixes, and a gift shop carrying wildflower-emblazoned products.

Vermont Wildflower Farm

STOWE★

Population 3,433
Map of Principal Sights
Tourist Office ☎ 802-253-7321

As Route 108 winds through this small village, situated at the foot of Stowe's distinctive landmark, Mt. Mansfield, the slender white spire of Christ Community Church comes into view. The valley's exceptionally long snow season and abundance of Swiss-style chalets, lodgings and restaurants account for Stowe's sobriquet, "the ski capital of the east."

During the winter up to 8,000 skiers use the trail systems on the slopes of Stowe's two interconnected mountains, **Mt. Mansfield** (4,393ft), Vermont's highest peak, and **Spruce Peak** (3,320ft). In the summer, Stowe features horseback riding, hiking, swimming, mountain climbing, theater and concerts. *Maps and information on area recreation available at the Green Mountain Club, Rte. 100 in Waterbury Center, south of Stowe ☎ 802-244-7037.*

Colorful shops, galleries and restaurants line Stowe's Main Street. Serving the townspeople since 1895, **Shaw's General Store** is a local institution, offering a wide variety of outdoor clothing, sporting goods, footwear and household supplies.

SIGHTS *3hrs*

Trapp Family Lodge – *Take Rte. 108 north 2mi, then turn left at the Trapp Family sign in front of the white church.* The Trapp family of *Sound of Music* fame chose this setting for their home because it reminded them of their native Austria. The mountain resort comprises a Tyrolean chalet-style lodge, guest houses and condominiums. It offers 30mi of cross-country skiing trails.

■ **Stowe Recreation Path**

Traversing as it does dairy pastures, wildflower meadows and wooden bridges on the West Branch River, this 5mi paved trail through the Green Mountains has garnered awards for its superb design. The path begins in back of the village's Community Church and ends on Brook Road. Views from the trail are particularly beautiful in spring and fall. Cyclists, in-liners and walkers find the trail a delight. *For specifics: Stowe Area Assn.* ☎ *800-24-STOWE.*

★★ **Mt. Mansfield** – From the summit there is a sweeping **view**★★ of the entire region, including JAY PEAK to the northeast, LAKE CHAMPLAIN and the Adirondacks of New York to the west and THE WHITE MOUNTAINS of New Hampshire to the east. On a clear day, Montreal can be seen to the north.

During the 1930s, when a skier had to climb the mountain before skiing down, Stowe's unplowed toll road was the only ski trail on Mt. Mansfield. Today a network of well-groomed ski and hiking trails lace the mountain's slopes.

Mt. Mansfield Auto Road – *Rte. 108, 7mi north of Stowe. Open mid-May–mid-Oct daily 9am–5pm. $12/car.* ☎ *802-253-3500. www.stowe.com.* The Auto Road *(toll)* is a 4.5mi gravel road that leads to the summit.

Mt. Mansfield Gondola – *Rte. 108, 8mi north of Stowe. Operates mid-Jun–mid-Oct daily 10am–5pm. $10.* ♿ ☎ *802-253-3500. www.stowe.com.* The eight-passenger gondola lift provides access to the Cliff House near the summit.

Bingham Falls – *.5mi north of the Auto Rd. there is a path (difficult to find) to the right that leads through the woods to the falls.* The west branch forms a series of waterfalls here as it spills through a ravine.

★★ **Smugglers Notch** – *Rte. 108, 7mi north of Stowe; closed in winter. Exercise caution when proceeding between the large roadside boulders that have split from the walls of the notch.* The road linking Stowe and Jeffersonville is extremely narrow and climbs rapidly as it twists through the rugged scenic notch (2,162ft) between Mt. Mansfield and Spruce Peak. The forest admits little light, even on a bright day. Smugglers Notch earned its name because of the slaves and contraband items that were smuggled from the US into Canada through this pass during the War of 1812.

★ **Ben & Jerry's Ice Cream Factory** Kids
Rte. 100, 9mi south of Stowe in Waterbury. Open Jul–Aug daily 9am– 8pm. Jun daily 9am–5pm. Sept–Oct daily 9am–6pm. Rest of the year daily 10am–5pm. Closed Jan 1, Thanksgiving Day, Dec 25. ✗ ♿ ☎ *802-882-1260. www.benjerry.com.* Now a Vermont landmark and headquarters for the nationally recognized gourmet ice cream company, this playful building, with its Holstein polka dots, reflects the fun-loving, "caring capitalism" approach of its founders Ben Cohen and Jerry Greenfield. The two men began their business in 1977 with a $5 correspondence course on ice-cream making. In 1978 they opened their first scoop shop in a renovated Burlington gas station. Their products are now sold worldwide, with 1998 sales totaling $209 million. Tours *(30min, $2)* include a movie *(10min)* on the history of the company, a look at the production process and samples of the flavors of the day.

Mist Grill
92 Stowe St. in Waterbury. ☎ *802-244-2233.* Ensconced within an 1807 gristmill overlooking Thatcher Brook Falls, this pleasant country bistro and bakery daily beckons those in search of breakfast and lunch. Griddle cakes with maple cured ham or smoked bacon, boiled grapefruit with maple syrup or apple pie with cheddar cheese are proffered from 7:30am. The bakery opens at 6:30am for roasted coffees, pastries and artisan breads. On Friday and Saturday, dinner is served and on Sunday a hearty supper.

Cold Hollow Cider Mill
On Route 100 in Waterbury. ☎ *802-244-8771.* You can't miss this commercial compound en route to Stowe. The retail shop is stocked with apple-derived products, Vermont cheeses, jams, condiments, all kinds of maple syrup concoctions, salsas and sauces. A cider jelly manufacturing facility and a bakery are on the premises and the cider mill contains an operational press *(visitors can view a video on cider-making).* Free samples of cider, cheeses and jellies can be found in almost every corner.

Moss Glen Falls – *Rte. 100, 3mi north of Stowe. From Rte. 100, take Randolph Rd., then the first right to the small parking area.* A short trail leads to the falls and continues somewhat steeply *(not well marked)* upstream to a brook where it is possible to take a dip in the cool water.

Alpine Slide – Kids *Spruce Peak. Rte. 108, 8.5mi north of Stowe. Open mid-Jun–mid-Oct daily 10am–5pm. $8. ☎ 802-253-3500. www.stowe.com.* Stowe is one of the ski areas in New England where an alpine slide operates on the mountain slopes during the mild seasons.

WINDSOR

Population 3,714
Map of Principal Sights
Tourist Office ☎ 802-674-5910

This historic town on the banks of the Connecticut River was the birthplace of Vermont in 1777. Representatives meeting here that year agreed upon the state's official name, declared Vermont an independent republic and drew up its first constitution—the first constitution in the nation to prohibit slavery and grant the right to vote without regard to property ownership or individual wealth.
In the 19C, the hydraulic pump, the coffee percolator and other inventions were developed in Windsor, which today is a center for the machine tool industry.

SIGHTS

Constitution House – *16 N. Main St. Open late May–mid-Oct Wed–Sun 11am–5pm. $2. ♿ ☎ 802-828-3051. www.cit.state.vt.us.* Delegates, meeting in this old tavern in July 1777, drew up Vermont's first constitution. Exhibits arranged in the tavern rooms describe the development of the state's constitution and include examples of early Vermont crafts.

Vermont State Craft Center in Windsor – *Main St. Open year-round Mon–Thu 10am–5pm, Fri & Sat 9am–6pm, Sun 11am–5pm. ♿ ☎ 802-674-6729.* Located in Windsor House, a restored 19C Greek Revival hotel, the center features the work of Vermont's finest craftspeople. Pottery, weavings, jewelry, leather goods, glassware and food products are among the hundreds of original items displayed in the retail galleries on the first and second floors.

American Precision Museum – *196 Main St. Open late May–Oct daily 10am–5pm. $5. ♿ ☎ 802-674-5781. www.americanprecision.org.* This cavernous brick building was constructed as the Robbins and Lawrence Armory (1846), an innovative machine mill where interchangeable-parts manufacturing was first widely used. The museum displays a large collection of precision machine tools and firearms that trace the history of American industrialization techniques from the mid-19C through the mid-20C.

Windsor-Cornish Covered Bridge – *South of the Constitution House; after two sets of lights, turn left.* Spanning the Connecticut River between New Hampshire and Vermont, this is the longest covered bridge (460ft) in New England.

WOODSTOCK★★

Population 3,212
Map of Principal Sights
Tourist Office ☎ 802-457-3555

A touch of urban elegance has characterized this pretty village since the 18C, when it was selected as the Windsor County seat. Businessmen, lawyers, doctors and teachers settled here during the next 200 years, building frame, brick and stone dwellings and shops that reflected the wealth of the community. A lack of industrial development in the 19C and the devotion of the town's residents to Woodstock's architectural heritage have ensured the preservation of the gracious 18C and 19C structures bordering the village green and lining Elm, Pleasant and Central Streets.

Historical Notes

Established in 1761 by settlers from Massachusetts, Woodstock developed quickly after it was selected as the county seat. Mills were built on the outskirts of town, and tradesmen, working in shops surrounding the village green, provided most of the goods needed for daily living. Woodstock was self-sufficient and prosperous. During the heyday of the 19C water cures, the village became a fashionable vacation spot. In 1934 skiers experimenting with a Model T motor and a piece of cable on a hill near

Mt. Tom *(outside Woodstock)* developed the nation's first ski tow. Twenty years later, a poma lift, then more modern lifts such as chairs and aerial trams, were adopted by Vermont's burgeoning ski industry. While the ski tow devised 50 years ago near Mt. Tom is still remembered for the role it played in the history of skiing in the US, today the most modern equipment is used at **Suicide Six**, a ski area nearby.
The **Woodstock Inn**, facing the village green, was opened in 1969. The hotel's lodging and conference facilities attract business travelers as well as tourists. **F.H. Gillingham & Sons** has been the town's general store since 1886 and stocks handmade Vermont products as well as hardware, housewares and specialty foods.

SIGHTS *2hrs*

To enjoy Woodstock, stroll along **Elm** and **Pleasant Streets**, browse in the emporiums and galleries on **Central Street** and walk across the covered bridge *(in the middle of town)* that spans the Ottauquechee River. The Town Crier bulletin board, located near the corner of Elm and Central Streets, posts notices of auctions, flea markets and other community events.

The Green – The oval village green is fringed with buildings of different styles: Federal mansions, the Greek Revival **Windsor County Courthouse** and the Romanesque-style **Norman Williams Library**, which is being expanded.

Dana House Museum – *26 Elm St. Open late May–Oct Mon–Sat 10am–5pm, Sun noon–4pm. $1. ☎ 802-457-1822.* Constructed in 1807 by the merchant Charles Dana, this Federal-style dwelling was occupied until 1942 by members of the Dana family. The Woodstock Historical Society uses it to house collections of locally made furniture, antique maps of the area, toys, clocks and clothing. A tasteful 1998 addition contains an exhibit on the history of the town's architecture, industry and preservationist activity. The research library is open to the public.

★★ **Billings Farm and Museum** – Kids *River Rd. Follow Elm St., cross the bridge, turn right, then .2mi on River Rd. Open May–Oct daily 10am–5pm. Thanksgiving weekend, Dec weekends & Dec 26 & 31 10am–4pm. $7. ♿ ☎ 802-457-2355. www.billingsfarm.org.* The complex is both an operating modern-day dairy farm and a museum depicting life on a Vermont farm in 1890. The farm was established in 1871 by lawyer/businessman **Frederick Billings**, whose interest in animal husbandry and conservation led him to stock the farm with purebred Jersey cattle. The Billings' herd, a prizewinner over the years, continues to earn blue ribbons to this day.
The 1890 **farmhouse**, restored and appointed with period furniture, features tile-decorated fireplaces and a basement creamery *(daily demonstrations of butter making)*. Life-size displays in several restored barns illustrate the daily and seasonal activities performed by a 19C Vermont family. Visitors can view an Academy Award nominated (1999) film *A Place in the Land (30min)*, which examines the property's role in the history of conservation in the US.
Located in the fields just below the farmhouse, a 19C garden features a variety of vegetables and flowers.

★★ **Marsh-Billings-Rockefeller National Historic Site** – *Across the street from the Billings Farm and Museum. Visit by guided tour (1hr 30min) only, May–Oct. ☎ 802-457-3368.* Opened in June 1998, Vermont's first national historic site centers on a meticulously preserved, art-filled Queen Anne mansion and the conservation efforts of three of its residents: the prescient environmentalist George

■ Woodstock's Watering Holes

Bentley's *(3 Elm St. ☎ 802-457-3232)* has been a local favorite for more than 20 years. Its dark-wooded interior lends a clubby atmosphere to the place. Lunch, dinner and Sunday brunch are served daily as well as breakfast, in the cafe. There's dancing every Saturday night and the restaurant's own custom-brewed ale, a large wine selection and Vermont microbrews. Tucked away next to the Dana House, **The Prince & the Pauper** *(24 Elm St. ☎ 802-457-1818)* serves a prix-fixe dinner daily (which includes appetizer, salad and entrée) as well as à la carte selections. There's also a Sunday brunch featuring international cuisine such as Ravioli del Giorno, Korean grilled beef, Coquille St. Jacques, Scandinavian eggs benedict and more. For morning coffee, a light lunch or Sunday brunch, pick a patio spot or take a linen-covered table in the bakery at **Pane e Salute** *(61 Central St. ☎ 802-457-4882)*. Tuscan pizza, pasta, traditional regional breads, biscotti, panettone, cornetti and other Italian cakes and pastries are tempting treats at this Euro-style cafe. Espresso to mocha lattes, teas, wine and beer are available.

Perkins Marsh, author of *Man and Nature* (1865); Frederick Billings, founder of the Billings Farm *(above)*; and Billings' granddaughter Mary French Rockefeller, who, with her husband, Laurance, sustained the farm and property from the mid- to late 20C. American landscape paintings by such renowned artists as Thomas Cole, Albert Bierstadt and Asher B. Durand deck the house's sumptuous interior and illustrate art and the conservation movement's influence on each other.

EXCURSIONS

★ **Plymouth** – *14mi southwest of Woodstock by Rtes. 4 & 100A. See Entry Heading.*

★ **Quechee Gorge** – *6mi east of Woodstock on Rte. 4.* Quechee Gorge, formed over thousands of years by the erosive action of the Ottauquechee River, is spanned by the Route 4 highway bridge. The sheer walls of the gorge rise approximately 165ft from the river below. The gorge is best seen from the bridge on Route 4.
A trail, steep in sections *(round-trip 1.5mi)*, leads to the bottom of the gorge, a popular swimming area *(in season)*. Hikers can park at the gift shop on the east side of the bridge.

Simon Pearce Restaurant

The Mill in Quechee. ☎ *802-295-1470.* After visiting the Simon Pearce retail store, have lunch or dinner in the airy, country-styled dining room with its expansive arched windows and sleek wooden tables and chairs, or on the outdoor deck overlooking the falls of the Ottauquechee River. Homemade soups, salads and breads as well as seafood, beef, veal and duck are presented on attractive Mill-manufactured dinner service. Beverages are served in hand-blown glassware. *Dinner reservations advised.*

Two miles beyond the gorge, in the appealing village of **Quechee**, is the popular **glass shop** of designer Simon Pearce. Housed in the town's historic 150-year-old woolen mill on the edge of the river, the retail store allows visitors to watch glassblowers and potters at work *(open year-round daily 9am–9pm; closed Thanksgiving Day & Dec 25;* ✗ ☎ *802-295-2711; www.simonpearce.com).*

Silver Lake State Park – *In Barnard, 10mi north of Woodstock by Rte. 12. Open mid-May–Labor Day daily 9am–9pm. $2 (Jun 75¢).* △ ♿ ☎ *802-234-9451. www.vtstateparks.com.* The park, within walking distance of Barnard village, contains a small lakefront beach, picnic area, country store and campsites set in a pine grove.

Joseph Smith Memorial – *Between Sharon & Royalton, 25mi north of Woodstock. From I-89 take Exit 2, then follow Rte. 14 north from Sharon. Turn right onto Dairy Hill Road for 2mi. Open year-round daily 9am–7pm.* ♿ ☎ *802-763-7742.* A lovely drive along the White River from the village of Sharon marks the approach to the birthplace of the founder of The Church of Jesus Christ of Latter-day Saints (the Mormons). Here, on an expansive hilltop overlooking the Green Mountains, a granite shaft (38.5ft) designates the farmsite where **Joseph Smith** (1805-1844), the Vermont native who went on to establish one of America's major religions, was born. Attractive stone buildings contain a visitor center and exhibits on Smith and the Mormon Church, which is headquartered in Salt Lake City, Utah. A video presentation *(12min)* and guided tours *(45min)* are offered to visitors.

Practical
Information

Calendar of Events

Below is a selection of New England's most popular annual events; some dates may vary from year to year. For detailed information contact local tourism (☎ numbers listed under blue entry headings in the main section of this guide) or state tourism offices.

Date	Event	Location
Spring		
3rd Mon in Apr	Boston Marathon	Boston (MA)
	Patriots' Day Celebrations	Lexington & Concord (MA)
May–Jun	Art of the Northeast	New Canaan (CT)
	MooseMainea	Moosehead Lake Region (ME)
mid-May	Dogwood Festival	Fairfield (CT)
	Sheep & Wool Festival	New Boston (NH)
mid-May, Jul & Sept	Brimfield Outdoor Antiques Show	Brimfield (MA)
late May	Lilac Sunday	Shelburne (VT)
late May–mid-Jun	Gaspee Days Festival	Cranston & Warwick (RI)
Memorial Day weekend	Lobsterfest	Mystic (CT)
Summer		
early Jun	Yale-Harvard Regatta	New London (CT)
mid-Jun	Festival of Historic Houses	Providence (RI)
	Market Square Days Celebration	Portsmouth (NH)
mid-Jun–Aug	Williamstown Theater Festival	Williamstown (MA)
mid–late Jun	American CraftFair	West Springfield (MA)
late Jun	St. Peter's Fiesta	Gloucester (MA)
	Block Island Race Week	Block Island (RI)
	Seacoast Jazz Festival	Portsmouth (NH)
	Harborfest	Boston (MA)
late Jun–late Aug	Berkshire Theater Festival	Stockbridge (MA)
next to last Tue & Wed in Jun	Windjammer Days	Boothbay Harbor (ME)
Jun–late Aug	Jacob's Pillow Dance Festival	Becket (MA)
Jul–late Aug	Tanglewood Music Festival	Lenox (MA)
Jul–Aug	Royal Lipizzan Stallions	North Hero (VT)
early Jul	Riverfest	Hartford (CT)
early to mid-Jul	International Tennis Hall of Fame Grass Court Championships	Newport (RI)
Jul 4	Bristol Civic, Military & Fireman's Parade	Bristol (RI)
1st weekend after Jul 4th	Great Schooner Days	Rockland (ME)
2nd weekend in Jul	Vermont Quilt Festival	Northfield (VT)
mid-Jul	Open House Tour	Litchfield (CT)
	Newport Music Festival	Newport (RI)
late Jul	Friendship Sloop Days	Rockland (ME)
	Blessing of the Fleet	Galilee (RI)
	Black Ships Festival	Newport (RI)
each Fri in Aug	Pilgrim Progress Procession	Plymouth (MA)
early Aug	Lobster Festival	Rockland (ME)
	Craftsmen's Fair	Sunapee (NH)
	Southern Vermont Craft Fair	Manchester (VT)
2nd weekend in Aug	JVC Jazz Festival	Newport (RI)
mid-Aug	Mystic Outdoor Art Festival	Mystic (CT)
	Retired Skippers Race	Castine (ME)

Fall

Sept–early Oct	**South Mountain Concert Festival**	*Pittsfield (MA)*
early Sept	**Tuna Tournament**	*Galilee & Narragansett (RI)*
	Vermont State Fair	*Rutland (VT)*
	Woodstock Fair	*South Woodstock (CT)*
mid-Sept	**Eastern States Exposition**	*West Springfield (MA)*
	Highland Games at Loon Mountain	*Lincoln (NH)*
mid-Sept–mid-Oct	**Stratton Arts Festival**	*Stratton (VT)*
late Sept	**Banjo Contest**	*Craftsbury Common (VT)*
	Old Time Fiddlers Contest	*Barre (VT)*
late Sept–early Oct	**Northeast Kingdom Fall Foliage Festival**	*Northeast Kingdom (VT)*
last weekend in Sept	**Old Fashioned Harvest Market**	*Underhill (VT)*
Halloween week	**Haunted Happenings**	*Salem (MA)*
	Pumpkin Festival	*Keene (NH)*
Thanksgiving Day	**Pilgrim Progress Procession**	*Plymouth (MA)*

Winter

mid-Dec	**Torchlight Parade**	*Old Saybrook (CT)*
mid-Jan	**Annual Winter Carnival**	*Stowe (VT)*
late Jan–Feb	**Chinese New Year Parade**	*Boston (MA)*
Feb	**Dartmouth Winter Carnival**	*Hanover (NH)*
early–mid-Feb	**World Championship Sled Dog Derby**	*Laconia (NH)*
mid-Feb–mid-Mar	**Vermont Mozart Festival**	*Burlington (VT)*
early Mar	**New England Spring Flower Show**	*Boston (MA)*

Vermont State Fair, Rutland

The following symbols are used throughout this section:

🆕 New England   ⓒ Connecticut   ⓜ Maine   ⓜ Massachusetts

ⓡ Rhode Island   ⓝ New Hampshire   ⓥ Vermont

See the Entry Headings *(see Index)* for detailed practical information about:

The Berkshires, Block Island, Boston, Cape Cod, Martha's Vineyard, Monhegan Island, Mount Desert Island, Nantucket Island, Northern Maine, Portland and the **White Mountains**.

Planning the Trip

Tourist Information

State tourism offices provide information and brochures on points of interest, seasonal events and accommodations, as well as road and city maps. In this guide, local tourism office telephone numbers are listed (if available) under the blue entry headings. Information centers are indicated on maps by the 🚹 symbol.

State	Tourism Offices	☎
ⓒ	**Dept of Economic & Community Development** 505 Hudson St. Hartford CT 06106 www.ctbound.org	860-270-8080 800-282-6863 (US & Canada)
ⓜ	**Maine Tourism Association** PO Box 396 Kittery ME 03904 www.mainetourism.com	207-439-1319 800-533-9595 (US & Canada)
ⓜ	**Office of Travel & Tourism** 10 Park Plaza, Suite 4510 Boston MA 02116 www.massvacation.com	617-973-8500 800-227-6277 (US & Canada)
ⓝ	**Office of Travel & Tourism Development** PO Box 1856 Concord NH 03301-1856 www.visitnh.gov	603-271-2665 800-386-4664
ⓡ	**State Tourism Division** 1 W. Exchange St. Providence RI 02903 www.visitrhodeisland.com	401-222-2601 800-556-2484 (US & Canada)
ⓥ	**Department of Tourism & Marketing** 6 Baldwin St., Drawer 33 Montpelier VT 05633-1301 www.travel-vermont.com	802-828-3237 800-837-6668

Tips for Special Visitors

Children – Throughout this guide, sights of particular interest to children are indicated with a 🅺🅸🅳🆂 symbol. Many museums and other attractions offer special children's programs and resource centers. Most attractions throughout New England offer discounted admission to visitors under 18 years of age. In addition, various hotels offer family discount packages, and many restaurants provide a children's menu.

Travelers with Disabilities – Federal law requires that businesses (including hotels and restaurants) provide access for the disabled, devices for the hearing impaired, and designated parking spaces. Many public buses are equipped with wheelchair lifts; many hotels have rooms designed for visitors with special needs. For further information, contact the state access office: ⓒ ☎ 860-418-6047 ⓜ ☎ 207-626-2774 ⓜ ☎ 413-545-5353 ⓝ ☎ 603-271-6895 ⓡ ☎ 401-222-3731 ⓥ ☎ 802-241-2400.

National Parks – All national parks have restrooms and other facilities for the disabled (such as wheelchair-accessible nature trails or tour buses). Disabled persons are eligible for the Golden Access Passport *($10, must be US citizen)*, which entitles the carrier to free admission to all national parks and a 50% discount on user fees (campsites, boat launches); contact the National Park Service, Office of Public Inquiry, PO Box 37127, Washington DC 20013-7127 ☎ 202-208-4747.

State Parks – Some state parks offer permanently disabled persons a discount on campsites and day-use fees at state-operated facilities; contact the appropriate state parks and recreation office *(p 309)*. Requests for discounts must include proof of identification and disability.

Transportation – **Train travel: Amtrak** publishes a handy book *Access Amtrak*. Passengers who will need assistance should give 24hr-advance notice ☏ 800-872-7245 or 800-523-6590 (TDD). **Bus travel:** Disabled riders are encouraged to notify **Greyhound** 48hrs in advance by calling ☏ 800-231-2222 *(US only)* or 800-345-3109 (TDD). *Greyhound Travel Policies* is published annually for customers who require special assistance. **Rental cars:** Reservations for hand-controlled cars should be made well in advance. For information about travel for individuals or groups, contact the Society for the Advancement of Travel for the Handicapped, 347 5th Ave., Suite 610, New York NY 10016 ☏ 212-447-7284.

Senior Citizens – Many of New England's attractions, parks, hotels and restaurants offer discounts to visitors age 62 and older (proof of age may be required). Discounts on lodging, car rentals and other travel-related services are available to members of the National Council of Senior Citizens, 8403 Colesville Rd., Suite 1200, Silver Spring MD 20910 ☏ 301-578-8800. Discounts are also available to members of the American Assn. of Retired Persons (AARP), 601 E St. NW, Washington DC 20049 ☏ 202-434-2277.

When to Go

A resort area for more than a century, New England continues to attract vacationers to its mountains and shores in every season. **Summer** months are generally mild. Daytime temperatures along the coast and in the north average 70 to 80°F (21 to 27°C); in the central area they rarely climb above 90°F (32°C), July being the warmest month. Summer nights tend to be cool and comfortable.

Average Daily Temperatures

State	January	July
Connecticut	27°F (–2.5°C)	73°F (23°C)
Maine	16°F (–9°C)	67°F (19°C)
Massachusetts	26°F (–3°C)	70°F (21°C)
New Hampshire	13°F (–10°C)	60°F (15°C)
Rhode Island	30°F (–1°C)	71°F (21.5°C)
Vermont	16°F (–9°C)	70°F (21°C)

In the north, the long summer days begin to fade into the clear, crisp days of autumn by late August. **Indian summer** (a period of warm, mild weather in late autumn or early winter) is considered the glory of New England and often is accompanied by the spectacle of blazing autumn color. Foliage reports *(p 311)* track the procession of color as it advances from the northern regions southward. In autumn the countryside teems with activity, including country fairs, auctions and flea markets.

Skiers and other snow enthusiasts await the long New England **winter**, typically lasting from late November through April. Daytime temperatures in the south and along the coast average 20° to 30°F (–7° to –1°C). In the north and at higher elevations,

Metcalf Pond, Vermont

temperatures may stay below 0°F (−18°) for 60 days annually. Snowfall is heavier in the higher elevations, with an annual average of 60in/154cm, the greatest snowfall occurring in January. There are more than 100 ski areas in the region, and opportunities abound for ice-skating and snowmobiling as well. New England's infamous "**Northeaster**" storms, typically lasting two to three days, can dump 10 or more inches (25cm) of snow in a single day.

The **spring** thaw, a mixture of warm days and cold nights, brings forth budding flowers, often peeking through an unexpected layer of snow, and is the perfect weather for the cultivation of maple syrup.

Most attractions are open from Memorial Day to mid-October only (except in large cities), although some sights extend their season from mid-April through late October.

International Visitors

Planning the Trip

Embassies/Consulates – Visitors from outside the US can obtain information from the tourism agencies listed in the chapter titled "Planning the Trip," or from the nearest US embassy or consulate in their country of residence.

Selected US Embassies

Australia	Moonah Place,	
	Yaralumla ACT 2600	(02) 6-214-5600
Canada	100 Wellington St.,	
	Ottawa ON K1P 5T1 Canada	613-238-4470
Japan	10-5, Akasaka 1-Chome, Minato-Ku (107)	
	Unit 45004, Box 258,	
	APO AP 96337-0001	(81) 3-3224-5000
Mexico	Paseo de la Reforma 305,	
	Colonia Cuauhtemoc, 06500 Mexico	(52) 5-211-0042
United Kingdom	24/31 Grosvenor Square, W. 1A 1AE,	
	PSC 801 Box 40, FPO AE 09498-4040	(44) 71-499-9000

Entry Requirements – Citizens of countries participating in the Visa Waiver Pilot Program (VWPP) are not required to obtain a visa to enter the US for visits of fewer than 90 days. For more information, contact the US consulate in your country of residence. Citizens of nonparticipating countries must have a visitor's visa. Upon entry, nonresident foreign visitors must present a valid passport and round-trip transportation ticket. Canadian citizens are not required to present a passport or visa to enter the US, although identification and proof of citizenship may be requested (a passport or Canadian birth certificate and photo identification are usually acceptable). Naturalized Canadian citizens should carry their citizenship papers. Inoculations are generally not required, but check with the US embassy or consulate before departing.

Customs – All articles brought into the US must be declared at the time of entry. **Exempt** from customs regulations: personal effects; one liter of alcoholic beverage *(providing visitor is at least 21 years old)*; either 200 cigarettes, 50 cigars or 2 kilograms of smoking tobacco; and gifts *(to persons in the US)* that do not exceed $100 in value. **Prohibited items:** plant material; firearms and ammunition *(if not intended for sporting purposes)*; and meat and poultry products. For further information regarding US Customs, contact the US embassy or consulate before departing. It is also recommended that visitors contact the customs service in their country of residence to determine reentry regulations.

Health Insurance – The US does not have a national health program. Before departing, visitors from abroad should check with their health care insurance to determine if it covers doctor's visits, medication and hospitalization in the US. Prescription drugs should be properly identified and accompanied by a copy of the prescription.

General Information

Driving in the US – Visitors bearing valid driver's licenses issued by their country of residence are not required to obtain an International Driver's License to drive in the US. Drivers must carry vehicle registration and/or rental contract and proof of automobile insurance at all times. Rental cars in the US are usually equipped with automatic transmission, and rental rates tend to be less expensive than overseas. **Gasoline** is sold by the gallon *(1 US gallon = 3.8 liters)* and is cheaper than in most other countries. Gas stations are usually found in clusters on the edge of a city, or where two or more highways intersect. Self-service gas stations do not offer car repair, although many sell standard maintenance items. **Road regulations** *(p 306)* in the US require that vehicles be driven on the right side of the road. Distances are posted in miles (1 mile = 1.6 kilometers). Travelers are advised to obey posted speed limit signs.

Electricity – Electrical current in the US is 110 volts AC, 60 Hz. Foreign-made appliances may need voltage transformers and North American flat-blade adapter plugs (available at specialty travel and electronics stores).

Emergency Assistance – In all major US cities, dial **911** to call the police, ambulance or fire department. Emergencies may also be reported by dialing 0 for the operator.

Mail – First-class postage rates within the US: letter 33¢ (1oz), postcard 20¢. Overseas: letter 60¢ (1/2 oz), postcard 50¢. Letters and small packages can be mailed from most hotels. Stamps and packing material can be purchased at post offices, grocery stores and businesses offering postal and express shipping services *(see Yellow Pages of phone directory under "Mailing Services" or "Post Offices")*. Most post offices are open Monday–Friday 9am–5pm; some are open Saturday 9am–noon.

Money – Most banks are members of the network of Automatic Teller Machines (ATMs), allowing visitors from around the world to withdraw cash using bank cards and major credit cards. ATMs can usually be found in banks, airports, grocery stores and shopping malls. To inquire about ATM service, locations and transaction fees, contact your local bank, Cirrus ☎ 800-424-7787 or Plus ☎ 800-843-7587.

Credit Cards and Traveler's Checks – Most banks will cash **traveler's checks** and process cash advances on major credit cards with proper identification. Traveler's checks are accepted at most stores, restaurants and hotels. To report a lost or stolen **credit card**: American Express ☎ 800-528-4800; Diners Club ☎ 800-234-6377; MasterCard ☎ 800-627-8372 or the issuing bank; Visa ☎ 800-336-8472.

Currency Exchange – Most main offices of national banks will exchange foreign currency and charge a small fee for this service; contact main or branch offices for exchange information and locations. Boston's Logan International Airport has several currency exchange offices **(Travelex World Wide Money)** ☎ 800-445-0295. **Thomas Cook Currency Services** ☎ 800-287-7362 and **American Express Travel Services** ☎ 800-297-3429 operate exchange offices throughout New England.

Taxes and Tipping – *p 308*. Prices displayed or quoted in the US do not generally include the **sales tax**. Sales tax is added at time of purchase and is not reimbursable as in other countries (it can sometimes be avoided if the buyer requests purchased items be shipped to another country). In the US it is customary to give a **tip** (a small gift of money) for services received from restaurant servers, porters, hotel maids and taxi drivers.

Smoking Regulations – Many cities throughout New England have ordinances that prohibit smoking in public places or confine smoking to designated areas.

Telephones/Telegrams – Instructions for using **public telephones** are listed on or near the phone. Some public telephones accept credit cards, and all will accept long-distance calling cards. For **long-distance** calls in the US and Canada, dial 1+area code+number. To place an **international call**, dial **011**+country code+number. To place a **collect call** (person receiving call pays charges), dial **0**+area code+number and tell the operator you are calling collect. If it is an international call, ask for the overseas operator. For local telephone number information, dial **0** for the operator.
The cost for a local call from a pay phone is 20¢–35¢ *(any combination of nickels, dimes or quarters)*. The charge for numbers preceded by **900** can range anywhere from 50¢ to $15 per minute. Most hotels add a surcharge for local and long-distance calls. Telephone numbers that start with **1-800** or **1-888** are toll-free *(no charge)* and may not be accessible outside of North America.
You can send a **telegram** or money, or have money telegraphed to you, via the Western Union system ☎ 800-325-6000.

Temperature and Measurement – In the US temperatures are measured in degrees Fahrenheit and measurements are expressed according to the US Customary System of weights and measures.

Equivalents

Degrees Fahrenheit	95°	86°	77°	68°	59°	50°	41°	32°	23°	14°
Degrees Celsius	35°	30°	25°	20°	15°	10°	5°	0°	–5°	–10°

1 inch = 2.54 centimeters	1 quart = 0.946 liters
1 foot = 30.48 centimeters	1 gallon = 3.785 liters
1 mile = 1.609 kilometers	1 pound = 0.454 kilograms

Time Zone – New England is on Eastern Standard Time (EST), 5hrs behind Greenwich Mean Time. Daylight Saving Time *(clocks advanced 1hr)* is in effect for most of the US from the first Sunday in April until the last Sunday in October.

Getting There and Getting Around

By Air – Most flights to New England stop at La Guardia or JFK International airports in New York, or Logan International Airport in Boston before making connecting flights to the principal New England airports: Bradley International (**Hartford** CT), Bangor International (**Bangor** ME), Portland International (**Portland** ME), Manchester Airport (**Manchester** NH) and T.F. Green State Airport (**Providence** RI).

By Train – With access to over 44 communities in New England, the Amtrak rail network offers a relaxing alternative for the traveler with time to spare. Advance reservations are recommended. First class, coach and sleeping accommodations are available; fares are comparable to air travel. The New England Express travels from New York City to Boston in just over five hours. Travelers from Canada should ask their local travel agents about Amtrak/Via Rail connections. **All-Aboard Pass** allows up to 45 days travel nationwide (limited to three stops). **USARailPass** *(not available to US or Canadian citizens or legal residents)* offers unlimited travel within Amtrak-designated regions at discounted rates; 15- and 30-day passes are available. Schedule and route information: ☎ 800-872-7245 *(North America only; outside North America, contact your local travel agent).*

By Bus – Greyhound, the largest bus company in the US, offers access to most communities in New England at a leisurely pace. Overall, fares are lower than other forms of public transportation. **Ameripass** allows unlimited travel for 7, 14, 30 or 60 days. Advance reservations suggested. Consult "Planning the Trip" for information for disabled riders. Schedule and route information: ☎ 800-231-2222 *(US only).*

By Car – New England has an extensive system of well-maintained major roads. In remote areas, minor roads tend to be unmarked and may be confusing. It is advisable to plan itineraries along numbered state routes and interstates. Exercise caution when driving in mountainous areas or on back roads. Roads tend to be narrow, steep and twisting; many are unpaved. Observe cautionary road signs and posted speed limits.

Rental Cars – Most large rental car agencies have offices at major airports and in the larger cities in New England. A major credit card and valid driver's license are required for rental (some agencies also require proof of insurance). Drop-off charges may apply if a vehicle is returned to a location other than where it was rented.

Rental Company	☎ Reservations	Rental Company	☎ Reservations
Alamo	800-327-9633	**Hertz**	800-654-3131
Avis	800-331-1212	**National**	800-328-4567
Budget	800-527-0700	**Thrifty**	800-331-4200
Dollar	800-421-6868		

(toll-free numbers may not be accessible outside of North America)

Road Regulations – The maximum speed limit on major freeways is 65mph (105km/h) in rural areas and 55mph (90km/h) in and around cities (in Connecticut and Rhode Island, maximum speed limits are 55mph). Speed limits range from 30 to 40mph (45-65km/h) within cities, and average 20 to 30mph (30-45km/h) in residential areas. Use of **seat belts** is mandatory for all persons in the car in all states except New Hampshire (required only for passengers under 18 years of age) and Connecticut. In Connecticut, seat belt use is mandatory for all persons 16 or under; for persons over 16, seat belt use is mandatory only in the front seat. In Rhode Island children from 4 to 5 years of age must ride *in the backseat* with a seat belt on.
Child safety seats are required in Vermont, Connecticut and Massachusetts for children under 5 years (or 40lbs and below in Connecticut); they are required in Maine, Rhode Island and New Hampshire for children under 4 years (seats available from most rental car agencies). **School bus** law in effect for the six-state area requires motorists to bring vehicles to a full stop when red lights on a school bus are activated. Unless otherwise posted, it is permissible to turn right at a red traffic light after coming to a complete stop. Parking spaces identified with ♿ are reserved only for disabled persons. Anyone parking in these spaces without proper identification is subject to ticketing.

Turnpikes – Principal toll roads in New England are: I-95 connecting with I-495 from York to Augusta, Maine; I-95 from the Massachusetts border to Portsmouth, New Hampshire; I-90 (Massachusetts Turnpike) from the New York/Massachusetts state border to Boston; Route 3 from Nashua to Manchester, and I-93 from Manchester to Concord, New Hampshire.

In Case of Accident – If you are involved in an accident resulting in personal or property damage, you must notify the local police and remain at the scene until dismissed. If blocking traffic, vehicles should be moved if possible.

Accommodations

Luxury **hotels** are generally found in major cities, **motels** in clusters on the edge of town, or where two or more highways intersect. In rural areas motels are found on roads frequently traveled by tourists. **Bed and breakfasts** (B&Bs) can be found in residential areas of cities and villages.

Local tourist offices provide detailed accommodation information (telephone numbers listed under blue entry titles in the main section of this guide). In season and during weekends, advance reservations are recommended. Always advise reservations clerk of late arrival; rooms, even though reserved, might not always be held after 6pm otherwise. Off-season and weekday rates are usually lower than seasonal and weekend rates. Many New England facilities offer either the American Plan (three meals included) or the Modified American Plan (breakfast and dinner included).

Hotels/Motels – Major hotel chains with locations throughout New England include:

Best Western	800-528-1234	Howard Johnson	800-446-4656
Comfort Inn	800-228-5150	Marriott	800-228-9290
Days Inn	800-325-2525	Radisson	800-333-3333
Hampton Inn	800-426-7866	Ramada Inn	800-272-6232
Holiday Inn	800-465-4329	Westin Hotels	800-228-3000

(toll-free numbers may not be accessible outside of North America)

Accommodations range from luxury hotels to budget motels. Rates vary with season and location; rates tend to be higher in cities and in coastal and vacation areas. Many hotels and motels offer packages (including meals, passes to local sights and access to facility-sponsored events) and weekend specials. Amenities include television, restaurant, swimming pool, and smoking/non-smoking rooms. The more elegant hotels also offer in-room dining and valet service.

Bed and Breakfasts/Country Inns – Many B&Bs are privately owned and located in historic homes. Breakfast is usually included; private baths are not always available. Smoking indoors may not be allowed.

Some inns have been in operation since colonial times. Inns often include a restaurant that serves three meals a day. The price of breakfast may not be included in the lodging fee, as it is with B&Bs.

Many inns and B&Bs participate in one-day and weekend inn-to-inn tours for bikers, hikers and cross-country skiers. Some establishments may charge a 10-15% gratuity (inquire when reserving). ☞ Maine: for a free copy of *Lodging and Dining Guide,* contact the Maine Innkeepers Assn., 305 Commercial St., Portland ME 04101 ☎ 207-773-7670.

Dianne Dietrich Leis

Longfellow's Wayside Inn, Sudbury, Massachusetts

Reservations services – 🔵 Nutmeg B&B Agency, PO Box 1117, West Hartford CT 06127 ☎ 860-236-6698 or 800-727-7592 or www.bnb-link.com 🔵 Bed & Breakfast of Maine, 377 Gray Rd., Falmouth, ME 04105 ☎ 207-797-5540 🔵 Bed & Breakfast Rhode Island, PO Box 3291, Newport RI 02840 ☎ 401-849-1298 or 800-828-0000 or www.visitnewport.com/bedandbreakfast 🔵 Vermont Centerpoint, VT 05048 ☎ 800-449-2745. 🔵 Destinnations, 572 Rte. 28, West Yarmouth, MA 02673 ☎ 508-790-0566 or www.destinnations.com.

Hostels – A simple, low-cost alternative to hotels and inns, hostels average $12–$17/night; amenities include community living room, showers, laundry facilities, full-service kitchen and dining room, and dormitory-style rooms (blankets and pillows are provided, but guests are required to bring their own linens). Membership cards are recommended. **American Youth Hostels**, POBox 37613, Washington DC 20013-7613 ☎ 202-783-6161.

Camping – Campsites are located in national and state parks, national forests and in private campgrounds. Amenities range from full RV hook-ups to rustic backcountry sites. Most camping areas provide recreational and sporting amenities. Advance reservations are recommended from mid-May through mid-October. **Wilderness camping** is available on most public lands. Topographic maps of most wilderness areas are available. Contact desired location or state tourism offices for further information.

Farm Vacations – Host farms allow paying visitors the opportunity to participate in the daily activities of a working farm. Rates vary from $28 to $60/night. For more information, contact: 🔵 Dept. of Agriculture, 765 Asylum Ave., Hartford CT 06105 ☎ 860-713-2569 🔵 Maine Farm Vacation B&B Assn., RR3, 377 Gray Rd., Falmouth, ME 04105 ☎ 207-797-5540 🔵 Dept. of Food & Agriculture, 100 Cambridge St., Boston, MA 02202 ☎ 617-727-3018 ext. 175 🔵 Dept. of Agriculture, PO Box 2042, Concord NH 03302 ☎ 603-271-2505. 🔵 Vermont Farm Vacations Dept. of Agriculture, 116 State St., Drawer 20, Montpelier VT 05620 ☎ 802-828-2416.

Basic Information

Business Hours – Mon–Fri 9am or 10am–5pm; some retail shops may stay open until 9pm on Thursday. Shopping centers: Mon–Sat 9:30am–8pm or 9pm, Sun 11am–6pm. Banking hours: Mon–Thur 10am–3pm or 4pm, Fri 10am–5pm; some banks close later on Friday. Banks in larger cities may open on Saturday morning.

Liquor Laws – The legal age for purchase and consumption of alcoholic beverages is 21 throughout New England; proof of age may be required. Liquor stores and many grocery and drug stores sell liquor. Almost all grocery stores sell beer and wine. Alcoholic beverages may be sold during the following hours: 🔵 Mon–Sat 8am–8pm; 🔵 Mon–Sat 6am–1am, Sun 9am–1am; 🔵 locally regulated, times vary; 🔵 daily 6am–11:45pm; 🔵 Jun–Oct Mon–Sat 7am–11pm (rest of the year 10pm) 🔵 daily 6am–midnight.

Major Holidays – Most banks and government offices in the New England states are closed on the following legal holidays *(many retail stores and restaurants remain open on days shown with *)*:

Holiday	States Observing	Date
New Year's Day	🔵	January 1
Martin Luther King's Birthday*	🔵	3rd Monday in January
Presidents' Day*	🔵	3rd Monday in February
Town Meeting Day	🔵	1st Tuesday in March
Patriots' Day	🔵 🔵	3rd Monday in April
Memorial Day	🔵	Last Monday in May or May 30
Independence Day	🔵	July 4
Victory Day	🔵	2nd Monday in August
Bennington Battle Day	🔵	August 16
Labor Day	🔵	1st Monday in September
Columbus Day*	🔵	2nd Monday in October
Election Day	🔵	2nd Tuesday in November
Veterans Day*	🔵	November 11
Thanksgiving Day	🔵	4th Thursday in November
Christmas Day	🔵	December 25

Taxes and Tipping – State taxes vary from state to state *(chart below)*. Local taxes may be applicable and also vary within the states. It is customary in restaurants to tip the server 15–20% of the bill. At hotels, porters should be tipped $1 per suitcase, and hotel maids $1 per night of stay. Taxi drivers are usually tipped 15% of the fare.

State Sales Tax

State	General Tax	Room Tax	Restaurant Tax	Exemptions
⊕	6%	12%	6%	Clothing purchases under $50, grocery items
⊕	6%	7%	7%	Grocery items
⊕	5%	5.7–9.7%	5%	Clothing purchases under $175, grocery
⊕	none	8%	8%	None
⊕	7%	12%	7%	Clothing and grocery items
⊕	5%	9%	9%	Grocery items

Telephones – **Emergencies** (police, fire, ambulance): dial **911**. Instructions for using public telephones are listed on or near the phone. The cost of a local call is 20–35¢. Public telephones are located in many public places, hotel lobbies, convenience stores and along major highways. For **area codes** of major cities, consult the front pages of the local phone directory or dial 0 for directory assistance.

Sports and Recreation

SELECTED STATE PARKS

	▲	!	🐟	🐠

⊕ Connecticut

State Parks Division
79 Elm St.
Hartford CT 06106 ☎ 860-424-3200

Park	▲	!	🐟	🐠
Gillette Castle SP		•		
Housatonic Meadows SP	•	•		•
Kent Falls SP	•		•	
Macedonia Brook SP	•	•		•
Sleeping Giant SP	•	•		•
Talcott Mountain SP		•		

⊕ Maine

Bureau of Parks and Land
22 State House Station
Augusta ME 04333 ☎ 207-287-3821

Park	▲	!	🐟	🐠
Baxter SP	•	•	•	•
Camden Hills SP	•	•		
Cobscook Bay SP	•	•		•
Crescent Beach SP			•	•
Grafton Notch SP		•		•
Mt. Blue SP	•	•	•	•
Popham Beach SP			•	•
Quoddy Head SP		•		
Rangeley Lake SP	•		•	•
Sebago Lake SP	•	•	•	•
Two Lights SP				
Wolfe's Neck Woods SP		•		

⊕ Massachusetts

Division of Forests and Parks
100 Cambridge St., 19th Floor
Boston MA 02202 ☎ 617-727-3180

Park	▲	!	🐟	🐠
Halibut Point SP		•		•
Natural Bridge SP		•		•
Nickerson SP	•	•	•	•
Skinner SP		•		
Western Gateway Heritage SP				

SELECTED STATE PARKS

△   !   ~   ~

New Hampshire

Division of Parks & Recreation
PO Box 1856
Concord NH 03302 ☎ 603-271-3556

	Camping	Hiking	Swimming	Fishing
Lake Francis SP	•			•
Monadnock SP	•	•		
Mt. Sunapee SP		•	•	
Rhododendron SP		•		
Rye Harbor SP				•
Wallis Sands SP			•	
Wellington SP		•	•	
White Lake SP	•	•	•	•

Rhode Island

Department of Parks and Recreation
2321 Hartford Ave.
Johnston RI 02919 ☎ 401-277-2632

	Camping	Hiking	Swimming	Fishing
Brenton Point SP				•
Colt SP		•		•
Fort Adams SP				•

Vermont

Department of Forests, Parks & Recreation
103 S. Main St.
Waterbury VT 05671 ☎ 802-241-3660

	Camping	Hiking	Swimming	Fishing
Branbury SP	•	•	•	
Button Bay SP	•		•	
Lake St. Catherine SP	•	•	•	
Silver Lake SP	•		•	
Woodford SP	•	•	•	

△ camping; ! hiking; ~ swimming; ~ fishing

SPORTS

Hiking/Biking – Many trail systems lace the region. State and local parks provide opportunities for hiking and biking. The **Long Trail** (265mi) in Vermont runs north to south along the Green Mountains from the Canadian to the Massachusetts border; the **Appalachian Trail** extends in New England from Mt. Katahdin in Maine to the Connecticut/New York border. **Acadia National Park** offers 35,000 acres of moderately easy hiking trails. The wilderness trails of 202,000-acre **Baxter State Park** and 772,000-acre **White Mountain National Forest** are more challenging. In addition, 455mi of former railroad tracks throughout New England have been converted into paved and dirt paths for bikers and pedestrians (contact **Rails-to-Trails Conservancy**, 1100 17th St. NW, 10th Floor, Washington DC 20036 ☎ 202-331-9696 for maps and information). **Llama tours** provide a novel way to enjoy the terrain while allowing these gentle creatures to carry the meals and gear: Northern Vermont Llama Co., Rd. 1, Box 544, Waterville VT 05492 ☎ 802-644-2257; Telemark Inn's Llama Treks, RFD 2, Box 800, Bethel ME 04217 ☎ 207-836-2703 http://telemarkinn.com.

When hiking in the backcountry, stay on marked trails. Taking shortcuts is dangerous and causes erosion. If hiking alone, notify someone of your destination and proposed return time.

Bicycles are prohibited on most unpaved trails. Riders should stay on paved paths and roads (on public roads, stay to the right and ride in single file). Bicyclists are encouraged to wear helmets and other protective gear.

Both hikers and bicyclists are cautioned to be well equipped (including detailed maps of the areas to be explored) and alert to weather conditions, particularly in higher elevations. For more information on trails and on local mountain biking regulations, contact local tourism offices.

Tours and Trail Information – ⬛ New England Hiking Holidays, PO Box 1648, North Conway NH 03860 ☎ 800-869-0949 or 603-356-9696. Cycle America PO Box 485, Cannon Falls MN 55009 ☎ 800-245-3263 or 507-263-2665. Appalachian Mountain Club, 5 Joy St., Boston MA 02108 ☎ 617-523-0636. Appalachian Trail Conference, PO Box 807, Harpers Ferry, WV 25425 ☎ 304-535-6331.

Back Country Excursions, 42 Woodward Rd., Parsonsfield ME 04047 ☎ 207-625-8189. Bike Vermont Inc., Box 207, Woodstock VT 05091 ☎ 800-257-2226 or 802-457-3553. Vermont Bicycle Touring, PO Box 711, Bristol VT 05443 ☎ 802-453-4811. Vermont Department of Forests, Parks & Recreation, 103 S. Main St., Building 10 South, Waterbury VT 05671 ☎ 802-241-3655. Green Mountain National Forest, Supervisor, 231 N. Main St., Rutland VT 05701 ☎ 802-747-6700. The Green Mountain Club, 4711 Waterbury Stowe Rd., Waterbury Center VT 05677 ☎ 802-244-7037.

Hunting and Fishing – With an abundance of game and fish (including deer, moose and trout), New England is a hunting and angling paradise. Licenses are required to hunt and fish in all six states. Nonresident fishing licenses are available in fishing supply stores (some offer rental equipment). Nonresident hunting licenses tend to be considerably more expensive than resident licenses. Many fish are in season year-round, whereas most game can only be hunted seasonally. If being transported, a rifle or shotgun must be unloaded (no permit required; some states require it to be in a secure case). Contact the following agencies for additional information (including regulations on transporting game out of state): Department of Environmental Protection, Wildlife Division, 79 Elm St., Hartford CT 06106 ☎ 860-424-3011. Department of Inland Fisheries and Wildlife, 41 State House Station, Augusta ME 04333 ☎ 207-287-2871. *Maine Guide to Hunting and Fishing*, published by the Maine Tourism Assn. *(p 302)*. Division of Fisheries and Wildlife, Field Headquarters, Westboro MA 01581 ☎ 508-792-7270. Fish & Game Department, 2 Hazen Dr., Concord NH 03301 ☎ 603-271-3421. Division of Fish & Wildlife, Government Center, Tower Hill Rd., Wakefield RI 02879 ☎ 401-789-3094. Department of Fish and Wildlife, 103 South Main St., Building 10 South, Waterbury VT 05671 ☎ 802-241-3700.

Ocean Swimming – Beaches along the coast of New England are generally clean and sandy; several are rocky, the beaches a mixture of sand with pebbles (walking barefoot may be uncomfortable). Summer water temperatures vary: Connecticut and Rhode Island waters range from 65° to 75°F (18° to 24°C); in southern Massachusetts (including Cape Cod), water temperatures average 65° to 75°F (18° to 24°C); northern Massachusetts, New Hampshire and Maine waters average a brisk 50° to 65°F (10° to 18°C). Excellent surfing can be found along the Rhode Island, Massachusetts and Maine coastlines. Swimmers should be aware of the occasional riptide or undertow (strong underlying currents that pull seaward away from shore). Many New England communities employ lifeguards seasonally. Care should be taken when swimming at an unguarded beach. Children should be supervised at all times.

RECREATION

Antiquing – Displayed in elegant Boston shops or simple roadside stands along rural roadways, New England antiques will delight both the seasoned and novice collector in variety and quality. **Auctions**, typically listed in Thursday and weekend editions of local newspapers, are a bargain hunter's dream.
The following organizations provide dealer listings: Vermont Antiques Dealers' Assn. directory, c/o James Harley, Yellow House Antiques, RR1, Box 155, Reading VT 05062 (include two stamped, self-addressed envelopes). *Antique Hunter's Guide to Route 7*, A&L Travel Guides, PO Box 488, Waitsfield VT 05673 ☎ 802-496-3062. Maine Antique Dealers' Assn. directory, c/o Priscilla Hutchinson PO Box 301, Wiscasset ME 04578 (include stamped, self-addressed envelope). New Hampshire Antiques Dealers' Assn. 585 Concord Rd., Northfield, NH 03276 ☎ 603-286-7506.

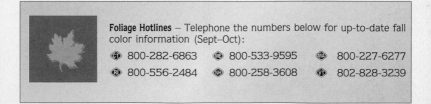

Foliage Hotlines – Telephone the numbers below for up-to-date fall color information (Sept–Oct):

800-282-6863   800-533-9595   800-227-6277

800-556-2484   800-258-3608   802-828-3239

Fall Foliage Tours – *maps pp 10-13*. New England's grand foliage season traditionally begins in early September along the Canadian border and higher elevations, and moves progressively southward until the end of October. Advance reservations (two to three months) are recommended for accommodations. Lovely views can be seen on most rural routes. Many tour companies offer weekend packages that include accommodations and guided tours.

A Vermont Farm

Farmers' Markets – During the New England harvest (mid- to late June through early October), many farmers sell fresh-grown produce at modest prices at roadside stands. Visitors can also pick their own fruits and vegetables *(for a small fee)* at farms open to the public. Contact the following agencies for a list of roadside stands and "pick your own" farms: ⊕ Dept. of Agriculture, Marketing Division, 765 Asylum Ave., Hartford CT 06105 ☎ 860-713-2569. ⊕ Dept. of Food & Agriculture, Bureau of Markets, 100 Cambridge St., Boston, MA 02202 ☎ 617-727-3018. ⊕ Dept. of Agriculture, PO Box 2042, Concord NH 03302 ☎ 603-271-2505. ⊕ Dept. of Agriculture, 116 State St., Drawer 20, Montpelier VT 05620 ☎ 802-828-2416.

Maple syrup is harvested in the spring. Farmers collect sap from maple trees in groves commonly called sugar bushes and boil down the watery substance into syrup. Visitors are welcome at a number of sugarhouses (to obtain list, contact the Vermont Dept of Agriculture, 116 State St., Drawer 20, Montpelier VT 05620 ☎ 802-828-2416 or the New Hampshire Dept. of Agriculture, PO Box 2042, Concord NH 03302 ☎ 603-271-2505). **Country fairs** offer a lively opportunity to view (and purchase) prize livestock, produce and local crafts.

Historic Tours – The following organizations offer their members free admission to their historic properties in New England: ⊕ ⊕ ⊕ ⊕ ⊕ Society for the Preservation of New England Antiquities, 141 Cambridge St., Boston MA 02114 ☎ 617-227-3956, yearly dues $35; ⊕ Antiquarian and Landmarks Society, 66 Forest St., Hartford CT 06105 ☎ 860-247-8996, yearly dues $30; National Trust for Historic Preservation (sights located nationwide), 1785 Massachusetts Ave., NW, Washington DC 20036 ☎ 202-588-6000, yearly dues $20.

Whale Watching – Because of the abundance of plankton, whales can be seen in large numbers on their migration route from the Caribbean to Greenland and Newfoundland from early spring to mid-October, primarily along the Stellwagen Bank (27mi east of Boston) in the Gulf of Maine.

Selected Cruise Companies

Company	Location	☎	Season
🦞 Massachusetts			
Boston Harbor Cruises	Boston	617-227-4321	May–mid-Oct
New England Aquarium	Boston	617-973-5281	Apr–Oct
Cape Ann Whale Watch	Gloucester	508-283-5110	May–mid-Oct
Captain Bill's Whale Watch	Gloucester	508-283-6995	May–Oct
Seven Seas Whale Watching	Gloucester	508-283-1776	May–mid-Oct
Yankee Whale Watch	Gloucester	508-283-0313	Apr–Oct
Hyannis Whale Watcher Cruises	Hyannis	508-362-6088	Apr–Oct
Captain John Boats	Plymouth	508-746-2643	Apr–Oct
Cape Cod Cruises	Provincetown	508-747-2400	Apr–Oct
Provincetown's Portuguese Princess Whale Watch	Provincetown	508-487-2651	Apr–Oct
East India Cruise Co.	Salem	508-741-0434	May–Oct
🦞 Maine			
Acadian Whale Watcher	Bar Harbor	207-288-9794	May–Oct
Whale Watcher, Inc.	Bar Harbor	207-288-3322	late May–late Oct

Puffins – Puffins can be seen in their summer colonies in the Gulf of Maine on Easter Egg Rock, Matinicus Rock and Machias Seal Island usually between June and early August (prime viewing time: July). On-land viewing is allowed only on Machias Seal Island by the following companies (binoculars recommended): Cap'n Fish's Boat Cruises, Boothbay Harbor ☎ 207-633-3244; Hardy Boat Cruises, New Harbor ☎ 207-677-2026.

Winter Activities

Skiing – The primary ski areas in New England are the Green Mountains of Vermont and the White Mountains of New Hampshire; there are also excellent ski resorts in northwestern Maine, western Connecticut and the Berkshires of Massachusetts. Many ski area communities offer a variety of accommodations including major hotel chains, B&Bs and alpine lodges. Discount packages for stays of 3 or more days, which can include lift tickets, equipment rental, meals and transportation to the slopes, are often available.

Radio stations throughout the northeast report local ski conditions. Most ski resorts have snow-making equipment.

Cross-Country Skiing – Many local parks and recreation departments maintain trail systems through recreation areas and forests. Always ask permission before skiing on private land. Some of the trail systems have warming huts, while others offer cabins with sleeping accommodations. Most backcountry trails are ungroomed.

Killington, Vermont

Vermont Dept. of Tourism & Marketing

State	Downhill	Cross-Country
 New Hampshire	800-258-3608	800-262-6660
Rhode Island		401-222-2601
Vermont	802-229-0531	802-828-3239

Snowmobiling – New England offers enthusiasts miles of maintained trails on both public and private lands. Many outfitters *(below)* provide guided tours and rental equipment.

The Vermont Assn. of Snow Travelers (VAST) maintains a 3,500mi trail system for its members that extends from the northern to the southern border of the state. VAST, PO Box 839, Montpelier VT 05601 ☎ 802-229-0005. Snowmobile Assocs., PO Box 80, Augusta ME 04332 ☎ 207-622-6983.

Trail Information – Office of State Parks & Recreation *(p 309)* Trails Bureau, Division of Parks & Recreation *(p 310)*. Snowmobile Assn. Inc., 722 Rte. 3A, Bow NH 03304 ☎ 603-224-8906. State Tourism Division *(p 302)*.

Dogsledding – This ancient mode of transportation offers a unique way to view the beauty of Maine's winter wilderness. Trips vary from one-hour excursions to day and overnight trips. **Mahoosuc Mountain Adventures** (Bear River Rd., Newry ME 04261) offers day and overnight trips in the Rangley Lakes region ☎ 207-824-2073. **White Howling Express** (PO Box 147, Stratton ME 04982) provides hour-long rides at Sugarloaf Ski Center near Farmington ☎ 207-246-4461. **Moose Country Dogsled Trips** (191 North Dexter Rd., Sangerville, ME 04479) offers two- to five-hour trips in the Moosehead Lake region ☎ 207-876-4907.

Selected Ski Areas	City	☎	Vertical Drop (ft)	Total Runs	Downhill Trails Beginner	Downhill Trails Intermediate	Downhill Trails Advanced	Cross Country Trails
❄ **Connecticut** / area code: 860								
Cedar Brook	West Suffield	668-5026						10km
Mohawk Mountain	Cornwall	672-6100	660	23	20%	60%	20%	8km
Mount Southington	Southington	628-0954	425	14	33%	33%	33%	
White Memorial Foundation	Litchfield	567-0857						56km
Woodbury Ski & Racquet	Woodbury	203-263-2203	300	14	33%	33%	33%	20km
❄ **Maine** / area code: 207								
Big Squaw Mtn.	Greenville	695-1000	1,750	18	33%	33%	33%	
Saddleback	Rangley	864-5671	1,826	41	33%	33%	33%	40km
Sugarloaf	Farmington	237-2000	2,820	126	28%	32%	40%	95km
Sunday River Ski	Newry Resort	824-3000	2,340	126	25%	35%	40%	
❄ **Massachusetts** / area code: 413								
Butternut Basin	Great Barrington	528-2000	1,000	22	20%	60%	20%	7km
Brodie Mountain	New Ashford	443-4752	1,250	40	30%	45%	25%	25km
Mt. Tom Ski Area	Holyoke	536-0416	680	15	20%	60%	20%	
❄ **New Hampshire** / area code: 603								
Attitash	Bartlett	374-2368	1,750	60	20%	47%	33%	
Balsams/Wilderness	Dixville Notch	255-3951	1,000	15	25%	50%	25%	90km
Black Mountain	Jackson	383-4490	1,150	40	30%	40%	30%	
Bretton Woods	Bretton Woods	278-5000	1,500	30	30%	43%	27%	90km
Cannon Mountain	Franconia	823-5563	2,146	38	21%	53%	26%	
Franconia Inn	Franconia	823-5542						65km
Gunstock	Gilford	293-4341	1,400	45	12%	68%	20%	50km
Highland Mtn. Ski Area	Tilton	286-2414	800	21	40%	30%	30%	Yes
Jackson Ski Touring Foundations	Jackson	383-9355						154km
King Ridge	New London	526-6966	850	23	57%	22%	22%	
Loon Mountain	Lincoln	745-8111	2,100	43	25%	50%	25%	35km
McIntyre	Manchester	624-6571	169	4	50%	50%		Yes
Mt. Cranmore	N. Conway	356-5543	1,200	40	22%	53%	25%	Yes
Mt. Sunapee	Sunapee	763-2356	1,510	38	24%	62%	14%	
Mt. Washington Ski Touring	Intervale	356 9920						20km
Nordic Skier	Wolfeboro	569-3151						40km
Norsk Cross-Country Center	New London	526-4685						90km
Pat's Peak	Henniker	428-3245	710	20	38%	30%	32%	20km
Ragged Mountain	Danbury	768-3475	1,250	32	30%	40%	30%	15km
Sugar Shack Nordic Village	Thornton	726-3867						32km
Sunset Hill Nordic Center	Sugar Hill	823-5522						30km
Temple Mountian	Peterborough	924-6949	600	16	40%	40%	20%	40km
Waterville Valley	Waterville Valley	236-8311	2,020	52	20%	60%	20%	105km
Wildcat Mountain	Jackson	466-3326	2,100	31	20%	45%	35%	
Windblown Cross-Country	New Ipswich	878-2869						40km

315

Selected Ski Areas			Vertical Drop (ft)	Total Runs	Downhill Trails			Cross Country Trails
City	☎				Beginner	Intermediate	Advanced	

◉ **Rhode Island** / area code: 401

Yawgoo Valley	Exeter	294-3802	260	12	60%	20%	20%	

◉ **Vermont** / area code: 802

	City	☎	Vertical Drop	Total Runs	Beginner	Intermediate	Advanced	Cross Country
Ascutney Mountain Resort	Brownsville	484-7711	1,530	47	26%	39%	35%	32km
Blueberry Hill	Goshen	247-6735						60km
Bolton Valley	Bolton	434-6400	1,625	48	28%	49%	23%	100km
Brattleboro Outing Club	Brattleboro	254-4081						25km
Bromley	Manchester	824-5522	1,334	42	39%	36%	28%	
Burke Mountain	East Burke	626-3305	2,000	31	25%	45%	30%	95km
Catamount Family Ctr.	Williston	879-6001						12km
Craftsbury Nordic	Craftsbury Common	586-7767						120km
Edson Hill Manor	Stowe	253-8954						25km
Green Mountain	Randolph	728-5575						35km
Green Trails	Brookfield	276-3412						34km
Hazen's Notch Center	Montgomery	326-4708						45km
Hermitage	Wilmington	464-3511						50km
Hildene	Manchester	362-1788						18km
Jay Peak	Jay	988-2611	2,153	64	20%	55%	25%	20km
Killington	Killington	800-621-6867	3,150	205	36%	32%	32%	
Lake Morey Inn	Fairlee	333-4311						12km
Mad River Glen	Waitsfield	496-3551	2,000	44	30%	30%	40%	
Meadow Brook Inn	Landgrove	824-6444						26km
Middlebury College	Wilmington	464-3333	1,700	133	20%	60%	20%	
Mt. Snow/Haystack								
Mountain Meadows	Killington	775-7077						50km
Mountain Top	Chittenden	483-6089						110km
Okemo	Ludlow	228-4041	2,150	98	30%	50%	20%	26km
Prospect Ski Mountain	Woodford	442-2575						40km
Rikert's	Ripton	388-2759						42km
Round Barn Farm	Waitsfield	496-2276						30km
Sitzmark	Wilmington	464-3384						40km
Snow Bowl	Middlebury	388-4356	1,200	13	23%	54%	23%	
Stowe Mountain Resorts	Stowe	253-3000	2,360	47	16%	59%	25%	70km
Stratton	Stratton Mtn.	297-2200	2,003	90	35%	37%	28%	70km
Sugarbush	Warren	583-6300	2,650	112	23%	48%	29%	25km
Suicide Six	Woodstock	457-6661	650	19	33%	33%	33%	
Topnotch	Stowe	253-8585						Yes
Trapp Family Lodge	Stowe	253-8511						55km
Viking Center	Londonderry	824-3933						40km
White House	Wilmington	464-2135						43km
Wild Wings	Peru	824-6793						24km
Wilderness Trails	Quechee	295-7620						18km
Woodstock	Woodstock	457-2114						60km

Index

New Haven — City, town, region or other point of interest
Revere, Paul — *Person, historic event or term*
Accommodations — Practical information

Place and sight names are followed by state abbreviations: CT Connecticut, ME Maine, MA Massachusetts, NH New Hampshire, RI Rhode Island, VT Vermont. Selected sights in Boston, Hartford and Providence are listed under those headings. **State parks** are listed on pages 309 and 310. **Maps** are listed on page 9.

A

Acadia Natl. Park *ME* 95
Accommodations 307
Adam, Robert 31, 35
Adams, John 203
Adams, John Quincy 203
Adams, Samuel 117, 129, 181
Alcott, Amos Bronson 171, 176
Alcott, Louisa May 127, 171
Allagash Wilderness Waterway *ME* 92
Allen, Ethan 22, 269, 270, 273
American Clock and Watch Museum 57
American Revolution 22, 116, 152, 170, 180, 251
American Textile History Museum *MA* 183
America's Cup 252
America's Stonehenge *NH* 224
Amherst College *MA* 197
Andover *MA* 183
Anheuser-Busch Hamlet *NH* 226
Antiquarian and Landmarks Society 312
Appalachian Gap *VT* 277
Appalachian Mountains 16
Appalachian Trail 55, 78, 279, 310
Architecture 30
Arethusa Falls *NH* 240
Arlington *VT* 279
Arnold, Benedict 22, 67, 273
Arundel *ME* 89
Attucks, Crispus 119
Augusta *ME* 76
Austin, Henry 64, 102

B

Bangor *ME* 76
Bar Harbor *ME* 94
Barnet Center *VT* 285
Barnstable *MA* 165
Barnum, Phineas T. 44, 241
Barre *VT* 270

Basketball Hall of Fame *MA* 209
Bath *ME* 77
Battleship Cove *MA* 175
Baxter State Park *ME* 78
Ben & Jerry's Ice Cream Factory *VT* 293
Benjamin, Asher 32, 127, 128
Bennington *VT* 270
Bennington, Battle of 22, 270
Bennington College *VT* 271
Berkshires, The *MA* 111
Bethel *ME* 80
Bierstadt, Albert 36
Blackstone, William 116, 129, 247
Block Island *RI* 248
Blue Hill *ME* 82
Boothbay Harbor *ME* 82
Boston
  Acorn Street 127
  African Meeting House 128
  Arlington Street 138
  Arnold Arboretum 148
  Back Bay 135
  Bay Village 148
  Beacon Hill 122
  Beacon Street 125, 138
  Boston Athenaeum 125
  Boston Center for the Arts 148
  Boston Common 129
  Boston Museum of Science 145
  Boston Pops 120
  Boston Public Library 136
  Boylston Street 139
  Bunker Hill Monument 147
  Charles Street 127
  Cheers Pub 138
  Chestnut Street 127
  Children's Museum 145
  Chinatown 148
  Christian Science Center 140
  City Hall 131
  Commonwealth Avenue 137
  Computer Museum 145
  Copley Place 139
  Copley Square 135
  Copp's Hill Burying Ground 133
  Cruises 134
  Custom House 131
  Esplanade 138
  Faneuil Hall 131
  Franklin Park Zoo 148
  Freedom Trail 128

  Georges Island 134
  Harrison Gray Otis House 128
  Hynes Convention Center 140
  Institute of Contemporary Art 146
  Isabella Stewart Gardner Museum 23, 144
  John F. Kennedy Library and Museum 146
  John Hancock Tower 136
  Joy Street 128
  King's Chapel 129
  Logan Airport 123
  Long Wharf 134
  Louisburg Square 127
  Marlborough Street 138
  Mt. Vernon Street 127
  Museum of Fine Arts 23, 140
  New England Aquarium 133
  Newbury Street 137
  North End 132
  Old City Hall 130
  Old Corner Bookstore 130
  Old Granary Burying Ground 129
  Old North Church 133
  Old South Meeting House 130
  Old State House 130
  Old West Church 128
  Park Street Church 129
  Paul Revere House 132
  Paul Revere Mall 132
  Pinckney Street 127
  Prudential Center 139
  Public Garden 139
  Quincy Market 132
  Revere Street 127
  Rowes Wharf 134
  Smith Court 128
  South End 148
  St. Stephen's Church 132
  State House 125
  Subway 123
  Tea Party Ship 134
  Theater District 120
  Trinity Church 136
  Union Street 132
  Waterfront 133
Boston Marathon 124, 137
Boston Massacre 117, 130
Boston Tea Party 117, 134
Bowdoin College *ME* 83
Bradford, William 39, 199, 200
Brandeis University *MA* 149
Brandon Gap *VT* 273
Brattleboro *VT* 274
Bretton Woods *NH* 240

317

Manufacture Française des Pneumatiques Michelin
Société en commandite par actions au capital de 2 000 000 000 de francs
Place des Carmes-Déchaux – 63000 Clermont-Ferrand (France)
R.C.S. Clermont-Fd B 855 200 507

Michelin et Cie, Propriétaires-éditeurs, 1999
Dépôt légal novembre 1999 – ISBN 2-06-156909-9 – ISSN 0763-1383

Printed in the EU 11-99/1
Photocompositeur : Nord-Compo à Villeneuve-d'Ascq
Impression : IME, Baume-les-Dames
Brochage : AUBIN, Ligugé

Illustration de la couverture par Richard BATSON